FOURTH EDITION

MASS MEDIA LAW

FOURTH EDITION

MASS MEDIA LAW

Don R. Pember
University of Washington—Seattle

wcb
Wm. C. Brown Publishers
Dubuque, Iowa

Book Team
Editor *Stan Stoga*
Developmental Editor *Edgar J. Laube*
Production Editor *Barbara Rowe Day*
Designer *Mary K. Sailer*
Permissions Editor *Vicki Krug*
Product Manager *Marcia Stout*

wcb group

Wm. C. Brown *Chairman of the Board*
Mark C. Falb *President and Chief Executive Officer*

wcb

Wm. C. Brown Publishers, College Division
G. Franklin Lewis *Executive Vice-President, General Manager*
E. F. Jogerst *Vice-President, Cost Analyst*
George Wm. Bergquist *Editor in Chief*
John Stout *Executive Editor*
Beverly Kolz *Director of Production*
Chris C. Guzzardo *Vice-President, Director of Marketing*
Bob McLaughlin *National Sales Manager*
Craig S. Marty *Manager, Marketing Research*
Julie A. Kennedy *Production Editorial Manager*
Marilyn A. Phelps *Manager of Design*
Faye M. Schilling *Photo Research Manager*

Cover photo by Kay Chernush/The Image Bank.

Interior design and cover design by Michael Warrell.

CONTENTS

3 LIBEL 108

4 INVASION OF PRIVACY 210

8   OBSCENITY   408

9   COPYRIGHT   452

10   REGULATION OF ADVERTISING   494

PREFACE

Mass media law is today more visible to the average person than at anytime in the past century. Libel law was propelled into the headlines by two widely publicized lawsuits against "60 Minutes" (the William Westmoreland case) and *Time* magazine (the Ariel Sharon case). Significant publicity was also given to a lawsuit by Carol Burnett against *National Enquirer* and an action against a popular men's magazine by a former Miss Wyoming. The press itself has kept the law of libel in the public eye by significantly publicizing what it often describes as the onslaught of libel actions and the accompanying "mega-verdicts" against the press.

Protests against what some consider pornographic material were manifest as well in the mid-1980s with the Meese Commission attacking the sale and distribution of popular mens' magazines, and a group of parents (many of whom happened to be the wives of members of Congress) attacking popular song lyrics and music videos. Attempts at press censorship for political or military reasons were also widely publicized, from the time the president permitted the armed forces to leave American reporters at home while the military invaded the "Caribbean stronghold" of Grenada to the point in mid-1986 when CIA director William Casey asked for the prosecution of several publications for supposedly revealing secrets about U.S. surveillance systems.

Americans seem more concerned than ever before about the intrusion by the press into the lives of the famous, and the not-so-famous, victims of crimes and terrorist acts. While not necessarily articulated as such by the average man and woman, such concern is the focus of much of the law of privacy. Finally, throughout the nation, citizens and government agencies are seeking to abridge such practices as the cablecasting of erotic R-rated movies, the broadcast of commercials for beer and wine, the advertising of tobacco products, and the telecasting of election projections before the polls have closed.

None of the issues outlined above is new; but rarely have members of the general public been so informed on such matters. The mass media, used to publishing and broadcasting news about a wide variety of social and political issues, suddenly finds its own behavior a public issue as well.

This book is an attempt to outline the law as it pertains to the mass media in America. It is not intended to teach people to practice law. Most lawyers are far more interested in process than substance, and this book focuses exclusively upon the substance of the law. It is written for persons who some day intend to work as journalists, broadcasters, or advertising copywriters. It is also written for others who are interested in the law and how it affects the press in America.

Chapter 1 of the text acquaints students with American law and the American legal system. Chapter 2 focuses upon a broad range of freedom of expression issues, including the history and development of this concept in the United States. Students' free speech rights are also considered, and a discussion of the 1986 ruling involving a suggestive political speech by a Washington state high school student is included in this section.

The chapter on libel, Chapter 3, is the longest and most detailed in the book. Significant court decisions have been handed down recently, including two important rulings in mid-1986: *Philadelphia Newspapers* v. *Hepps,* a case involving the truth or falsity of a libelous remark; and *Anderson* v. *Liberty Lobby,* a case involving the very important summary judgment process. Material on invasion of privacy has been updated in Chapter 4, and the actions by the Reagan administration to frustrate the press in its quest for information about government are outlined in Chapter 5. Reporters who are called to testify at trials or before grand juries sometimes still seek to keep the names of their news sources confidential, and this issue (and the matter of contempt of court, the legal threat often used against reporters in such instances) is outlined in Chapter 6.

Whether or not judges can close pretrial hearings and trials to the press and the public was the most persistent media law problem in the early 1980s. Decisions by the U.S. Supreme Court and lower federal courts in 1985 and 1986 significantly clarified these issues, as is noted in Chapter 7. The law regarding obscenity remains as murky as ever, as you will note by reading Chapter 8. Attempts to regulate pornography, rather than the more explicitly defined obscenity, have only added to the confusion on these matters. Two important copyright rulings that were unresolved when the third edition of this text went to press in 1983 have been settled by the U.S. Supreme Court. Other interesting developments in copyright law were also generated in the past three years. All of this material is in Chapter 9.

Chapter 10 reflects the continuing de-emphasis upon the regulation of advertising by the federal government, as well as the continued emergence of the so-called commercial speech doctrine. The ruling by the U.S. Supreme Court in 1986 in *Posadas de Puerto Rico Associates* v. *Tourism Company of Puerto Rico* reflects directly on the First Amendment and advertising, the focus of the commerical speech doctrine. And Chapter 11 reflects the continuing movement toward the deregulation of broadcasting. Important developments in the regulation of cable television, including court rulings granting at least limited First Amendment rights beyond those possessed by over-the-air broadcasters to the cablecasters and the passage of the Cable Communications Policy Act of 1984, are included in this chapter. Finally, the regulation of mass media as businesses is the focus of the final chapter in the book, a topic that includes a discussion of joint-operating agreements, a means by which newspapers can avoid prosecution under the antitrust laws for what are clearly violations of these statutes.

As with earlier editions, this book contains a bias in favor of freedom of expression. I believe this is perhaps the single most important right we residents of the United States possess today. Make no mistake about it, there is currently in America a rising tide of calls for increased censorship. Voices in the federal government, voices in the extreme religious right, and voices even in the feminist community all ask for increased restrictions upon what may be published, circulated and read. The call for censorship has worn many disguises in our history; regardless of its clothing or its plaintive pitch, censorship remains an anathema to both the democratic form of government and the development of the human spirit.

At the same time, it becomes seemingly harder for those of us who stand in support of the mass media and their news gathering activities to defend some behaviors characteristic of a few in the press. There is no attempt in this book to justify the often intrusive behavior of some reporters, especially those armed with cameras and microphones, to exploit the victims of crime and tragedy. Similarly, no special pleadings are contained in these pages to defend the bad taste sometimes shown by reporters and editors in publicizing what many in a civilized nation are embarrassed to talk about in private. Students need to remember that this text outlines the limits of the law, not the boundaries of sensitivity, good taste, or general civility.

As always, there are many persons responsible for the publication of a book beside the author. Teachers of mass media law who have used this text have provided many valuable suggestions, many of which are incorporated into the text. I would especially like to thank the people who read the manuscript and provided suggestions for its revision: Terry Bales, Santa Ana College; Sam Danna, Loyola University; David Eshelman, Central Missouri State University; William McCavitt, Indiana University of Pennsylvania; David Pritchard, University of Indiana; Paul Siegel, Illinois State University; and William Steng, Oklahoma State University. Teaching colleagues at the University of Washington have also been helpful. The Wm. C. Brown publishing team, including Stan Stoga, Edgar Laube, Michael Warrell, Karen Doland, Barbara Day, and Vicki Krug, have given me all the support an author can expect. My students, who use the book, have provided insight (by questioning statements in the book) and inspiration (by telling me they find the text highly useful). Finally, the Pember clan, Diann, Alison, and Brian, all of whom have stuck with a husband and father who has too often uttered, "No I can't do that, I have to work on the book now," deserve high praise and thanks for "hanging in there" through the duration of the revision.

Don R. Pember
Seattle, Washington

FOURTH EDITION

MASS MEDIA LAW

1 THE AMERICAN LEGAL SYSTEM

Probably no nation is more closely tied to the law than the American Republic. From the 1770s, when in the midst of a war of revolution we attempted to legally justify our separation from the motherland, to the 1980s, when citizens of the nation attempt to resolve weighty moral, political, social, and environmental problems through the judicial process, and during the more than two hundred years between, the American people have showed a remarkable faith in the law. One could write a surprisingly accurate history of this nation using reports of court decisions as the only source. Not that what happens in the courts reflects everything that happens in the nation; but as has been observed by Alexis de Tocqueville and others, political issues in the United States often end up as legal disputes. Beginning with the sedition cases in the late 1790s, which reflected the political turmoil of that era, one could chart the history of the United States from adolescence to maturity. As the frontier expanded in the nineteenth century, citizens used the courts to argue land claims and boundary problems. Civil rights litigation in both the midnineteenth and midtwentieth centuries reflects a people attempting to cope with racial and ethnic diversity. Industrialization brought labor unions, workmen's compensation laws, and child labor laws, all of which resulted in controversies that found their way into the courts. As mass production developed and large manufacturers began to create most of the consumer goods used, judges and juries had to cope with new laws on product safety, honesty in advertising, and consumer complaints.

Americans have protested nearly every war the nation has fought—including the Revolutionary War. The record of these protests is contained in scores of court decisions. And as some young people refuse to register under the selective service laws of the 1980s, their protests will be recorded in judicial records when prosecutions occur. Prohibition and the crime of the twenties and the economic woes of the thirties both left residue in the law. In the United States, as in most other societies, law is a basic part of existence, as necessary for the survival of civilization as are economic systems, political systems, cultural achievement, and the family.

This chapter has two purposes: to acquaint readers with the law and to present a brief outline of the legal system in the United States. Students who study mass media law frequently face the serious difficulty of studying a special area of law without having an understanding of the law and the court system in general, a situation somewhat like a medical student studying neurosurgery before taking work in anatomy, basic medicine, and surgical techniques. While this chapter is not designed to be a comprehensive course in law and the judicial system—such material can better be studied in depth in an undergraduate political science course—it does provide sufficient introduction to understand the remaining eleven chapters of the book.

The chapter opens with a discussion of the law, giving consideration to the five most important sources of the law in the United States, and moves on to the judicial system, including both the federal and state court systems. A summary of judicial review and a brief outline of how both criminal and civil lawsuits are started and proceed through the courts are included in the discussion of the judicial system. ♦

SOURCES OF THE LAW

There are almost as many definitions of law as there are people who study the law. Some people say that law is any social norm or any organized or ritualized method of settling disputes. Most writers on the subject insist that it is a bit more complex, that some system of sanctions is required before law exists. John Austin, a nineteenth-century English jurist, defined law as definite rules of human conduct with appropriate sanctions for their enforcement. He added that both the rules and the sanctions must be prescribed by duly constituted human authority. Roscoe Pound, an American legal scholar, has suggested that law is really social engineering—the attempt to order the way people behave. For the purposes of this book, it is probably more helpful to consider the law to be a set of rules that attempt to guide human conduct and a set of formal, governmental sanctions that are applied when those rules are violated.

Scholars still debate the genesis of "the law." A question that is more meaningful and easier to answer is, What is the source of American law? There are really five major sources of the law in the United States: the Constitution, the common law, the law of equity, the statutory laws, and the rulings of various executive and administrative bodies and agencies. Historically we can trace American law to Great Britain. As colonizers of much of the North American continent, the British supplied Americans with an outline for both a legal system and a judicial system. In fact, because of the many similarities between British and American law, many people consider the Anglo-American legal system to be a single entity. Today in the United States our federal Constitution is the supreme law of the land. Yet when each of these five sources of law is considered separately, it is more useful to begin with the earliest source of Anglo-American law, the common law.

The Common Law

The **common law,** which developed in England during the two hundred years after the Norman Conquest in the eleventh century, is one of the great legacies of the British people to colonial America. During those two centuries the crude mosaic of Anglo-Saxon customs was replaced by a single system of law worked out by jurists and judges. The system of law became common throughout England; it became the common law. It was also called the common law to distinguish it from the ecclesiastical (church) law prevalent at the time. Initially, the customs of the people were used by the king's courts as the foundation of the law, disputes were resolved according to community custom, and governmental sanction was applied to enforce the resolution. As such, the common law was, and still is, considered "discovered law." It is law that has always existed, much like air and water. When a problem arises, the court's task is to find or discover the proper solution, to seek the common custom of the people. The judge doesn't create the law; he or she merely finds it, much like a miner finds gold or silver.

This, at least, is the theory of the common law. Perhaps at one point judges themselves believed that they were merely discovering the law when they handed down decisions. As legal problems became more complex and as the law began to be professionally administered (the first lawyers appeared during this era and eventually professional judges), it became clear that the common law reflected not so much the custom of the land as the custom of the court—or more properly, the custom of the judges. While judges continued to look to the past to discover how other courts had decided, given similar facts (precedent is discussed in a moment), many times judges were forced to create the law themselves.

This common-law system was the perfect system for the American colonies. Like most Anglo-Saxon institutions, it was a very pragmatic system aimed at settling real problems, not at expounding abstract and intellectually satisfying theories. The common law is an inductive system of law in which a legal rule is arrived at after consideration of a great number of specific instances of cases. (In a deductive system the rules are expounded first and then the court decides the legal situation under the existing rule.) Colonial America was a land of new problems for British and other settlers. The old law frequently did not work. But the common law easily accommodated the new environment. The ability of the common law to adapt to change is directly responsible for its longevity.

Fundamental to the common law is the concept that judges should look to the past and follow earlier court precedents. The Latin expression for the concept is this: *Stare decisis et non quieta movere* (to stand by past decisions and not disturb things at rest). **Stare decisis** is the key phrase: let the decision stand. A judge should resolve current problems in the same manner as similar problems were resolved in the past. When Barry Goldwater sued publisher Ralph Ginzburg for publishing charges that the conservative Republican senator was mentally ill, was paranoid, the judge most certainly looked to past decisions to discover whether in previous cases such a charge had been considered defamatory or libelous. There are ample precedents for ruling that a published charge that a person is mentally ill is libelous, and Senator Goldwater won his lawsuit (*Goldwater* v. *Ginzburg,* 1969).

At first glance one would think that under a system that continually looks to the past, the law can never change. What if the first few rulings in a line of cases were bad decisions? Are we saddled with bad law forever? Fortunately, the law does not operate quite in this way. While following **precedent** is the desired state of affairs (many people say that certainty in the law is more important than justice), it is not always the proper way to proceed. To protect the integrity of the common law, judges have developed several means of coping with bad law and with new situations in which the application of old law would result in injustice.

Imagine for a moment that the newspaper in your hometown publishes a picture and story about a twelve-year-old girl who gave birth to a seven-pound son in a local hospital. The mother and father do not like the publicity and sue the newspaper for invasion of privacy. The attorney for the parents finds a precedent (*Barber* v. *Time,* 1942) in which a Missouri court ruled that to photograph a patient in a hospital room against her will and then to publish that picture in a news magazine is an invasion of privacy.

Now does the existence of this precedent mean that the young couple will automatically win their lawsuit? that the court will follow the decision? No, it does not. For one thing, there may be other cases in which courts have ruled that publishing such a picture is not an invasion of privacy. In fact in 1956 in the case of *Meetze* v. *AP,* a South Carolina court made just such a ruling. But for the moment assume that *Barber* v. *Time* is the only precedent. Is the court bound by this precedent? No. The court has several options concerning the 1942 decision.

First, it can *accept* the precedent as law and rule that the newspaper has invaded the privacy of the couple by publishing the picture and story about the birth of their child. Second, the court can *modify* or change the 1942 precedent by arguing that *Barber* v. *Time* was decided more than forty years ago when people were more sensitive about going to a hospital, since a stay in a hospital was often considered to reflect badly on a patient, but that hospitalization is no longer a sensitive matter to most people. Therefore, a rule of law restricting the publication of a picture of a hospital patient is unrealistic, unless the picture is in bad taste or needlessly embarrasses the patient. Then its publication is an invasion of privacy. If not, the publication of such a picture is permissible. In our imaginary case, then, the decision turns on what kind of picture and story the newspaper published: a pleasant picture that flattered the couple? or one that mocked and embarrassed them? If the court rules in this manner, it *modifies* the 1942 precedent, making it correspond to what the judge perceives to be contemporary life.

As a third option the court can argue that *Barber* v. *Time* provides an important precedent for a plaintiff hospitalized because of disease—as Dorothy Barber was. But that in the case before the court, the plaintiff was hospitalized to give birth to a baby, a different situation: Giving birth is a voluntary status; catching a disease is not. Consequently the *Barber* v. *Time* precedent does not apply. This practice is called *distinguishing the precedent from the current case,* a very common action.

Finally, the court can *overrule* the precedent. In 1941 the United States Supreme Court overruled a decision made by the Supreme Court in 1918 regarding the right of a judge to use what is called the summary contempt power (*Toledo Newspaper Co.* v. *U.S.,* 1918). This is the power of a judge to charge someone with being in contempt of court, to find that person guilty of contempt, and then to punish him or her for the contempt—all without a jury trial. In *Nye* v. *U.S.* (1941) the High Court said that in 1918 it had been improperly informed as to the intent of a measure passed by Congress in 1831 that authorized the use of the summary power by federal judges. The 1918 ruling was therefore bad, was wrong, and was reversed. (Fuller explanation of summary contempt as it applies to the mass media is given in chapter 6.) The only courts that can overrule the 1942 decision by the Missouri Supreme Court in *Barber* v. *Time* are the Missouri Supreme Court and the United States Supreme Court.

Obviously the preceding discussion oversimplifies the judicial process. Rarely is a court confronted with only a single precedent. And whether or not precedent is binding on a court is often an issue. Lower federal courts are bound to follow precedents from the appellate court in their circuit or region (see pages 27–29) and from the Supreme Court of the United States. But when focusing upon state law, the courts in the fifty separate states are bound to follow only the court rulings or precedents that have been generated within each state. A court in Arkansas, for example, need only look to the precedents from other Arkansas courts when deciding an issue that involves only Arkansas law. It might be useful to look to court decisions in other states that have similar laws or have had similar cases. But the Arkansas courts are not bound by these other state rulings. Because mass media law is so heavily affected by the First Amendment, state judges are frequently forced to look outside their borders to precedents developed by the federal courts. A state court ruling on a question involving freedom of speech and freedom of the press is necessarily governed by federal court precedents on the same subject.

Lawyers and law professors often debate just how important precedent really is when a court makes a decision. Some persons have suggested what is called the "hunch theory" of jurisprudence. Under this theory a judge or justice decides a case based on instinct or a feeling of what is right and wrong and then seeks out precedents to support the decision.

The imaginary invasion-of-privacy case just discussed demonstrates that the common law can have vitality, that despite the rule of precedent a judge is rarely bound tightly by the past. There is a saying, Every age should be the mistress of its own law. This saying applies to the common law as well as to all other aspects of the legal system.

It must be clear at this point that the common law is not specifically written down someplace for all to see and use. It is instead contained in the hundreds of thousands of decisions handed down by courts over the centuries. Many attempts have been made to summarize the law. Sir Edward Coke compiled and analyzed the precedents of common law in the early seventeenth century. Sir William Blackstone later expanded Coke's work in the monumental *Commentaries on the Law of England.* More recently, in such works as the massive *Restatement of Torts* the task was again undertaken, but on a narrower scale. Despite these compilations, in the eyes of some European attorneys the common law remains "the law nobody knows" because it is not spelled out neatly in a statute book or administrative edict.

Courts began to keep records of their decisions centuries ago. In the thirteenth century unofficial reports of cases began to appear in Year Books, but they were records of court proceedings in which procedural points were clarified for the benefit of legal practitioners, rather than collections of court decisions. The modern concept of fully reporting the written decisions of all courts probably began in 1785 with the publication of the first British Term Reports.

While scholars and lawyers still uncover the common law using the case-by-case method, it is fairly easy today to locate the appropriate cases through a simple system of citation. The cases of a single court (such as the United States Supreme Court or the federal district courts) are collected in a single **case reporter** (such as the *United States Reports* or the *Federal Supplement*). The cases are collected chronologically and fill many volumes. Each case collected has its individual **citation,** which reflects the name of the reporter in which the case can be found, the volume of that reporter, and the page on which the case begins (fig. 1.1). For example, the citation for the decision in *Adderly* v. *Florida* (a freedom-of-speech case) is 385 U.S. 39 (1966). The letters in the middle (U.S.) indicate that the case is in the *United States Reports,* the official government reporter for cases decided by the Supreme Court of the United States. The number 385 refers to the specific volume of the *United States Reports* in which the case is found. The last number (39) gives the page on which the case appears. Finally, 1966 provides the year in which the case was decided. So, *Adderly* v. *Florida* can be found on page 39 of volume 385 of the *United States Reports.*

If you have the correct citation, you can easily find any case you seek. Locating all citations of the cases apropos to a particular problem—such as a libel suit—is a different matter and is a technique taught in law schools. A great many legal encyclopedias, digests, compilations of the common law, books, and articles are used by lawyers to track down the names and citations of the appropriate cases.

Figure 1.1 Reading a case
citation

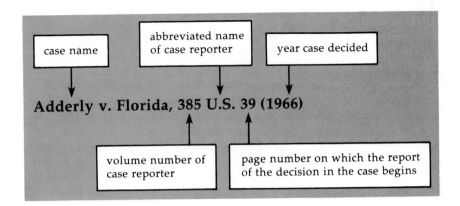

There is no better way to sum up the common law than to quote Oliver
Wendell Holmes (*The Common Law*, published in 1881):

> The life of the law has not been logic; it has been experience. The felt
> necessities of the time, the prevalent moral and political theories, intuitions of
> public policy, avowed or unconscious, even the prejudices which judges share
> with their fellow-men, have had a good deal more to do than syllogism in
> determining the rules by which men should be governed. The law embodies
> the story of a nation's development through many centuries, and it cannot be
> dealt with as if it contained only the axioms and corollaries of a book of
> mathematics. In order to know what it is, we must know what it has been, and
> what it tends to become. . . . The very considerations which judges most
> rarely mention, and always with an apology, are the secret root from which
> the law draws all the juices of life. I mean, of course, considerations of what is
> expedient for the community concerned.

The Law of Equity

The common law is not the only legal legacy the British provided the American people. The law of **equity,** as developed in Britain beginning in the fourteenth and fifteenth centuries, is also a remnant of our British heritage and is
the second basic source of the law in the United States. Equity was originally
a supplement to the common law and developed side by side with the common
law. During the 1300s and 1400s the king's courts became rigid and narrow.
Many persons seeking relief under the common law for very real grievances
were often turned away because the law did not provide a suitable remedy for
their problems. In such instances the disappointed litigant could take the
problem to the king for resolution, petitioning the king to "do right for the
love of God and by way of charity." According to legal scholar Henry Abraham
(*The Judicial Process*), "The king was empowered to mold the law for the
sake of 'justice,' to grant the relief prayed for as an act of grace." Soon the
chancellor, the king's right-hand man, set up a special office or court to settle

the kinds of problems that the king's common law courts could not resolve. At the outset of the hearing, the aggrieved party had to establish that there was no adequate remedy under the common law and that a special court was needed to hear the case. The office of the chancellor soon became known as the Court of Chancery. Decisions were made on the basis of conscience or fairness or "equity."

British common law and equity law were American law until the Revolution in 1776. After independence was won, the basic principles of common law in existence before the War of Revolution were kept because the cases remained acceptable precedent. After some hesitation, equity was accepted in much the same way. While present-day United States courts can consider decisions made in British courts after the Revolution, they are not bound by these decisions. For example, when the law of privacy is discussed, it will be seen that the decisions of British courts were often cited by American judges in the early development of privacy law, but were rarely fully accepted.

Initially there was a separate **court of equity, or chancery,** in Great Britain. But today in Great Britain and the United States, the same court hears cases both in equity and under the common law. Depending upon the kind of judicial relief sought by the plaintiff, the judge applies either the common law or the rules of equity.

The rules and procedures under equity are far more flexible than those under the common law. Equity really begins where the common law leaves off. Equity suits are never tried before a jury. Rulings come in the form of **judicial decrees,** not in judgments of yes or no. Decisions in equity are (and were) discretionary on the part of judges. And despite the fact that precedents are also relied upon in the law of equity, judges are free to do what they think is right and fair in a specific case.

Equity provides another advantage for troubled litigants—the restraining order. A judge sitting in equity can order preventive measures as well as remedial ones. Individuals who can demonstrate that they are in peril, or about to suffer a serious irremediable wrong, can usually gain a legal writ such as an injunction or a restraining order to stop someone from doing something. Generally a court issues a temporary restraining order until it can hear arguments from both parties in the dispute and decide whether an injunction should be made permanent.

In 1971 the federal government asked the federal courts to restrain the *New York Times* and the *Washington Post* from publishing what have now become known as the Pentagon Papers (this case is discussed in greater detail in chapter 2). This case is a good example of equity law in action. The government argued that if the purloined documents were published by the two newspapers the nation would suffer irremediable damage; that foreign governments would be reluctant to entrust the United States with their secrets if those secrets might someday be published in the public press; that the enemy would gain valuable defense secrets. The federal government argued further that it would do little good to punish the newspapers after the material had been published since there would be no way to repair the damage. The federal district court temporarily restrained both newspapers from publishing the material while the case was argued—all the way to the Supreme Court of the United States. After two weeks of hearings, the High Court finally ruled that publication could continue, that the government had failed to prove that the nation would be damaged (*New York Times Co.* v. *U.S.,* 1971).

Prior to the Revolution, Americans were also bound by laws made by their colonial legislatures as well as by the British Parliament. Following independence, the British statutes passed by Parliament were no longer applicable in the United States; instead the residents of the new nation were bound by the laws of their own local, federal, and state legislatures. Legislation is therefore the third great source of United States law.

Statutory Law

Today there are legislative bodies of all shapes and sizes. The common traits they share are that they are popularly elected and that they have the authority to pass laws. In the beginning of our nation, legislation, or statutory law, really did not play a very significant role in the legal system. Certainly many laws were passed, but the bulk of our legal rules were developed from the common law and from equity law. After 1825 statutory law began to play an important role in our legal system, and it was between 1850 and 1900 that a greater percentage of law began to come from legislative acts than from common-law court decisions. Today, most American law comes from various legislatures: Congress, state legislatures, city councils, county boards of supervisors, township boards, and so forth. In fact, legislative action produces the greatest volume of American law in the 1980s.

Several important characteristics of statutory law can best be understood by contrasting them with common law. First, **statutes** tend to deal with problems affecting society or large groups of people, in contrast to common law, which usually deals with smaller, individual problems. (Some common-law rulings affect large groups of persons, but this occurrence is rare.) It should also be noted in this connection the importance of not confusing common law with constitutional law. Certainly when judges interpret the Constitution they make policy that affects us all. However, it should be kept in mind that the Constitution is a legislative document voted upon by the people and is not "discovered law" or "judge-made law."

Second, statutory law can anticipate problems, and common law cannot. For example, a state legislature can pass a statute that prohibits publication of the school records of a student without prior consent of the student. Under the common law the problem cannot be resolved until a student's record has been published in a newspaper or broadcast on television and the student brings action against the medium to recover damages for the injury incurred.

Third, the criminal laws in the United States are all statutory laws—common-law crimes no longer exist in this country and have not since 1812. Common-law rules are not precise enough to provide the kind of notice needed to protect a criminal defendant's right to due process of law.

Fourth, statutory law is collected in codes and law books, instead of in reports as is the common law. When a proposal or bill is adopted by the legislative branch and approved by the executive branch, it becomes law and is integrated into the proper section of a municipal code, a state code, or whatever. However, this does not mean that some very important statutory law cannot be found in the case reporters.

Passage of a law is rarely the final word on the subject. Courts become involved in the process of determining what that law means. While a properly constructed statute sometimes needs little interpretation by the courts, judges are frequently called upon to rule upon the exact meaning of ambiguous phrases and words. The resulting process is called **statutory construction** and is a very important part of the law. Even the simplest kind of statement often needs interpretation. For example, a prohibition stating "it is illegal to distribute an obscene newspaper" is filled with ambiguity. What does *distribution* mean? Can an obscene newspaper be sent through the mail? distributed from house to house? passed out on street corners? Are all of these actions prohibited? What constitutes a newspaper? Is any printed matter a newspaper? Is any printed matter published regularly a newspaper? Are mimeographed sheets and photocopied newsletters considered newspapers? Of course, implicit is the classic question with which courts have wrestled in this country for nearly a century, What is obscenity?

Usually a legislature tries to leave some kind of trail to help a judge find out what the law means. For when judges rule on the meaning of a statute, they are supposed to determine what the legislature meant when it passed the law (the legislative intent), not what they think it should mean. Minutes of committee hearings in which the law was discussed, legislative staff reports, and reports of debate on the floor can all be used to help a judge determine the legislative intent. Therefore when lawyers deal with statutes, they frequently are forced to search the case reporters to find out how the courts interpreted a law in which they are interested.

Constitutional Law

Great Britain does not have a written **constitution.** The United States does have a written constitution, and it is an important source of our law. In fact, there are many constitutions in this country: the federal Constitution, state constitutions, city charters, and so forth. All of these documents accomplish the same ends. First, they provide the plan for the organization of the government. Next, they outline the duties, responsibilities, and powers of the various elements of government. Finally, they usually guarantee certain basic rights to the people, such as freedom of speech and freedom to peaceably assemble.

Legislative bodies may enact statutes rather easily by a majority vote. It is far more difficult to adopt or change a constitution. State constitutions are approved or changed by a direct vote of the people. It is even more difficult to change the federal Constitution. An amendment may be proposed by a vote of two-thirds of the members of both the United States House of Representatives and the Senate. Alternatively, two-thirds of the state legislatures can call for a constitutional convention for proposing amendments. Once proposed, the amendments must be approved either by three-fourths of the state legislatures or by three-fourths of the constitutional conventions called in all the states. Congress decides upon which method of ratification or approval is to be used. Because the people have an unusually direct voice in the approval and change of a constitution, constitutions are considered the most important source of United States law.

One Supreme Court justice described a constitution as a kind of yardstick against which all the other actions of government must be measured to determine whether the actions are permissible. The United States Constitution is the supreme law of the land. Any law or other constitution that conflicts with the United States Constitution is unenforceable. A state constitution plays the same role for a state: a statute passed by the Michigan legislature and signed by the governor of that state is clearly unenforceable if it conflicts with the Michigan constitution. And so it goes for all levels of constitutions.

While constitutions tend to be short and infrequently amended, the process of determining what specific areas of these documents mean and whether a specific law or government action violates a certain constitutional provision is a laborious one, usually taking hours and hours and days and days of court time. Consequently, with the exception of the bare-bones documents themselves, the case reporters are once again the repository for the constitutional law that governs the United States.

Twenty-six amendments are appended to the United States Constitution. The first ten of these are known as the Bill of Rights and provide a guarantee of certain basic human rights to all citizens. Included are freedom of speech and freedom of the press, rights you will come to understand more fully in future chapters.

The federal Constitution and the fifty state constitutions are very important when considering mass-media law problems. All fifty-one of these charters contain provisions, in one form or another, that guarantee freedom of speech and freedom of the press. Consequently, any government action that affects in any way the freedom of individuals or mass media to speak or publish or broadcast must be measured against the constitutional guarantees of freedom of expression. There are several reasons why a law limiting speaking or publishing might be declared unconstitutional. The law might be a direct restriction on speech or press that is protected by the First Amendment. For example, an order by a Nebraska judge that prohibited the press from publishing certain information about a pending murder trial was considered a direct restriction on freedom of the press (see *Nebraska Press Association* v. *Stuart,* chapter 7). A criminal obscenity statute or other kinds of criminal laws might be declared unconstitutional because they are too vague. A law must provide adequate notice to a person of ordinary intelligence that his or her contemplated conduct is prohibited by the law. An Indianapolis pornography ordinance that made it a crime to publish pornographic material was declared void, at least in part, because the law's definition of pornography was not specific enough. The law defined pornography as including depictions of "the subordination of women." It is almost impossible to settle in one's own mind upon a single meaning or understanding of that term, noted Judge Sarah Barker (see *American Booksellers Association* v. *Hudnut,* chapter 8). A statute might also be declared to be unconstitutional because it violates what is known as the overbreadth doctrine. A law is overbroad, the Supreme Court said many years ago, if it does not aim specifically at evils within the allowable area of government control but sweeps within its ambit other activities that constitute an exercise of protected expression. Struthers, Ohio, an industrial community where many people worked at night and slept during the day, passed an ordinance that forbade knocking on the door or ringing the doorbell at a residence in order to deliver a handbill. The Supreme Court ruled that the ordinance was overbroad, that the city's objective could be obtained by passing an ordinance making it an offense for any person to ring a doorbell of a householder who had, through a sign or some other means, indicated that he or she did not wish to be disturbed. As written, however, the law prohibited persons from distributing handbills to all persons—to those who wanted to see and read them as well as those who did not (see *Martin* v. *Struthers,* chapter 2). So there are many reasons why a court might declare a law to be an unconstitutional infringement upon the guarantees of freedom of speech and press.

Administrative Rules

By the latter part of the nineteenth century in the United States, not only had the simple idyllic life of the eighteenth century slipped away, but also the job of governing had become much more complex. Congress was being asked to resolve questions going far beyond such simple matters as budgets, wars, treaties, and the like. Technology created new kinds of problems for the Congress to resolve. Many such issues were complex and required specialized knowledge and expertise which the Congress lacked and could not easily acquire, had it wanted to. Federal agencies were therefore created to deal with these problems.

For example, regulation of the railroads that traversed the nation created numerous problems in the late nineteenth century. Since questions concerning use of these railroads fell within the commerce power of the Congress, that deliberative body was given the task of resolving this complex issue. But railroad regulation involved serious technical matters, and competent regulation required a high level of expertise. To deal with these problems, Congress created the first **administrative agency,** the Interstate Commerce Commission (ICC). This agency was established by legislation and funded by Congress. Its members were appointed by the president and approved by the Congress. Each member served a fixed term in office. The agency was independent of the Congress, the president, and the courts. Its task was (and is) to regulate commerce between the states, a matter that concerned pipelines, shipping, and transportation. The members of the board presumably were somewhat expert in the area before appointment and of course became more so during the course of their term.

Today hundreds of such agencies exist at both federal and state levels. Each agency undertakes to deal with a specific set of problems that are too technical or too large for the legislative branch to handle. Typical is the Federal Communications Commission (FCC), which was created by Congress in 1934. Its task is to regulate broadcasting in the United States, a job that Congress has really never attempted. Its members must be citizens of the United States and are appointed by the president. The single stipulation is that at any one time no more than three of the five individuals on the commission can be from the same political party. The Senate must confirm the appointments.

Congress sketched the broad framework for the regulation of broadcasting in the Federal Communications Act of 1934, and this act is used by the agency as its basic regulatory guidelines. The agency also creates much law itself in administration of the 1934 act. In interpreting provisions, handing down rulings, developing specific guidelines, and the like, the FCC has developed a sizable body of regulations that bind broadcasters. For example, the Federal Communications Act of 1934 states that broadcasters must operate in the public interest, convenience, or necessity. The FCC holds that one aspect of operation in the public interest is to air all sides of a controversial issue to make certain that the audience has access to the full range of opinion on the topic. This general rule gradually emerged during the past forty years as the Fairness Doctrine, a full-blown set of rules created by the FCC that carry the force of law. Broadcasters who fail to live up to these rules can be fined or (rarely) have their license to broadcast taken away.

Persons dissatisfied with rulings by the FCC can go to court and seek a reversal of the commission action. But courts are strictly limited in their power when reviewing decisions by administrative agencies, and can overturn a commission ruling or any other action by an administrative agency in only these limited circumstances: (1) if the original act that established the commission is unconstitutional, (2) if the commission exceeds its authority, (3) if the commission violates its own rules, or (4) if there is no evidentiary basis whatsoever to support the ruling. The reason for these limitations is simple: These agencies were created to bring expert knowledge to bear on complex problems, and the entire purpose for their creation would be defeated if judges with no special expertise in a given area could reverse an agency ruling merely because they had a different solution to a problem.

The case reporters contain some law created by the administrative agencies, but the reports that each of these agencies themselves publish contain much more such law. These reports are also arranged on a case-by-case basis in chronological order. A citation system similar to that used for the case reporters is used in these reports.

As the problems that governments must deal with become more complicated and more numerous, administrative agencies seem to proliferate, and more and more of our law comes from such agencies.

There are other sources of American law. Executives—a governor, a president, a mayor—have the power to make law, in some circumstances, through executive order. The five sources just discussed—common law, law of equity, statutory law, constitutional law, and rules and regulations by administrative agencies—are the most important, however, and are of most concern in this book. First Amendment problems fall under the purview of constitutional law. Libel and invasion of privacy are matters generally dealt with by the common law and the law of equity. Obscenity laws in this country are statutory provisions (although this fact is frequently obscured by the hundreds of court cases in which judges attempt to define the meaning of obscenity). And of course the regulation of broadcasting and advertising falls primarily under the jurisdiction of administrative agencies.

While this section provides a basic outline of the law and is not comprehensive, the information is sufficient to make upcoming material on mass media law understandable.

SUMMARY

There are five important sources of American law. The common law is the oldest source of our law, having developed in England more than six hundred years ago. The law became common throughout Great Britain and reflected the customs of the people. It was easily transported to the New World, and its pragmatic philosophy was highly useful on the rapidly developing North American continent. Fundamental to the common law is the concept that judges should look to the past and follow earlier court rulings called precedents. *Stare decisis* (let the decision stand) is a key concept. But judges have developed the means to change or adapt the common law by modifying, distinguishing, or overruling precedent case law. The common law is not written down in a law book but is collected in volumes that contain the reports of legal decisions. Each case is given its own legal identity through a system of numbered citations.

Equity law, the second source of American law, developed because in some instances the common law was simply too rigid to fairly resolve the real grievances of British subjects. The rules and procedures of equity are far more flexible than those of the common law and permit a judge (equity cases are never heard before a jury) to fashion a solution to unique or unusual problems. A court is permitted under equity law to restrain an individual or a corporation or even a government from taking an action. Under the common law a court can only attempt to compensate the injured party for the damage that results from the action.

Today the greatest volume of American law is generated by Congress, legislatures, city and county councils, and myriad other legislative bodies. This legislation, called statutory law, is the third important source of American law. All criminal laws are statutes. Also, statutes usually deal with problems that affect great numbers of people, and statutes can anticipate problems, whereas the common law cannot. All statutes are collected in codes or statute books. Courts become involved in the development of statutes when they are called upon to interpret the meaning of the words and phrases contained in a statute. Most American law is generated by legislative bodies.

Constitutions, the fourth source of our law, take precedence over all other American law. The United States Constitution is the supreme law of the land. Other laws, whether they spring from common law, equity, legislative bodies, or administrative agencies, cannot conflict with the provisions of the Constitution. Courts are often called upon to interpret the meaning of the provisions of our constitutions (one federal and fifty state constitutions) and through this process can often make these seemingly rigid legal prescriptions adaptable to contemporary problems.

There are thousands of administrative agencies, boards, and commissions in the nation that produce rules and regulations. This administrative law, the fifth source of American law, usually deals with technical and complicated matters requiring levels of expertise that members of traditional legislative bodies do not normally possess. Members of these agencies and commissions are usually appointed by presidents or by governors or mayors, and the agencies are supervised and funded by legislative bodies. Their tasks are narrowly defined, and their rulings, while they carry the force of law, can always be appealed.

THE JUDICIAL SYSTEM

This section gives an introduction to the court system in the United States. Since the judicial branch of our three-part government is the field upon which most of the battles involving communications law are fought, an understanding of the judicial system is essential.

It is technically improper to talk about the American judicial system. There are fifty-one different judicial systems in the United States, one for the federal government and one for each of the fifty states. While each of these systems is somewhat different from all the others, the similarities among the fifty-one systems are much more important than the differences. Each of the systems is divided into two distinct sets of courts—trial courts and appellate courts. Each judicial system is established by a constitution, federal or state. In each system the courts act as the third branch of a common triumvirate of government: a legislative branch, which makes the law; an executive branch, which enforces the law; and a judicial branch, which interprets the law.

Facts Versus the Law

Common to all judicial systems is the distinction between trial courts and appellate courts, and it is important to understand this distinction. Each level of court has its own function: basically, **trial courts** are fact-finding courts and **appellate courts** are law-reviewing courts. Trial courts are the courts of first instance, the place where nearly all cases begin. Juries sit in trial courts, but never in appellate courts. Trial courts are empowered to consider both the facts and the law in a case. Appellate courts consider only the law. The difference between facts and law is significant. The facts are what happened. The law is what should be done about the facts.

The difference between facts and law can be emphasized by looking at an imaginary libel suit that might result when the *River City Sentinel* publishes a story about costs at the Sandridge Hospital.

Ineffective Medications Given to Ill, Injured
SANDRIDGE HOSPITAL OVERCHARGING PATIENTS ON PHARMACY COSTS

Scores of patients at the Sandridge Hospital have been given ineffective medications, a three-week investigation at the hospital has revealed. In addition, many of those patients were overcharged for the medicine they received.

The *Sentinel* has learned that many of the prescription drugs sold to patients at the hospital had been kept beyond the manufacturer's recommended storage period.

Many drugs stored in the pharmacy (as late as Friday) had expiration dates as old as six months ago. Drug manufacturers have told the *Sentinel* that medication used beyond the expiration date, which is stamped clearly on most packages, may not have the potency or curative effects that fresher pharmaceuticals have.

Hospital spokesmen deny giving patients any of the expired drugs, but sources at the hospital say it is impossible for administrators to guarantee that none of the dated drugs were sold to patients.

In addition, the investigation by the *Sentinel* revealed that patients who were sold medications manufactured by Chaos Pharmaceuticals were charged on the basis of 1985 price lists despite the fact that the company lowered prices significantly in 1986.

The Sandridge Hospital sued the newspaper for libel. When the case got to court, the first thing that had to be done was to establish what the facts were—what happened. Both the hospital and the newspaper presented evidence, witnesses, and arguments to support its version of the facts. Several issues had to be resolved. In addition to the general questions of whether the story had been published and whether the hospital had been identified in the story, the hospital had to supply evidence that its reputation had been injured, that its good name had been damaged, that the story was false, and that the newspaper staff had been extremely careless or negligent in the publication of the report. The newspaper will seek to defend itself by attempting to document the story or raise the defense that the report was privileged in some way. Or the newspaper may argue that even if the story is mistaken, it was the result of an innocent error, not negligence on the part of the staff.

All this testimony and evidence establishes the factual record—what actually took place at the hospital. When there is conflicting evidence, the jury decides whom to believe (in the absence of a jury, the judge makes the decision). Suppose the hospital is able to prove by documents that pharmacists in fact had removed the dated medicine from their shelves and simply stored it to return to the manufacturers. Further, the hospital can show that while it did overcharge some patients for Chaos products, it quickly refunded the excess charge to these patients. Finally, attorneys for the hospital demonstrate that the story was prepared by an untrained stringer for the newspaper who used but a single source—a pharmacist who had been fired by Sandridge for using drugs while on the job—to prepare the story and failed to relate to readers the substance of the evidence (which it had when the story was published) presented by the hospital in court. In such a case, a court would likely rule that the hospital had carried its burden of proof, and that no legitimate defense exists for the newspaper. Therefore, the hospital wins the suit. If the newspaper is unhappy with the verdict, it can appeal.

In an appeal, the appellate court does not establish a new factual record. No more testimony is taken. No more witnesses are called. The factual record established by the jury or judge at the trial stands. The appellate court has the power in some kinds of cases (libel suits that involve constitutional issues, for example) to examine whether the trial court properly considered the facts in the case. But normally it is the task of the appellate court to determine whether the law has been applied properly in light of the facts established at the trial. Perhaps the appellate might rule that even with the documentary evidence it presented, the hospital failed to prove that the newspaper story was false. Perhaps the judge erred in allowing certain testimony into evidence or refused to allow a certain witness to testify. Nevertheless, in reaching an opinion the appellate court considers only the law; the factual record established at the trial stands.

What if new evidence is found or a previously unknown witness comes forth to testify? If the appellate court believes that the new evidence is important, it can order a new trial. However, the court itself does not hear the evidence. These facts are given at a new trial.

The important differences between trial and appellate courts have now been pointed out. Other differences will undoubtedly emerge as the specific structure of each court system is discussed.

In the discussion that follows, the federal court system and its methods of operating are considered first, and then some general observations about state court systems are given, based on the discussion of the federal system.

The Federal Court System

The Congress has the authority to abolish every federal court in the land, save the Supreme Court of the United States. The United States Constitution calls for but a single federal court, the Supreme Court. Article III, Section 1 states: "The judicial power of the United States shall be vested in one Supreme Court." The Constitution also gives Congress the right to establish inferior courts if it deems these courts to be necessary. And Congress has, of course, established a fairly complex system of courts to complement the Supreme Court.

The jurisdiction of the federal courts is also outlined in Article III of the Constitution. The jurisdiction of a court is its legal right to exercise its authority. Briefly, federal courts can hear the following cases:

1. Cases that arise under the United States Constitution, United States law, and United States treaties
2. Cases that involve ambassadors and ministers, duly accredited, of a foreign country
3. Cases that involve admiralty and maritime law
4. Cases that involve controversies when the United States is a party to the suit
5. Cases that involve controversies between two or more states
6. Cases that involve controversies between a state and a citizen of another state (we must remember that the Eleventh Amendment to the Constitution states that a state must give its permission before it can be sued)
7. Cases that involve a controversy between citizens of different states

While special federal courts have jurisdiction that goes beyond this broad outline, these are the circumstances in which a federal court may normally exercise its authority. Of the seven categories of cases just listed, categories one and seven account for most of the cases getting to federal court. For example, disputes that involve violations of the myriad federal laws and disputes that involve constitutional rights such as the First Amendment are heard in federal courts. Also, disputes between citizens of different states—what is known as a diversity of citizenship matter—are heard in federal courts. It is very common, for example, for libel suits and invasion of privacy suits against publishing companies to start in federal courts rather than in state courts. If a citizen of Arizona should be libeled by *Time* magazine, the case would very likely be tried in a federal court in the state of Arizona, rather than in a state court. The magazine would look at the tribunal as a more neutral court. But the federal court would still follow Arizona law when hearing the case.

The Supreme Court

The Supreme Court of the United States is the oldest federal court, having been in operation since 1789. The Constitution does not establish the number of justices who will sit on the High Court. That task is left to the Congress. In 1789 the Congress passed the first judiciary act and established the membership of the High Court at six: a chief justice and five associate justices. This number was increased to seven in 1807, to nine in 1837, and to ten in 1863. The Supreme Court had ten members until 1866, when Congress ruled that only seven justices would sit on the high tribunal. Since 1869 the Supreme Court has had eight associate justices and the chief justice of the United States. (Note the title: not chief justice of the Supreme Court, but the chief justice of the United States.)

No attempt to change the size of the Court has occurred since the 1930s, when President Franklin Roosevelt, unhappy about the manner in which it treated some of his New Deal legislation, proposed enlarging the Court. Publicly, Roosevelt argued that serving on the Court was arduous and that the work load for the older judges had become onerous. He sought the power to appoint one new justice for every justice over seventy years of age, to a limit of fifteen justices on the High Court. The public response to the president's plan was strongly negative, and the measure never came to a vote in the Senate. But the president won in the end when James McReynolds, one of the Court's staunchest New Deal foes, retired and Roosevelt was able to appoint a jurist more of his own philosophical bent as a replacement. In addition, following the announcement of the president's judiciary plan, the High Court handed down a ruling that seemed to indicate that one of the formerly anti-New Deal justices (Owen Roberts) had changed his position regarding the president's social and economic programs. Despite a political defeat, Roosevelt got his legislation, and in the end he appointed nine men to the High Court, more than any president except Washington.

The Supreme Court exercises both original and appellate jurisdictions. Under its **original jurisdiction,** which is established in the Constitution, the Supreme Court is the first court to hear a case and acts much like a trial court in ascertaining facts and deciding law. But original jurisdiction is rarely exercised. Legal scholar Henry Abraham reports in *The Judicial Process* that between 1789 and 1979, the High Court rendered decisions under the original jurisdiction clause of the Constitution in only one hundred forty-eight cases. Because the High Court is strictly limited by the Constitution to exercise its original jurisdiction in a few specific instances, and because Congress has given the lower federal courts concurrent jurisdiction with the Supreme Court in those specific instances, few persons begin their lawsuits at the Supreme Court.

The primary task of the Supreme Court is as an appellate tribunal, hearing cases already decided by lower federal courts and state courts of last resort. The appellate jurisdiction of the Supreme Court is established by the Congress, not by the Constitution. A case will come before the Supreme Court of the United States for review in one of two principal ways: on a direct appeal or by way of a writ of certiorari. The certification process is a third way for a case to get to the High Court, but this process is rarely used today. In fact, according to Abraham, the Court hears more cases via its original jurisdiction than through certification. A case may be certified for review when a lower federal court, such as a court of appeal, seeks instructions from the Supreme Court on a legal question. For example, in 1963 the Court of Appeals in the Fifth Circuit certified a question to the Supreme Court about its power to hold Mississippi Governor Ross Barnett in contempt of court. The lower court wanted to know whether its contempt citation against Barnett and Lt. Governor Paul Johnson, Jr., required a trial by jury. The High Court said no (*U.S. v. Barnett*).

In some instances a litigant has a right, guaranteed by federal statute, to carry an appeal to the Supreme Court. This is called a **direct appeal.** In what kinds of instances? Here are three examples:

1. A federal court of appeals has ruled that a state statute violates the United States Constitution or conflicts with a federal law. The state has a right to appeal this decision to the Supreme Court.

2. A federal court declares an act of Congress to be unconstitutional. The United States government has a right to appeal this ruling to the United States Supreme Court.

3. A state court rules that a state law violates the United States Constitution. The state has a right to appeal that decision to the United States Supreme Court.

On the basis of what has been said so far, it appears that the Supreme Court must hear a case that comes to it on direct appeal. This is not true. Since 1928 the Supreme Court has had the right to reject such an appeal "for want of a substantial federal question." About 90 percent of the cases that come before the High Court through the direct appeal process are rejected. So despite the fact that a litigant may appear to have a statutory right to appeal a decision by a lower court to the Supreme Court, the High Court has the power to reject the appeal if the members of the tribunal do not feel that significant legal issues have been presented in the lawsuit.

The much more common way for a case to reach the nation's High Court is via a **writ of certiorari.** No one has the right to such a writ. It is a discretionary order issued by the Court when it feels that an important legal question has been raised. Litigants using both the federal court system and the various state court systems can seek a writ of certiorari. The most important requirement that must be met before the Court will even consider issuing a writ is that a petitioner exhaust all other legal remedies. While there are a few exceptions, this generally means that if a case begins in a federal district court, the trial level court, the **petitioner** must first seek a review by a United States Court of Appeals before bidding for a writ of certiorari. The writ can be sought if the Court of Appeals refuses to hear the case or sustains the verdict against the petitioner. All other legal remedies have then been exhausted. In state court systems every legal appeal possible must be made within the state before seeking a review by the United States Supreme Court. This usually means going through a trial court, an intermediate appeals court, and finally the state supreme court.

When the Supreme Court grants a writ of certiorari, it is ordering the lower court to send the records to the High Court for review. Each request for a writ is considered by the entire nine-member Court, and an affirmative vote of four justices is required before the writ can be granted. The High Court rejects most of the petitions it receives. Again, work load is the key factor. Certain important issues must be decided each term, and the justices do not have the time to consider thoroughly most cases for which an appeal is sought. Term after term, suggestions to reduce the Court's work load are made. At the time this chapter was being prepared Congress was contemplating the establishment of a national appellate court as a five-year experiment to reduce the work load at the Supreme Court. Former Chief Justice Warren Burger pushed the idea of establishing a kind of two-tiered Supreme Court, with the lower tier (the national appellate court) handling what might be considered more routine appeals to give the upper tier (the Supreme Court) more time to focus upon more important, policy-oriented cases. There was, however, a great reluctance in the Congress and the nation to establishing the upper level appellate court. All citizens believe that they should have the right to appeal to the Supreme Court; even if the appeal will probably be rejected, and even if the Court may never hear the case, the right to make the appeal should remain.

Hearing a Case

While the operation of state and federal appellate courts varies from state to state and court to court, these courts have a good deal in common in the way in which they hear and decide a case. So by examining how the Supreme Court operates, we can also learn quite a bit about how other appellate courts operate.

The first thing the Court does is to decide whether it will hear a case, either on appeal or via a writ of certiorari. Once a case is accepted, the attorneys for both sides have the greatest burden of work during the next few months. Oral argument on the case is scheduled, and both sides are expected to submit **legal briefs**—their legal arguments—for the Court to study before the hearing. The greatest burden at this point is on the party seeking appeal, since he or she must provide the Court with a complete record of the lower court proceedings in the case. Included are trial transcripts, lower-court rulings, and all sorts of other materials.

Arguing a matter all the way to the Supreme Court takes a long time, often as long as five years—sometimes longer—from initiation of the suit until the Court gives its ruling. James Hill brought suit in New York in 1953 against Time, Inc., for invasion of privacy. The United States Supreme Court made the final ruling in the case in 1967 (*Time v. Hill,* 1967).* Even at that the matter would not have ended had Hill decided to go back to trial, which the Supreme Court said he must if he wanted to collect damages. He chose not to.

After the nine justices study the briefs (or at least the summaries provided by their law clerks), the **oral argument** is held. For a generation schooled on Perry Mason and Owen Marshall, oral argument before the Supreme Court (or indeed before any court) must certainly seem strange. For one thing, the attorneys are strictly limited as to how much they may say. Each side is given a brief amount of time, often no more than an hour or ninety minutes, to present its arguments. In important cases "friends of the court" (**amici curiae**) are allowed to present briefs and to participate for thirty minutes in the oral arguments. For example, the American Civil Liberties Union often seeks the friend status in important civil rights cases.

Deciding a Case

After the oral argument, which of course is given in open court with visitors welcome, is over, the members of the High Court move behind closed doors to undertake their deliberations. No one is allowed in the discussion room except members of the Court itself—no clerks, no bailiffs, no secretaries. The discussion, which often is held several days after the arguments are completed, is opened by the chief justice. Discussion time is limited, and by being the first speaker the chief justice is in a position to set the agenda, so to speak, for each case—to raise what he or she thinks are the key issues. Next to speak is the justice with the most seniority, and after him or her, the next most senior justice. The Court usually has an average of seventy-five items or cases to dispose of during one conference or discussion day; consequently, brevity is valued. Each justice has just a few moments to state his or her thoughts on the matter.

*The Bibliography at the end of each chapter supplies additional information about the sources and legal cases cited in the text. An explanation of how to locate a given case using its citation is provided on pages 8–9.

After discussion, a tentative vote is taken and recorded by each justice in a small, hinged, lockable docket book. In the voting procedure the junior justice votes first; the chief justice, last.

Under the United States legal system, which is based so heavily upon the concept of court participation in developing and interpreting the law, a simple yes-or-no answer to any legal question is hardly sufficient. More important than the vote, for the law if not for the **litigant,** are the reasons for the decision. Therefore the Supreme Court and all courts that deal with questions of law prepare what are called opinions in which the reasons, or rationale, for the decision are given. One of the justices voting in the majority is asked to write what is called the **Court's opinion.** If the chief justice is in the majority, he or she selects the author of the opinion. If not, the senior associate justice in the majority makes the assignment. Either the chief justice or the senior associate justice can write the opinion.

Opinion writing is a difficult task. Getting five or six or seven people to agree to yes or no is one thing; getting them to agree upon why they say yes or no is something else. The **opinion** must therefore be carefully constructed. After it is drafted, it is circulated among all Court members, who make suggestions or even draft their own opinions. The opinion writer incorporates as many of these ideas as possible into the opinion to retain its majority backing. While all this is done in secret, historians have learned that rarely do court opinions reflect solely the work of the writer. They are more often a conglomeration of paragraphs and pages and sentences from the opinions of several justices.

A justice in agreement with the majority who cannot be convinced to join in backing the Court's opinion has the option of writing what is called a **concurring opinion.** This means that the justice agrees with the outcome of the decision but does so for different reasons than those of the majority.

Justices who disagree with the majority can also write an opinion, either individually or as a group, called a **dissenting opinion.** Dissenting opinions are very important. Sometimes, after the Court has made a decision, it becomes clear that the decision was not the proper one. The issue is often litigated again by other parties who use the arguments in the dissenting opinion as the basis for a legal claim. If enough time passes, if the composition of the Court changes sufficiently, or if the Court members change their minds, the High Court can swing to the views of the original dissenters. This is what happened in the case of *Nye* v. *U.S.* (noted earlier) when the High Court repudiated a stand it had taken in 1918 and supported instead the opinion of Justice Oliver Wendell Holmes, who had vigorously dissented in the earlier decision.

Finally, it is possible for a justice to concur with the majority in part and to dissent in part as well. That is, the justice may agree with some of the things the majority says but disagree with other aspects of the ruling. This kind of stand by a justice, as well as an ordinary concurrence, frequently fractures the Court in such a way that in a six-to-three ruling only three persons subscribe to the Court's opinion, two others concur, the sixth concurs in part and dissents in part, and three others dissent. Such splits by the members of the Court have seemingly become more common in recent years. In several key mass-media law decisions (*Gannett* v. *DePasquale,* 1979 and *Island Trees* v. *Pico,* 1982, for example) such disarray has left substantial confusion among persons vitally interested in the issues.

The Supreme Court can dispose of a case in two other ways. A **per curiam** (by the court) **opinion** can be prepared. This is an unsigned opinion drafted by one or more members of the majority and published as the Court's opinion. Per curiam opinions are not common, but neither are they rare.

Finally, the High Court can dispose of a case with a **memorandum order**— that is, it just announces the vote without giving an opinion. Or the order cites an earlier Supreme Court decision as the reason for affirming or reversing a lower-court ruling. This device is quite common today as the work load of the High Court increases. In cases with little legal importance and in cases in which the issues were really resolved earlier, the Court saves a good deal of time by just announcing its decision.

One final matter in regard to voting remains for consideration: What happens in case of a tie vote? When all nine members of the Court are present, a tie vote is technically impossible. However, if there is a vacancy on the Court, only eight justices hear a case. Even when the Court is full, a particular justice may disqualify himself or herself from hearing a case. When a vote ends in a tie the decision of the lower court is affirmed. No opinion is written. It is almost as if the Supreme Court had never heard the case.

During the circulation of an opinion, justices have the opportunity to change sides, to change their vote. The number and membership in the majority may shift. It is not impossible for the majority to become the minority if one of the dissenters writes a particularly powerful dissent that attracts support from members originally opposed to his opinion. This event is probably very rare. Nevertheless, a vote of the Court is not final until it is announced on decision day, or opinion day. The authors of the various opinions—court opinions, concurrences, and dissents—publicly read or summarize their views. Printed copies of these documents are handed out to the parties involved and to the press.

Are lower courts bound to follow United States Supreme Court decisions? The answer to that is yes and no. Since the Supreme Court is the supervisor of the federal courts, lower federal courts are bound closely by the High Court rulings. Still, occasionally lower federal courts are reluctant to follow the lead of the High Court.

The Supreme Court is not empowered to make a final judgment when it reviews a state court decision. All it can do, as Henry Abraham writes in *The Judicial Process,* is "to decide the federal issue and remand it to the state court below for final judgment 'not inconsistent with this opinion.' " However, new issues can be raised at the lower level by the state courts, and the opportunity to evade the ruling of the Supreme Court always exists. One study undertaken by the *Harvard Law Review* showed that of 175 cases remanded to state courts between 1941 and 1951, 22 of the litigants who won at the High Court level ultimately lost in the state courts following the High Court ruling. As pointed out earlier, because courts operate on a case-by-case basis, the opportunity for defiance beyond the instant case is real.

Finally, courts have no real way to enforce decisions and must depend upon other government agencies for enforcement of their rulings. The job normally falls to the executive branch. If perchance the president decides not to enforce a Supreme Court ruling, no legal force exists to compel him to do so. If former President Nixon, for example, had chosen to refuse to turn over the infamous Watergate tapes after the Court ruled against his arguments of executive privilege, no other agency could have forced him to give up those tapes.

At the same time, there is one force that usually works to see that court decisions are carried out: it is that vague force called public opinion or what political scientists call "legitimacy." People believe in the judicial process; they have faith that what the courts do is probably right. This does not mean that they always agree with court decisions, but they do agree that the proper way to settle disputes is through the judicial process. Jurists help engender this spirit or philosophy by acting in a temperate manner. The Supreme Court, for example, has developed means that permit it to avoid having to answer highly controversial questions in which an unpopular decision could weaken its perceived legitimacy. The justices might call the dispute a political question, a **nonjusticiable matter,** or they may refuse to hear a case on other grounds. When the members of the Court sense that the public is ready to accept a ruling, they may take on a controversial issue. School desegregation is a good example. In 1954 the Supreme Court ruled in *Brown* v. *Board of Education* that segregated public schools violated the United States Constitution. The foundation for this ruling had been laid by a decade of less momentous desegregation decisions and executive actions. By 1954 the nation was prepared for the ruling, and it was generally accepted, even in most parts of the South. The legitimacy of a court's decisions, then, often rests upon prudent use of the judicial power.

Other Federal Courts   The United States Supreme Court is the most visible, perhaps the most glamorous (if that word is appropriate), of the federal courts. But it is not the only federal court nor even the busiest. There are two lower echelons of federal courts, plus various special courts, within the federal system. These special courts, such as the Court of Military Appeals, Court of Claims, Customs Court, and so forth, were created by the Congress to handle special kinds of problems.

Most business in the federal system begins and ends in a district court. This court was created by Congress by the Federal Judiciary Act of 1789, and today in the United States there are nearly one hundred such courts staffed by 515 judges. Every state has at least one United States district court. Some states are divided into two districts: an eastern and western district or a northern and southern district. Individual districts often have more than one judge, sometimes many more than one. The Southern District of New York (a veritable hotbed of litigation), for example, has twenty-seven judges at work full time. Other metropolitan areas frequently have six or eight district judges.

When there is a jury trial, the case is heard in a district court. It has been estimated that about half the cases in United States district courts are heard by a jury.

At the intermediate level in the federal judiciary are the twelve United States courts of appeal. These courts were also created by the Federal Judiciary Act of 1789. Until 1948 these courts were called circuit courts of appeal, a reflection of the early years of the republic when the justices of the Supreme Court "rode the circuit" and presided at the courts-of-appeal hearings. While the title Circuit Courts of Appeal is gone, the nation is still divided into circuits, each of which is served by one court of appeal:

First Circuit: Maine, Massachusetts, New Hampshire, Rhode Island, and Puerto Rico

Second Circuit: Connecticut, New York, and Vermont

Third Circuit: Delaware, New Jersey, Pennsylvania, and Virgin Islands

Fourth Circuit: Maryland, North Carolina, South Carolina, Virginia, and West Virginia

Fifth Circuit: Texas, Mississippi, and Louisiana

Sixth Circuit: Kentucky, Michigan, Ohio, and Tennessee

Seventh Circuit: Illinois, Indiana, and Wisconsin

Eighth Circuit: Arkansas, Iowa, Minnesota, Missouri, Nebraska, North Dakota, and South Dakota

Ninth Circuit: Alaska, Arizona, California, Hawaii, Idaho, Montana, Nevada, Oregon, Washington, Guam, and Northern Mariana Islands

Tenth Circuit: Colorado, Kansas, New Mexico, Utah, Oklahoma, and Wyoming

Eleventh Circuit: Alabama, Florida, Georgia, and the Canal Zone

The twelfth circuit is unnumbered and is known as the Court of Appeals for the District of Columbia.

The courts of appeal are appellate courts, which means that they hear appeals from lower courts and other agencies exclusively. These courts are the last stop for nine out of ten cases in the federal system. Each circuit has nine or more judges. While all judges can hear a single case—**sitting en banc** it is called—more commonly three judges hear a case. It is possible for two judges to hear a case, but this is unusual. In a case of great importance, all the judges hear the case, as in the Pentagon Papers case, when in both the Second Circuit Court and the District of Columbia Circuit Court, all members of the court heard the appeals from the two district courts.

Federal Judges

All federal judges are appointed by the president and must be confirmed by the Senate. The appointment is for life. The only way a federal judge can be removed is by impeachment. Nine federal judges have been impeached: Four were found guilty by the Senate, and the other five were acquitted. Impeachment and trial is a long process and one rarely undertaken.

Political affiliation plays a distinct part in the appointment of federal judges. Democratic presidents usually appoint Democratic judges, and Republican presidents appoint Republican judges. Nevertheless, it is expected that nominees to the federal bench be competent jurists. This is especially true for appointees to the courts of appeal and to the Supreme Court. The Senate must confirm all appointments to the federal courts, a normally perfunctory act in the case of lower-court judges. More careful scrutiny is given nominees to the appellate courts. The Senate has rejected twenty-one men nominated for the Supreme Court either by adverse vote or by delaying the vote so long that the appointment was withdrawn by the president or the president left office and the new chief executive nominated a different individual.

American presidents have used various schemes to select justices to the Supreme Court, but normally most presidents ask the American Bar Association to approve a list of potential nominees. In selecting a justice to the High Court the president obviously seeks a person who reflects some of the president's personal philosophy. Because so many different kinds of issues confront the Court, to find someone who is both "right" on all the issues and professionally competent is virtually impossible. A potential nominee may have the same philosophy on law-and-order issues but may take a stance opposite the president's on labor matters and antitrust law.

While district judges must live in the community in which they work and are therefore clearly sensitive to some public pressure, judges of the courts of appeal and the justices of the Supreme Court are quite isolated from public pressure. Hence, philosophy can change when an individual reaches the Court; judges and justices mature or change in many directions. Liberal President John Kennedy named Justice Byron White to the Supreme Court, but Justice White more often than not has taken the conservative position in recent years. On the other hand conservative President Dwight Eisenhower appointed former Chief Justice Earl Warren and Justice William Brennan, two of the Court's most outstanding liberals in the last half of the twentieth century. It is difficult to predict just which way an appointee will move after reelection or reappointment is no longer a factor.

The State Court System The constitution of every one of the fifty states either establishes a court system in that state or authorizes the legislature to do so. The court system in each of the fifty states is somewhat different from the court system in all the other states. There are, however, more similarities than differences among the fifty states.

The **trial courts** (or court) are the base of each judicial system. At the lowest level are usually what are called courts of limited jurisdiction. Some of these courts have special functions, like a traffic court, which is set up to hear cases involving violations of the motor-vehicle code. Some of these courts are limited to hearing cases of relative unimportance, such as trials of persons charged with misdemeanors, or minor crimes, or civil suits where the damages sought fall below $1,000. The court may be a municipal court set up to hear cases involving violations of the city code. Whatever the court, the judges in these courts have limited jurisdiction and deal with a limited category of problems.

Above the lower-level courts normally exist trial courts of general jurisdiction similar to the federal district courts. These courts are sometimes county courts and sometimes state courts, but whichever they are, they handle nearly all criminal and civil matters. They are primarily courts of original jurisdiction; that is, they are the first courts to hear a case. However, on occasion they act as a kind of appellate court when the decisions of the courts of limited jurisdiction are challenged. When that happens, the case is retried in the trial court—the court does not simply review the law. This proceeding is called hearing a case de novo.

A **jury** is most likely to be found in the trial court of general jurisdiction. It is also the court in which most civil suits for libel and invasion of privacy are commenced (provided the state court has jurisdiction), in which prosecution for violating state obscenity laws starts, and in which many other media-related matters begin.

Above this court may be one or two levels of appellate courts. Every state has a supreme court, although some states do not call it that. In New York, for example, it is called the Court of Appeals, but it is the High Court in the state, the court of last resort. Formerly a supreme court was the only appellate court in most states. As legal business increased and the number of appeals mounted, the need for an intermediate appellate court became evident. Therefore, in more than one-half of the states there is an intermediate court, usually called the court of appeals. This is the court where most appeals end. In some states it is a single court with three or more judges. More often, numerous divisions within the appellate court serve various geographic regions, each division having three or more judges. Since every litigant is normally guaranteed at least one appeal, this intermediate court takes much of the pressure off the High Court of the state. Rarely do individuals appeal beyond the intermediate level.

State courts of appeal tend to operate in much the same fashion as the United States courts of appeal, with cases being heard by small groups of judges, usually three at a time.

Cases not involving federal questions go no further than the High Court in a state, usually called the supreme court. This court—usually a seven- or nine-member body—is the final authority regarding the construction of state laws and interpretation of the state constitution. Not even the Supreme Court of the United States can tell a state supreme court what that state's constitution means. For example, in 1976 the United States Supreme Court ruled that the protection of the First Amendment did not include the right to distribute materials, demonstrate, or solicit petition signatures at privately owned shopping centers (*Hudgens* v. *NLRB*—this case is discussed fully on page 102). In 1980, however, the Supreme Court refused to overturn a decision by the California Supreme Court which declared that students had the right under the California constitution to solicit signatures for a pro-Israeli petition at a private shopping center in Cambell, California. Justice William Rehnquist wrote for the unanimous United States Supreme Court that perhaps the free-speech guarantee in the California constitution is broader than the First Amendment. In any case, the California High Court was the final authority on the state's constitution (*Pruneyard Shopping Center* v. *Robins*).

State supreme court judges—like most state judges—are usually elected. Normally the process is nonpartisan, but because they are elected and must stand for reelection periodically, state court judges are generally a bit more politically motivated than their federal counterparts. In some states the judges or justices are appointed, and a few states have experimented with a system that both appoints and elects. Under this scheme, called the **Missouri Plan,** the state's High-Court judges (and sometimes all judges) are appointed to the bench by the governor from a list supplied by a nonpartisan judicial commission. After a one-year term, the judge must stand before the people during a general election and win popular support. The voter's ballot asks "Shall Judge Smith be retained in office?" If Judge Smith wins support, his next term is usually a long one, up to twelve years. If support is not forthcoming, a new person is selected to fill the seat for one year, and at the end of the term the judge must seek voter approval.

The advantages of the Missouri Plan are appointment of a qualified person initially and eventual citizen participation in the selection process.

Judicial Review

One of the most important powers of courts and at one time one of the most controversial is the power of **judicial review**—that is, the right of any court to declare any law or official governmental action invalid because it violates a constitutional provision. We usually think of this in terms of the United States Constitution. However, a state court can declare an act of its legislature to be invalid because the act conflicts with a provision of the state constitution. Theoretically, any court can exercise this power. The Circuit Court of Lapeer County, Michigan, can rule that the Environmental Protection Act of 1972 is unconstitutional because it deprives citizens of their property without due process of law, something guaranteed by the Fifth Amendment to the federal Constitution. But this action isn't likely to happen, because a higher court would quickly overturn such a ruling. In fact, it is rather unusual for any court—even the United States Supreme Court—to invalidate a state or federal law on grounds that it violates the Constitution. Less than 130 federal statutes have been overturned by the courts in the nearly two-hundred-year history of the United States. During the same period, about 950 state laws and state constitutional provisions have been declared invalid. Judicial review is therefore not a power that the courts use excessively. In fact, a judicial maxim states: When a court has a choice of two or more ways in which to interpret a statute, the court should always interpret the statute in such a way that it is constitutional.

Judicial review is extremely important when matters concerning regulations of the mass media are considered. Because the First Amendment prohibits laws that abridge freedom of the press and freedom of speech, each new measure passed by the Congress, by state legislatures, and even by city councils and township boards must be measured by the yardstick of the First Amendment. Courts have the right, in fact have the duty, to nullify laws and executive actions and administrative rulings that do not meet the standards of the First Amendment. While many lawyers and legal scholars rarely consider constitutional principles in their work and rarely seek judicial review of a statute, attorneys who represent newspapers, magazines, broadcasting stations, and motion-picture theaters constantly deal with constitutional issues, primarily those of the First Amendment. The remainder of this book will illustrate the obvious fact that judicial review, a concept at the very heart of American democracy, plays an important role in maintaining the freedom of the American press, even though the power is not included in the Constitution.

Lawsuits

The final topic which needs to be understood before mass media law itself is considered is what happens in a lawsuit. The brief discussion of the process which follows is simplified as much as possible. Many good books on the subject are available for persons interested in going further into the intricacies of lawsuits (some are listed in the Bibliography at the end of the chapter).

The party who commences a civil action is called the **plaintiff,** the person who brings the suit. The party against whom the suit is brought is called the **defendant.** In a libel suit the person who has been libeled is the plaintiff and is the one who starts the suit against the defendant—the newspaper, the magazine, the television station, or whatever. To file a civil suit is a fairly simple process. A civil suit is usually a dispute between two private parties. The government offers its good offices—the courts—to settle the matter. A government can bring a civil suit such as an antitrust action against someone, and an individual can bring a civil action against the government. But normally a civil suit is between private parties. (In a criminal action, the government always initiates the action.)

To start a civil suit the plaintiff first picks the proper court, one that has jurisdiction in the case. Then the plaintiff presents the charges in the form of a **civil complaint.** The plaintiff also summons the defendant to appear in court to answer the charges. If the defendant chooses not to answer the charges, he or she normally loses the suit by default. After the complaint is filed, a hearing is scheduled. Then the plaintiff prepares a more detailed set of charges and arguments called **pleadings,** a very formal written statement of the charge and the remedy sought. Usually the remedy involves money damages.

The defendant then prepares his or her own set of pleadings, which constitute an answer to the plaintiff's charges. If there is little disagreement at this point about the facts—what happened—and that a wrong has been committed, the plaintiff and the defendant might settle their differences out of court. The defendant might say, "I guess I did libel you in this article, and I really don't have a very good defense. You asked for $15,000 in damages, would you settle for $7,500 and keep this out of court?" The plaintiff might very well answer yes, because a court trial is costly and takes a long time, and the plaintiff can also end up losing the case. Smart lawyers try to keep their clients out of court if possible and settle matters in somebody's office.

If there is disagreement, the case is likely to continue. A common move for the defendant to make at this point is to file a motion to dismiss, or a **demurrer.** In such a motion the defendant says this to the court: "I admit that I did everything the plaintiff says I did. On June 5, 1986, I did publish an article in which he was called a socialist. But, Your Honor, it is not libelous to call someone a socialist." The plea made then is that even if everything the plaintiff asserts is true, the plaintiff is not legally wronged. The law cannot help the plaintiff. The court might grant the motion, in which case the plaintiff can appeal. Or the court might refuse to grant the motion, in which case the defendant can appeal. If the motion to dismiss is ultimately rejected by all the courts up and down the line, a trial is then held. It is fair play for the defendant at that time to begin argument of the facts, in other words to deny that his newspaper published the article containing the alleged libel.

Before the trial is held, the judge may schedule a conference between both parties in an effort to settle the matter before starting the formal hearing or at least to narrow the issues so that the trial can be shorter and less costly. If this move fails, the trial goes forward. If the facts are agreed upon by both sides and the question is merely one of law, a judge without a jury hears the case. There are no witnesses and no testimony, only legal arguments before the court. If the facts are disputed, the case can be tried before either a jury or, again, only a judge. Note that both sides must waive the right to a jury trial. In this event, the judge becomes both the fact finder and the lawgiver. Now, suppose that the case is heard by a jury. After all the testimony is given, all the evidence is presented, and all the arguments are made, the judge instructs the jury in the law. Instructions are often long and complex, despite attempts by judges to simplify them. **Judicial instructions** guide the jury in determining guilt or innocence if certain facts are found to be true. The judge will say that if the jury finds that X is true and Y is true and Z is true, then it must find for the plaintiff, but if the jury finds that X is not true, but that R is true, then it must find for the defendant.

After deliberation the jury presents its **verdict,** the action by the jury. The judge then announces the **judgment of the court.** This is the decision of the court. The judge is not always bound by the jury verdict. If he or she feels that the jury verdict is unfair or unreasonable, the judge can reverse it and rule for the other party. Needless to say this happens rarely.

If either party is unhappy with the decision, an appeal can be taken. At that time the legal designations change. The person seeking the appeal becomes the **appellant,** or **petitioner.** The other party becomes the **appellee,** or **respondent.** The name of the party initiating the action is listed first in the name of the case. For example: Smith sues Jones for libel. The case name is *Smith* v. *Jones*. Jones loses and takes an appeal. At that point Jones becomes the party initiating the action and the case becomes *Jones* v. *Smith*. This change in designations often confuses novices in their attempt to trace a case from trial to final appeal. If Jones wins the appeal and Smith decides to appeal to a higher court, the case again becomes *Smith* v. *Jones*.

The end result of a successful civil suit is usually awarding of money **damages.** Sometimes the amount of damages is guided by the law, as in a suit for infringement of copyright in which the law provides that a losing defendant pay the plaintiff the amount of money he or she might have made if the infringement had not occurred, or at least a set number of dollars. But most of the time the damages are determined by how much the plaintiff seeks, how much the plaintiff can prove he or she lost, and how much the jury thinks the plaintiff deserves. It is not a very scientific means of determining the dollar amount.

A **criminal suit** is like a civil suit in many ways. The procedures are more formal, are more elaborate, and involve the machinery of the state to a greater extent. The state brings the charges, usually through the county or state prosecutor. The defendant can be apprehended either before or after the charges are brought. In the federal system persons must be indicted by a **grand jury,** a panel of twenty-one citizens, before they can be charged with a serious crime. But most states do not use grand juries in that fashion, and the law provides that it is sufficient that the prosecutor issue an **information,** a formal accusation. After being charged, the defendant is arraigned. An **arraignment** is the formal reading of the charge. It is at the arraignment that the defendant makes a formal plea of guilty or not guilty. If the plea is guilty, the judge then gives the verdict of the court and passes sentence, but usually not immediately, for presentencing reports and other procedures must be undertaken. If the plea is not guilty, a trial is then scheduled.

Some state judicial systems have an intermediate step called a preliminary hearing or preliminary examination. The preliminary hearing is held in a court below the trial court, such as a municipal court, and the state has the responsibility of presenting enough evidence to convince the court—only a judge—that a crime has been committed and that there is sufficient evidence to believe that the defendant might possibly be involved.

In both a civil suit and a criminal case, the result of the trial is not enforced until the final appeal is exhausted. That is, a money judgment is not paid in civil suits until defendants exhaust all of their appeals. The same is true in a criminal case. Imprisonment or payment of a fine is not required until the final appeal. However, if the defendant is dangerous or if there is some question that the defendant might not surrender when the final appeal is completed, bail can be required. Bail is money given to the court to ensure appearance in court.

SUMMARY

There are fifty-one different judicial systems in the nation: one federal system and one for each of the fifty states. Courts within each of these systems are divided into two general classes—trial courts and appellate courts. In any lawsuit both the facts and the law must be considered. The facts or the factual record is an account of what happened to prompt the dispute. The law is what should be done to resolve the dispute. Trial courts determine the facts in the case; then the judge applies the law. Appellate courts, using the factual record established by the trial court, determine whether the law was properly applied by the lower court and whether proper judicial procedures were followed. Trial courts exercise original jurisdiction almost exclusively; that is, they are the first courts to hear a case. Trial courts have very little discretion over which cases they will and will not hear. Appellate courts exercise appellate jurisdiction almost exclusively; that is, they review the work done by the lower courts when decisions are appealed. While the intermediate appellate courts (i.e., courts of appeal; the appellate division) have limited discretion in the selection of cases, the High Courts (supreme courts) in the states and the nation generally have the power to select the cases they wish to review.

Federal courts include the Supreme Court of the United States, the courts of appeal, the United States district courts, and several specialized tribunals.

These courts have jurisdiction in all cases that involve the United States Constitution, United States law, and United States treaties; in disputes between citizens of different states; and in several less important instances. In each state there are trial-level courts and a court of last resort, usually called the supreme court. In about half of the states there are intermediate appellate courts as well. State courts generally have jurisdiction in all disputes between citizens of their state that involve the state constitution or state law.

Judicial review is the power of a court to declare a statute, regulation, or executive action to be a violation of the Constitution and invalid. Because the First Amendment to the United States Constitution guarantees the rights of freedom of speech and freedom of the press, all government actions that relate to the communication of ideas and information face potential scrutiny by the courts to determine their validity.

There are two basic kinds of lawsuits—civil suits and criminal suits. A civil suit is normally a dispute between two private parties in which the government offers its good offices (the courts) to resolve the dispute. The person who initiates the civil suit is called the plaintiff; the person at whom the suit is aimed is called the defendant. A plaintiff who wins a civil suit is normally awarded money damages.

A criminal case is normally an action in which the state brings charges against a private individual, who is called the defendant. A defendant who loses a criminal case can be assessed a fine, jailed, or in extreme cases executed. A jury can be used in both civil and criminal cases. The jury becomes the fact finder and renders a verdict in a case. But the judge issues the judgment in the case. In a civil suit a judge can reject any jury verdict and rule in exactly the opposite fashion, finding for either plaintiff or defendant if the judge feels the jury has made a serious error in judgment. Either side can appeal the judgment of the court. In a criminal case the judge can take the case away from the jury and order a dismissal, but nothing can be done about an acquittal, even an incredible acquittal, as Charles Rembar notes in his book *The Law of the Land*. While a guilty defendant may appeal the judgment, the state is prohibited from appealing an acquittal.

As stated at the outset, this chapter is designed to provide a glimpse, only a glimpse, of both our legal system and our judicial system. The discussion is in no way comprehensive, but it provides enough information to make the remaining eleven chapters meaningful. The chapter is not intended to be a substitute for a good political science course in the legal process. Students of communications law are at a distinct disadvantage if they do not have some grasp of how the systems work and what their origins are.

The United States legal and judicial systems are old and tradition-bound. But they have worked fairly well for these last two hundred years. In the final analysis the job of both the law and the men and women who administer it is to balance the competing interests of society. How this balancing act is undertaken comprises the remainder of this book. The process is not always easy, but it is usually interesting.

BIBLIOGRAPHY

Here is a list of some of the sources that have been helpful in the preparation of chapter 1:

Books

Abraham, Henry. *The Judicial Process.* 4th ed. New York: Oxford University Press, 1980.
_____. *The Judiciary: The Supreme Court in the Governmental Process.* 3d ed. Boston: Allyn & Bacon, 1973.
American Law Institute. *Restatement of the Law of Torts.* St. Paul, Minn.: American Law Institute, 1939.
Blackstone, William. *Commentaries on the Laws of England.* Edited by St. George Tucker. Philadelphia: W. Y. Birch & Abraham Small, 1803.
Franklin, Marc A. *The Dynamics of American Law.* Mineola, N. Y.: Foundation Press, 1968.
Holmes, Oliver W. *The Common Law.* Boston: Little, Brown & Co., 1881.
Pound, Roscoe. *The Development of the Constitutional Guarantees of Liberty.* New Haven: Yale University Press, 1957.
Rembar, Charles. *The Law of the Land.* New York: Simon and Schuster, 1980.
Roche, John P. *Courts and Rights.* 2d ed. New York: Random House, 1966.

Cases

Barber v. *Time,* 159 S.W.2d 291 (1942).
Branzburg v. *Hayes,* 408 U.S. 665 (1972).
Gannett v. *DePasquale,* 99 S.Ct. 2898 (1979).
Goldwater v. *Ginzburg,* 414 F.2d 324 (1969).
Hudgens v. *NLRB,* 424 U.S. 507 (1976).
Island Trees v. *Pico,* 102 S.Ct. 2799 (1982).
New York Times Co. v. *U.S.,* 403 U.S. 713 (1971).
Nye v. *U.S.,* 313 U.S. 33 (1941).
Pruneyard Shopping Center v. *Robins,* 447 U.S. 74 (1980).
Time v. *Hill,* 385 U.S. 374 (1967).
Toledo Newspaper Co. v. *U.S.,* 242 U.S. 402 (1918).
U.S. v. *Barnett,* 376 U.S. 681 (1964).

FREEDOM OF THE PRESS

When people reach the final years of their lives, they often ponder how people will remember them. What aspects of their characters and their contributions to society will people cherish? What will be quickly forgotten? So too is it with nations. Historians outline the important contributions made by ancient Greece and Rome, by imperial Spain, and by the British Empire. What will historians consider the outstanding contributions of America and Americans? William O. Douglas, former associate justice of the Supreme Court of the United States, suggests that United States technology will not be the most memorable aspect of the nation's life. Instead, it will be our experiment with freedom of expression, an experiment shared with other Western democracies. Freedom of speech and freedom of the press—they are the achievements people will look upon with awe in eons to come.

No one knows whether Justice Douglas will be right. Clearly the attempt by Western democracies during the past three centuries to construct societies based upon the freedom to speak, the freedom to publish, and the freedom to criticize the government is a remarkable effort. Perhaps even more remarkable is that the experiment has worked so well. The guarantee of freedom of expression can be found in the constitution of nearly every nation. Only in a few countries such as the United States, however, are the people and the government dedicated to making the ideal come true.

The purpose of this chapter is to sketch a broad outline of the meaning of freedom of the press in the United States today. Freedom of the press is an element in all aspects of mass media law—libel, invasion of privacy, obscenity, regulation of broadcasting, and so forth. Indeed, in any area in which the law touches mass media, the First Amendment is a material consideration. At the same time, broader general principles defining freedom of expression have been fashioned by the courts in the past half-century. It is these broader principles that we will focus upon in chapter 2. ◆

HISTORICAL DEVELOPMENT

Before freedom of the press can be defined, however, a brief look at the roots of the idea, roots that wind through many centuries, is necessary. Freedom of the press is not, and was not, exclusively an American idea. We did not invent the concept—in fact, no one invented it. Like Topsy, it just grew from crude beginnings that can be traced back to Plato and Socrates. The concept developed more fully during the past four hundred years. The modern history of freedom of the press really began in England during the sixteenth and seventeenth centuries as printing developed and grew. Today the most indelible embodiment of the concept is the First Amendment to the United States Constitution, forged in the last half of the eighteenth century by the men who built upon their memory of earlier experiences. To understand the meaning of freedom of the press and freedom of speech, it is necessary to understand the meaning of censorship, for viewed from a negative position freedom of expression can be simply defined as the absence of censorship. To understand censorship it is necessary to look first at the experience of the British who fought to be free from the yoke of government control of printing more than five centuries ago.

Freedom of the Press in England

When William Caxton set up the first British printing press in Westminster in 1476, his printing pursuits were restricted only by his imagination and ability. There were no laws governing what he could or could not print—he was completely free. For five centuries Englishmen and Americans have attempted to regain the freedom that Caxton enjoyed, for shortly after he started publishing, the British Crown began the control and regulation of printing presses in England. Printing developed during a period of great religious struggle in Europe, and it soon became an important tool in that struggle. Printing presses made communication with hundreds of persons fairly easy and in doing so gave considerable power to small groups or individuals who owned and/or could use a printing press.

The British government soon realized that unrestricted publication and printing could seriously dilute its own power. Information is a powerful tool in any society, and the individual or individuals who control the flow and content of the information received by a people exercise considerable control over those people. The printing press broke the Crown's monopoly of the flow of information, and therefore control of printing was essential.

In his study of censorship of the British press during the three hundred years between the establishment of printing in England and the American Revolution, Frederick Siebert (*Freedom of the Press in England*) lists several means used by the Crown to limit or restrict the press. Criticism of the government or of the king or of the great men of the realm was called sedition or **seditious libel** and was considered a serious crime. Whether the criticism was truthful was immaterial. In fact, for many years British courts considered truthful criticism of the government more harmful than untruthful criticism, since untruthful criticism was easier to deny. Truthful criticism could more easily stir the people to dissatisfaction and anger.

The press in England was licensed as well until the 1690s. **Licensing** meant prior censorship, since all printers were forced to get prior approval to publish from the Crown or the Church. **Bonding** ensured that printers followed the rules. Printers were required to put up large sums of money before they were allowed to print. If they violated the law or failed to assist the government in enforcing the law, they forfeited the money and were out of business until they raised another **bond.** The British government granted patents and monopolies to certain printers in exchange for their cooperation in publishing only acceptable material and for their assistance in locating printers who broke the law by printing without permission or by printing seditious material. For their help these printers were granted exclusive rights to publish various categories of books such as spellers, Bibles, and grammar books.

These restraints were just some of the means used by the British between 1476 and 1776 to control printing. While most authorities considered British press control quite effective, this control did not go unchallenged. Men of ideas—writers, philosophers, even statesmen—argued for the rights of free British subjects to enjoy freedom of expression: the right to print without prior restraint and the right to criticize the government and the Church without punishment. Some notions regarding freedom of expression emerged from that amorphous doctrine referred to as "the natural rights philosophy." This philosophy, which developed in Europe in the late seventeenth and early eighteenth centuries, asserts that man is a rational, thinking creature and by virtue of the laws of nature may claim certain rights against the state, such as freedom of expression. The growth of democratic government also spurred men to challenge government censorship, for it was strongly believed that democracy would surely fail without guarantees of freedom of expression. The flow of information within the society was the essential lubricant of the democratic process. So a mixture of philosophy and pragmatism fueled the protests against government control of the press.

The men who drafted the United States Constitution were well acquainted with these ideas, as well as with British censorship and control of the press. In addition, the founding fathers could draw upon firsthand experience of British control of the press in the American colonies.

Freedom of the Press in Colonial America

There were laws in the United States restricting freedom of the press for almost thirty years before the first newspaper was published. As early as 1662, statutes in Massachusetts made it a crime to publish anything without first getting prior approval from the government, twenty-eight years before Benjamin Harris published the first—and last—edition of *Publick Occurrences.* The second and all subsequent issues of the paper were banned because Harris had failed to get permission to publish the first edition, which contained material construed to be criticism of British policy in the colonies, as well as a report that scandalized the Massachusetts clergy because it said the French king took immoral liberties with a married woman (not his wife).

Despite this inauspicious beginning, American colonists had a much easier time getting their views into print (and staying out of jail) than their counterparts in England. There was censorship, but American juries were reluctant to convict printers prosecuted by the British colonial authorities. The colonial governments were less efficient than the government in England. Also, the British had only limited control over the administration of government in many of the colonies.

The British attempted to use sedition laws to control the press in America but did not attempt to organize guilds or printing monopolies. Licensing, which died in England in 1695, continued until the 1720s in the colonies. In 1723 the government of Massachusetts forbade printer James Franklin to publish the *New England Courant* or any similar newspaper or pamphlet without government supervision. Franklin, who was Benjamin Franklin's older brother, had angered officials by charging in his newspaper that the colonial government was ineffective in protecting coastal communities from raids by bands of pirates. This restraint was the dying gasp of licensing in America.

The few taxes on the press were legitimate taxes levied to raise revenues, not to censor the press. The taxes were generally ignored by publishers and printers. The most widely known tax, the Stamp Act of 1765, succeeded only in increasing disgust toward and hatred of Parliament and the king. The stamps were poorly distributed, not being available in many communities. Newspaper publishers, who were supposed to buy the stamps and affix one to each copy of papers printed and sold, devised a multitude of schemes to avoid the tax. Some publishers removed the nameplate (the name of the paper) from the first page and declared they no longer published newspapers, but pamphlets, which were not subject to the tax. Others defied the law with little fear of retribution.

Government censorship of the press was widely publicized throughout the colonies for the first time when John Peter Zenger was tried for seditious libel in 1735. However, this was not the first time the Crown had attempted to use sedition law to silence the American press. Professor Harold L. Nelson reports that at least four sedition cases were tried prior to the Zenger trial (*American Journal of Legal History*, 1959).

The Zenger trial has attained an important place in American political mythology in the 250 years since it concluded. Unfortunately, the importance of both the man and the trial have been exaggerated with the passage of time. This is not to say that what John Peter Zenger and his attorneys accomplished was unimportant. But it was the recalcitrant jury of American yeomen that really deserves an accolade. The trial should probably stand as a monument to the jury system, if it is to be remembered at all.

John Peter Zenger was an immigrant printer who was prosecuted because the newspaper he published, the *New York Weekly Journal,* contained statements that were critical of both Governor William Cosby and the state government. The *Journal* was sponsored by Lewis Morris and James Alexander, political opponents of the unpopular state governor. Morris was a wealthy politician who had his envious eye on the money that could be made from land speculation by the man who sat in the governor's mansion.

The first edition of the *New York Weekly Journal* appeared on November 5, 1733. The attacks on Cosby in subsequent editions were relentless, and in November 1734 Zenger found himself in jail, accused of printing and publishing seditious libels that "tended to raise factions and tumults in New York, inflaming the minds of the people against the government, and disturbing the peace." Since Zenger was one of only two printers in the colony (the other printed a progovernment newspaper), Morris and Alexander had to get him out of jail if they were to continue publication of the *Journal*.

A court-appointed attorney, John Chambers, prepared to defend Zenger as the trial opened in August 1735. He was ably assisted by Andrew Hamilton, a fifty-nine-year-old Scots attorney and a renowned criminal lawyer whose interest in the case led him to come from Philadelphia to participate in the defense. There was little dispute that Zenger had published what eighteenth-century law defined as seditious libels against the governor and the government. For this he should have been convicted under British law. But Zenger's attorneys appealed to the conscience of the jury and argued that the law was wrong. No man should be imprisoned or fined for publishing criticism of the government that was truthful and fair. The jury agreed and found the German printer not guilty. In doing so the jurymen ignored the law; it was a simple case of what is called "a jury revolt."

There are three important facts to remember about the case. First, the law of seditious libel did not change because of the jury verdict. Following the Zenger case it was still considered a crime to criticize the government in New York. Second, the outcome of this case and others forced government prosecutors to reconsider the usefulness of sedition laws as a means of silencing opposition to the government. We can find no records of sedition trials in the colonial courts following the *Zenger* case. Finally, the trial of John Peter Zenger was widely publicized both in this country and in England, and became a rallying point for foes of government censorship of the press. James Alexander published an account of the trial that was widely circulated. It was through such publicity that the case began to take on its stature as an event somewhat larger than life.

After Zenger's trial, government strategy changed. Rather than haul printers and editors before juries often hostile to the state, the government hauled printers and editors before legislatures and state assemblies that were usually hostile to journalists. The charge was not sedition, but breach of parliamentary privilege or contempt of the assembly. There was no distinct separation of powers then, and the legislative body could order the printer to appear, question him, convict him, and penalize him. The same kinds of criticism that had previously provoked a sedition trial now resulted in a trial before a colonial assembly. Only the basis of the charge was changed. In a contempt hearing the printer was now accused of questioning the authority of the assembly, detracting from its honor, affronting its dignity, or impeaching its behavior, rather than of arousing general dissatisfaction among the people. Professor Nelson estimates that probably a large number of persons were brought before legislatures on such charges, but much more research is needed before all that happened during that period is known. We do know that repression of this kind was powerful and not uncommon.

Yet despite these potent sanctions occasionally levied against publishers and printers, the press of this era was remarkably robust. Researchers who have painstakingly read the newspapers and pamphlets and handbills produced in the last half of the eighteenth century are struck by the seeming lack of concern for government retribution or censorship. Historian Leonard Levy notes in a recent book, *Emergence of a Free Press,* the seeming paradox uncovered by scholars who seek to understand the meaning of freedom of expression during that era. "To one [a scholar] whose prime concern was law and theory, a legacy of suppression [of the press] came into focus; to one who looks at newspaper judgments on public men and measures, the revolutionary controversy spurred an expanding legacy of liberty," he wrote.

But the appearance of such freedom can be deceptive, as political scientist John Roche points out in his book *Shadow and Substance,* for the community often exerted tremendous pressure upon anyone who expressed an unpopular idea. The belief of many persons that freedom was the hallmark of society in America ignores history, Roche argues. In colonial America the people simply did not understand that freedom of thought and expression meant freedom for the other fellow also, particularly for the fellow with hated ideas. Roche points out that colonial America was an open society dotted with closed enclaves—villages and towns and cities—in which citizens generally shared similar beliefs about religion and government and so forth. Citizens could hold any belief they chose and could espouse that belief, but personal safety depended upon the people in a community agreeing with a speaker or writer. If they didn't, the speaker then kept quiet or moved to another enclave where the people shared his ideas. While there was much diversity of thought in the colonies, there was often little diversity of belief within towns and cities, according to Roche.

they kiss ass like its' part of their diet

The propaganda war that preceded the Revolution is a classic example of the situation. In Boston, the Patriots argued vigorously for the right to print what they wanted in their newspapers, even criticism of the government. Freedom of expression was their right, a God-given right, a natural right, a right of all British subjects. Many persons, however, did not favor revolution or even separation from England. Yet it was extremely difficult to publish such pro-British sentiments in many American cities after 1770. Printers who published such ideas in newspapers and handbills did so at their peril in many instances. In cities like Boston the printers were attacked, their shops were wrecked, and their papers were destroyed. Freedom of the press was a concept with limited utility in many communities for colonists who opposed revolution once the Patriots had moved the populace to their side. In other cities where the pro-British citizens held the upper hand, colonists seeking independence published in fear for their safety.

The plight of the pro-British printer in Boston in the 1770s was not a unique chapter in American history. Such community censorship still exists today in all parts of the nation. Ask the druggist who seeks to sell *Playboy* or *Penthouse* magazine in his suburban pharmacy. Ask the small-town theater owner who wants to show a rather explicit R-rated film. Ask the small-town newspaper editor who seeks to publish the names of local men who have been arrested for soliciting an act of prostitution. Ask the television station manager who seeks to telecast a controversial documentary on abortion. The cure for these ills is education and maturity. An educated person understands that a free society cannot long tolerate even the informal suppression of freedom of expression. A tolerance of censorship can develop that makes a people an easy prey for dictatorship. A mature citizen understands that the right to disagree about ideas and values and religious beliefs is the essence of a democracy. And no individual's freedom is secure unless the freedom of all is ensured.

SUMMARY

Freedom of the press is a part of the great Anglo-American legal tradition, but it is a right that has been won only through many hard-fought battles. The British discovered the power of the press in the early sixteenth century and devised numerous schemes to restrict publication. Criticism of the government, called seditious libel, was outlawed. Licensing or prior censorship was also common. In addition, the Crown for many years used an elaborate system of patents and monopolies to control printing in England.

While under British law for more than one hundred years, American colonists enjoyed somewhat more freedom of expression than did their counterparts in England. Censorship laws existed before the first printing press arrived in North America, but they were enforced erratically or not at all. Licensing ended in the United States colonies in the 1720s. There were several trials for sedition in the colonies, but the acquittal of John Peter Zenger in

1735 by a recalcitrant jury ended that threat. Colonial legislatures and assemblies then attempted to punish dissident printers by using their contempt power. By the time the American colonists began to build their own governments in the 1770s and 1780s, they had the history of a three-hundred-year struggle for freedom of expression upon which to build.

THE FIRST AMENDMENT

In 1781, even before the end of the Revolutionary War, the new nation adopted its first constitution, the Articles of Confederation. The Articles provided for a loose-knit confederation of the thirteen colonies, or states, in which the central or federal government had little power. The Articles of Confederation did not contain a guarantee of freedom of expression. In fact, it had no bill of rights of any kind. The men who drafted this constitution did not believe such guarantees were necessary. Under these articles states were the most powerful political entities; the national government had few prerogatives. Guarantees of freedom of expression were already a part of the constitutions of most of the thirteen states. The citizens of Virginia, for example, had adopted a new constitution that contained a declaration of rights in June 1776, five years before the Articles of Confederation were written. Freedom of the press was guaranteed as a part of that declaration of rights. Other states soon followed Virginia's lead.

But the system of government created by the Articles of Confederation did not work very well. In the hot summer of 1787, each of the thirteen states sent a handful of its best men to Philadelphia to revise or amend the Articles, to make fundamental changes in the structure of the government.

The New Constitution

It was a remarkable group of men; perhaps no such group has gathered before or since. The members were merchants and planters and professional men, and none were full-time politicians. As a group these men were by fact or inclination members of the economic, social, and intellectual aristocracy of their respective states. These men shared a common education centered around history, political philosophy, and science. Some of them spent months preparing for the meeting—studying the governments of past nations. While some members came to modify the Articles of Confederation, many others knew from the start that a new constitution was needed. In the end that is what they produced, a new governmental charter. The charter was far different from the Articles in that it gave vast powers to a central government. The states remained supreme in some matters, but in other matters they were forced to relinquish their sovereignty to the new federal government.

No official record of the convention was kept. The delegates deliberated behind closed doors as they drafted the new charter. However, some personal records remain. We do know, for example, that inclusion of a bill of rights in the new charter was not discussed until the last days of the convention. The Constitution was drafted in such a way as not to infringe upon state bills of rights. When the meeting was in its final week, George Mason of Virginia indicated his desire that "the plan be prefaced with a Bill of Rights. . . . It would give great quiet to the people," he said, "and with the aid of the state declarations, a bill might be prepared in a few hours." Few joined Mason's call. Only one delegate, Roger Sherman of Connecticut, spoke against the suggestion. He said he favored protecting the rights of the people when it was necessary, but in this case there was no need. "The state declarations of rights are not repealed by this Constitution; and being in force are sufficient." He said that where the rights of the people are involved Congress could be trusted to preserve the rights. The states, voting as units, unanimously opposed Mason's plan. While the Virginian later attempted to add a bill of rights in a piecemeal fashion, the Constitution emerged from the convention and was placed before the people for ratification without a bill of rights.

The new Constitution was not without opposition. The struggle for its adoption was hard fought. The failure to include a bill of rights in the document was a telling complaint raised against the new constitution. Even Thomas Jefferson, who was in France, lamented, in a letter to his friend James Madison, the lack of a guarantee of political rights in the charter. When the states finally voted on the new constitution, it was approved, but only after supporters in several states had promised to petition the first Congress to add a bill of rights.

James Madison was elected from Virginia to the House of Representatives, defeating James Monroe for the House seat only after promising his constituents to work in the first Congress toward adoption of a declaration of human rights. When Congress convened, Madison worked to keep his promise. He first proposed that the new legislature incorporate a bill of rights into the body of the Constitution, but the idea was later dropped. That the Congress would adopt the declaration was not a foregone conclusion. There was much opposition, but after several months, twelve amendments were finally approved by both houses and sent to the states for ratification. Madison's original amendment dealing with freedom of expression states: "The people shall not be deprived or abridged of their right to speak, to write or to publish their sentiments and freedom of the press, as one of the great bulwarks of liberty, shall be inviolable." Congressional committees changed the wording several times, and the section guaranteeing freedom of expression was merged with the amendment guaranteeing freedom of religion and freedom of assembly. The final version is the version we know today:

> Congress shall make no law respecting an establishment of religion, or prohibiting the free exercise thereon; or abridging the freedom of speech, or of the press; or the right of the people peaceably to assemble, and to petition the Government for a redress of grievance.

The concept of the "first freedom" has been discussed often. Historical myth tells us that because the amendment occurs first in the Bill of Rights it was considered the most important right. In fact, in the Bill of Rights presented to the states for ratification, the amendment was listed third. Amendments one and two were defeated and did not become part of the Constitution. The original First Amendment called for a fixed schedule that apportioned seats in the House of Representatives on a ratio many persons thought unfair. The Second Amendment prohibited senators and representatives from altering their salaries until after a subsequent election of representatives. Both amendments were rejected, and amendment three became the First Amendment.

Passage of the last ten amendments did not occur without struggle. Not until two years after being transmitted to the states for approval did a sufficient number of states adopt the amendments for them to become part of the Constitution. Connecticut, Georgia, and Massachusetts did not ratify the Bill of Rights until 1941, a kind of token gesture on the 150th anniversary of its constitutional adoption. In 1791 approval by these states was not needed, since only three-fourths of the former colonies needed to agree to the measures.

Freedom of Expression in the Eighteenth Century

What did the First Amendment mean to the people who supported its ratification in 1790? This is not an idle question. The Bill of Rights was, after all, approved by a vote of the people in the several states. By their votes of approval, they enacted into the supreme law of the land their definitions of such rights as freedom of the press. Technically, the definition of freedom of the press approved by the nation when the First Amendment was ratified in 1791 is what is guaranteed today. To enlarge or narrow that definition requires another vote of the people, a constitutional amendment.

But most people today consider this notion so much legalistic poppycock. The nation has changed dramatically in two hundred years. Television, radio, and film did not exist in 1790, for example. Does this mean that the guarantees of the First Amendment should not apply to these mass media? Of course not. Our Constitution has lasted for two hundred years because it has been somewhat elastic. The United States Supreme Court, our final arbiter on the meaning of the Constitution, has helped adapt the document to changing times.

Still, it is important that we respect the document that was adopted almost two hundred years ago. If we stray too far from its original meaning, the document may become meaningless; there will be no rules of government. Anarchy will be but a step away.

So what did the First Amendment mean in 1790? One theory, held by most scholars until about twenty-five years ago, is that freedom of expression included the right to be free from **prior restraint** (prior censorship) and the right to criticize the government without fear of punishment. Freedom from prior restraint was supposedly guaranteed to all British subjects, as well as

American subjects, even before the Revolution. Sir William Blackstone, a British legal scholar, published a major four-volume summary of the common law between 1765 and 1769. In this summary, *Commentaries on the Law of England,* Blackstone defined freedom of expression as "laying no previous restraints upon publication." Today we call that no prior censorship.

In addition to prohibiting prior censorship, the First Amendment also precludes punishment of persons who criticize the government, according to many American legal scholars. After all, they argue, one of the reasons for the Revolution was to rid the nation of the hated British sedition law. The First Amendment surely must guarantee unrestricted political discussion.

This latter view was strongly challenged in 1960 in a book entitled *Legacy of Suppression* by historian Leonard Levy. Levy argued, with considerable supporting evidence, that the common legal definition of freedom of the press in 1790 included only freedom from prior censorship. The crime of seditious libel remained intact following the adoption of the First Amendment and was not philosophically challenged until the late 1790s during the fierce debate over the constitutionality of the Alien and Sedition Laws of 1798 (see pages 55–56 for a discussion of these laws). Freedom of the press, then, had a limited meaning for the generation that drafted the First Amendment.

Levy revised this thesis somewhat in 1985 in his revised edition of *Legacy of Suppression,* which he titled *The Emergence of a Free Press.* His ideas had been seriously challenged by scholars who had actually looked at the publications that appeared during this era and noted a robust press that was not afraid to criticize the government. Levy too looked at the newspapers and pamphlets produced during the era and was forced to conclude that the press that existed at that time seemed to have little fear of prosecution for seditious libel. Levy has now concluded that while the law of sedition in fact remained in force after the adoption of the First Amendment and the press was technically bound by this restriction, in fact publishers and printers ignored this law with few serious consequences. Hence the paradoxical situation of "nearly unfettered press practices in a [political] system characterized by legal fetters," Levy notes. The truth is that we probably still don't really know what freedom of the press meant to American citizens two hundred years ago.

The written residue of the period reveals only a partial story. Undoubtedly, in 1790 the First Amendment's guarantee of freedom of expression meant different things to different people. In fact, one can speculate that the inherent vagueness in the constitutional guarantee enhanced its chances of being adopted. The First Amendment could mean almost anything a citizen wanted it to mean. A more specific definition might have prompted heated debate and endangered passage of the First Amendment. This is not to say that there was no definition of freedom of expression in 1790. On the contrary, there were probably many definitions. There was probably little consensus on the exact meaning of the concept, even among those who adopted the First Amendment.

Freedom of
Expression Today

If we are not certain what the First Amendment meant in 1790, do we know what it means today? More or less. The First Amendment means today what the Supreme Court of the United States says it means. Certainly many people often disagree with the definition of freedom of expression rendered by the High Court. But from the standpoint of the law—and that is what this book is about—the Supreme Court defines the meaning of the First Amendment to the Constitution.

The Supreme Court is a collection of nine justices, not a single individual. Consequently, at any given time there can be nine different definitions of freedom of expression. This has never happened—at least, not on important issues. What has happened is that groups of justices have subscribed to various theoretical positions regarding the meaning of the First Amendment. These theories of the meaning of the First Amendment help justices shape their vote on a question regarding freedom of expression. These theories have changed during the past sixty years, the point at which the First Amendment first came under serious scrutiny by the Supreme Court. It is rare that the justices themselves develop such theories. Most theories are proposed by persons outside the court: legal scholars, lower court judges, even philosophers. At some point a jurist finds a comfortable theory and uses it to assist in interpreting the First Amendment.

Legal theories are sometimes like amorphous wraiths—difficult to handle. Judge Learned Hand, a distinguished American jurist, referred to the propagation of legal theory as "shoveling smoke." With such cautions in mind, we will attempt to identify five important First Amendment theories or strategies that have been used or are used today to help judges develop a practical definition of freedom of expression.

Absolutist Theory: The First Amendment declares that "no law" shall abridge the freedom of speech or of the press. "No law" means *no law.* Speech and press are absolutely protected from interference by the government. There are no exceptions. This is what was intended by the men who drafted the First Amendment.

No more than two Supreme Court justices—Hugo Black and William Douglas—have subscribed to this position. Critics of the absolutist theory argue that the key words in the First Amendment are "freedom of speech and press," not "no law." The freedom to speak and publish was not an absolute freedom in 1790; limits to this freedom were accepted by the people. What the amendment means, then, is that "no law" may abridge the limited protection given to the rights to speak and publish. If speech and press were to be protected absolutely, the First Amendment would have been written this way: "Congress shall pass no law abridging speech and press." The absolutist theory has received little public support because it lacks the recognition that other important human rights often conflict with freedom of speech and press.

Ad hoc balancing theory: Freedom of speech and press are two of a number of important human rights we value in this nation. These rights often conflict. When conflict occurs, it is the responsibility of the court to balance the freedom of expression with other values. For example, the government must maintain the military to protect the people from aggression. To function, the military must maintain security about many of its weapons, plans, and movements. Imagine that the press seeks to publish information about a secret weapon system. The right to freedom of expression must be balanced with the need for secrecy in the military.

This theory is called *ad hoc* balancing because the scales are erected anew in every case; the meaning of the freedom of expression is determined solely on a case by case basis. Freedom of the press might outweigh the need for the government to keep secret the design of its new rifle, but the need for secrecy about a new fighter plane might take precedence over freedom of expression.

Ad hoc balancing is really not a theory; it is a strategy. Developing a definition of freedom of expression on a case-by-case basis leads to uncertainty. Under *ad hoc* balancing we will never know what the First Amendment means except as it relates to a specific, narrow problem (e.g., the right to publish information about a new army rifle). If citizens cannot reasonably predict whether a particular kind of expression might be protected or prohibited, they will have the tendency to play it safe and keep silent. This will limit the rights of expression of all persons. Also, *ad hoc* balancing relies too heavily in its final determination on the personal biases of the judge or justices who decide a case.

Preferred position balancing theory: Freedom of expression is the foundation of the United States system of government. Without our ability to speak and publish freely, all other rights have little meaning. Of what value is the right to be free from illegal police searches if complaints about the police after such searches have been made cannot be published? Because it is so important, freedom of expression must be given a preferred status when balanced against other rights. Operationally this means that whenever balancing between freedom of expression and some other interest takes place, a court will presume that the limitation upon freedom of speech or freedom of the press is illegal. It is the responsibility of the persons who seek to block the speech or publication to convince a court that their interests should be given preference. For example, imagine that the navy seeks to block the publication of information about a new fighter plane. The navy must prove to the court that the publication of this material will be harmful to the national interests. Those who seek to publish the material are not obliged to convince the court that publication of the matter will be harmless or that the people have a right to see this information. The burden of proof falls on the navy.

Today, courts use this theory more than any other. While it retains some of the negative features of *ad hoc* balancing, by tilting the scales in favor of freedom of expression it adds somewhat more certainty to our definition of freedom of expression. By basing this balancing strategy upon a philosophical foundation (the maintenance of all rights is dependent upon free exercise of speech and press), it becomes easier to build a case in favor of the broad interpretation of freedom of expression under the First Amendment.

Meiklejohnian theory: Philosopher Alexander Meiklejohn presented the legal community with a rather complex set of ideas about freedom of expression in the late 1940s *(Free Speech and Its Relation to Self-Government)*. Meiklejohn looked at the First Amendment in a pragmatic manner and argued that freedom of expression is worth little as an abstract concept; that its primary value is as a means to an end. That end is successful self-government. Freedom of speech and press are protected in the Constitution so that our system of democracy can function, and that is the only reason they are protected. Expression that relates to the self-governing process must be protected absolutely by the First Amendment. There can be no government interference with such expression. Expression that does not relate to the self-governing process is not protected absolutely by the First Amendment. The value or worth of such speech must be balanced by the courts against other rights and values.

Critics of this theory argue in a telling fashion that it is not always clear whether expression pertains to self-government (public speech) or to other interests (private speech). While not providing the specific definition sought by critics, Meiklejohn argued that a broad range of speech is essential to successful self-government. He included speech-related education (history, political science, geography, etc.), science, literature, and many other topics. This theory has been subscribed to by some members of the Supreme Court of the United States, most notably Justice William Brennan. American libel law was radically changed when Brennan led the Supreme Court to give First Amendment protection only to libels published about government officials and others who attempt to lead public policy, a purely Meiklejohnian approach to the problem.

Access theory: In the mid-1960s some legal scholars suggested that the First Amendment includes the right of the people to gain access to the mass media to publish or present their own views and ideas. Development of this theory was prompted by economic trends in the nation, which showed a rapidly diminishing number of newspapers. Surely the First Amendment means more than simply the right of rich publishers to print their views. The First Amendment gives the average citizen the right to speak and publish freely. To make this right mean something, newspapers should be forced to open up their news columns to persons with ideas and views different from their own.

The Supreme Court unanimously rejected this notion in 1974 in *Miami Herald* v. *Tornillo*. Chief Justice Warren Burger, writing for the Court, said that the choice of material to go into a newspaper, and the decisions made as to limitations on the size of the paper and to content and treatment of public issues and public officials are decisions that must be made by the editors. The First Amendment does not give the government the right to force a newspaper to publish the views or ideas of a citizen. The *Tornillo* case sounded the legal death knell for this access theory for print media. See *South Wind Motel* v. *Lashutka* (1983) for an example of how courts have rejected the access theory since the *Tornillo* ruling.

However, the access theory was a potent justification for the regulation of broadcasting. The Federal Communication Commission has in the past justified its regulation of the content of broadcasting on the theory that the airwaves belong to the people and that all persons really have a right to see and hear programs that reflect a diverse range of ideas. As Justice White said in the famous case of *Red Lion Broadcasting* v. *FCC* (1969), "It is the right of the public to receive suitable access to social, political, esthetic, moral, and other ideas and experiences, which is crucial here." Using this argument as a foundation, the government has justified the application of the Fairness Doctrine and other rules that can force broadcasters to carry certain kinds of programming. As we will note in chapter 11, this philosophy of broadcast regulation is being undercut today by many factors.

The five theories or strategies just outlined guide jurists across the nation as they attempt to fathom the meaning of these seemingly simple thirteen words: "Congress shall make no law abridging freedom of speech or of the press." In the remainder of this book, we will attempt to tell you what the courts—using these theories—say the First Amendment means. It is appropriate that we begin that discussion now.

SUMMARY

The nation's first constitution, the Articles of Confederation, did not contain a guarantee of freedom of speech and press, but nearly all state constitutions provided for a guarantee of such rights. Citizens insisted that a written declaration of rights be included in the Constitution of 1787, and a guarantee of freedom of expression was a part of the Bill of Rights that was added to the national charter in 1791.

There is a debate within the legal-historical community over the meaning of the First Amendment when it was drafted and approved in the late eighteenth century. Some persons argue that it was intended to block both prior censorship and prosecution for seditious libel. Others argue that it prohibits only prior censorship. We will probably never know what the guarantee of freedom of expression meant to the persons who drafted it, but it is a good bet that citizens had a wide variety of interpretations of the First Amendment when they voted to approve it.

The meaning of the First Amendment today is largely determined through interpretation by the Supreme Court of the United States. Jurists use legal theories to guide them in determining the meaning of the Constitutional guarantee that "Congress shall make no law abridging freedom of speech or of the press." Five such theories are (1) absolutist theory, (2) *ad hoc* balancing theory, (3) preferred position balancing theory, (4) Meiklejohnian theory, and (5) public access theory. Theories two, three, and four have the most supporters on the Supreme Court, and all the theories have assisted members of the High Court to shape the meaning of the First Amendment.

SEDITIOUS LIBEL AND THE RIGHT TO CRITICIZE THE GOVERNMENT

The First Amendment of the United States Constitution states:

Congress shall make no law respecting an establishment of religion, or prohibiting the free exercise thereof; or abridging the freedom of speech, or of the press; or the right of the people peaceably to assemble, and to petition the Government for a redress of grievances.

The essence of a democracy is the participation by citizens in the process of government. At its most basic level, this participation involves selecting leaders for the nation, the state, and the various local governments through the electoral process. Popular participation also includes examination of government and public officials to determine their fitness for serving the people. Discussion, criticism, and suggestion all play a part in the orderly transition of governments and elected leaders. The right to speak and print, then, is inherent in a nation governed by popularly elected rulers.

Whether the rights of free expression as defined in 1790 included a broad right to criticize the government, this kind of political speech has emerged as a central element of our modern understanding of the First Amendment.

The right to discuss the government, the right to criticize the government, the right to oppose the government, the right to advocate the change of the government—all of these dimensions of free speech and free press are at the center of our political philosophy today. But this has not always been the case. Even today we are sometimes troubled when asked to decide just how far an individual can go in criticizing or opposing the government. Can the use of force or violence be advocated as a means of changing the government? Can a citizen use the essence of democracy, free expression, to advocate the violent abolition of democracy and the establishment of a repressive state in which the rights of free speech and free press would be denied? Americans familiar with the history of the past two hundred years know these are more than academic questions. Some of the fiercest First Amendment battles have been fought over exactly these issues. Indeed, the new nation was less than ten years old when its resolve regarding freedom of expression was first put to the test. The results of the test were not encouraging.

In 1798 John Adams was in his third year as president. As Washington's successor he was also the head of the nation's first political party, the Federalist party. This was the party that favored a strong national government, the party that many believed was somewhat antidemocratic. Arrayed against the Federalists was the party of Thomas Jefferson, the Republican or Democratic-Republican or Jeffersonian party.

The young nation was experiencing difficulties with the French in 1798. Some Federalist politicians said that war was imminent. This event was unlikely, even though the impact of the democratic ideas generated by the French Revolution clearly stirred some segments of the American population. The Republican press used the Federalist fear of the French to make political hay. The Republican editors, many of whom were French sympathizers and some of whom were French aliens, rarely missed an opportunity to attack President Adams and other Federalist leaders. Opposition to the Federalist government and the Federalist president aligned the Republican journalists with the French in the eyes of some of the Federalist leaders. Remember that the newspapers of this era were tied closely to political parties and sought to interpret news and events in terms of political affairs. Editorial attacks were often vicious as compared with the genteel press of the late twentieth century.

No one will ever know whether John Adams really feared war with France and sought to stifle dissent in order for the nation to present a united front to Europe or whether the trouble with France was a convenient excuse to muzzle some of his political enemies. In either case Adams approved of the efforts of some extremists in the Federalist party to curb the power of the aliens, the Republicans, and the Republican press. In 1798 the Federalist Congress passed four laws known today as the **Alien and Sedition Acts of 1798.** The first three acts dealt with aliens: the period of residence for naturalization was extended from five to fourteen years, and the president was given the power to apprehend, restrain, and deport aliens whom he deemed to be dangerous. The sedition law was aimed directly at the Jeffersonian press. It forbade false, scandalous, and malicious publications against the United States government, the Congress, and the president. The new law also punished persons who sought to stir up sedition or urged resistance to federal laws. The punishment was a fine of as much as $2,000 and a jail term of not more than two years.

Truth was a defense in a prosecution brought under the new law, and the jury was given the power to determine whether the words were seditious. However, these safeguards proved ineffective. The courts insisted that the defendant had to prove that his statements or opinions were true. This was a reversal of the normal criminal law presumption of innocence in which the state must prove that the words are false and scandalous. Since the trials were normally held in communities dominated by Federalists, both the judge and jury were highly sensitive to criticism of the Federalist government.

The fifteen prosecutions under the law ranged from ludicrous to absurd. Speaking for the Republican party were five major newspapers in Philadelphia, Boston, New York, Richmond, and Baltimore. The editors of four of the five newspapers were prosecuted, as well as the editors of four lesser Republican newspapers. Even Congressmen did not escape. Matthew Lyon, a Republican member of Congress from Vermont, was prosecuted for publishing an article in which he asserted that under President Adams, "every consideration of the public welfare was swallowed up in a continual grasp for power, in an unbounded thirst for ridiculous pomp, foolish adulation and selfish avarice." He also printed a letter written by a friend that suggested the president be committed to a madhouse. For these offenses against the government, Congressman Lyon was fined $1,000 and spent four months in jail. While he was in jail, he was reelected to Congress.

Far from inhibiting dissent, Adams succeeded only in generating dissension among many persons who were formerly his supporters. The constitutional issues raised by the law never reached the Supreme Court, although the validity of the measure was sustained by Federalist judges and by three Federalist Supreme Court justices hearing cases on the circuit. The people, however, acted as a kind of court and voted Adams out of office in 1800, replacing him with his Republican foe, Thomas Jefferson. Other factors prompted public dissatisfaction with the Massachusetts nationalist to be sure, but unpopularity of the alien and sedition laws cannot be underestimated. The Sedition Act expired in 1801. Jefferson pardoned all persons convicted under it, and Congress eventually repaid most of the fines.

Several lessons emerge from the experience under that set of laws. Foremost is the proposition that the First Amendment does nothing, in and of itself, to guarantee freedom of expression. The people and the courts must support the proposition before it becomes workable. In 1798 the courts were staffed with Federalists who were basically sympathetic to the law, and juries sympathetic to the Federalist cause could also be drawn quite easily. In 1798 the defense of truth did not help much when it was framed in such a way as to force the defendant to prove the truth of his assertions.

We discovered that in 1798 there was little consensus on what freedom of the press really meant. Some of the best writing ever on the topic was published during this period as the Republicans attempted to define free expression in a way that tolerated a broader range of governmental criticism. Tracts by men like Tunis Wortman, forgotten by most scholars for more than 150 years, have emerged in the second half of the twentieth century and offer legal scholars profound insight into how freedom of expression and stability of the government can be balanced.

Another lesson is that the nation's first peacetime sedition law left such a bad taste that another peacetime sedition law was not passed until the Smith Act of 1940.

Our brief consideration of this episode also shows that Americans (to their probable chagrin) were not really so different from their colonial forebears on the issue of free expression, that an American president and a Congress could be as ignorant of the importance of freedom of speech as a British king and parliament.

The conflict between political criticism and freedom of expression was not dormant for the next 115 years, but neither was it at the forefront of public discussion. Debate on freedom of expression arose again during the period in which abolitionist publishers worked to end slavery in the United States. Between 1830 and 1840 some states and members of the federal government made serious efforts to stop the circulation of abolitionist newspapers on the grounds that they tended to incite slave revolt. The legal moves were defeated in northern states, and the Congress, instead of bowing to President Andrew Jackson's request to ban these publications from the United States mail, insisted that local postmasters had to deliver all mail, even if it contained abolitionist sentiments. Informal pressure was far more effective in stifling publication and circulation of abolitionist newspapers. This was especially true in the South, where community pressure was a far more effective censor, despite the existence of laws in a few states making circulation of some abolitionist tracts punishable by death. During the antebellum period, freedom of expression in most of the South meant freedom to discuss or publish only the views with which a community did not disagree.

In the North the issue of liberty of the press received a substantial airing during debates over censorial statutes in many state legislatures. However, because slavery did not touch the lives of many northerners, persons living north of the Mason-Dixon line found it easier to stand behind a more expansive definition of freedom of expression.

Freedom of expression was an issue during the Civil War also. Some newspapers were temporarily closed in the North. The government effectively screened most war news published in the press, and Lincoln showed little sensitivity to civil liberties on some occasions. Still, the war was a national crisis of unprecedented proportions, and one way or another most persons were intimately involved in the war. Freedom of the press paled somewhat when placed next to the life-and-death struggle many persons suffered.

The right to criticize the government did not again become a controversial issue in this nation until after the turn of the century, when the political "isms" of the late 1800s (socialism, anarchism, syndicalism) fused with the war in Europe. The safety of the nation appeared to be at stake, and repression once again seemed to be the proper answer.

In the late nineteenth century hundreds of thousands of Americans began to realize that democracy and capitalism were not going to bring the prosperity promised by some obscure national compact. The right to pursue happiness did not assure that one would find it. The advancing rush of the new industrial society left many Americans behind, and they were unhappy. Some of the more dissatisfied persons wanted to do something about the situation and proposed new systems of government and advanced new economic theories. The specter of revolution arose in the minds of millions of Americans. Emma Goldman, Big Bill Haywood, and Daniel DeLeon represented salvation and hope to their tens of thousands of followers, but they represented a violent change in the comfortable status quo to many other thousands of Americans. Hadn't the radicals caused a riot in 1886 in Chicago? Hadn't they killed President McKinley in 1901? Hadn't they planted bombs along the West Coast and in the Northwest? Didn't they advocate general strikes? Didn't they want to take over the plants and factories and let the workers control production? With this threat lurking in the background, the United States found a real live bogeyman in 1917, when the nation went to war against Germany—to win the war that would make the world safe for democracy.

Sedition in the Twentieth Century

The history of sedition law in the United States during and since World War I centers upon the struggle by courts at all levels to fashion some kind of test that permitted the government to protect itself from damaging criticism without stifling expression, which is protected by the First Amendment. Beginning with cases that grew out of dissent against the war in Europe, through cases in the early 1970s, federal courts, especially the Supreme Court, have made numerous attempts to develop a satisfactory test or formula. In the following section these attempts are outlined through a discussion of many of the major cases that raised this difficult problem. But before the cases can be discussed, it is necessary to look briefly at the period that many regard as the most repressive in the history of the nation, the World War I era.

World War I is probably the most unpopular war this nation has fought, except for the Vietnam conflict of the sixties and seventies. The war was a replay of the imperial wars of the seventeenth and eighteenth centuries in Europe, except that it was fought with deadly new weapons. Patriots were thrilled that the United States was finally asked to fight in the big leagues. Farmers and industrialists saw the opportunity for vast economic gains. The military believed that no more than six months or so were needed to clean up what many called at the outset "that lovely little war." So most of the "ins" liked the idea of going to war. But most of the "outs" hated it because they had to fight the war, because many were born in nations now our enemies, and because a war always signals the beginning of a period of internal political repression for the "outs". When persons who opposed the war in an organized way spoke out against it, their opposition became just another excuse for suppression, fines, and jail.

Suppression of freedom of expression reached a higher level during World War I than at any other time in our history. Government prosecutions during the Vietnam War, for example, were minor compared with government action between 1918 and 1920. Vigilante groups were active as well, persecuting when the government failed to prosecute.

Two federal laws were passed to deal with persons who opposed the war and United States participation in it. In 1917 the **Espionage Act** was approved by the Congress and signed by President Woodrow Wilson. The measure dealt primarily with espionage problems, but some parts were aimed expressly at dissent and opposition to the war. The law provided that it was a crime to willfully convey a false report with the intent to interfere with the war effort. It was a crime to cause or attempt to cause insubordination, disloyalty, mutiny, or refusal of duty in the armed forces. It also was a crime to willfully obstruct the recruiting or enlistment service of the United States. Punishment was a fine of not more than $10,000 or a jail term of not more than twenty years. The law also provided that material that violated the law could not be mailed.

In 1918 the **Sedition Act,** an amendment to the Espionage Act, was passed, making it a crime to attempt to obstruct the recruiting service. It was criminal to utter or print or write or publish disloyal or profane language that was intended to cause contempt of or scorn for the federal government, the Constitution, the flag, or the uniform of the armed forces. Penalties for violation of the law were imprisonment for as long as twenty years and/or a fine of $10,000. Approximately two thousand offenders were prosecuted under these espionage and sedition laws, and nearly nine hundred were convicted. Offenders who found themselves in the government's dragnet were usually aliens, radicals, publishers of foreign-language publications, and other persons who opposed the war.

In addition the United States Post Office Department censored thousands of newspapers, books, and pamphlets. Some publications lost their right to the government-subsidized second-class mailing rates and were forced to use the costly first-class rates or find other means of distribution. Entire issues of magazines were held up and never delivered, on the grounds that they violated the law (or what the postmaster general believed to be the law). Finally, the states were not content with allowing the federal government to deal with dissenters, and most adopted sedition statutes, laws against criminal syndicalism, laws that prohibited the display of a red flag or a black flag, and so forth.

While the Congress adopted measures making it a crime to oppose the government or to oppose the recruiting service, the courts were given the task of reconciling these laws with the guarantee of freedom of expression in the

First Amendment. The courts, ultimately the Supreme Court, had to specifically define what kinds of words were protected by the First Amendment and what kinds of words were outside the range of protected speech. The United States had been in the war but a short time when the case that would become the Supreme Court's first opportunity to reconcile the First Amendment and outlaw political speech began.

The Philadelphia Socialist party authorized Charles Schenck, the general secretary of the organization, to publish 15,000 antiwar leaflets. These were distributed through the party's bookshop and mailed directly to young men who had been drafted. The publication urged the young inductees to join the Socialist party and work for the repeal of the selective service law, told the young men that the law was a violation of the Thirteenth Amendment, which abolished slavery, and told the draftees that they were being discriminated against because certain young men (Quakers and clergymen) did not have to go to war. The pamphlet also described the war as a cold-blooded and ruthless adventure propagated in the interest of the chosen few of Wall Street. Schenck and other party members were arrested, tried, and convicted of violating the Espionage Act. The socialists appealed to the High Court, asserting that the law denied them the right of freedom of speech and freedom of the press. Justice Oliver Wendell Holmes wrote the opinion in this important case (*Schenck* v. *U.S.,* 1919). Holmes initially asserted that the main purpose of the First Amendment is to prevent prior censorship, although he conceded that the amendment might not be confined to that. In ordinary times, such pamphlets might have been harmless and considered protected speech. "But the character of every act depends upon the circumstances in which it is done. . . . The question in every case is whether the words used, are used in such circumstances and are of such a nature as to create a clear and present danger that they will bring about the substantive evils that Congress has a right to prevent. It is a question of proximity and degree."

Translated, this is what Holmes's proposition means. Congress has a right to outlaw certain kinds of conduct that can be harmful to society. Words, as in publications or public speeches, that can result in persons undertaking the illegal conduct can also be outlawed, and publishers or speakers can be punished without infringing upon First Amendment rights. How great must be the connection between the forbidden conduct and the words? Holmes said the words must create a "clear and present danger" that the illegal activity will result.

Needless to say, in Holmes's view the requisite clear and present danger of obstructing the recruiting service existed in the *Schenck* case, and the conviction was upheld. In two other Espionage Act cases, also decided in the spring of 1919, Holmes wrote the opinion for the Court and used the clear-and-present-danger test to affirm the convictions of Jacob Frohwerk, editor of a

German-language newspaper (*Frohwerk* v. *U.S.,* 1919) and Eugene V. Debs, leader of the American Socialist party during World War I (*Debs* v. *U.S.,* 1919). The requisite clear and present danger existed in both cases, Holmes said.

Political liberals in the nation were left in considerable dismay upon reading Holmes's opinion in the *Schenck* case. The aging jurist was regarded as a great civil libertarian, but his formulation of the clear-and-present-danger test allowed little room for what most American liberals regarded as protected expression. There is some evidence that Justice Holmes was sadly underprepared in First Amendment law when he wrote the opinion. An even more interesting theory has been proposed by Stanford University scholar Jeremy Cohen, who suggests that Holmes may not have viewed the legal controversy primarily as a First Amendment case. Cohen suggests that Holmes's long background as a state judge and other factors set his mind to view the dispute in the *Schenck* case with strong judicial deference to legislative policy making. Should the legislature or the courts make policy on this issue? Holmes may have asked himself. One needs only to look at Holmes's writing and his previous court opinions to determine the answer to the question, writes Cohen. The courts should not interfere with legislature in such policy matters.

Holmes was sharply criticized by many civil libertarians following the *Schenck* ruling. Some suggest that he was re-educated in constitutional law by a few of his friends during the subsequent summer (*see* Ragan article, *Journal of American History,* in the Bibliography on page 105).

Regardless, in November 1919, when the Court decided its first appeal of a conviction under the Sedition Act, Holmes split with the majority and wrote a moving dissent in defense of freedom of expression.

In *Abrams* v. *U.S.* (1919) the High Court upheld the convictions of five young radicals who protested the movement of American troops into the Soviet Union and called for a general strike to stop the production of munitions and arms. In writing for the majority, Justice John Clarke wrote that the leaflets published by the defendants "obviously intended to provoke and to encourage resistance to the United States in the war." Whether they intended to hurt the United States was not at issue. "Men must be held to have intended, and to be accountable for, the effects which their acts were likely to produce." As Professor Fred D. Ragan notes: "Thus Clarke employed criteria used by Holmes earlier in the year . . . to sustain the conviction."

Holmes, on the other hand, joined his colleague Louis Brandeis in the dissent. The jurist wrote that the ultimate good desired is better reached by free trade in ideas, that the best test of truth is the power of a thought to get accepted in the marketplace. "That, at any rate, is the theory of our Constitution," he wrote. Holmes then argued that nobody could seriously believe that the silly leaflet published by the five defendants would hinder the war effort.

He turned his back on notions of probable or indirect interference with the prosecution of the war. To be guilty of resistance meant direct and immediate opposition to some effort by the United States to prosecute the war. There was no evidence of that here, Holmes concluded.

Holmes's change of heart did not spell the demise of the clear-and-present-danger test. It was used in other sedition cases by the High Court. However the only instances in which a majority of the High Court subscribed to the test were to uphold convictions under various sedition laws. Holmes and Brandeis used the test often to argue that the requisite clear and present danger was missing, that the utterances or published materials were protected by the First Amendment. These arguments, it should be noted, were in dissenting opinions.

The *Gitlow* Ruling

The next sedition case of significance during the postwar era was *Gitlow* v. *New York* (1925). Many scholars argue that this decision by the Supreme Court ranks as one of the most important civil rights decisions of the twentieth century, despite the fact that defendant Benjamin Gitlow lost his First Amendment appeal. Gitlow and three other persons were arrested, tried, and convicted of publishing and distributing a pamphlet that, the state of New York argued, advocated the violent overthrow of the government—a violation of the New York Criminal Anarchy Law. The pamphlet, the *Left Wing Manifesto,* was a dreadfully dull thirty-four-page political tract on revolution and social and economic change. In his book *Free Speech in the United States,* Zechariah Chafee, a renowned legal scholar of Harvard University, accurately notes, "Any agitator who read these thirty-four pages to a mob would not stir them to violence, except possibly against himself. This manifesto would disperse them faster than the riot act." Nevertheless Gitlow was sentenced to ten years in prison. In his appeal to the High Court, he argued that the state criminal anarchy statute violated his freedom of expression guaranteed by the United States Constitution. In making this plea, Gitlow was asking the Court to overturn a ninety-two-year-old precedent.

In 1833 the Supreme Court of the United States ruled that the Bill of Rights, the first ten amendments to the United States Constitution, were applicable only in protecting citizens from actions of the federal government (*Barron* v. *Baltimore,* 1833). Chief Justice John Marshall ruled that the people of the United States established the United States Constitution for their government, not for the government of the individual states. The limitations of power placed upon government by the Constitution applied only to the government of the United States. In fact, while considering the adoption of the Bill of Rights in 1789, the U.S. Senate rejected a resolution that would have applied to the states as well as the federal government the limits on government action contained in the ten amendments. Applying this rule to the First Amendment meant that neither Congress nor the federal government could abridge freedom of the press, but that the government of New York or the government of Detroit could interfere with freedom of expression without violating the guarantees of the Constitution. The citizens of the individual states or cities could erect their own constitutional guarantees in state constitutions or city charters. Indeed, such provisions existed in many places.

As applied to the case of Benjamin Gitlow, then, it seemed unlikely that the First Amendment (which prohibited interference by the federal government with freedom of speech and press) could be erected as a barrier to protect the radical from prosecution by the state of New York. Yet this is exactly what the young socialist argued.

Gitlow's attorneys, especially Walter Heilprin Pollak, did not attack Chief Justice Marshall's ruling in *Barron* v. *Baltimore* directly; instead they went around it. Pollak constructed his argument upon the Fourteenth Amendment to the Constitution, which was adopted in 1868, thirty-five years after the decision in *Barron* v. *Baltimore*. The attorney argued that there was general agreement that the First Amendment protected a citizen's right to liberty of expression. The Fourteenth Amendment says in part, "no state shall deprive any person of life, liberty or property, without due process of law. . . ." Pollak asserted that included among the liberties guaranteed by the Fourteenth Amendment is liberty of the press as guaranteed by the First Amendment. Therefore, a state cannot deprive a citizen of the freedom of the press that is guaranteed by the First Amendment without violating the Fourteenth Amendment. By jailing Benjamin Gitlow for exercising his right of freedom of speech granted by the First Amendment, New York State denied him the liberty assured him by the Fourteenth Amendment. Simply, then, the First Amendment, as applied through the Fourteenth Amendment, prohibits states and cities and counties from denying an individual freedom of speech and press.

The High Court had heard this argument before, but apparently not as persuasively as Mr. Pollak presented it. In rather casual terms Justice Edward Sanford made a startlingly new constitutional pronouncement: "For present purposes we may and do assume that freedom of speech and of the press—which are protected by the First Amendment from abridgement by Congress—are among the fundamental personal rights and 'liberties' protected by the due process clause of the Fourteenth Amendment from impairment by the states."

Despite this important ruling, Gitlow lost his case. Justice Sanford said that the New York law was warranted and did not violate the First Amendment nor the Fourteenth Amendment. Sanford then went on to outline his own rather novel interpretation of Holmes's clear-and-present-danger test. He said that in passing the Espionage Act, the Congress forbade certain deeds—interference with the recruiting service, for example. In such instances when the defendant is charged with using words to promote the forbidden deeds, the courts must decide whether the language used by the accused creates a clear and present danger for bringing about the forbidden deeds. In other words, does the defendant's pamphlet create the danger that persons will in fact interfere with the recruiting service?

However, in this case, Sanford said, the New York legislature outlawed certain words—that is, words advocating violent overthrow of the government are forbidden. The clear-and-present-danger test does not apply, he said. The only issue the court has to decide is, Do the words in question, in this case the *Left Wing Manifesto,* fall within the class of forbidden words, words that advocate violent overthrow of the government? The court has no power to determine in such a case if in fact the defendant's pamphlet creates the danger of a violent revolt. It is sufficient that the state has outlawed such words. Only if the judgment of the legislature is completely without foundation can the court interfere. In this case the legislature's action is warranted: Gitlow's pamphlet falls within the category of proscribed words—ten years in jail!

Holmes and Brandeis vigorously dissented, arguing that it was absurd to think that Gitlow's small band of followers posed any danger at all to the government. "It is said that this manifesto was more than a theory," Holmes wrote, "that it was an incitement. Every idea is an incitement. . . . The only difference between the expression of an opinion and an incitement in the narrower sense is the speaker's enthusiasm for the result." The argument was to no avail. After three years in prison, Gitlow was pardoned by Governor Alfred Smith.

The importance of the *Gitlow* case is that the High Court acknowledged that the Bill of Rights places limitations upon the actions of states and local government, as well as upon the federal government. The *Gitlow* case states that freedom of speech is protected by the Fourteenth Amendment. In later cases the Court placed freedom of the press, freedom of religion, freedom from self-incrimination, and freedom from illegal search and seizure under the same protection. Today, virtually all of the rights outlined in the Bill of Rights are protected via the Fourteenth Amendment from interference by states and cities, as well as by the federal government. The importance of the *Gitlow* case cannot be underestimated. It truly marked the beginning of attainment of a full measure of civil liberties for the citizens of the nation. It was the key that unlocked an important door.

Sedition in the Twenties

The Sanford interpretation of the clear-and-present-danger test was next used two years later when the Supreme Court reviewed the prosecution by California of sixty-year-old philanthropist Anita Whitney for threatening the security of the state (*Whitney* v. *California,* 1927). Miss Whitney, the niece of Justice Stephen J. Field, who served on the Supreme Court from 1863 to 1897, joined the Socialist party in the early 1920s. At a convention in Chicago, the chapter to which Miss Whitney belonged seceded from the Socialist party and formed the Communist Labor party. The Communist Labor party held a convention in Oakland to which Miss Whitney was a delegate. She worked hard as a delegate to ensure that the new party worked through political means to capture political power, but the majority of delegates voted instead for the party to dedicate itself to gaining power through revolution and general strikes in which the workers would seize power by violent means. After this convention Miss Whitney was not active in the party, but she was nevertheless arrested three weeks after the Oakland convention and charged with violating the California Criminal Syndicalism Act, which prohibited advocacy of violence to change the control or ownership of industry or to bring about political change.

Following her conviction she appealed to the High Court, arguing that the law violated the guarantees of freedom of expression. Justice Edward Sanford, writing for the majority, again ruled that the clear-and-present-danger test did not apply, that the California state legislature outlawed certain kinds of words that it deemed a danger to public peace and safety, and that the Court could not hold that the action was unreasonable or unwarranted. There was therefore no infringement upon the First Amendment.

This time Holmes and Brandeis concurred with the majority, but only, Brandeis said, because the constitutional issue of freedom of expression had not been raised sufficiently at the trial to make it an issue in the appeal. (If a legal issue is not raised during a trial it is difficult for an appellate court to later consider the matter.) In his concurring opinion, Brandeis disagreed sharply with the majority regarding the limits of free expression. In doing so he added flesh and bones to Holmes's clear-and-present-danger test. Looking to the *Schenck* decision, the justice noted that the Court had agreed that there must be a clear and imminent danger of a substantive evil that the state has the right to prevent before an interference with speech can be allowed. Then he went on to describe what he believed to be the requisite danger (*Whitney* v. *California*):

> To justify suppression of free speech there must be reasonable ground to fear that serious evil will result if free speech is practiced. There must be reasonable ground to believe that the danger apprehended is imminent. There must be reasonable ground to believe that the evil to be prevented is a serious one. Every denunciation of existing law tends in some measure to increase the probability that there will be violation of it. Condonation of a breach enhances the probability. Expressions of approval add to the probability. Propagation of the criminal state of mind by teaching syndicalism increases it. Advocacy of law-breaking heightens it further. But even advocacy of violation, however reprehensible morally, is not a justification for denying free speech where the advocacy falls short of incitement, and there is nothing to indicate that the advocacy would be immediately acted on. The wide difference between advocacy and incitement, between preparation and attempt, between assembling and conspiracy, must be borne in mind. In order to support a finding of clear and present danger it must be shown either that immediate serious violence was to be expected or was advocated, or that the past conduct furnished reason to believe that such advocacy was then contemplated.

Brandeis concluded that if there is time to expose through discussion the falsehoods and fallacies, to avert the evil by the process of education, the remedy to be applied is more speech, not enforced silence.

This truly is a clear-and-present-danger test that even the most zealous civil libertarian can live with. And this is the test that many mistakenly confuse with Holmes's original pronouncement. Unfortunately, this version of the clear-and-present-danger test has never found its way into a majority opinion in a sedition case.

Before the last two important sedition cases decided during this century are discussed, it should be noted that in 1927 the Supreme Court first struck down a state sedition conviction because the defendant's federal constitutional rights had been violated (*Fiske* v. *Kansas,* 1927). In Kansas a man named Fiske was arrested, tried, and convicted of violating that state's criminal anarchy statute. He was an organizer for the International Workers of the World (IWW), a radical union group. The evidence the state used against him was the preamble to the IWW constitution, which discussed in vague terms the struggle between workers and owners and the necessity for workers to take control of the machinery of production and to abolish the wage system. No mention was made of violence, but the state supreme court upheld the conviction on the grounds that despite the lack of specific reference to violence, it was possible for the jury to read between the lines in light of the reputation of the IWW. The United States Supreme Court reversed the conviction because there was no evidence on the record to support the conviction. There was no suggestion in the testimony that Fiske used anything but lawful methods, and thus the conviction was "an arbitrary and unreasonable exercise of the police power of the state, unwarrantably infringing upon the liberty of the defendant." While this was a terribly small victory and no major liberal interpretation of the First Amendment was announced, as Zechariah Chafee (*Free Speech in the United States*) notes, "the Supreme Court for the first time made freedom of speech mean something."

The Smith Act

The Congress adopted the nation's first peacetime sedition law in 1798 and approved the second law in 1940, when it ratified the **Smith Act,** a measure making it a crime to advocate the violent overthrow of the government, to conspire to advocate the violent overthrow of the government, to organize a group that advocates the violent overthrow of the government, or to be a member of a group that advocates the violent overthrow of the government.

The Smith Act, which was aimed at the Communist party, was drafted by Congressman Howard Smith of Virginia and Congressman John McCormack of Massachusetts. It received little publicity while Congress considered it, and many months elapsed before civil libertarians realized that the act had been passed. Among others Zechariah Chafee (*Free Speech in the*

United States) writes, "Not until months later did I for one realize this statute contains the most drastic restriction on freedom of speech ever enacted in the United States during peace."

A small band of Trotskyites, members of the Socialist Workers party, were prosecuted and convicted under the Smith Act in 1943, but not until 1948 did a federal grand jury indict twelve of the nation's leading Communists for advocating the violent overthrow of the United States government. The trial began in January 1949 and lasted nine months. Eleven defendants (one became sick during the trial and was excused temporarily) were convicted, including Eugene V. Dennis, one of the party leaders in the United States. Trial judge Harold Medina told the jury that the statute did not prohibit discussing the propriety of overthrowing the government by force or violence, but "the teaching and advocacy of action for the accomplishment of that purpose by language reasonably and ordinarily calculated to incite persons to such action." In other words, the Smith Act prohibited the teaching or advocacy of action aimed at the violent overthrow of the government.

The convictions were appealed all the way to the Supreme Court, and in *Dennis* v. *U.S.* (1951) the High Court once again was called upon to outline the limitations that might be constitutionally applied against persons who oppose the government. In arguing that the Smith Act violated the guarantees of freedom of speech and press in the First Amendment, the defendants raised the almost thirty-year-old clear-and-present-danger test as a barrier to the prosecution. The actions of this small band of Communists did not represent a clear and present danger to the nation, they argued. Chief Justice Fred Vinson wrote the opinion for the Supreme Court in the seven-to-two ruling that upheld the constitutionality of the federal sedition law. In considering the clear-and-present-danger test, Vinson could have chosen to adopt the crabbed view of freedom of expression enunciated by Holmes in the *Schenck* case, or he could have followed Brandeis's more liberal exposition of the test from the *Whitney* decision. Vinson ended up creating a new test, which fell politically somewhere between the tests outlined by Holmes in 1919 and Brandeis in 1927.

Vinson first insisted that the evil involved in the case (the evil which Congress has the right to prevent) was a substantial one, the overthrow of the government. That was the professed aim of the Communists, no doubt, but it was not very realistic. That does not matter, Vinson wrote, rejecting the contention that success or probability of success is the criterion, "Certainly an attempt to overthrow the Government by force, even though doomed from the outset because of inadequate numbers or power of the revolutionists, is a sufficient evil for Congress to prevent. The damage which such attempts create both physically and politically to a nation makes it impossible to measure the validity in terms of the probability of success, or the immediacy of a successful attempt." However, Vinson equated advocacy of overthrow with actual attempt at overthrow. It could be asked, How likely is it that the words spoken or written by the defendants would lead even to an attempted overthrow? Vinson's opinion was a far cry from Justice Brandeis's statement in *Whitney*. Recall Brandeis's words: "But even advocacy of violation (of the law), however reprehensible morally, is not a justification for denying free speech where the advocacy falls short of incitement and there is nothing to indicate that the advocacy would be immediately acted upon. The wide difference between advocacy and incitement, between preparation and attempt, between assembling and conspiracy, must be borne in mind."

Vinson outlined the test used by Judge Learned Hand when the Second United States Court of Appeals sustained the conviction of the eleven Communists. "In each case [courts] must ask whether the gravity of the 'evil,' discounted by improbability, justifies such invasion of free speech as is necessary to avoid the danger." Vinson said, "We adopt this statement of the rule."

The clear-and-probable-danger test really says little more than the original Holmes clear-and-present-danger test if Holmes's exposition in the *Debs, Frohwerk,* and *Schenck* cases are added. If the gravity of the evil is considered, Holmes said that the evil must be substantive or serious. Hand said that the probability of what might occur must be considered. What might occur? Might the overthrow succeed? Might the overthrow be attempted? Might the words lead someone to attempt an overthrow? What kind of danger are we trying to avoid? The issue is so unclear.

One could speculate that if the clear-and-present-danger test as articulated by Justice Brandeis had been applied in this case, the convictions would have gone out the window. The danger was not clear, nor was it present. However, in the atmosphere of 1951, such was not likely. We were in the midst of both a cold war with the Soviet Union and a hot war with the North Koreans and Communist Chinese, and as was said previously, the Supreme Court (all courts for that matter) is a political body at least to some extent.

Chief Justice Vinson made one additional important observation. Almost in passing, he noted that the Smith Act is aimed at advocacy, not at discussion.

After the government's success in the *Dennis* case, more prosecutions were initiated against Communists in the United States. Seven separate prosecutions were started in 1951, three in 1952, one in 1953, and five more during the next three years. One trial begun in late 1951 involved the top Communist leadership on the West Coast. At the trial after hearing both sides, Judge William C. Mathes told the jury that any advocacy dealing with the forcible overthrow of the government and presented with a specific intent to accomplish the overthrow is illegal under the Smith Act. This is about what Vinson said in the *Dennis* case. The defendants appealed their conviction, and six years later, in 1957, the Supreme Court voted five to two to reverse the convictions (*Yates* v. *U.S.,* 1957). On what grounds? Several factors influenced the reversal in *Yates* v. *U.S.,* but the basic reason was that Judge Mathes failed to distinguish between the advocacy of forcible overthrow as an abstract doctrine and the advocacy of action aimed at the forcible overthrow of the government. The Smith Act reaches only advocacy of action for the overthrow of government by force and violence, Justice John Marshall Harlan wrote for the court. "The essential distinction," Harlan notes, "is that those to whom the advocacy is addressed must be urged to do something now or in the future, rather than merely to believe in something." How specific must this advocacy of action be? It does not have to be immediate action; it can be action in the future. But it must be an urging to do something: form an army, blow up a bridge, prepare for sabotage, train for street fighting, and so forth.

The government was unprepared to meet this new burden of proof. Far more evidence is needed to prove that someone has urged people to do something than to prove that someone has merely urged them to believe something. All but one of the cases pending were dismissed. The defendants in the single case that was tried were set free on an evidentiary issue (*Bary* v. *U.S.*, 1957) and were never retried. In fact, there has not been a single successful prosecution for advocacy of violent overthrow since the *Yates* decision. One successful prosecution under the membership clause of the Smith Act has occurred, but it was in 1961 (*Scales* v. *U.S.*, 1961).

To his credit, Justice Harlan did not attempt to apply either the clear-and-present-danger test or the clear-and-probable-danger test. This consideration wasn't necessary, since the constitutionality of the law was not the heart of the appeal in the *Yates* case as it was in *Dennis*.

Few sedition trials have occurred since 1957. In 1969, the Supreme Court once again looked at a state sedition law in *Brandenburg* v. *Ohio* (1969). In this case a Ku Klux Klan leader was prosecuted by the state of Ohio for advocating unlawful methods of terrorism and crime as a means of accomplishing industrial and political reform. The High Court voided his conviction on the grounds that the Ohio law failed to distinguish between the advocacy of ideas and the incitement to unlawful conduct. In its per curiam opinion the Court said, "The constitutional guarantees of free speech and free press do not permit a State to forbid or proscribe advocacy of the use of force or of law violation except where such advocacy is directed to inciting or producing imminent lawless action or is likely to incite or produce such actions." This opinion comes close to the way Louis Brandeis outlined the clear-and-present-danger test in 1927 in the *Whitney* case.

The famous Holmes test is not dead by any means. It still lives, for example, in criminal contempt law, where the High Court has fashioned it into a workable test to protect both courts and defendants from the interference of the mass media in the judicial process. If it is not dead, the test is certainly lifeless with regard to sedition law, partly because sedition law is not nearly so robust as it was forty years ago. The Communists long since ceased to be an internal threat in this nation.

The federal government chose not to use sedition laws in prosecuting protestors and dissidents during the Vietnam War. Instead, the government used rather exotic conspiracy laws and still enjoyed little success. The Smith Act is still on the books, and it probably could have been used against some antiwar leaders. But it was not. The law is not popular today. Sedition laws are not popular today. When people feel little direct threat to their well-being, they are willing to exercise a remarkable range of tolerance for unpopular ideas and suggestions. Unpopular or unorthodox speakers and writers are written off as kooks, which in many cases they are. However, should there occur another serious war, a deep depression that causes loss of confidence in the government, or some other situation in which people feel threatened, what could happen is difficult to predict.

SUMMARY

Within eight years of the passage of the **First Amendment**, the nation adopted its first (and most wide-ranging) sedition laws, the Alien and Sedition Acts of 1798. Many leading political editors and politicians were prosecuted under the laws, which made it a crime to criticize both President John Adams and the national government. While the Supreme Court never did hear arguments regarding the constitutionality of the laws, several justices of the Supreme Court presided at sedition act trials and refused to sustain a constitutional objection to the laws. The public hated the measures. John Adams was voted out of office in 1800 and was replaced by his political opponent and target of the sedition laws, Thomas Jefferson. The laws left such a bad taste that the federal government did not pass another sedition law until World War I, 117 years later.

Sedition prosecutions in the period of 1915–1925 were the most vicious in the nation's history as war protestors, socialists, anarchists, and other political dissidents became the target of government repression. It was during this era that the Supreme Court began to interpret the meaning of the First Amendment. In a series of rulings stemming from the World War I cases, the High Court fashioned what is known as the clear-and-present-danger test to measure state and federal laws and protests and other expressions against the First Amendment. The test was rigid and was never used to overturn a lower-court conviction, although in 1927 Justice Louis D. Brandeis did fashion a broad and liberal interpretation of the clear-and-present-danger test in his dissent in the case of *Whitney* v. *California*. In 1925 the Court ruled that the guarantees of freedom of speech apply to actions taken by all governments, that freedom of speech under the First Amendment protects individuals from censorship by all levels of government, not just from actions by the federal government. This pronouncement in *Gitlow* v. *New York* opened the door to a much broader protection of freedom of expression in the nation.

The nation's most recent sedition law was adopted in 1940. The Smith Act, as it is known, prohibits the advocacy of the violent overthrow of the government. Following a series of trials and two Supreme Court rulings in the 1950s, the law has become a relatively benign prohibition. The High Court ruled in 1957 in *Yates* v. *U.S.* that to sustain a conviction under the Smith Act, the government must prove that the defendants advocate specific violent or forcible action toward the overthrow of the government. The government found it impossible to do this in the 1950s, and the Smith Act has not been invoked to punish an act of expression for more than twenty-five years.

PRIOR RESTRAINT

The great compiler of the British law, William Blackstone, defined freedom of the press in the 1760s as freedom from "previous restraint," or **prior restraint.** Regardless of the difference of opinion on whether the First Amendment is intended to protect political criticism, most students of the constitutional period agree that the guarantees of freedom of speech and press were intended to bar the government from exercising prior restraint. Despite the weight of such authority, the media in the United States in the 1980s still faces instances of prepublication censorship. The issue is clearly not completely settled.

Prior censorship, or prior restraint, is probably the most insidious kind of government control. Speakers and publishers are stopped before they can speak or print. The people are not allowed to discover what was going to be said or published. We are denied the benefit of these ideas or suggestions or criticisms.

Prior censorship is difficult to define, as scores of laws and government actions hold the potential for a kind of prior restraint. In privacy law, for example, it is possible under some statutes to stop the publication of material that illegally appropriates a person's name or likeness. In extreme cases the press can be stopped from publishing information it has learned in a criminal case. The two instances just mentioned, as well as others, will be discussed fully in later, more appropriate sections of this book. The purpose of this section is to outline those kinds of prior restraint that seem to fall outside the boundaries of other chapters in the book. We will therefore discuss injunctions against public nuisances, laws that place limits on when and where materials may be distributed, cases involving national security matters, and other topics.

The Supreme Court did not consider the issue of prior restraint until more than a decade after it had decided its first major sedition case. In 1931, in *Near* v. *Minnesota,* the Court struck an important blow for freedom of expression.

City and county officials in Minneapolis, Minnesota, brought a legal action against Jay M. Near and Howard Guilford, publishers of the *Saturday Press,* a small weekly newspaper. Near and Guilford were reformers whose purpose was to clean up city and county government in Minneapolis. In their attacks upon corruption in city government, they used language that was far from temperate and defamed some of the town's leading government officials. Near and Guilford charged that Jewish gangsters were in control of gambling, bootlegging, and racketeering in the city and that city government and its law enforcement agencies did not perform their duties energetically. They repeated these charges over and over in a highly inflammatory manner.

Minnesota had a statute that empowered a court to declare any obscene, lewd, lascivious, malicious, scandalous, or defamatory publication a public nuisance. When such a publication was deemed a public nuisance, the court issued an injunction against future publication or distribution. Violation of the injunction resulted in punishment for contempt of court.

In 1927 County Attorney Floyd Olson initiated an action against the *Saturday Press.* A district court declared the newspaper a public nuisance and "perpetually enjoined" publication of the *Saturday Press.* The only way either Near or Guilford would be able to publish the newspaper again was to convince the court that their newspaper would remain free of objectionable material. In 1928 the Minnesota Supreme Court upheld the constitutionality of the law, declaring that under its broad police power the state can regulate public nuisances, including defamatory and scandalous newspapers.

The case then went to the United States Supreme Court, which reversed the ruling by the state supreme court. The nuisance statute was declared unconstitutional. Chief Justice Charles Evans Hughes wrote the opinion for the Court in the five-to-four ruling, saying that the statute in question was not designed to redress wrongs to individuals attacked by the newspaper. Instead, the statute was directed at suppressing the *Saturday Press* once and for all. The object of the law, Hughes wrote, was not punishment but censorship—not only of a single issue, but also of all future issues—which is not consistent with the traditional concept of freedom of the press. That is, the statute constituted prior restraint, and prior restraint is clearly a violation of the First Amendment.

One maxim in the law holds that when a judge writes an opinion for a court, he should stick to the problem at hand, that he should not wander off and talk about matters that do not really concern the issue before the court. Such remarks are considered **dicta,** or words that do not really apply to the case. These words, these dicta, are never really considered an important part of the ruling in the case. Chief Justice Hughes's opinion in *Near* v. *Minnesota* contains a good deal of dicta.

In this case Hughes wrote that the prior restraint of the *Saturday Press* was unconstitutional, but in some circumstances, he added, prior restraint might be permissible. In what kinds of circumstances? The government can constitutionally stop publication of obscenity, the government can stop publication of material that incites people to acts of violence, and it may prohibit publication of certain kinds of materials during wartime. Hughes admitted, on the other hand, that defining freedom of the press as the only freedom from prior restraint is equally wrong, for in many cases punishment after publication imposes effective censorship upon the freedom of expression.

Near v. *Minnesota* stands for the proposition that under American law prior censorship is permitted only in very unusual circumstances; it is the exception, not the rule. Courts have reinforced this interpretation many times since 1931. Despite this considerable litigation, we still lack a complete understanding of the kinds of circumstances in which prior restraint might be acceptable under the First Amendment, as a series of recent cases (some of which are concerned with national security) illustrate.

Austin v. *Keefe*

A case that to some extent reinforced the *Near* ruling involved the attempt of a real-estate broker to stop a neighborhood community action group from distributing pamphlets about him (*Organization for a Better Austin* v. *Keefe,* 1971). The Organization for a Better Austin was a community organization in the Austin suburb of Chicago. Its goal was to stabilize the population in the integrated community. Members were opposed to the tactics of certain real estate brokers who came into white neighborhoods, spread the word that blacks were moving in, bought up the white-owned homes cheaply in the ensuing panic, and then resold them at a good profit to blacks or other whites. The organization received pledges from most real estate firms in the area to stop these blockbusting tactics. But Jerome Keefe refused to make such an agreement. The community group then printed leaflets and flyers describing his activities and handed them out in Westchester, the community in which Keefe lived. Group members told the Westchester residents that Keefe was a "panic peddler" and said they would stop distributing the leaflets in Westchester as soon as Keefe agreed to stop his blockbusting real estate tactics. Keefe went to court and obtained an injunction that prohibited further distribution by the community club of pamphlets, leaflets, and literature of any kind in Westchester on the grounds that the material constituted an invasion of Keefe's privacy and caused him irreparable harm. The Organization for a Better Austin appealed the ruling to the United States Supreme Court. In May 1971 the High Court dissolved the injunction. Chief Justice Warren Burger wrote, "The injunction, so far as it imposes prior restraint on speech and publication, constitutes an impermissible restraint on First Amendment rights." He said that the injunction, as in the *Near* case, did not seek to redress individual wrongs, but instead sought to suppress on the basis of one or two handbills the distribution of any kind of literature in a city of 18,000 inhabitants. Keefe argued that the purpose of the handbills was not to inform the community, but to force him to sign an agreement. The chief justice said this argument was immaterial and was not sufficient cause to remove the leaflets and flyers from the protection of the First Amendment. Justice Burger added (*Austin* v. *Keefe):*

> Petitioners [the community group] were engaged openly and vigorously in making the public aware of respondent's [Keefe's] real estate practices. Those practices were offensive to them, as the views and practices of the petitioners are no doubt offensive to others. But so long as the means are peaceful, the communication need not meet standards of acceptability.

The *Keefe* case did a good job of reinforcing the High Court's decision in *Near* v. *Minnesota.*

Pentagon Papers Case

While it is more famous, another 1971 decision is not as strong a statement in behalf of freedom of expression as either *Near* or *Keefe*. This is the famous Pentagon Papers decision (*New York Times Co.* v. *U.S.; U.S.* v. *Washington Post,* 1971). While the political implications of the ruling are very important, the ruling itself is legally quite unsatisfying.

The case began in the summer of 1971 when the *New York Times,* followed by the *Washington Post* and a handful of other newspapers, began publication of a series of articles based on a top-secret forty-seven-volume government study entitled "History of the United States Decision-Making Process on Vietnam Policy." The day after the initial article on the Pentagon Papers appeared, Attorney General John Mitchell asked the *New York Times* to stop publication of the material. When the *Times's* publisher refused, the government went to court to get an injunction to force the newspaper to stop the series. A temporary restraining order was granted as the case wound its way to the Supreme Court. Such an order was also imposed upon the *Washington Post* after it began to publish reports based on the same material.

At first the government argued that the publication of this material violated federal espionage statutes. When that assertion did not satisfy the lower federal courts, the government argued that the president had inherent power under his constitutional mandate to conduct foreign affairs to protect the national security, which includes the right to classify documents secret and top secret. Publication of this material by the newspapers was unauthorized disclosure of such material and should be stopped. This argument did not satisfy the courts either, and by the time the case came before the Supreme Court, the government argument was that publication of these papers might result in irreparable harm to the nation and its ability to conduct foreign affairs. The *Times* and the *Post* consistently made two arguments. First, they said that the classification system is a sham, that people in the government declassify documents almost at will when they want to sway public opinion or influence a reporter's story. Second, the press also argued that an injunction against the continued publication of this material violated the First Amendment. Interestingly, the newspapers did not argue that under all circumstances prior restraint is in conflict with the First Amendment. Defense attorney Professor Alexander Bickel argued that under some circumstances prior restraint is acceptable, for example, when the publication of a document has a direct link with a grave event that is immediate and visible. Former Justice William O. Douglas noted that this was a strange argument for newspapers to make—and it is. Apparently both newspapers decided that a victory in that immediate case was far more important than to establish a definitive and long-lasting constitutional principle. They therefore concentrated on winning the case, acknowledging that in future cases prior restraint might be permissible.

On June 30 the High Court ruled six to three in favor of the *New York Times* and the *Washington Post*. The Court did not grant a permanent injunction against the publication of the Pentagon Papers, but the ruling was hardly the kind that strengthened the First Amendment. In a very short per curiam opinion, the majority said that in a case involving the prior restraint of a publication, the government bears a heavy burden to justify such a restraint. In this case the government failed to show the Court why such a restraint should be imposed upon the two newspapers. In other words, the government failed to justify its request for the permanent restraining order.

The decision in the case rested upon the preferred position First Amendment theory or doctrine (see page 51). The ban on publication was *presumed* to be an unconstitutional infringement upon the First Amendment. The government had to prove that the ban was needed to protect the nation in some manner. If such evidence could be adduced, the Court would strike the balance in favor of the government and uphold the ban on the publication of the articles. But in this case the government simply failed to show why its request for an injunction was vital to the national interest. Consequently, the high court denied the government's request for a ban on the publication of the Pentagon Papers on the grounds that such a prohibition was a violation of the First Amendment. Note: The Court did not say that in all similar cases an injunction would violate the First Amendment. It did not even say that in this case an injunction was a violation of the First Amendment. It merely said that the government had not shown why the injunction was needed, why it was not a violation of the freedom of the press. Such a decision is not what one would call a ringing defense of the right of free expression.

In addition to the brief unsigned opinion from the majority, the chief justice and each of the eight associate justices wrote short individual opinions. They were not very instructive, but should be noted anyway.

Justices Black and Douglas clung to the absolutist theory and argued that they could conceive of no circumstance under which the government can properly interfere with freedom of expression. Debate on public questions must be open and robust, Justice Douglas wrote. Justice William Brennan echoed the Court's opinion: there was no proof that the publication of the papers would damage the national security or the nation. Justice Potter Stewart agreed and attacked the notion of classifying public documents and excessive secrecy in government. "For when everything is classified," he wrote, "then nothing is classified, and the system becomes one to be disregarded by the cynical or the careless, and to be manipulated by those intent on self-protection or self-promotion."

Justice Byron White supported the notion that the government lacked the evidence needed to sustain an injunction. But Justice White added that he believed the publication of the material would damage the national interest, and if the government chose to bring the newspapers back to court for criminal prosecution for violating an espionage statute, he could surely support a conviction. These last remarks are another example of dicta. The last member of the majority, Justice Thurgood Marshall, said he did not believe the president has the right to classify documents in the first place, that Congress has consistently rejected giving the executive this power, and that consequently the Court should not support such questionable authority.

All three of the dissenters, Chief Justice Warren Burger, Justice John M. Harlan, and Justice Harry Blackmun, complained that there had not been sufficient time to properly consider the case. The issues were too important for such a rush to judgment, Justice Burger said, noting his dissent was not based upon the merits of the case. Harlan and Blackmun did dissent on the merits. Harlan argued that foreign relations and national security are both concerns of other branches of the government, and the Court should accept the government's assertions in this case—even without evidence—that disclosure of the material in the Pentagon Papers would substantially harm the government. Justice Blackmun wanted to send the case back to the trial courts for fuller exposition of the facts and to allow the government more time to prepare its case.

What many people at first called the case of the century ended in a fizzle, at least with regard to developing First Amendment law. The press won the day; the Pentagon Papers were published. But thoughtful observers expressed concern over the ruling. A majority of the Court had not ruled that such prior restraint was unconstitutional—only that the government had failed to meet the heavy burden of showing such restraint was necessary in this case.

Progressive
Magazine Case

The fragile nature of the Court's holding became clear in early 1979 when the government again went to court to block the publication of material it claimed could endanger the national security (*U.S.* v. *Progressive*, 1979). Freelance writer Howard Morland had prepared an article, entitled "The H-Bomb Secret: How We Got It, Why We're Telling It." The piece was scheduled to be published in the April edition of the *Progressive* magazine, a seventy-year-old political digest founded by Robert M. LaFollette as a voice of the progressive movement.

Morland had gathered the material for the article from unclassified sources. After completing an early draft of the piece, he sought technical criticism from various scholars. Somehow a copy found its way to officials in the federal government. With the cat out of the bag, *Progressive* editor Erwin Knoll sent a final draft to the government for prepublication comments on technical accuracy. The government said the piece was too accurate and moved into federal court to stop the magazine from publishing the story.

The defendants in the case argued that all the information in the article was in the public domain, that any citizen could have gotten the same material by going to the Department of Energy, federal libraries, and the like. Other nations already had this information or could easily get it. Experts testifying in behalf of the magazine argued that the article was a harmless exposition of some exotic nuclear technology.

The government disagreed. It said that while some of the material was in the public domain much of the data were not publicly available. Prosecutors and a battery of technical experts argued that the article contained a core of information that had never before been published. The United States also argued that it was immaterial where Morland had gotten his information and whether it had come from classified or public documents. Prosecutors argued that the nation's national security interest permitted the classification and censorship of even information originating in the public domain if, when such information is drawn together, synthesized, and collated, it acquires the character "of presenting immediate, direct and irreparable harm to the interests of the United States." The United States was arguing, then, that some material is automatically classified as soon as it is created if it has the potential to cause harm to the nation. The information in Morland's article met this description, prosecutors argued.

It fell to United States District Judge Robert Warren to evaluate the conflicting claims and reach a decision on the government's request to enjoin the publication of the piece. In a thoughtful opinion in which Warren attempted to sort out the issues in the case, he agreed with the government that there were concepts in the article not found in the public realm—concepts vital to the operation of a thermonuclear bomb. Was the piece a do-it-yourself-guide for a hydrogen bomb? No, Warren said, it was not. "A number of affidavits make quite clear that a sine qua non to thermonuclear capability is a large, sophisticated industrial capability coupled with a coterie of imaginative, resourceful scientists and technicians." But the article could provide some nations with a ticket to bypass blind alleys and help a medium-sized nation to move faster in developing a hydrogen bomb.

To the *Progressive*'s argument that the publication of the article would provide people with the information needed to make an informed decision on nuclear issues, Warren wrote, "This Court can find no plausible reason why the public needs to know the technical details about hydrogen bomb construction to carry on an informed debate on this issue."

Looking to the legal issues in the case, Warren said he saw three differences between this case and the *Pentagon Papers* ruling of 1971. The Pentagon Papers themselves were a historical study; the Morland article was of immediate concern. In the *Pentagon Papers* case there had been no cogent national security reasons advanced by the government when it sought to enjoin the publication of the study. The national security interest is considerably more apparent in the *Progressive* case, Warren noted. Finally, the government lacked substantial legal authority to stop the publication of the Pentagon Papers. The laws raised by the government were vague, not at all appropriate. But Section 2274 of the Atomic Energy Act of 1954 is quite specific in prohibiting anyone from communicating or disclosing any restricted data to any persons "with reasons to believe such data will be utilized to injure the United States or to secure an advantage to any foreign nation." Section 2014 of the same act defined restricted data to include information on the design, manufacture, or utilization of atomic weapons.

Warren concluded that the government had met the heavy burden of showing justification for prior restraint. The judge added that he was not convinced that suppression of the objected-to technical portions of the article would impede the *Progressive* in its crusade to stimulate public debate on the issue of nuclear armament. "What is involved here," Warren concluded, "is information dealing with the most destructive weapon in the history of mankind, information of sufficient destructive potential to nullify the right to free speech and to endanger the right to life itself."

When the injunction was issued, the editors of the *Progressive* and their supporters inside and outside the press vowed to appeal the ruling—to the Supreme Court if necessary. Yet there was a distinct uneasiness among even many persons who sided with the publication. Judge Warren had done a professional job of distinguishing this case from the *Pentagon Papers* ruling. There were important differences. The membership on the High Court had changed as well. Black and Douglas, both of whom had voted against the government in 1971, had left the Court, as had Harlan who had voted with the government. Some newspapers, the *Washington Post* and the *New York Times*, for example, expressed the fear that a damaging precedent could emerge from the Supreme Court if the *Progressive* case ultimately reached the high tribunal.

Then in September of 1979, as the *Progressive* case began its slow ascent up the appellate ladder, a small newspaper in Madison, Wisconsin, published a story containing much of the same information as was in the Morland article. When this occurred, the Department of Justice unhappily withdrew its suit against the *Progressive* (*U.S.* v. *Progressive*, 1979). The confrontation between the press and the government in the Supreme Court was averted. Many journalists expressed relief.

But the victory in the *Progressive* case was bittersweet at best. The publication of the article had been enjoined. A considerable body of legal opinion had supported the notion that the injunction would have been sustained by the Supreme Court, rightly or wrongly. Prior restraint, which had seemed quite distant in the years succeeding *Near* v. *Minnesota* and in the afterglow of the press victory in the *Pentagon Papers* case, took on realistic and frightening new proportions.

Since the Progressive case the federal government has made several new attempts to restrict the flow of information relating to the national security via prior restraints of one sort or another. The administration of President Ronald Reagan has gone to incredible lengths to block the flow of information on a wide range of subjects to the American press and the American people. Many of these actions will be outlined in chapter 5 when access to information is discussed. We will focus only on three instances of prior restraint at this point.

For decades employees of the Central Intelligence Agency have had to sign agreements at the time they are hired in which they promise not to publish "any information or material relating to the Agency, its activities or intelligence activities generally, either during or after the term of employment . . . without specific prior approval of the Agency." This gives the agency a right of prior censorship over any books or articles current or former CIA employees might seek to publish. Previous presidential administrations have vigorously enforced this provision (see *U.S.* v. *Marchetti, 1972*) and in 1980 the U.S. Supreme Court, ignoring the obvious First Amendment questions involved, approved of such enforcement by dealing with the matter as a contractual problem rather than a constitutional one. In *Snepp* v. *U.S.* the High Court ruled that sanctions could be imposed against a former agent who sought to publish a book without getting the CIA's prior approval because the agent had breached his "valid CIA employment agreement."

In January of 1983 the White House budget office proposed a modification in its circular A–122 that would prohibit all persons and organizations who receive federal grants from speaking out on public affairs issues. The revision, which constitutes a prior censorship of millions of people, was only slightly modified before it was adopted in 1984.

On March 11, 1983 the president issued National Security Decision Directive 84, which required all government employees with access to "sensitive compartmentalized information" to sign contracts that subject them to official censorship. "If they wish to publish a book, an article, or even submit a letter to the editor containing any 'information' related to 'intelligence'—a category vast enough to take in most of the domain of national security—they must first show it to the government for review, and, if need be, alteration, not only while in office but for the rest of their lives," wrote Walter Karp in *Harper's* magazine in November of 1985. This directive would cover 128,000 employees, it was learned. President Reagan decided in February of 1984 to hold the censorship provisions of the directive in abeyance, but did not revoke the order, even after the Senate had voted 56 to 34 against the lifetime censorship provisions. Such censorship contracts constitute serious prior censorship, but are justified by the government as a means of limiting damaging leaks of important information. The State Department reports, however, that the total number of damaging leaks conveyed through the writings of government officials during the five years preceding the development of the presidential directive was zero—not one.

The government exercised another blatant form of prior censorship in the autumn of 1983 when it barred reporters from accompanying the U.S. forces that invaded the tiny Caribbean island of Grenada. This was not the first time the government had censored reporters who attempted to cover a war. In both world wars and the Korean conflict the press acceded to censorship, but journalists were allowed on the scene to report the action. Reporters even accompanied Allied forces when they invaded Europe on D-Day in 1944, one of the most secret military operations of all time. Little censorship, however, was exercised during the Vietnam War, and many in the military were unhappy about this.

The Grenada invasion marked the first time the press was left at home. The president permitted the military commander of the operation to decide whether reporters went or stayed in this country as the operation began, and he opted to keep the press at home for the first 48 hours of the invasion. Many believe the intense distrust of the press that developed among many military men during the war in Southeast Asia was largely responsible for this decision in 1983; the generals and admirals still don't trust reporters, whom they blame in part for the United States' having lost the war in Vietnam. Clearly, some civilians in the administration agreed with this point of view. Secretary of State George Schultz said, "It seems as though the reporters are always against us. . . , seeking to report something that's going to screw things up."

Considerable public outcry followed the revelation that reporters were barred from accompanying the invading U.S. forces. The operation itself was not a model of military perfection, and many argued that the public needs to know just how well prepared and well trained the U.S. forces are. Others simply decried the censorship of this important information on general philosophical grounds. Under public pressure Secretary of Defense Caspar Weinberger formed a panel on press-military relations under the leadership of retired army Major General Winant Sidle. The Sidle panel recommended that in the future a pool of reporters, that is a small group of journalists, should accompany the military on all future missions, secret or not, and should share the information they obtain with others in the press. The pool was developed in 1984, and the use of the reporting pool was tested twice during mock military operations. The first test was a failure, but a test in mid-1985 worked well, according to both the military and the reporters involved.

The pool was activated for the U.S. attack on Libya in mid-April in 1986. Eight reporters and photographers boarded a U.S. aircraft carrier in the Mediterranean Sea shortly after attack aircraft from that vessel bombed targets in Libya. Reporters in the pool got first-hand reports on the attack from pilots and others. "In general, the pool worked well," said Charles Lewis, AP Washington Bureau Chief.

The issue of prior restraint arose again in May of 1986 when CIA Director William Casey threatened to initiate prosecution of *The Washington Post, The Washington Times, The New York Times, Time,* and *Newsweek* if stories about U.S. intelligence gathering capabilities were published. The stories were generated while the government was prosecuting Ronald Pelton, a former intelligence specialist with the National Security Agency, for selling secrets to the Russians. The stories focused upon a top secret U.S. eavesdropping operation against the Soviet Union, something Pelton had apparently revealed to the Russians. Casey met with two senior editors at *The Washington Post* and threatened to invoke a thirty-five-year-old federal law that makes it a crime to reveal information about American ciphers, code-breaking, and other communication intelligence functions. *The Post* ultimately published a version of the story, but without three paragraphs containing a description of the interception device. President Reagan called *Post* publisher Katherine Graham and personally asked that the material be deleted. The Justice Department, which had never used the 1950 law cited by Casey to prosecute a journalist, said it was very reluctant to prosecute any reporter under the statute, and the issue died away as the Pelton trial ended.

All the newspapers and magazines had gotten the information about the eavesdropping capability legally. Reporters argued that the government used a double standard by invoking the classification of material to try to block the publication or broadcast of stories. When the government wanted to prove a point or make a case for its own action (as when President Reagan revealed that American intelligence agencies had eavesdropped on communications between Libyan officials and their agents in Germany prior to the bombing of the discotheque in Germany which prompted the air attacks against that African nation) it never hesitated to declassify material. But it uses classification to block the flow of information that is sometimes embarrassing to the government, journalists argue.

While national security issues are frequently the source of prior restraint problems, other issues can provoke authorities to the application of restraint. In 1942, in the case of *Chaplinsky* v. *New Hampshire*, the Supreme Court identified one category of speech in which the application of prior censorship is not necessarily a violation of the First Amendment. Justice Frank Murphy wrote:

> There are certain well-defined and narrowly limited classes of speech, the *prevention* [emphasis added] and punishment of which have never been thought to raise any constitutional problems. These include . . . fighting words—those which by their very utterance inflict injury or tend to incite an immediate breach of the peace. It has been well observed that such utterances are no essential part of any exposition of ideas, and are of such slight social value as a step to the truth that any benefit that may be derived from them is clearly outweighed by the social interest in order and morality.

In the *Chaplinsky* case a Jehovah's Witness who sought to distribute pamphlets denouncing religion as a fraud in Rochester, New Hampshire, angered citizens. When warned by a law officer of the danger to his safety, the Witness called the marshal a "God-damned racketeer" and a "damned Facist." He was convicted of violating a state statute that forbade any person to "address any offensive, derisive, or annoying words, to any other person who is lawfully in any street or other public place, nor call him by any offensive or derisive name."

The prohibition of this kind of verbal assault is permissible so long as the statutes are carefully drawn and do not permit the application of the law to protected speech. Also, the "fighting words" must be used in a personal, face-to-face encounter—a true verbal assault. In 1972 the Supreme Court ruled that laws on the subject must be limited to words "that have a direct tendency to cause acts of violence by the person to whom, individually, the remark is addressed" (*Gooding* v. *Wilson*, 1972).

The 1977 confrontation in Skokie, Illinois, between Nazi protesters and city officials presents a contemporary example of a multitude of free-speech problems, including the so-called fighting-words doctrine. In 1976 members of the National Socialist party said they planned to peacefully demonstrate in Skokie, a community with a large Jewish population, to protest the racial integration of nearby Chicago schools. The protest was prohibited by village officials, who said the Nazis had failed to obtain $350,000 worth of liability and property damage insurance as required by a Skokie Park District ordinance.

After the Nazis announced that they planned to protest against the insurance ordinance, the village obtained a temporary restraining order blocking the demonstration and then adopted three new ordinances regarding public marches and protests. In addition to the insurance requirements, the village ruled that a member of a political party cannot march in a military-style uniform and ruled that it is not permissible to disseminate material intended to incite racial hatred. State and federal courts in Illinois invalidated all the ordinances, ruling that they were discriminatory or abridged constitutionally protected rights of free speech (*Collin* v. *Smith*, 1978; *Village of Skokie* v. *National Socialist Party*, 1978).

The Illinois Supreme Court, in refusing to enjoin the display of the swastika and other Nazi symbols, rejected the contention that such display constituted "fighting words" sufficient "to overcome the heavy presumption against the constitutional validity of a prior restraint" (*Village of Skokie* v. *National Socialist Party*, 1978). "Peaceful demonstrations cannot be totally precluded solely because that display [of the swastika] may provoke a violent reaction by those who view it. . . . A speaker who gives prior notice of his message has not compelled a confrontation with those who voluntarily listen."

In *Handbook of Free Speech and Free Press*, authors Jerome Barron and C. Thomas Dienes suggest two key questions in determining whether so-called fighting words might be suppressed. First, is there imminent danger of disorder? Second, does the speaker use provocative language that constitutes fighting words or that incites his audience to a clear and present danger of disorder? Both questions must be answered in the affirmative before the speech can reasonably be restrained.

Freedom of Expression in Schools

The prior restraint of speech and press in schools is also permissible in several circumstances, some of which run closely parallel with the fighting-words doctrine. The starting point for any discussion of First Amendment rights of students is *Tinker* v. *Des Moines Independent School District*, a 1969 U.S. Supreme Court ruling that for the first time extended the constitutional rights of free expression to students. But the court placed some limits on student speech and press rights as well, noting that "conduct by the student, in class or out of it, which for any reason—whether it stems from time, place, or type of behavior—materially disrupts classwork or involves substantial disorder or invasion of the rights of others is, of course, not immunized by the constitutional guarantee of freedom of speech."

The Supreme Court added little more to an understanding of this issue between 1969 and 1986. Five cases came to the court on petitions for certiorari. But the court refused to grant the writ four times and dismissed the fifth case as moot when it was learned the plaintiff had graduated from high school. Consequently, the lower federal courts, especially the courts of appeal, had to develop the *Tinker* rule on their own. And this resulted in serious inconsistency among the circuits, according to an article in the *Michigan Law Review*. In one case a federal appeals court invalidated high school rules requiring the prior submission of a student newspaper because the rules were vague, too broad, and failed to provide a prompt review and appeals procedure (*Baughman* v. *Freienmuth,* 1973). In another case an appellate court ruled that a college president could not cut off funds to a school newspaper that advocated segregation (*Joyner* v. *Whiting,* 1973). Another appellate court overturned the expulsion of a student for distributing, without approval, an underground newspaper critical of school authorities because there was no evidence that the distribution of the paper would cause a substantial disruption of school activities (*Scoville* v. *Board of Education,* 1970).

On the other hand, an appellate court upheld the right of school authorities to stop the distribution of a voluntary survey of student sexual attitudes and experiences and publication of the results of this survey when psychologists suggested that some students would experience some level of stress from confronting some of the questions in the survey (*Trachtman* v. *Anker,* 1977). Another appellate court ruled that "Writers on a high school newspaper do not have an unfettered constitutional right to be free from prepublication review" (*Nicholson* v. *Board of Education,* 1982).

In 1986, the Supreme Court handed down its second ruling regarding the First Amendment rights of students. In a 7–2 ruling, the High Court said it was permissible for a Spanaway, Washington, high school to suspend a student who had used sexual metaphor and innuendo in a speech to a school assembly to tout the virility of a candidate for student government office. Some of the six hundred students who attended the assembly responded to the speech with hooting and yelling. While Chief Justice Burger, who wrote the Court's opinion, at one point called the speech obscene, nothing in Matthew Fraser's short speech met the legal definition of obscenity (see chapter 8). In fact, the speech was reprinted in stories about the case in many newspapers and magazines.

Burger stressed, in his opinion, the marked distinction between the Tinker case, which focused upon a political message, and the purely sexual content of Fraser's speech. "The undoubted freedom to advocate unpopular and controversial views in schools and classrooms must be balanced against the society's countervailing interest in teaching students the boundaries of socially appropriate behavior," the Chief Justice wrote. The schools could reasonably conclude, he said, that the essential lessons of civil, mature conduct cannot be conveyed in a school that tolerates "lewd, or offensive speech." Burger added that the "pervasive sexual innuendo in Fraser's speech was plainly offensive to both teachers and students. Dissenter Justice John Paul Stevens questioned whether "a group of judges who are at least two generations and three thousand miles away from the scene of the crime" were as well qualified as Fraser to determine whether the speech would offend his contemporaries, who went on to elect the candidate for whom he spoke. (*Bethel School District* v. *Fraser,* 1986)

From these and other seemingly contradictory decisions, several criteria have emerged that suggest the circumstances under which student free-speech rights may be denied. The first is the original Tinker standard; school officials may regulate expression that "materially disrupts classwork or involves substantial disorder." Courts have interpreted disruption to mean "a physical disruption which constitutes a substantial material threat to the orderly operation of the campus." And the fear of substantial disruption must be based on what the courts have called "substantial reliable information," not merely intuition. Schools can limit expression that may invade the rights of others. This standard generally refers to problems of libel or invasion of privacy. The school can also block the publication or distribution of material that could result in tort liability for the school itself. A school can be held responsible, for example, for material that is published in a school newspaper or yearbook.

School officials, in light of the Fraser ruling by the U.S. Supreme Court, are given generally wide latitude in blocking or punishing speech or publications that they consider sexually provocative or offensive. The Fraser case provides few guidelines in this regard and lower courts will surely have to draw some boundaries to protect the legitimate First Amendment interests of high school students. Whether the Fraser ruling will be applicable to college and university administrators is an open question, since Chief Justice Burger seemed to be especially concerned in his opinion about the damage Fraser's speech might cause to the less mature students, some of whom were not yet fourteen years old. Burger's concern is surely not applicable to the eighteen-year-old college freshman.

Clearly, any school can limit any kind of speech or press that any other government can limit, such as material that could incite violent or illegal actions, endanger national security or is legally obscene. And, apparently the courts are willing to permit the schools to censor student newspapers that carry advertisements for drug paraphernalia on the grounds that the sale and use of such paraphernalia may endanger the health or safety of students (see *Williams* v. *Spencer,* 1980). Schools can also insist that the distribution of student newspapers and other handouts be carried out at a reasonable time, in a reasonable place, in a reasonable manner.

A commonly asked question regarding schools and the control of the student press focuses upon funding. Can a school attempt to control a newspaper by threatening to remove the funding of the publication? A 1983 case involving the University of Minnesota's *Minnesota Daily* provides some answers to this question. At the end of the 1978–79 school year the *Minnesota Daily* published its Finals Edition, which offended literally thousands of persons on and off the Twin Cities campus. "The newspaper," wrote University of Minnesota journalism professor Don Gillmor, "through sexual gabble and toilet talk, was designed to irritate Third World students, Blacks, Jews, feminists, gays, lesbians and Christians." Through what it called an exclusive interview with Jesus Christ, the newspaper "revealed" to readers that Christ was a druggie, a bootlegger, a lecher, and a homosexual, for example.

The newspaper, the university administration and the board of regents were inundated with complaints from all segments of the state's population. Hundreds of students were upset enough to begin a drive to change the student-fee support system for the newspaper. The *Daily* is typical of many university newspapers in that a small portion of student activity fees—in this case $2 per semester—was automatically given to the newspaper. It was suggested that students should be given the right to choose not to support the newspaper. The regents liked this idea as well, and despite the advice of two review committees, which recommended just the opposite, voted in 1980 for a refundable fee system that would permit students to refuse to financially support the newspaper. A court case resulted and in 1983 the Eighth U.S. Court of Appeals ruled that the regents' action violated the First Amendment. If the fee system had been changed, the court said, simply to respond to student complaints of being coerced into supporting views in the newspaper that they opposed, there would be no problem. But the *Daily* carried a wide variety of views, something for virtually everyone on campus. More importantly, it was clear under the circumstances that the fee system was changed because the regents were unhappy with the 1979 Finals Edition. "Several Regents testified that one of the reasons that they voted in favor of the resolution was that students should not be forced to support a paper which was sacrilegious and vulgar," the court noted. The heavy political pressure on the regents and their two resolutions deploring the content in the Finals Edition added weight to the conclusion that they were attempting to punish the newspaper. Finally, the University of Minnesota has several state campuses, but the fee-support system was changed only on the Twin Cities campus, home of the offending newspaper. "Our study of the record . . . leaves us with the definite and firm conviction that this change in funding would not have occurred absent the public hue and cry that the *Daily's* offensive contents provoked. Reducing the revenues available to the newspaper is therefore forbidden by the First Amendment," the court concluded (*Stanley* v. *McGrath,* 1983).

Reducing the financial support for a student newspaper is clearly something a school administrator or school board can do—but only if it is done for the proper reasons. Any hint that censorship is behind the reduction could result in such an action running afoul of the First Amendment.

Book Banning

Another school censorship problem arose in the early 1980s and quickly became a serious legal issue. The banning of books in libraries—primarily school libraries—reached epidemic levels in 1981 and 1982. A survey by the American Library Association reported that the number of challenges to books in libraries tripled to nearly 1,000 during 1981. Conservative groups have been active in banning attempts, but other individuals not usually associated with this problem are active as well. Black parents in several areas, for example, urged a ban on Mark Twain's *The Adventures of Huckleberry Finn* because of what they felt was racist language. The most common reason would-be censors give to justify removing books from library shelves is that a book is unsuitable for minors because of its vulgarity or its description of sexual behavior, according to the *New York Times*. But these censors also condemn the depiction of unorthodox family arrangements; speculations about Christ; sexual explicitness, even in a biological context; unflattering portraits of American authority; criticisms of business and corporate practices; and radical political ideas.

Censorship activities have focused upon a wide variety of books, according to the survey sponsored by the Association of American Publishers, the American Library Association, and the Association for Supervision and Curriculum Development and reported in the *New York Times*. Some of the books most commonly attacked by censors are:

Jaws by Peter Benchley

Several books by Judy Blume, a best-selling children's author

The Pill Versus the Springhill Mine Disaster and other novels by Richard Brautigan

Manchild in the Promised Land by Claude Brown

Kramer Versus Kramer by Avery Corman

Catch-22 by Joseph Heller

Sons by Evan Hunter

Valley Forge by MacKinlay Kantor

One Flew Over the Cuckoo's Nest by Ken Kesey

The Thorn Birds by Colleen McCullough

The Godfather by Mario Puzo

One Day in the Life of Ivan Denisovitch by Aleksander Solzhenitsyn

The American Heritage Dictionary

The Dictionary of American Slang

Trial of the Catonsville Nine by Daniel Berrigan

Our Bodies, Ourselves by the Boston Women's Health Book Collective

The Art of Loving by Erich Fromm

Boss: Richard J. Daley of Chicago by Mike Royko

The Electric Kool-Aid Acid Test by Tom Wolfe

Also included in the list of frequently censored books are *A Farewell to Arms, 1984, Brave New World, The Catcher in the Rye, The Merchant of Venice, The Grapes of Wrath, Huckleberry Finn,* and *Stuart Little.*

Most school boards were woefully unprepared for the pressure generated by parents and community groups to remove books from the shelves of libraries. While book banning has occurred as a periodic nuisance over the past two hundred years, the problem has rarely reached the courts. Consequently, little law exists on the subject to advise library supervisors or school boards. It took only a few years for a case to reach the Supreme Court of the United States during this round of book censorship.

Members of the Board of Education of the Island Trees School District in Eastern New York removed nine books from the high school library. Included among the banished books were *The Fixer* by Bernard Malamud, *Slaughterhouse Five* by Kurt Vonnegut, *The Naked Ape* by Desmond Morris, *Soul on Ice* by Eldridge Cleaver, and the *Best Short Stories by Negro Writers.* Student Council President Steven Pico and four other students challenged this action in the United States district court. They argued that their First Amendment rights to read these books had been violated. But United States District Judge George Pratt rejected these arguments and ruled that a school board has the right to remove books that are irrelevant, vulgar, and immoral and in bad taste. The First Amendment was not violated by such action, Pratt ruled, citing a seven-year-old Second United States Court of Appeals decision (*President's Council District 25 v. Community School Board,* 1972). The judge's ruling came on the board of education's motion for summary judgment. No trial was ever held to establish the facts, including the school board's motives for removing these volumes (*Pico v. Island Trees,* 1979).

The Second United States Court of Appeals reversed Judge Pratt's order and ordered the district court to hold a trial. The court stood by its earlier decision that permitted school authorities to remove vulgar or immoral books from the school library. But Steven Pico and the other students should have been given a chance at trial to persuade the court that the school board's ostensible justification for removing the books (that they were in bad taste, vulgar, etc.) was merely a pretext for the suppression of freedom of speech. The board could not ban the books if their decision to remove them was based on their political or moral disagreement with the content of the works.

In March 1982 the Supreme Court heard arguments in the case and three months later handed down one of the least-satisfying rulings in many years. On the bottom line the High Court affirmed the court of appeals and returned the case to district court for trial. However the High Court was fractured into several groups, and seven different opinions were written.

The Court's opinion was written by Justice William Brennan. A school board cannot, under the First Amendment, remove books from a school library simply because it disapproves of the political ideas or philosophies expressed in the books, wrote Justice Brennan. Books may be removed if they are persuasively vulgar or if they are educationally unsuitable. But the First Amendment guarantees to students a right to receive ideas, and the board of education cannot interfere with that right simply because it disagrees with those ideas. Brennan mustered the support of Justices Thurgood Marshall and John Stevens behind his opinion.

Justice William Blackmun concurred with all of Brennan's opinion except his reference to a "right to receive ideas," a controversial notion Brennan has promulgated in recent years. Blackmun said he based his opinion on a principle narrower and far more basic than the right to receive ideas. The state may not suppress exposure to ideas for the sole purpose of suppressing exposure to those ideas, he wrote. The fifth vote in the five-to-four decision came from Justice Byron White, who seemed dismayed at Brennan's exploration of constitutional issues. A trial was needed, he said, to find out what motivated the removal of the books. When the facts are established, he wrote, the Court can develop constitutional law on the matter.

Chief Justice Warren Burger and Justices Lewis Powell, William Rehnquist, and Sandra O'Connor all dissented. All the dissenting opinions reflected the position that it was the responsibility of the school board, not of a federal court, to run the school. "The plurality [Brennan, Marshall, Blackmun, and Stevens] concludes that the Constitution requires school boards to justify to its teenage pupils the decision to remove a particular book from a school library," Burger wrote. Other dissenters echoed Burger's complaint.

The ruling was particularly unsatisfactory because the Court failed to provide any clear guidance on an issue that is plaguing scores of school libraries across the nation. The splits within the Court left even a careful reader of the decision with little certainty about how the Court would act in a subsequent case. Four justices said school boards cannot remove books from a library for political or moral reasons; four justices said school boards can remove books for any reason; and Justice White refused to say where he stands on the issue. "We should not decide constitutional questions until it is necessary to do so," he wrote. Even the language in the Court's opinion lacks clarity. Brennan said that a book can be removed from the shelves if it is "persuasively vulgar" or "educationally unsuitable." What do these terms mean?

No court decision since 1982 has helped to clarify the meaning of the ruling in *Pico*. The High Court's decision clearly established a First Amendment right of access to the information in books already held in secondary school libraries. School boards no longer have the broad discretion once exercised to remove works they personally find offensive. And school boards must exercise great caution to assure that when they are operating in what they consider the best interests of their students, they do not tread on educationally relevant information, noted Donald J. Dunn in an article in the *Law Library Journal*. But work still needs to be done, for the Supreme Court has not dispelled all the confusion surrounding the book removal issue. Other courts, if not the Supreme Court, will have to refine the broad and even vague standards enunciated in *Pico* before the issue will be clearly resolved.

Other forms of prior restraint also emerge from time to time as government attempts to control one kind of publication or another. An interesting case developed in the early 1980s, when the Securities and Exchange Commission (SEC), a federal agency that regulates the investment business in the nation, attempted to block the publication of a newsletter published by an investment advisor named Christopher Lowe. Lowe had been convicted on three different occasions of serious misconduct in connection with investment advisors' businesses. Pursuant to the Investment Advisors Act of 1940, the SEC revoked Lowe's registration as an investment advisor. But Lowe continued to publish his investment newsletter on a regular basis and sent it to paying subscribers. The SEC then attempted to stop the publication of the newsletter, arguing that because Lowe was not a registered investment advisor, his publication of the newsletter was a violation of the law.

The Investment Advisors Act of 1940 clearly makes it illegal for any unregistered individual to use the mails or any other means or "instrumentality of interstate commerce in connection with his or her business as an investment advisor." But the law contains an exception for the publisher of any "bonafide newspaper, news magazine or business or financial publication of general and regular circulation." Lowe made two arguments. He first asserted that the First Amendment blocked the SEC from stopping his publication. Failing that, he argued that his newsletter was a bonafide newspaper and hence exempt from the restrictions in the act. The U.S. Court of Appeals ruled against Lowe (*SEC* v. *Lowe,* 1984), but the Supreme Court reversed this ruling. The High Court did not even consider the First Amendment challenge. There is a maxim in the law that judges should consider constitutional questions last, after they have attempted to resolve the issue in other ways. That is what the Supreme Court did as Justice Stevens, speaking for a unanimous Court, ruled that Lowe's newsletter was a bonafide newspaper and exempt from the restrictions in the act. "Investment newsletters that offer disinterested investment advice to paid subscribers on a regularly scheduled basis fall within the bonafide newspaper exemption to the registration requirements of the Investment Advisors Act," Stevens wrote. Responding to government concerns about Lowe's past illegal activities Stevens noted that the term "bonafide" describes the publication, not the publisher. "Hence, Lowe's unsavory past does not prevent his newsletter from being bonafide" (*Lowe* v. *SEC,* 1985).

SUMMARY

While virtually all American legal scholars agree that the adoption of the First Amendment in 1791 was designed to abolish prior restraint in this nation, prior censorship still exists by virtue of an opinion of the Supreme Court in

1931. In *Near* v. *Minnesota* Chief Justice Charles Evans Hughes ruled that while prior restraint is unacceptable in most instances, there are times when it must be tolerated if the republic is to survive. The most vivid example cited by Hughes is the prior restraint of the publication of information that may assist the enemy during wartime. Hughes's "wartime" exception has been translated today to mean a "national security" exception, and in recent years in two important cases the press has been stopped from publishing material that courts believed to be too sensitive. While the Supreme Court finally permitted the *New York Times* and the *Washington Post* to publish the so-called Pentagon Papers, the newspapers were blocked for two weeks from printing the material. And in the end the High Court merely ruled that the government had failed to make its case, not that the newspapers had an absolute right to publish the material. The *Progressive* magazine was enjoined from publishing an article about the hydrogen bomb. Only the publication of the material by a small newspaper in Wisconsin thwarted government efforts to permanently stop publication of the material.

Chief Justice Hughes said in 1931 that prior restraint is also permissible in instances in which a speaker or publisher is attempting to incite violence. The Supreme Court has developed a "fighting-words" doctrine, which has been applied in several instances to block expression that might incite others to violence, although in recent cases involving a protest by members of the Nazi party in Illinois, both federal and state courts have ruled that members of an audience have an obligation to restrain themselves, and expression cannot be prohibited merely because the speaker has chosen to appear before a volatile group.

Schools must live by the First Amendment. So long as expression does not substantially and materially interfere with the requirements of appropriate discipline in the operation of the schools, invade the rights of others, subject the school to liability, or violate other laws that restrict adults as well, students may speak and publish freely, subject only to other community and state laws, such as libel or invasion of privacy statutes. High school administrators, however, have additional power to control sexually offensive speech on publications. There is however a new threat to freedom of expression in the schools as a wave of book banning has hit school libraries. A plurality of the Supreme Court ruled in 1982 that the removal of books from the shelves of school libraries cannot be motivated because school members disagree with the political ideas or philosophies in the books. Books can be removed, however, if they are considered persuasively vulgar or educationally unsuitable. The Court was badly split in the decision and the ruling was murky. The issue remains to be clarified.

TIME, PLACE, AND MANNER RESTRICTIONS

Justification of the previously noted instances of prior restraint—both inside and outside the schools—was based on the content of the article or the speech; that is, what was written or said provoked the prior censorship. Prior censorship can also be justified, however, on the basis of where or when a particular expression is scheduled to occur. In these instances the content of the publication or speech is not considered material in determining whether the prior restraint is justified or whether it is prohibited by the First Amendment. Such rules are called **time, place, and manner restrictions** and focus on when, where, or how the expression is to be made public. Sometimes these rules involve the need for licenses prior to the public distribution of printed matter; sometimes restrictions on door-to-door solicitation are concerned. In all cases, however, courts insist that such rules be applied without regard to the content of the publication or message. For example, when the city of Brentwood, Tennessee, adopted a rule that said that commercial handbills could not be delivered in any public place but that newspapers, political, and religious material could be delivered in this manner, the Tennessee Supreme Court invalidated the ordinance because it was not content neutral (*H & L Messengers* v. *Brentwood*, 1979). Similarly, a federal district court in New Mexico ruled that an Alamogordo city ordinance that exempted religious and charitable organizations from a general ban on door-to-door solicitation was invalid because it allowed the city manager discretion in determining what is and what is not a religious cause. This is a content consideration (*Weissman* v. *Alamogordo*, 1979).

Consideration of such time, place, and manner rules by the Supreme Court dates to the 1930s.

Public Forums

The preeminent judicial ruling on the question of the validity of licensing laws is the case of *Lovell* v. *Griffin* decided by the nation's High Court in 1938. The city of Griffin, Georgia, had an ordinance that prohibited distribution of circulars, handbooks, advertising, and literature of any kind without first obtaining written permission from the city manager. Under the law, the city manager had considerable discretion as to whether to give permission. Alma Lovell was a member of the Jehovah's Witnesses religious sect, an intense and ruggedly evangelical order that suffered severe persecutions in the first half of this century. But the Witnesses doggedly continued to spread the Word, passing out millions of leaflets and pamphlets and attempting to proselytize anyone who would listen. Laws like the distribution ordinance were common in many communities in the United States and were directed at stopping the distribution of material by groups such as the Witnesses.

Alma Lovell didn't even attempt to get a license before she circulated pamphlets, and she was arrested, convicted, and fined fifty dollars for violating the city ordinance. When she refused to pay the fine, she was sentenced to fifty days in jail. At the trial the Jehovah's Witnesses freely admitted the illegal distribution, but argued that the statute was invalid on its face because it violated the First Amendment guarantees of freedom of the press and freedom of religion.

On appeal the Supreme Court agreed that the law did indeed violate freedom of the press. Chief Justice Charles Evans Hughes wrote, "We think that the ordinance is invalid on its face" because it strikes at the very foundation of freedom of the press by subjecting it to license and censorship. The city argued that the First Amendment applies only to newspapers and regularly published materials like magazines. The High Court disagreed, ruling that the amendment applies to pamphlets and leaflets as well: "These indeed have been historic weapons in the defense of liberty, as the pamphlets of Thomas Paine and others in our own history abundantly attest. The press in its historic connotation comprehends every sort of publication which affords a vehicle of information and opinion."

Lawyers for Griffin also argued that the First Amendment was not applicable because the licensing law said nothing about publishing, but only concerned distribution. Again the Court disagreed, noting that liberty of circulation is as essential to freedom of expression as liberty of publication. Chief Justice Hughes wrote, "Without the circulation, the publication would be of little value."

Public Streets

Nineteen months after the *Lovell* decision the Supreme Court decided a second distribution case, a case that involved licensing laws in four different cities. The four cases were decided as one (*Schneider* v. *New Jersey*, 1939). A Los Angeles ordinance prohibited the distribution of handbills on public streets on the grounds that distribution contributed to the litter problem. Ordinances in Milwaukee, Wisconsin, and Worcester, Massachusetts, were justified on the same basis—keeping the city streets clean.

An Irvington, New Jersey, law was far broader, prohibiting street distribution or house-to-house calls unless permission was first obtained from the local police chief. The police department asked distributors for considerable personal information and could reject applicants the law officers deemed not of good character. This action was ostensibly to protect the public against criminals.

Justice Owen Roberts delivered the opinion of the Court, which struck down each of the four laws. Justice Roberts said that a city can enact regulations in the interest of public safety, health, and welfare, but not regulations that interfere with the liberty of the press or freedom of expression. He then gave some examples of what he meant, examples that have proved most helpful in framing such ordinances. Cities, he said, have the responsibility to keep the public streets open and available for the movement of people and property, and laws to regulate the conduct of those who would interfere with this legitimate public problem are constitutional (*Schneider v. New Jersey*, 1939):

> For example, a person could not exercise this liberty [of free expression] by taking his stand in the middle of a crowded street, contrary to traffic regulations, and maintain his position to the stoppage of all traffic; a group of distributors could not insist upon a constitutional right to form a cordon across the street and to allow no pedestrian to pass who did not accept a tendered leaflet; nor does the guarantee of freedom of speech or of the press deprive a municipality of power to enact regulations against throwing literature in the streets.

These kinds of activities, Roberts said, bear no relationship to the freedom to speak, write, print, or distribute information or opinion. The justice closed by saying that the High Court characterized freedom of speech and freedom of the press as fundamental personal rights and liberties: "The phrase is not an empty one and was not lightly used. . . . It stresses, as do many opinions of this Court, the importance of preventing the restriction of enjoyment of these liberties."

A somewhat different dimension of this same problem arose in a Connecticut case in which, again, members of Jehovah's Witnesses faced criminal prosecution under an ordinance that limited the solicitation of funds (*Cantwell v. Connecticut*, 1940). Jesse Cantwell and his two sons attempted to carry their religious message along the streets of a heavily Catholic neighborhood in New Haven, Connecticut. They were arrested for violating a state law that prohibited the solicitation of money by a religious group without first gaining approval from the local public official whose job it was to decide whether the religious cause in question was a "bona fide object of charity" and whether it conformed to "reasonable standards of efficiency and integrity." The Supreme Court tossed out the law as a violation of the First Amendment. For the unanimous Court, Justice Roberts wrote that the state could, in order to protect its citizens from fraudulent solicitations, require strangers in the community to establish identity and authority to act for the cause they purport to represent before permitting any solicitation in the community. And the state could pass rules setting reasonable regulatory limits on the time of day solicitations could be made (no solicitations before 9 A.M. or after 10 P.M., for example):

> But to condition the solicitation of aid for the perpetuation of religious views or systems upon a license, the grant of which rests in the exercise of a determination by state authority as to what is a religious cause, is to lay a forbidden burden upon the exercise of liberty protected by the Constitution.

Airports

Each of these three cases concerned restrictions of expression in the so-called public forum—public streets and parks. Other recent cases have focused on this same problem. Airports, for example, have become a popular place for solicitors for various religious and political causes. Milwaukee County was one of many governing bodies that tried to restrict such solicitation on the grounds that the passageways and corridors at General Billy Mitchell Field were too narrow and crowded to allow such activity. The United States District Court for Eastern Wisconsin ruled that the county airport is a public forum and that county rules that require prior permission before any solicitation can take place violate the First Amendment: "Crowded conditions may require restrictions to ensure the efficient operation of the airport," the court ruled. But such conditions did not justify sweeping rules that totally excluded solicitation by many persons and groups (*International Society for Krishna Consciousness* v. *Wolke*, 1978). Other courts have made similar rulings with regard to airport regulations.

State Fairs

In a similar manner the United States Supreme Court ruled that officials of the Minnesota State Fair can regulate solicitations on the fair grounds during the annual summer event. Anyone who seeks to sell or distribute merchandise or even hand out written material is required to work from booths rented for a small fee from fair officials. Booths are provided on a first-come, first-serve basis, and the rule applies to everyone—commercial, nonprofit, and charitable organizations—equally. The International Society for Krishna Consciousness challenged the rule, arguing it violated their religious freedom as well as their freedom of expression. Justice White and four other members of the High Court disagreed.

White reiterated that in order for a time, place, and manner rule to be acceptable it must (1) be content neutral, (2) serve a significant governmental interest, and (3) leave ample alternative channels for the communication of the information. The Minnesota State Fair rules are content neutral; they apply to all equally. The state has a strong interest in maintaining the orderly movement of crowds at the fairgrounds. The grounds are small, only 125 acres; crowds are heavy, up to 160,000 persons on a weekend day. The fairgrounds are not like a public street, White said, which is always open and normally uncongested. Finally, the members of the Society for Krishna Consciousness can perform their ritualistic solicitation outside the fairgrounds. Members can mingle with the crowds on the grounds, talk with people, and propagate their views. They can even have a booth on the fairgrounds. There are alternative means to communicate their information. "The Minnesota State Fair is a limited public forum in that it exists to provide a means for a great number of exhibitors temporarily to present their products or views . . . to a large number of people in an efficient fashion," Justice White wrote. Considering these limits, the rules are reasonable (*Heffron* v. *International Society*, 1981).

Justice Brennan and three other members of the Court agreed that rules that confined selling goods and literature and the solicitation of funds to the booths are permissible. They would have struck down, however, the portion of the rules that prohibit the distribution of literature on the grounds, arguing that this certainly does not exacerbate crowd-control problems.

Restrictions regarding the placement of news racks on city streets have also been scrutinized by the courts in recent years. So long as these rules do not discriminate unfairly against one particular publication or one kind of publication, rules that limit the number of racks on any one corner are generally considered permissible time, place, and manner restrictions. Glendale, California, for example, adopted an ordinance that said that no more than eight news racks could be on a public sidewalk in a space of 200 feet in any direction within the same block of the same street. In setting priorities to determine which publications could use the limited number of news racks, the city gave preference to "newspapers of general circulation for Los Angeles County." The county code defined a newspaper of general circulation as one with a subscription list of paying customers and that has been published at least weekly within the district for at least three years. Also, according to the code, a newspaper of general circulation must have substantial distribution and contain at least 25 percent news in each edition. Papers not meeting this description were given a lower priority under the city ordinance. Because its paper did not contain at least 25 percent news, the Socialist Labor party challenged the ordinance as a violation of the First Amendment. The California Court of Appeals rejected the challenge. The court said:

> When the law, ordinance, or other rule is aimed directly at pure speech or content, it is examined for constitutionality by strait and narrow measures and almost no interference is allowed. On the other hand, when only the mechanical means or particular time or place of dissemination is involved, some reasonable limitation is recognized.

The court said sidewalk space is limited; the city has an obligation to allocate it. The ordinance was not intentionally aimed at the Socialist Labor party paper, but at any publication that did not contain 25 percent news. The preference for newspapers of general circulation is "simply a means of balancing the problem of public demand and its supply" (*Socialist Labor Party* v. *Glendale*, 1978).

A Texas civil court of appeals ruled that a city of Houston ordinance that made it unlawful for persons to sell newspapers from street corners to passing motorists was unconstitutional. The problem the ordinance sought to solve was a real one. There was considerable traffic congestion at downtown streets; the newspaper hawkers, often either quite young or quite old, stood on medians in the roadway to sell the newspapers to persons in automobiles stopped temporarily in traffic. This means of selling was dangerous to both motorists and to the salespersons. Still, the city ordinance went too far, the court said. "The city has banned newspaper sales by persons of all ages to occupants of all motor vehicles located on public property, including residential neighborhoods, regardless of the time of day or night, and regardless of whether the cars are moving, standing, parked or even not in the traffic lanes," the court noted. As such the law was too broad. While the city might fashion a ban on such selling on congested downtown streets during rush hours, the ordinance went too far and interfered with protected freedoms (*Houston Chronicle* v. *Houston,* 1981).

Clifton, New Jersey, attempted to go further than both Glendale and Houston and prohibit all newspaper vending machines on city sidewalks. The city said it was responding to the growing proliferation of newspaper racks, a phenomenon common in virtually every city as more and more national publications like *USA Today* and the *Wall Street Journal* attempt to capture street sales. A New Jersey superior court threw out the city's ordinance, stating there was no evidence to support the claim that the newsracks impeded the flow of pedestrian traffic. "Government may reasonably regulate the time, place or manner of the expression of speech, provided the regulation is content neutral, is narrowly tailored to serve a significant governmental interest, and leaves open ample alternative channels of communication," the court ruled. The Clifton ordinance was not narrowly tailored and did not further any substantial government interest (*Passaic Daily News* v. *Clifton,* 1985).

Several states and cities have attempted to regulate the placement of billboards, with mixed results. The problem in such regulation is coping with the rights of store owners to advertise their businesses. The dilemma is best illustrated by a 1981 United States Supreme Court ruling on a San Diego billboard ordinance. The ordinance prohibited all outdoor advertising except on-site commercial signs that promoted goods or services offered by businesses on the premises. That is, owners of hardware stores could erect on their property signs that advertised materials sold in the hardware store. Acknowledging that the ban was prompted by substantial state interests in the aesthetic quality of the city and in traffic safety, the Supreme Court nevertheless struck down the city law. The flaw in the ordinance was the broad exemption granted for on-site commercial speech. "Insofar as the city tolerates billboards at all," Justice White wrote in the plurality Court opinion, "it cannot choose to limit their content to commercial messages." The law is not content neutral; it reaches into the realm of protected speech, he wrote. To be constitutional, then, the ordinance must allow noncommercial (Save the Whales, Abortion Is a Crime, etc.) on-site billboards as well. A total ban on billboards, if properly justified, might also be acceptable (*Metromedia* v. *San Diego,* 1981; see also *Donnelly* v. *Campbell,* 1980; *Metromedia* v. *Baltimore,* 1982; and *Norton* v. *Arlington Heights,* 1982).

Other Public Forums

Public streets, airports, and state fairs are some of the public forums that have been discussed thus far in relation to permissible time, place, and manner rules. In the early 1980s federal courts were asked to examine two other communication forums and to determine (1) whether they were public forums and (2) whether decisions made regarding their use violated the First Amendment. The forums were mailboxes and public television stations.

For nearly fifty years the Congress has prohibited deposit of unstamped mailable matter in a letter box in front of someone's home. The rule was adopted in 1934 when the postal service was losing revenues because many organizations and businesses were hand delivering circulars, letters, bills, and other mailable material and depositing them in homeowners' mailboxes. The law is justified today by the government on three grounds:

1. The law protects postal revenues.
2. The law facilitates the efficient and secure delivery of the mail.
3. The law promotes a mail patron's privacy.

Number one has just been discussed. A mailbox filled with nonstamped junk can crowd out real mail, slowing the delivery of the mail. Thieves can use the delivery of circulars as a ruse to examine the contents of a mailbox and then steal checks and other valuable material. Finally, the mail received by an individual should be private, not exposed to other persons who are hand delivering circulars or other matter.

The postal regulation was challenged by the Council of Greenburgh Civic Association, which delivered pamphlets and notices to local residents by placing them in mailboxes. The local postmaster ordered the practice stopped. The council said the postal regulation violated their rights under the First Amendment. The Supreme Court disagreed in a seven-to-two ruling. In his majority opinion Justice William Rehnquist rejected the notion that a mailbox is a public forum. He wrote that a mailbox was much like a military base, a jail or a prison, or the advertising space in a city transit system. "In all these cases, this Court recognizes that the First Amendment does not guarantee access to property simply because it is owned or controlled by the government," Rehnquist wrote. "It is a giant leap from the traditional 'soap box' to the letter box designated as an authorized depository of the United States mails, and we do not believe the First Amendment requires us to make that leap," he added. Because the mailbox is not a public forum, there is no need to evaluate whether the statute is a reasonable time, place, and manner rule. However, Rehnquist added, there are ample reasons to support the law, even if the mailbox were considered a public forum. He cited the government's justifications for the law (see one through three above). He also noted that there are numerous alternative means that the civic council could use to communicate information to residents. Justices Brennan and White said that they believed the mailbox to be (or at least be like) a public forum, but that the rules were reasonable. Marshall and Stevens dissented (*Postal Service* v. *Council,* 1981).

While a mailbox may not be a public forum, a federal district court in Texas ruled that a public television station is a public forum and cannot refuse to broadcast a controversial program. KUHT-TV, the public station licensed to the University of Houston, chose not to broadcast "Death of a Princess" in late 1980. The program is about a Saudi Arabian princess who had a non-sanctioned love affair with a young man and was subsequently executed. The Saudi government put pressure on the United States State Department to block the showing of the film in the United States. The station managers of KUHT-TV said they did not want to show the program because it was offensive and in bad taste and that it could interfere with the school's long friendship and contractual relationships with the Saudi Arabian government. Viewers protested, and when no relief was granted, a federal court suit was initiated to force KUHT-TV to show the film. The United States district court ruled that the station is a public forum and failure to broadcast the film was a prior restraint. "The people of this country have a First Amendment right to see and hear without having their sights and sounds subjected to the censorship of those wrapped in the cloak of the state . . . ," the court ruled (*Barnestone v. University of Houston,* 1981).

The district court ruling was appealed to the Fifth United States Court of Appeals. Another panel of Fifth Circuit judges had ruled three months earlier that the refusal of the Alabama Educational Television Commission to show "Death of a Princess" was not a prior restraint. In the Alabama case the judges ruled that a station's decision not to show the film was a programming decision and that, "it would demean the First Amendment to find that it required a public referendum on every programming decision made every day by every public television station solely because the station is owned and partially funded by the state government." Citing the *Postal Service* case (pages 97–98), the court said that a piece of property does not become a public forum just because it is owned or controlled by the government. "It is only when the government has created a public forum dedicated to public use that a right of access may obtain," the court added (*Muir v. Alabama Educational Television Commission,* 1981).

When *Barnestone v. University of Houston* reached the Fifth United States Court of Appeals, the decision was reversed because the panel of judges said they felt bound by the decision in the Alabama case. Shortly thereafter, however, it was announced that an en banc panel of the Fifth Circuit would rehear both the *Barnestone* case and the *Muir* case. The cases were reargued before all twenty-two judges in the circuit, and in October 1982 a majority ruled that public television stations are free—like commercial broadcasting stations—to make editorial judgments on the basis of content in selecting programs to broadcast. The court acknowledged that the First Amendment was designed to protect the press from government interference, not vice versa. Still, the court ruled, "The First Amendment does not preclude the government from exercising editorial control over its own medium of expression. To find that the government is without First Amendment protection is not to find that the government is prohibited from speaking or that private individuals have the right to limit or control the expression of the government. Even without First Amendment protection government may participate in the marketplace of ideas and contribute its own views to those of other speakers," the court added (*Muir* v. *Alabama Educational Television Commission*, 1982).

Private Forums

The cases just noted concern public forums. Courts have generally tolerated more restrictions upon expression exercised in private forums—shopping centers and private residences, for example. Residential distribution and solicitation have consistently been a vexing problem as the rights of freedom of expression are measured against the rights of privacy and private property.

Private Homes

In 1943 the Supreme Court faced an unusual ordinance adopted by the city of Struthers, Ohio, which totally prohibited door-to-door distribution of handbills, circulars, and other advertising materials. The law also barred anyone from ringing doorbells to summon householders for the purpose of distributing literature or pamphlets.

Justice Hugo Black wrote the opinion for the majority in the divided Court. He said the arrest of Thelma Martin, another Jehovah's Witness, for ringing doorbells in behalf of her religious cause was a violation of her First Amendment rights. Door-to-door distributors can be a nuisance and can even be a front for criminal activities, Justice Black acknowledged. Further, door-to-door distribution can surely be regulated, but it cannot be altogether banned. It is a valuable and useful means of the dissemination of ideas and is especially important to those groups that are too poorly financed to use other expensive means of communicating with the people. Black said a law that makes it an offense for a person to ring the doorbell of householders who have appropriately indicated that they are unwilling to be disturbed would be lawful and constitutional. However, the city of Struthers cannot by ordinance make this decision on behalf of all its citizens—especially when such a rule clearly interferes with the freedom of speech and of the press. "The right of freedom of speech and press has broad scope. The authors of the First Amendment knew that novel and unconventional ideas might disturb the complacent, but they chose to encourage a freedom which they believed essential if vigorous enlightenment was ever to triumph over slothful ignorance" (*Martin* v. *City of Struthers*, 1943).

Nearly ten years later, in 1951, the High Court was confronted with still another case of door-to-door solicitation. This case, however, concerned solicitation of subscriptions for nationally circulated magazines (*Breard* v. *Alexandria*, 1951). The Alexandria, Louisiana, ordinance in question prohibited door-to-door solicitation for sale of goods, wares, or merchandise without the prior consent or invitation of the homeowner. Jack H. Breard, who was employed by a Pennsylvania magazine subscription company, appealed his conviction all the way to the Supreme Court on the grounds that the law violated his First Amendment rights. This time the divided Court ruled against the solicitor, stating that the restriction was not a violation of the First Amendment.

Justice Stanley Reed distinguished the early cases from the *Breard* case by arguing that *Breard* was a case of door-to-door sale of wares, not of propagation of ideas or religious faith. "This kind of distribution is said to be protected because the mere fact that money is made out of the distribution does not bar the publications from First Amendment protection. We agree that the fact that periodicals are sold does not put them beyond the protection of the First Amendment. The selling, however, brings into the transaction a commercial feature," Reed wrote. He added that there are many other ways to sell magazines besides intruding upon the privacy of a householder through door-to-door techniques. Justices Black, Douglas, and Vinson disagreed with Justice Reed, arguing that the High Court had turned its back on earlier free expression decisions. "The constitutional sanctuary for the press must necessarily include liberty to publish and circulate. In view of our economic system, it must also include freedom to solicit paying subscribers," Black wrote. The jurist added that homeowners could themselves place the solicitor on notice by using a sign that they did not wish to be disturbed.

The majority opinion in the *Breard* case, which distinguishes commercial solicitation and distribution from noncommercial solicitation and distribution, has been seriously undercut recently by the Supreme Court's rulings that commercial speech is also entitled to the protection of the First Amendment (these rulings are discussed in chapter 10). For example, the Third United States Court of Appeals recently invalidated a township ordinance that prohibited the distribution of advertising matter without first getting consent of the homeowner. *Ad World,* which publishes *Piggy Back,* a sixteen-page tabloid that is filled mostly with advertising but that also carries a few community announcements and bits of consumer information, challenged the ordinance. The court ruled, "The line between commercial and noncommercial speech cannot be drawn by some magic ratio of editorial to advertising content. The important question is whether the publication as a whole relates solely to the economic interests of the speaker and its audience." The court said that an ordinance aimed at "purely commercial advertising" might be constitutional, but only if the community can justify the need for such a law. Doylestown Township argued that the accumulation of free newspapers on a doorstep might tip off burglars that the homeowner is out of town. But the township offered no evidence to support this argument. Also the township failed to show why the homeowner should not be called upon to request that delivery be stopped if the delivery of *Piggy Back* was not desired (*Ad World* v. *Doylestown,* 1982).

Shopping Centers

The problem of dealing with distribution of materials at privately owned shopping centers has also been a troubling one. In 1968, in *Amalgamated Food Employees Local 590* v. *Logan Valley Plaza,* the Supreme Court ruled that the shopping center was the functional equivalent of a town's business district and permitted informational picketing by persons who had a grievance against one of the stores in the shopping center. Four years later in *Lloyd Corp.* v. *Tanner* (1972), the Court ruled that a shopping center can prohibit the distribution of handbills on its property when the handbilling is unrelated to the shopping center operation. Protesters against nuclear power, for example, cannot use the shopping center as a forum. Persons protesting against the policies of one of the stores in the center, however, can use the center to distribute materials.

In 1976 the Supreme Court recognized the distinctions it had drawn between the rules in the *Logan Valley* case and the rules in the *Lloyd Center* case for what they were—restrictions based on content. The distribution of messages of one kind was permitted, while the distribution of messages about something else was banned. In *Hudgens* v. *NLRB* (1976), the High Court ruled that if, in fact, the shopping center is the functional equivalent of a municipal street, then restrictions based on content cannot stand. But rather than to open the shopping center to the distribution of all kinds of material, *Logan Valley* was overruled, and the Court announced that "only when . . . property has taken all the attributes of a town" can property be treated as public. Distribution of materials at private shopping centers can be prohibited.

Just because the First Amendment does not include within its protection of freedom of expression the right to circulate material at a privately owned shopping center does not mean that such distribution might not be protected by legislation or by a state constitution. That is exactly what happened in California. In 1974 in the city of Campbell, California, a group of high school students took a card table, some leaflets, and unsigned petition forms to the popular Pruneyard Shopping Center. The students were angered by a recent anti-Israel United Nations' resolution and sought to hand out literature and collect signatures for a petition to send to the president and Congress. The shopping center did not allow anyone to hand out literature, speak, or gather petition signatures, and the students were quickly chased off the property by a security guard. They filed suit in court, and in 1979 the California Supreme Court ruled that the rights of freedom of speech and petitioning are protected under the California Constitution, even in private shopping centers, as long as they are "reasonably exercised." (*Robins* v. *Pruneyard Shopping Center,* 1979) The shopping center owners appealed the ruling to the U.S. Supreme Court, arguing that the High Court's ruling in *Lloyd* v. *Tanner* prohibited the states from going further in the protection of personal liberties than the federal government. But six of the nine justices disagreed, ruling that a state is free to adopt in its own constitution individual liberties more expansive than those conferred by the federal constitution (*Pruneyard Shopping Center* v. *Robins,* 1980).

Since 1980, courts in Washington, Massachusetts, and New York have ruled that under their state constitutions, citizens could exercise rights of free expression at private shopping centers, according to an unpublished master's thesis by Kenneth Schiffler at the University of Washington. Courts in Pennsylvania and New Jersey have ruled that persons have a right to exercise rights of free expression on the grounds of private colleges. Schiffler points out that this is one indication of a growing tendency for state courts to use their own constitutions rather than the federal constitution as a basis for expanding rights of free speech and press. We will encounter other instances of this tendency in future chapters.

Finally, in an interesting decision that focused upon the mail rather than upon the mailbox, the Supreme Court ruled that the New York Public Service Commission could not restrict the content of inserts Consolidated Edison, a private utility company, put in billing envelopes. The utility company used the inserts to promote the value of nuclear power to its customers. The commission passed a regulation prohibiting utilities from using bill inserts to discuss political matters, including the desirability of future development of nuclear power. Justice Powell, who wrote the seven-to-one ruling, said the regulation was not content neutral. "The First Amendment means that government has no power to restrict expression because of its message, its ideas, its subject matter or content," he wrote. In addition, the state was hard pressed to outline a compelling or substantial state interest it was attempting to protect through such a regulation (*Consolidated Edison* v. *Public Service Commission, 1980*).

As noted previously, other examples of prior restraint can be found within the law. Films may be censored before they are shown, for example (see chapter 6). Under certain circumstances the press may be prohibited from publishing material that might prejudice a defendant's chance for a fair trial (see chapter 7). Such examples will be noted as other aspects of mass media law are discussed.

SUMMARY

The prior restraint of expression is permissible under what are known as time, place, and manner regulations. That is, the government can impose reasonable regulations about when, where, and how individuals or groups may communicate with other persons. Time, place, and manner rules apply to both public forums (settings owned or controlled by a government, such as a public street or an airport) and private forums (privately owned settings, such as residences and shopping centers). In order to be constitutional, time, place, and manner restraints must meet certain criteria:

1. The regulation must be content neutral; that is, application of the rule cannot depend upon the content of the communication.

2. The regulation must serve a substantial governmental interest, and the government must justify the rule by explicitly demonstrating this interest.
3. There cannot be total prohibition of the communication. The speakers or publishers must have reasonable alternative means of presenting their ideas or information to the public.
4. The rules cannot be broader than they need to be to serve the governmental interest. For example, the government cannot stop the distribution of literature on all public streets if it only seeks to stop the problem of congestion on public streets that carry heavy traffic.

BIBLIOGRAPHY

Here is a list of some of the sources that have been helpful in the preparation of chapter 2:

Books

Alexander, James. *A Brief Narrative on the Case and Trial of John Peter Zenger.* Edited by Stanley N. Katz. Cambridge, Mass.: Harvard University Press, 1963.

Barron, Jerome, and Dienes, C. Thomas. *Handbook of Free Speech and Free Press.* Boston: Little, Brown & Co., 1979.

Chafee, Zechariah. *Free Speech in the United States.* Cambridge: Harvard University Press, 1941.

Fellman, David. *The Limits of Freedom.* New Brunswick, N. J.: Rutgers University Press, 1959.

Gerald, J. Edward. *The Press and the Constitution.* Minneapolis, Minn.: University of Minnesota Press, 1948.

Jensen, Merrill. *The Articles of Confederation.* Madison, Wis.: University of Wisconsin Press, 1966.

———. *The Making of the American Constitution.* New York: Van Nostrand Reinhold Co., 1964.

Levy, Leonard. *Freedom of Speech and Press in Early American History.* New York: Harper & Row, Harper Torchbooks, 1963.

———. *Emergence of a Free Press.* New York: Oxford University Press, 1985.

Meiklejohn, Alexander. *Free Speech and Its Relation to Self-Government.* New York: Harper & Brothers, 1948.

Miller, John C. *Crisis in Freedom.* Boston: Little, Brown & Co., 1951.

Peterson, H. C., and Fite, Gilbert. *Opponents of War, 1917–1918.* Seattle: University of Washington Press, 1957.

Roche, John P. *Shadow and Substance.* New York: Macmillan Co., 1964.

Rutland, Robert. *The Birth of the Bill of Rights.* Chapel Hill: University of North Carolina Press, 1955.

Siebert, Frederick. *Freedom of the Press in England, 1476–1776.* Urbana: University of Illinois Press, 1952.

Smith, James Morton. *Freedom's Fetters.* Ithaca, N. Y.: Cornell University Press, 1956.

"Administrative Regulation of the High School Press," 83 *Michigan Law Review* 625, 1984.

Articles

Dunn, Donald J. "*Pico* and Beyond: School Library Censorship Controversies," 77 *Law Library Journal* 435, 1984–85.

Gillmor, Donald M. "The Fragile First," 8 *Hamline Law Review* 277, 1985.

Karp, Walter. "Liberty Under Siege," *Harper's* 53, November, 1985.

Nelson, Harold L. "Seditious Libel in Colonial America," 3 *American Journal of Legal History* 160, 1959.

Pember, Don R. "The Pentagon Papers Decision: More Questions Than Answers." 48 *Journalism Quarterly* 403, 1971.

_____. "The Smith Act as a Restraint on the Press." 10 *Journalism Monographs* 1, 1969.

Ragan, Fred D. "Justice Oliver Wendell Holmes, Jr., Zechariah Chafee, Jr., and the Clear and Present Danger Test for Free Speech: The First Year, 1919." 53 *Journal of American History* 24, 1971.

Cases

Abrams v. *U.S.*, 250 U.S. 616 (1919).
Ad World v. *Doylestown*, 672 F.2d 1136 (1982).
Amalgamated Food Employees Local 590 v. *Logan Valley Plaza*, 391 U.S. 308 (1968).
Barnestone v. *University of Houston*, 660 F.2d 137 (1981).
Barron v. *Baltimore*, 7 Pet. 243 (1833).
Bary v. *U.S.*, 248 F.2d 201 (1957).
Baughman v. *Freienmuth*, 478 F. 2d 1345 (1973).
Brandenburg v. *Ohio*, 395 U.S. 444 (1969).
Breard v. *Alexandria*, 341 U.S. 622 (1951).
Cantwell v. *Connecticut*, 310 U.S. 296 (1940).
Chaplinsky v. *New Hampshire*, 315 U.S. 568 (1942).
Collin v. *Smith*, 578 F.2d 1197, cert. den. 99 S.Ct. 291 (1978).
Consolidated Edison v. *Public Service Commission*, 447 U.S. 529 (1980).
Debs v. *U.S.*, 249 U.S. 211 (1919).
Dennis v. *U.S.*, 341 U.S. 494 (1951).
Dickey v. *Alabama*, 273 F. Supp. 613 (1967).
Donnelly v. *Campbell*, 639 F.2d 6 (1980).
Fiske v. *Kansas*, 274 U.S. 380 (1927).
Frasca v. *Andrews*, 463 F. Supp. 1043 (1978).
Fraser v. *Bethel School District*, 106 S.Ct. 3159 (1986).
Frohwerk v. *U.S.*, 249 U.S. 204 (1919).
Gitlow v. *U.S.*, 268 U.S. 652 (1925).
Gooding v. *Wilson*, 405 U.S. 518 (1972).
H. & L. Messengers v. *Brentwood*, 577 S.W. 2d 444 (1979).
Heffron v. *International Society*, 101 S.Ct. 2559 (1981).
Houston Chronicle v. *Houston*, 630 S.W.2d 927 (1982).
Hudgens v. *NLRB*, 424 U.S. 507 (1976).
International Society for Krishna Consciousness v. *Wolke*, 453 F. Supp. 869 (1978).
Island Trees v. *Pico*, 102 S.Ct. 2799 (1982).
Jacob v. *Board of School Commrs*, 490 F.2d 601 (1973).
Joyner v. *Whiting*, 477 F. 2d 456 (1973).
Lloyd Corp. v. *Tanner*, 407 U.S. 551 (1972).
Lovell v. *Griffin*, 303 U.S. 444 (1938).
Lowe v. *SEC*, 105 S.Ct. 2557 (1985).
Martin v. *City of Struthers*, 319 U.S. 141 (1943).
Metromedia v. *Baltimore*, 538 F. Supp. 1183 (1982).
Metromedia v. *San Diego*, 101 S.Ct. 2882 (1981).

Miami Herald v. *Tornillo,* 418 U.S. 241 (1974).

Muir v. *Alabama Educational TV Commission,* 656 F.2d 1012 (1981); 688 F.2d 1033 (1982).

Near v. *Minnesota,* 383 U.S. 697 (1931).

New York Times Company v. *U.S.; U.S.* v. *Washington Post,* 713 U.S. 403 (1971).

Nicholson v. *Board of Education,* 682 F.2d 858 (1982).

Norton v. *Arlington Heights,* 433 N.E.2d 198 (1982).

Organization for a Better Austin v. *Keefe,* 402 U.S. 415 (1971).

Passaic Daily News v. *Clifton,* 491 A.2d 808 (1985).

Pico v. *Island Trees,* 747 F.Supp. 387 (1979); revd. 638 F.2d 404 (1980).

President's Council District 25 v. *Community School Board,* 457 F.2d 566 (1972).

Pruneyard Shopping Center v. *Robins,* 447 U.S. 74 (1980).

Red Lion Broadcasting v. *FCC,* 395 U.S. 367 (1969).

Robins v. *Pruneyard Shopping Center,* 592 P.2d 341 (1979).

Scales v. *U.S.,* 367 U.S. 203 (1961).

Schenck v. *U.S.,* 249 U.S. 47 (1919).

Schneider v. *New Jersey,* 308 U.S. 147 (1939).

Scoville v. *Board of Education,* 425 F.2d 10 (1970).

Snepp v. *U.S.,* 100 S.Ct. 763 (1980).

Socialist Labor Party v. *Glendale,* 82 Cal. App.3d 722 (1978).

Stanley v. *McGrath,* 719 F.2d 279 (1983).

Tinker v. *Des Moines School District,* 393 U.S. 503 (1969).

Trachtman v. *Anker,* 563 F.2d 512 (1977).

U.S. v. *Progressive,* 467 F. Supp. 990 (1979).

Village of Skokie v. *National Socialist Party,* 373 N.E.2d 21 (1978).

Weissman v. *Alamogordo,* 472 F. Supp. 425 (1979).

Whitney v. *California,* 274 U.S. 357 (1927).

Williams v. *Spencer,* 622 F.2d 1200 (1980).

Yates v. *U.S.,* 354 U.S. 298 (1957).

U.S. v. *Marchetti,* 466 F.2d·1309 (1972).

3 LIBEL

Defamation, or **libel,** is probably the most common legal problem
journalists face today. In simple terms libel is the publication or broadcast
of a statement that injures someone else's reputation, lowers that person's
esteem in the community. The very nature of contemporary journalism
creates a fertile soil for the growth of libel problems.

A modern American news medium carries an immense amount of
information about a huge number of people. Each item carries the potential
for a libel action. News, by definition, is a report of something unusual or
out of the ordinary, and frequently this report contains facts, accusations,
innuendo, or references that are negative or critical of someone. While
journalists attempt to use care in the preparation of news reports, some
practices of modern journalism exacerbate the problem of libel for the
press.

Every news medium faces deadlines, a time when the news must be
prepared for publication or broadcast. But the rush to get a story completed
before press time or air time creates an atmosphere in which a careless
error is more likely to occur. And carelessness is at the root of the
publication of most stories that result in successful libel actions. Headlines
create problems for American newspapers as well. The headline writer is
forced to compress often complicated information into a few words. This
frequently results in confusion for the reader and sometimes exaggerates
charges carried in the story, resulting in the publication of libel. Journalists
are aggressive seekers of information, and during the last fifteen years the
emphasis by many in journalism on investigative reporting has resulted in
the publication of stories that are embarrassing and even harmful to many
influential people. Such exposés, by their nature, usually harm someone's
reputation and this, in turn, often results in a libel case. Finally, the
publication and broadcast of news is a complex process. A story generated
by a newspaper reporter, for example, goes through many hands before it is
ultimately published. Each person who handles the story has the
opportunity to change it in such a way that it results in defaming someone.
A word is accidently dropped, changing *not* guilty to guilty; names are
transposed, resulting in the victim becoming the perpetrator of a crime; or
letters are transposed or changed so the phrase "he vied to gain support
from the commission" becomes "he lied to gain support from the
commission." People in the news business frequently blame such errors on
gremlins who inhabit all newsrooms, printing plants, and broadcasting
studios.

The potential for causing a libel has been and remains a part of the
working environment of every American journalist. But libel suits seem to
be a special problem today. Surely more and more people are aware of libel,

largely because of the publicity given to libel actions brought by well-known persons against well-known mass media. Carol Burnett won a $200,000 libel judgment against the *National Enquirer*. More recently General William Westmoreland, former commander of U.S. troops in Vietnam, sued CBS for $120 million over what he called defamatory statements in a 1982 documentary. And former Israeli defense minister Ariel Sharon sued *Time* magazine for $50 million after the magazine published a story that Sharon said falsely accused him of encouraging a 1982 massacre by Lebanese Phalangists. Both Westmoreland and Sharon lost their libel suits; and neither case established any important legal principles. Nevertheless, the public was treated to front-page stories and nightly television news reports on both trials for many weeks.

Some persons argue that more libel suits are being filed today than ever before; other people dispute this assertion and argue that it only seems like more are being filed because libel suits are more widely publicized. There is no dispute, however, that libel judgments—the money paid out to plaintiffs who win—are much bigger today than ever before. Plaintiffs don't hesitate to sue for many millions of dollars, and juries don't hesitate to award multimillion-dollar judgments, according to studies done by the Libel Defense Resource Center. Between 1980 and 1983, for example, the average jury award in a news media libel case was $2.2 million. Until 1980 there had been only one million-dollar libel award in our history.

Why are jury awards so high today? Why are libel suits seemingly more common? There are several plausible answers. Law Professor Rodney Smolla suggests that libel law, as well as other areas of tort law, has recently undergone a relaxation of rules that formerly prohibited recovery for purely emotional or psychic damage rather than for injury to reputation. Today, Smolla contends in an article in the *University of Pennsylvania Law Review,* the bulk of money paid out in damage awards in defamation suits is to compensate for psychic injury, rather than to compensate for any objectively verified damage to one's community standing. Such damages are easier to collect and will generally be larger, since the defense has little ability to challenge the assertion that harm has been caused. This trend in libel law, Smolla notes, parallels a corresponding trend in our culture, the growing preoccupation of many (maybe most) Americans with the discovery and nourishment "of various formulations of the individual self"—in other words, the growth of the so-called me generation. Smolla writes,

> Contemporary America's attitude toward a defamed plaintiff is likely to reflect society's increased expenditure of money and effort first at finding and then to nurturing the inner self. One does not go to significant personal expense in an effort to define a self image, and then sit idly by as that work is publicly undone by "60 Minutes" or the *National Enquirer.*

Others suggest that a generally anti-press mood in America today often puts the jury on the side of the libel plaintiff. People tend to think reporters are intrusive and arrogant, and a libel suit is a good way to force journalists to pay for their perpetually bad manners. Others think the press is too powerful, but accountable to no one, an echo of the attacks made upon the mass media by former vice-president Spiro Agnew in the early seventies. Politicians may be dangerous, but they can be tossed out of office. However, the public has little say in the appointment or firing of a network anchorperson or a local editor. Public opinion polls consistently show that most persons have a fairly low regard for journalists in both the print and broadcast media. And many persons are unhappy with the news being brought into their homes each day, finding it too negative, too critical, too anti-this or -that. Gannett Co. chairman Al Neuharth noted recently that "it is the constant negative tone that is getting the public down on the press and paves the way for demagogues on the left and the right to rally people against the press. . . ."

Finally, and perhaps most importantly, the law of libel has moved in the past twenty-five years from a fairly easily understood common law tort to a highly complex legal scheme that is deeply infused with constitutional considerations. It is often very difficult for a jury of citizens to understand the complex nature of the law when they are asked to deliberate in a libel case. Jury instructions are often poorly drafted, according to an unpublished study undertaken by University of Washington doctoral student Linda Lawson, thus adding to the confusion. The instructions are poorly drafted because trial judges are often confused about the law. Years ago, before the law became as complex as it is today, libel attorney and author Paul Ashley wrote in his handbook *Say It Safely:*

> Significant segments of the law of libel are unique—dissimilar from legal rules with which lawyers and judges are most familiar. Libel cases are relatively few in number. Judges are not ordinarily experienced in the practical application of the esoteric concepts of privilege and fair comment essential to the preservation of freedom of speech and, in turn, of a free society.

But concepts like privilege and fair comment are relatively easy to understand when compared with newer libel concepts such as actual malice and limited public figure and neutral reportage. The law is simply rife with opportunities for both trial judges and juries to foul up. And they do foul up. News media defendants lose six out of every ten libel suits decided by juries. But seventy-five percent of these rulings are later overturned by appellate courts, which are generally better capable of dealing with the complexities of modern libel law. In an additional 10 percent of the cases, the jury's damage award is substantially reduced.

Why has the law become so complicated? The introduction in 1964 of constitutional restrictions upon the application of the law of libel is certainly one reason, as you will note as you read this chapter. But the inability of the Supreme Court of the United States to agree upon basic positions in the law has also resulted in problems. The attempt by the Burger Court to delineate libel law has been marked by rulings with multiple opinions; that is, the nine justices producing three or even four different opinions in a case, with a plurality of only three or four subscribing to the court's opinion. The High Court seems badly split over some basic aspects of modern libel law, as will be noted when we consider some fundamentals of libel later in this chapter. While some justices, like William Brennan and Thurgood Marshall, believe that it should be more difficult for people to sue for libel, others like former Chief Justice Burger and Justice Byron White, have suggested that it should be easier for many plaintiffs to sue and have called for a reevaluation of some basic constitutional libel principles (see *Dun & Bradstreet* v. *Greenmoss,* 1985). This causes immense confusion in the lower courts.

The greater number of highly visible libel suits and larger libel judgments have had a deleterious impact upon the American press. The large libel judgments have hit the press hard in the pocketbook. The *Alton* (Illinois) *Telegraph,* for example, was almost forced into bankruptcy when it lost a $9.2 million libel judgment to a local contractor. The paper ultimately settled the suit for $1.4 million and survived the ordeal. But the actual cost of the judgment is really a minor problem as compared with the cost of defending the libel suit. You need only pay a judgment if you lose a libel suit, and the press ultimately wins the vast majority of libel suits. But you must pay defense costs whether you win or lose. The typical libel suit that goes to trial and is then appealed will cost the newspaper or broadcasting station $150,000 in attorney's fees and court costs. The *Westmoreland* v. *CBS* lawsuit, which required 2½ years of preparation and 18 weeks in court, cost the network—which won the case at a trial when Westmoreland finally withdrew his suit—in excess of $2 million, according to most estimates. *The Washington Post* has spent almost the same amount defending a lawsuit entered by Mobil Oil president William Tavoulareas.

These high costs have had a devastating impact upon the press. Small newspapers, magazines, and broadcasting stations are being forced to give up running some stories that might provoke a libel suit, even a suit without merit. *The Washington Post* recounted the story of Jack Fraser, publisher of the tiny *Bastrop* (Texas) *Advertiser & County News,* who recently decided not to publish a letter to the editor complaining about a fight at a local country-club bar in which a normally mild-mannered local politician began verbally abusing his fellow drinkers. "Five or ten years ago I would have run it, but now I couldn't take that chance," Fraser said, fearing a libel action. And Irvin Lieberman, publisher of four weekly newspapers in the suburbs of Philadelphia, told reporter David Zucchino that he has stripped his newspapers of much of their aggressiveness and vitality. He has stopped publishing investigative news stories, after having been sued for libel eleven times in a seven-year period. The suits, he said, taxed his time, finances, resources, and morale. "It was injurious to my health and to my role as a family breadwinner," said Lieberman of the litigation. "I finally had to make a choice: I decided to abandon my obligation to the First Amendment and run my newspapers as businesses," he added, noting he hasn't been sued since.

Defending a libel suit consumes a lot of money; it also consumes a lot of time. Working to defend a libel suit often becomes a full-time job for reporters involved in the case, taking them off the street for months at a time. And the problems of self-censorship affect big media as well as small. In 1984 Senator Paul Laxalt sued the *Sacramento Bee* for $25 million for publishing a story that suggested that more than $2 million was illegally skimmed from a Carson City, Nevada, casino owned by Laxalt and others. *Newsweek,* CBS, and ABC all had stories in preparation on the same allegation. The networks pulled their stories and *Newsweek* ended up printing a "correction" worked out between the magazine and the senator's lawyers, stating that the magazine did not "intend to adopt as its own the story on Senator Laxalt or to impugn the senator's reputation." *Newsweek* later ran a story on the lawsuit against the *Bee.*

The self-censorship that is taking place in the press because of a fear of having to pay the costs of defending a libel action is not a healthy situation. Many solutions have been put forth in an attempt to try to quell the outbreak of libel actions and high libel judgments. But none appeared to provide a significant answer to the problem. Fred Friendly, former CBS news president and now a professor of journalism at Columbia, said he believes that broadcasters could avoid many lawsuits by providing an opportunity for those who feel treated unfairly by newscasts or documentaries to answer back on the air. CBS did this in the 1950s after Ed Murrow on "See It Now" had broadcast a scathing attack on Senator Joseph McCarthy. The junior senator from Wisconsin was given thirty minutes to reply to the broadcast, and no lawsuit ever resulted. Friendly produced the "See It Now" series for Murrow and CBS. "Broadcasters have got to find a way to ventilate criticisms of them," says Friendly. "The problem is, they think they're trapped because time is so expensive. But if it costs them $300,000 to put on a half hour, that's the price they've got to pay. Not paying that is to invite another one of these suits and another and another."

The New York Times suggests that the press should not only offer those offended an opportunity to air their side of the issue, but that the press should be more willing to correct errors itself and criticize others in the media who do not. The newspaper was critical of *Time* magazine for failing to acknowledge it had erred in its story on Ariel Sharon, even after a jury had found that the story contained falsehoods. "To deserve the extraordinary protections of American law, *Time* and all of journalism needs a stronger tradition of mutual and self-correction. The more influential the medium, the greater the duty to offer a place for rebuttal, complaint, correction and reexamination. Beating the arrogance rap is even more important than escaping one for libel," the editors wrote in 1985.

A change in the law was proposed in Congress in 1985. A measure, proposed by Representative Charles E. Schumer of New York and scheduled for hearings in 1986, would eliminate all monetary damages in libel suits filed by public officials and public figures against the mass media and would eliminate punitive damages in other libel actions. The public official or public figure could only win a declaratory judgment that the published or broadcast story was false and caused damage. In addition, Schumer's bill would allow the prevailing party in the lawsuit to collect attorney's fees. Now it is rare for a defendant that wins a suit to collect the cost of his or her defense in the case. The bill contains other provisions that would limit the sting of libel as well. Reaction to the proposal has been mixed in Congress, and some observers, such as *Baltimore Sun* reporter Lyle Denniston who applauds the measure, think it might be unconstitutional because it wipes out a right that individuals currently have under existing law. No Congressional action had been taken on the measure as this chapter was being prepared.

Some libel defendants have tried to gain court costs and attorney's fees from the plaintiff after winning a lawsuit. But judges seem generally reluctant to make such an award, fearing it would deter a truly injured plaintiff from suing for libel. Other defendants have filed a counterclaim against a libel plaintiff. McClatchy Newspapers, publishers of the *Sacramento Bee,* filed a counterclaim for violation of First Amendment rights and abuse of process against Senator Paul Laxalt after he sued the *Bee* for libel. McClatchy sought $6 million in damages. But a U.S. district court threw out the countersuit, saying it failed to state a cause of action. In 1985 NBC won a $200,000 judgment against Lyndon H. Larouche when it filed a counterclaim against Larouche's libel action. The network charged that Larouche interfered with its attempt to gather news (*Larouche* v. *NBC*, 1985).

Whether any of these proposals will actually stem the tide of libel actions against the press remains to be seen. In time the number of suits and size of judgments may simply diminish naturally. But reporters, editors, and broadcasters—and even advertising copywriters and public relations specialists—must constantly be on guard for libel problems. The best weapon is knowledge, an understanding of the law. That is what is provided in the remainder of this lengthy but very important chapter. ◆

LAW OF DEFAMATION

The law of defamation is ancient; its roots can be traced back several centuries. Initially the law was an attempt by government to establish a forum for persons involved in a dispute brought about by an insult or by what we today call a defamatory remark. One man called another a robber and a villain. The injured party sought to avenge his damaged reputation. A fight or duel of some kind was the only means of gaining vengeance before the development of libel law. It was obvious that fights and duels were not satisfactory ways to settle such disputes, so government offered its "good offices" to solve these problems. Slowly the law of defamation evolved.

Today the process of going to court to avenge one's honor is highly institutionalized. In addition, some scholars in the field suggest that the purpose of the law has subtly changed as well. While protection of reputation still remains a primary objective of the law of defamation, the law is also seen as a means of gaining press accountability. Standards of responsible journalism and professional conduct are frequently applied to the press in determining liability, and in this way society and the government, via the court system, are taking a role in defining acceptable journalistic practices.

In other parts of the world, different schemes are used to accomplish similar ends. In continental Europe libel suits are uncommon. When a newspaper defames a person, that person has the right—under law—to strike back, using the columns of the same newspaper to tell his side of the story; so to speak, to blast the writer or the editor. This right is called the right of reply, and it exists in the United States in a far less advanced form, as is noted near the end of this chapter. Many people favor the notion; that is, letting the parties fight it out in print or by broadcast. They say it is far better to set out after the truth in this fashion than to rattle the chains on the courthouse door every time an insult is flung in the public press.

Parts of the law of libel do not really concern journalists. In this chapter the discussion of the law of libel is generally confined to those areas of the law that are important to reporters, editors, and broadcasters, and some aspects of libel law are not included. For example, the law of defamation regarding private communications as opposed to public communications differs somewhat. What a newspaper can legally do is somewhat different from what an employer writing a job evaluation for an employee can legally do. Defamation contained in personal letters, credit reports, job evaluations—a whole range of relatively private communications—is treated somewhat differently in the eyes of the law. The focus of this chapter is defamation in the mass media; that is, public communication libel.

Additionally, it must be remembered that libel law is essentially state law. It is possible to describe the dimensions of the law in broad terms that transcend state boundaries, and that is what this chapter attempts to do. But important variations in the law from state to state exist, as will be demonstrated later in this chapter in the discussion of fault requirements. It is important for students to focus on the specific elements of the law in their states after gaining an understanding of the general boundaries of the law.

Another complex problem in the law has to do with whether a communication is a libel (written defamation) or a **slander** (an oral defamation). The law in many states distinguishes between the two. The problem was simple one hundred years ago. Because of the state of technology, a public communication, one meant for a wide audience, was a printed communication—a newspaper, magazine, or handbill. Therefore a law that dealt with libel more harshly than with slander made sense; libel caused more severe damage. A libel lasted longer than a slander since a libel was printed, more people saw it, and it was generally considered to be planned defamation, not words accidentally spoken in the heat of argument. Film, radio, and television have made these distinctions meaningless. If a performer defames someone on "The Tonight Show," despite the fact that the defamation is not printed, the defamation still has immense impact and is heard by millions. Today it is a general rule that a published defamation, whether it is in a newspaper, on radio or television, in the movies, or what have you, is a libel. And libel rules apply.

The purpose of this chapter is to give journalists guidance and rules to apply in the process of gathering, writing, and publishing and broadcasting the news. People who want to learn to litigate a lawsuit should go to law school. This author's goal is to keep reporters and broadcasters out of libel suits or at least to keep them from losing libel suits.

The chapter is divided into two basic parts. The first section deals with the nature of a defamation suit: definitions of libel, what a plaintiff must prove in a libel suit, words that tend to be defamatory, and so forth. The second section outlines the various defenses—legal excuses for publishing defamatory matter—for a libel suit.

ELEMENTS OF LIBEL

There are many definitions of defamation, and they are all about the same. A few typical definitions follow.

In their book *Libel,* Phelps and Hamilton include this definition:

> Defamation is a communication which exposes a person to hatred, ridicule, or contempt, lowers him in the esteem of his fellows, causes him to be shunned, or injures him in his business or calling.

The legal encyclopedia *Corpus Juris* defines libelous words as follows:

> . . . words which have a tendency to disgrace or degrade the person or hold him up to public hatred, contempt, ridicule or cause him to be shunned and avoided; the words must reflect on his integrity, his character, and his good name and standing in the community. . . . The imputation must be one

which tends to affect the plaintiff in a class of society whose standard of opinion the court can recognize. It is not sufficient, standing alone, that the language is unpleasant and annoys and irks plaintiff and subjects him to jests or banter, so as to affect his feelings.

The new edition of the *Restatement of Torts* (2nd ed.), a compilation by the American Law Institute of what it thinks the common law says, defines libel this way:

. . . a communication which has the tendency to so harm the reputation of another as to lower him in the estimation of the community or to deter third persons from associating with him.

Here is a shorter definition: Defamation is any communication that holds a person up to contempt, hatred, ridicule, or scorn.

Each of the four preceding definitions reveals common and important elements of defamation:

1. Defamation is an action that damages the reputation of a person, but not necessarily the individual's character. Your character is what you are; your reputation is what people think you are. Reputation is what the law protects. A person without a reputation cannot be libelled. The Alabama Supreme Court ruled that a libel plaintiff, a prison inmate who had five convictions on theft charges and was declared a habitual criminal, could not possibly show damage to his reputation; he had no reputation. He was libel proof. The suit was based on a published statement that the inmate's lawsuit against the state was "frivolous." (*Cofield* v. *Advertiser Co.,* 1986).

2. To be actionable defamation, the words must actually damage a reputation. There must be some harm done to the individual's reputation. Without proof of this harm, the party who claims injury should not be able to recover damages for the injury. As noted previously, however, juries in the 1980s seem to be awarding damages to plaintiffs who have suffered only personal, emotional harm.

3. At least a significant minority of the community must believe that the plaintiff's reputation has been damaged, but the minority must not be an unrepresentative minority. A Delaware superior court ruled that it was not defamatory for a television newscaster to refer to a convict as "an alleged FBI informant." The plaintiff complained that the statement hurt his reputation among his fellow prisoners at the state penitentiary. Conceding that the "informant" label might harm his prison reputation, the court ruled that "it is not one's reputation in a limited community in which attitudes and social values may depart substantially from those prevailing generally which an action for defamation is designed to protect." The public in general would not

think any less of the plaintiff for being an informant for the FBI (*Saunders* v. *WHYY-TV,* 1978). To summarize this point: The defamation must lower a person's reputation in the eyes of a significant number of people, and unless unusual circumstances exist, these people must fairly reflect representative views.

Persons can be injured through a libel in numerous ways. The statement may simply hurt their reputation, or it may be that lowering their reputation deprives them of their right to enjoy social contacts, which is a fancy way of saying that their friends don't like them any more or their friends want to avoid them. A man's or woman's ability to work or hold a job or make a living may be injured. A person need only be injured in *one* of these three ways to have a cause of action for libel. If plaintiffs can show actual harm in any one of these areas, chances are good they will recover some damages. That is one of the reasons libel law exists—to compensate the plaintiff for injury. There are other reasons. A libel suit can help vindicate the plaintiff, help restore the damaged reputation. A victorious plaintiff can point a finger at the newspaper or television station and say, "See, they were wrong, they lied, they made an error." A damage judgment is also considered punishment for the defendant. Editors and broadcasters who have to pay a large damage award may be more cautious in the future. It can stand also as an example to other journalists to avoid such behavior.

Any living person can bring a suit for civil libel. If a dead person is libeled, relatives cannot sue in the name of the deceased. However, as noted in the last section of this chapter, it is possible (but highly improbable) for the state to bring a criminal libel action against the publisher of a defamation against a person who has died. Note, however, that if a living person is defamed, brings suit, and then dies before the matter is settled by the court, it is possible in some states that have what are called **survival statutes** for relatives to continue to pursue the lawsuit (see *MacDonald* v. *Time,* 1983, and *Canino* v. *New York News,* 1984), for example. A business corporation can sue for libel, as can a nonprofit corporation, if it can show that it has lost public support and contributions because of the defamation. There is a division in judicial opinion about whether unincorporated associations like labor unions and political action groups can sue for libel. Some court rulings say no; others say yes. Find out what the law is in your state. Cities, counties, agencies of government, and governments in general cannot bring a civil libel suit. This question was decided years ago and is settled law (see *City of Chicago* v. *Tribune Co.,* 1923). Nevertheless, every now and then an angry public official brings an action against the media in the name of the city or state rather than sue as an individual. In 1979 the United States Department of Justice filed a lawsuit charging the city of Philadelphia, its mayor, Frank Rizzo, and various police officials with violating the civil rights of many citizens by pursuing policies of police abuse and brutality. After the *Washington Post* published an account of the lawsuit, the city of Philadelphia brought a libel action against the newspaper. The federal district court ruled that the city could not maintain an action for libel. "A governmental entity is incapable of being libeled," Judge Fullam ruled (*City of Philadelphia* v. *Washington Post,* 1979). Neither can relatives of defamed persons sue simply because they are relatives. If you call John Smith a fraud, John's brother Homer cannot sue just because he is related to John.* It is a different story if Homer can show that the libel reflects on him. For example, if you call John Smith illegitimate, the charge reflects directly on his parents, and they can sue.

PROVING THE INITIAL ELEMENTS

In a libel suit, as in any kind of lawsuit, certain tasks fall to the plaintiff and certain tasks fall to the defendant. Since the plaintiff initiates the suit, he or she bears the burden of getting the case started. In a libel suit the plaintiff is charged with establishing four elements, and without proof of these elements the case will be dismissed even before it really starts. The four conditions that the plaintiff must prove are as follows:

1. That the libelous communication was published
2. That the plaintiff was identified in the communication
3. That the communication is defamatory in some way
4. That the libelous matter was published due to neglect or disregard or carelessness, that its publication is not simply the result of an honest error

Each of these elements will be considered in detail shortly, but a brief introduction is appropriate first. Proof of publication, identification, and defamation is usually quite mechanical. The plaintiff either was identified or was not identified, for example. All plaintiffs must prove these three elements.

The fault requirement, the last of the four elements listed earlier, is probably applicable only to those libel suits brought against mass media defendants (see *Columbia Sussex* v. *Hay,* 1981 and *Mutafis* v. *Erie Insurance Exchange,* 1985; but see also *Nodar* v. *Galbreath,* 1985 for example). The courts have not finally resolved this issue. Since this book is about mass media law, and we know that proof of fault is required before a plaintiff can win a libel action against a newspaper or magazine or broadcasting station, we will consider some evidence of fault to be a required part of the plaintiff's case.

The fault requirement is the most complicated of the four elements. The kind of fault that must be proved by the plaintiff, whether the defamation results from simple negligence by the reporter or from deliberate disregard of

---

*John Smith, Jane Adams, Frank Jones, Professor LeBlanc, KLOP, the *River City Sentinel, Scam* magazine, and the like, are my fictional creations and are used to illustrate specific points I wish to make when actual case law either does not exist or is unknown to me.

the truth, depends upon who the plaintiff is and in which state the lawsuit is filed. Many persons consider the fault requirement to be a libel defense. But since the burden of proving fault rests with the plaintiff, it is more properly considered an element of the plaintiff's case than a part of the defendant's case. The defendant's obligations do not technically begin until the injured party has established publication, identification, defamation, and fault.

As a part of the fault requirement, virtually all plaintiffs must prove that the libelous allegations are false. For more than twenty years, plaintiff's who under the law are considered public officials or public figures (terms we will define with some precision later, see pages 147–64) have had to prove that the libelous material was false. But the law regarding other libel plaintiffs—so-called private persons—tended to vary from state to state and was frequently ambiguous. In 1986 the U.S. Supreme Court ruled that all persons suing a mass medium for libel must prove that the damaging statements are false, at least when the statements focus upon "matters of public concern" (*Philadelphia Newspapers* v. *Hepps,* 1986). Justice Sandra Day O'Connor, who wrote the opinion for the five-person majority, did not define "matters of public concern." It is probable, however, that the term will be construed broadly and encompass all but the highly frivolous news and information published and broadcast in the public press. One suspects that the rule could even be applied to serious drama or sports as well. But court decisions in the next decade will clarify this rule. If a private-person plaintiff sues for the publication of defamatory statements that are not considered by the court to focus upon matters of public concern, the plaintiff need not prove the statements false, only that they were published through the negligence of the defendant. But as a practical matter, it seems difficult to imagine that a plaintiff can prove that the material was published due to negligence without also showing that the material is false.

| Publication | Before the law recognizes a statement or comment as a civil libel (**criminal libel** is different; see page 203), the statement must be published. In the eyes of the law, **publication** occurs when one person, in addition to the writer and the person who is defamed, sees or hears the material.* Think of the situation as a kind of triangle. The writer or broadcaster (ultimately the defendant) is |

*This statement may confuse some people who see it as a contradiction of an earlier statement that to be defamatory something must lower an individual's reputation in the eyes of a significant minority of the community. It is not a contradiction. Publication is what is being discussed here: how many people must see something before the law considers it to have been published. The earlier remark refers to damage to an individual: how many people must think less of a person upon hearing or reading the statement. It is necessary for the plaintiff to convince the court that a significant number of people in the community think less of him or her because of the libelous remark, but it is not necessary that the plaintiff show that these people have actually seen the libelous remark, only that they would think less of the plaintiff if they had seen it.

at the first point; the subject of the defamatory statement (ultimately the plaintiff) is at the second point; and a third person is at the third point. All three are necessary for a libel suit. The issue of publication becomes a real problem in defamation via private communication. You send a nasty letter to someone and a secretary opens it first by mistake. Is that publication? You dictate a letter to your secretary. Is that publication? (In both instances the law answers with a resounding "it depends.") In defamation by the mass media, publication is virtually presumed, however. In fact, some cases are on record in which courts ruled that if a statement was published in a newspaper or broadcast over television, it is presumed that a third party saw it or heard it (*Hornby* v. *Hunter*, 1964).

Technically, every republication of a libel is a new libel. Judge Leon Yankwich *(It's Libel or Contempt If You Print It)* wrote more than two decades ago:

> In brief, the person who repeats a libel assumes responsibility for the statement and vouches for its truth as though it had been of his own making or on his own information, no matter how emphatically the qualifying words show that the statement is made on the basis of a source other than the writer himself.

If the *River City Sentinel* is being sued for libel for calling John Smith a communist and the *Ames Daily Gazette* informs its readers about the suit and notes that the *Sentinel* called Smith a communist, the *Gazette* has republished the libel. A more common problem under republication has to do with one of the great myths of American journalism called attribution. A great many people erroneously presume that a publication is not responsible for a libelous statement so long as the statement is attributed to a third person. For example, it is clear that it is libelous for a newspaper to say that John Smith shot and killed his wife's lover. It is just as libelous, however, for a newscaster to report that "according to police Smith shot and killed his wife's lover," or that "Captain Jack Jones or Prosecutor Webley Webster said that Smith shot and killed his wife's lover." The attribution does not help. The newscaster has republished the libel, and the law treats the bearer of tales in the same manner that it treats the author of tales. (But see pages 182–83 for a discussion of qualified privilege which often is applicable as a libel defense in such situations.)

Because of the republication rule, nearly everybody in the chain of production of a news story is technically liable in a lawsuit. The reporter is liable: he or she wrote the story and published it by giving it to the editor. (In fact, more and more reporters are being named defendants in libel suits.) The editor passes it along after checking it (another publication); the copy editor does the same. The story goes to the composing room, and the printers and the newspaper carriers—every one of them—are technically republishing the libelous remark. The law releases vendors of publications from liability unless it can be shown they had knowledge of the defamatory content. The other people at the newspaper really are not worth suing; they do not have any money to speak of. So the publication is sued.

Identification

The second element in a libel suit is **identification:** the injured party must be identified. All sorts of nasty things can be published about anonymous people, but as soon as someone is named, or identified in some other way, a libel suit can result. Not all readers have to recognize the person about whom you write. Not even the majority of readers need know to whom you refer. Some authorities say it is sufficient if only a single person can identify the subject of the story.*

A person can be identified in a number of ways. He or she can be named; the Knave of Hearts stole the tarts. A photograph without a name is considered identification. A person can be identified by a pen name, by a nickname, by initials, and even by a pencil or pen drawing. Circumstances can sometimes point the finger at someone. Several years ago a New York gossip columnist wrote, "Palm Beach is buzzing with the story that one of the resort's richest men caught his blonde wife in a compromising spot the other day with a former FBI agent." A man named Frederick Hope sued the Hearst Corporation (for whom the columnist worked) for libel. Hope, who was a former member of the Federal Bureau of Investigation (FBI), convinced the jury that the article identified him. He had recently joined the county attorney's staff and had been given considerable local publicity. His background as a former FBI man was given special prominence. He was also able to show that he was the only former G-man who ran with Palm Beach high society. Hope claimed that many of his friends would put these two facts together and know that the columnist referred to him. Hope won a $58,000 judgment (*Hope* v. *Hearst Corp.,* 1961).

It is also possible to put two stories together to make an identification. Imagine that this story was broadcast on Monday: "A fugitive wanted by the FBI for bank robbery was injured today when the automobile in which he was riding was struck by a train." No name appears here, so there is no problem. Tuesday's story appears to be safe as well: "John Smith who was severely injured yesterday when the automobile in which he was riding was struck by a train. . . ." Smith can put two stories together and claim that he has been identified as the fugitive and bank robber.

*This situation should not be confused with damage to the plaintiff. Only one person has to see a story for it to have been published. Some authorities (e.g., Phelps and Hamilton) also say that only one person has to identify the plaintiff. However, when a judge and jury consider whether the material is defamatory and damaging to the plaintiff, they must decide whether the statement can lower the plaintiff's reputation in the eyes of a significant minority of the community.

If a libelous statement does not make an explicit identification, then the plaintiff must prove that the defamatory words refer to him. This is not usually an insurmountable burden, and reporters must be extremely careful when making identification in a news story, especially if business affiliations are included in a story. Comments about an executive of a corporation, the president, for example, may reflect on the prestige of the firm and give rise to cause of action by the corporation. The corporation must prove, however, that the comments about the management discredit the business in some way.

One of the most common problems in libel is careless identification that results in a case of mistaken identity. Years ago the *Washington Post* ran a story about a District of Columbia attorney named Harry Kennedy who was brought back from Detroit to face charges of forging a client's name. The attorney charged was Harry P. L. Kennedy, a man who used his middle initials when he gave his name. The *Post* left out the middle initials. Harry F. Kennedy, another District of Columbia attorney who did not use his middle initial in business, sued the newspaper and won a substantial judgment (*Washington Post* v. *Kennedy,* 1924). That was sloppy journalism.

Most journalists learn early that complete identification is required when an individual in a news story is discussed. The identification should include the name, John Smith; the address, 2185 Pine Street; the age, 34; and if possible the occupation, carpenter. This complete identification clearly separates this John Smith from any other John Smith in the area. Complete identification protected the now defunct *Washington Star* newspaper in a lawsuit brought by a man who was erroneously named a suspect in a shooting. When prominent physician Michael Halberstam was shot in the nation's capital, the *Star* reported that police had arrested a suspect named "Jerry Summerlin, 22, of the 5500 block of Dana Place N.W." This address is just a block from Dr. Halberstam's home in the District of Columbia. The *Star* also reported that the suspect had been hit by the victim's car and was in the District General Hospital. The assailant was really Bernard Welch, who refused to provide any identification to police. The court ruled that Summerlin had not been libeled because he had not been identified. Summerlin was not twenty-two years old, lived in Silver Springs, Maryland, and was not in the District General Hospital after the shooting. In fact the *Star* had got everything correct in its identification of the shooting suspect except the name. By adding the details of identification, the newspaper saved itself from a libel judgment (*Summerlin* v. *Washington Star,* 1981).

The number of suits that result from mistaken identity is high, and most are preventable. One thing a young reporter should learn immediately is to not take anyone's word for an identification. If the police tell you they have arrested John Smith of Pine Street, you should double-check their statement. Numerous means of checking are available: city directories, utility company records, and so forth. Because they compound the error, newspapers, broadcasting stations, and magazines are sometimes held responsible even for errors that result from official blunders.

The most troublesome question regarding identification is group identification. Can the members of a group sue when the group as a whole is libeled? The answer to this question is not completely clear. If the group is massive, there can be no suit. In a recent suit, the New York Supreme Court ruled that several nonprofit Puerto Rican community organizations could not bring a libel action based on the remark "nine hundred-thousand Puerto Ricans live in New York and they're all on food stamps." The court ruled that such remarks aimed at ethnic or racial groups in general do not cause direct, focused harm to individual group members. (*Puerto Rican Legal Defense Fund* v. *Grace,* 1983). If the group is small—a three-man zoning board is corrupt— each member can sue. The group is small enough so that each member can be clearly identified. What about a middle-sized group? The *Restatement of Torts* (2nd ed.) says this:

> One who publishes defamatory matter concerning a group or class of persons is subject to liability to an individual member of it, but only if (A) the group or class is so small that the matter can reasonably be understood to refer to the individual or (B) the circumstances of publication reasonably give rise to the conclusion that there is particular reference to him.

According to the *Restatement,* publication of defamatory statements about groups having more than twenty-five members is safe. Circumstances and what is said play a big part in this question. Several years ago employees of Neiman-Marcus department store in Dallas sued the publisher of a book entitled *USA Confidential* for statements in the book about the store's sales staff and models. The author of the book charged that the models and salesgirls were call girls and that most of the salesmen in the menswear department were homosexual. Only nine models were employed in the store, and that suit was uncontested. The store had twenty-five menswear salesmen. The article said most were "fairies," and the court allowed recovery for several individual salesmen. However, there were more than three hundred salesgirls in the store, and the federal court said the group was too large. "No reasonable man would take the writer seriously and conclude from the publication a reference to any individual saleswomen," the judge ruled (*Neiman-Marcus* v. *Lait,* 1952).

Recent case law on the issue of group identification tends to support the notion that courts seem reluctant to find liability unless it is quite clear that the specific plaintiff has been identified, as the following cases show.

A doctor of osteopathy sued a magazine in 1984 after it published an article urging readers who were ill to see a medical doctor, not an osteopath. "A D.O.'s [doctor of osteopathy] training is similar to that of an M.D.'s, but in most of their schools and hospitals the standard of training is still below that of the M.D. institutions," the article said. The court ruled that the statement did not injure the plaintiff, it injured his profession. "Whatever aspersions are cast by the publication fall upon the profession of osteopathy, and not upon a small or identifiable group within the class of osteopaths," the Oklahoma Supreme Court noted (*McCullough* v. *Cities Service*, 1984).

A U.S. district court in Minnesota ruled that statements in Peter Matthiessen's book, *In the Spirit of Crazy Horse*, about "FBI agents" did not identify Agent David Price, who sued Viking Press, the publisher of the book, for defamation. The group "FBI agents" is too large, the court said (*Price* v. *Viking Press*, 1985).

The question in a Massachusetts newspaper, "Is it true that a Bellingham cop locked himself and a female companion in the back of a cruiser in a town sandpit and had to radio for help?" did not specifically identify any single member of the community's twenty-one-member police department (*Arcand* v. *Evening Call*, 1977). There was no liability.

Finally, a federal court ruled that a small group of editors and reporters for the Manchester *Union-Leader* newspaper could not maintain a lawsuit against the *Boston Globe* because of critical comments published in the *Globe* about the New Hampshire publication. The *Union-Leader*, which was published for many years by William Loeb, a very controversial figure in journalism, was described in a *Globe* editorial as "probably the worst newspaper in America." The *Globe* said that Loeb "runs a newspaper by paranoids for paranoids." Three editors and twenty-four other employees including some reporters brought suit against the *Globe*, but a United States district court in Massachusetts dismissed the action. "Defamation of a large group gives rise to no civil action on the part of an individual member of the group unless he can show special application of the defamatory matter to himself," the court ruled. Three hundred twenty-five persons were employed at the newspaper. The group was too large. Admitting that the general references to the paper probably hurt the editors more than other employees because they were ostensibly responsible for what appeared in the *Union-Leader*, the court ruled that no special application or particular reference to these three persons could be inferred from the general criticism of the newspaper (*Loeb* v. *Globe Newspaper*, 1980).

Despite these victories by the press, caution is urged upon reporters who describe even a very large group in a defamatory manner. Caution is especially appropriate if only a small number of the defamed group live in the community. If the charge is made that all astrologers are frauds and there is only one astrologer in the community, the remark can be dangerous. The plaintiff could convince a sympathetic jury that he or she has been severely harmed by the remark. Saying "all" members of a group are corrupt is worse than saying "most" members are corrupt. Saying "most" is worse than saying "some," and saying "some" is worse than saying "one or two." This is a particularly unsettled area of the law, and the journalist must remember that ultimately the suit will be decided by a judge and jury who may neither look at the issue in the same manner as the journalist nor be particularly sympathetic to the charges made by the journalist.

Defamation

The third element in the plaintiff's case are the words themselves. There are two kinds of defamatory words. The first kind consists of words that are libelous on their face, words that obviously can damage the reputation of any person. Words like *thief, cheat,* and traitor are libelous per se—there is no question that they are defamatory.

The second kind of words are innocent on their face and become defamatory only if the reader or viewer knows other facts. To say that Jane Adams had a baby appears safe enough. But if the reader knows that Ms. Adams is not married, then the words are libelous.

The distinction between these two kinds of words used to be more important than it is now. At one time plaintiffs had to prove they were specifically harmed by the words in the second category, sometimes called "libel per quod." Damage was presumed from the words in the first category, often called "libel per se." All libel plaintiffs must prove harm of some kind today. Yet in some states the plaintiff suing for the so-called libel per quod must meet a more rigorous fault requirement than the plaintiff suing for libel per se. For example, in some jurisdictions the libel plaintiff suing on the basis of words that appear innocent on their face (libel per quod) must prove that the defendant was grossly negligent in publishing the statement, whereas the plaintiff suing for words that are plainly defamatory must show only simple **negligence.** (The meanings of the various fault requirements are discussed on pages 165–74.)

A description of the kinds of words that are libelous is codified (by statute) in most states. These laws are most general, however, describing kinds of words (words that hold someone up to ridicule, hatred, scorn, etc.), rather than specific words. Only by looking at the numerous court decisions in libel law can one get a fairly good picture of the specific kinds of words that can be libelous. Even then the process is imprecise.

There is another problem. The meanings people attach to words change over time. Socialists were once feared and hated, and the word was defamatory. It is doubtful that calling someone a Socialist today would be libelous. Labeling someone a Communist was and is defamatory, except during the period between 1942 and 1945 when the Communists were our allies in World War II. The term *slacker* seems harmless enough today, but in World War I *slacker* had a derogatory meaning; the word described someone who sought to avoid military service.

At a libel trial a judge and jury are supposed to consider words in light of their ordinary meanings unless the evidence is persuasive that the defendant meant something else when the statement was published. As a general rule it is for the judge to decide whether an ambiguous statement can convey a defamatory meaning and for the jury to decide whether in fact the statement does convey that meaning. A judge can dismiss a suit without a trial if he or she believes the words cannot be considered defamatory. By letting a case go to the jury, the judge is only ruling that a jury could find that the words are defamatory. For example, an Australian researcher sued *Science* magazine for publishing an article that he argued impugned his integrity. The story focused upon hearings held by the Food and Drug Administration about the safety of Bendectin, a drug taken by pregnant women to relieve nausea. William G. McBride, an expert in the study of agents that can cause abnormalities in the development of embryos, testified against the drug at the hearing. The magazine noted that the panel was not impressed with McBride's testimony and then noted that he had been paid $5,000 a day to testify in a civil action brought against the manufacturers of the drug by a woman in Orlando, Florida. The magazine noted that the drug manufacturer paid its expert witnesses only $250 to $500 a day during the trial. Actually McBride was paid only $1,116 per day. But the magazine publishers argued that the assertion that McBride was paid $5,000 a day was not libelous, even though it was wrong. A trial judge agreed and dismissed the suit. However, the United States Court of Appeals for the District of Columbia ruled that the statement was ambiguous and certainly could convey a defamatory meaning. "It is possible that a reader might conclude that plaintiff's case [the suit against the drug manufacturer] was so weak they had to pay that much to get any expert to testify, and hence that Dr. McBride's testimony was for sale." A jury should decide the question, the court ruled (*McBride* v. *Merrell Dow*, 1984).

A person may be defamed in any number of ways. Simply saying that Robert Smith is the illegitimate child of John and Mary Smith is defamatory. The parents have been defamed. Implication can be used: John and Mary Smith have been married for six years and have a seven-year-old son named Robert. Some journalists think that if they do not spell out a situation, but just drop subtle hints, they are on safe ground. In Massachusetts a libel case resulted when a newspaper reporter thought something was wrong and tried to say so subtly. Here is part of the story:

> The Veterans Hospital here suspected that 39-year-old George M. Perry of North Truro, whose death is being probed by federal and state authorities, was suffering from chronic arsenic poisoning.
> State police said the body of Perry, and of his brother, Arthur, who is buried near him, would probably be exhumed from St. Peter's Cemetery in Provincetown.

George Perry died in the VA hospital last June 9, 48 hours after his tenth admission there. . . . His brother, who lived in Connecticut and spent two days here during George's funeral, died approximately a month later. About two months later, in September, George's mother-in-law, 74-year-old Mrs. Mary F. Mott, who had come to live with her daughter, died too. Her remains were cremated.

While the story lacked a good deal in journalistic clarity, an Ellery Queen or a Perry Mason is not needed to get the gist of what the reporter was saying. Mrs. Perry murdered her husband, her brother-in-law, and her mother. Lizzie Borden strikes again! The insinuations are that Arthur died after visiting the plaintiff's home and that the mother had "died too." Isn't it too bad that her remains were cremated? This story cost the Hearst Corporation, publishers of the *Boston Record,* $25,000 (*Perry* v. *Hearst Corp.,* 1964).

A libel suit cannot be based on an isolated phrase wrenched out of context. The article as a whole must be considered. A story about baseball's legendary base stealer, Maury Wills, might contain the sentence "Wills might be the best thief of all time," referring to his base-stealing ability. Wills cannot sue on the basis of that single sentence. The story itself makes it clear the kind of thievery the writer is discussing. Nevertheless, a libelous remark in a headline—even though it is cleared up in the story that follows—can be the basis for a libel suit.

Also, a headline cannot go beyond the story and say more than the story says. In Mississippi recently, *The Commercial Dispatch* newspaper published a story about three men who had pleaded guilty to charges of illegally transferring cattle from one county to another without having the animals tested for a bacterial disease. But the headline on the story said, "Three Plead Guilty to Cattle Theft." That the true facts were contained in the story did not immunize the newspaper from a successful libel suit based upon headline, according to the Mississippi Supreme Court. (*Whitten* v. *Commercial Dispatch,* 1986).

A federal court in Seattle ruled that reader habits can also be material in a libel case. Suit was brought against the *Seattle Post-Intelligencer* for a story it published about the redemption of a home mortgage by a local attorney. The headline and the first four or five paragraphs suggested that the attorney had done something illegal or unethical. The remainder of the story—which was about fifty paragraphs long and jumped from page to page after leaving the front page—explained that what the attorney had done was not illegal or unethical, that his actions were fair and aboveboard. The court admitted expert testimony on reader habits, which indicated that people tend not to finish such long stories, that many people stop reading as soon as the story is continued on the inside pages of a newspaper. The plaintiff argued that in the minds of most readers, the libelous opinion created by the first part of the story was not corrected, since they did not finish the story. The jury awarded the attorney $100,000 in damages (*McNair* v. *Hearst Corp.,* 1974).

Factual statements can obviously be defamatory. What about an opinion? "I think Mayor Frank Jones is doing a rotten job of running this city." An opinion cannot be defamatory. In 1974, in a very important case, the Supreme Court of the United States ruled (*Gertz* v. *Welch,* 1974):

> Under the First Amendment there is no such thing as a false idea. However pernicious an opinion may seem, we depend for its correction not on the conscience of judges and juries but on the competition of other ideas.

The revised *Restatement of Torts* states that an opinion statement can be defamatory only if "it also expresses, or implies the assertion of a false and defamatory fact which is not known or assumed by both parties to the communication." We will talk much more about statements of opinion when we examine the defense of fair comment.

The next one hundred pages of this book could be a kind of Sears Roebuck catalog of defamatory words, but such an enumeration here is a waste of time. Instead, we will consider specific examples of the kinds of words that in the past were held to be defamatory. These examples should permit you to generalize about specific remarks. Simply ask this question when you evaluate whether something is defamatory: Will the people in the community think less of this person after I publish this story than they do before I publish it? If the answer is yes, then the statement, remark, or comment is probably defamatory.

Accusation of a Crime

Probably the category of words responsible more than any other for the greatest number of libel suits pertains to crime and criminal acts. Any imputation that a man or woman has done something illegal—from murder to jaywalking—is libelous. The statement can be a straightforward charge: John Smith is an arsonist or John Smith was convicted of arson. The imputation can be indirect: John Smith makes his living using matches and gasoline. The statement might note only that John Smith has spent much of his life in jail because fire fascinates him. A description might be used: John Smith went to the Fuddle Paint Company, poured gasoline on an outside wall, and then lit a match. Maybe John has a nickname—John the Torch. Each of these statements and many more you can think of accomplish the same end: they defame poor John Smith.

It is also libelous to call John an "alleged arsonist," which points out another great myth of journalism. According to the dictionary, to allege means "to assert without proof." The police assert that John is an arsonist, and by calling him an alleged arsonist the journalist republishes the libel the police officer uttered. Republication of a libel is a new libel.

A serious problem faced by the reporter who writes or broadcasts about crime is lack of knowledge about the meaning of criminal terms. Not every killing is a homicide or murder. When John Smith kills his wife, he might be acting in self-defense. Calling him a murderer creates a problem. Be certain the term used does not go beyond the action.

The *Calvin* (Okla.) *Chronicle* was angered when a federal district judge, fearful of the impact of intense prejudicial publicity, changed the venue for the trial of a state official. In an editorial the newspaper noted that "State Treasurer Leo Winters and all the other people are just as guilty in Guymon on the panhandle, Idabel in Southeastern Oklahoma, Bartlesville in the Northeast, Lawton in the Southwest, or right smack in downtown Oklahoma City." Winters sued for libel, and the state supreme court ruled that the charge that he was guilty of a crime was libelous per se (*Winters* v. *Morgan,* 1978).

Sexual Slurs

It has been said that the United States is a nation overly concerned with sex. Sexual references, comments about sexual morality, sexual abnormality, and so forth, all constitute bases for libel suits. Supposedly, we are in the midst of a sexual revolution, but many people are not aware of the fact. For a woman to be sleeping with a man to whom she is not married may be perfectly normal in some parts of our society, but is still not acceptable behavior in other parts of our society. If such a charge were made against a woman, a libel suit would probably stand. Woman's virtue is strongly protected by our courts via the libel suit. Any charge made in any fashion that a woman may be unchaste or may not be virtuous is dealt with harshly by a court. Charges of rape come within this category as well.

Similarly, comments about sexual abnormality are dangerous. John is gay or John is queer, Jane is a lesbian, Frank is an exhibitionist—all are defamatory remarks. Caution must be exercised as well in stories about less exotic sexual concerns: calling a man impotent can be libelous. Charges of wife swapping and failure to fulfill "marital obligations" are also defamatory.

Personal Habits and Characteristics

Much of a person's reputation is concerned with personal habits. Is he honest, ethical, and kind? Does he pay his bills on time or is he a deadbeat? Is she clean, does she drink too much liquor, does she use cocaine, does she smoke pot? Statements regarding all such behaviors have been and will continue to be the subjects of libel suits. To call a man dishonest is defamatory. Likewise are charges that he is unkind to his children and unethical in the way he conducts his financial affairs. She drinks too much, she is a drunkard, she is always potted or smashed, she is an alcoholic, she is a member of Alcoholics Anonymous, she is on the juice, she was arrested for drunken driving—all of these charges are libelous. The same is true of statements regarding the use of drugs and marijuana. A good credit rating is very important today; therefore any charge that reflects on financial standing—the Smiths live beyond their means, they are broke, they don't pay their bills, they owe money all over town—is defamatory.

Reporters must be wary of many other aspects of personal characteristics. Imputation that a person has a certain kind of disease can be dangerous. What kinds of diseases? Not a cold or the flu: anyone can have these disorders.

Syphilis, gonorrhea, and genital herpes—euphemistically called social diseases—suggest a kind of loose sexual behavior and uncleanliness frowned upon by many people. Diseases that cause a person to be shunned—contagious diseases such as smallpox, infectious hepatitis, or even the widely publicized AIDS—are examples.

In an interesting decision by a United States circuit court of appeals, a former Philadelphia Eagles football player lost a libel suit based on the published erroneous assertion that he had contracted polycythemia vera, an abnormal cell condition that can precipitate dangerous clotting of blood. The court ruled that polycythemia vera is not a loathesome disease, not contagious, and not attributed in any way to socially repugnant conduct. As such, the charge was not defamatory (*Chuy* v. *Philadelphia Eagles,* 1979).

Mental illness is another dangerous area. To say that someone is crazy or insane or nuts is defamatory. We are becoming a bit more sophisticated in this area. While fifty years ago the charge that someone had a nervous breakdown was probably defamatory, today such a charge is probably safe unless the plaintiff can prove that the charge caused some special harm, such as the loss of a job.

Religion and Politics

If a person professes to belong to a specific faith, a charge that reflects on his or her commitment to or acceptance by that faith can be defamatory. To say that a Catholic was denied the right of Holy Communion is a serious charge, for to most people it suggests some ghastly kind of behavior by the excommunicant. The same rule applies to political and patriotic affiliations. To charge that a person had been stripped of citizenship is defamatory. Charging someone with being a traitor or a spy or with urging sedition or anarchy or revolution are all defamatory statements.

It can be libelous to ridicule someone, to make that person appear foolish. Ridicule is a difficult area to describe because not all ridicule is defamatory. Many humorous stories about people have been ruled to be safe. Newspapers are frequently the victims of false obituaries, and generally courts rule that such stories are not libelous to the person alleged to have died (*Cohen* v. *New York Times,* 1912). In one case the false obituary had the deceased lying in state in a saloon (*Cardiff* v. *Brooklyn Eagle,* 1948). Other humorous kinds of accounts are generally protected.

A plaintiff sued the *New York Post* for the intentional infliction of emotional distress when the newspaper mistakenly published a death notice. But the New York Court of Appeals has defined this emerging tort very narrowly, ruling that recovery could only be based on defamation and malicious prosecution, willful and outrageous humiliation intentionally inflicted by conduct exceeding all bounds usually tolerated by decent society, or deliberate harrassment. Publication of the death notice was not libelous, the New York Supreme Court ruled, nor did it meet the other two criteria (*Rubenstein* v. *New York Post,* 1985).

There has been concern expressed by some persons in journalism that the emerging tort, intentional infliction of emotional distress, may become a serious problem for the press. But a study by lawyer Terrance C. Mead, published in the *Washburn Law Journal,* suggests such fear might not be warranted at the present. An examination of tort actions brought against the mass media during a five-year period showed substantial increases in both the number of libel and privacy cases, but only a modest increase in the number of emotional distress actions. Mead said his study demonstrated that tort law was in flux, but added, "The cases also indicate, though one action might stand while another falls due to particular circumstances, the infliction of emotional distress tort need not raise fears of opening a huge new area of claims." The difficulty in pleading such a claim—as noted above—make libel and privacy more attractive to most plaintiffs, Mead said.

Ridicule which can be libelous is that which makes the plaintiff appear to be uncommonly foolish, which carries a kind of sting that hurts. Everyone must die, and therefore a false obituary really says nothing derogatory about the plaintiff. It is just a joke at his expense. But a story in a New England newspaper about a man so thrifty that he built his own casket and dug his own grave was ruled to be libelous ridicule. The story made the man appear to be foolish, weird, and unnatural. A fifty dollar judgment was awarded (*Powers* v. *Durgin-Snow Publishing Co.,* 1958). How can reporters tell the difference between the two kinds of stories? The distinction is often very difficult. Extreme care is needed to avoid problems.

Business Reputation

Thus far the kinds of charges that can injure almost all persons, hurt their reputations, cause them to lose friends, have been discussed. The law goes beyond these limits in protecting some individuals; it goes to the point of protecting both men and women in their businesses or occupations. Any comment that injures a person's ability to conduct a business or occupation successfully can be considered defamatory. For example, comments about business ethics can be defamatory. Sid, a butcher, sells tainted meat. Archie, a mechanic, overcharges his customers. Similarly, statements about competence to do a job can be defamatory. Milton lacks the skill to be an architect. Doris, a nurse, cannot tell a bedpan from a baby bottle. Comments about honesty, about the financial solvency of a business person—anything that tends to impair an individual's means of making a livelihood or discredits the individual in his or her business or profession—can be the basis for a successful libel suit.

Because reputation is an essential element in the success of many professional persons, such a person is probably more easily defamed and more likely to sue than a typical working man or woman. In fact, Professor Marc Franklin of Stanford University recently reported, following his study of more than five hundred libel suits, that professional people were one of six groups of people responsible for two-thirds of all the libel suits filed in the United States. The other groups were business managers, government employees, law enforcement personnel, corporations, and public officials. Teachers, doctors, journalists, businessmen, lawyers, and many other persons are very easily defamed by comments about their business or occupation. Yet such persons are not above honest criticism; journalists should not totally abdicate their role as consumer protectors. James Southard, an antique automobile dealer and the creator of something called Classic Car Investments, sued *Forbes* magazine for what he said amounted to questioning his integrity as a businessman. *Forbes* did an article on the growing field of investment in classic cars that was critical of speculators and promoters. It discussed Southard's plan to develop an investment program in classic automobiles, which he hoped to sell to doctors, lawyers, and corporations. The magazine quoted Southard as saying, "The value of those cars never goes down, so you're guaranteed to make money." Writer Alvin Butkus then noted, "If he made claims like that for stocks, Southard would be in the soup. But there is no Securities and Exchange Commission for classic cars." Southard said Butkus's statement implied he was unethical, that he had violated federal securities laws, that he was selling unregistered securities. The Fifth U.S. Court of Appeals disagreed and said that the meaning placed on the statement by Southard was farfetched. The article at worst, the court ruled, suggested that the plaintiff was puffing the value of an investment in classic cars to an extent beyond what was permitted in marketing of securities. "The fundamental message was caveat emptor [buyer beware] to potential customers of Southard and others in his business. . . . It lacks the element of personal disgrace necessary for defamation" (*Southard v. Forbes,* 1979).

The law also provides some other exceptions. For example, the law does not presume that people think that business or professional people are perfect. Therefore, to report that a professional person or a business person has made an error is not always defamatory. It depends upon how the statement is made. If the statement merely suggests that the individual made an isolated mistake—Dr. John Smith operated on Jane Adams yesterday to remove a sponge he had failed to remove during an earlier operation on Ms. Adams—it is probably not libelous. However, if the published comment suggests a pattern of incompetence—this is the fifth time in the past two years Dr. Smith has had to operate a second time to remove a surgical tool left in a patient—the statement clearly is defamatory. Be careful in this area. Recourse to this rule is never an excuse for clumsy or careless journalism. This rule (called by some the **single-mistake rule**) is not constructed upon an unassailable foundation (see *Hentell* v. *Knopf,* 1982, for an example of how this rule can protect a libel defendant).

One other group of "business persons" can sue if they are improperly criticized: government officials and politicians. Charges of corruption, bribery, vote buying, gross dereliction of duty, and graft can all stand as the basis for a successful libel action. Accusing a judge of being biased and unfair, accusing the head of the street department of improperly maintaining the public roads, and accusing a public official of selling out to the mob are all defamatory charges. (As will be noted later, it is much harder for government officials to win a libel suit than it is for a private business person.)

While a person's general reputation is fairly nebulous, the individual's right to earn a living, practice a profession, successfully operate a business, and so forth, are quite specific. Courts are prone to protect such individuals from unwarranted attack. Journalists and broadcasters must exercise caution in dealing with such subjects, lest they inadvertently damage that right.

About a Business

In addition to damaging a person, a defamatory statement can injure a business or corporation. A corporation can maintain a lawsuit when it believes its credit has been damaged or its reputation has been hurt. The same kinds of words that can defame an individual can also defame a corporation or business. Any assertion that the corporation has engaged in criminal activity, is dishonest, has ties to organized crime, lacks integrity, fails to pay its bills on time, and so forth, can be libelous. Corporations can be hurt in other ways as well.

An assertion that the corporation makes unsafe products—not that the products are unsafe, but that the corporation deliberately produces unsafe products to cut costs—can result in a libel suit. Statements that reflect on the company's labor policies—management runs a real sweatshop, takes advantage of its workers, violates labor laws—are libelous. Attacks on fiscal integrity (better not buy a car from Acme Motors because chances are good that the company won't be around next year to fix the car when it breaks down) are defamatory. An assertion that DooDad Industries does not maintain safe working conditions or that the company makes illegal political contributions or that it cheats its customers is libelous to that business.

Some authorities assert that making derogatory statements about persons who manage a business, who work at a business, or who are customers of a business can also be used as the basis for a defamation suit. The law is not settled in this area. Publishing nasty things about the president and vice-president of DooDad Industries will not give the corporation the right to sue unless it can be proved that such statements actually damaged the reputation of the company. Reporting that DooDad employees are "a bunch of louts" might also serve as the basis for a damage suit if the company can prove that the charge somehow reflects on the corporation's ability to hire the proper people.

There is little chance, however, that a corporation can sue merely because of actions or behavior of its customers. Several years ago Louis Stillman sued Paramount Pictures for the remark in the motion picture *Country Girl* that punch-drunk fighters frequented Stillman's Gym in New York City.

Stillman argued that the remark reflected upon him and his business. The court disagreed (*Stillman* v. *Paramount Pictures,* 1957). Proprietors of public businesses have no control over the kinds of persons who use their establishments. Therefore, readers should not think anything less of Stillman because punch-drunk fighters might be training in his gym. Another example of the problem is a story saying that for the second time in two weeks a fight broke out at a local tavern last night. Again, the proprietor does not have much control over who drinks in his tavern and what happens when they drink. Any implication that the owner of the place encourages this kind of behavior, condones it, fails to call authorities after it starts, and so forth, will of course change the nature of the remark and can be libelous (see also *Namlod, Ltd* v. *Newsday,* 1984).

About a Product

Criticism of a product falls into a different legal category called "disparagement of property." While such criticism is often called **trade libel,** it is not really libel at all, but product disparagement. What is the difference? A plaintiff finds it significantly harder to win a trade libel case than to win a garden-variety libel suit. First, consider some examples of trade libel. Bango rifles fail to eject empty cartridges. Crumo bread gets stale in one day. DooDad motorcycles fail to stop within a safe distance. The remarks are aimed at the products, not at the companies. There is no implication that the manufacturer intentionally makes a bad product, tries to cheat customers, or conducts its business fraudulently. DooDad may make the best motorcycles it can make; they just turn out to be unsafe.

Since the company itself is not presumed to be hurt, the law raises some stiff barriers to a successful trade libel suit. First, the plaintiff, the manufacturer of the product, must prove that the statement is untrue. Proof is difficult, but not too difficult for the kinds of statements just given. If DooDad is able to demonstrate to the court that some of its motorcycles brake to a stop within a safe distance, the company then shows the falsity of the charge. It is much safer to refer to individual products. For example, rather than say that DooDad motorcycles do not stop safely, report that of the ten motorcycles tested none stopped safely or that of the Bango rifles tested, none ejected cartridges properly. The manufacturer will then have to refute this evidence, not merely find examples of the product that are in good working order.

Next, the plaintiff will have to show special damage—actual monetary loss because of the comments. Loss of orders attributable to the unfavorable report is such evidence, and testimony from potential customers who failed to purchase the maligned product because of the comment can be used to support the damage claim. Finally, the plaintiff has to prove that the false remarks were motivated by ill will, bad feeling, or gross carelessness. The plaintiff can prove this if he or she can show that the negative remarks were published "to get him (or her)" and that the writer doesn't like him or her. The plaintiff might also be able to prove that the writer was grossly negligent in checking the truth of the statement. Before the plaintiff can collect for trade libel, all three charges must be proved: falsity, damage, and malicious motives or extreme carelessness.

Evaluate the following three statements on the basis of the foregoing discussion of trade libel:

1. DooDad autos are superior to Acme cars.
2. Acme cars stop running after about one year.
3. Acme cars stop running after about one year because the company has a plan to force customers to buy a new car every year.

Is statement one libelous? It contains no libel, no disparagement, no anything. Nothing negative was said about Acme; only a positive statement about DooDad cars was made. Statement two? This statement is trade libel, an attack upon the product. Statement three? Here we have garden-variety libel. The comment states that Acme purposefully sells automobiles that break down after one year and reflects upon the integrity of the business itself.

Banks and Insurance Companies

One other point should be made before we leave this topic. In addition to the protections businesses and corporations have against libel, many states have laws that prohibit critical and untrue comments about banks, insurance companies, and other such organizations. What these laws are designed to do is to protect such organizations from attack upon their fiscal integrity to avoid turning customers against them and destroying them. After all, a bank has only its fiscal integrity and other people's money to sell.

Suits under such statutes are rare, but occasionally they do occur. And then the newspaper or broadcasting station soon discovers that the many protections the press enjoys in a libel suit often do not apply when a suit is brought under such a law. Check the insurance laws and the banking laws in your state. If such laws exist, find out how the courts interpreted the laws. This check might save a lot of grief some time in the future.

SUMMARY

A plaintiff bears the initial burden of proof in a libel suit and must prove:

1. That the libel was published
2. That the plaintiff was identified
3. That the words were defamatory

Publication can be established if the plaintiff can show that one additional person besides the plaintiff and the defendant has seen the material. An individual can be identified for purposes of a libel suit by a name, nickname, or photograph or even through a report of circumstances. Statements made about a very large group of people cannot be used as the basis for a libel suit by a single member of that group. However, if the group is smaller, all the members might be able to sue for comments made about the entire group. A statement is defamatory if it lowers the reputation of the injured party. The most common kinds of defamatory statements reflect such matters as suggestions of criminal behavior or sexual impropriety, comments about personal habits or characteristics, statements reflecting upon patriotism or political beliefs, and reports about competence and qualifications in an individual's occupation or business. Corporations and other businesses can be defamed; the manufacturer of a product that has been criticized can sue for product disparagement.

THE FAULT REQUIREMENT

The fault requirement, the final element in the plaintiff's case, is a relatively new element in libel litigation. Since the mid-1960s **public persons**—that is, persons in the public eye—have had to prove an element of fault when they sue mass media defendants. **Private persons** have had to prove fault since 1974. The fault requirement places a significant additional burden upon the plaintiff in a libel suit and offers important additional protection to the defendant. For example, Ariel Sharon was able in 1985 to prove the first three elements of libel in his suit against *Time* magazine. In addition, he was able to convince the jury that the defamatory statement was false. But the jury ruled that the former Israeli defense minister had failed to prove fault; he had not shown that *Time* magazine editors acted with actual malice. The magazine won the case. Proof of fault is not only required for a plaintiff to win a suit, but the level or kind of fault the plaintiff can prove is also an important element of determining damages (see pages 199–202).

The fault requirement has a kind of dual nature that makes it both indispensable to the plaintiff's libel case and a privilege used by the defense. In some regards it can be considered to fit naturally as a requisite that must be met by the plaintiff along with the demonstration of publication, identification, and defamation. Yet it is also a prerogative raised by defendants to protect themselves from a libel suit. In this regard it has many of the characteristics of a defense to libel. The dual nature of this requirement is recognized in this book by placing the discussion of fault, including consideration of private and public persons and the meaning of fault, between the outline of the plaintiff's case and the defenses to libel.

Proof of Falsity

As noted earlier, most libel plaintiffs must prove the falsity of the defamatory statements as part of proving fault. Historically, words challenged in court as being libelous were presumed to be false. The defendant, the publisher of the libel, carried the burden of proving the truth of the assertions. But in 1964 the Supreme Court embarked on a long process of what is now known as the "constitutionalization of the law of libel" that is, the application of the First Amendment to libel. In a case called *New York Times* v. *Sullivan,* the Supreme Court ruled that persons who held public office must not only show that they were the target of a damaging libelous comment, but that that comment was published by the defendant with the knowledge that it was false or with reckless disregard of whether it was true or false.

Later it was ruled that plaintiffs classified as public figures must also meet this same fault requirement. Requiring that a plaintiff prove that a statement was made with knowledge of its falsity or with reckless disregard of the truth would seem also to require the simultaneous determination that the statement in question was false, even though the members of the Supreme Court did not specifically say this. Slowly but surely lower courts reached the conclusion that the burden of proving the truth or falsity of a statement—at least in those lawsuits where public officials and public figures were plaintiffs—had shifted to the plaintiff.

In 1974 the high court ruled that even persons who are not public officials or public figures had to prove some measure of fault in a libel action, at least that the defendant was negligent in publishing the defamatory statement. Proving negligence on the part of the defendant seemingly also implies prior or simultaneous proof that the damaging statement was false. But the lower courts were much slower to reach this conclusion. In 1986 the Supreme Court decided the matter for them by ruling in *Hepps* v. *Philadelphia Inquirer* that all persons suing the mass media for a damaging statement that involves "matters of public concern" must prove that the statement is false. So the burden of proof has dramatically shifted from the defendant, who formerly had to prove the truth of the libelous assertions, to the plaintiff, who now must prove the falsity of the assertions. We don't yet know whether this rule covers all libel plaintiffs or even all libel plaintiffs suing the mass media. The court said the rule applies at least in those instances when the damaging statement concerns a matter of public concern. But the court did not suggest how narrowly or how broadly the words "public concern" are to be interpreted.

In reversing the burden of proof with regard to the proof of the truth or falsity of a defamatory charge, the Supreme Court did not change the law regarding what is legally a truthful statement and what is not. For centuries, defendants have attempted to prove in court the veracity of the allegations they have published or broadcast. There are ample precedents that remain as useful now as they were prior to the ruling by the High Court in the Philadelphia Newspapers case. The plaintiff must now use this case law to attempt to convince the judge or jury that the defamatory statements are false. Failing to do that, the court must rule for the defendant.

The first rule of proving truth or falsity is that the evidence presented in court must go to the heart of the libelous charge.

The proof must be direct and explicit. If there is conflicting evidence, the fact finder—the judge or the jury—will decide who is telling the truth. Every word of a defamatory charge need not be truthful, only the part that carries the gist or the sting.

What the court is looking for is substantial truth. For example, a Michigan newspaper published that a land developer had been "Charged in Shopping Mall Fraud." The story said Harlan Orr had been charged with fifteen counts of fraud, outlined what it called his "phony shopping mall investment scheme," and referred to his behavior as an "alleged swindle." Orr sued for libel. He admitted that the basic facts of the story were true: he had been charged with five counts of the sale of unregistered stock, with eight counts of failure to disclose information, and two acts of deceit. Orr had told potential investors in his scheme that J.C. Penney Company had already leased space in his proposed shopping center. That was not true. What Orr objected to was the use of the words "fraud," "swindle," and "phony" scheme. The United States Court of Appeals for the Sixth Circuit overturned a jury verdict in behalf of Orr and ruled that the article was substantially true. The word *fraud* is an accurate and appropriate description of a violation of the Michigan security laws, the court said. The word *swindle* is a common colloquialism for the term *defraud*. The J.C. Penney scheme was "phony." The court admitted that the words in the story could mean more; they could mean a "flimflam." But they could be used also to mean what Orr had done (*Orr* v. *Argus Press,* 1978).

Extraneous errors do not always equal falsity. The *Ashtabula Telegraph* reported that George C. Horvath had been arrested with several other persons in a drug raid. The reporter talked with various police agencies in gathering information on the story and learned that Horvath was supposedly funneling the money earned from the sale of the drugs back into his businesses, Horvath Service and All-Seasons Nursery. But in fact his father, George J. Horvath, owned the businesses. George C. had worked at the businesses and was even perceived by some to be the owner. George J. Horvath sued for libel. He said that there were falsehoods in the story, that George C. did not own the businesses, and that the business was named All-Seasons Archery, not All-Seasons Nursery. Everything else was true. The Ohio court of appeals ruled that the gist of the article was true and that the two minor errors did not distract from the story. The article was true under the law (*Horvath* v. *Ashtabula Telegraph,* 1982).

But the story must have some truth to it. Two men were apprehended at the Galleria Shopping Center in Little Rock, Arkansas, after police had received a call that a design store was being robbed. The two men were handcuffed, searched, placed in a patrol car, and taken to the police station. The action was videotaped by reporters from KARK-TV. The police made no comment to the reporters at the scene, and a clerk in the store gave the reporter what was later described as a "vague response." Nevertheless, KARK told the viewers of the "10 O'Clock News" that quick action by police had stopped a robbery at the Custom Design store. "Details are sketchy, however it appears that two suspects backed their car up to the store in order to rob it. For a time, the two men allegedly held a store clerk hostage," the broadcaster reported, as videotape of the incident was telecast. In fact, police had released the two men at 9 P.M., an hour earlier, after deciding no robbery attempt had even taken place. Reporters had not followed up on the apprehension and went on the air with little more than rumors. The station attempted to use truth as a defense; two men were apprehended. But the Supreme Court of Arkansas refused to permit the tactic. Literal truth is not necessary, the court noted. Only the gist of the libel need be true. But in this story nothing was true. There was no robbery attempt, no hostage-taking; the plaintiffs were involved in no crime whatsoever (*KARK-TV* v. *Simon,* 1983).

How does the court evaluate the truth of the charge? The jury does this with guidance from the judge. The judge will probably give the jury a test to use in evaluating the evidence against a defamatory charge. One of the commonly used tests comes from a 1934 New York case, *Fleckstein* v. *Friedman.* Defendant Benny Friedman, a former all-star professional football player, charged that some of the players in the National Football League were sadists and bullies. Friedman named names in his *Collier's* magazine story, and one of the players identified, William Fleckstein, sued.

In attempting to prove the truth of the charge, Friedman demonstrated some of the tactics used by these rough players. In instructing the jury in this case, the judge said:

> . . . a workable test of truth is whether the libel as published would have a different effect on the mind of the reader from that which the pleaded truth would have produced. When truth is so near to the facts as published that fine and shaded distinctions must be drawn and words pressed out of their ordinary usage to sustain a charge of libel, no legal harm has been done.

In simpler terms this is what the court said: After reading the article, readers were left with a certain opinion of William Fleckstein, a negative opinion since he was called a bully and a sadist in the story. Now, if persons who had not seen the story had a similar opinion of Fleckstein after seeing the evidence Friedman presented in court, Friedman had then succeeded in proving his charges. Today this test would be applied to the plaintiff's proof of falsity. If the proof offered by the plaintiff in court leaves a different impression in the minds of the jurors than the published defamation has left, this would likely constitute proof of falsity.

One more point should be stressed about truth and falsity. Correctly quoting someone or accurately reporting what someone else has told you does not necessarily constitute publishing a truthful statement. Imagine that John Smith tells a reporter that the police chief changes arrest records of certain prisoners to simplify their getting bail and winning acquittal. This charge, attributed to John Smith, is contained in the reporter's story which is subsequently published. The police chief sues for libel. It is not sufficient for the reporter to prove merely that the statement in the story was an accurate copy of what Smith said. Even if the reporter's story contained an exact duplicate of Smith's charge, truth can be sustained only by proving the substance of the charge, that the police chief has altered arrest records. It is the truth of the libelous charge that is at issue, not merely of the accuracy of the quote in the story. Accuracy, then, is not always the same thing as truth.

SUMMARY

The plaintiff in lawsuits against the mass media must prove the falsity of damaging statements on matters of public concern. The evidence presented in court must go to the heart of the libelous charge; it must relate to the gist or the basic substance of the libel. Minor errors in a story will not necessarily result in a finding of falsity.

Proof of Fault

Proving the falsity of the defamatory statements is simply the first hurdle the plaintiff must cross in proving fault. It must be remembered that in proving fault in a libel suit, that is, in proving that the newspaper or magazine or broadcasting station was careless or reckless in allowing the libelous material to be published, both the plaintiff and the defendant have a role. The plaintiff must convince the judge and/or jury that the publication or broadcasting station was indeed at fault, that it was negligent or careless. The defendant on the other hand, must try to convince the court either that there was no negligence or that the highest possible level of fault needs to be proved; that is, the defendant will argue that the plaintiff needs to prove that the publication of the story resulted from something more serious than simple carelessness—that it was published because of reckless disregard for the truth. The defendant wants to make the plaintiff's task as difficult as possible. Given this perspective, two sets of questions need to be considered. First, what is the fault requirement for private persons? What is the fault requirement for public persons? How does the law distinguish between private and public persons? Second, how have the courts defined the various levels of fault? And how can such fault be proved by plaintiffs?

Two generalizations are useful as guidelines in understanding fault:

1. Private persons who sue the media for defamation must at least prove that the material was published through negligence. **Negligence** is defined in the law as conduct that creates an unreasonable risk of harm. Another way of describing this concept is that something published negligently was published *without* the exercise of reasonable care by the defendant.

2. Public persons who sue the media for defamation because of the publication or broadcast of stories about their public conduct must normally prove that the defendant exhibited **actual malice** when the material was published. Actual malice is defined in the law as publishing the material with the knowledge that it is false or publishing the material with a reckless disregard for the truth.

Both of these generalizations need important qualification and clarification, and that is the purpose of the bulk of this section.

Throughout almost its entire history, the tort of libel has been governed by a standard called "strict liability." **Strict liability** means that if you harm someone, you are responsible for that harm, regardless of how it happened to come about. You could have undertaken every possible effort to ensure that no harm would result from your action; nevertheless, if someone is hurt, the responsibility is yours. In the law of libel this meant that even though editors attempted to verify a story in every possible way, even though they exercised every caution normally exercised by careful journalists, even though there was no doubt at all in their minds that the story was accurate and truthful, if the story defamed someone, the newspaper was liable for damages.

In 1964 the Supreme Court of the United States ruled that in libel law the doctrine of strict liability violated the First Amendment insofar as the defamatory statement concerned government officials and focused upon their official conduct. The dispute from which the ruling sprang was played against the vivid backdrop of the civil rights struggle in the South. In some ways the result of the lawsuit was a recognition by the Supreme Court that while for all practical purposes the law of **seditious libel** had become impotent by the last half of the twentieth century, government leaders could use civil libel actions to accomplish the goals of sedition law: to quiet criticism of the government.

In the early 1960s important segments of the American press took a strong stand in support of the passage and enforcement of civil rights laws. In Alabama five government officials attempted to retaliate against the press by filing a series of lawsuits against the *New York Times* for three million dollars.

The material upon which the suits were based was not even a news article; it was an editorial advertisement (an advertisement that promoted an idea rather than a product or commercial service). A civil rights group, the

Committee to Defend Martin Luther King and the Struggle for Freedom in the South, had placed the advertisement. In the narrative part of the full-page advertisement, charges were leveled at various Alabama government leaders. While it was basically true, the advertisement was nevertheless peppered with small factual errors. These errors proved to be the downfall of the *Times* in an Alabama state court, where the newspaper lost the first suit brought by Montgomery, Alabama, Police Commissioner L. B. Sullivan. Sullivan won a $500,000 judgment—all that he asked for—and this ruling was affirmed by the state supreme court. One must remember that as much as anything, the case against the *Times* allowed Alabamians to vent their pipes, which had been filling with steam ever since that (according to prevailing Southern thought) "damned, liberal [radical, communist] New York scandal sheet" had taken a leadership role in seeking passage and enforcement of federal civil rights guidelines in the South. The political implications of this case are beyond the scope of this text, but should not be overlooked. The *New York Times* appealed the decision to the Supreme Court of the United States and won a unanimous reversal of the judgment. In reversing the Alabama state courts in the case of *New York Times Co.* v. *Sullivan* (1964), the Supreme Court changed the law of libel forever.

Under the traditional law of libel the newspaper was in serious trouble. There had been publication and identification, and the words were clearly defamatory. The story contained numerous false statements. Traditional libel defenses were inapplicable. But Justice William Brennan and his eight colleagues on the High Court did not apply the traditional law of libel. Sullivan was not a typical plaintiff; he was a government officer. The defamation did not concern his private life; it focused on his role as police commissioner. The Court ruled therefore that because of the nature of this suit, because of the immense First Amendment implications, plaintiff Sullivan should carry an added burden of proof. He should show that the publication of the advertisement was made with actual malice. Actual malice was defined as knowledge of falsity or reckless disregard of whether the story was truthful. Sullivan, then, had to show that the *New York Times* published the advertisement with knowledge that some of its charges were false or that the newspaper exhibited reckless disregard as to whether the charges were true.

The Court's decision can be explained on three bases. First, this libel case was really a kind of seditious libel case. A government official was criticized for the manner in which he conducted his public office. He sued for civil libel and won. The *New York Times* was punished for criticizing the government. Punishment for criticism of government is the essence of sedition. It matters little that the punishment comes in the form of a money judgment that must be paid to the government official as opposed to a fine that must be paid into the public treasury. The results are the same; others will be more cautious in their comments about those who control the government. With the exception of the **Smith Act,** which is aimed at prohibiting the advocacy of action toward the violent overthrow of the government (see pages 66–70), sedition has been effectively abolished in this country. In *New York Times Co. v. Sullivan,* the Supreme Court simply made it much harder (but not impossible) for government officials to accomplish the goals of sedition law through civil libel suits.

Members of the Court also said they were concerned that these kinds of lawsuits might have an impact upon debate about political issues. Quoting numerous earlier High Court opinions, Brennan wrote (*New York Times Co. v. Sullivan,* 1964):

> The general proposition that freedom of expression upon public questions is secured by the First Amendment has long been settled by our decisions. The constitutional safeguard, as we have said, "was fashioned to assure the unfettered interchange of ideas for the bringing about of political and social changes desired by our people. . . ." The maintenance of the opportunity for free political discussion to the end that government may be responsive to the will of the people and that changes may be obtained by lawful means, an opportunity essential to the security of the Republic. . . . "The First Amendment," said Judge Learned Hand, "presupposes that right conclusions are more likely to be gathered out of a multitude of tongues, than through any kind of authoritative selection."

Thus, Brennan wrote, this case is considered against the background of a profound national commitment to the principle that debate on public issues should be uninhibited, robust, and wide open.

Turning to the fact that there were errors in the publication, Brennan asserted, "Erroneous statement is inevitable in free debate, and it must be protected if the freedoms of expression are to have the 'breathing space' that they need . . . to survive." Whatever is added to the field of libel, the associate justice noted, is taken from the field of free debate. This concept—traditional concern with maintaining free debate—formed the philosophical basis for the decision.

Finally, as a public official, a government leader, Sullivan voluntarily took a position for which criticism was common, usual, and, indeed, expected. As a servant of the public one must expect to be criticized, sometimes quite strongly. In a way, he had asked for criticism. Also, as a public official and a politician he had easy access to the press to respond to criticism. Whereas a private person whose reputation has been damaged may have no recourse but to go to court to win vindication, Sullivan could give as good as he got. He could deny the charges in the public press; he could make countercharges. In short, he had access to an effective means of rebuilding his damaged reputation without relying upon a libel suit, which, as we have noted, can have a serious impact upon the freedom of expression.

These reasons are the pillars upon which the *Sullivan* decision rested. In taking this stand the Court followed a course of action that a handful of states had adopted years earlier. In 1908 the Kansas Supreme Court ruled that public officials and candidates for public office must carry a more rigorous burden of proof than private citizens to sustain a libel judgment in order to preserve the immense public benefit gained from free and robust debate (*Coleman* v. *MacLennan,* 1908). The *Sullivan* case amplified and extended this ruling to every state in the Union. Henceforth, public officials had to prove actual malice in order to sustain a civil libel suit.

In 1966 a federal court extended much of the reasoning of the *Sullivan* ruling to persons it called "public figures" in the case of *Pauling* v. *Globe-Democrat.* The plaintiff in this case was Linus Pauling, a Nobel Prize-winning physicist who was very active in the movement to ban atmospheric testing of nuclear weapons. Pauling had never held public office and could not in any sense be considered a public official. Yet in the libel suit that resulted when the *St. Louis Globe-Democrat* incorrectly published that the Nobel laureate had been convicted of contempt of Congress, the United States Eighth Court of Appeals ruled that as a "public figure" Pauling must prove that the story was published with actual malice (*Pauling* v. *Globe-Democrat,* 1966). The rationale?

> Professor Pauling, by his public statements and actions, was projecting himself into the arena of public controversy and into the very vortex of the discussion of a question of pressing public concern. He was attempting to influence the resolution of an issue which was important, which was of profound effect, which was public, and which was internationally controversial.

Conscious that important public debate frequently involves persons not in government and that the threat of a libel suit could interfere with such debate, the Court ruled that the First Amendment protects this kind of discussion. One year later in *AP* v. *Walker* and *Curtis Publishing Co.* v. *Butts,* the Supreme Court accepted this argument and made the actual malice fault requirement applicable to public figures as well.

It was not until 1974 that the Supreme Court further extended the development of the fault requirement. In a case that will be discussed often for other reasons, *Gertz* v. *Welch,* the Court ruled that henceforth private persons would no longer be able to sue for libel unless they, too, were able to demonstrate that the media were in some way at fault in publishing the story. Justice Lewis Powell said that states must require that nonpublic persons prove that the defendant is, at the very least, negligent. States can, however, ask private persons to prove a greater degree of fault. That is, under the ruling in

Gertz, states can insist that all libel plaintiffs—not just public officials and public figures—prove actual malice, or anything between simple negligence and actual malice. Negligence is the minimum requirement, but state courts can ask for proof of a higher degree of fault.

By early 1986 courts in most of the fifty states had explicitly or implicitly selected a level of a fault to apply when a private person sues a media defendant, and all but a handful had chosen to use the negligence standard. Courts in Colorado (*Walker* v. *Colorado Springs Sun, Inc.,* 1975), Indiana (*AAFCO Heating and Air Conditioning Co.* v. *Northwest Publications, Inc.,* 1974), and New York (*Chapadeau* v. *Utica Observer-Dispatch, Inc.,* 1975) have clearly selected a higher standard of fault. Courts in Michigan, which originally selected a higher standard, seemingly changed their minds and will now apply a negligence standard also (see *Rouch* v. *Enquirer & News of Battle Creek,* 1984).

The simple way to find whether your state has adopted a negligence requirement, a slightly higher level of fault such as gross negligence, or actual malice is to locate the most recent state supreme court libel rulings. Within the text of these cases will be found the level of fault applicable to private-person plaintiffs in your jurisdiction.

Thus far, we can summarize the fault requirement in this manner: When a newspaper, magazine, broadcasting station, or other kind of mass media defendant is sued for libel, the plaintiff must prove fault. A plaintiff who is considered a private person must prove at least that the defendant acted in a negligent manner in publishing the libel; that is, the defendant did not exercise reasonable care. In some states the private-person plaintiff is required to prove an even higher level of fault than negligence—that the publisher of the libel acted in a grossly negligent manner. In all states a plaintiff who is a public person must prove to the court that the publisher of the libel acted with actual malice; that is, the publisher had knowledge that the material was false and still published it or the publisher acted in reckless disregard of the truth. Remember, the standards of fault are incremental. Simple negligence is simple carelessness, fairly easy to prove. Gross negligence is acting in a very irresponsible manner and is somewhat more difficult to prove. Actual malice is knowing that information is false but still publishing it or acting with little concern for determining what the truth may be. This is normally very difficult to prove. Please note that all these levels of fault are discussed in much greater detail on pages 165 through 173. Let us now take up the important question of the differences between private persons and public persons as defined by the courts.

PRIVATE PERSONS VERSUS PUBLIC PERSONS

Whenever a court takes a common description and attempts to shape it into a legal concept, much confusion results. Such is the case with the private-person-versus-public-person dichotomy in the law of libel. A majority of the United States Supreme Court has seemingly settled upon a rationale that has been cited consistently over the past two or three years to justify the distinction the Court has drawn in applying the fault requirement differently to private persons than to public persons. The rationale has two parts. First, public persons are somewhat less vulnerable to injury from defamatory statements because they enjoy a much higher degree of access to the press to rebut or deny the libelous statements. The only recourse for a private person is a lawsuit; a public person can use the press to respond to and deny the charges, to correct the errors. Hence, private persons need more protection; the press needs to be more careful when it writes about private persons.

Second, and probably more important, public persons are less deserving of protection than other persons because public persons have voluntarily exposed themselves to the increased risk of injury by moving into the public spotlight. Public persons do this by running for government office, attempting to lead public opinion upon important issues, or working publicly toward the resolution of important societal issues. The avowed goal of the Supreme Court is to protect the integrity of the debate that results when society attempts to resolve important issues; in order that such debate be open and free, the threat of libel actions must be minimized. Hence, because of the higher fault requirements, it is more difficult for a public person to win a libel suit (see *Gertz* v. *Welch,* 1974; *Time, Inc.* v. *Firestone,* 1976; *Wolston* v. *Reader's Digest,* 1979; and *Hutchinson* v. *Proxmire,* 1979).

Who is a private person? Who is a public person? Stating the rationale for distinguishing between plaintiffs who are private persons and plaintiffs who are public persons is far easier than outlining the legal distinction between these two kinds of plaintiffs. We must rely upon often incomplete or ambiguous criteria provided by the courts to define whether a particular person in a particular case is a private person or a public person. This latter point is very important. When you attempt to determine whether a plaintiff is a public or private person, always evaluate the plaintiff in relationship to the facts in the libel case. It is very likely that a person who might be considered a public person in one case might not be considered a public person in another libel suit.

Who Is a Public Person?

The courts have classified public persons into these three categories:

1. Public officials
2. All-purpose public figures
3. Limited public figures

Two questions must be asked to determine whether a libel plaintiff should be considered a public official.

1. Who is this plaintiff; that is, what kind of job does this person have?
2. What was the allegedly libelous story about?

Let us consider these questions separately.

A public official is someone who works for a government and draws a salary from the public payroll. Included are persons from the president of the United States to a patrolman on a beat. Yet not all persons who are government employees qualify as public officials under the law of libel. In 1966 when the Supreme Court was confronted with a lawsuit from a former director of a county ski area, Justice Brennan attempted to define those persons in government who would fall under the rubric public official. "It is clear," he wrote, "that the 'public official' designation applies at the very least to those among the hierarchy of government employees who have or appear to the public to have substantial responsibility for or control over the conduct of governmental affairs" (*Rosenblatt* v. *Baer,* 1966). Brennan added that the person must hold a position that invites public scrutiny of the person holding it, entirely apart from the scrutiny and discussion occasioned by the particular charges in the controversy.

This latter dimension is terribly important. The Supreme Court demonstrated this in 1979 when it refused to consider the research director of a public mental hospital to be a public official. There could be little doubt that Ronald Hutchinson was a well-paid public employee. In addition to his state salary, he was the recipient of about a half-million dollars in public funds for his research on aggression in animals. Senator William Proxmire, who apparently thought the expenditure of public money on such research was wasteful and foolish, named the public agencies that funded the scientist's research recipients of one of his Golden Fleece awards for making a "monkey out of the American taxpayer." In the libel suit that followed, the Supreme Court ruled that there was little public interest in Hutchinson's job before he was made the butt of Proxmire's joke. Chief Justice Burger said that those charged with defamation cannot by their own conduct create their own defense by making the plaintiff a public person (*Hutchinson* v. *Proxmire,* 1979). In other words, Hutchinson's position was not one that invited public scrutiny, apart from the scrutiny and discussion caused by the defamatory charges.

State courts have not always followed this rule to the letter. In *Press* v. *Verran* (1978) the Tennessee Supreme Court ruled that a junior state social worker was a public official because her job carried with it "duties and responsibilities affecting the lives, liberty, money or property of a citizen or that may enhance or disrupt his enjoyment of life. . . ." The Washington Supreme Court in 1979 said that the administrator of a small county motor pool, who worked without direct supervision, had two assistants, and could independently spend up to $500 of county money on open charge accounts at several local parts dealers, was a public official. "The public quite naturally has a legitimate and continuing interest in how local tax revenues are spent by those county employees vested with the power to utilize the public purse," wrote Chief Justice Robert Utter for the court (*Clawson* v. *Longview Publishing Co.,* 1979). The defamation in this case was an allegation that the plaintiff had used small amounts of county funds to repair private vehicles. Similarly, police officers, who are relatively low-level government employees, have frequently been held to be public officials because they hold the power of life and death over the citizens in a community (see *Malerba* v. *Newsday,* 1978).

It is safe to conclude that any government employee who stands for election periodically is a public official in the eyes of the law. As just noted, appointed officials can also meet the established criteria. The appointed Attorney General of the United States is undoubtedly a public person; similarly, the appointed head of a large public utility qualifies. Since 1964 courts have held that judges, senators, state legislators, mayors, school board members, teachers, city tax assessors, and many others are public officials.

What about a consulting firm that advises a government on a controversial but important government policy question? The Iroquois Research Institute was hired by Fairfax County, Virginia, to evaluate the historical and archeological value of an island in the Potomac River on which the county hoped to construct water-intake facilities. Lowes Island was the subject of a great zoning controversy in the community, and when Iroquois reported that the work could be done without harming the island, the research institute became the focus of sharp criticism. The *Loudoun* (Va.) *Times Mirror* published a story that challenged the competence of Iroquois researchers, and a libel suit followed. The Fourth United States Court of Appeals ruled that the consulting firm could not be considered a public official in terms of the libel suit. The court said that the institute made no recommendations to the county, participated in no policy determinations, and exercised no discretion. In short, it had no control over the conduct of governmental affairs. "Its position was not of such apparent importance that the public has an independent interest in its qualifications," the court ruled. The court conceded that in some instances a consultant employed by the government entity can be classified a public official, but not this time (*Artic* v. *Loudoun Times Mirror,* 1980).

The context in which the defamation occurs is often important. A planner with a state geological survey office might not normally hold a position that invites public scrutiny. But if this person is appointed by the governor to conduct a study of the feasibility of constructing three nuclear power plants near the state capital, this special assignment brings with it closer public scrutiny. In such a case a person who was not a public official might suddenly become one in terms of libel law.

This leads to the second question in determining who is a public official in a libel suit: What is the nature of the supposedly libelous story?

A person who works for the government in a position of authority may not be termed a public official for the purposes of a lawsuit if the allegedly libelous story does not pertain either (1) to the plaintiff's official conduct—the manner in which the official conducts the official public role or (2) to the plaintiff's general fitness to hold public office.

Stories that fall under category 1 are obvious. These stories focus upon how well or how badly public officials handle their job. Stories in category 2 are far more troublesome for journalists.

If the mayor is drunk when he attempts to preside at a meeting of the city council, his personal habits directly affect his fitness for office. But what if the mayor has a serious drinking problem that does not visibly affect his work? And what if a newspaper erroneously reports, following the mayor's arrest for drunken driving, that it was the third arrest for such an offense? Will the mayor be forced to prove actual malice in the libel suit that follows? This is a tough question. As a rule of thumb, the lower persons are on the scale of public officialdom, the more their private lives will be protected by the law. Because of the immense responsibilities, almost everything the president of the United States does reflects upon his fitness to hold the job. The private life of a United States senator is probably less open to public scrutiny than the private life of a president, but more investigation of the senator's private life will be permitted than of the life of an elected prosecutor of Clinton County, Michigan.

Public Figures

The concept of the public figure was introduced into libel law in the mid-1960s. However it was not until 1974 that the category was divided into two subcategories by the Supreme Court. Initially, in his opinion in *Gertz* v. *Welch* (1974), Justice Lewis Powell attempted to outline the essence of the public-figure category:

> Hypothetically, it may be possible for someone to become a public figure through no purposeful action of his own, but the instances of truly involuntary public figures must be exceedingly rare. For the most part those who attain this status have assumed roles of especial prominence in the affairs of society.

Powell then noted that there were two separate categories of persons who might be classified public figures:

> Some [persons] occupy positions of such pervasive power and influence that they are deemed public figures for all purposes. More commonly, those classed as public figures have thrust themselves to the forefront of particular public controversies in order to influence the resolution of the issues involved. In either event, they invite attention and comment.

While Justice Powell's dichotomy makes sense on paper, the courts have had a devil of a time identifying persons who fall into Justice Powell's all-purpose public figure category. Television personality Johnny Carson was considered a total public figure in a lawsuit (*Carson* v. *Allied News*, 1976); so was conservative writer and gadfly William F. Buckley (*Buckley* v. *Littel*, 1976). Singer Wayne Newton was recently declared to be an all-purpose public figure by a federal district court in his libel action against NBC (*Newton* v. *NBC*, 1985). It has been speculated that someone like Lee Iacocca or Jane Fonda *might* be total public figures. In *Handbook of Free Speech and Free Press*, Barron and Dienes suggest: "It is almost as if the courts are saying that a plaintiff will have to be totally exposed to constant media attention in order to be classified as a total public figure." The two authors suggest the key to be instant national recognition and constant media exposure.

On a national level this definition of a general or all-purpose public figure is probably accurate, but there is another way of looking at the problem: the general notoriety of a person within the area in which the libel is circulated. It is quite probable that there are persons in small communities who might have the status of total public figures. Consider the woman who lives in a community of 6,500 persons. She was formerly the mayor, has served on the school board in the past, and has been a perennial choice for president of the Parent-Teacher Association. She is the president of the largest real estate company in town, is a director on the board of the local bank, and owns the local pharmacy and dry cleaner's. She is active in numerous service clubs, is a leader in various civic projects, and is instantly recognizable on the street by virtually all of the town's residents. Her family founded the town 150 years earlier. If she is libeled in a community newspaper whose circulation remains almost exclusively in the community, it could be argued persuasively that this woman is a total public figure in the community. (See *Steere* v. *Cupp*, 1979, where the Kansas Supreme Court ruled such an individual was a total or all-purpose public figure.) In 1982, the Montana Supreme Court ruled that investment and commodity adviser Larry Williams was an all-purpose public figure for his libel suit based on a Democratic Party press release that erroneously charged that he had been under federal indictment for political dirty tricks. The court listed the following activities by Williams, which convinced the court that he was an all-purpose public figure: he published an investment advisory service; he wrote three books on stocks; he was the subject of an article in *Forbes* magazine and another article in the *Wall Street Journal;* he frequently gave speeches and ran unsuccessfully for the United States Senate; he was chairman of the Republican Party in Montana; and he was an active member of the National Taxpayers Union (*Williams* v. *Pasma*, 1982).

But what if the publication being sued circulates outside the local community, as well, to persons who may not be familiar with the plaintiff? This question arose in 1985 in a libel suit by businessman George Martin against the *Chariho Times* in Rhode Island. Martin was clearly well known in the village of Shannock, where he owned and had developed a considerable amount of property over a period of fifteen years. The *Times* was widely read by the three hundred residents of the village, and a trial court ruled that Martin was a local all-purpose public figure. On appeal Martin argued that the newspaper had three thousand subscribers, a far larger readership than just among the village residents by whom he was so well known. The Rhode Island Supreme Court, noting that Martin's fame had spread beyond the Shannock Village limits, added that "very few individuals will be known to all subscribers or purchasers of any publication." Wally Butts and Major General Edwin Walker were not known to all subscribers of the *Saturday Evening Post,* yet were declared to be public figures by the Supreme Court, the Rhode Island justice noted, recalling that famous 1967 decision (see pages 168–70). "It is sufficient to attain a public figure status that the plaintiff should have been known to a substantial portion of the publication's readership," the court ruled. And Martin met this test (*Martin* v. *Wilson Publishing,* 1985).

Regardless of these examples, few persons fall into the category of all purpose public figure. Far more important for journalists is Justice Powell's second category, the limited public figure. The Supreme Court has spent more time since 1974 on defining who is and who is not a limited public figure than on any other aspect of libel law. The High Court wrote opinions in four libel suits in the five years following the *Gertz* ruling, and in three of the four cases a central question was whether the plaintiff was a limited public figure (*Time, Inc.* v. *Firestone,* 1976; *Wolston* v. *Reader's Digest,* 1979; and *Hutchinson* v. *Proxmire,* 1979). The fourth case was *Herbert* v. *Lando* (1979), which focused upon the discovery procedures in a libel action. When the essential elements are extracted from *Gertz* and the three subsequent public figure cases, certain basic criteria in the definition of a limited public figure emerge.

In *Gertz* v. *Welch* plaintiff Elmer Gertz was a well-known and widely respected Chicago attorney who had gained prominence in civil rights disputes in that city. He had written several books and articles, and on many occasions had served on commissions and committees in Chicago and Cook County. When a young man was slain by a Chicago police officer, Gertz agreed to represent the family in a civil action against the officer. The policeman had been tried and convicted of murder in the shooting, but Gertz played no role in that criminal action. His only role in the entire matter was as an attorney representing the family in the action for civil damages. He became the subject of a vicious attack by *American Opinion,* a magazine published by the John Birch Society, which accused him of being a communist fronter, a Leninist, and the architect of a frame-up against the police officer. It also charged that Gertz had a long police record.

In the libel suit that followed, the Supreme Court ruled that despite his prominence in the civil rights area, Elmer Gertz was not a public figure for the purposes of this lawsuit. The words of Justice Powell stand as an important guideline (*Gertz* v. *Welch,* 1974):

> It is preferable to reduce the public figure question to a more meaningful context by looking to the nature and extent of an individual's participation in the particular controversy giving rise to the defamation.

The key phrase is "extent of an individual's participation in the particular controversy giving rise to the defamation." To be a limited public figure, the plaintiff must be shown to have played a prominent role in the particular controversy giving rise to the defamation, the controversy prompting publication of the defamatory statement or comment. Gertz would have been a limited public figure if the dispute in the case had involved civil rights in Chicago. He would have had to prove actual malice in such circumstances. But the particular controversy that gave rise to the article in *American Opinion* was the murder of the young man and the subsequent trial of the police officer. Gertz was not an important participant in that issue. He was simply acting as an attorney—which is his profession—in representing the family of the youth in a civil action. He was acting as a private individual and as such had only to prove simple negligence.*

Two years later the Court ruled that a socially prominent Palm Beach woman was not a public figure with regard to the divorce action in which she was involved. The case, *Time, Inc.* v. *Firestone* (1976), resulted from a short notice published in *Time* magazine that Russell Firestone was granted a divorce from his wife on grounds of extreme cruelty and adultery. Firestone was in fact granted a divorce from his wife, but on grounds that neither member of the couple was "domesticated." Mary Alice Firestone sued *Time* for libel, claiming she had been called an adulteress. *Time* argued that her prominence in the Palm Beach community made her a public figure. On the record she clearly appeared to be a public figure, a leading member of the "Four Hundred of Palm Beach society," an "active member of the sporting set," a person whose activities attracted considerable public attention. She even maintained a clipping service to keep track of her publicity. The divorce case became a *cause celebre* in the community, prompting forty-three articles in a Miami newspaper and forty-five stories in the Palm Beach newspapers. She held several press conferences during the course of the seventeen-month legal dispute.

---

*The case of *Gertz* v. *Welch,* which began in 1969, finally ended in the summer of 1982 when a $400,000 judgement against *American Opinion* was upheld by the Seventh United States Court of Appeals (*Gertz* v. *Welch,* 1982).

Nevertheless, the Supreme Court refused to acknowledge that Mary Alice Firestone was a public figure in the context of the divorce case, the subject of the *Time* article that was defamatory. Justice William Rehnquist wrote:

> Respondent did not assume any role of especial prominence in the affairs of society, other than perhaps Palm Beach society, and she did not thrust herself to the forefront of any particular public controversy in order to influence the resolution of the issues involved in it.

Time argued that because the trial was well publicized, it must be considered a public controversy and Mary Alice Firestone a public person. "But in doing so," Justice Rehnquist wrote, "petitioner seeks to equate 'public controversy' with all controversies of interest to the public." The Justice said that a divorce proceeding is not the kind of public controversy referred to in *Gertz*. While there was public interest in the proceedings, the case was not an important public question.

Rehnquist also pointed out that Mrs. Firestone was not a voluntary participant in the divorce proceeding. She was forced to go into public court to dissolve her marriage. Whether individuals have voluntarily thrust themselves into the public spotlight is probably not a controlling issue in most cases. But Justice Powell did write in the *Gertz* decision, "it may be possible for someone to become a public figure through no purposeful action of his own, but the instances of truly involuntary public figures must be exceedingly rare. For the most part those who attain this status have assumed roles of especial prominence in the *affairs of society* [author's emphasis]."

The meaning of *Gertz* and *Firestone* was reemphasized in 1979 in two rulings by the Supreme Court that clearly indicated that the High Court intended the limited-public-figure category to be narrow. In both cases, *Hutchinson* v. *Proxmire* and *Wolston* v. *Reader's Digest,* the Supreme Court reversed rulings by lower federal courts, rulings that had declared that the plaintiffs were in fact limited public figures.

The facts in the *Hutchinson* case were mentioned earlier. The plaintiff was the research director at a public mental hospital in Michigan. He was also the recipient of about $500,000 in federal grants to support his research on animal aggression. Believing that such research was unimportant, Senator William Proxmire bestowed his monthly Golden Fleece Award on several federal agencies that had funded Hutchinson's research for nearly seven years. In the process the Wisconsin lawmaker accused Hutchinson of putting the "bite" on the American taxpayer and making "a monkey" out of the American people. Hutchinson sued.

Chief Justice Burger refused to consider the plaintiff a public figure. He said there was no controversy about the research until Proxmire's defamatory comments about Dr. Hutchinson. The scientist did not thrust himself or his views into a public dispute or issue. In fact, Burger said, the defendants "have not identified such a particular controversy; at most they point to concern about general public expenditures." Hutchinson, the chief justice noted, at no time assumed any role of public prominence in the broad question of concern about expenditures. The researcher, then, had no part in the controversy that gave rise to the defamation, according to Burger. Simply taking public money to do research is not enough to make a person like Hutchinson into a public figure, the Court ruled. "If it were, everyone who received or benefited from the myriad public grants for research could be classified as a public figure. . . ."

Finally, the chief justice drew upon the basic rationale for the distinction between private and public persons and said that "we cannot agree that Hutchinson had such access to the media that he should be classified as a public figure." His access, Burger noted, was limited to responding to Proxmire's announcement of the Golden Fleece Award. The decision of the Court was eight to one in favor of Hutchinson, and the single dissenting vote by Justice Brennan was based solely on how the Court had responded to another question, not to the public-figure issue.

The facts in the *Wolston* case are somewhat more complicated. Ilya Wolston was identified in a 1974 book, *KGB: The Secret World of Soviet Agents,* as a Soviet agent. His description as such stemmed from events that had taken place nearly twenty years earlier when a federal grand jury in New York State was investigating the activities of Soviet agents in the United States. Wolston's aunt and uncle, Myra and Joe Soble, were well-publicized American Communists who were arrested in January 1957 and charged with spying. Wolston himself was interviewed by the Federal Bureau of Investigation (FBI) and testified several times before the New York grand jury. In July 1958 he failed to respond to yet another grand jury subpoena. His failure to appear was publicized in the press. He said he had not testified because he was in a state of mental depression. Later he changed his mind and offered to give testimony. He subsequently pleaded guilty to a charge of contempt and was sentenced to three years' probation. During the six weeks between the time he refused to testify and his sentencing, fifteen news stories were published about Ilya Wolston in New York and Washington newspapers. He was never indicted for espionage.

Wolston's libel suit was based on his misidentification in the *KGB* book published by *Reader's Digest*. The publication argued that because of his contempt conviction in 1958, Wolston was a limited public figure for purposes of a discussion of Soviet agents and espionage. Eight members of the Supreme Court disagreed. Justice William Rehnquist, writing for the majority, argued that Wolston did not "inject" himself into any controversy, that he was dragged into the controversy when the government pursued him during the investigation of Soviet agents. "The mere fact that petitioner voluntarily chose not to appear before the grand jury, knowing that his action might be attended by publicity, is not decisive on the status of public figure," Rehnquist said. The justice noted that Wolston played a minor role in whatever controversy there might have been over Soviet espionage, that he had never talked about this matter with the press. "We decline to hold that his mere citation for contempt rendered him a public figure for purposes of comment on the investigation of Soviet espionage."

Rehnquist stressed that Wolston had made no effort to influence the public on the resolution of any issue. The plaintiff did not in any way seek to arouse public sentiment in his favor or against the investigation. Quoting his own opinion in the *Firestone* (1976) case, Rehnquist wrote:

> While participants in some litigation may be legitimate "public figures," either generally or for the limited purpose of that litigation, the majority will more likely resemble respondent [Mary Firestone or Ilya Wolston], drawn into a public forum largely against their will in order to attempt to obtain the only redress available to them or to defend themselves against actions brought by the state or by others.

The question now is, what can we learn from the language in these Supreme Court rulings? Three basic points seem to emerge:

1. Limited public figures normally must voluntarily step into the public spotlight. The Court said it would be exceedingly rare for someone to be an involuntary public figure. Such instances as rising to deny charges made against you and going to court to end a marriage or to defend yourself from government charges do not represent voluntary behavior. They represent a response to the behavior of someone or something else.

2. A limited public figure is someone who plays a role in the resolution of an important public or social issue. A messy divorce, an investigation of aggression in animals, a charge of contempt for failure to testify before a grand jury are not the kinds of "affairs of society" that the Court considers to be important. One gets the impression that the justices are looking to the discussion of social issues (abortion, discrimination), economic issues (taxpayers' revolt, city budget), educational problems (busing, minimum competency requirements), governmental rulings (censorship, arms control), and the like, to find the kinds of persons they would consider limited public figures. A public controversy might be defined as a controversy in which the resolution of the issues will affect the general public or at least a wider group of persons than those individuals involved in the controversy.

3. There must have been some attempt by the plaintiff to influence public opinion in the resolution of these issues. This speaks to the basic point made by Justice Powell in the *Gertz* case—the nature and extent of the individual's participation in the particular controversy

giving rise to the defamation. In *Hutchinson* the issue was wasteful expenditures, but Dr. Hutchinson had said little, if anything, about that before being libeled by Senator Proxmire. Similarly, Ilya Wolston had said nothing about the issue of Soviet agents in this country—which is what the defendant contended was the issue in *Wolston* v. *Reader's Digest* (1979).

Inherent in an attempt to influence the outcome of a public issue is the ability of the plaintiff to get access to the mass media. The plaintiff generally must have some means of speaking out on the issue or of responding to criticism. Also, the media cannot create the controversy by defaming the plaintiff and then argue that the role of the plaintiff is important to the resolution of the issue. These are the key points, then, in determining whether an individual is a limited public figure:

1. There must be an important public controversy.
2. The plaintiff must inject himself or herself voluntarily into the controversy.
3. The plaintiff must attempt to influence public opinion about the resolution of the issue and have some access to the press to accomplish this feat.

While the members of the U.S. Supreme Court have apparently decided who they believe is or is not a public figure, the standards articulated by justices on the High Court have frequently caused utter confusion in the lower courts. What follows is a review of some lower court rulings that demonstrate how other justices and judges have tried to apply the standards enunciated by the nation's High Court. But these lower court rulings are really more illustrative than useful as precedents. Anyone seeking to determine answers to fault questions (i.e., who is a limited public figure?) should look to rulings by applicable U.S. Courts of Appeal or their own state supreme court. If all else fails, the opinions of the U.S. Supreme Court may be consulted.

Attorney William Denny worked for the Koehring Company of Wisconsin for fifteen years before he resigned in 1969 to go into private practice. In 1974 he became visibly involved in a campaign by dissident stockholders to oust the management of Koehring, whose stock had plummeted in price between 1969 and 1974 from $45 per share to $5 per share. *Business Week,* in its story on the stockholders' dispute, erroneously reported that Denny had been fired from Koehring. Denny sued for libel, and the Wisconsin Supreme Court ruled that he was not a public figure for purposes of the libel action because there was no public controversy. The court defined a public controversy as one that, when resolved, will have an impact upon more than the immediate participants in the controversy. This was a stockholders' fight; its outcome would have no impact upon the general public (*Denny* v. *Mertz,* 1980; see also *Levine* v. *CMP Publications,* 1984).

In a similar decision a United States district court in New York ruled that no public controversy existed in a lawsuit by a writer against an erotic magazine that had erroneously identified the picture of a woman in a sexual orgy as the writer. "A public controversy is a dispute that in fact has received public attention because its ramifications will be felt by persons who are not direct participants." The plaintiff was not a public figure in this case, despite the fact she was a celebrated novelist (*Lerman* v. *Chuckleberry Publications,* 1981).

The Delaware Supreme Court recently declared that an inventor who invited the press to a demonstration of an automobile that ran on compressed air was not a public figure. The Delaware *News Journal* made an error in a story about the demonstration, which had taken place in 1977. The newspaper argued that Ronald Re, the inventor, was a public figure because he had thrust himself into the public spotlight to try to resolve the energy crisis by demonstrating an automobile he had designed that did not need gasoline. But the state's high court disagreed, stating that the energy crisis was merely a matter of public concern and interest, not a controversy, which the court said must involve a dispute. Many people are trying to find a way to save energy, the court said. There is surely public interest in this issue. But it is not a public controversy as defined by the leading U.S. Supreme Court rulings (*Gannett* v. *Re,* 1985).

When KSL-TV broadcast a news segment on animal cruelty in 1974, the station identified W. Garth Seegmiller as a rancher who failed to take care of his horses. The station charged that a number of the animals were malnourished and two had died. The story contained several errors and Seegmiller sued. KSL argued that cruelty to animals was an important public issue. The Utah Supreme Court agreed with that argument, but declared that the plaintiff was not a voluntary participant in attempting to resolve the controversy. "On the contrary, he was plucked by the defendant from the anonymity of private life and thrust against his will into the limelight," the state's high court noted. Even if he had been guilty of a misdemeanor, the court ruled, that fact by itself would not be sufficient to compel the conclusion that he is a public figure" (*Seegmiller* v. *KSL-TV,* 1981).

A book-banning controversy arose at San Rafael High School in California when the members of an Elks lodge complained about a textbook being used in an American government class. The book was used in a unit on political philosophies and contained writings from the underground of the sixties, articles on revolution, drugs, and sex. The board of education held several public meetings to discuss the issue. Teacher Virginia Franklin, who taught the class, testified at the meetings, but took no other part in the dispute. The *Elks Magazine* published a story on the controversy, but erroneously reported that teacher Franklin had been fired from a previous job for "teaching the same sort of rot." In the libel suit that followed, the California court of appeals rejected the magazine's contention that Franklin was a public figure. Her only voluntary overt act had been to order several copies of the book for the class. Her testimony was mandated by the school district. "There is no showing that appellant [Franklin] ordered the book for the purpose of inciting controversy. She declares without contradiction that she did not anticipate controversy. It is not clear that, but for the vigorous reaction of Lodge 1108 [the Elks] there would ever have been a controversy," the court noted (*Franklin* v. *Lodge 1108,* 1979). (Please note that in other cases teachers have been declared to be public officials. See *Johnson* v. *Corinthian Television,* 1978, Oklahoma Supreme Court, for example.)

Finally, the Tenth United States Court of Appeals ruled in 1981 that the political aide for a United States Senate candidate was not a public figure in his libel action against then incumbent Senator Frank Moss. G. Andrew Lawrence worked for candidate Orrin Hatch in 1976 as a private consultant in political polling, strategy, voter targeting, volunteer organizations, advertising, fund raising, and speech writing. He came to Utah to work for Hatch in September 1976 after working in the early seventies on Vice-President Spiro Agnew's staff and for the General Services Administration (GSA). Charges of improper conduct were brought against Lawrence while he worked at GSA, but these charges were dropped after he resigned. He then became an independent political consultant.

During the 1976 campaign Frank Moss charged that Lawrence had been Spiro Agnew's "bagman," someone who "picked up the money Spiro Agnew would get." When Lawrence sued for libel, Moss contended that the political consultant was a public figure. The United States Court of Appeals said no. His participation in Hatch's political campaign may have made Lawrence newsworthy, but that fact did not transform him into a public figure. At no time did Lawrence thrust himself into public prominence in order to resolve important public controversies. He participated behind the scenes. The statements he made on public controversies were made in private for his employer, Orrin Hatch. It is the plaintiff's status that is the controlling factor, "not the nebulous interest of the public in a matter with which he is inconspicuously involved," the court ruled (*Lawrence* v. *Moss,* 1981).

More often than not, courts do find that libel plaintiffs are public figures. Here are some cases in which plaintiffs have been ruled to be public figures. Try to note the differences between these cases and the earlier examples.

An attorney who was a former state legislator and who was appointed guardian of an estate that became the center of controversy was deemed to be a limited public figure by the Idaho Supreme Court. A trial judge ruled that the plaintiff's management of the estate had been negligent. Consequently, the state's High Court ruled, Glenn Bandelin was "a pivotal figure in the controversy regarding the accounting of the estate that gave rise to the defamation. . . ." (*Bandelin* v. *Pietsch,* 1977).

A United States district court in the District of Columbia ruled that the question of protein supplements in the human diet was a question of public concern and that consequently, the president of a firm selling such tablets was a limited public figure for the purposes of a libel suit against the *Washington Post*. An article in the newspaper identified the plaintiff as someone who was making lots of money selling the tablets to athletes. When the plaintiff promoted and sold the dietary supplements, he was voluntarily injecting himself into a public controversy, the court ruled (*Hoffman* v. *Washington Post*, 1977).

In 1980 the United States Court of Appeals in the District of Columbia ruled that Eric Waldbaum, former head of the nation's second largest consumer cooperative, was a public figure with regard to a story about his dismissal as president of that organization. The court ruled that Waldbaum had played an active role in attempting to bring consumer-related issues before the public through the media and was a limited public figure in his role with the cooperative (*Waldbaum* v. *Fairchild Publications*, 1980). The Second United States Court of Appeals ruled in 1980 that John Yiamouyiannis, long an outspoken foe of the fluoridation of public water supplies, was a limited public figure in a lawsuit he brought against Consumers Union for criticizing him and his research on the subject (*Yiamouyiannis* v. *Consumers Union*, 1980).

Finally, in one of the most interesting cases in many years, the Sixth United States Court of Appeals ruled in 1981 that a woman who had become a public figure during a celebrated trial in 1931 was still a public figure in relationship to that event. Victoria Price Street was the chief witness against the so-called Scottsboro Boys in a sensational rape trial in Alabama. In a National Broadcasting Company (NBC) dramatization of the long legal struggle, the viewer is left with the strong impression that Victoria Street falsely accused the young men of rape. NBC thought that Mrs. Street was dead. When she sued for libel, the television network argued that she was a limited public figure in connection with the Scottsboro Boys trial. The plaintiff conceded that she may have been a public figure during the trial, but pointed out that that was forty years ago. The court of appeals sided with the network, ruling that "once a person becomes a public figure in connection with a particular controversy, that person remains a public figure thereafter for purposes of later commentary or treatment of that controversy" (*Street* v. *NBC*, 1981). Mrs. Street appealed the decision to the Supreme Court of the United States, which accepted the case. But before arguments were heard, NBC and Mrs. Street agreed upon an out-of-court settlement. Apparently NBC was fearful that it would lose the case in the Supreme Court.

The precedent of *Street* v. *NBC*, that a former public figure remains a public figure for purposes of commentary or retelling of the original controversy, is still law in the Sixth United States judicial circuit (Kentucky, Michigan, Ohio, and Tennessee). In 1984 the Mississippi Supreme Court made a similar ruling in *Newsom* v. *Henry,* stating that a man who ran for public office in 1967, lost the race, and retired from public life was still a public figure in the 1980s for purposes of a libel contained in a story about the 1967 election (*Newsom* v. *Henry,* 1984).

Businesses as Public Figures

Businesses and corporations have, on occasion, been deemed to be limited public figures. It is difficult, however, to discern a real pattern in the court opinions in this area. In 1980 the Third United States Court of Appeals ruled that a company accused of misrepresentation was a limited public figure because it advertised low-priced, inspected, ungraded, frozen, tenderized, boxed beef in a very unusual manner, which attracted great public attention to itself (*Steaks Unlimited* v. *Deaner,* 1980). In another case the Bose Corporation was deemed to be a limited public figure in a lawsuit against *Consumer Reports* magazine over a review of Bose stereo speakers because the audio equipment manufacturer advertised the speakers in a highly unconventional manner that precipitated a public discussion of the merits of the product. The *Consumer Reports* article that criticized the speaker system did not create a controversy, the court ruled. Bose had done this by using a market strategy that emphasized the unconventional design of the 901 speakers (*Bose* v. *Consumers Union,* 1981). So when a company attempts to draw attention to itself in an unusual way, it may become a limited public figure.

On the other hand, simply doing business in a normal manner—even if it involves advertising and promotion—does not turn a business into a public figure. Thomas Jadwin promoted a double tax-exempt no-load bond mutual fund he had developed by placing ads in newspapers, distributing thirteen thousand copies of the fund prospectus and sales literature, and issuing more than two dozen press releases. But the Minnesota Supreme Court ruled in 1985 that he was not a public figure for purposes of a lawsuit based on a newspaper article about the fund because his accomplishments and activities "are not unlike countless other finance professionals. . . ." Soliciting media attention for such an offering is normal, the court said. "To hold, in effect, that soliciting public investment automatically transforms any small businessman into a public figure would, in our view, expand the category beyond the limits contemplated by Gertz" (*Jadwin* v. *Minneapolis Star,* 1985). The First United States Court of Appeals made a similar ruling in 1980. *The Boston Globe* published four articles critical of commercial fishing boats manufactured by the Bruno and Stillman Company. A libel suit followed and the court ruled that the company was not a public figure. There had been no controversy or public discussion about the boats before the libelous stories were published. "The mere selling of products itself cannot easily be deemed a public controversy," the court said (*Bruno and Stillman* v. *Globe Newspapers,* 1980).

Another criterion has been used to establish whether or not a business is a limited public figure. In 1984 a United States district court in Kansas ruled that the Beech Aircraft Co. was a limited public figure for the purposes of a libel suit against the *Aviation Consumer Magazine,* which had published a story about Beech aircraft that had been involved in accidents. The court said that "The defamatory statements relate to part of Beech's business that is federally regulated and arose in the context of a federal investigation." By entering into a regulated activity like the manufacture of aircraft, the company, in essence, invited public scrutiny, the court said (*Beech Aircraft* v. *National Aviation Underwriters,* 1984). But the Supreme Court of Oregon did not even consider the rationale that a regulated business is a public figure when it ruled that the Bank of Oregon was not a limited public figure for purposes of a lawsuit against the *Williamette Week* newspaper. "There simply is no public controversy into which plaintiffs arguably thrust themselves. Merely opening one's doors to the public, offering stock for public sale, advertising, etc., even if considered a thrusting of one's self into matters of public interest, is not sufficient to establish a public figure," the court ruled. *Williamette Week* had suggested that the bank was wrongfully diverting depositors' money and credit to another bank customer, something federal regulators of the banking industry would certainly find interesting. But the court did not discuss this aspect of the case (*Bank of Oregon* v. *Independent News,* 1985).

There is reason for caution, then, when communicating about businesses, even those that have a high visibility in the marketplace. Conducting business in a normal, albeit public manner, is not sufficient to make a corporation or company into a limited public figure. And there is no guarantee that even heavily regulated business, like banks, attain this status simply by virtue of being regulated.

An outline of these cases was presented to give you some insight into how the courts have applied the criteria established by the Supreme Court to determine whether a libel plaintiff is a limited public figure. The simplest way to determine whether a particular individual would be considered a public figure is to apply the test given us by Justice Powell. Determine the extent and the nature of the individual's participation in the controversy giving rise to the defamation. What is the controversy? How did the plaintiff get involved in the controversy? What was the plaintiff's role in the controversy? The answers to these questions will normally lead to the correct answer.

OTHER PUBLIC FIGURES

While the states have with near unanimity accepted the Supreme Court's invitation in *Gertz* to establish liability on a showing of negligence when the plaintiff is a private person, many lower courts have refused to define a public figure in the constricted fashion the Supreme Court adopted in *Firestone, Wolston, and Proxmire.* Individual decisions abound that appear to be out of line with mainstream of the law (see *Maule* v. *New York Magazine,* 1980, for example). An entire line of cases has developed that seems to suggest that in most circumstances professional athletes, members of the underworld, and entertainers will be deemed to be public figures in libel actions based on statements that relate to their chosen professions. Such plaintiffs do not meet the three-part limited-public-figure test outlined earlier in the chapter. Yet courts have ruled that where persons have chosen to engage in professions that draw them regularly into regional and national view and lead to fame and notoriety in the community, even if they have no ideological thesis to promulgate, they invite general public discussion (see *Chuy* v. *Philadelphia Eagles,* 1979 and *Rosanova* v. *Playboy,* 1976, aff'd 1978). Additionally, the courts have ruled that if society chooses to direct massive public attention to a particular sphere of activity, those who enter that sphere inviting attention must overcome the *Times* standard.

A good example of this emerging definition of a public figure is found in the case of *Marcone* v. *Penthouse,* a 1985 ruling by the Third U.S. Court of Appeals. Frank Marcone is a Philadelphia lawyer who gained great notoriety by representing members of national motorcycle gangs when they ran afoul of the law. But he enjoyed socializing with members of the Pagans as well and was indicted for participating in illegal drug trafficking. In a libel action against *Penthouse* magazine, which made a slight error in a story written about Marcone, the Court of Appeals ruled that Marcone was a public figure because of his status. Surely, Marcone did not thrust himself into the public spotlight by attempting to resolve an important public controversy. But the court said that multiple factors—including his legal representation of the gang members, his indictment on drug charges, and the fact that he went on trips and socialized with gang members—when added together, pushed Marcone into the public-figure category. Intense media attention was engendered through this behavior and it does not matter than Marcone did not desire the status of a public person. "The purpose of the First Amendment would be frustrated if those persons and activities that most require public scrutiny could wrap themselves in a veil of secrecy and thus remain beyond the reach of public knowledge," the court said (*Marcone* v. *Penthouse,* 1985).

It is important to note the difference between this case and others. Unlike Elmer Gertz, Frank Marcone not only represented clients, he also spent a great deal of time with them. And the clients were notorious. And unlike Ilya Wolston, Frank Marcone voluntarily engaged in a course of conduct that involved him with organized crime, was not a passive respondent to a legal process, the court noted. This emerging status test for public figures is surely a tentative standard at this time and is probably limited to only a few kinds of persons. But it is clearly a positive development for the mass media in the quest for broader libel protections.

SUMMARY   Under the fault requirement all persons who sue a mass medium for libel must prove that the defendant was somehow at fault in publishing the defamatory material, that the publication (or broadcast) did not result from an innocent error. What the courts call a "public person" must normally prove that the defendant acted with actual malice in publishing the libel; that is, the defendant knew the material was false but still published it or exhibited reckless disregard for the truth. What the courts define as "private persons" must prove at least that the defendant acted negligently, that is, in such a way as to create an unreasonable risk of harm. The courts have ruled that there are three kinds of "public persons:"

1. *Public officials:* Persons who work for a government in a position of authority, who have substantial control over the conduct of governmental affairs, and whose position in government invites independent public scrutiny beyond the general public interest in the qualifications and performance of all government employees. Libelous comments must focus upon the plaintiff's official conduct (the manner in which the plaintiff conducts his or her job) or upon the plaintiff's general fitness to hold public office.
2. *All-purpose public figures:* Persons who occupy persuasive power and influence in the nation or in a community, persons who are usually exposed to constant media attention.
3. *Limited public figures:* Persons who voluntarily inject themselves into an important public controversy in order to influence public opinion regarding the resolution of that controversy. The key elements are
   a. Public controversy, the resolution of which must affect more persons than simply the participants. The outcome must have an impact upon people in a community.
   b. Plaintiffs who voluntarily thrust themselves into this controversy. An individual who has been drawn involuntarily into a controversy created by someone else (such as the press) is not a limited public figure.
   c. Plaintiffs who attempt to influence the outcome of the controversy, to shape public opinion on the subject. This implies that a plaintiff has some access to the mass media to participate in the public discussion surrounding the controversy.

Additionally, highly visible persons engaged in professional sports or underworld activities have been deemed to be limited public figures by virtue of their occupational status.

THE MEANING OF FAULT

We have attempted to establish which persons must prove negligence and which persons must prove actual malice. It is now time to explore the meaning of those terms as they pertain to the fault requirement. What is negligence? What is actual malice?

Negligence

Negligence is a term that has been commonly used in tort law for centuries, but has only recently been applied to libel law. In simple terms, negligence implies the failure to exercise ordinary care. In deciding whether to adopt the negligence or the stricter actual malice fault requirements, state courts are providing their own definitions of the standard. Washington State adopted a "reasonable care" standard. Defendants are considered negligent if they do not exercise reasonable care in determining whether a statement is false or will create a false impression (*Taskett* v. *King Broadcasting,* 1976). The Tennessee Supreme Court has adopted a "reasonably prudent person test": What would a reasonably prudent person have done or not have done in the same circumstance? Would a reasonably prudent reporter have checked the truth of a story more fully? Would such a reporter have waited a day or so to get more information? Would a reasonably prudent reporter have worked harder in trying to reach the plaintiff before publishing the charges? (See *Memphis Publishing Co.* v. *Nichols,* 1978.) In Arizona, negligence has been defined as conduct that creates unreasonable risk of harm. "It is the failure to use that amount of care which a reasonably prudent person would use under like circumstances," the Arizona Supreme Court ruled (*Peagler* v. *Phoenix Newspapers,* 1976).

Negligence may result from many kinds of behavior. A reporter who trusts an inherently untrustworthy source may be deemed to be negligent. Failure by a reporter to check statements in a story that he or she does not understand may be ruled to be negligent behavior. Misreading a file or not including all the pertinent information from a file when preparing a story could be deemed to be a failure to exercise reasonable care. Carelessness in handling a news story might also result in a finding of negligence. A Washington State newspaper reporter who was covering a trial left the courthouse while jury deliberations were underway late on a Friday afternoon. Back at the newspaper the reporter prepared a story that stated that the jury had found the defendant guilty and told the editor to publish it in Saturday's newspaper, but only if the guilty verdict, which was expected, was handed down. The jury verdict came in—not guilty. But the reporter's erroneous story was accidently published. This could clearly be considered negligence.

There are a growing number of cases defining negligence, some of which are quite helpful. Here is a sample of how the courts are defining a failure to exercise reasonable care. The Massachusetts Supreme Judicial Court ruled in

1985 that a newspaper or broadcasting station is not negligent when it publishes or broadcasts a story carried by the Associated Press or United Press International without first independently verifying allegations contained in the story. The two wire services are recognized throughout the industry as trustworthy, accurate news sources, and requiring independent verification of wire service stories would place too heavy a burden on the press. Of course, if it appears likely that the story probably contains an error, the publication or broadcasting station should undoubtedly try to verify the report (*Appleby* v. *Daily Hampshire Gazette,* 1985).

Courts have been reluctant to find negligence when a reporter bases a story on the report of a normally reliable "official" source. A Florida court of appeals ruled that a story based upon an inaccurate report from an immigration officer was not published negligently. The same officer had provided consistently accurate information in the past (*Karp* v. *Miami Herald,* 1978). In 1977 the Philadelphia Police Department arrested two brothers, John and Tyrone Mathis, for attempted bank robbery. The police supplied pictures of the suspects to the *Philadelphia Daily News,* but the photograph identified as John Mathis by the police was not the same John Mathis arrested in connection with the attempted bank robbery. The John Mathis incorrectly identified as an attempted bank robber sued for libel, but the United States District Court for Eastern Pennsylvania ruled that there was no evidence that the newspaper was negligent—the publication was an accurate report of an inaccurate government report (*Mathis* v. *Philadelphia Newspapers,* 1978).

The South Carolina Supreme Court ruled that the failure of a reporter to examine a public judicial record when writing about a criminal case could be negligence. The plaintiff in the case had been arrested with four other men and charged with pirating stereo audio tapes. Two months later four of the men arrested pleaded guilty to the charges, but the charges were dismissed against the plaintiff. The newspaper published a story saying that the plaintiff had also pleaded guilty to the charges. The reporter had gotten his information about the case in a telephone conversation with the prosecuting attorney. The attorney testified that he had given the reporter the correct information. Six days elapsed between the dismissal of charges and the erroneous story. The South Carolina High Court concluded that the correct information was available to the reporter in the court records and that he could have looked at this material before publishing the story. He instead chose to rely upon a telephone conversation and in doing so got the story fouled up. The jury could readily conclude that the reporter was negligent, the court ruled (*Jones* v. *Sun Publishing,* 1982).

The North Carolina Court of Appeals ruled that failure to retract a libelous statement is not evidence of fault of any kind (*Walters* v. *Sanford Herald,* 1976). But the Arizona Supreme Court ruled that it was reasonable to expect a reporter to attempt to verify charges made by two former employees of the Phoenix Better Business Bureau about a local automobile dealer. The former employees charged the businessman with misrepresentation in advertising. The reporter did not attempt to verify the statements by calling the Better Business Bureau to determine the truth of the charges. This was negligent conduct, the court ruled (*Peagler* v. *Phoenix Newspapers,* 1976).

The definition of the term *negligence* will undoubtedly vary from state to state and possibly from judge to judge within a state. It is going to be some time before any kind of broad, consistently applied guidelines emerge. The United States Supreme Court will be of little help in this case, as it appears to be the intention of the Court to leave the matter to the states.

While the uncertainty in this area of the law exists, reporters and editors need to put a premium on *reasonable caution.* Newspapers and broadcasting stations should attempt to develop their own standards of care, and these should be applied in publishing and broadcasting the news. The Tennessee Supreme Court noted in 1978 that the negligence standard was *not* a "journalistic malpractice test" (*Memphis Publishing Co.* v. *Nichols,* 1978). Liability will be based upon a departure from supposed standards of care set by publishers themselves. Reporters need to become better bookkeepers and undertake to keep records on how and when they investigate the veracity of libelous charges. The key term is "good faith effort." So long as the press makes a good faith effort to establish the truth or falsity of libelous charges, it does not appear that negligence will be a serious problem.

As noted previously, other states have chosen to adopt other standards. The gross irresponsibility or gross negligence standard of New York falls somewhere between simple negligence and actual malice, which will be discussed shortly. Courts in New York have defined gross irresponsibility as acting with a degree of awareness of the probable falsity of the published statements (*Chapadeau* v. *Utica Observer-Dispatch, Inc.,* 1975). That is, the reporter or editor or broadcaster probably had some degree of knowledge that the material that was going to be published or broadcast was false. This would be harder for a plaintiff to prove, obviously, than that the defendant did not exercise reasonable care.

Actual Malice

Defining actual malice is somewhat easier than defining who is and who is not a public figure or public official. In *New York Times Co.* v. *Sullivan* (1964) Justice Brennan defined actual malice as "knowledge of falsity or reckless disregard of whether the material was false or not." The two parts of this definition should be considered separately.

Knowledge of Falsity

"Knowledge of falsity" is a fancy way of saying "lie." If the defendant lied and the plaintiff can prove it, actual malice has then been shown. But plaintiffs are rarely in a position to show that the defendant lied. Furthermore, not many defendants, at least not many mass media defendants, lie. However, this did occur on one occasion. In 1969 Barry Goldwater was able to convince a federal court that Ralph Ginzburg published knowing falsehoods about him during the 1964 presidential campaign in a "psychobiography" carried in Ginzburg's *Fact* magazine. Ginzburg sent questionnaires to hundreds of psychiatrists asking them to analyze Goldwater's mental condition. Ginzburg published only those responses that agreed with the magazine's predisposition that Goldwater was mentally ill and changed the responses on other questionnaires to reflect this point of view. Proof of this conduct, plus evidence of other kinds of similar practices, led the court of appeals to conclude that Ginzburg had published the defamatory material with knowledge of its falsity (*Goldwater* v. *Ginzburg,* 1969; see also *Morgan* v. *Dun & Bradstreet, Inc., 1970*).

Reckless Disregard for the Truth

A few months after the initial decision in the *Sullivan* case, the Supreme Court defined reckless disregard for the truth in a **criminal libel** action (*Garrison* v. *Louisiana,* 1964) as "a high degree of awareness of probable falsity" of the material or statements. In 1968, in *St. Amant* v. *Thompson,* the High Court said that before a court can conclude that reckless disregard for the truth exists, "there must be sufficient evidence to permit the conclusion that the defendant in fact entertained serious doubts as to the truth of his publication." Failure to investigate in and of itself is not sufficient evidence to prove actual malice, wrote Justice White.

Both are good definitions of reckless disregard for the truth, but they are not much help to the working journalist who needs a more practical measure of reckless disregard. The Supreme Court has to an extent provided that as well. Look at *New York Times Co.* v. *Sullivan,* for example. All that was required to check the truth of the charges made in the advertisement that ultimately became the basis for the libel suit was for someone to compare the assertions in the advertisement with clippings in the newspaper's files, a simple matter. Yet the Court in that case did not indicate that such a check was really called for. There was no reason for the advertising staff to doubt the veracity of the claims in the document. The newspaper had every reason to believe that the charges contained in the advertisement were true.

A better practical definition of reckless disregard evolved from the cases of *Curtis Publishing Co.* v. *Butts* and *AP* v. *Walker* (1967). In developing the criteria that follow, Justice Harlan said he was attempting to determine whether the plaintiffs in these cases had seriously departed from the standards of responsible reporting. He did not call his opinion a definition of reckless disregard. Some of the other members of the Court did, however, refer to these standards as a measure of reckless disregard, and so have many lower federal and state courts.

These two appeals came before the Supreme Court at about the same time and were joined and decided as one case. In the first case Wally Butts, the athletic director at the University of Georgia, brought suit against the *Saturday Evening Post* for an article it published alleging that Butts and University of Alabama football coach Paul "Bear" Bryant had conspired prior to the annual Georgia-Alabama football game to "fix" the contest. The *Post* obtained its information from a man who said that while making a telephone call, he had been accidentally plugged into a phone conversation between Butts and Bryant. George Burnett, who had a criminal record, told the *Post* editors that he had taken careful notes. The story was based on these notes.

In the other case Major General (retired) Edwin Walker, a political conservative and segregationist from Texas, brought suit against the Associated Press (AP) and a score of publications and broadcasting stations for publishing the charge that he led a mob of white citizens against federal marshals who were attempting to preserve order at the University of Mississippi during the crisis over the enrollment of James Meredith. The AP report, which was wrong, was filed by a young AP correspondent on the scene.

The court ruled that in the *Butts* case the *Post* had exhibited highly unreasonable conduct in publishing the story but that in the *Walker* case no such evidence was present. Again, it is important to note that while Justice John Marshall Harlan did not call the conduct reckless disregard at the time, most authorities accept these cases as good indicators of what the court means by reckless disregard. Look at the details of each case.

In the *Butts* case the story was not what would be called a hot news item. It was published months after the game occurred. The magazine had ample time to check the report. The source of the story was not a trained reporter, but a layman who happened to be on probation on a bad-check charge. The *Post* made no attempt to investigate the story further, to screen game films to see if either team had made changes in accord with what Bryant and Butts supposedly discussed. Many persons were supposedly with Burnett when he magically overheard this conversation and none were questioned by the *Post*. The magazine did little, then, to check the story, despite evidence presented at the trial that one or two of the editors acknowledged that Burnett's story needed careful examination.

In the *Walker* case different circumstances were present. It was a hot story, one that had to get out on the wires right away. It was prepared in the "heat of battle" by a young, but trained, reporter who in the past had given every indication of being trustworthy. All but one of the dispatches from the correspondent said the same thing: Walker led the mob. So there was internal consistency. Finally, when General Walker's previous actions and statements are considered, the story that he led a mob at Ole Miss was not terribly out of line with his prior behavior. There was nothing to cause AP to suspect that the story was wrong as, for example, would be a report that the Archbishop of New York led a mob down Fifth Avenue. A red light should signal those kinds of instances that should suggest further checking because the story doesn't sound very likely.

When all this is sorted out, three key factors emerge:

1. Was the publication of the story urgent? Was it a hot news item? Or was there sufficient time to check the facts in the story fully?
2. How reliable was the source of the story? Should the reporter have trusted the news source? Was the source a trained journalist? Should the editor have trusted the reporter?
3. Was the story probable? Or was the story so unlikely that it cried out for further examination?

These factors make up a fairly good operational definition of reckless disregard and are the kinds of considerations a court might take a close look at in determining the reasonableness of the conduct of an editor or a broadcaster.

By combining the two conceptual definitions from *Garrison* and *St. Amant* and the practical guidelines from *Butts* and *Walker,* you should have a pretty good idea of the meaning of actual malice. The standard from *St. Amant,* the requirement of evidence that the defendant in fact entertained serious doubts as to the truth of the material, is a significant burden for the plaintiff to overcome. In addition, in bringing forward evidence to prove to the jury that the defendant did "entertain serious doubts," the plaintiff must meet a rigorous burden of proof. The normal evidentiary test in civil suits—the plaintiff must prove with a preponderance of evidence—has been abandoned in cases involving the *Times* rule. Instead the plaintiff must prove with "convincing clarity," must bring forth "clear and convincing evidence," that there was reckless disregard. If there is doubt in a juror's mind, the vote must be for the defendant. This standard strengthens the *Times* rule additionally.

Lower courts have had some of the same kinds of difficulties applying the actual-malice guidelines as they have had in applying the limited-public-figure guidelines. But standards do exist—even though contradictory decisions, especially from state courts, are not uncommon. It is obvious, for example, that reckless disregard for the truth is not the same thing as a sloppy journalistic error. When the *St. Louis Globe-Democrat* inadvertently attributed a city alderwoman's admission that she had had two abortions to another alderwoman who was a strong opponent of abortion, the Missouri Supreme Court ruled the error negligent, but not actual malice. The reporter gave the correct facts to a rewrite man over the telephone, but somehow the rewrite man, who was working on a close deadline, botched the story. The emphasis placed on the close deadline by the Missouri court reflects Justice Harlan's opinions in the *Butts* and *Walker* cases (*Glover* v. *Herald Co.,* 1977). Other courts have focused upon these dimensions as well.

A New Mexico radio station broadcast false charges against a deputy sheriff that it had gained from interviews with confidential informants. The state's court of appeals ruled that the failure to investigate these charges before broadcasting them did not itself demonstrate actual malice (*Ammerman v. Hubbard,* 1977). Quoting the *Restatement of Torts* (2nd ed.) the court said:

> Availability of sufficient time and opportunity to investigate the truth of the statement is a significant factor in determining whether the publisher was negligent, and it may have some relevance in determining whether the publisher acted with reckless disregard as to truth or falsity.

The Eleventh U.S. Court of Appeals ruled evidence of actual malice existed when the Liberty Lobby published a story in its *Spotlight* magazine claiming that the CIA was planning to frame Howard Hunt, a man involved in the Watergate mess of the 1970s, for the assassination of John Kennedy. The story ran on page one with a headline, "CIA TO NAIL HUNT FOR KENNEDY KILLING." It was written by Victor Marchetti, a former CIA agent who had had serious legal difficulties with the agency when he attempted to publish a book about his experience as an agent without first getting the CIA's approval (see pages 79–80). The article even suggested that Hunt may have had something to do with a plane crash that killed his wife because, the article said, she was about to leave him and even turn on him. The article said the CIA had evidence that Hunt was in Dallas on November 22, 1963, the day Kennedy was shot. This was an error, which the Liberty Lobby admitted at the trial. Hunt admitted he was a public figure. Was there evidence of actual malice?

The court said there was. The source of the story was a man with a reason to dislike the CIA who therefore should not have been trusted without considerable questioning. Editors had made no independent attempt to verify the story and did not question Marchetti about the article; they trusted him, they said. The story was not hot news; *Spotlight* had the article weeks before it was published. The story was inherently improbable. The editors said they believed it; not that Hunt had killed Kennedy, but that the CIA would try to frame him. But the court said the jury does not have to believe the editors' professions of belief. The jury could conclude that only a reckless man would believe and circulate such a story (*Hunt* v. *Liberty Lobby,* 1983). The District of Columbia U.S. Court of Appeals made a similar point recently with regard to the arguments of editors that they believed a story that turned out to be false (see *Liberty Lobby* v. *Jack Anderson,* 1984).

In 1984 the United States Supreme Court ruled that it was not actual malice when an engineer at *Consumer Reports* magazine knowingly changed the wording of the results of a test panel that had evaluated an audio speaker system, even though his testimony that he didn't think he had changed the meaning of the statement was unbelievable. *Bose Corporation* v. *Consumer's*

Union, (1984) is better known for its ruling that federal appeals courts, when reviewing findings of actual malice in a libel action, must exercise their own judgment in determining whether actual malice was actually shown with convincing clarity and not be restricted by an erroneous standard of review used by a lower court. But the High Court did speak to the question of actual malice as well. In its review of the Bose 901 speakers, *Consumer Reports* magazine said the sound from the speakers "tended to wander about the room." This statement was written by engineer Arnold Seligson, who supervised the test. But the listener panel had actually said that the sound tended to move along the wall, in front of and between the two speakers. At the trial Seligson testified that he believed the two statements meant the same thing. The district court found this testimony incredible and said that Seligson obviously knew he had changed the meaning of the statement. This was evidence of actual malice. The Supreme Court disagreed, saying Seligson's testimony, in and of itself, was not evidence, of actual malice. "He had made a mistake," Justice John Paul Stevens wrote, "and when confronted with it he refused to admit it and steadfastly attempted to maintain that no mistake had been made— that the inaccurate was accurate. That attempt failed, but the fact that he made the attempt does not establish that he realized the inaccuracy at the time of publication."

What happens when the plaintiff in a lawsuit denies the truth of the libelous allegations before they are printed, but the newspaper publishes the story anyway? Is this actual malice? A United States district court in Tennessee ruled that it is not. Trucker Aubrey Roberts called the *Tennessean* newspaper and told reporter Albert Cason that he had been harrassed by a Tennessee highway patrolman. Roberts said he had made some unflattering comments about the patrolman over his citizens-band radio. This apparently angered Trooper Mike Dover. Roberts claimed Dover buzzed his truck in his highway patrol helicopter. The truck Roberts was driving was pulled over, and the trucker was put into the backseat of a patrol car that had arrived to assist Dover. Roberts reported that the patrolmen rolled up all the windows in the car and turned on the car heater full blast. It was a very hot day. After a short time in the steamy patrol car, Roberts was released. Reporter Cason said he believed Roberts's story because the trucker was so upset and because it would be very hard for someone to make up such a farfetched story. But Cason held the story until he had talked to Dover. Dover denied most of the story, insisting that Roberts had been stopped for speeding, but he could not explain why the trucker was not ticketed if he had been speeding. The story was published as Roberts had told it to the reporter.

Dover sued for libel. The police officer, who admittedly was a public official, argued that because he had told the reporter that the story was not true but the story was published anyway, this was evidence of actual malice.

Reporters and editors at the newspaper knew the story was false and still published it, Dover argued. The court disagreed. Dover's denial of the charges, standing alone, was not sufficient to sustain the inference that the reporter knew the charges were false. "To require that a reporter withhold such a story or face potential liability for defamation because a police officer denies a citizen's allegations of misconduct is exactly the type of self-censorship the *New York Times* rule was intended to avoid," the court noted. Police are always likely to have different stories from citizens in these kinds of cases. It is true that the reporter might have done other things to more fully check the story. "Indeed, such efforts might have resulted in a better news story. However, it cannot be said on this record that any failure of Cason or the *Tennessean* to make such further prior investigation constitutes proof sufficient to present to a jury a question on actual malice," the court concluded (*Roberts* v. *Dover,* 1981).

The California Supreme Court added another dimension to the matter of prior denial of libelous allegations in 1984 in its ruling in *Reader's Digest* v. *Marin County Superior Court.* The plaintiff in the case was Charles Dederich, the head of Synanon, an organization highly prominent in the seventies for its professed rehabilitation of drug users. But Synanon was attacked as a fraud later in the decade by many in the news media and by others. Dederich and Synanon threatened to bring almost one thousand libel suits when the reputation started to sour and actually brought suit in many cases. A small newspaper, the *Point Reyes Light,* received a Pulitizer Prize for a series of articles exposing Synanon, and in 1981 the *Reader's Digest* published a story about the newspaper, a story that charged Synanon and Dederich with intimidation and assault. Dederich sued *Reader's Digest* and suggested that the magazine's editor should have known the story was false because of all the lawsuits he had initiated against other publications that had made similar charges. This is evidence of actual malice, Dederich said. The court disagreed and ruled that previous lawsuits and even a threat of a lawsuit "may give a publication pause, but it would not necessarily lead it to doubt the truthfulness of its articles or its sources."

The fault requirement has done much in the past two decades to ease the burden of libel suits. This is especially true with regard to publication about persons in government and persons who attempt to lead or shape public opinion. The presumed function of the press, after all, is to educate and inform the public on such issues. Freedom to undertake this role is important, and simple relief from the threat of libel action will enhance the undertaking.

SUMMARY

In a lawsuit against a mass medium, a private person must prove that the defendant was at least negligent in publishing the defamatory matter. Negligence has been defined as the failure to exercise reasonable care or as acting in such a way as to create a substantial risk of harm. In some states, in some cases private persons will be required to prove more than simple negligence. They may be required to prove gross negligence, which is a standard that implies a greater degree of carelessness on the part of the defendant. An individual who has been declared to be a public person for the purposes of a libel suit must prove actual malice. Actual malice is defined as knowledge of falsity or reckless disregard of the truth. Transmitting a story with the knowledge of its falsity means that the publishers of the story knew it was not true but still communicated it to the public. To prove reckless disregard for the truth, the plaintiff must show that the publisher of the defamation had a "high degree of awareness of the probable falsity of the material" when it was published or that the publisher in fact "entertained serious doubts about the truth of the material" before it was published. The courts have established a set of three criteria that are used to help determine whether material was published with reckless disregard of the truth. The jurists tend to look at these factors:

1. Whether there was time to investigate the story or whether the material had to be published quickly
2. Whether the source of the information appeared to be reliable and trustworthy
3. Whether the story itself sounded probable or farfetched

If the item was hot news, if the source was a trained journalist, and if the information in the story sounded probable, there can be no finding of reckless disregard. However, if there was plenty of time to investigate, if the source of the material was questionable, or if the information in the story sounded completely improbable, courts are more likely to permit a finding of reckless disregard for the truth.

SUMMARY JUDGMENT

No attempt is made in this book to teach anyone how to try a libel suit; students need to go to law school to find that out. But even journalists should know about one procedural matter in a libel suit. This is called "a motion for **summary judgment.**" After plaintiffs have made all their allegations in a lawsuit, but before the actual trial has begun, defendants can ask the court for a summary judgment. The United States Court of Appeals for the District of Columbia described a summary judgment in this way (*Nader* v. *deToledano,* 1979):

> . . . a summary judgment should be granted if (1) taking all reasonable inferences in the light most favorable to the nonmoving party [the plaintiff in this case], (2) a reasonable juror, acting reasonably, could not find for the nonmoving party, (3) under the appropriate burden of proof.

This is a good outline, but by using an example we can assist in translating it for nonlawyers. John Smith is sued by Jane Adams for libel. After Ms. Adams has presented all her allegations and arguments to the court, and after the court gives her the benefit of the doubt in any instance that might be questionable, if the judge believes that a juror could not possibly rule in her favor, the judge can grant a summary judgment for the defendant. The defendant would win without going to trial.

The summary judgment has proved especially useful in libel suits since 1964, when the Supreme Court raised the constitutionally mandated "actual malice" fault requirement for public persons. Whether or not there was actual malice in a case was considered a "constitutional fact" that could be determined by a judge. This was not necessarily a jury question. Therefore, if the plaintiff in the lawsuit could bring forth no evidence at all of actual malice, the judge could dismiss the suit on a motion for summary judgment. As more and more persons fell under the rubric of public person and more and more cases hinged upon the finding of actual malice, motions for summary judgments became commonplace in libel suits. And they were granted with some regularity. With the growing commonality of libel suits, summary judgments are more important than ever before for the press in a libel action. Judge Sarokin of the U.S. District Court in New Jersey explained this importance in a 1985 libel ruling;

> Possibly the giants of the industry have both the finances and the stamina to run the risk in such situations [the threat of a libel suit]. But the independent will of smaller magazines, newspapers, television and radio stations undoubtedly bends with the spectre of a libel action looming. Even if convinced of their ultimate success on the merits, the costs of vindication may soon be too great for such media defendants to print or publish that which may entail any risk of a court action. If that is the result, it is a sorry state of affairs for the media, and, more important, for the country. Therefore, probably more than any other type of case, summary judgments in libel actions should be readily available and granted where appropriate. (See *Schiavone Construction* v. *Time,* 1985.)

Granting summary judgments to libel defendants is somewhat controversial. Warren Burger, former chief justice of the United States, attempted to discourage lower courts from granting summary judgments in cases in which actual malice is a question. In a footnote to his opinion in *Hutchinson* v. *Proxmire* the chief justice noted that "proof of actual malice calls a defendant's state of mind into question . . . and does not lend itself to summary disposition." Burger raised an issue that many persons—especially plaintiffs' attorneys—think is real and important. Can a court adequately determine a defendant's state of mind—whether the person in fact entertained serious doubts as to the truth of the material—without a trial in which the adversary process can be conducted to hopefully unearth material facts? While footnotes in Supreme Court opinions are not to be taken lightly, lower courts seemed to largely ignore the chief justice's suggestion. And the U.S. Supreme Court itself seemingly rejected Burger's admonition when it ruled in mid-1986 that libel suits filed by public officials and public figures in federal courts must be dismissed before the trial via summary judgment unless the evidence suggests that the plaintiff can prove libel and fault with convincing clarity (*Anderson v. Liberty Lobby,* 1986). Attorneys for newspapers and other mass media hailed the 6–3 ruling as one that would encourage district court judges to dispose of weak libel claims at early stages of litigation. And this could ultimately result in lessening the libel pressure against the press.

Now it is time to turn to the subject of the defenses to libel suits. A libel defense can be defined as a legally acceptable reason for publishing something that is defamatory. There are many different kinds of defenses, some very old and some relatively new. The libel defenses considered here are truth, privileged communication, fair comment, consent, and right of reply. The applicability of each defense in a particular case is determined by the facts in the case—what the story is about, how the information was gained, the manner in which it was published. Before looking at the substantive defenses, it is appropriate to consider the one remedy offering a defendant complete immunity in a libel action—the statute of limitations.

STATUTE OF LIMITATIONS

For nearly all crimes and most civil actions there is a **statute of limitations.** Courts do not like stale legal claims. They have plenty of fresh ones to keep them busy. Prosecution for most crimes except homicide and kidnapping must be started within a specified period of time. For example, in many states if prosecution is not started within seven years after an armed robbery is committed, the robber cannot be brought to trial. He or she is home free. (However, the robber can still be prosecuted for failing to pay income tax on money taken from a bank, but that is another story.)

The duration of the statute of limitations for libel actions differs from state to state, varying from one to six years. In most states the duration is one or two years. What this means is that a libel suit must be started within one or two years following publication of the offending material. The date of publication on a newspaper determines when the duration of the statute begins. In television and radio the statute of limitation begins on the day the program is telecast or broadcast. Magazines pose a somewhat different problem. The publication date on the magazine rarely coincides with the date the publication is actually distributed. Magazines dated November are usually distributed in October, sometimes even in late September. Courts have ruled that the statute of limitations begins on the date that a magazine is distributed to a substantial portion of the public. *Time* magazine was sued in New Jersey, which has a one-year statute of limitations, for an article published in an issue dated February 18, 1980. The suit was filed on February 17, 1981. But the magazine proved that a substantial portion of the magazine had been distributed to subscribers and newsstands before February 17, 1980. The United States district court ruled that the statute of limitations had expired by February 17, 1981 (*MacDonald* v. *Time,* 1981). In a similar suit Don Wildmon failed in his attempt to sue *Hustler* magazine for an article published in the November 1978 issue. Wildmon filed his suit on October 9, 1979, but the magazine proved that the November 1978 issue of *Hustler* had gone on sale on October 3, 1978, and subscriber copies had been mailed one to two weeks earlier. The United States district court dismissed the suit because the one-year statute of limitations in Mississippi had expired (*Wildmon* v. *Hustler,* 1980).

The libel republication rule can be a factor in considering the statute of limitations. In many states buying a back issue of a publication is considered new publication, and the statute of limitations starts over. More and more jurisdictions have rejected this rule and substituted the single publication rule. This rule states that the entire edition of a newspaper or magazine is a single publication and that isolated sales in the months or years to come do not constitute republication. Therefore the statute of limitations starts on the day the edition hit the newsstands and ends one or two or three years later. The statute cannot be reactivated by a later sale. About one-half of the states have this progressive rule. Find out if your state does.

Is it possible for a plaintiff who has not filed a libel suit within the statute of limitations in his home state to file an action in another state that has a longer statute of limitation? The answer is yes, so long as the libel has been circulated in this other state. The Supreme Court clarified this question in two 1984 rulings, *Keeton* v. *Hustler* and *Clader* v. *Jones.* Kathy Keeton, a resident of New York, sued *Hustler* magazine, an Ohio corporation, for libel in the state of New Hampshire. *Hustler* challenged the action, arguing that the suit should be brought in New York or Ohio but not New Hampshire, which has a six-year statute of limitations. Only about fifteen thousand copies of the one-million-plus circulation of the magazine are sold in New Hampshire, the defendant argued. The U.S. Court of Appeals ruled that the plaintiff had too tenuous a contact with New Hampshire to permit the assertion of personal jurisdiction in that state, but the Supreme Court unanimously reversed the ruling. *Hustler's* regular circulation of magazines in New Hampshire is sufficient to support an assertion of jurisdiction in a libel action, Justice William Rehnquist wrote. "False statements of fact harm both the subject of the falsehood and the readers of the statement: New Hampshire may rightly employ its libel laws to discourage the deception of its citizens," the justice continued. The state may extend its concern to the injury that in-state libel causes within New Hampshire to a nonresident, he added (*Keeton* v. *Hustler,* 1984).

The same day, the High Court ruled that California courts could assume jurisdiction in a case brought by a California resident against the authors of a story that was written and published in a newspaper in Florida but circulated in California. Shirley Jones sued Ian Calder and John South for an article they wrote and edited in Florida and that was then published in *National Enquirer*. The *Enquirer* has a national circulation of about five million and distributes about 600,000 copies each week in California. A trial court ruled that Jones could certainly sue the publishers of the *Enquirer* in California, but not the reporters. Requiring journalists to appear in remote jurisdictions to answer for the contents of articles upon which they worked could have a chilling impact upon the First Amendment rights of reporters and editors, the court said. But again a unanimous Supreme Court disagreed, with Justice Rehnquist noting that the article was about a California resident who works in California. Material for the article was drawn from California sources and the brunt of the harm to both the career and the personal reputation of the plaintiff will be suffered in California, he added. "An individual injured in California need not go to Florida to seek redress from persons who, though remaining in Florida, knowingly cause the injury in California," Rehnquist wrote. The justice said that the potential chill on protected First Amendment activity stemming from libel actions is already taken into account in the constitutional limitations on the substantive law governing such suits. "To reinforce those concerns at the jurisdictional level would be a form of double counting," he said (*Calder* v. *Jones,* 1984).

SUMMARY

A libel suit must be started before the statute of limitations expires. Each state determines how long this period will be. In most states it is one, two, or three years. A libel suit started after the expiration of the statute of limitations will be dismissed.

TRUTH

Traditionally, truth has been regarded as an important libel defense that completely protected defendants in lawsuits for defamation. To use this defense, the defendant was required to prove the truth of the libelous allegations he or she published. Truth is still a defense in a libel action, but surely has lost much of its importance in light of recent rulings that most libel plaintiff's carry the burden of proving a defamatory allegation to be false as a part of proving that the defendant was at fault (see pages 137–38). In those few instances when a private-person plaintiff sues for a libelous statement that does not focus on something of public concern and does not have to show the falsity of the matter as a part of proving negligence, the libel defendant can escape liability in the case by showing that the defamatory matter is true. But the defendant carries the burden of proof; truth becomes a defense. The same rules apply to proving truth that apply to proving falsity, only they are reversed. The defendant must show that the allegations are substantially true. Extraneous errors will not destroy the defense. See pages 138–41 to refresh your memory on these matters.

PRIVILEGED COMMUNICATIONS

Traditionally in the United States we value robust debate as a means of discovering those elusive truths that we continually pursue. The law takes pains to protect this debate, making sure that speakers are not unduly punished for speaking their minds. Article 1, Section 6, of the federal Constitution provides that members of the Congress are immune from suits based on their remarks on the floor of either house. This is called a privilege. The statement in question is referred to as a privileged communication.

Absolute Privilege

Today, privilege attaches to a wide variety of communications and speakers. Anyone speaking in a legislative forum—congressmen and -women, senators, state representatives, city councilmembers, and so forth—enjoys this privilege. Even the statements of witnesses at legislative hearings are privileged. But the comments must be made in the legislative forum. The Supreme Court ruled in 1979 that while a speech by a senator on the floor of the Senate would be wholly immune from a libel action, newsletters and press releases about the speech issued by the senator's office would not be protected by the privilege. Only that speech which is "essential to the deliberations of the Senate" is protected, and neither newsletters to constituents nor press releases are parts of the deliberative process (*Hutchinson* v. *Proxmire,* 1979).

Similarly, the privilege attaches to communications made in judicial forums—courtrooms, grand jury rooms, and so forth. Judges, lawyers, witnesses, defendants, plaintiffs, and all other persons are protected so long as the remark is uttered during the official portions of the hearing or the trial. Finally, persons who work in the administrative and executive branches of government enjoy privilege as well. Presidents, mayors, governors, department heads—official communications or official statements by these kinds of persons are privileged. In 1959 in *Barr* v. *Mateo* the Supreme Court suggested that the privilege applies to any publication by government officials that is in line with the discharge of their official duty. This case involved a press release from a department head explaining why two federal employees had been fired. "A publicly expressed statement of the position of the agency head," the Court ruled, "announcing personnel action which he planned to take in reference to the charges so widely disseminated to the public was an appropriate exercise of the discretion which an officer of that rank must possess if the public service is to function effectively."

More recently the court of appeals in New York State ruled that a press release issued by an assistant attorney general concerning the investigation of possible fraudulent activities by fund raisers was protected from a lawsuit by privilege. The court said that since the attorney general as an executive official enjoys absolute privilege while exercising the functions of his office, the same privilege applies to his subordinates, who exercise delegated powers (*Gautsche* v. *New York,* 1979). The difference in the treatment of the assistant attorney general by the New York court and Senator Proxmire by the United States Supreme Court over essentially the same item—a press release—stems from the different roots of the privilege. Congressional privilege stems directly from the United States Constitution and is limited by the constitutional language. The privilege applied to the state attorney general stems from the common law. Also, the functions of the two offices are different. Senators are supposed to deliberate and make legislative policy. Reporting to the public on the results of an official investigation is one of the governmental functions of an attorney general.

The privilege just discussed is an **absolute privilege.** The speaker cannot be sued for defamation on the basis of such a remark. A similar kind of a privilege applies also to certain kinds of private communications. Discussions between an employer and an employee are privileged; the report of a credit rating is privileged; a personnel recommendation by an employer about an employee is privileged. These kinds of private communications remain privileged so long as they are not disseminated beyond the sphere of those who need to know.

Qualified Privilege

What is called **qualified privilege** goes far beyond the absolute immunity granted to speakers at public and official meetings and the conditional immunity applied to certain types of private communication. The press is granted a qualified or conditional privilege to report what happens at official governmental meetings and other meetings open to the public. This is how the privilege is outlined in the second edition of the *Restatement of Torts:*

> The publication of defamatory matter concerning another in a report of any official proceeding or any meeting open to the public which deals with matters of public concern is conditionally privileged if the report is accurate and complete, or a fair abridgement of what has occurred.

This means that a libel suit premised upon such a publication will not stand. While technically the press has no special privileges in the law of defamation, in actual operation of the law this privilege is invoked so infrequently on behalf of anyone other than the press that it is generally regarded to be a privilege of the press. In fact, this privilege is sometimes called the privilege of the reporter, as opposed to the absolute immunity noted earlier, which is referred to as the privilege of the participant.

There is much to discuss about this privilege. Perhaps the most important point that needs to be made is that it is a *conditional* privilege; that is, the privilege of the reporter works as a defense in a libel suit only if certain conditions are met. First, the privilege applies only to reports of certain kinds of meetings, generally meetings of governmental bodies, public meetings on issues of public importance, and other public proceedings. Second, the privilege applies only to reports that are a fair and accurate or truthful summary of what occurred at the meeting. Some states still enforce a rule that the publication of a privileged communication must be motivated by a desire to inform the public and cannot be motivated by ill will, a desire to hurt the plaintiff. But this rule is changing and is really not considered a condition of the application of the privilege in most jurisdictions any longer (see *Schiavone* v. *Time,* 1983).

The defendant bears the burden of proving that the privilege applies to the libelous material. The court determines whether the particular occasion (meeting or proceeding) is privileged. The jury determines whether the defendant's story is a fair and accurate report. Each of these elements needs closer scrutiny. Let us, therefore, focus now on meetings and proceedings said to be privileged.

The privilege applies at the very least to reports of all official proceedings of a governmental agency. Some authorities contend that it also applies to all public meetings at which matters of public concern are discussed (more on this in a moment). The qualified privilege applies to official proceedings of the legislative branch of government, to the judicial branch, and to the executive branch. Let's look at each briefly.

Legislatures

Quite obviously, the privilege applies to meetings of organizations such as Congress, state legislatures, city councils, county councils, and so forth. The privilege also applies to the reports of meetings of committees of such organizations, as well as to stories about petitions, complaints, and other communications received by these bodies. The only requirement that must be met with regard to this aspect of the privilege is that the official body, such as a city council, must officially receive the complaint or petition before the privilege applies. If the Citizens for Cleaner Streets bring to a city council meeting a petition charging the street superintendent with incompetence and various and sundry blunders in his job, publication of these charges is privileged as soon as the city council officially accepts the petition. Nothing has to be done with the document. It must merely be accepted.

The privilege likely applies to stories about the news conferences of members of a legislative body following a session, to stories about what was said during a closed meeting by the body, and to what was said during an informal gathering of legislators before or after the regular session. If what is said or what occurs during these kinds of events is of great public interest and there is a compelling public need to know, the privilege then likely applies.

The privilege of the reporter also applies to actions that take place in judicial forums: testimony and depositions of witnesses, arguments of attorneys, pronouncements of judges, and so forth. Stories about trials, decisions, jury verdicts, court opinions, judicial orders and decrees, and grand jury indictments are all protected by the privilege.

Probably the most serious problem a reporter on the court beat has to face is what to do when a lawsuit is initially filed. Under our legal system a lawsuit is started when a person files a complaint with a court clerk and serves a summons on the defendant. The complaint is filled with charges, most of which are usually libelous. Can a reporter use that complaint as the basis for a story?

The states are divided on this question. In some states a complaint is not considered privileged until a judge takes some kind of action on the lawsuit. This action may only be the scheduling of an appearance by the litigants, or it may be more. But a judge must get involved in the matter before the complaint becomes a privileged document. In other states the complaint becomes privileged as soon as it has been filed with the court clerk and a summons has been issued. It is important for you to determine which rule governs civil complaints in your state. The simplest way to do this is to look for opinions on this question in cases decided by your state high court.

Stories about those parts of the judicial process that are closed to public view are not protected by the privilege. Frequently, court sessions for juveniles and divorce proceedings are closed in order to further a public policy. The legislature or the courts feel obligated to discourage publicity about what occurs during such hearings. A few years ago the *New York Daily News* published a series of articles about a sensational divorce case, one in which the wife accused the husband of keeping a harem of women in a private plane that he used for business (and pleasure?) trips. When the husband sued the newspaper for libel, the *Daily News* argued that it had taken its report directly from court records and trial testimony.

In New York, however, divorce proceedings are closed to the public. The state's High Court ruled that the legislature deemed it to be in the public interest to close divorce proceedings to public scrutiny (*Shiles* v. *News Syndicate Co.,* 1970):

> Since, then, such matrimonial actions were and are not proceedings which the public had the right to hear and see, it follows—and it has been consistently held—that the privilege generally accorded to reports of judicial proceedings is unavailable to reports of matrimonial actions.

Government Executives and Administrators

Reports of the statements and proceedings conducted by mayors, department heads, and other persons in the administrative and executive branches of government are generally privileged. The best guideline is that the privilege is confined to stories about actions or statements that are official in nature, the kinds of things that are substantially "acts of state." By law administrators are required to prepare certain reports and to hold certain hearings, and the privilege certainly covers stories on these activities. Although not required by law, other actions are unmistakably part of the job. Reports on these affairs are undoubtedly protected as well. The California Supreme Court, for example, recently ruled that a report on organized crime prepared for the state attorney general by a special commission was a privileged document once it was released to the press and public (*Kilgore* v. *Younger,* 1982). A report of the Pennsylvania Crime Commission was ruled to be privileged by a federal court in Maryland (*D'Alfonso* v. *A.S. Abell Co.,* 1984). Even stories based on confidential government documents that focused on possible government misconduct were declared to be privileged under Massachusetts law (*Ingerere* v. *ABC,* 1984).

Reports of police activities also fall under the heading of executive actions, but the privilege is applied sparingly here. It is fairly well settled that a report that a person has been arrested and charged with a crime is privileged. The arrest and charge is a public kind of event. All the additional information the police and prosecutor are wont to give the press—how the crime was committed, statements by witnesses, circumstances surrounding the arrest—is clearly not protected by the privilege. The police really go beyond their authority in making such statements and frequently defame the suspect in the process. There is some indication that the privilege is expanding in this area, however. *Time* magazine published an article that described an individual as a "capo [chief] in his Mafia family." The story summarized information from Federal Bureau of Investigation investigatory documents that *Time* had obtained legally. The Third United States Court of Appeals ruled that this information is protected by a qualified privilege (*Medico* v. *Time,* 1981).

Other Public Concerns

The privilege of the reporter is not confined only to those instances of reporting official government proceedings. For example, an Idaho court ruled that the privilege applied to a story about a meeting called by citizens to protest the actions of a judge. It clearly was not an official meeting, but concerned important public business, the conduct of a public official. The court said, "There is a general doctrine that what is said at a public meeting, at which any person of the community or communities involved might have attended and heard and seen for himself, is conditionally privileged for publication" (*Borg* v. *Boas,* 1956).

The *Restatement of Torts* (2d ed.) says that reports of what occurs at meetings open to the public at which matters of public concern are discussed are privileged. Paul Ashley, libel authority and author of *Say It Safely* (1976), wrote that the privilege probably applies to a public meeting even though admission is charged, so long as everyone is free to pay the price. "By supplying them with information about public events," Ashley writes, "the publisher is acting as the 'eyes and ears' of people who did not attend."

In such a circumstance, the report of a public meeting, the key element undoubtedly is the subject of debate. Was it of public concern? Was it of limited public concern? Was it a purely private matter? Using the standard of public concern, we can look at some kinds of nonofficial public meetings and try to determine whether the privilege applies.

1. Meeting of local Rotary Club: probably of private concern; not privileged
2. Meeting of board of directors of United Fund: of public concern; privileged
3. Meetings of local bar association or medical society: of limited public concern; privileged
4. Meeting of stockholders of General Motors Company: about private business and of private concern; not privileged
5. Meeting of county Democratic party: of public concern; privileged

At this point how far the privilege will extend in protecting nonofficial public meetings cannot be said. Traditionally each state handles this problem differently, and therefore you should seek guidance from local statutes and court decisions. The privilege is clearly extended to gatherings outside the official governmental sphere.

Neutral Reportage

The privilege has grown in another direction in some parts of the country with the development of what many libel authorities call the defense of **"neutral reportage."** One thing that must be remembered about neutral reportage is that it is by no means accepted as a legitimate defense in all states, or even in most states.

The neutral reportage privilege developed most directly from an interesting suit in New York State concerning the annual Audubon Society Christmas bird count. The *New York Times* printed charges made by an official of the Audubon Society that any scientist who argues that the continued use of the pesticide DDT has not taken a serious toll of bird life is "someone who is being paid to lie about it or is parroting something he knows little about." The implication was, of course, that certain scientists were being paid by the pesticide industry to lie about the impact of the chemicals on wildlife. The *Times* story included the names of several scientists given to the reporter by Robert Arbib, the official at the Audubon Society. Some of these scientists sued for libel, but the Second Circuit Court of Appeals ruled the story published by the *Times* containing the libelous charges was privileged, even though reporter John Devlin might have believed the charges made by Arbib were false when he published them. The court called the privilege "neutral reportage" and described it in the following manner (*Edwards* v. *National Audubon Society,* 1977):

> When a responsible prominent organization like the National Audubon Society makes serious charges against a public figure, the First Amendment protects the accurate and disinterested reporting of those charges, regardless of the reporter's private views regarding their validity. What is newsworthy about such accusations is that they were made. . . . The public interest in being fully informed about controversies that often rage around sensitive issues demands that the press be afforded the freedom to report such charges without assuming responsibility for them. We must provide immunity from defamation where the journalist believes, reasonably and in good faith, that his report accurately conveys the charges made.

In simple terms the neutral reportage rule may be stated this way: publication of an accurate account of information about a public figure from a reliable source by a reporter who doubts the truth of the assertions is still privileged. When charges are made by responsible agencies or persons, the public should hear these charges, even when the journalist doubts their veracity. It is newsworthy that the charges have been made; that fact alone might add materially to the public debate on the issue.

As applied in a handful of courts since the *Edwards* case the neutral reportage privilege seems to have four distinct requirements:

1. The story must be newsworthy; it must be of public interest.
2. The individual who has been libeled must be a public figure.
3. The reporter must accurately report the libelous charges *and* present all sides of the controversy.
4. The publication must play the role of an impartial transmitter of information and not espouse the libelous charges.

A United States district court recently denied the application of the neutral reportage privilege in a libel suit because the target of the charges was not a public figure (*Dresbach* v. *Doubleday,* 1982). The Second United States Court of Appeals ruled the neutral reportage inapplicable in a case in which the defendant publication not only inaccurately reported the charges against the public figure, but also vigorously supported these charges in a personal attack upon the plaintiff. Obviously, the reportage ceased to be neutral (*Cianci* v. *New Times,* 1980).

Neutral reportage remains a limited privilege. In 1985, for example, the South Dakota Supreme Court rejected neutral reportage as a defense (*Janklow* v. *Viking Press,* 1985). Other courts have taken similar action (see *Dickey* v. *CBS,* 1978; *Postill* v. *Booth Newspapers,* 1982; and *Hellman* v. *McCarthy,*

1984). Other courts have accepted it (see, for example, *Orr* v. *Lynch,* 1978; *Krauss* v. *Champaign News Gazette,* 1978; *Wade* v. *Stocks,* 1981; *El Amin* v. *Miami Herald,* 1983; and *Palmer* v. *Seminole,* 1983). Probably the Supreme Court of the United States will be asked to decide upon the viability of the defense. Until such a definitive ruling, neutral reportage remains a creative effort in a few jurisdictions to expand the range of permissible reporting.

Abuse of Privilege

Whether qualified privilege applies to a particular story is only part of the problem. The privilege can also be destroyed if the story in question is not a fair and accurate or true report of what took place. *Fair* means balanced. If at a public meeting speakers both attack and defend John Smith, the story should reflect both the attack and the defense. A story that focuses just on the charges is not fair, and the privilege will have been abused. Similarly, if the story concerns a continuing kind of an affair—a legislative hearing, a trial, and so forth—in which testimony is given for several days, the press is obligated to publish stories about each day's events if the privilege is to be used. There has to be balance. If a story about a civil suit based upon the charges listed in the complaint is prepared, it is important to get the defendant's response as well. Balance is the key.

An accurate or true report means just that; it should honestly reflect what took place or what was said. An attorney named Frank Marcone was indicted in Pennsylvania for giving money to other persons to invest in drug trafficking, such as buying marijuana. The indictment was later dismissed. *Penthouse* magazine published a story in which it said that Marcone had "contributed down payments of up to $25,000 on grass transactions. Charges against him were dropped because he cooperated with further investigations." *Penthouse* argued this was a privileged story, since it relied upon the grand jury indictment, a privileged document. But an indictment is an allegation or charge that someone has done something. *Penthouse* reported that Marcone had in fact provided money for drug purchases. The story was not a fair and accurate report of the indictment. The magazine could have said Marcone had been indicted for providing money to purchase drugs or that there were allegations that he had provided money to purchase drugs. The story as published went beyond the official document (*Marcone* v. *Penthouse,* 1982).

Small errors in the story will not destroy the privilege. When a California newspaper reported on a tax fraud trial it stated that the defendant in the case had failed to report $436,000 in taxable income. Actually, the plaintiff's gross income, not his taxable income, was $436,000. The California Court of Appeals ruled that this small error did not destroy the privilege (*Jennings*

v. *Telegram-Tribune,* 1985). Attorney F. Lee Bailey wrote in a book that Lawrence D. Murray, a former San Francisco assistant district attorney, was arrested for driving under the influence of alcohol and for assault and battery of police officers. In fact Murray was arrested for being intoxicated in a public place and resisting arrest. "The slight inaccuracy in the details will not prevent a judgment for the defendant," a federal judge ruled, "if the inaccuracy does not change the complexion of the affair so as to affect the reader of the article differently than the actual truth would." The error in Bailey's book was a small one (*Murray* v. *Bailey,* 1985).

The fact finder will determine whether or not the defendant has fairly summarized the report or the testimony. In 1983 Brown and Williamson, a cigarette manufacturer, sued Chicago broadcast journalist Walter Jacobson for libel when he attacked the company in a program on WBBM-TV. Jacobson used as the foundation of his story a Federal Trade Commission report on the tobacco industry. The FTC document focuses upon a report from a market-research firm about the development of an advertising strategy that portrays smoking cigarettes as a kind of illicit pleasure in an effort to make smoking more attractive to young smokers. Brown and Williamson rejected this illicit pleasures strategy, but the FTC concluded that the company adopted "many of the ideas contained in this report in the development of a Viceroy advertising campaign." A Brown and Williamson internal report called the "Viceroy Strategy" is cited by the FTC as evidence. The commission, quoting from the B & W Viceroy report, describes the company's advertising strategies. The "Viceroy Strategy" report did not refer to young smokers or "starters," but did discuss an advertising campaign featuring "young adults in situations that the vast majority of young people would probably experience and in situations demonstrating adherence to a 'free and easy, hedonistic lifestyle.' " Jacobson reported that Brown and Williamson used an advertising strategy that tried to hook children on cigarettes, "to addict children to poison," basing his statements on the FTC report. The Seventh U.S. Court of Appeals ruled that a jury should decide whether the television journalist's comments were a fair and accurate summary of the FTC report (*Brown and Williamson* v. *Jacobson and CBS,* 1983). In the autumn of 1985, a jury in Chicago ruled that Jacobson's comments were not an accurate summary of the report and awarded the cigarette maker more than $5 million in damages.

The story should also be in the form of a report. If defendants fail to make it clear that they are reporting something that was said at a public meeting or repeating something that is contained in the public record, the privilege may be lost. The law says the reader should be aware that the story is a report of what happened at a public meeting or at an official hearing or is taken from the official record. These facts should be noted in the lead and in the headline if possible, as noted in the following example.

The U.S. Court of Appeals for the District of Columbia recently ruled that qualified privilege did not apply to a magazine summary of statements contained in an official report from the National Transportation Safety Board. The report is an official record; it is clearly covered by the reporter's privilege. But the statements in the magazine gave readers no clue that they were in fact a summary of an official document. "The challenged [defamatory] assertion is simply offered as historical fact without any particular indication of its source," the court said. The reader was left with the impression that the author of the article reached the conclusion contained in the defamatory allegations based upon his own research (*Dameron* v. *Washingtonian*, 1985).

Finally, the privilege protects only that part of a story based on an official proceeding or a public record or report. Anything added to the story from outside these sources will not be protected by the qualified privilege.

The privilege of the reporter is a very important defense and protects the press in a large percentage of the stories that are printed or telecast. Privilege is much easier to use than truth, since all the defendant must prove is that the event, meeting, or report was in fact a privileged occasion and the story was a fair and true report.

SUMMARY

The publication of defamatory material in a report of a public meeting, legislative proceeding, or legal proceeding or in a story that reflects the content of an official government report is conditionally privileged. The privilege extends to the meetings of all public bodies, to all aspects of the legal process, to reports and statements issued by members of the executive branch of government, and even to nonofficial meetings of the public in which matters of public concern are discussed. Such reports cannot be the basis for a successful libel suit as long as the report presents a fair (balanced) and accurate (truthful) account of what took place at the meeting or what is contained in the record.

FAIR COMMENT

Fair comment is another kind of privilege. It permits the journalist to express defamatory opinions on matters of public interest. The key words are *opinions* and *public interest*. Once again the law allows the press valuable protection when it concerns itself with matters of importance to readers and viewers. By its very nature an opinion is not subject to proof or to test by evidence. An opinion is a subjective statement that reflects the speaker's tastes, values, or sensitivities. There is no way to prove its truth or falsity. The privilege of the reporter that has just been discussed is often limited in its application by the kinds of proceedings and reports to which it is applicable.

The roots of fair comment are deep. British courts long ago recognized the need for some means of permitting critical views and opinions to be aired. Lord Ellenborough summed up the basis of the defense of fair comment in the early nineteenth century (*Tabart* v. *Tipper*, 1808):

> Liberty of criticism must be allowed, or we should have neither purity of taste nor of morals. Fair discussion is essentially necessary to the truth of history and the advancement of science. That publication, therefore, I should never consider as a libel which has for its object not to injure the reputation of any individual, but to correct misrepresentations of fact, to refute sophistical reasoning, to expose a vicious taste in literature or to censure what is hostile to morality.

More recently the Supreme Court has noted that the privilege of fair comment rests within the First Amendment as well. Writing in *Gertz* v. *Welch* Justice Powell noted:

> We begin with the common ground. Under the First Amendment there is no such thing as a false idea. However pernicious an opinion may seem, we depend for its correction not on the conscience of judges and juries, but on the competition of other ideas.

On the same day the *Gertz* ruling was handed down, the Supreme Court ruled that naming some postal workers "scabs" during a labor dispute was protected. The expression of such an opinion, even in the most pejorative terms, the court said, is protected (*Old Dominion Branch No. 496, National Association of Letter Carriers* v. *Austin,* 1974). Opinion, then, will be protected.

By granting constitutional protection to statements of opinion, the Supreme Court clearly enhanced the libel defense of fair comment. But has the First Amendment entirely absorbed this defense as well? That is a question that has not yet been answered but is certainly troublesome. Fair comment is a common law defense that is applicable only if the defendant has met a series of requirements. The comment must focus upon a subject of public interest, for example. It should reflect upon the public rather than private life of the targets of the defamation. The comment should have a factual basis. Only if these guidelines have been followed will the defense of fair comment work under the common law. But Justice Powell's opinion in *Gertz* says nothing about requirements; it simply says there is no such thing as a false idea, that false opinion must be corrected by other ideas, not by judges and juries. And this has left the trial judges confused. Is any opinion protected, regardless of whether it focuses upon a subject of public interest or whether there is a factual base? Or are the traditional requirements for the defense still valid? The law is simply not clear enough to answer that question. In this section we will outline the traditional requirements of the fair comment defense, without assuming that a trial court will insist they exist before protecting a statement of opinion. A defendant who, in publishing an opinion, has followed the guidelines that follow, will surely be protected under fair comment and the First Amendment.

Statement of Opinion

Regardless of whether the First Amendment has absorbed fair comment or not, only statements of opinion will be protected. Statements of fact are still subject to a successful libel suit. Opinion or fact? While this may seem like a simple distinction, it is not. In fact, American courts have spent considerable time in the last five years attempting to develop a test to distinguish between the two kinds of statements.

Some courts have attempted to use a simple test to try to distinguish between fact and opinion: Can the statement be proved? This test works well for some kinds of statements. John robbed a bank—obviously a statement of fact because it can be proved. Or John is ugly—a statement of opinion because it cannot be proved. But what about the statement John is a fascist? What does this mean? Such words do not easily lend themselves to proof (see *Buckley* v. *Littell,* 1976). So courts have developed other, more complex tests to try to distinguish between fact and opinion.

By early 1986 a test developed by Judge Starr of the U.S. Court of Appeals for the District of Columbia in 1984 seemed to be gaining use in other federal courts. The test was developed by Starr in a case called *Ollman* v. *Evans* in which a professor of political science sued columnists Rowland Evans and Robert Novak for calling him a Marxist and speculating that his appointment as chairman of the department of politics and government at the University of Maryland might lead to the use of the classroom for indoctrination, rather than education.

Starr outlined four criteria to be used to determine whether the defamatory statements were protected opinion or statements of fact:

1. What is the common usage or meaning of the language? What do the words mean in their ordinary usage? Do the words have sufficiently specific meaning to convey facts?

2. To what degree are the statements verifiable? Can they be proved? Some statements are simply incapable of being judged true or false and reflect opinions about personal taste, aesthetic judgments, or religious belief.

3. What is the specific context in which the statement occurs? "The degree to which a statement is laden with factual content or can be read to imply facts depends upon the article or column, taken as a whole, of which the statement is a part," Starr wrote. The language of an entire column may signal, for example, that a single statement that may appear factual when standing alone, is actually a statement of opinion.

4. The broader social and journalistic contexts into which the language falls should also be considered. "Some types of writing or speech by custom or convention signal to readers or listeners that what is being read or heard is likely to be opinion, not fact," Starr wrote. Rhetoric is exaggerated in labor disputes. Political debate is usually exaggerated as well. And the world of sports provokes opinions from many persons about the relative merits of individual performers. The journalistic context should also be considered. Readers and viewers expect to find factual statements in the news columns and in broadcast news reports. On the other hand, they expect to find opinions in editorials, editorial columns, reviews, and commentary.

Applying his test to the facts in *Ollman,* Judge Starr ruled that the objectionable material was opinion, not fact. The statements were contained in an editorial column on the "OP Ed" page of the newspaper. Readers don't consider such material factual hard news. In the column itself the authors made it clear they were not setting forth specific conclusions, but simply raising questions. The cautionary language suggests that the statements should be treated as opinion. Words like *Marxist* and *political activist* are simply not words that have specific factual meaning today, Starr said (*Ollman* v. *Evans,* 1984).

This test has been criticized by some as being as subjective as the simple true/false test outlined above. Indeed, the *Ollman* case was decided by a 6-to-5 vote of the court of appeals, which heard the case (for a second time) en banc, and not even all those who voted with Judge Starr subscribed to his entire test. But other courts have started to use the Ollman test. In March of 1985 the Second U.S. Court of Appeals used parts of the test to determine whether comments made about a restaurant called Mr. Chow were fact or opinion. The reviewer complained that the sweet-and-sour pork contained more dough than meat, that the rice was soaking in oil, that the pancakes were the thickness of a finger, and that other things weren't right as well. Looking at the context of the statements, the court noted that restaurant reviews are well-recognized as vehicles for opinion, not facts. The words used suggest opinion as well—the fried rice was too oily or the meat was too doughy. Finally, only one of the objectionable statements properly lent itself to a test of truth or falsity. The matter of the amount of oil in which rice should be fried or the thickness of pancakes or the amount of dough in sweet-and-sour pork are questions of personal taste, the court said. But the statement that the Peking Duck was made up of only one dish instead of the traditional three does lend itself to proof (*Mr. Chow* v. *Ste. Jour. Azur S.A.,* 1985).

The Eighth U.S. Court of Appeals applied the Ollman test in *Janklow* v. *Newsweek,* a suit brought by William Janklow against the magazine for suggesting that the former South Dakota attorney general had prosecuted Sioux activist Dennis Banks to gain revenge because of a personal feud. The trial court ruled that the comments were opinion, but the court of appeals overturned this decision. But upon a motion by *Newsweek,* the court of appeals agreed to rehear the case en banc and by a 7–3 vote ruled that the language in the magazine article was opinion, not statements of fact. The defamatory allegations lacked the precision of facts and were not really verifiable. The words could be read in several plausible ways. While the report was in the news columns of the weekly news magazine, the court noted that magazines like *Newsweek* and *Time* have a tradition of more colorful or feisty language than a daily newspaper. This freer style should signal to readers that opinion should be expected. Finally, the general context of the remarks was the discussion of how well or how badly government officials carry out their duties, a subject that lies at the heart of the First Amendment. Robust and vigorous debate must be expected in this arena, the court said (*Janklow* v. *Newsweek,* 1986).

The Ollman test is surely not the only way to determine whether something is opinion or fact. Other judges have generated, and will continue to generate, their own criteria. A state supreme court could, for example, generate its own guidelines that would bind courts in that state. Has the supreme court in your state done that already?

Nevertheless, most tests will look something like the Ollman test, consider the words themselves, the ability to verify the statements, and probably the context of the remarks. The determination of whether a comment is fact or opinion must be made, whether or not the Gertz ruling and the First Amendment protection for opinion have completely absorbed the common law defense of fair comment. Now let us look at the other traditional requirements, probably applicable only if the traditional fair-comment defense is applied.

Legitimate Public Interest

The next requirement is that the comment must concern something of legitimate public interest. The courts have granted a wide range of topics that are fair game for comment. Educational, charitable, and religious institutions are eligible for comment, as are quasi-public organizations such as bar associations, medical societies, and other professional groups. Manufacturers who place products on the market must expect criticism; businesses that cater to the public, such as restaurants, theaters, and galleries, are subject to the same treatment. Any solicitation for public support, such as an advertisement, is fair game, as are artistic and creative efforts such as movies, plays, operas, books, paintings, recitals, comic strips, and television and radio programs. The work of journalists and broadcasters may be commented upon. The performances of those who seek to entertain the public—actors, musicians, athletes, and the like—are also considered legitimate targets for fair comment. In the 1930s a football coach sued a newspaper for its criticism of his team and his coaching abilities. The court found little sympathy for the plaintiff (*Hoeppner* v. *Dunkirk Printing Co.,* 1930):

> When the plaintiff assumed the position of . . . coach to the football team of the Dunkirk High School, he was no exception to the habits and customs which have become a part of the game. His work and the play of his team were matters of keen public interest; victories would be heralded, defeats condemned. The same enthusiasm which welcomed the home-coming of the Roman conqueror now finds expression in the plaudits of the bleachers and the grandstand. The conquered now appear not in chains, but what may be far worse, amidst ridicule and derision—the boos of the crowd.

More recently, the Illinois court of appeals ruled that when the chairman of a university department described the scholarship of one of the faculty members in the department as "neither the quantity nor the quality of . . . work [that] justifies a grant of tenure" that it was a fair comment. It was an opinion on the man's public work. "Once published material is placed into the stream of ideas and it cannot be defamation when that material is critiqued, be it by a reviewer or a superior" (*Byars* v. *Kolodziej,* 1977). A broad range of subjects, then, come under the purview of the privilege.

If a statement of opinion is focused on an individual, the courts will generally require that the comment deal with the public rather than private aspects of the individual's life. That is, while Elvis Presley's performances may have been legitimate targets of criticism, his private life was not. Similarly, while a book might be the fair subject even of scathing critical analysis, fair comment is no license to undertake scathing criticism of the author or the author's life. A very old case makes the point best. The plaintiff was a lecturer and teacher named Oscar Lovell Triggs. After a series of lectures by Triggs in New York, the *New York Sun* editorially attacked Triggs's public performance and his public pronouncements. These were fair game. But the newspaper went further and criticized the plaintiff because he and his wife took a year to name their baby. This attack was upon his personal life and could not be excused as a fair comment (*Triggs* v. *Sun Printing and Publishing Association,* 1904). To quote Lord Ellenborough about another case (*Carr* v. *Hood,* 1808), "Every man who publishes a book commits himself to the judgment of the public and any one may comment upon his performance. If the commentator does not step aside from the work, . . . he exercises a fair and legitimate right."

It is very likely that even if a court ruled that the First Amendment protection for opinion had absorbed fair comment, that court would still insist upon some kind of public interest test before ruling that the opinion was completely protected. So opinion statements about purely personal matters may be outside the range of protected speech, whether or not the fair comment defense is applied.

Offensive Hyperbole

The opinion does not need to be temperate. As a federal court once noted, an opinion can be good, bad, or indifferent, immature, premature, or ill-founded. A newspaper in Alaska once called the late Drew Pearson "the garbage man of the Fourth Estate." The court permitted this comment (*Pearson* v. *Fairbanks Publishing Co.,* 1966). Decades ago the *Des Moines Leader* published this review of a vocal trio, the Cherry Sisters (*Cherry* v. *Des Moines Leader,* 1901):

> Effie is an old jade of 50 summers, Jessie is a frisky filly of 40, and Addie, the flower of the family, a capering monstrosity of 35. Their long skinny arms, equipped with talons at the extremities, swung mechanically, and anon waved frantically at the suffering audience. The mouths of their rancid features opened like caverns, and sounds like the wailing of damned souls issued therefrom. They pranced around the stage with a motion that suggested a cross between the danse du'ventre and fox trot—strange creatures with painted faces and hideous mien. Effie is spavined, Addie is stringhalt, and Jessie, the only one who showed her stockings, has legs with calves as classic in their outlines as the curves of a broom handle.

This review was considered fair comment.

Wealthy real estate developer Donald Trump sued the *Chicago Tribune* when its architecture critic called Trump's plan to build a 150-story building in New York City a "Guinness Book of World's Records architecture proposal." Paul Gapp said the 150-story building "would be one of the silliest things anyone could inflict on New York or any other city" and said Trump's suggestion that his building would balance the World Trade Center located on the other side of Manhattan was "eyewash." A United States district court said the prose was a highly subjective personal judgment and consequently protected opinion (*Trump* v. *Chicago Tribune,* 1985).

The *Barre* (Vt.) *Times Argus* was sued for libel when it quoted one political candidate who called his opponent "a horse's ass, a jerk, an idiot and paranoid." The Vermont Supreme Court ruled that the words may be insulting, abusive, unpleasant, and objectionable, but they are opinions protected by the First Amendment (*Blovin* v. *Anton,* 1981).

Finally, the Louisiana Supreme Court refused to permit recovery for libel when a devastating review of a prominent restaurant was published in the *New Orleans States Item.* Reviewer Richard Collin began his review of the Maison de Mashburn, "T'aint Creole, t'aint Cajun, t'aint French, t'aint country American, t'aint good." He said the food was hidden under a melange of "hideous sauces" and called the menu a "travesty of pretentious amateurism." He described the oysters as "a ghastly concoction," the poached trout "trout a la green plague," and said that "most of the food tastes as if the conceptions were wrong to begin with." And there was more. But the review was an opinion, the court said, and the restaurant was a public commercial establishment (*Mashburn* v. *Collin,* 1977). It was fair comment.

Factual Basis

Under the common law the defense of fair comment is only applicable when readers or viewers of or listeners to the defamatory opinion statement have access to facts upon which the statement is based. In other words, if a movie critic says a film is lousy, the worst of the year, readers should be given some facts about the film that prompted the reviewer's opinion. Based on these facts the reader might disagree with the reviewer's opinion and choose to see the film. And that is what the defense of fair comment is really all about—giving people an opportunity to form and express their own opinions.

If a judge subscribes to the notion that the First Amendment has absorbed the defense of fair comment, that any and every opinion is fully protected, there is no need for the writer or broadcaster to support the opinion with facts. But if the traditional defense of fair comment is applied, the people who read or view the defamatory opinion will have to be exposed to some facts in one of two ways. First, the article or broadcast that contains the opinion might also contain some facts. To wit:

> In 1982 Mayor Robert Allen bought six road graders for the city, none of which were needed or used. Two years later he spent $500,000 of the people's money upon an auditorium which stands vacant 350 nights a year. Last year he sent four of his staff to Europe to study how mass transit is operated there, and three of the cities his staff visited have no mass transit system. Mayor Allen has been squandering taxpayers' money for too long; he is wasteful and pays little heed to need for fiscal caution.

The opinion—that Allen has been squandering taxpayers' money—was supported by the factual statements in the first part of the story.

But the facts do not have to be actually outlined so long as both parties to the communication—the writer and the readers, for example—know the facts or can assume their existence. The *Wilmington* (Del.) *News-Journal,* in an editorial about a local public official who had just pled guilty to a charge of official misconduct, added this sentence: "Other men in quite recent local memory abused their offices and forfeited their right to them: former County Director Melvin A. Slawik. . . ." Slawik had pleaded guilty three years earlier to a charge of obstruction of justice. He sued the newspaper for libel, but the Delaware Supreme Court ruled the phrase "abused their offices" was an opinion protected by fair comment. What about facts to support the opinion?

The court ruled that since Slawik's departure from office had received intensive publicity when it occurred, the facts upon which the newspaper's opinion were based were well known in the community (*Slawik* v. *News-Journal,* 1981).

What if the facts are not stated and are not well known? In such a circumstance it is unlikely that the defense of fair comment will work. Why? It is argued that in such a case the reader or viewer is left with an impression that the writer or broadcaster knows something bad about the plaintiff—something that has not been stated. This suggestion of negative facts is defamatory; it is defamation.

For example, the *New York Times* published a story in 1978 about entertainer Phoebe Snow. Quoting singer-writer Janis Ian, the author of the story described Ms. Snow in this way: "She is also paranoid. . . . Her record company and her manager all screwed her at once." Phoebe Snow's manager sued for defamation. The court acknowledged that the statement that Phoebe Snow was "screwed" by her manager was an opinion, a rather colorful way of saying that he treated Ms. Snow unfairly. That is fine. But the facts upon which this conclusion was drawn were not stated in the article, nor could it be assumed that all readers knew what the writer was referring to. Saying that she had been "screwed" by her manager implied the existence of negative, defamatory facts, the court ruled. "If the author represents that he has private, firsthand knowledge which substantiates the opinions he expresses, the expression of opinion becomes as damaging as an assertion of fact," the court ruled (*Rand* v. *New York Times,* 1978).

The New Mexico court of appeals reached the same opinion in a 1981 ruling involving a weekly newspaper. The weekly, in its criticism of a competing newspaper, reported that the competitor "actually printed a piece by rabid environmentalist Jack Kutz, who used to send us letters so violent we turned them over to the police." Kutz sued for libel. The court ruled that the phrase "rabid environmentalist" was protected opinion but that the reference to violent letters implied that the newspaper's editors had private, negative defamatory facts about Kutz to support the opinion that he was a rabid environmentalist. None of this information was in the article to allow readers to make up their minds about Kutz. The court of appeals sent the case back for trial (*Kutz* v. *Independent Publishing,* 1981).

SUMMARY

The defense of fair comment has existed for centuries to protect the publication of opinion, but recently there is reason to believe the defense has been absorbed into the First Amendment through a 1974 Supreme Court decision, *Gertz* v. *Welch,* which ruled that there is no such thing as a false idea. If the First Amendment protection of opinion is absolute, as some suggest, any statement that is an opinion may be published without fear of a successful libel suit. The only question in the case is whether the comment is indeed an opinion or a statement of fact. The specific words used in the statement, whether the assertions are subject to proof, the context of the statement, and other matters are all important to the determination of whether or not a phrase is a statement of opinion or a statement of fact. But if the defense of fair comment is still viable and is applied in a libel suit, then the defendant will have to meet additional requirements. The libelous statement must focus on a matter of public interest and must have a factual base. If the facts are not stated or well known, the defense of fair comment will not work. In this way the public has the ability to develop its own opinion about the individual or the issue. If the facts are not stated or are not well known, the defense of fair comment will not work. The court will presume that the defendant harbored negative and defamatory information about the subject of the critical opinion, and this suggestion to the readers or listeners is defamatory.

CONSENT

There are two additional libel defenses. Both defenses have been used on occasion to successfully ward off a libel suit, but their foundations are tenuous. They have been accepted in some courts and rejected in other courts. Reliance upon either of them as the only defense is therefore not advised. However, both make excellent backup defenses, to be used with privilege or fair comment. The two defenses are **consent** and **right of reply.**

As one authority notes, an otherwise actionable defamation may be privileged if the plaintiff consented to its publication. Imagine that Frank Jones, a reporter for the *River City Sentinel,* hears rumors that John Smith is a leader of organized crime. Jones visits Smith and tells him that he has heard these rumors. Then Jones asks Smith if he cares if the rumors are published in the newspaper. Smith says it is OK with him, and Jones writes and publishes the story. In this instance Smith consented to publication of the defamation.

Now this event is not too likely to happen, is it? Cases of consent are extremely rare. Courts insist that the plaintiff either know or have a good reason to know the full extent of the defamatory statement in advance of its publication before consent can be said to exist.

At least one authority (Phelps and Hamilton) has suggested that while the kind of direct consent just noted is difficult to obtain, indirect consent is a viable defense. Indirect consent means that individuals were informed of the defamatory charges against them and were asked to comment upon the charges. The logic behind this defense is that if the newspaper publishes the response to the charges, it must publish the charges as well. For example, let us look at Smith and Jones again. Frank Jones tells John Smith that the police have called Smith "a big-time gangster." Jones says he is going to print the charge and then asks Smith, "Would you care to comment on the charge?" Smith denies the charge and claims that he is a legitimate businessman. He calls the man who made the charge a liar. Again, the logic of the defense suggests that if Smith's denial is printed, the charge that he denies must also be printed.

This reasoning may be logical, but few courts have accepted it. On record are one or two cases in which this kind of indirect consent by itself worked to defeat a libel suit (*Pulverman* v. *A. S. Abell Co.,* 1956). A very imaginative judge is needed to accept these arguments.

This does not mean, however, that it is not good policy to get a comment from the defamed party before the story is published. The facts may be wrong, and the subject of the story can then point out errors and save the newspaper from a suit. Even if the story is correct, the reporter's attempt to get both sides of the story, to discover the truth, will impress a jury if a suit does result. The reporter's efforts will demonstrate that there was no malice in printing the story, that the reporter honestly sought the truth, and that the plaintiff was given a chance to explain the charges. This policy is far more effective than giving the plaintiff the chance to reply after having been defamed. At that point, the offer looks like an afterthought. Similarly, even if the subject of the story cannot be reached, it is good policy for the journalist to tell readers that an effort was made to contact the person or that the person refused to comment. A reporter can have no worse experience than to testify in a libel suit that he or she made no attempt to contact the plaintiff before printing the story. "You mean you didn't even try to find out from the plaintiff whether the charges were true or not? You didn't have the decency to make a simple phone call?" the plaintiff's attorney will ask as the jury sits up attentively.

Indirect consent can help in a defense, but it is rare indeed for it to defeat a libel suit when standing by itself. As with other defenses, publication of materials for malicious reasons, and not for public enlightenment, can invalidate the protection.

RIGHT OF REPLY

Right of reply is a better defense than consent, is used more often, and is somewhat more substantial. The basis of right of reply is simple: The one who has been libeled may answer in kind. John Smith calls Steve Wilson a cheat, a fraud, and a common thief. Wilson has the right to answer Smith in kind. He can defame Smith in response.

The right of reply is based on the broader concept of self-defense; in fact, it is often referred to as *the* self-defense. As in self-defense, right of reply does have limitations. If a woman walks down the street and someone begins to pepper her with a peashooter, she has the right to stop her assailant, to protect herself. She does not have the right to pull out a .44-magnum pistol and pump three or four slugs into her attacker. Her defense then far exceeds the threat of the original attack. The same is true in a libel case. If a woman has been defamed, she may respond in kind. She may defame her attacker, but her reply cannot exceed the provocation; she cannot hit back harder than she was hit.

In a famous lawsuit two American journalists assailed one another in print. Newsman Quentin Reynolds suggested that columnist Westbrook Pegler had once called a third journalist, Heywood Broun, a liar. This bothered Broun, Reynolds wrote, to the extent that he could not sleep. Broun became ill and finally died. Pegler was incensed by this comment, claiming it charged him with moral homicide. So he attacked Reynolds, calling him sloppy, a sycophant, a coward, a slob, and a four-flusher. Pegler accused Reynolds of public nudism, of being a war profiteer, and of being an absentee war correspondent. Pegler also attacked the deceased Broun, calling him a liar and someone who made his living by controversy.

In the libel suit that followed, Pegler raised the defense of right of reply. The court agreed that Pegler's comments about Broun bore a resemblance to a reply but determined that the columnist had gone too far in his attack on Quentin Reynolds. This portion of the article had no conceivable relationship to a reply. Reynolds was awarded $175,000 from Pegler, the *New York Journal-American,* and the Hearst Corporation (*Reynolds* v. *Pegler,* 1955).

The right of reply can in the right circumstances work as a defense. Where does the press fit in? Many authorities argue that the press has the right to carry the reply and remain immune from suit. In several cases it was held that where the plaintiff's charge was made in a newspaper, the newspaper was privileged to carry the defendant's reply (*Fowler* v. *New York Herald,* 1918). Otherwise the right of reply is of no avail to the defendant; no one would be able to see or read the reply if the defendant were denied use of the press. Similarly, it was held that the reply can even be carried in a newspaper or a medium different from the medium used for the attack.

In *Cases and Materials on Torts,* law professor Harry Kalven writes:

> The boundaries of this privilege are not clearly established and it gives rise to questions amusingly reminiscent of those raised in connection with self-defense: How vigorous must the plaintiff's original aggression have been? Must the original attack itself have been defamatory? What if it [the original attack] is true or privileged? How much verbal force can the defendant use in reply? Can he defend third parties?

Questions like these continue to reduce the true effectiveness of the defense of right of reply. It is useful as a second defense, to back up either the privilege of the reporter or of fair comment, perhaps. Beyond this use its value is limited, at least at this point.

DAMAGES

If the court gets to the point in a libel suit of assessing **damages,** it is obvious that the plaintiff has met all requirements, including proving fault, and that none of the defenses just outlined have worked. How damages are assessed is not an essential piece of information for a journalist to carry; yet some feeling for the subject is useful. Libel law operates with four kinds of damages today. In each instance, before any damages can be awarded, the plaintiff must prove one thing or another to the court.

Actual Damages	The most common libel damages are called **actual damages,** or damages for actual injury. Plaintiffs have to convince the jury that they have suffered actual harm. What kind of harm? Not physical harm, obviously. The best definition of actual damages (as they are now defined) comes from the *Gertz* case. Justice Powell wrote that actual injury is not limited to out-of-pocket loss or money loss, which is how many authorities defined actual damages prior to this decision. Powell said, "Indeed, the more customary types of actual harm inflicted by defamatory falsehood include impairment of reputation and standing in the community, personal humiliation, and mental anguish and suffering." This statement is a very broad definition of actual damage. How can someone prove that he or she has suffered mental anguish? What is evidence of personal humiliation? These are very hard questions to answer. Libel damages have never been precise, and this formulation does not promise additional precision. The plaintiff has to bring evidence of some kind of injury. The jury will be the key factor in making the determination of how much harm and how much damage.

In 1985 the Supreme Court made a ruling in *Dun & Bradstreet* v. *Greenmoss Builders* that somewhat modified the High Court's 1974 *Gertz* v. *Welch* ruling on damages. In the Dun and Bradstreet ruling, the court relieved a heavy burden of proof from private persons who were suing for libel on the basis of statements that do *not* focus upon an issue of public concern.* These changes are reflected in the summaries below.

Special Damages	**Special damages** are specific items of pecuniary loss caused by published defamatory statements. Special damages must be established in precise terms, much more precise terms than those for the actual damages just outlined. If a plaintiff can prove that he or she lost $23,567.19 because of the libel, that amount is then what the plaintiff can ask for and what will likely be awarded if he or she can convince the jury of the validity of the case. Special damages represent a specific monetary, and only monetary loss as the result of the libel. Most plaintiffs do not seek special damages. However, in some cases special damages are all that can be sought. In trade libel, for example, the only award a plaintiff can get is special damages.
Presumed Damages	Presumed damages are damages that a plaintiff can get without proof of injury or harm. A public person plaintiff or a private person plaintiff suing for a libelous statement that focuses on a matter of public concern can only be awarded presumed (sometimes called general or compensatory damages) on

---

*Some people have viewed the ruling in *Dun & Bradstreet* in a far broader fashion. But it is this author's belief, based on the consensus of authorities, that the ruling applies only to the matter of damages, not to the question of fault generally.

a showing of actual malice, knowledge of falsity, or reckless disregard of the truth. However, a private person suing on the basis of a libelous statement that focuses on a private matter and not a public concern, need only show negligence to collect presumed damages.

Punitive Damages

Lawyers used to call **punitive damages,** or exemplary damages, the "smart money." Punitive damage awards are usually very large. The other kinds of damages just discussed are designed to compensate the plaintiff for injury. Punitive damages are designed to punish defendants for their misconduct and to warn other persons not to act in a similar manner.

A public person plaintiff or a private person plaintiff suing for a libelous statement that focuses on a matter of public concern can only win punitive damages upon a showing of actual malice, knowledge of falsity, or reckless disregard for the truth. A private person suing for libel based on remarks made about a private matter, and not a public concern, can win punitive damages on a showing of negligence.

Punitive damages are the most onerous aspect of any libel suit, and many persons think they are grossly unfair. Consequently, some state courts have abolished punitive damages—regardless of a showing of actual malice. Massachusetts (see *Stone* v. *Essex County Newspapers,* 1975) and Washington (see *Taskett* v. *King Broadcasting,* 1976) are two such states.

One additional point should be made clear about damages. All plaintiffs can attempt to prove actual malice in the hope of getting punitive and presumed damages, and it is only if they meet this burden that they can collect the smart money.

Retraction Statutes

The phrase "I demand a retraction" is common in the folklore of libel. What is a **retraction?** A retraction is both an apology and an effort to set the record straight. Let us say you blow one as an editor. You report that Jane Adams was arrested for shoplifting, and you are wrong. In your retraction you first tell readers or viewers that Jane Adams was not arrested for shoplifting, that you made a mistake. Then you might also apologize for the embarrassment caused Ms. Adams. You might even say some nice things about her. At common law a prompt and honest retraction is usually relevant to the question of whether the plaintiff's reputation was actually harmed. After all, you are attempting to reconstruct that part of her reputation which you tore down just the day before. She might have difficulty proving actual harm.

A good example of correction, or retraction, occurred about five years ago and involved, of all things, *Playboy's Book of Wines.* The slick-paper wine book erroneously charged on page 63 that a leading Italian winery, Bolla Vineyards, doctored its wine. As one writer noted, "All hell broke loose" when the American distributor of Bolla wines saw the reference. Playboy Press reached an agreement with the vintners in which it called back all five thousand copies of the book already distributed, sliced the two offending pages out of those copies, and replaced them with two new pages containing flattering references to Bolla, stopped publication of the book until corrections could be made, and issued multiple apologies. In late 1983 Random House recalled almost 60,000 copies of a biography of Barbara Hutton, entitled *Poor Little Rich Girl*, because of errors in the book about one of the physicians who treated the heiress to the Woolworth fortune. This largest book recall in history was an extreme measure, but it was necessary to prevent a possible lawsuit.

In the several states that have retraction statutes, a plaintiff must give the publisher an opportunity to retract the libel before a suit may be started. If the publisher promptly honors the request for a retraction and retracts the libelous material in a place in the newspaper as prominent as the place in which the libel originally appeared, the impact will reduce and in some instances cancel any damage judgment the plaintiff might later seek in a lawsuit. Failure to seek a retraction limits the plaintiff's right to bring a lawsuit against the publisher. About thirty-one states have retraction laws of one kind or another.

In an unusual case the Montana Supreme Court declared that state's retraction statute to be unconstitutional. The court ruled that the state constitution guarantees that the state courts shall be open to every person who seeks a remedy for any injury to person, property, or character. The court ruled that a retraction is not a remedy in the terms intended in the constitution. Consequently, the state's statute, under which persons who fail to seek a retraction are not permitted to sue for libel, denied citizens the remedy promised by the state constitution (*Madison* v. *Yunker,* 1978).

Retraction laws make good sense. It is the truth we seek, after all; a successful libel suit results in lining the plaintiff's pocket, but it is not very effective in correcting the errors in people's minds resulting from publication of the defamation.

SUMMARY

To collect damages in a libel suit, plaintiffs must demonstrate to the court that there was actual harm to their reputations. These are called *actual damages.* If plaintiffs can demonstrate specific items of monetary loss, *special damages* may be awarded. Plaintiffs may also seek to win *punitive damages.* In nearly thirty-one states, a timely retraction of the libel can reduce damages significantly and even lessen the likelihood of a libel suit. These rules are governed by state laws called *retraction statutes.*

CRIMINAL LIBEL   Since this book is for persons in the media or persons who plan to work in the media, there is really little reason to spend time discussing criminal libel. But it is there and is difficult to ignore. So here are a few well-chosen words on the subject.

The bulk of this chapter deals with civil libel—one person suing another for defamation. In most states, however, libel can be a crime as well. That is, there are criminal libel statutes, laws that make certain kinds of defamation a crime. For the most part these laws go unused today. They are relics of the past. In some states, in the South especially, recent instances of criminal libel prosecution have occurred. In the 1980s most states are not very interested in taking on someone else's troubles and suing for libel. A prosecutor has very little to gain from such an action. In fact, he or she would probably be roundly criticized for instituting criminal libel charges. In an age when people are mugged, robbed, raped, and murdered with alarming frequency, damage to an individual's reputation—or even to the reputation of a large number of persons—somehow does not seem too serious. Moreover, individuals who have been harmed already have recourse—a civil suit. Several years ago in New York, a judge stated this proposition very well (*People* v. *Quill,* 1958):

> The theory, in simplest terms, is that when an individual is libeled, he has an adequate remedy in a civil suit for damages. The public suffers no injury. Vindication for the individual and adequate compensation for the injury done him may be obtained as well in the civil courts. Thus the rule has always been that the remedy of criminal prosecution should only be sought where the wrong is of so flagrant a character as to make a criminal prosecution necessary on public grounds.

Despite the fact that they are not used, criminal libel statutes remain on the books in most states. In Louisiana the law is defined in this manner:

> Defamation is the malicious publication or expression in any manner, to any one other than the party defamed, of anything which tends:
>   (1) To expose any person to hatred, contempt, ridicule or to deprive him of the benefit of public confidence or social intercourse; or
>   (2) To expose the memory of one deceased to hatred, contempt or ridicule; or
>   (3) To impair any person, corporation or association of persons in his or their business occupations.
>   Whoever commits the crime of defamation shall be fined not more than $3,000 or imprisoned for not more than one year or both.

As you can see, the crime of defamation is very similar to the tort of defamation: a person can get into trouble in both instances by doing about the same thing. It can be seen from the statute quoted that it is possible to criminally libel a dead person. Since the deceased cannot sue to protect their own good names, it only makes sense to allow the state to intercede. Criminal libel differs from civil libel in several other ways as well.

First, in a few states criminal libel is tied to causing or potentially causing a breach of the peace. This charge used to be quite common. If a publication, speech, or handbill so provoked the readers or listeners that violence became possible or did in fact occur, criminal libel charges might result. In 1966 the United States Supreme Court undermined most of the "breach of the peace" statutes, as well as the actions of those states that brought criminal libel actions under the common law. The case was *Ashton* v. *Kentucky* and involved a mining dispute in Hazard, Kentucky. An agitator was arrested for circulating a pamphlet that contained articles attacking the chief of police, the sheriff, and a newspaper editor, among others. At the criminal libel trial, the judge defined the offense as "any writing calculated to create a disturbance of the peace, corrupt public morals or lead to any act, which when done, is indictable."

The Supreme Court reversed the conviction. Writing for a unanimous court, Justice William O. Douglas said the crime, as defined by the trial court, was too general and indefinite. It left the standard of responsibility—whether something is illegal or not—wide open to the discretion of the judge. Also, Douglas noted, the crime is determined not by the character of the person's words, not by what that person says or writes, but rather by the boiling point of those who listen to or read those words. The law makes someone a criminal simply because his or her neighbors have no self-control and cannot refrain from violence. This decision was an important factor, but only one factor, in the passing of "breach of the peace" as an aspect of criminal libel. It is extremely rare for such a case to occur today.

In the past it was possible to criminally libel a large group or race of people. The Supreme Court upheld such a law in 1952, a law that made it a crime to libel any race, color, creed, or religion. The case originated in Illinois where a white racist named Joseph Beauharnais distributed insulting literature at a time when blacks were attempting to integrate the white Chicago suburb of Cicero. Beauharnais's words were strong at a time when police and other officials had their hands full keeping the peace. He was arrested, tried, and fined $200 for his pamphleteering.

Beauharnais argued that his conviction violated the First Amendment. In a five-to-four vote, the Court upheld the conviction on the grounds that libelous utterances are not within the protection of the First Amendment. Justice Felix Frankfurter wrote that if an utterance directed at an individual may be the object of criminal penalties, the High Court could not then deny the right of a state to make criminal as well such utterances aimed at a well-defined group (*Beauharnais* v. *Illinois,* 1952).

The rationale for this decision was eroded, if not completely undercut, by the *New York Times* decision: Libelous utterances are protected by the First Amendment in an increasing number of instances. There is serious doubt in the minds of most press-law scholars whether the *Beauharnais* ruling remains viable today. It is very likely, given the opportunity, that the Supreme Court would overturn that decision.

The High Court has heard one criminal libel case since the *Sullivan* ruling. The Court ruled in *Garrison* v. *Louisiana* (1964) that when the defamation of a public official is the basis for a criminal libel suit, the state has to prove actual malice on the part of the defendant; that is, knowledge of falsity, reckless disregard for the truth, or falsity of the matter. Justice Brennan wrote that the reasons that persuaded the Court to rule that the First Amendment protected criticism of public officials in a civil libel suit apply with equal force in a criminal libel suit. "The constitutional guarantees of freedom of expression compel application of the same standard to the criminal remedy," he added. However, the question of what the Court would do with a group libel suit of the kind it faced in 1952 is still not answered.

Criminal libel is not a real problem for journalists and broadcasters. Within the few criminal libel cases on record since World War II, cases in which the media were the defendants can be counted on one hand. Normally the action is brought against the writer of the article or the speaker of the words, not against the medium publishing the comments.

As was noted at the beginning of this chapter, libel is probably the most common legal problem most journalists and broadcasters face today. Unlike difficulties with courts and problems in getting information from the government, which occur infrequently, the fear of publishing a libel is something the press lives with day in and day out. Virtually every story contains the potential for a libel suit.

The press is much better protected today than it was twenty-three years ago before the *New York Times* decision. The *Sullivan* ruling has helped the press in many ways. In the past, plaintiffs with only the remote possibility of victory were lured to court by the possibility of large windfall judgments. Recent cases have made the smart money tougher to get. Also, infusion of good, solid First Amendment idealism and logic into the law has made judges at all levels far more sensitive to the needs of the press. These events have been very helpful. While "freedom of the press" may be legally vague, a judge or jury who think about the First Amendment is likely to be more receptive to the arguments of the defense.

BIBLIOGRAPHY   *Here is a list of some of the sources that have been helpful in the preparation of chapter 3:*

Books   American Law Institute. *Restatement of the Law of Torts.* 2d ed. Philadelphia: American Law Institute, 1975.

Ashley, Paul. *Say It Safely.* 5th ed. Seattle: University of Washington Press, 1976.

Gregory, Charles O., and Kalven, Harry, Jr. *Cases and Materials on Torts.* 2d ed. Boston: Little, Brown & Co., 1969.

Hansen, Arthur. *Libel and Related Torts.* New York: Publishers Association Foundation, 1969.

Phelps, Robert, and Hamilton, Douglas. *Libel.* New York: Macmillan Co., 1966.

Prosser, William L. *Handbook of the Law of Torts.* St. Paul, Minn.: West Publishing Co., 1963.

Thomas, Ella C. *The Law of Libel and Slander.* Dobbs Ferry, N.Y.: Oceana Publications, 1963.

Yankwich, Leon R. *It's Libel or Contempt If You Print It.* Los Angeles: Parker & Sons Publications, 1950.

Articles   Anderson, David A. "Libel and Press Self-Censorship," 53 *Texas Law Review* 422, 1975.

"Defamation Law in the Wake of *Gertz* v. *Welch, Inc.,*" 69 *Northwestern University Law Review* 960, 1975.

Frakt, Arthur N. "Evolving Law of Defamation: *New York Times Co.* v. *Sullivan* to *Gertz* v. *Welch, Inc.,* and Beyond," 6 *Rutgers Camden Law Journal* 471, 1975.

Franklin, Marc A. and Bussel, Daniel. "The Plaintiff's Burden in Defamation: Awareness and Falsity," 25 *William and Mary Law Review* 825, 1984.

Mead, Terrance C., "Suing Media for Emotional Distress: A Multi-Method Analysis of Tort Law Evolution," 23 *Washburn Law Journal* 24, 1983.

Smolla, Rodney A. "Let the Author Beware: The Rejuvenation of American Law of Libel," 132 *Univ. of Pennsylvania Law Review* 1, 1983.

"Torts: Libel," 41 *Brooklyn Law Review* 389, 1974.

Cases   *AAFCO Heating and Air Conditioning Co.* v. *Northwest Publications, Inc.,* 321 N.E.2d 580 (1974).

Ammerman v. *Hubbard,* 572 P.2d 1258 (1977).

Anderson v. *Liberty Lobby,* 106 S.Ct. 2505 (1986).

Appleby v. *Daily Hampshire Gazette,* 395 Mass 2 (1985).

Arcand v. *Evening Call,* 567 F.2d 1163 (1977).

Artic v. *Loudoun Times Mirror,* 624 F.2d 518 (1980).

Ashton v. *Kentucky,* 384 U.S. 195 (1966).

Bandelin v. *Pietsch,* 563 P.2d 395 (1977).

Bank of Oregon v. *Independent News,* 693 P.2d 35 (1985).

Barr v. *Mateo,* 353 U.S. 171 (1959).

Beauharnais v. *Illinois,* 343 U.S. 250 (1952).

Beech Aircraft v. *National Aviation Underwriters,* 11 MLR 1401 (1984).

Blouin v. *Anton,* 431 A.2d 489 (1981).

Borg v. *Boas,* 231 F.2d 788 (1956).

Bose v. *Consumers Union,* 508 F. Supp. 1249 (1981), rev'd. 629 F.2d 189 (1982), aff'd 10 MLR 1625 (1984).

Brown and Williamson v. *Jacobson and CBS,* 713 F.2d 262 (1983).

Bruno and Stillman v. *Globe Newspapers,* 633 F.2d 583 (1980).

Buckley v. Littell, 539 F.2d 882 (1976).
Byars v. Kolodziej, 363 N.E.2d 628 (1977).
Calder v. Jones, 104 S.Ct. 1482 (1984).
Canino v. New York News, 10 M.L. Rept. 1852 (1984).
Cardiff v. Brooklyn Eagle, 75 N.Y.S.2d 222 (1948).
Carr v. Hood, 1 Camp. 355 (1808).
Carson v. Allied News, 529 F.2d 206 (1976).
Chapadeau v. Utica Observer-Dispatch, Inc., 341 N.E.2d 569 (1975).
Cherry v. Des Moines Leader, 86 N.W. 323 (1901).
Chuy v. Philadelphia Eagles, 595 F.2d 1265 (1979).
Cianci v. New Times, 639 F.2d 54 (1980).
City of Chicago v. Tribune Co., 139 N.E.2d 86 (1923).
City of Philadelphia v. Washington Post, 482 F. Supp. 897 (1979).
Clawson v. Longview Publishing Co., 589 P.2d 1223 (1979).
Cohen v. New York Times, 138 N.Y.S. 206 (1912).
Coleman v. MacLennan, 98 P.2d 281 (1908).
Columbia Sussex v. Hay, 627 S.W.2d 270 (1981).
Columbo v. Times-Argus Association, 380 A.2d 80 (1977).
Curtis Publishing Co. v. Butts and *AP v. Walker,* 388 U.S. 130 (1967).
Dameron v. Washingtonian, 779 F.2d 736 (1985).
D'Alfonso v. A.S. Abell Co., 10 M.L. Rept. 1663 (1984).
Denny v. Mertz, 318 N.W.2d 141 (1980).
Dickey v. CBS, 583 F.2d 1221 (1978).
Dilorenzo v. New York Times, 4 M.L. Rept. 2230 (1979).
Dresbach v. Doubleday, 8 M.L. Rept. 1793 (1982).
Dun & Bradstreet v. Greenmoss, 105 S.Ct. 2939 (1985).
Edwards v. National Audubon Society, 556 F.2d 113 (1977).
El Amin v. Miami Herald, 9 M.L. Rept. 1079 (1983).
Farnsworth v. Tribune Co., 253 N.E.2d 408 (1969).
Fleckstein v. Friedman, 195 N.E. 537 (1934).
Fowler v. New York Herald, 172 N.Y.S. 423 (1918).
Franklin v. Lodge 1108, 97 Cal. App.3d 915 (1979).
Gannett v. Re, 496 A.2d 553 (1985).
Garrison v. Louisiana, 379 U.S. 64 (1964).
Gautsche v. New York, 415 N.Y.S.2d 280 (1979).
Gertz v. Welch, 94 S.Ct. 2997 (1974).
Glover v. Herald Co., 549 S.W.2d 858 (1977).
Goldwater v. Ginzburg, 414 F.2d 324 (1969).
Hellman v. McCarthy, 10 M.L. Rept. 1789 (1984).
Hentell v. Knopf, 8 M.L. Rept. 1908 (1982).
Herbert v. Lando, 441 U.S. 153 (1979).
Hoeppner v. Dunkirk Printing Co., 172 N.E. 139 (1930).
Hoffman v. Washington Post, 433 F. Supp. 600 (1977).
Hope v. Hearst Corp., 294 F.2d 681 (1961).
Hornby v. Hunter, 385 S.W.2d 473 (1964).
Horvath v. Ashtabula Telegraph, 8 M.L. Rept. 1657 (1982).
Hunt v. Liberty Lobby, 720 F.2d G31 (1983).
Hutchinson v. Proxmire, 99 S. Ct. 2675 (1979).
Ingerere v. ABC, 11 M.L. Rept. 1227 (1984).
Jadwin v. Minneapolis Star, 367 N.W.2d 476 (1985).
Janklow v. Newsweek, 759 F.2d 644(1985).

Janklow v. Newsweek, 788 F.2d 1300 (1986).
Janklow v. Viking Press, 378 N.W.2d 875 (1985).
Jennings v. Telegram-Tribune, 210 Cal. Rept. 485 (1985).
Johnson v. Corinthian Television, 583 P.2d 1101 (1978).
Jones v. Sun Publishing, 292 S.E.2d 23 (1982).
KARK-TV v. Simon, 656 S.W.2d 702 (1983).
Karp v. Miami Herald, 359 So.2d 580 (1978).
Keeton v. Hustler, 104 S.Ct. 1473 (1984).
Kilgore v. Younger, 180 Cal. Rptr. 657 (1982).
Krauss v. Champaign News Gazette, 375 N.E.2d 1362 (1978).
Kutz v. Independent Publishing, 638 P.2d 1088 (1981).
Larouche v. NBC, 11 M.L. Rept. 1655 (1985).
Lawrence v. Moss, 639 F.2d 635 (1981).
Lerman v. Chuckleberry Publications, 521 F. Supp. 228 (1981).
Levine v. CMP Publications, 738 F.2d 660 (1984).
Liberty Lobby v. Jack Anderson, 746 F.2d 1563 (1984).
Loeb v. Globe Newspaper, 489 F. Supp. 481 (1980).
MacDonald v. Time, 7 M.L. Rept. 1981 (1981).
MacDonald v. Time, 554 F. Supp. 1053 (1983).
McBride v. Merrell Dow, 717 F.2d 1460 (1984).
McCullough v. Cities Service, 676 P.2d 833 (1984).
McNair v. Hearst Corp., 494 F.2d 1309 (1974).
Madison v. Yunker, 589 P.2d 126 (1978).
Malerba v. Newsday, 406 N.Y.S.2d 552 (1978).
Marcone v. Penthouse, 533 F. Supp. 353 (1982), 754 F.2d 1072 (1985).
Martin v. Wilson Publishing, 497 A.2d 322 (1985).
Mashburn v. Collin, 355 So.2d 879 (1977).
Mathis v. Philadelphia Newspapers, 455 F. Supp. 406 (1978).
Maule v. New York Magazine, 429 N.Y.S.2d 891 (1980).
Medico v. Time, 634 F.2d 134 (1981).
Memphis Publishing Co. v. Nichols, 569 S.W.2d 412 (1978).
Michigan Conservation Clubs v. CBS, 665 F.2d 110 (1981).
Morgan v. Dun & Bradstreet, Inc., 421 F.2d 1241 (1970).
Mr. Chow v. Ste. Jour. Azur S.A., 759 F.2d 219 (1985).
Murray v. Bailey, 11 M.L. Rept. 1369 (1985).
Mutafis v. Erie Insurance Exchange, 775 F.2d 593 (1985).
Myers v. Boston Magazine, 403 N.E.2d 376 (1980).
Nader v. deToledano, 408 A.2d 31 (1979).
Namlod, Ltd. v. Newsday, 11 M.L. Rept. 1057 (1984).
Neiman-Marcus v. Lait, 13 F.R.D. 311 (1952).
Newsom v. Henry, 443 So. 2d 817 (1984).
Newton v. NBC, 12 M.L. Rept. 1252 (1985).
New York Times Co. v. Sullivan, 376 U.S. 254 (1964).
Nodar v. Galbreath, 462 So.2d 803 (1985).
Old Dominion Branch No. 496, National Association of Letter Carriers v. Austin, 94 S.Ct. 2770 (1974).
Ollman v. Evans, 750 F.2d 970 (1984).
Orr v. Argus Press, 586 F.2d 1108 (1978).
Orr v. Lynch, 401 N.Y.S.2d 897 (1978).
Palmer v. Seminole, 9 M.L. Rept. 2151 (1983).
Pauling v. Globe-Democrat, 362 F.2d 188 (1966).
Peagler v. Phoenix Newspapers, 547 P.2d 1074 (1976).

Pearson v. *Fairbanks Publishing Co.*, 413 P.2d 711 (1966).
People v. *Quill*, 177 N.Y.S.2d 380 (1958).
Perry v. *Hearst Corp.*, 334 F.2d 800 (1964).
Philadelphia Newspapers v. *Hepps*, 106 S.Ct. 1558 (1986).
Postill v. *Booth Newspapers*, 325 N.W.2d 511 (1982).
Powers v. *Durgin-Snow Publishing Co.*, 144 A.2d 294 (1958).
Press v. *Verran*, 589 S.W.2d 435 (1978).
Price v. *Viking Press*, 625 F.Supp. 641 (1985).
Puerto Rican Legal Defense Fund v. *Grace*, 9 M.L. Rept. 1514 (1983).
Pulverman v. *A. S. Abell Co.*, 228 F.2d 797 (1956).
Rand v. *New York Times*, 4 M.L. Rept. 1556 (1978).
Reader's Digest v. *Marin County Superior Court*, 11 MLR 1065 (1984).
Reynolds v. *Pegler*, 223 F.2d 429 (1955).
Roberts v. *Dover*, 525 F. Supp. 987 (1981).
Rosanova v. *Playboy*, 411 F.Supp 440 (1976), aff'd 580 F.2d 859 (1978).
Rosenblatt v. *Baer*, 383 U.S. 75 (1966).
Rouch v. *Enquirer & News of Battle Creek*, 357 N.W. 794 (1984).
Rubenstein v. *New York Post*, 488 N.Y.S.2d 331 (1985).
St. Amant v. *Thompson*, 390 U.S. 727 (1968).
Saunders v. *WHYY-TV*, 382 A.2d 257 (1978).
Schiavone v. *Time*, 569 F.Supp. 614 (1983).
Schiavone Construction v. *Time*, 619 F.Supp. 684 (1985).
Seegmiller v. *KSL-TV*, 626 P.2d 968 (1981).
Shiles v. *News Syndicate Co.*, 261 N.E.2d 251 (1970).
Slawik v. *News-Journal*, 428 A.2d 15 (1981).
Southard v. *Forbes*, 588 F.2d 140 (1979).
Steaks Unlimited v. *Deaner*, 623 F.2d 624 (1980).
Steere v. *Cupp*, 602 P.2d 1267 (1979).
Stevens v. *Sun Publishing Co.*, 240 S.E.2d 812 (1978).
Stillman v. *Paramount Pictures*, 147 N.E.2d 741 (1957).
Stone v. *Essex County Newspapers*, 330 N.E.2d 161 (1975).
Street v. *NBC*, 645 F.2d 1227 (1981).
Summerlin v. *Washington Star*, 7 M.L. Rept. 2460 (1981).
Tabart v. *Tipper*, 1 Camp. 350 (1808).
Taskett v. *King Broadcasting*, 546 P.2d 81 (1976).
Time, Inc. v. *Firestone*, 96 S.Ct. 958 (1976).
Triggs v. *Sun Printing and Publishing Association*, 71 N.E. 739 (1904).
Trump v. *Chicago Tribune*, 616 F.Supp. 1434 (1985).
Wade v. *Stocks*, 7 M.L. Rept. 2200 (1981).
Waldbaum v. *Fairchild Publications*, 627 F.2d 1287 (1980).
Walker v. *Colorado Springs Sun, Inc.* 538 P.2d 450 (1975).
Walters v. *Sanford Herald*, 228 S.E.2d 766 (1976).
Washington Post v. *Kennedy*, 3 F.2d 207 (1924).
Wasserman v. *Time, Inc.*, 424 F.2d 920 (1970).
Weaver v. *Pryor-Jeffersonian*, 569 P.2d 967 (1977).
Whitten v. *Commercial Dispatch*, 487 So.2d 843 (1986).
Wildmon v. *Hustler*, 508 F. Supp. 87 (1980).
Williams v. *Pasma*, 9 M.L. Rept. 1004 (1982).
Wilson v. *Scripps-Howard*, 642 F.2d 371 (1981).
Winters v. *Morgan*, 576 P.2d 1152 (1978).
Wolston v. *Reader's Digest*, 99 S.Ct. 2701 (1979).
Yiamouyiannis v. *Consumers Union*, 619 F.2d 932 (1980).

4 INVASION OF PRIVACY

Privacy: How much do we have? Every person seems to give up a little more privacy as each year passes. Each of us gives up considerable privacy to fully participate in our buy-now-pay-later, opinion-research-oriented, fully insured, credit-card, big-government, security-conscious society. There are people who have withdrawn from this kind of society to live in a cabin in a remote wilderness. But most modern Americans refuse to give up the comforts that modern life provides.

Privacy is a very difficult concept to define. It has many meanings. One individual may say that he believes in the right of privacy, but also believes that the police have the right to wiretap telephone conversations. A shopowner may assert that she stands behind the right of privacy, but is reluctant to give up the television cameras that scan every nook and cranny of the shop in an effort to discourage shoplifting. The government is supposed to help citizens protect their privacy; yet governments at all levels seriously invade our privacy by gathering massive amounts of data on private citizens for a variety of reasons, good and bad.

In 1888 in *Treatise on the Law of Torts,* Thomas M. Cooley defined privacy as "the right to be let alone." More recently privacy was defined as the right of individuals to control information about themselves. The right of privacy was first proposed as a narrow legal right in 1890. However, as Professor Edward J. Bloustein writes in "Privacy as an Aspect of Human Dignity," "What began at the turn of the century as a limited private right to prevent undue and unreasonable publicity concerning private lives has now developed into an extraordinarily broad constitutional right, the limits of which are still not clear."

Today **invasion of privacy** encompasses a wide range of behavior that includes wiretapping, illegal surveillance, misuse of information by retail credit agencies, use of two-way mirrors in department store dressing rooms, and collection of private information by researchers, banks, and government agencies. The mass media are also frequently accused of invasion of privacy. This chapter is about invasion of privacy by the press, by radio and television, and by the motion-picture industry.

As you will come to understand by reading this chapter, the legal right to privacy imposes a minimum of restrictions upon the newsgathering activities of the press. Most courts and legislatures have simply refused to limit the legitimate gathering, publication, and broadcast of information that is of importance or interest to the public. So legally, the right of privacy is not a major impediment to reporters and editors who seek to tell us about what is going on in the world.

Yet invasions of privacy by the press are still viewed by a substantial number of Americans as one of society's most vexing problems. They complain, often legitimately, about the microphone shoved in the face of the victim of a crime or the witness to a tragedy; the insensitive questions to persons who have suffered some serious personal loss; the photos of grief-stricken relatives of persons killed in accidents or acts of terrorism; and the often needless repetition of personal details about an individual who has been inadvertently thrust into the news through some unlikely quirk of fate. These Americans perceive reporters and editors and newscasters as an insensitive lot, persons who trade on the tragedy and sorrow of the unfortunate to sell newspapers or attract viewers.

For the press, then, problems of invasion of privacy go beyond the law. What is legally permissible may not be viewed as ethical or proper in our contemporary society. Those who work in the mass media must be extremely sensitive to these issues. Legitimate news must be reported, sometimes with all the tragic details. But each story must be weighed on its own merits, and the members of the press must consider not only the legal problems that are faced by invading personal privacy, but also the damage that is wrought to the press as an important societal institution through the sometimes thoughtless publicity given to purely private matters.

The chapter opens with a brief history of the law of privacy. Then each of the four ways in which the media can run afoul of the law for invasion of privacy is discussed, and the defenses for each kind of invasion of privacy are outlined. It is important to remember this point. Invasion of privacy by the media really involves four distinct legal wrongs: (1) **appropriation** of an individual's name or likeness for commercial purposes without first getting consent, (2) **intrusion** upon a person's solitude, (3) **publication of private information** about a person, and (4) publication of false information about a person, or putting someone in a **false light.** Each area has defenses that the press may erect in an effort to ward off a plaintiff's lawsuit. The defenses that work for one kind of invasion of privacy suit are generally not effective in defending another kind of suit for invasion of privacy. The defense of newsworthiness, for example, can be used to stop a suit for the publication of private information, but the defense normally will not work in a suit based upon intrusion. It is best to think of invasion of privacy as four separate legal problems, each with its own defenses.

Despite its apparent similarity to libel, the law of privacy is far less mature than its older tort cousin. In fact, from the standpoint of the centuries-old common law system, privacy is downright modern. Unlike most other areas of the law, we can say specifically that a legal remedy for invasion of privacy was first advocated less than one hundred years ago.

The concept of privacy is old, but the law of privacy is young, growing out of the dramatically changing social conditions of the late nineteenth century, the era that spawned present-day urban United States. The Industrial Revolution brought crowded cities and reduced space to a premium, and at the same time the American press changed profoundly. In the fight for circulation, the mass press of the big cities undertook new schemes to attract readers. It is perhaps an understatement to note that this was not journalism's finest hour.

While privacy was something that people enjoyed and sought, it was not something with which our legal system could cope. There was no legal right to privacy, no law that guaranteed the right to be left alone. In 1890 two young lawyers proposed in the *Harvard Law Review* ("The Right to Privacy") that such a law should exist. One of the pair, the prominent Boston attorney Samuel D. Warren, was annoyed at what he described as the gossipy, snoopy Boston press, which frequently focused on the social activities of the Warren family. Warren sought the aid of his former law partner, former Harvard Law School classmate and close friend, Louis D. Brandeis, in preparing a plea for the legal recognition of the right to be let alone.

The pair argued, "Instantaneous photographs and newspaper enterprise have invaded the sacred precincts of private and domestic life; and numerous mechanical devices threaten to make good the prediction that 'what is whispered in the closet shall be proclaimed from the house-tops.'" Warren and Brandeis said they were offended by the gossip in the press, which they said had overstepped in every direction the obvious bounds of propriety and decency:

> To satisfy a prurient taste the details of sexual relations are spread broadcast in the columns of the daily papers. To occupy the indolent, column upon column is filled with idle gossip, which can only be procured by intrusion upon the domestic circle. . . .
> The common law has always recognized a man's house as his castle, impregnable, often, even to its own officers engaged in the execution of its commands. Shall the courts thus close the front entrance to constituted authority, and open wide the back door to idle or prurient curiosity?

To stop this illicit behavior, the two young lawyers proposed that the courts recognize the legal right of privacy; that is, citizens should be able to go to court to stop such unwarranted intrusions and also secure money damages for the hardship they suffered from such prying and from publication of private material about them.

To a modern observer, the Boston press does not appear to be nearly so scandalous as the charges Warren and Brandeis suggested. One gets the distinct impression that Mr. Warren was an overly sensitive individual. The article also appears to have been Warren's idea. He sought help from Brandeis, who was indeed a legal scholar. Brandeis later went on to a distinguished career as a jurist. Despite the eloquence of their plea, the Warren and Brandeis proposal initially fell on deaf ears. Thirteen years passed before any state recognized the legal right of privacy. In 1903 New York passed a privacy statute that guaranteed its citizens protection from invasion of their privacy, but the statute contained a far different concept of privacy than that proposed in 1890. What the New York law did was prohibit commercial exploitation of the name or picture of any citizen.

From these rather humble beginnings more than ninety years ago, privacy law has grown until today it is an important segment of our legal rights. The courts or the legislatures in virtually all the states have recognized the legal claim of invasion of privacy. Most states have recognized the right to privacy through the common law. At least eight states—New York, Nebraska, Rhode Island, Utah, Virginia, Wisconsin, Massachusetts, and Oklahoma—have recognized the right to privacy through a statute, but often these statutes grant a narrower protection for privacy than the common law. In 1984 the Minnesota Court of Appeals in *House* v. *Sports Films* (1984) ruled that Minnesota does not recognize the right to privacy, citing an earlier state supreme court ruling (*Hendry* v. *Conner,* 1975). But one suspects that this situation will change, either through legislative action or a subsequent supreme court ruling.

But the recognition of a right merely states a legal conclusion. It does not, by itself, provide a full set of legal principles that can be used to grant relief to a plaintiff. The law has grown over the past nearly one hundred years by fits and starts. It has a somewhat ragged profile. Some parts of the right to privacy bear little resemblance to the plan proposed by Warren and Brandeis in 1890. In fact the right to privacy today contains dimensions that have little to do with what we traditionally think of as privacy. As noted previously, invasion of privacy today encompasses not just one, but four, legal wrongs. They are different and should be thought of as separate wrongs. Let us briefly summarize these four wrongs and then study each of them in depth.

The first kind of invasion of privacy is called appropriation and is defined as taking a person's name, picture, photograph, or likeness and using it for commercial gain without permission. This is technically the only right of privacy guaranteed in some of the states that have privacy statutes. The laws are limited to outlawing this one kind of behavior. But as a matter of fact, judicial construction of these laws has allowed them to encompass many of the other aspects of invasion of privacy as well.

Intrusion is the second type of invasion of privacy, an area of the law growing rapidly today, and is what most people think of when invasion of privacy is mentioned. Intrusion upon the solitude and into the private life of a person is prohibited.

The law prohibits publication of private information—truthful private information—about a person. What is truthful private information? Gossip, substance of private conversations, and details of a private tragedy or illness have all been used as the basis of a suit.

Finally, the publication of any false information about a person can result in a privacy suit, whether the material is defamatory or not. The fourth area of the law is an outgrowth of the first, the appropriation area. Maybe both should be in a single category, but they are probably easier to understand when they are considered separately.

Some people have said that a law of privacy is really not needed. Several years ago law professor Frederick Davis ("What Do We Mean by Right to Privacy?") wrote, "Indeed, one can logically argue that the concept of a right of privacy was never required in the first place, and that its whole history is an illustration of how well-meaning but impatient academicians can upset the normal development of the law by pushing it too hard."

One can make a persuasive argument that Davis is right. The appropriation area of the law really deals with a property right and would probably fit more comfortably as part of the law of literary property, product disparagement, trademark protection, and the like. Intrusion is really more akin to the law of trespass. False information is very close to defamation. Publication of private information—the only truly unique aspect of the law—has enjoyed such limited success that it might be abandoned altogether with little loss. Control of this kind of behavior might better be left to public opinion and the conscience of reporters and editors, as Professor Zechariah Chafee once suggested.

Regardless of whether it is legally logical, the law of privacy does exist; it is a part of our legal system. Persons in the media must be constantly aware of it. The number of privacy suits seems to increase a little each year. A considerable number of cases are settled in favor of the plaintiff. For better understanding of the law, each of the four types or kinds of invasion of privacy is discussed at length in the pages that follow. ◆

APPROPRIATION   Appropriation is the oldest, and in many ways the least ambiguous, of the four types of invasion of privacy. Two of the earliest cases remain good examples of this area of the law:

1. In 1902 young Abigail Roberson of Albany, New York, awoke one morning to find her picture all over town on posters advertising Franklin Mills Flour. Twenty-five thousand copies of the advertisement had been placed in stores, warehouses, saloons, and other public buildings. Abigail said she felt

embarrassed and humiliated, that she suffered greatly from this commercial exploitation, and she therefore sued for invasion of privacy. But she lost her case, and the state's High Court ruled (*Roberson* v. *Rochester Folding Box Co.,* 1902):

> . . . an examination of the authorities leads us to the conclusion that the so-called "right of privacy" has not yet found an abiding place in our jurisprudence, and, as we view it, the doctrine cannot now be incorporated without doing violence to settled principles of law by which the profession and the public have long been guided.

Following this decision a great controversy arose in New York, led by the press, much of which expressed outrage at the way the court had treated Abigail. The controversy settled on the state legislature, which during the following year, 1903, adopted the nation's first privacy law. The statute was very narrow; that is, it prohibited a very specific kind of conduct. Use of an individual's name or likeness without the individual's consent for advertising or trade purposes was made a minor crime. In addition to the criminal penalty, the statute allowed the injured party to seek both an injunction to stop the use of the name or picture and money damages. This was the first privacy statute.

2. Two years later Georgia became the first state to recognize the right of privacy through the common law. Paolo Pavesich, an Atlanta artist, discovered that a life insurance company had used his photograph in newspaper advertisements. Pavesich's photograph was used in a before-and-after advertisement to illustrate a contented, successful man who had bought sufficient life insurance. A testimonial statement was also ascribed to the artist. He sued for $25,000 and won his case before the Georgia Supreme Court, which ruled (*Pavesich* v. *New England Mutual Life Insurance Co.,* 1905)

> . . . the form and features of the plaintiff are his own. The defendant insurance company and its agents had no more authority to display them in public for the purpose of advertising the business . . . than they would have had to compel the plaintiff to place himself upon exhibition for this purpose.

Before the ramifications of this aspect of the law are discussed, let us ask the question, For what are plaintiffs compensated in an invasion of privacy suit? What is their damage? In a libel case the reputation is damaged, a fairly invisible injury. But in a privacy suit the damage is even more invisible: the damage is the humiliation, embarrassment, and general bother that an ordinary person might experience from invasion of privacy. In other words, the damage is personal. The right of privacy is a personal right.

Use of Name or Likeness

Everybody knows what a name is, and it is therefore unnecessary to dwell on that term. It should be noted, however, that stage names, pen names, pseudonyms, and so forth, count the same as real names in the eyes of the law. If the name of rock star Elton John is used in an advertisement for dental floss without his permission, the suit cannot be defended on the basis that since Elton John's real name is Reginald Kenneth Dwight, his "name" was not appropriated illegally. It should also be noted that the law of privacy protects only people's names. Company names, trade names, and corporate names are not protected. Only people enjoy the right of privacy. Businesses, corporations, schools, and other "things" are not protected under the law. However, the use of a trade name like Kodak or Crest can create other serious legal problems.

What is a likeness? Obviously a photograph, a painting, and a sketch—anything that suggests to readers and viewers that the plaintiff is pictured—are likenesses. Federal courts in New York State ruled recently that a sketch of a black man sitting in the corner of a boxing ring was, for purposes of an invasion-of-privacy suit, the "likeness" of former heavyweight champion Muhammed Ali. The boxer looked a little like Ali, and the photograph was accompanied by a verse that referred to the boxer as "the Greatest" (*Ali* v. *Playgirl,* 1978). ABC Records lost the right-to-privacy suit brought by classical guitarist Jean Pierre Jumez over an album cover. As part of a promotional scheme to attract the attention of young people, ABC packaged Jumez's record in an album that depicted a bearded man playing a guitar. The hairy-legged individual, whose face was obscured, was dressed in a tuxedo jacket but wore no pants. Jumez contended record buyers would think the picture was of him. "Any sufficiently clear representation of a living person is violative of the [New York] statute if it is used for commercial purposes without the subject's consent," the court ruled. Since the face of the man was obscured, record buyers could not tell whether the picture was of Jumez or not. But since the artist's name was on the album cover, people might surely believe Jumez was the individual in the picture (*Jumez* v. *ABC Records,* 1978).

Whether or not a likeness or representation of a plaintiff has been appropriated is often a jury question. Susan Cohen sued a cosmetics maker in 1984 after the firm published an ad containing what Cohen said was a photo of herself and her daughter bathing in a stream while nude. But only the backs and the sides of the bathers can be seen, and the company argued no appropriation had taken place because the plaintiffs were not identifiable. Cohen's husband said he recognized his wife and daughter, as did friends of the family. A lower court dismissed the suit, ruling that the plaintiff's identities cannot be determined from the picture. But the Appellate Division of the New York Supreme Court overturned the dismissal. The requirement that a portrait or picture of a plaintiff be appropriated "does not require that there be an identifiable facial representation as a prerequisite to relief," the court said. A jury should decide whether the advertisement contains a recognizable likeness (*Cohen* v. *Herbal Concepts,* 1984).

Does using a look-alike in an advertisement constitute appropriating someone's likeness? Barbara Reynolds, a woman who bears a striking resemblance to Jackie Kennedy Onassis, was featured in a Christian Dior ad, along with movie reviewer Gene Shalit, model Shari Belafonte, and actress Ruth Gordon. Reynolds was dressed and made up to look like Onassis, who sued, arguing her likeness had been appropriated for the advertisement. The New York Supreme Court agreed, ruling that the law prohibits the use of a representation "which conveys the essence and likeness of an individual." Reynolds complained that she cannot be stopped from using her own face in advertisements. The court said she could use her own face, but she could be stopped from appearing when she was attempting to convey the appearance of someone else, someone much better known. But what about her artistic career? Reynolds asked. "While some imitators may employ artistry in the use of voice, gesture and facial expression, a mere similarity of features is no more artistry than the mimicry of the Monarch butterfly by its look-alike, the Viceroy butterfly. To paint a portrait of Jacqueline Kennedy Onassis is to create a work of art; to look like Jacqueline Kennedy Onassis is not," the court said (*Onassis* v. *Christian Dior,* 1984).

What are advertising and trade purposes? While minor differences exist among the states—especially among the states with statutes—a general guideline can be set down: advertising or trade purposes are commercial uses; that is, someone makes money from the use. Here are examples of the kinds of actions that are clearly commercial use:

1. Use of a person's name or photograph in an *advertisement* on television, on radio, in newspapers, in magazines, on posters, on billboards, and so forth
2. Display of a person's photograph in the window of a photographer's shop to show potential customers the quality of work done by the studio
3. A testimonial falsely suggesting that an individual eats the cereal or drives the automobile in question

In Utah recently a broadcaster announced the name of a person on the "Dialing for Dollars" television feature. The individual sued, arguing that the program was simply an advertising device used by the station to attract viewers and that since no consent had been given for the use of the name over the air, the use was an invasion of privacy. The Utah Supreme Court agreed with the plaintiff, declaring that the name had been used to promote a commodity—the television station (*Jeppson* v. *United Television,* 1978).

What about this argument? A newspaper runs a photograph of John Smith on the front page after his car rolled over several times during a high-speed police pursuit. Smith sues for invasion of privacy, arguing that his picture on the front page of the newspaper attracted readers to the paper, resulted in the sale of newspapers, and therefore was used for commercial or trade purposes. Despite the arguments of many persons—even today—courts have consistently rejected this claim.

This plea was first made in 1907 by a New Yorker who objected to having his picture appear on the front page of the *New York World*. The state supreme court rejected the argument, noting that surely the intent of the state legislature was not to prohibit a newspaper or magazine from publishing a person's name or picture in a single issue without his consent (*Moser* v. *Press Publishing Co.*, 1908). Two years later another New York court reiterated this stand, ruling that advertising and trade purposes referred to commercial use, not to the dissemination of information (*Jeffries* v. *New York Evening Journal*, 1910). The United States Supreme Court has ruled that the fact that newspapers and books and magazines are sold for profit does not deny them the protection of liberty of expression (*Time, Inc.* v. *Hill*, 1967).

Anyone who has worked in journalism for very long knows that material created for promotional or trade purposes is often published or broadcast under the guise of news or information. A newspaper, for example, may publish what appears to be a newsworthy column on new products. In reality the material is an advertisement for these new products. In these instances the courts will rule that the publication was made to further a trade purpose, and an invasion of privacy suit will often stand. But the courts scrutinize these cases quite closely and offer considerable leeway to the press. For example, *Seventeen* magazine features what it calls its make-over section each month. Teenage girls are given clothing, cosmetics, and considerable advice to use to try to improve their appearance. The article accompanying the before-and-after pictures discusses the make over, and the brand names of products are prominently mentioned. The teenagers are paid and are supposed to sign permission forms, but one young woman inadvertently did not sign a model release. She sued and argued that her name and likeness had been appropriated for trade purposes. She lost. A court ruled that the article about grooming, makeup, and clothing was newsworthy to the teenage audience at which it was aimed. Mention of the brand names of products was incidental to the article and pictures (*Lopez* v. *Triangle Communications*, 1979).

A professional model argued that the use of a picture of her modeling a jacket in the "Best Bets" column of the *New York* magazine was an illegal appropriation of her likeness for advertising purposes. The column features short articles and photos about new and unusual products and services, and the photo of the model carried this caption:

> Yes Giorgio—From Giorgio Armani. Based on his now classic turn on the bomber jacket, this cotton-twill version with "fun fur" collar features the same cut at a far lower price—about $225. It'll be available in the stores next week. Henry Post Bomber Jacket/Barney's, Bergdorf Goodman, Bloomingdale's.

The plaintiff said this was an advertisement and that in order to get a product featured in the "Best Bets" column, a merchant had to advertise in the magazine. The New York Court of Appeals disagreed that use of the photo was an appropriation, ruling that the "newsworthiness exception applies not only to reports of political happenings and social trends, but also to news stories and articles of consumer interest, including developments in the fashion world." The plaintiff argued that she certainly was not newsworthy. The court said that was immaterial—the jacket she modeled was newsworthy (*Stephano* v. *News Group Publications,* 1984).

Perhaps the one striking exception to this broad general rule that virtually any information article is excluded from an appropriation suit is the use of a name or picture in a pornographic magazine or book. Some courts find this objectionable and will permit an appropriation suit to succeed. For example, the use of the plaintiff's nude photograph in a book entitled *World Guide to Nude Beaches and Recreation* was deemed to be an appropriation because, the court said, the book was merely an excuse to disseminate pornographic pictures (*Creel* v. *Crown Publishers,* 1985). This is an irrational exception in the law but is the kind of exception that is possible when judges are given the power to determine what is and what is not "information of public interest."

The law of privacy, like all law, contains narrow exceptions to general rules, and what follows is one of them. Despite what has just been said, there is a category of advertisements in which use of a person's name or picture without consent is not an invasion of privacy. These are advertisements for media—newspapers, television, and magazines—that are otherwise protected by freedom of expression. The use of a person's name or picture in such an advertisement will not result in liability, provided that the picture or name had been used earlier in a news or information story. Here is an example from a real case.

The controversy that sparked this rule involved actress Shirley Booth. She was photographed in Jamaica, and the picture was published in a feature story in *Holiday* magazine. *Holiday* then used the same picture to advertise the magazine itself. The full-page advertisement told readers that the picture was typical of the material appearing in *Holiday* magazine and urged people to advertise in the periodical or subscribe to *Holiday*. Ms. Booth did not object to her photograph in the feature story, only to its use in the subsequent advertisement. The courts, however, refused to call the use an invasion of privacy. The New York Supreme Court ruled that the strength of a free press depends upon economic support from advertisers and subscribers, and hence a publication or broadcasting station must promote itself. Since the picture in this case was first used in an information story, its subsequent use in a promotion for the magazine was really only "incidental" to its original use and was merely to show the quality and content of the magazine. The picture was not used to sell spaghetti or used cars. Hence the use did not constitute an invasion of privacy (*Booth* v. *Curtis Publishing Co.,* 1962).

In advertisements promoting itself, a newspaper or magazine can re-publish stories and photographs that contain the names and pictures of people—private citizens as well as celebrities. The key word is *republish;* the material must first have been used as a news or information item in the publication (see *Lawrence* v. *A.S. Abell Co.,* 1984). The publication can even use these photographs in television advertisements, as *New York* magazine did with the picture of Betty Friedan. She sued but lost, with the U.S. District court ruling that "under New York law, an advertisement, the purpose of which is to advertise the article, shares the privilege enjoyed by the article, if the article itself was unobjectionable" (*Friedan* v. *Friedan,* 1976).

A television station can put together a montage of news clips from stories it has broadcast and use the montage as a promotion. A television station can even take brief photographic segments from an upcoming news or information program and use them in promotions to advertise the show.

A commercial advertiser cannot republish a news story or use news film in its advertising if these items contain names or recognizable faces without running the risk of liability. If there was a fire at the Acme Furniture Store, and the local newspaper wrote a long story about it that contained the names of fire fighters, employees, witnesses, and so forth, Acme could not republish this story in its Fire Sale advertisements unless it first deleted the names of the persons mentioned and covered up the faces of any persons identifiable in the photographs. The exception to the general rule applies only to advertisements for the mass media that contain pictures or names previously used in informational or news stories.

How far can a medium go in republishing or broadcasting stories and photographs for promotional purposes? While there are obviously limits, the courts have granted considerable leeway. Former professional quarterback Joe Namath sued *Sports Illustrated* when the magazine used a 1969 Super Bowl photograph of Namath (which it had previously published) to promote subscriptions to the magazine. This was an incidental republication of the picture, the court ruled (*Namath* v. *Sports Illustrated,* 1976). But performer Cher won a lawsuit against *Forum* magazine when it used her picture to promote an edition of the magazine. The promotional advertisements stated that Cher endorsed the magazine, which was not true. A United States district court in California ruled that the use of the performer's name and picture went much further than establishing the news content and the quality of the periodical. The advertising was not merely incidental to the original publication. Complicating the case was the fact that *Forum* had illegally obtained the interview with Cher, but that was not a material factor in the court's ruling (*Cher* v. *Forum International,* 1982).

Consent as a Defense   The law prohibits only the unauthorized use of a name or picture. In those states that have privacy statutes, the law specifically requires that the consent be a written authorization from the subject. In the remainder of the states, the law is more ambiguous on the question. Nevertheless, defendants are forced to prove they do have written consent if and when a lawsuit arises. Therefore, it only makes sense to obtain written consent. An example of a standard consent or release form appears on page 224.

The problems that can arise from the defense of consent are numerous, and in each case they are more severe when written consent has not been obtained. For example, it is always possible for the person to withdraw consent after it has been given. Columbia Broadcasting System prepared a fictional television drama about the kidnapping of Jackie Gleason. Gleason played himself in the story, and an actor played the part of Gleason's manager. The manager's real name was used in the script. Suddenly the manager decided after the program was filmed that he did not want his name included in the program. Despite the fact that he had worked on the play for many weeks, planning and writing, a New York court said that inclusion of the plaintiff's name in the film against his will constituted an invasion of privacy (*Durgom v. CBS,* 1961). While this suit falls under category four of invasion of privacy, the rules are the same for both appropriation and falsehood. Columbia Broadcasting was therefore forced to write the plaintiff out of the script and reshoot part of the production.

Had the network gained written consent from the subject, and had it paid the plaintiff for using his name in the play, he would have found it much harder—if not impossible—to revoke consent at the last minute. Written consent has a distinct advantage. The safest rule is to always get written consent. Photographers especially are advised to carry copies of a standard release form in their gadget bags so that when that once-in-a-lifetime picture comes along, the one they are certain to sell for $10,000, they can obtain written consent from the subject on the spot.

There are times when even written consent does not work as a defense, and the media must be aware of such situations:

1. Consent given today may not be valid ten years hence, especially if it is gratuitous oral consent. In Louisiana a man named Cole McAndrews gave permission to the owner of a health spa to use his before-and-after pictures in advertisements for the gym. But the owner, Alvin Roy, waited ten years to use the photographs, and in the interim McAndrews's life had changed considerably. He sued Roy, who argued that it was McAndrews's responsibility to revoke the consent if he no longer wanted the pictures used. But a Louisiana court of appeals agreed instead with the plaintiff. Judge Robert D. Jones wrote (*McAndrews* v. *Roy,* 1961):

> We are of the opinion that it would be placing an unreasonable burden on the plaintiff to hold he was under duty to revoke a gratuitous authorization given many years before. As the defendant was the only person to profit from the use of the pictures then, under all the circumstances, it seems reasonable that he should have sought renewal of the permission to use the old pictures.

Reauthorization is needed when a name or photograph is used many years after consent was first given. A professional actor in New York gave the manufacturer of artificial Christmas trees permission to use his picture in a commercial for one year. When the commercial was used after one year, he sued for appropriation, and the New York High Court sustained his privacy suit against the challenge by the defendant that only an action for breach of contract should be permitted (*Welch* v. *Mr. Christmas Tree,* 1982).

2. Some persons cannot give consent. A teenage girl is perfect to appear in an Acme Shampoo advertising campaign. She agrees to pose and signs a release authorizing use of her picture in the advertisements. The pictures are great, the advertisements are great, everything is great—until notice arrives that the model is suing for invasion of privacy! But she signed the permission form. Right. But she was only sixteen years old, and under the law minors cannot give consent. Parental consent is required in such instances. If parents or guardians do give consent for the use of a minor's name or picture, under the common law in many states it is possible for the minors to revoke that consent when they reach the legal age. When Brooke Shields was ten years old, a photographer was given permission by Brooke's mother to use a picture he had taken of the child model. The Appellate Division of the New York Supreme Court ruled that Brooke could revoke that consent when she became an adult (*Shields* v. *Gross,* 1982). But the state's High Court reversed this ruling. The court of appeals said it recognized that such a revocation was possible under the common law, but the New York state privacy statute specifically permits parents to give written consent on behalf of a minor child. The statute, the court said, derogates, or rejects, the common law rule. Brooke Shields had no recourse, since her mother had previously given written permission for the use of the photograph (*Shields* v. *Gross,* 1983).

Other people are unable to give consent as well. Columbia Broadcasting System (CBS) was sued on behalf of David Delan by his guardian for including the young man in its film "Any Place But Here," a documentary about mental illness. Delan had been hospitalized for more than five years as a psychotic at the Creedmor State Hospital in New York. He was legally incompetent to sign a consent form, and the network failed to gain a signed release from a physician. A psychologist gave CBS permission to film David, but the New York state law specifically requires the signature of a medical doctor on the release agreement before patients in the state's mental hospitals can be photographed or interviewed (*Delan* v. *CBS,* 1981). CBS ultimately prevailed in the case when the Appellate Division of the New York Supreme Court ruled that the broadcast was not made for advertising or trade purposes, and therefore consent from David Delan was not required (*Delan* v. *CBS,* 1983). But the point made by the trial court is well taken. Persons who are unable to give consent because, for one reason or another, they are wards of the state are risky subjects for publications or broadcasts that are made for advertising or trade purposes.

It is important to know that the person from whom consent is obtained is legally able to give consent.

3. Finally, consent to use a photograph of a person in an advertisement or on a poster cannot be used as a defense if the photograph is materially altered or changed. Several years ago a well-known and well-paid New York fashion model posed for pictures to be used in an advertising campaign for a bookstore. After the photography session, model Mary Jane Russell signed this standard release form:

> The undersigned hereby irrevocably consents to the unrestricted use by Richard Avedon [the photographer], advertisers, customers, successors, and assigns, of my name, portrait, or picture for advertising purposes or purposes of trade, and I waive the right to inspect or approve such completed portraits, pictures, or advertising matter used in connection therewith.

It sounds as though she signed her life away, and with regard to the pictures Avedon took she did. However, the bookstore sold one of the photographs to a maker of bed sheets. The bedding manufacturer had a reputation for running sleazy advertising and consequently had trouble getting first-class models to pose for advertising pictures. The manufacturer substantially retouched the Avedon photographs, changing the context. Mary Jane Russell sued for invasion of privacy, but the manufacturer answered her by telling the court that the model had given irrevocable consent for anyone to use those pictures, that she had waived her right to inspect the completed pictures and the advertising, and so forth.

The court agreed that Mary Jane had given up her right of privacy with regard to the pictures Avedon took. But the picture used by the sheet maker in its advertising was not the same picture taken by Avedon. It had been altered. And Mary Jane won her case. Justice Matthew Levy of the New York Supreme Court wrote (*Russell* v. *Marboro Books*, 1959):

> If the picture were altered sufficiently in situation, emphasis, background, or context, I should think that it would no longer be the same portrait, but a different one. And as to the changed picture, I would hold that the original written consent would not apply and that liability would arrive when the content of the picture has been so changed that it is substantially unlike the original.

What is substantial alteration? It probably means something other than minor retouching, but how much retouching is permissible before a privacy suit can accrue is difficult to say. This is one of the few cases on this legal point. Persons who want to retouch a photograph should be careful, even when they have written consent. They might change the picture sufficiently so that the consent would not apply.

The reference to altering the context of a picture arose recently in New York when a model sued and won after her seminude photograph was used to advertise an allegedly obscene movie. She had signed a release permitting the use of her photograph for "any purpose whatsoever," but the New York Supreme Court ruled that "any purpose whatsoever" does not include a "degrading use" (*Dittner* v. *Troma,* 1980).

Right of Publicity

In 1953, a distinguished American jurist, Jerome Frank, noted in an appropriation case that some plaintiffs might indeed be embarrassed and humiliated to see their name or face used to promote cornflakes or shampoo. Yet other plaintiffs, Frank argued, were not upset because they were humiliated; they were angry because they had not been paid for the commercial exploitation of their name or likeness (*Haelan Laboratories, Inc., v. Topps Chewing Gum,* 1953). Judge Frank identified what he called the "right of publicity," the right of persons to control the commercial exploitation of their name or likeness. The logic behind this assertion is that persons have a property right in their name just as they can have a property right in a book or a piece of land.

The relative youth and somewhat ambiguous state of the law of privacy resulted in most courts ignoring Judge Frank's ideas for many years. However, recently several jurisdictions have accepted the idea of this property right ancillary to the right of privacy.

Right of publicity cases generally involve persons who have developed a significant property right in their name through their exploits. Athletes, entertainers, writers, and other celebrities have all argued that the use of their name without consent and without compensation deprived them of rightful income. In cases in 1967 and 1970, courts ruled that several professional athletes, like Arnold Palmer and Jack Nicklaus, have the right to enjoy the fruits of their own industry free from unjustified interference and that celebrities have a legitimate proprietary interest in their public personality. These cases involved the use of the athletes' names and pictures in board games without compensation or permission (*Palmer* v. *Schonhorn Enterprises,* 1967, and *Uhlaender* v. *Henricksen,* 1970). A judge noted that the celebrity's "identity, embodied in his name, likeness, statistics and other personal characteristics, is the fruit of his labors and a type of property." However, in New Jersey a court said that even noncelebrities enjoy a property right in their identity when it ruled that a real estate company could not use a family's name and picture in its advertisements without permission (*Canessa* v. *J. I. Kislak,* 1967). "However little or much plaintiff's likeness and name may be worth," the judge wrote, "defendant, who has appropriated them for his commercial benefit, should be made to pay for what he has taken. . . ."

Some courts have simply refused to recognize the claims of the right of publicity. When comedian Pat Paulsen announced his candidacy for president in 1968, unauthorized campaign posters of the comedian were published. Paulsen sued, claiming appropriation of his likeness (*Paulsen* v. *Personality Posters*, 1968). But the court refused to compensate the entertainer, arguing that by declaring for president, even in jest, he had lost his right to privacy regarding his picture (see also *Man* v. *Warner Brothers,* 1970).

In its only ruling on the subject, the Supreme Court of the United States left many observers bewildered when it ruled that it is a violation of the right to publicity for a television station to broadcast news film of an entertainer's entire performance (*Zacchini* v. *Scripps-Howard Broadcasting Co.,* 1977). In a case that clearly proves the old judicial maxim that hard cases make bad law, the High Court overturned a decision by the Ohio Supreme Court and ruled that Hugo Zacchini, "The Human Cannonball," had indeed been harmed by the broadcast. The case was a hard one for at least two reasons. Zacchini's performance—being shot out of a cannon into a net—took only about fifteen seconds and consequently fit neatly into a small segment on a thirty-minute newscast. Obviously, such is not the case with most performers. Also, Zacchini had specifically asked the television station employees not to film the act, which was playing at a local county fair. A cameraman filmed it anyway. Zacchini argued that the television broadcast hurt his ability to make a living. Why should people pay to get into the fair to see his act if they had seen it on the television news? Justice Byron White and four other members of the Court agreed. The broadcast of the film of Zacchini's *entire* performance posed a substantial threat to the economic value of that performance, Justice White wrote. It went to the heart of his ability to earn a living as an entertainer, he added. Yet the ruling raised more questions than it answered. In previous right-of-publicity cases, the defendant had gained monetarily by exploiting the plaintiff's name or likeness. Yet in this case the television station had made no monetary gain from showing the short film of Zacchini being shot from a cannon. The cannon shot was a news item, like an automobile accident or a street parade.

White made the point that the station televised the *entire act*. But what does this mean? Zacchini took several minutes to do his act—adjusting the net, preparing to get into the cannon, building the suspense. The film lasted but fifteen seconds and included only the actual cannon shot. Would a newspaper be prohibited from publishing a detailed word description of the feats of Zacchini? If Zacchini were seriously injured in performing this stunt, could the accident be safely filmed? The dissenters in the case argued strongly—but to little avail—that the important question to be decided was not whether Zacchini's *entire act* was broadcast, but the purpose for which the film was used. Had the station filmed the shot, promoted it, built a show around it, and got advertisers to pay money to sponsor it? Such action would clearly be exploitation of Zacchini. But this was a routine newscast, Justice Powell noted. There was no violation of any right.

The Zacchini case will probably have little impact upon the emerging—and often confusing—right of publicity. White's ruling was based largely on the fact that the television station telecast the *entire act*. Since few performers have such abbreviated acts, there seem to be few persons who could use the ruling as a precedent in a similar suit.

The right of privacy is a personal right and generally ends upon the death of the individual. But the right of publicity—based upon a theory of property rights—does not necessarily terminate upon death. In some instances it may be passed on to benefit the heirs, like any other part of the estate. The law on this question, which has only been raised recently, is currently being decided on a state-by-state basis. In about eight states legislation has been adopted. In Kentucky, for example, a 1984 law states that the name or likeness of a person who is a public figure shall not be used for commercial profit for a period of fifty years from the date of death without the written consent of the heirs. Tennessee and California have similar laws, and statutes in Florida, Nebraska, Oklahoma, Utah, and Virginia all speak in some way to the question of the rights of heirs.

Litigation of this question in other states has produced a ragged profile for the law, one that seems to be heading in three different directions. In some states, courts have ruled that the right to publicity is not descendible; it may not be passed on to heirs (see *Reeves* v. *United Artists*, 1983, for example). In other states, courts have ruled that the right of publicity may be passed on to heirs, but only if the deceased had attempted to exploit this right while he or she was alive. In other words, the public figure had to have capitalized on his or her fame to create the property right to pass on to the heirs. This is the direction in which the California law was proceeding prior to the adoption of a state statute (see *Lugosi* v. *Universal*, 1979 and *Acme* v. *Kuperstock*, 1983). Finally, some state courts have ruled that the right may be passed on to heirs, regardless of whether the deceased attempted to exploit it while he or she was alive (see *The Martin Luther King Center* v. *American Heritage Products*, 1982).

Large advertising agencies have routinely sought permission from estates to insure that clients are not embarrassed by lawsuits. After IBM chose Charlie Chaplin's Little Tramp character to promote its line of personal computers, the company sought a license from the owner of the rights, Bubbles, Inc., before beginning the campaign. Licensing fees can be very expensive, according to an article in *The New York Times*, sometimes as much as $10,000 for the use of a character or likeness in one sixty-second commercial. It is advisable for anyone seeking to use the name or likeness of a dead celebrity in an advertisement to gain permission from the heirs. While the courts and legislatures in most states have not yet decided whether or not the right to publicity is descendible, the clear trend is toward protecting that right for use by the heirs.

SUMMARY

Appropriation of a person's name or likeness for commercial or trade purposes without permission is an invasion of privacy. Use of an individual's photograph, a sketch of the person, a nickname, or a stage name are all considered use of a name or likeness. However, the publication of news and information in magazines, books, newspapers, and news broadcasts is not considered a trade purpose, even though the mass medium may make a profit from such publication. Consequently, persons who are named or pictured in news stories or other such material cannot sue for appropriation. Also, a news medium may republish or rebroadcast news items or photographs already carried as news stories in advertising for the mass medium to establish the quality or kind of material carried by the medium.

Anyone who seeks to use the name or likeness of an individual for commercial or trade purposes should gain written consent from that person. Even written consent may be invalid as a defense in an invasion of privacy suit if the consent was given many years before publication, if the person from whom the consent was gained cannot legally give consent, or if the photograph or other material that is used is substantially altered.

Courts have also recognized what is known as the right to publicity. Right to publicity actions are most often instituted by well-known persons who believe the unauthorized use of their name or likeness has deprived them of an opportunity to reap financial gain by selling this right to the user. The United States Supreme Court has ruled that it is a violation of the right to publicity for a television news station to broadcast an entertainer's complete act without permission, even if this is done in the context of a news broadcast. In some states the right to publicity can be passed on to heirs like any other piece of property, which means that a performer's estate can control the use of his or her name and likeness after the performer's death.

INTRUSION

The intrusion category is what a lot of people think of when they hear the phrase "right to privacy." Wiretapping, using cameras with telephoto lenses, peeping-Tom actions, bugging rooms, and using supersensitive microphones and hidden transmitters are the kinds of behavior that many people—especially people outside the press—associate with violations of the right to privacy. This kind of behavior does occur, people are caught, and lawsuits do result. Until recently such suits were simply not brought against mass-media defendants. Even now such litigation is relatively rare.

The press does not often go in for this kind of snooping, or at least does not get caught frequently. Probably, the earliest known intrusion case involving the press occurred in 1926 when a reporter for the *Washington* (D.C.) *Herald* stole a picture from the home of Mrs. Louise Peed, who had nearly died from asphyxiation when a gas jet was carelessly left open in the home of a friend she was visiting. The court held the newspaper responsible because it had published the plaintiff's picture, not because it had stolen the picture (*Peed* v. *Washington Times Co.,* 1927). A similar suit in Los Angeles a few years later failed altogether (*Metter* v. *Los Angeles Examiner,* 1939).

The *Peed* case points out a very important aspect of intrusion in invasion of privacy. In appropriation cases and in cases based upon publication of private information or publication of falsehoods, the legal wrong occurs when the picture or story is published. It must be published. A photographer who takes a picture of a skier, enlarges it to eight-by-ten inches, and hangs it on his or her kitchen wall has not invaded the skier's privacy. If the photographer were to publish the picture in an advertisement, for example, appropriation, an illegal invasion of privacy, then occurs. If a newspaper reporter uncovers private information about a teacher's life but keeps the information confidential, no invasion of privacy occurs. Only when the reporter publishes this information might a lawsuit succeed.

In intrusion, however, the legal wrong is committed as soon as the intrusion takes place, whether or not the fruits of the intrusion are published. If your home is bugged, someone intrudes upon your privacy. Invasion of privacy occurred regardless of whether the content of the overheard conversations are published. If a reporter breaks into a private office and copies information from a private file, his act would probably be considered an invasion of privacy, an intrusion.

Intrusion cases are not too common. Those that have occurred seem to fall into a handful of categories. Here are some examples of the kinds of intrusion problems faced by the mass media.

Publication of Material Obtained Through Intrusion

In two cases in the late sixties, federal courts in Washington, D.C., established the principle that a news medium that publishes material obtained via intrusion by someone not connected with the medium cannot be held liable for the intrusion. In the two instances, the late newspaper columnist Drew Pearson obtained documents from private files of the Liberty Lobby, a right-wing, public-interest group in Washington, and from the files of former Connecticut Senator Thomas Dodd. Employees of both Dodd and Liberty Lobby took the files from the private offices, made copies of them (which were given to Pearson), and then returned the purloined files. In both cases the court ruled that the publishers could not be held responsible for the actions of the intruders (*Liberty Lobby* v. *Pearson,* 1968; *Pearson* v. *Dodd,* 1969).

Judge J. Skelly Wright wrote in the *Dodd* case:

> If we were to hold appellants liable for invasion of privacy on these facts, we would establish the proposition that one who receives information from an intruder, knowing it has been obtained by improper intrusion, is guilty of a tort. In an untried and developing area of tort law, we are not prepared to go so far, . . .

This principle was supported in 1978 by a Maryland circuit court when several former and current members of the University of Maryland basketball team sued the *Baltimore Evening Star* for publishing an article that revealed portions of their academic records. Somebody gave the newspaper the information. There was no evidence presented that the reporters had either personally inspected the records or asked someone else to do it. Consequently, no suit could be maintained by the athletes on the intrusion theory (*Bilney* v. *Evening Star,* 1979).

Possessing Stolen Property

There is, however, another aspect of intrusion that can result in a problem for a journalist. If a reporter has original files that belong to someone else, a suit based on the doctrine of conversion could possibly be maintained. Conversion means to unlawfully convert someone else's property for your own use. This is property law and would be applicable only if journalists have the actual files—someone else's property—in their possession. In both the *Dodd* and *Liberty Lobby* cases just noted, the plaintiffs attempted to sue for conversion, but columnist Pearson did not have the original files, only copies of those files. Hence, no conversion had occurred.

In California the publisher and a reporter of the *Los Angeles Free Press* were found guilty of possession of stolen goods after they bought a list of names of undercover narcotic agents stolen from the attorney general's office. Art Kunkin and Robert Applebaum were freed upon appeal to the state's high court, but only because there was insufficient evidence to prove that they had known the list was stolen when they purchased it (*People* v. *Kunkin,* 1973). If the state could have adduced any evidence at all that the pair had knowledge that the list was stolen, the conviction would have stood. As it was, the thief was a former employee of the attorney general's office, and Kunkin and Applebaum said they thought he still worked for the attorney general. The thief also asked that they return the list to him after it was copied, presumably to return it to the proper file, the two journalists said.

This whole area of the law is gray. Of course, if employees of the publication are the intruders, liability might result, depending upon whether they acted on their own or at the employer's suggestion. In any case, intruders are always liable if they are caught, regardless of what use is made of the purloined material.

Journalists should ask tough questions of their sources of documents and files. Did you steal it? Did you copy it illegally? If a jury can be convinced that the journalist knew it was obtained illegally, or should have known it was obtained illegally (secret files, for example, can normally only be obtained illegally), a suit based on property law, not on privacy, might then in fact hold up.

News Gathering

While reporters may not engage in stealing or breaking and entering, they sometimes undertake other kinds of intrusions. These intrusions are harder to define, and generally involve the use of snooper aids; that is, hidden cameras, telephoto lens, and hidden microphones.

No broad, general proposition can be stated here, and we must rely instead upon examples. Hopefully, as more and more cases are litigated, the gaps will be filled and a rule formulated. Reporters have the right to photograph persons in public places, even when they do not know they are being photographed. These people are present in a public, not a private, place and are visible to anyone passing by. A ruling by the Eighth United States Circuit Court of Appeals supports this proposition. An attorney who was jailed for drunken driving became angry when jailed and began hitting and banging on the cell door, hollering and cursing and calling police officers names. The sounds were recorded by a television reporter, who played them during a newscast. The attorney sued for invasion of privacy, but the appellate court ruled that there was no zone of privacy in a jail cell. The court ruled that the reporter "could not be prevented from reporting the statements he could so easily overhear aurally; use of a device to record them cannot create a claim for privacy when one would not otherwise exist." The court noted that undoubtedly the plaintiff had not made his boisterous outbursts with any expectation of privacy at all (*Holman* v. *Central Arkansas Broadcasting*, 1979).

On record is a case in which harassment, not invasion of privacy, was charged. The photographer was Ron Galella, whose whole life seemed to revolve around taking pictures of Jacqueline Kennedy Onassis. He went everywhere she went, blocked her path, made a general nuisance of himself. When he was not around Mrs. Onassis, he followed the Kennedy children. In one instance his penchant for getting close almost resulted in a serious accident for young John Kennedy when the horse he was riding bolted after being frightened by Galella. The Secret Service, which guards the Kennedy children and Mrs. Onassis, went to court to stop Galella. A federal court enjoined the photographer from coming within twenty-four feet of Mrs. Onassis and within thirty feet of the children, from blocking their movement in any way, from doing anything that might put them in danger or might harass, alarm, or frighten them and from entering the children's play area at school (*Galella* v. *Onassis,* 1973). In 1982 a United States district court in New York found Galella in contempt of court for violating this order on twelve separate occasions. The photographer faced a severe fine and possible imprisonment (*Galella* v. *Onassis,* 1982).

The lawsuit against Galella was based on harassment. Could an invasion of privacy suit for intrusion have worked as well for Mrs. Onassis? No. Taking pictures on a public street or in a public schoolyard is not considered an intrusion. In an intrusion suit the courts will ask, Was there any legitimate expectation of privacy or solitude for the plaintiff when the photograph was taken? There can be none in a public setting. What can be seen on a public street or in a public park is open to public scrutiny.

A pharmacist in Seattle, Washington, sued KING-TV for invasion of privacy after the television station photographed the interior of his pharmacy through the front window. The druggist had been charged with cheating the state out of Medicaid funds. He refused to talk with reporters after the charges were made, so the KING-TV camera operator placed the camera against the outside of the store's front window and photographed the druggist as he talked on the telephone. The filming was done from the exterior of the building, from a place open to the public. The court ruled that an intrusion must be something that the general public would not be free to view. In this case any passerby could have seen what was recorded on film by the KING-TV camera operator. There was no unwarranted intrusion (*Marks* v. *King Broadcasting,* 1980).

There are some instances when an invasion of privacy suit based upon photography may very well stand. For example, imagine that a homeowner has a fenced-in yard with a pool. The pool area is hidden from public view by a fence and foliage. Surely someone at pool side would legitimately enjoy the expectation of privacy. But a photographer climbs a nearby hill and using a supertelephoto lens takes photographs of persons swimming in the pool. This action could very likely be considered an intrusion. Or imagine that a photographer films the interior of a home through a crack in the draperies while standing on private property surrounding the home. This is a scene that a passerby would not see. This, too, is fertile ground for an intrusion suit. Many problems also surround the use of hidden cameras and recording devices, as the next series of cases readily demonstrates.

A disabled veteran and journeyman plumber named A. A. Dietemann practiced healing using clay, minerals, and herbs. Dietemann practiced his strange version of medicine in his home. It was there that two *Life* magazine reporters who had agreed to work with Los Angeles law enforcement people visited the healer. Jackie Metcalf and William Ray pretended they were married, and Ms. Metcalf complained of a lump in her breast. Dietemann diagnosed the ailment as due to rancid butter she had eaten eleven years, nine months, seven days previously. While the "doctor" examined Ms. Metcalf, Ray photographed him with a secret camera. The conversation between the reporters (who did not reveal that they were reporters) and the healer was also broadcast via a hidden microphone to investigators waiting in a car outside.

Dietemann was arrested weeks later and charged with practicing medicine without a license. *Life* photographers took more pictures at the time of the arrest, and in an article on medical quackery included those pictures with pictures taken by the hidden camera. Dietemann sued for invasion of privacy. *Life* magazine said the pictures were informational and newsworthy and were protected. The court agreed that the pictures were indeed newsworthy but ruled that the photos taken with the hidden camera had been obtained by intruding upon Dietemann's privacy. The magazine had the right to publish the pictures; the publication did not constitute an invasion of privacy. It was the use of the secret camera and microphone that turned the relatively routine news-gathering venture into an illegal intrusion into Dietemann's privacy. Judge Shirley Hufstedler wrote (*Dietemann v. Time, Inc.,* 1971):

> One who invites another into his home or office takes a risk that the visitor may not be what he seems, and that the visitor may repeat all he hears and observes when he leaves. But he does not and should not be required to take the risk that what is heard and seen will be transmitted by photography or recording, or in our modern world, in full living color and hi-fi to the public at large or any segment of it that the visitor might select.

Recognizing that news gathering is an integral part of news dissemination, Judge Hufstedler said she still did not believe there was a need to use mechanical devices in gathering information:

> The First Amendment is not a license to trespass, to steal, or to intrude by electronic means into the precincts of another's home or office. It does not become such a license simply because the person subjected to the intrusion is reasonably suspected of committing a crime.

The magazine protested, saying the story was simply an example of good investigative reporting. Judge Hufstedler was unimpressed:

> Investigative reporting is an ancient art; its successful practice long antecedes the invention of miniature cameras and electronic devices. The First Amendment has never been construed to accord newsmen immunity from torts or crimes committed during the course of news gathering.

The facts in the *Dietemann* case are significant. And as more and more intrusion cases are decided, this ruling stands out as an unusual, not typical decision; one tied very closely to the unusual facts in this case. The reporters were in the plaintiff's home, almost as uninvited visitors, taking secret pictures and making a clandestine recording of the conversation. Cases since 1971 demonstrate the narrow bases of the Dietemann ruling.

In 1975 Arlyn Cassidy and several other Chicago police officers were acting as undercover agents, investigating massage parlors in the city. The owner of one massage parlor where police previously had made arrests believed he was being harassed by the lawmen and invited a television news camera crew to come in and secretly film an encounter between an undercover agent and a model at the parlor. The camera was set up behind a two-way mirror and was filming when officer Cassidy came in, paid thirty dollars for deluxe lingerie modeling, and subsequently arrested the girl for solicitation. Three other agents came into the room at about the same time the television news crew burst through another door, filming as they left the building. The officers sued the station for intrusion, using the *Dietemann* case as precedent.

But the Illinois appellate court ruled in favor of the journalists, distinguishing the *Dietemann* case in some important ways. First, Cassidy and the other plaintiffs were public officers acting in the line of duty as the filming took place. Second, the film crew was not in a private home, but in a public business. And third, the crew was on hand at the invitation of the operator of the premises. "In our opinion," the court ruled, "no right of privacy against intrusion can be said to exist with reference to the gathering and dissemination of news concerning discharge of public duties" (*Cassidy* v. *ABC,* 1978).

In 1979 a Kentucky circuit court ruled that it was not an intrusion when a young woman, at the instigation of a newspaper, secretly recorded a conversation she had with an attorney. Kristie Frazier met with attorney John T. McCall after she was indicted on a drug charge. According to Ms. Frazier, the attorney said he would guarantee that he could get her "off the hook" if she could come up with $10,000. He said he would return $9,000 if he failed to have her set free. Setting a fee in a criminal case in such a manner is considered unethical conduct for an attorney.

Ms. Frazier, who apparently was no stranger to legal problems, recognized the unusual fee arrangement and went to the offices of the *Louisville Courier-Journal*. Reporters were interested in Ms. Frazier's allegations against McCall but were unwilling to take her word for what had been said in the private conversation. They gave her a small tape recorder and told her to propose a second meeting with McCall—to try to trap him into repeating what he had said earlier. McCall repeated his proposal, Ms. Frazier recorded it secretly, and the *Courier-Journal* published the transcript. McCall sued for intrusion, but lost.

The court distinguished *Dietemann* by noting that Frazier—who may or may not have been an agent of the newspaper—was in McCall's office at his invitation. There was no intrusion into McCall's private affairs because they were also the affairs of Ms. Frazier. "A lawyer, an officer of the court, discussing in a public court with a potential client, is not in seclusion within the meaning of the law," the court ruled. "Human dignity demands the rights of privacy be enforced, but when the rights of privacy encroach upon the most sacred trust the public possesses, namely, the judicial system, then those rights must give way," the judge added (*McCall* v. *Courier-Journal*, 1979). The trial court ruling for the newspaper was upheld in March 1980 by the Kentucky court of appeals.

Cassidy and *McCall* have chipped away at some of the fears the press had after the *Dietemann* case. The California case must be viewed as a fairly narrow ruling. Remember, the intrusion in *Dietemann* took place in the plaintiff's home, and Anglo-American courts have protected a citizen's home from government intrusions for centuries. ("A man's home is his castle," ruled Lord Chief Justice Sir Edward Coke in the early seventeenth century.) Remember also that the reporters carried hidden electronic devices into the plaintiff's home. The courts have suggested that different rules apply in public places and in business offices, especially when public officers (such as police officers and attorneys, who are considered officers of the court) are being scrutinized in the performance of their duty.

A brief note; the surreptitious recording of a conversation may violate either federal or state law. Sandra Boddie sued ABC television for secretly videotaping and recording an interview she willingly gave to Geraldo Rivera for a segment on the program "20/20." She had refused to give the interview on camera. She sued for defamation and invasion of privacy and lost. But she also brought a civil action under the federal wiretap statute, which makes it illegal to "willfully intercept . . . any oral communication" for the purpose of committing any criminal or tortious act. ABC contended it did not intend to commit a crime or a tortious act, but the Sixth U.S. Court of Appeals ruled that a jury should decide whether or not the network acted with a purpose to injure Boddie (*Boddie* v. *ABC,* 1984). Also, many states require the consent of both parties to a conversation before it can be recorded. Check the law in your state.

Some persons have expressed concern that an intrusion may occur if a reporter poses as someone other than a reporter to gain a story. That is not likely; the fact that reporters posed as patients in the *Dietemann* case does not appear to be a material consideration. This conclusion is strengthened by the decision in *Rifkin* v. *Esquire,* 1982, when a United States district court in California ruled that no invasion of privacy took place when reporters posed as a friend of the plaintiff, Stan Rifkin, in order to get information about Rifkin from his friends and neighbors. The court said this did not constitute an intrusion upon plaintiff Rifkin's solitude.

Because intrusion is such a new area of the law, no good defenses have been developed. A heavy burden rests upon the plaintiff to prove that the behavior by the reporter or cameraman was in fact an intrusion, an invasion of privacy. If invasion of privacy can be established, there are no good "legal excuses" with which to defend this behavior. In addition to the legal problems involved, members of the press themselves have begun to raise ethical questions about such behavior. Defending illegal behavior on the grounds that it is in the public interest is an excuse that the American people seemed to reject when the members of the Nixon White House used it in 1973 and 1974. There are few causes that are "good enough" to justify illegal intrusion upon the privacy of others. Intrusion as an aspect of invasion of privacy should really not be a problem to journalists who conduct their business in an ethical fashion. Still, the paucity of good guidelines at this time can be somewhat frightening. Until there is more law to guide the press, journalists are advised to be guided by the common sense, conscience, and integrity one normally expects from responsible adults.

Trespass

An invasion of privacy suit for intrusion is one legal problem facing a reporter who pursues the news a bit too aggressively. Other intrusion-like situations must be understood. **Trespass,** the failure to respect authorized police barricades and the failure to obey the lawful order of a police officer can pose other equally serious problems for journalists. In the past ten years numerous reporters and news organizations have been convicted for failing to respect property lines. This line of trespass cases began in Florida in 1976. A photographer and a reporter were invited by police and fire officials into a house that had been gutted by fire. The owner of the house, who was not on the premises at the time of the fire, later brought suit for trespass against the journalists. The journalists were exonerated in this instance, but only because the homeowner had not objected at the time the newspaper people entered the home. The Florida Supreme Court said it was common custom for the press to inspect private premises after a serious fire or a crime and that this common custom constituted a kind of indirect consent to the trespass. But it was clear from the court's opinion that had the homeowner been at the scene of the fire and objected to the reporter and photographer coming on the property, common custom or not, the journalists would have been guilty of trespass (*Florida Publishing Co.* v. *Fletcher,* 1976).

As if to emphasize what could have happened to the reporters in Florida, a state court in New York sustained a trespass action against a broadcasting film crew stemming from an incident at an exclusive New York City restaurant. The news crew had been sent to visit various restaurants cited by local authorities for health code violations. The crew entered the restaurant with its cameras rolling and floodlights on. Although the proprietor of the restaurant commanded the reporters to leave, the journalists stayed with the cameras and continued to film until they were physically escorted from the premises. In the meantime, customers ducked under tables, and some fled without paying their bills.

The broadcasting company, CBS, attempted to defend its action by using the First Amendment as a shield to protect itself from the trespass suit. The court disagreed. "Clearly, the First Amendment is not a shibboleth before which all other rights must succumb," the judge ruled (*Le Mistral, Inc.* v. *CBS,* 1978):

> This Court recognizes that the exercise of the right of free speech and free press demands and even mandates the observance of the co-equal duty not to abuse such right, but to utilize it with right reason and dignity. Vain lip service to "duties" in a vacuous reality wherein "rights" exist, sovereign and independent of any balancing moral or social factor, creates a semantical mockery of the very foundation of our laws and legal system.

In a subsequent trespass action that mirrored the facts in *Fletcher,* the New York Supreme Court in Monroe County followed the *Le Mistral* precedent closely. A Humane Society investigator obtained a search warrant to enter a home whose occupants had been the object of numerous complaints of cruelty to animals. The investigator invited reporters and film crews from three television stations to accompany him in this foray. The journalists went inside the home, despite the protests of one of the occupants, filmed the interior of the home, and then broadcast the news story. In a lawsuit that followed, the television stations attempted to raise the defense of "implied consent through custom and usage" accepted by the Florida courts in the *Fletcher* case, but the New York court disagreed vigorously.

The so-called implied consent to enter a private home is a custom created by the press itself, the judge noted. "This is a boot-strapping argument," he said, that does not eliminate the trespass in this case. News people do not stand in any favored position with regard to trespass, the judge said. "If the news media were to succeed in compelling an uninvited and nonpermitted entry into one's private home whenever it chose to do so, this would be nothing less than a general warrant equivalent to the writs of assistance which were so odious to the American colonists," he added (*Anderson* v. *WROC-TV,* 1981).

Reporters in Oklahoma were found guilty of criminal trespass when they followed protestors into restricted areas during demonstrations at a nuclear facility. The Oklahoma Court of Criminal Appeals ruled that journalists enjoyed reasonable access to the events taking place in areas set aside by authorities for the press and for legal protests and did not need to trespass to get the story (*Stahl* v. *Oklahoma,* 1983). The fact that reporters could have legally viewed this news event without trespassing is an important element in this ruling. A federal court in Massachusetts ruled in 1982 that the government could not unreasonably limit press access to the scene of a tragic air crash. The National Transportation Safety Board opened the crash site to the press only one hour per day. The district court said the government had failed to establish a reason for such limited press access to the crash scene. The court cited two important elements in lifting the government ban. First, the crash site was on public, not private, property. The court said it might come to a different conclusion if private property were involved. Next, there was not an adequate and clear alternative means of access for the press to get the desired kinds of information and pictures about the crash. Reporters sought access to the site, not to the wreckage itself, the judge noted (*Westinghouse Broadcasting* v. *National Transportation Safety Board,* 1982).

The trespass problem is likely to be more common in the future and could become even more difficult to resolve. A Colorado district court judge recently noted that in the past the press has been afforded considerable First Amendment protection when disseminating the news, but very limited (if any) protection when gathering the news. But the judge asked, When a television reporter is standing in a field, instantly reporting a story with an electronic instant cam or live-action cam is that gathering or disseminating the news? The court suggested that charges of trespass should stand only if reporters were aware that they were committing a trespass and if the plaintiff suffered damage as a result of the trespass (*Allen* v. *Combined Communications,* 1981).

But a charge of trespass is not the only problem that faces a reporter in news gathering. The New Jersey Supreme Court recently upheld the disorderly person conviction of a press photographer who was charged with impeding a police officer in the performance of his duty at the scene of a serious traffic accident. The photographer was standing near the wreckage when the state trooper, who feared a fire might begin and who also wanted to preserve the accident scene for investigation, ordered the area cleared of spectators. The news photographer moved back five feet, but when he refused to move any farther, he was arrested.

The journalist, Harvey J. Lashinsky, argued that the state's disorderly person statute was inapplicable to him because he was a member of the press. The state's High Court disagreed, noting that "the constitutional prerogatives of the press must yield under appropriate circumstances to other important and legitimate interests." Acknowledging that the press does play a special role in society, the court nevertheless said that the photographer clearly impeded the officer by refusing his request to leave the area. While the officer was arguing with the journalist, he could have been giving assistance to the accident victims and beginning the investigation of the crash (*State* v. *Lashinsky,* 1979).

The brief discussion of these cases makes it clear that the courts will insist that reporters, like all other citizens, obey the law; their status as members of the press, which is granted protection under the First Amendment, is generally immaterial when they are called upon to account for their behavior while gathering news for publication and broadcast.

SUMMARY   Intruding upon an individual's solitude is an invasion of privacy. While the press is not often the subject of intrusion privacy suits, cases have occurred more often in recent years. An invasion of privacy takes place as soon as the intrusion has been made. Publication of the fruits of the intrusion is irrelevant in such cases. Journalists will not normally be held responsible for intrusion if they publish material that other persons have obtained through an intrusion. However, the journalist may be charged with the possession of stolen goods if in fact the material was stolen and the news person is aware of that fact.

Courts will not permit a successful intrusion suit based upon the recording of events that take place in public places. The court will permit a suit only if the plaintiff in the case can prove that at the time the intrusion was made, there was a "legitimate expectation of solitude"; that is, the plaintiff was in a place where he or she could expect to be alone. Courts are sensitive about protecting the privacy of a home and are likely to rule it is an intrusion to secretly film or record what occurs there. Courts are less sensitive about protecting what takes place in a business office.

In addition to the danger of intrusion suits, reporters are expected to obey other laws as they gather news. Unauthorized crossing of property lines can result in a criminal or civil trespass suit. Failure to obey the order of a police officer can result in a charge of disorderly conduct. The responsibility of gathering the news does not place journalists above the law.

PUBLICITY ABOUT PRIVATE FACTS

The most controversial aspect of the right of privacy in the current decade is that aspect of the law which penalizes the publication of private information about a person. The *Restatement of the Law of Torts* defines this section of the law this way:

> One who gives publicity to a matter concerning the private life of another is subject to liability to the other for invasion of his privacy, if the matter publicized is of a kind that
> a. would be highly offensive to a reasonable person, and
> b. is not of legitimate concern to the public.

This, of course, is the kind of privacy protection that Warren and Brandeis sought in 1890. Strangely, as we will see shortly, American courts have been most reluctant to curb this kind of journalism, for it touches at the very foundation of our long-held notions about freedom of the press. Most American judges find it difficult, if not impossible, to impose liability upon a newspaper or broadcasting station for the publication or broadcast of truthful information. This attitude has angered many persons, who suggest that members of the press use this freedom irresponsibly to probe and publicize intimate information about the famous and the not-so-famous or to prey upon the private lives of victims of crime and other tragedy. While most journalists don't do this, those who do have generated a strong antipress feeling among large and often vocal segments of the public. The reluctance of judges to rule for plaintiffs in these private facts cases has suggested to some scholars that this area of privacy has no real validity. But that is not the case, for occasionally judges are willing to draw the line. Reporters need to be aware of the guidelines that do exist, as generous as they are. Reporters also need to reflect upon their ethical and moral responsibilities as well as their legal liabilities.

Most courts use a two-step evaluation in considering whether this kind of invasion of privacy has occurred. This method also lends itself to presentation of a simple explanation of the law. First, the determination must be made that private facts about a person's life have indeed been publicized, which requires examination of two concepts: publicity and private facts. The information or facts publicized must be private, not known to other persons. And these facts must have been publicized. The plaintiff must prove both elements. If there *has been* publicity about private facts, a second evaluation must be made. The questions asked are, (1) Would this publicity be highly offensive to a reasonable person? and (2) Was the matter published of legitimate public concern? In this second stage, a kind of balancing process normally results, with the importance to the public of the revelation of the private material being weighed against how offensive the publication is to the plaintiff. While guidelines do exist, the balancing process often tends to be quite subjective, and matters of personal taste and sensitivity frequently play a role in the outcome. Reporters should spend time in considering how to present important but sensitive material in the least offensive manner.

This category of right to privacy can be best understood by considering each of the two elements of the law individually.

Publicity

The words *publicity* and *publication* mean different things in privacy law than they do in libel law. In defamation, *publication* means to communicate the material to a single third party. The word *publicity* in privacy law implies far more. It means that the material is communicated to the public at large or to a great number of people, making it certain that the facts will shortly become public knowledge. Needless to say this kind of publicity can usually be presumed when a story is published in a newspaper or broadcast over radio and television.

Private Facts

Before there can be an invasion of privacy, it must be demonstrated that the material publicized was indeed private. What happens in public is considered public information. A fan at a Pittsburgh Steeler football game urged a news photographer to take his picture. The photographer did, but when the photograph was published in *Sports Illustrated*, the fan sued for invasion of privacy, arguing that the photograph revealed that his trousers were unzipped and that this was quite embarrassing. The District Court for Eastern Pennsylvania ruled against the plaintiff, primarily because the picture was taken in a public place with the defendant's knowledge and encouragement. It was not private information (*Neff* v. *Time, Inc.,* 1976). Similarly, the United States Court of Appeals (D.C. circuit) refused to find liability for the broadcast of news film that showed two men on a public street being escorted by police officers. Plaintiff Darryl Harrison argued that the pictures were embarrassing because they portrayed him as being a criminal. But the court ruled that an action for invasion of privacy cannot be maintained for pictures of events that take place in public view. The photographer in this case was standing on a public sidewalk while he took the pictures (*Harrison* v. *Washington Post,* 1978). The Massachusetts court of appeals ruled that no privacy exists when a person is standing in a line at a government building. The plaintiff in the case was photographed while standing in a line of persons waiting to collect unemployment benefits at the state employment security office. "The appearance of a person in a public place necessarily involves doffing the cloak of privacy which the law protects," the court ruled (*Cefalu* v. *Globe Newspaper,* 1979; see also *Arrington* v. *New York Times,* 1982).

Three revelers at a San Francisco Exotic Erotic Halloween Ball brought suit against *Penthouse* when it published their pictures in the magazine. They complained they had not given permission to the photographer to take their pictures; in fact, they had not even known the pictures were taken. The California Court of Appeals said that was immaterial. It doesn't make the facts any less public. Thousands of other persons attending the ball saw the plaintiffs. These were not private facts (*Martin* v. *Penthouse,* 1986).

If a large segment of the public is already aware of supposedly intimate or personal information, it is not private. Oliver Sipple, a man who deflected a gun held by a woman who tried to assassinate President Gerald Ford, sued the *San Francisco Chronicle* after a columnist noted that Sipple was a homosexual and that that may be the reason Ford had never thanked his benefactor for his heroic act. But Sipple's suit failed, in part at least, because his sexual orientation was hardly a secret in San Francisco. The California Court of Appeals noted that Sipple routinely frequented gay bars, marched in parades with other homosexuals, openly worked for the election of homosexual political candidates and that many gay publications had reported stories about his activities in the homosexual community. That he was a homosexual was not a private fact, the court ruled (*Sipple* v. *Chronicle Publishing,* 1984).

In 1975 the United States Supreme Court ruled that the broadcast or publication of the name of a rape victim that was included in the public record during a criminal trial could not be considered an invasion of privacy. At that time, at least four states had statutes making the publication of such information an invasion of privacy. The rationale for such laws was generally accepted: nonpublication would save victims from embarrassment and might, in turn, encourage more women to report such incidents. Decreased reporting of names might therefore result in more prosecutions of rapists. There had been at least two decisions prior to the 1975 ruling upholding these laws (see, for example, *Nappier* v. *Jefferson Standard Life Insurance Co.*, 1963). When an Atlanta, Georgia, television station broadcast the name of a young woman who had been raped and murdered, her parents sued. In *Cox Broadcasting Co.* v. *Cohn* (1975), the United States Supreme Court overturned the Georgia state court ruling and held that the press cannot be held liable for invasion of privacy for reporting information already part of the public record. Justice Byron White noted that most persons depend upon the mass media for information about the operations of the government via public meetings and the public record. Judicial proceedings are an important part of our governmental system and are something in which the public has always expressed a great interest. By making judicial records and proceedings public, the state of Georgia must have concluded that the public interest was being served (*Cox Broadcasting Co.* v. *Cohn*, 1975):

> We are reluctant to embark on a course that would make public records generally available to the media but forbid their publication if offensive to the sensibilities of the supposed reasonable man. Such a rule would make it very difficult for the press to inform their readers about the public business and yet stay within the law. The rule would invite timidity and self-censorship and very likely lead to the suppression of many items that would otherwise be put into print and that should be made available to the public.

Quoting the latest revision of the *Restatement of Torts* (2nd ed.), which attempts to summarize the law of torts, the Court said, "There is no liability when the defendant merely gives further publicity to information about the plaintiff which is already public. Thus there is no liability for giving publicity to facts about the plaintiff's life which are matters of public record."

Since 1975 the impact of the decision in *Cox* v. *Cohn* has been felt nationwide. A 1982 New Jersey ruling is a good example. When the victim of a sexual assault in Willingboro, New Jersey, reported the crime, she asked police to keep her name and address confidential. The hospital at which she was treated routinely gave out her name, and a reporter for the *Burlington County Times* followed up the story by talking with a police officer who was investigating the case. Three stories were published about the incident, and in each the plaintiff was identified. Details of the attack were not included, however. In her invasion of privacy suit, the plaintiff argued that this case was different from *Cox* v. *Cohn* where the reporter got the information from an official court record. This story was obtained orally from a police officer. But the New Jersey Superior Court rejected the plaintiff's argument. "The fact that the story was derived directly from a person in charge of the investigation and not from a written record of such investigation . . . does not distinguish [this case from] *Cox* in the opinion of the court." The police officer was an official source, the court ruled. This was a matter of great public interest (*Griffith* v. *Rancocas Valley Hospital et al.,* 1982).

Despite the legal resolution of this issue in *Cox* v. *Cohn,* the publication of the name of a rape victim remains a controversial social question. Many persons ask that newspapers and broadcasting stations think about the harm that can result from such identification and balance that with the limited public good that derives from such publication or broadcast.

It is fair to say that the ruling in *Cox* v. *Cohn* stands for the broad proposition that any information taken from a public record will not be considered a private fact for purposes of an invasion of privacy suit. But a note of caution is justified. Governments keep all kinds of records, some of which are public, some of which are not. A reporter who has taken information from a government-held record that is not considered a public record may have difficulty arguing that the facts in question are publicly known, are not private facts (see *Patterson* v. *Tribune Co.,* 1962, for example).

Offensive Material

If the determination has been made that private facts about a person's life have been published, a court must then ask two subsequent questions:

1. Would the publication of the material offend a reasonable person?
2. Was the published material of legitimate public concern?

Frequently courts are faced with the real dilemma that while revelation of the material was extremely offensive and embarrassing, its publication, however, was of great importance for the public. Except in extremely unusual circumstances, the press will win such decisions. The judiciary places great weight upon the role of the press as an agent to inform and enlighten the public upon matters of interest and importance. Judges have ruled time and again that it is the responsibility of the press to bring such "newsworthy" information to the people. And courts have been hesitant to define narrow limits upon what the public needs to know or upon the kinds of information in which the people have a genuine interest. And remember, the publication of the material must be offensive to a reasonable person. The feelings of a hypersensitive person or someone who is especially sensitive do not count. Peggy Jo Fry sued the *Ionia* (Mich.) *Sentinel-Standard* for invasion of privacy when it reported that her husband and another woman had died in a fire that destroyed a cottage near Lake Michigan. The story mentioned that Ted Fry had been seen with Rita Hill at a tavern prior to the fire and related details about Fry's wife and children. The court ruled that these details were simply not highly offensive to a reasonable person (*Fry* v. *Ionia Sentinel-Standard,* 1980). Another

Michigan woman sued Knight-Ridder Newspapers after the *Miami Herald* published a story about the murder of her daughter. The plaintiff in the case was mentioned incidently in the story. It was noted that four of her six children were deaf and that she was a hardworking woman who had great faith in her daughter's ability to succeed in life. The court said such information is not offensive (*Andren* v. *Knight-Ridder Newspapers, 1984*).

Generally, if journalists stick to their job—reporting what is newsworthy—there is little to worry about. But privacy is an emotional subject. There are times when the revelation of details is highly offensive, and even seemingly newsworthy reports lose their immunity from a successful invasion of privacy suit.

Several years ago a woman with a rather unusual disorder—she ate constantly, but still lost weight—was admitted to a hospital. The press was tipped off and descended upon her room, pushed past the closed door, and took pictures against the patient's will. *Time* magazine ran a story about the patient, Dorothy Barber, whom in inimitable "*Time* style" it called "the starving glutton." Mrs. Barber sued and won her case. The judge said the hospital is one place people should be able to go for privacy (*Barber* v. *Time, Inc., 1942*). More than the privacy of the hospital visit influenced the ruling, because there are several decisions in which persons in hospitals have been considered to be the subject of legitimate concern and did not therefore enjoy the right to privacy. The story about the unusual disorder was surely offensive, almost mocking. The disorder was not contagious, and the implications for the general public were minimal. The *Time* story seemed to focus upon Mrs. Barber almost as if she were a freak, and in doing so the revelation of this information was highly offensive to any reasonable person.

A Georgia housewife took her two sons to the county fair and finally succumbed to their pressure to be taken through the fun house. As she left the building, an air jet blew Mrs. Flora Bell Graham's dress up over her head, and she was exposed from the waist down except for her underclothing. As fate would have it, a local photographer was nearby and captured the moment on film. The picture was featured in the Sunday edition of the local newspaper as a publicity piece for the fair. Mrs. Graham sued. By logical analysis one could suggest that she should not have won. The event took place in public. Many people saw her. She could not be readily identified in the picture because her dress was over her head. However, persons who knew the children, who were also in the picture, could make the connection between mother and children. Mrs. Graham did win (*Daily Times-Democrat* v. *Graham, 1962*). She had suffered an immense amount of embarrassment from the most intimate kind of revelation, and the public value of the photograph was extremely low.

More recently a woman successfully sued her plastic surgeon for publicly displaying "before and after" pictures of her at a department store presentation about plastic surgery and on a television appearance promoting the presentation. The plaintiff argued that only the members of her immediate family and a few close friends were aware she had undergone the cosmetic surgery. A jury ruled that the revelation of such personal medical facts was offensive to a reasonable person, and the United States Court of Appeals for the District of Columbia sustained the ruling (*Vassiliades* v. *Garfinckel's,* 1985). The court let the department store and other defendants off the hook because of evidence that the doctor had given assurances that he had consent to use the pictures.

Finally, the South Carolina Supreme Court recently affirmed a jury verdict against a newspaper that in publishing a story about teenage pregnancies had identified a young man—a minor—as the father of an illegitimate child. The teenage mother of the baby had given the reporter the father's name. The reporter talked to the young man who understood that the newspaper was doing a survey on teenage pregnancy. He said he was never told that his name might be used in the story. The newspaper argued that the information—including the boy's name—was of great public interest. The state supreme court said that was a jury question, and a jury ruled it was not of great public interest (*Hawkins* v. *Multimedia,* 1986).

| Legitimate Public Concern | While the four cases cited do not stand alone, they are unusual. Far more often courts rule that public concern over the issues involved outweighs any embarrassment to plaintiffs. Several factors have been cited in weighing the public concern or interest in a particular matter. |

In determining whether something is of public concern, courts have focused upon such factors as what the story is about, who the story is about, when the incidents described in the story took place, and sometimes where they took place. Factual stories, reports, or broadcasts that have great public interest have generally been protected in invasion of privacy suits. The courts have been really quite liberal in defining public interest, not as something people should read about but as something they do read about, something in which people are interested.

A twelve-year-old girl who gave birth to a baby (*Meetze* v. *AP,* 1956), the suffocation of two children in an old refrigerator (*Costlow* v. *Cuismano,* 1970), the sterilization of an eighteen-year-old girl (*Howard* v. *Des Moines Register,* 1979), the death of a young man from a drug overdose (*Beresky* v. *Teschner,* 1978), the activities of a bodysurfer (*Virgil* v. *Time,* 1975), and other subjects have all been ruled to be of legitimate concern and interest to the public. Even the seemingly frivolous subject of romance was declared to be newsworthy by a New York court that found no liability in the broadcast of a television film of a man and a woman walking hand in hand along Madison Avenue. The couple objected to being photographed; he was married to another woman, she was engaged to be married to another man. The court said that the film, used to show people behaving in a romantic fashion in order to explore the prevailing attitudes on this topic, is newsworthy (*DeGregorio* v. *CBS*, 1984). The courts have been most generous to the press in their understanding of American reading and viewing habits.

In a 1975 ruling in California, the Ninth United States Court of Appeals noted that "in determining what is a matter of legitimate public interest, account must be taken of the customs and conventions of the community; and in the last analysis what is proper becomes a matter of community mores" (*Virgil* v. *Time,* 1975). Thirty-five years earlier another federal judge noted that the public enjoyed reading about the problems, misfortunes, and troubles of their neighbors and other members of the community. "When such are the mores of the community, it would be unwise for a court to bar their expression in the newspapers, books, and magazines of the day," Judge Charles Clark wrote (*Sidis* v. *F-R Publishing Co.,* 1940).

Even the way a story is presented is normally not a factor: sensationalism and sensational treatment generally do not remove the protection of newsworthiness. Concerning the story of the suffocation of the two young children, the parents found the sensational treatment of the story as objectionable as the story itself. However, the court ruled that the manner in which the article was written was not relevant to whether the article was protected by the constitutional guarantees of free speech and free press—which, by the way, it was. In another case a Boston newspaper published a horrible picture of an automobile accident in which the bloodied and battered body of one of the victims was clearly visible and identifiable, and the court rejected the plaintiff's claim. The Massachusetts Supreme Court noted, "Many things which are distressing or may be lacking in propriety or good taste are not actionable" (*Kelley* v. *Post Publishing Co.,* 1951).

What the story is about, then, is an important aspect of determining whether it is newsworthy. American readers, viewers, and listeners are believed to have a wide range of interests that often focus on grotesque events and the tragedy, unhappiness, and misfortune of other persons.

Who the story is about is also taken into account in determining whether the material is of legitimate public concern. As in the law of libel, stories about public officials and persons who thrust themselves into the public eye are looked at much differently than are stories about private persons. A story that Mayor John Smith has a serious drinking problem would not be considered an invasion of privacy; the same story about barber Bill Brown might in fact be an invasion of privacy. How far can the press go in publishing details of the private life of so-called public persons? That is a difficult question to answer. Certainly the public status of the individual is important. Probably few details of the life of a president are considered private in terms of the law, but a circuit judge in a rural county, also an elected official, would probably enjoy considerably more privacy. In an interesting case in California, federal courts were asked to determine how far the press can go in looking into the private life of a public person.

The story focused upon Mike Virgil, widely regarded in southern California as one of the best bodysurfers along the Pacific Coast. *Sports Illustrated* decided to publish a feature on bodysurfing, and writer Curry Kirkpatrick chose to emphasize the prowess of Virgil. Virgil was known for his almost total disregard for personal safety and talked freely with the writer about his private life, as well as about his surfing. He told Kirkpatrick that he was reckless in private as well and described several incidents to demonstrate this attitude. These incidents included putting out a burning cigarette with his mouth, burning a hole in his wrist with a cigarette, diving headfirst down a flight of stairs, and eating live insects. But after the interview Virgil had second thoughts about the story and asked *Sports Illustrated* not to include the material about his private life. The magazine published the story as Kirkpatrick had written it, and Virgil sued. The Ninth Circuit Court of Appeals ruled that the line between private and public information "is to be drawn when the publicity ceases to be the giving of information to which the public is entitled, and becomes a morbid and sensational prying into private lives *for its own sake* [emphasis added]." In applying this standard to the Virgil case, the United States district court ruled that "any reasonable person reading the article would conclude that the personal facts concerning the individual were revealed in a legitimate journalistic attempt to explain his extremely daring and dangerous style of bodysurfing" (*Virgil* v. *Sports Illustrated,* 1976). Judge Thompson ruled that no one could reasonably conclude that these personal facts were included for any inherent morbid, sensational, or curiosity appeal they might have. If *Sports Illustrated* had published these personal details about Virgil without any other information, it might have been an invasion of privacy. But in the context of the story about his public life as a surfer, the publication was not an invasion of privacy.

Iowa courts used the same sort of standard when ruling that a story about a girl who had been sterilized when she was eighteen years old was not an invasion of privacy. The story focused upon the activities at a county juvenile home that had come under investigation by the state. As an example of what occurred there, the *Des Moines Register* recounted the story of a girl who was sterilized against her will because a psychiatrist reported to officials that she was "impulsive" and "hair-triggered" and would probably have sexual problems in the future. The girl's name was used, but was not prominent in the story. The court ruled that the paper had not pried into the girl's life simply to shock or outrage the community. The facts were presented to demonstrate to the community the kind of unethical, even illegal, activities taking place at the home. As such, the material was of legitimate public concern (*Howard* v. *Des Moines Register,* 1979). But was it necessary to use the victim's name in this story? Was it not possible for the newspaper to present this story to readers without identifying an unfortunate victim of this county home? The Iowa high court ruled it was legitimate to conclude that the name was an essential ingredient in the story (*Howard* v. *Des Moines Register,* 1979):

> In the sense of serving an appropriate news function, the disclosure [of the name] contributed constructively to the impact of the article. It offered a personalized frame of reference to which the reader could relate, fostering perception and understanding. Moreover, it lent specificity and credibility to the report. In this way the disclosure served as an effective means of accomplishing the intended news function. . . . Moreover, at a time when it was important to separate fact from rumor, the specificity of the report would strengthen the accuracy of the public perception of the merits of the controversy.

The Tenth United States Court of Appeals used this same argument to refute charges of invasion of privacy brought by a physician against the periodical *Medical Economics.* The story in the magazine was entitled "Who Let This Doctor in the O.R.? The Story of a Fatal Breakdown in Medical Policing," and described several patients of an anesthesiologist who suffered fatal or severely disabling injuries in the operating room. The article focused upon the lack of self-policing by physicians and the lack of disciplinary action by hospitals. To document these allegations the author of the story discussed the plaintiff anesthesiologist's psychiatric and related personal problems. Her picture and name were included in the story. While the plaintiff conceded the story was newsworthy, she argued that the publication of her photograph, name, and private facts revealing her psychiatric and marital histories added nothing to the story and were an invasion of privacy. The court disagreed, stating that the inclusion of the name and photograph strengthened the impact and credibility of the article. "They obviate any impression that the problems raised in the article are remote or hypothetical, thus providing an aura of immediacy and even urgency that might not exist had plaintiff's name and photograph been suppressed," the court said. The plaintiff's psychiatric and marital problems were connected to the newsworthy topic by the rational inference that her personal problems were the underlying causes of the acts of alleged malpractice (*Gilbert* v. *Medical Economics,* 1981).

What courts often look for in these kind of cases, then, is a nexus between the admittedly private and embarrassing information and the newsworthy subject of the story. How far the press can go in reporting the private life of public persons often depends not only upon what was said—how private the information is—but also upon why the material was used. When an individual's public life is explained, many parts of that person's private life are of legitimate public concern.

Since 1929 American courts have also recognized what might be called the "involuntary public figure" in privacy law. The Kentucky Supreme Court first noted such a person and gave this definition of the status (*Jones* v. *Herald Post Co.,* 1929):

> The right of privacy is the right to live one's life in seclusion, without being subjected to unwarranted and undesired publicity. In short, it is the right to be let alone. . . . There are times, however, when one, whether willing or not, becomes an actor in an occurrence of public or general interest. When this takes place he emerges from his seclusion, and it is not an invasion of his right of privacy to publish his photograph with an account of such occurrence.

The court later noted that private citizens can become "innocent actors in great tragedies in which the public has a deep concern." The scope, therefore, of the rubric involuntary public figure is wide. In Kansas City not too long ago, a young man was arrested by police outside the local courthouse on suspicion of burglary. Local television news cameramen filmed the arrest, and it was broadcast on televison that night. The young man, however, had been released by police, who admitted they had arrested the wrong man. An invasion of privacy suit followed, but the courts rejected it, stating that the plaintiff must show a serious, unreasonable, unwarranted, and offensive invasion of private affairs before recovery can be allowed (*Williams* v. *KCMO Broadcasting Co.,* 1971):

> In the case at bar, plaintiff was involved in a noteworthy event about which the public had a right to be informed and which the defendant [television station KCMO] had a right to publicize. This is true even though his involvement therein was purely involuntary and against his will.

An Illinois appeals court ruled in 1978 that a story that reported the death of a boy from an apparent drug overdose and then went on to outline details of the youth's life was not an invasion of privacy. The subject was of legitimate concern; in addition, the youth became an involuntary public figure by his actions within the drug culture in the community. "It is not necessary for an individual to actively seek publicity in order to be found in the public eye," the court ruled (*Beresky* v. *Teschner,* 1978).

There has been speculation that, given the opportunity, the United States Supreme Court would reject the so-called involuntary-public-figure rule in privacy law. The rationale behind this speculation rests upon the language of recent Supreme Court rulings in libel (*Firestone* v. *Time* and *Wolston* v. *Reader's Digest,* among others). In those decisions members of the High Court ruled that public figures in libel law must actively thrust themselves into the forefront of a public issue. They must voluntarily choose to be public figures by attempting to lead public opinion. But while libel law and invasion of privacy are similar in many respects, the argument that the Supreme Court will ultimately apply the same rules in privacy invasion appears to have little merit. There is a fundamental difference of crucial importance between a suit for libel and one for the publication of private facts. In the libel case the published material is false; in the privacy suit the material is truthful. This difference is critical. It is more likely that the Supreme Court would lessen the restrictions upon the publication of truthful material, as it did in the *Cox* case. The involuntary-public-figure rule has been a part of privacy law for more than fifty years, and it is unlikely the High Court would abandon it.

Persons who are thrust, even unwillingly thrust, into the public spotlight lose some of the protection of their right of privacy. How much privacy is lost? Probably only the privacy that protects that part of their life that has come into focus because of the event or incident. This line is not easy to draw. Imagine that John Smith, publisher of the *Daily Sentinel,* is arrested for violating the state unfair labor practices act. Under the guise of his status as an involuntary public figure, how far into his life can the press go? Can it report his extramarital affairs? that he has a gun fetish? that he cheats at cards? All these questions are hard to answer. Probably the answers depend upon the status of the person involved, the magnitude of the event, the scope of public interest, and the connection, or nexus, between these private personal matters and the newsworthy aspects of the story.

Sometimes the people who are close to public figures also lose some of their privacy. In 1971 in Pennsylvania the state High Court ruled that the *Saturday Evening Post* was not liable for the publication of the names of the children of an entertainer in a story relating that the entertainer, Lillian Corabi, was accused of masterminding a complex burglary (*Corabi* v. *Curtis Publishing Co., 1971*). The court said that "Tiger Lil" Corabi was a public figure and that anyone could legitimately publish her biography without consent and could include the names of the members of her family.

When a white southern civil rights leader published his autobiography, it was not an invasion of privacy to include information about his brother's wife, according to a United States district court. In *Brother to a Dragonfly,* author Will D. Campbell portrayed his life and his relationship to his deceased brother Joe, whom he regarded as a major inspiration in his life. Joe was a pharmacist who became addicted to drugs. This resulted in a dramatic change in his personality, and at times he seriously abused his wife, Carlyne, who was also mentioned several times in the book. She sued for invasion of privacy. "The fact that she [the plaintiff] was the wife of a close and influential family member of the author justifies her inclusion in the book," the United States district court ruled. "Joe's problems with drugs and the profound effect that had on the author justifies the extent of her inclusion" (*Campbell* v. *Seabury Press,* 1979).

Recounting the Past   A great number of privacy suits have resulted from both published and broadcast stories about people who were formerly in the public eye. In these cases the plaintiffs have consistently argued that the passing of time dims the public spotlight and that a person stripped of privacy because of great notoriety regains the protection of privacy after several years. Courts have not accepted this argument very often. The general rule is that once persons become public figures they pretty much remain public figures, despite attempts to avoid publicity. Two kinds of stories fall into this category: (1) stories that merely recount a past event (fourteen years ago today Walter Denton jumped off the Golden Gate Bridge and survived) and do not tell readers what the subject of the story does today and (2) stories that recount a past occurrence and attempt to focus as well on what the participant does today (fourteen years ago Walter Denton jumped off the Golden Gate Bridge and survived, and today he is principal of Madison High School).

Stories that fall in the first category are protected in almost every instance. In 1975 the Kansas Supreme Court, for example, ruled it was not an invasion of privacy when a newspaper republished in a "Looking Backward Column" a story that a police officer had been suspended and then fired in 1964 after a complaint from a citizen. The court said that "official misconduct is newsworthy when it occurs, and remains so for so long as anyone thinks it worth retelling." The court added, "Once these facts entered the public domain, they remained there . . . plaintiff could not draw himself like a snail into his shell" (*Rawlins* v. *The Hutchinson Publishing Co.,* 1975). And the Nevada Supreme Court ruled that the publication in 1978 of a story that recounted the arrest in 1955 of Ronald Montesano on a narcotics charge was not an invasion of privacy. The facts about Montesano were republished twenty-three years later in an article recounting the hit-and-run death of a Las Vegas police officer, an incident in which Montesano had been involved (*Montesano* v. *Las Vegas Review-Journal,* 1983). Such decisions are the rule.

The second kind of story is more problematic. There have been too few cases to establish a clear guideline. Some courts have clearly gone on record permitting the "where-are-they-now" kind of story. But even these judges have suggested that stories designed to purposely embarrass or humiliate a person because of his or her past conduct might not be tolerated under all circumstances (see *Kent* v. *Pittsburgh Press,* 1972; *Sidis* v. *F-R Publishing Co.,* 1940; and *Bernstein* v. *NBC,* 1955). There is a real risk in running a story about a local banker that includes the fact that he was arrested for car theft twenty years earlier. A judge may ask, Of what relevance is this information about past deeds? Surely if the man is running for public office, the public deserves to have this information. No privacy suit would stand in such a case. Oftentimes such stories are published or broadcast for inspirational reasons—see how this person pulled him- or herself up by the bootstraps and succeeded despite the odds. In such cases the subjects of the stories will usually consent to the use of this information because they are proud of their accomplishments. But if, for example, the editor publishes this information to hurt a banker because an application for a loan was rejected, a court may very well rule that an invasion of privacy has taken place. This is another area where the journalist has to exercise judgment and ask, Why am I publishing this embarrassing information? If there is good cause, the journalist will find the courts will bar an action for invasion of privacy.

Stories that relate past events are some of the most difficult to evaluate in terms of public interest and public information. For a time the courts in California promulgated an unusual rule and insisted that there must be a social value or social utility gained by recounting past events about a person's life (see *Briscoe* v. *Reader's Digest Association,* 1971). This rule is now all but dead (see *Forsher* v. *Bugliosi,* 1980).

The publication of private facts generates many lawsuits, but few are successful. The key to avoiding successful litigation in this area is for the news person to stick to reporting the news. It is when the journalist makes a foray into nonnewsworthy private lives of average persons in order to titillate or amuse readers or viewers that this area of invasion of privacy can prove extremely troublesome.

SUMMARY

It is an invasion of privacy to publicize private information about another person's life if the publication of this information would be embarrassing to a reasonable person and the information is not of legitimate public interest or concern. To publicize means to communicate the information to a large number of people. There is no liability for giving further publicity to information that is already considered public. The press is free, for example, to report even embarrassing and sensitive matters contained in public records. The information that is publicized must be considered offensive to a reasonable person; the law does not protect hypersensitive individuals.

Courts use many strategies to determine whether information has legitimate public concern. Stories that have great interest have legitimate public concern. Stories about both voluntary and involuntary public figures are normally considered of legitimate public concern. When private information is published or broadcast, it is important that there is a connection between the revelation of the embarrassing private information and the newsworthy aspects of the story. Embarrassing details about a person's private life cannot be publicized simply to amuse or titillate audiences. News stories that recount past events—including embarrassing details of an individual's life—are normally protected from successful privacy suits. However, courts will normally insist upon a good reason for attempting to relate these embarrassing past events to an individual's current life or work.

FALSE-LIGHT PRIVACY

The fourth category of invasion of privacy looks, at first glance, as if it has little to do with what we traditionally think of as privacy. It has nothing to do with digging into a person's past, taking pictures with a telephoto lens, or using someone's picture to advertise toothpaste. What this category of invasion of privacy bans is the publication of false information about a person. The law states that it is an invasion of privacy to publish material that puts an individual in a false-light. There are two qualifications to this rule. First, the published false information must be highly offensive to a reasonable person. Second, it must be shown—as in libel—that the publisher of the information was somehow at fault, exhibiting either actual malice or negligence (more about this later in this section).

False-light cases come in a wide variety of shapes and colors. Some involve blatant fictionalization of otherwise true stories; others result from simple errors in news stories. A false-light privacy suit surely resembles a defamation action. But it has one important difference. In order to maintain a libel action, the plaintiff must show that the material has damaged his or her reputation, that the material is in fact defamatory. In false-light cases the plaintiff must only show that the published material is considered highly offensive by a reasonable person. It is not unusual for a plaintiff to file both an action for invasion of privacy and libel at the same time. Some states, however, have rules that limit a plaintiff to one cause of action based on a single set of facts. The plaintiff must choose either libel or invasion of privacy. Let us first look at some typical examples of false-light invasion of privacy to try to develop some guidelines on the subject.

Fictionalization

Radio and television writers who dramatize true stories are commonly the victims of false-light suits. Years ago the National Broadcasting Company dramatized the heroism of a naval officer who, as a passenger on a flight from Honolulu to California, was responsible for saving many lives when the plane crash-landed at sea. The drama stuck to the hard facts of the story, but of course dialogue between passengers and crew was added. In addition, the naval officer was somewhat humanized; he smoked a cigarette and prayed before the crash. The court that heard the officer's privacy suit ruled that these embellishments constituted fictionalization and resulted in an invasion of privacy (*Strickler* v. *NBC,* 1958).

Newspapers and magazine writers have been caught when they dramatized true stories in the same manner by adding dialogue, changing the scene slightly, and so forth. A writer for a Philadelphia newspaper uncovered an interesting divorce suit involving a teenage couple. The boy married the girl only to spite her parents, who did not like him. The newspaper story described the couple as they secretly planned the marriage, as they walked to the justice of the peace, and so forth. Dialogue between the couple was invented. A suit resulted, and the newspaper lost the case because the story was written "in a style used almost exclusively by writers of fiction" (*Acquino* v. *Bulletin Co.,* 1959). Note, the court did not say that the story was fiction, because it was not. The basic facts were true, but they were presented in a fictional style.

Such opinions are not always the rule. Other courts in other cases have said that minor fictionalization, the creation of dialogue, does not constitute invasion of privacy in an otherwise true story (*Carlisle* v. *Fawcett Publishing Co.,* 1962). The foregoing examples point up the confused state of the law in this area.

The style of the fiction writer—putting heavy emphasis on descriptive detail, using dialogue, narrating the story from the subject's, rather than the writer's, point of view—is used increasingly today by some journalists. Writers such as Gay Talese, Tom Wolfe, Jimmy Breslin, Joan Didion, and Norman Mailer are leading the way in the exploration of stylized nonfiction writing, often called New Journalism. Nonfiction novels like Truman Capote's *In Cold Blood* and Joseph Wambaugh's *The Onion Field* demonstrate the journalistic power of this style. Yet, these writers clearly open themselves to lawsuits unless extreme care is taken.

The simplest way to avoid a suit for false-light, if the truth is embellished in any way, is to change the names of the characters in the story. This strategy will work in every case except in those stories that are about a specific person. It does not make much sense to do a character sketch about Mick Jagger if you must refer to him throughout the piece as John Smith because parts of the story are embellished or fictionalized.

On the opposite side of the fictionalization coin is the problem of using the name of a real person in what is clearly a work of fiction. What happens when a novel is about a fictional character named Judy Splinters and a real Judy Splinters exists? Can the real Ms. Splinters sue for invasion of privacy? The first point to remember is that the little notice in the front of the book— all characters in this book are fictional and any resemblance to persons living or dead is purely coincidental—does not help much. It is impossible to escape liability by merely saying you are not liable. If a man commits an illegal act, he is responsible for his action, regardless of the notices he may have published. If someone trips on a broken piece of cement in a sidewalk, it matters not that the owner of the property has a sign on the lawn declaring that the owner takes good care of his or her property and is not responsible for injuries to other persons.

Does Judy Splinters have a case? If only her name is used, she does not. The names of many people get into works of fiction. Such occurrences are coincidental. Liability does not accrue unless Judy can convince a jury that in fact she is the character in the book. She can do this by showing that more than her name is used, that other aspects of her identity are used as well.

For example, the author and publisher of a book entitled *Match Set* was sued by a woman who had the same name as the central character in the novel. Both women were named Melanie Geisler. The character in the novel is a female transsexual tennis player who is induced to participate in tennis fraud. The plaintiff in the case worked for a small publishing company for six months and was acquainted with the defendant author who also worked at the same company for a short time. The plaintiff and the fictional Melanie Geisler share many physical characteristics. The real Melanie Geisler argued that the similarity of names and physical descriptions, coupled with the fact that she and the author were acquainted for a short time, led many persons to believe the book was about her. The Second United States Court of Appeals ruled that a reasonable person could come to such a conclusion, rejected the defendant's motion for dismissal, and sent the case back for trial (*Geisler* v. *Petrocelli,* 1980). Some authors can face a problem even if the plaintiff does not have the same name as a character in the novel. In a Florida case a novelist knowingly used a real person with whom she was acquainted as the basis for a character in a book. She was sued for invasion of privacy and lost the case. The court ruled that because the character described in the novel was so unusual, many persons in the community recognized her even though the name had been changed (*Cason* v. *Baskin,* 1947).

Finally, what about novels like E. L. Doctorow's *Ragtime* in which famous people play an incidental part in a fictional story? The courts in at least one jurisdiction, New York, have ruled that such incidental use of the name and character of real notable people is not an invasion of privacy so long as it is evident to readers that the book is a work of fiction and that individuals named are included simply to add color to the book (*Hicks* v. *Casablanca,* 1978).

<table>
<tr><td>False Statements</td><td>Today most false-light cases do not involve blatant fictionalization. They instead result from news and feature stories that are either intentionally or unintentionally embellished. Typical of the first sort of case is one in which a writer for a national newspaper told his readers that a mystery surrounded the suicide death of a mother. The woman killed herself after murdering her children, and the writer said that police, family, and friends were baffled because she had been a happy, normal woman. Her husband sued, charging false light. He was able to show that the woman had a history of psychiatric care and mental illness. She was quite despondent before the incident, and her death was really not a mystery at all. The court ruled that the publication had put the woman in a false light (*Varnish* v. *Best Medium,* 1968).</td></tr>
</table>

Photographs are a more common source of false-light cases than are stories. The late, great *Saturday Evening Post* seemed to have a penchant for false-light cases, most of which involved photographs. Years ago the magazine published a picture of a little girl who was brushed by a speeding car in an intersection and lay crying in the street. The girl was the victim of a motorist who ignored a red traffic light, but in the magazine the editors implied that she had caused the accident herself by darting into the street between parked cars. The editors simply needed a picture to illustrate a story on pedestrian carelessness and plucked this one out of the files. The picture was totally unrelated to the story, except that both were about people being hit by cars. Eleanor Sue Leverton sued the *Post* and won. Judge Herbert F. Goodrich ruled that the picture was clearly newsworthy in connection with Eleanor's original accident (*Leverton v. Curtis Publishing Co.,* 1951):

> . . . but the sum total of all this is that this particular plaintiff, the legitimate subject for publicity for one particular accident, now becomes a pictorial, frightful example of pedestrian carelessness. This, we think, exceeds the bounds of privilege.

WJLA-TV in the nation's capital was sued in a case that graphically demonstrates how a broadcasting station or publication can and cannot use unrelated pictures to illustrate a story. The station broadcast a story on a new medical treatment for genital herpes. The report appeared on both the 6 P.M. and 11 P.M. newscasts. Both reports carried the same opening videotape of scores of pedestrians walking on a busy city street. Then the camera zoomed in on one woman, Linda Duncan, as she stood on a corner. Duncan turned and looked at the camera. She was clearly recognizable. On the 6 P.M. news there was no narration during this opening footage. The camera focused on the plaintiff Duncan and then the tape cut to a picture of the reporter, who was standing on the street, and said, "For the twenty million Americans who have herpes, it's not a cure." The remainder of the story followed. But for the 11 P.M. news, the reporter's opening statement was read by the news anchor as viewers watched the opening videotape, including the close-up of Linda Duncan. A defense motion to dismiss the privacy and defamation actions was granted as it related to the 6 P.M. newscast. The court said there was not a sufficient connection between pictures of the plaintiff and the reporter's statement. But the court denied a summary judgment relating to the 11 P.M. broadcast. "The coalescing of the camera action, plaintiff's action (turning toward the camera), and the position of the passerby caused plaintiff to be the focal point on the screen. The juxtaposition of this film and commentary concerning twenty million Americans with herpes is sufficient to support an inference that indeed the plaintiff was a victim," the court ruled. A jury should decide whether the connection was strong enough (*Duncan v. WJLA-TV,* 1984).

Sometimes an error simply occurs, and there is nothing anyone can do about it. One simple precaution can be taken to avoid false-light suits: refrain from using unrelated pictures to illustrate news stories. When the annual Christmas story warning readers to be wary of shoplifters in department stores is prepared, control the impulse to pull from the files a picture of people shopping and run it as artwork with the story. When a story warning older men to be wary of overexertion as they shovel the first snow lest they fall victim to a heart attack is published, do not use a file picture of a sixty-year-old man clearing his driveway. In both cases the juxtaposition of the story and the photograph implies a relationship that is not necessarily true.

Highly Offensive Material

Before a plaintiff can win a false-light case, the court must be convinced that the material that is false is highly offensive to a reasonable person. While there are on record a handful of cases where nonoffensive material was the basis for a successful false-light suit (see *Molony* v. *Boy Comics Publishers,* 1946), these cases are old and should not be regarded as authoritative today. Typical of modern decisions is the case of *Cibenko* v. *Worth Publishers.* The plaintiff is a New York–New Jersey Port Authority police officer whose photograph appeared in a college sociology text. In a section of the book entitled "Selecting the Criminals," the picture depicts a white police officer (Cibenko) in a public place apparently prodding a sleeping black with his nightstick. The caption for the picture states:

> The social status of the offender seems to be the most significant determinant of whether a person will be arrested and convicted for an offense and of the kind of penalty that will be applied. In this picture a police officer is preventing a black male from falling asleep in a public place. Would the officer be likely to do the same if the "offender" were a well-dressed, middle-aged white person?

Officer Cibenko claimed the photograph and caption made him appear to be a racist, and this was false. A United States district court in New Jersey disagreed and ruled that there was no offensive meaning attached to the photograph and caption, especially not a highly offensive meaning (*Cibenko* v. *Worth Publishers,* 1981).

The Fault Requirement

Since 1967 plaintiffs in false-light suits have been required to carry a fault requirement much like the one applied in libel cases. The case in which this fault requirement was applied to invasion of privacy was the first mass media invasion of privacy suit ever heard by the United States Supreme Court. In the early 1950s the James Hill family were held captive in their home for nearly twenty-four hours by three escaped convicts. The fugitives were captured by police shortly after leaving the Hill home. The incident became a widely publicized story. A novel, *The Desperate Hours,* was written about a similar incident, as were a play and a motion-picture script. *Life* magazine published a feature story about the drama, stating that the play was a reenactment of the ordeal suffered by the James Hill family. The actors were even taken to the home in which the Hills had lived (now vacant) and were photographed at the scene of the original captivity.

James Hill sued for invasion of privacy. He complained that the magazine had used his family's name for trade purposes and that the story put the family in a false light. *The Desperate Hours* did follow the basic outline of the Hill family ordeal, but it contained many differences. The fictional Hilliard family, for example, suffered far more physical and verbal indignities at the hands of the convicts than did the Hill family.

The family won money damages in the New York state courts, but the Supreme Court of the United States vacated the lower court rulings and sent the case back for yet another trial. The Hill family gave up at this point, and no subsequent trial was held.

Justice William Brennan, in a five-to-four ruling, declared that the family's name and photographs had not been used for trade purposes. Brennan reminded all concerned that informative material published in newspapers and magazines is not published for purposes of trade (see pages 218–19), even though these publications generally are considered profit-making businesses.

Turning to the false-light action, Brennan applied the same First Amendment standards he had developed in the *New York Times* v. *Sullivan* libel suit to this category of invasion of privacy litigation. "We hold that the constitutional protections for speech and press preclude the application of the New York [privacy] statute to redress false reports of matters of public interest in the absence of proof that the defendant published the report with knowledge of its falsity or in reckless disregard of the truth," he wrote. In the last twenty years, however, the Supreme Court has substantially modified the fault requirement in libel. Since 1974 and the case of *Gertz* v. *Welch,* the Supreme Court has insisted that public persons must prove actual malice to win a libel suit, but that states may permit private persons to win a libel judgment with proof of simple negligence, not actual malice. Six months after its ruling in *Gertz,* the Supreme Court issued a ruling in a false-light invasion of privacy case, *Cantrell* v. *Forest City Publishing Co.* In this case the High Court ruled that there was evidence to show that the defendant had acted with reckless disregard for the truth. But because the plaintiff had managed to bear the higher burden of proof in the case and was able to prove actual malice, the Supreme Court didn't decide whether the Gertz ruling had changed the law of privacy as well as the law of libel. "This case presents no occasion to consider whether a State may constitutionally apply a more relaxed standard of liability for a publisher or broadcaster of false statements injurious to a private individual under a false-light theory of invasion of privacy or whether the constitutional standard announced in *Time, Inc.* v. *Hill* applies to all false-light cases," wrote Justice Stewart for the court.

The Supreme Court has done nothing to clarify its stand on this issue since 1974. Consequently, lower federal and state courts have been forced to make rulings on their own in this area. And since the early 1980s, there seems to be a clear trend in favor of requiring the lower burden of proof for private person plaintiffs in false-light cases. The Fifth U.S. Court of Appeals adopted this rule in two cases in 1984, *Braun* v. *Flynt* and *Wood* v. *Hustler*. Some state courts have adopted this rule as well (see *Crump* v. *Beckley Newspapers,* 1984). The issue is not resolved by any means. But it appears that when given a choice, courts seem to follow the libel rules. Private individuals must prove only that the defendant acted negligently when placing them in a false light.

A plaintiff who is asked to prove fault in an invasion of privacy suit bears the same burden of proof as the libel plaintiff. Negligence, knowledge of falsity, and reckless disregard for the truth are all defined in the same manner. Here are three false-light cases in which the fault questions were considered:

1. In 1977 the defendant West Virginia newspaper published an article about women coal miners. Photos of the plaintiff were taken with her consent and used in the article. Two years later the same newspaper published another story about the problems faced by women who try to work in the mines, specifically their harrassment by male miners. The story told of women in Kentucky mines who had been stripped, greased, and sent out of the mine as part of an initiation rite; of a woman miner in Virginia who had been physically attacked twice while underground; and of a female miner in Wyoming who had been dangled off the edge of a 200-foot water tower while male miners suggested she quit her job. The newspaper used a photo of the plaintiff, taken but not published in 1977, to illustrate the article. The caption said "Women are entering mines as a regular course of action." Sue Crump complained that this put her in a false light. The West Virginia Court of Appeals refused to grant a summary judgment for the plaintiff and said a jury should decide whether publication of the photo had put Crump in a false light and, because she was a private person, whether the newspaper had acted negligently in publishing the photo with the story (*Crump* v. *Beckley Newspapers,* 1984).

2. In 1967 a bridge across the Ohio River between West Virginia and Ohio collapsed, killing forty-three people. Reporter Joe Eszterhas wrote a feature story about the family of one of the victims for the *Cleveland Plain-Dealer*. A year later Eszterhas revisited the scene of the tragedy and wrote a story about how the family was managing without their husband and father. The story contained several inaccuracies about the family's poverty and other matters. In addition, Eszterhas implied that he had seen and talked to the widow, described her, and told readers she said she had refused money from people in town and was reluctant to talk about the tragedy. In fact, the woman was not at home when the reporter made his second visit, and he did not see her. The Supreme Court said that evidence of these "calculated falsehoods" was sufficient proof of actual malice (*Cantrell* v. *Forest City Publishing Co.,* 1974). The reporter must have known, Justice Stewart wrote, that a number of statements in his story were untrue.

3. Sixty-seven-year-old James Kent was released from prison after twenty-seven years of incarceration on a murder charge. He had won a new trial, and the state chose not to reprosecute. Therefore, in the eyes of the law, Kent

was innocent of the murder he had been charged with. A story in the *Pittsburgh Press* on prison reform made a single-sentence reference to Kent as a man who had taken a life. He sued for publication of a false report, arguing that had the reporter checked with the prison officials, he would have discovered the facts—that Kent's conviction for murder had been overturned. The federal district court said that the story was not reckless disregard for the truth, it was not malice (*Kent v. Pittsburgh Press,* 1972):

> Obviously if Grochot [the reporter] had checked the court records relating to Kent, he could have discovered the reason for his release. Obviously too, however, he had no reason in the circumstances to entertain any doubts, quite apart from serious doubts, as to the matter of Kent's release.

SUMMARY

It is an invasion of privacy to publish false information that places an individual into what is called a false light. However, this false information must be considered offensive to a reasonable person. Also, the plaintiff must prove that the information was published negligently, with knowledge of its falsity or with reckless disregard for the truth.

One common source of false-light privacy suits is any drama that adds fictional material to an otherwise true story. The use of fictional rather than real names in such a drama will normally preclude a successful invasion of privacy suit. The coincidental use of a real name in a novel or stage play will not stand as a cause of action for invasion of privacy. Most false-light cases, however, result from the publication of false information about a person in a news or feature story. Pictures of persons who are not involved in the stories the pictures are used to illustrate frequently provoke false-light privacy suits.

To succeed in a false-light case, the plaintiff must demonstrate to the court that the publication of the false material offends a reasonable person. Also, the plaintiff must show that the material was published negligently, with knowledge that it was false or with reckless disregard of the truth.

Before the discussion of the right of privacy comes to an end, we need to recall a few points. First, remember that only people have the right of privacy. Corporations, businesses, and governments do not enjoy the legal right of privacy as such. Second, unlike libel, the law of privacy does provide that the plaintiff may seek an injunction to stop an invasion of privacy. This action is in addition to the right to seek money damages. However, it is difficult for a plaintiff to get an injunction. Courts are very hesitant to enjoin tortious conduct unless the plaintiff can show that the action will cause irreparable injury and that the tortious conduct will likely be continued. Such was the case in the *Galella-Onassis* suit. A plaintiff is far more likely to get an injunction in either an intrusion or an appropriation case than in a private-facts or false-light suit. Normally courts refuse to grant injunctions, because they believe an adequate legal remedy is available or because they believe that the injunction could constitute prior censorship in violation of the First Amendment. The plaintiff bears an immense burden in convincing a court that prior restraint is called for. While it is possible to get an injunction, it is difficult. Third, it is impossible to civilly libel a dead person, but a few state privacy statutes make it possible for an heir to maintain an action for invasion of privacy.

Although privacy law is not as well charted as libel law and although there are fewer privacy cases, suits for invasion of privacy are a growing menace to journalists. If journalists stick to the job of responsibly reporting the news, they may rest assured that the chance for a successful privacy suit is slim.

BIBLIOGRAPHY

Here is a list of some of the sources that have been helpful in the preparation of chapter 4:

Books

Pember, Don R. *Privacy and the Press*. Seattle: University of Washington Press, 1972.

Articles

Bloustein, Edward J. "Privacy as an Aspect of Human Dignity: An Answer to Dean Prosser." 39 *New York University Law Review* 962, 1964.

Davis, Frederick. "What Do We Mean by Right to Privacy?" 4 *South Dakota Law Review* 1, 1959.

Levine, Marla E. "The Right of Publicity as a Means of Protecting Performers' Style." 14 *Loyola of Los Angeles Law Review* 129, 1980.

Pember, Don R. "The Burgeoning Scope of Access Privacy and the Portent for a Free Press." 64 *Iowa Law Review* 1155, 1979.

Pember, Don R., and Teeter, Dwight L. "Privacy and the Press Since *Time, Inc.* v. *Hill.*" 50 *Washington Law Review* 57, 1974.

Prosser, William L. "Privacy." 48 *California Law Review* 383, 1960.

Sims, Andrew B. "Right of Publicity: Survivability Reconsidered." 49 *Fordham Law Review* 453, 1981.

Cases

Acme v. *Kuperstock*, 711 F.2d 1538 (1983).
Acquino v. *Bulletin Co.*, 190 Pa. Super. 528 (1959).
Ali v. *Playgirl*, 447 F. Supp. 723 (1978).
Allen v. *Combined Communications*, 7 M.L. Rept. 2417 (1981).
Anderson v. *WROC-TV*, 441 N.Y.S.2d 815 (1981).
Andren v. *Knight-Ridder Newspapers*, 10 M.L. Rept. 2109 (1984).
Arrington v. *New York Times*, 55 N.Y.2d 433 (1982).
Barber v. *Time, Inc.*, 159 S.W.2d 291 (1942).
Beresky v. *Teschner*, 381 N.E.2d 979 (1978).
Bernstein v. *NBC*, 232 F.2d 369 (1955).
Bilney v. *Evening Star*, 406 A.2d 652 (1979).
Boddie v. *ABC*, 731 F.2d 333 (1984).

Booth v. *Curtis Publishing Co.*, 11 N.Y.2d 907 (1962).

Braun v. *Flynt*, 726 F.2d 245 (1984).

Briscoe v. *Reader's Digest Association*, 483 P.2d 34 (1971).

Campbell v. *Seabury Press*, 614 F.2d 395 (1979).

Canessa v. *J. I. Kislak*, 235 A.2d 62 (1967).

Cantrell v. *Forest City Publishing Co.*, 95 S.Ct. 465 (1974).

Carlisle v. *Fawcett Publishing Co.*, 210 Cal. App.2d 733 (1962).

Cason v. *Baskin*, 159 Fla. 131 (1947).

Cassidy v. *ABC*, 377 N.E.2d 126 (1978).

Cefalu v. *Globe Newspaper*, 391 N.E.2d 935 (1979).

Cher v. *Forum International*, 7 M.L. Rept. 2593 (1982).

Cibenko v. *Worth Publishers*, 510 F. Supp. 761 (1981).

Cohen v. *Herbal Concepts*, 473 N.Y.S.2d 426 (1984).

Corabi v. *Curtis Publishing Co.*, 273 A.2d 899 (1971).

Costlow v. *Cuismano*, 311 N.Y.S.2d 92 (1970).

Cox Broadcasting Co. v. *Cohn*, 95 S.Ct. 1029 (1975).

Creel v. *Crown Publishers*, 11 M.L. Rept. 1541 (1985).

Crump v. *Beckley Newspapers*, 10 M.L. Rept. 2225 (1984).

Daily Times-Democrat v. *Graham*, 162 So.2d 474 (1962).

DeGregorio v. *CBS*, 43 N.Y.S.2d 922 (1984).

Delan v. *CBS*, 445 N.Y.S.2d 898 (1981); 458 N.Y.S.2d 608 (1983).

Dietemann v. *Time, Inc.*, 499 F.2d 245 (1971).

Dittner v. *Troma*, 6 M.L. Rept. 1991 (1980).

Duncan v. *WJLA-TV*, 10 M.L. Rept. 1395 (1984).

Durgom v. *CBS*, 214 N.Y.S.2d 752 (1961).

Florida Publishing Co. v. *Fletcher*, 340 So.2d 914 (1976).

Forsher v. *Bugliosi*, 608 P.2d 716 (1980).

Friedan v. *Friedan*, 414 F. Supp 77 (1976).

Fry v. *Ionia Sentinel-Standard*, 300 N.W.2d 687 (1980).

Galella v. *Onassis*, 487 F.2d 986 (1973); 533 F. Supp. 1076 (1982).

Geisler v. *Petrocelli*, 616 F.2d 636 (1980).

Gilbert v. *Medical Economics*, 665 F.2d 305 (1981).

Griffith v. *Rancocas Valley Hospital*, 8 M.L. Rept. 1760 (1982).

Haelan Laboratories, Inc. v. *Topps Chewing Gum*, 202 F.2d 866 (1953).

Harrison v. *Washington Post*, 391 A.2d 781 (1978).

Hawkins v. *Metromedia*, 12 M.L. Rept. 1878 (1986).

Hendry v. *Conner*, 303 Minn. 317 (1975).

Holman v. *Central Arkansas Broadcasting*, 610 F.2d 542 (1979).

Holmes v. *Curtis Publishing Co.*, 303 F. Supp. 522 (1969).

House v. *Sports Films*, 10 M.L. Rept. 2223 (1984).

Howard v. *Des Moines Register*, 283 N.W.2d 789 (1979).

Jeffries v. *New York Evening Journal*, 124 N.Y.S. 780 (1910).

Jeppson v. *United Television*, 580 P.2d 1087 (1978).

Jones v. *Herald Post Co.*, 18 S.W.2d 972 (1929).

Jumez v. *ABC Records*, 3 M.L. Rept. 2324 (1978).

Kelley v. *Post Publishing Co.*, 327 Mass. 275 (1951).

Kent v. *Pittsburgh Press*, 349 F. Supp. 622 (1972).

Le Mistral, Inc. v. *CBS*, 402 N.Y.S.2d 815 (1978).

Leverton v. *Curtis Publishing Co.*, 192 F.2d 974 (1951).

Liberty Lobby v. *Pearson*, 390 F.2d 489 (1968).

Lopez v. *Triangle Communications*, 421 N.Y.S.2d 57 (1979).

Lugosi v. *Universal*, 160 Cal. App.3d 323 (1979).

McAndrews v. *Roy*, 131 So.2d 256 (1961).

McCall v. *Courier-Journal*, 4 M.L. Rept. 2337 (1979); affd. 6 M.L. Rept. 1112 (1980).

Man v. *Warner Brothers*, 317 F. Supp. 50 (1970).

Marks v. *King Broadcasting*, 618 P.2d 572 (1980).

Martin v. *Penthouse*, 12 M.L. Rept. 2058 (1986).

The Martin Luther King Center v. *American Heritage Products*, 296 S.E.2d 697 (1982).

Meetze v. *AP*, 95 S.E.2d 606 (1956).

Metter v. *Los Angeles Examiner*, 95 P.2d 491 (1939).

Molony v. *Boy Comics Publishers*, 65 N.Y.S.2d 173 (1946).

Montesano v. *Las Vegas Review-Journal*, 9 M.L. Rept. 2266 (1983).

Moser v. *Press Publishing Co.*, 109 N.Y.S. 963 (1908).

Namath v. *Sports Illustrated*, 39 N.Y.2d 897 (1976).

Nappier v. *Jefferson Standard Life Insurance Co.*, 322 F.2d 502 (1963).

Neff v. *Time, Inc.*, 406 F. Supp. 858 (1976).

New Mexico v. *McCormack*, No. CR-81-215 (N. M.Dist. Ct., Eddy County, 1982).

Onassis v. *Christian Dior*, 10 M.L. Rept. 1859 (1984).

Palmer v. *Schonhorn Enterprises, Inc.*, 232 A.2d 458 (1967).

Patterson v. *Tribune Co.*, 146 So.2d 623 (1962).

Paulsen v. *Personality Posters*, 299 N.Y.S.2d 501 (1968).

Pavesich v. *New England Mutual Life Insurance Co.*, 122 Ga. 190 (1905).

Pearson v. *Dodd*, 410 F.2d 701 (1969).

Peed v. *Washington Times Co.*, 55 Wash. L. Rept. 182 (1927).

People v. *Kunkin*, 100 Cal. Rptr. 845 (1972); revd. 107 Cal. Rptr. 184 (1973).

Rawlins v. *The Hutchinson Publishing Co.*, 543 P.2d 288 (1975).

Reeves v. *United Artists*, 572 F. Supp. 1231 (1983).

Rifkin v. *Esquire*, 8 M.L. Rept. 1384 (1982).

Roberson v. *Rochester Folding Box Co.*, 171 N.Y. 538 (1902).

Russell v. *Marboro Books*, 183 N.Y.S.2d 8 (1959).

Shields v. *Gross*, 451 N.Y.S.2d 419 (1982); 58 N.Y.2d 338 (1983).

Sidis v. *F-R Publishing Co.*, 113 F.2d 806 (1940).

Sipple v. *Chronicle Publishing*, 154 Cal. App.3d 1040 (1984).

Stahl v. *Oklahoma*, 9 M.L. Rept. 1945 (1983).

State v. *Lashinsky*, 404 A.2d 1121 (1979).

Stephano v. *News Group Publications*, 11 M.L. Rept. 1303 (1984).

Strickler v. *NBC*, 167 F. Supp. 68 (1958).

Time, Inc. v. *Hill*, 385 U.S. 374 (1967).

Uhlaender v. *Henricksen*, 159 F. Supp. 1277 (1970).

Varnish v. *Best Medium*, 405 F.2d 608 (1968).

Vassiliades v. *Garfinckel's*, 492 A.2d 580 (1985).

Virgil v. *Time, Inc.*, 527 F.2d 1122 (1975); 424 F. Supp. 1286 (1976).

Welch v. *Mr. Christmas Tree*, 57 N.Y.2d 143 (1982).

Westinghouse Broadcasting v. *National Transportation Safety Board*, 8 M.L. Rept. 1177 (1982).

Williams v. *KCMO Broadcasting Co.*, 472 S.W.2d 1 (1971).

Wood v. *Hustler*, 736 F.2d 1084 (1984).

Zacchini v. *Scripps-Howard Broadcasting Co.*, 433 U.S. 562 (1977).

5

GATHERING INFORMATION: RECORDS AND MEETINGS

One of the truly revolutionary changes in American journalism in the past two hundred years has been the fundamental shift in emphasis in the American press from journals of opinion, commentary, and some small bits of "intelligence" to the predominance of publications that offer readers a steady diet of news and information. The "news" paper as we know it simply did not exist in the era of the founding of the republic. And the significant legal battles that faced the eighteenth-century editor developed over the right to criticize, ridicule, and even libel the government and government officials. Sedition law was the primary legal problem faced by leading journalists who used their newspapers and pamphlets to form and lead political opinion.

To the editor of the 1980s the law of sedition is about as relevant as a hand-operated printing press. News and information are today the lifeblood of most newspapers, many magazines, and significant sections of the radio and television industry. Gathering and publishing news about government and government officials has become the central task of many journalists.

Most journalists consider the press in the United States to be the eyes and ears of the people with regard to their government, a function often referred to as "a watchdog role." It is the responsibility of the press to inform the people about their government—whether it is operating efficiently, whether it is living up to its constitutional requirements, whether it is treating its citizens fairly, whether its officials are acting responsibly and honestly. This interest in reporting on the activities of government has grown markedly since the 1930s, most particularly since the social and political upheavals of the late sixties and early seventies. Paradoxically, as the journalist's appetite for reporting news of government has grown, so too has grown the societal interest in government secrecy and the right to privacy. The modern reporter who seeks to scrutinize the operation of government at any level is frequently faced with legal impediments that stem from the countervailing interests in secrecy and privacy.

Government secrecy is not a new idea, but it has blossomed with new vigor since World War II. Secrecy results from many conditions. The cold war of the fifties provoked government to actions inconsistent with an open, democratic society. In the name of national security, thousands and thousands of documents are classified as confidential or secret. Ten years ago *Science* magazine reported that nearly 14,000 persons in the federal government had the power to classify material. More than 4 million documents were classified each year, and the Departments of Defense, State, and Energy and the Central Intelligence Agency were the most prolific classifiers. Scientific data that relate in obscure ways to sophisticated weapon systems, military plans and procedures, maps, photographs, and documents and papers relating to foreign policy and strategic materials—all are sifted, stamped, and filed away beyond the view of the press or the public. The problem has grown considerably worse since 1980 and the election of Ronald Reagan as president. Reagan is extremely sensitive about America's adversaries gaining access to important military, diplomatic, and scientific secrets. And he has surrounded himself with a staff that can only be described as being paranoid about the problem. Hence, the administration has enacted and proposed everything from lie detector tests and prepublication review contracts for government employees to significantly tightening government information release policies (more on this on pages 275–77).

The tremendous growth of bureaucracy at all levels of government has also resulted in cutting off public access to many governmental processes and operations. In his classic analysis of bureaucracy as a form of social organization, Max Weber argued that preoccupation with secrecy is an inherent characteristic of administrative organizations. Weber asserted that this preoccupation is based partially on the functional need to keep certain phases of administrative operation a secret to maintain a competitive edge over rival administrative units. Weber also noted that it is not uncommon that this secrecy is transformed into an obsession; that is, an action begun simply as a means to achieve organizational objectives often becomes an end in itself.

The ineptness, dishonesty, and stupidity of some government officials are also conditions that provoke secrecy in government. An inefficient, unethical, or dishonest government official can find the cloak of secrecy a convenient means of covering up misfeasance or malfeasance in office.

The emergence of the right to privacy as an obstacle to gathering news and information about government is an even more recent phenomenon. Citizens of the United States have used the law of privacy as a means of redressing excesses by the press and others for nearly a century (this dimension of privacy is fully explored in chapter 4). As our government at all levels has become more entwined in our personal lives through massive programs of public assistance, education, financial aid, and health care, the amount of information the government possesses about individual citizens has dramatically increased. Similarly, as the scope of government regulation of business, industry, financial institutions, transportation, and other activities has enlarged, government knowledge about confidential business practices, manufacturing processes, and related matters has grown as well. And as this storehouse of information about both people and institutions has grown, government has more often raised the right of privacy of these citizens or institutions as a barrier to the scrutiny of its own operations.

The purpose of this chapter is to explore the problems of gathering news and information in a society that manifests a growing interest in secrecy and privacy but that at the same time gives at least lip service to a growing interest in watching government more closely than ever. The chapter has five main sections:

1. The right to gather information from government, which is implied or may be inferred from the common law and the First Amendment to the United States Constitution
2. Federal open records and open meetings laws
3. State open records and open meetings laws
4. Federal and state statutes that specifically preclude public access to information held by the government
5. Public and press access to evidence that is presented in a court of law

While this chapter is generally comprehensive in coverage of the federal statutes and guidelines, only an overview of state law is offered. But this does not mean that state law is not important. For most reporters state laws governing access to records and meetings are more important than federal laws because local journalists spend more time reporting on local and state governments. To be a successful reporter, a journalist must have a good working knowledge of state laws governing access to information. This knowledge is as much a part of the reporter's trade as a pencil or a notebook. A reporter without full knowledge of state laws governing access to information will simply not get all the information and news to which the public is entitled. We will all be losers. Information about state laws can be obtained from teachers and professors, from press organizations within the state (such as the Society of Professional Journalists and Women in Communication, Inc.), from attorneys who represent newspapers and broadcasting stations, and from the statutes and court decisions themselves. ◆

NEWS GATHERING, THE COMMON LAW, AND THE CONSTITUTION

Persons unacquainted with the legal problems involved in news gathering are usually startled to discover that there is no clear common law right to gather news or information. Despite the tradition of open government both in this country and in Great Britain, the common law provides only bare access to government documents and to meetings of public agencies. In Great Britain, where the common law developed, complete and total access to Parliament, for example, was not guaranteed until 1874, and even then the House of Commons could exclude the public by a majority vote. Initially the public was excluded because members of Parliament feared reprisal from the Crown for statements made during floor debate. Later this fear subsided, but secret meetings continued in order to prevent voters from finding out that many members of the legislative body were not faithful in keeping promises to constituents.

Secrecy in England had a direct impact upon how colonial legislatures conducted their business. The Constitutional Convention of 1787 in Philadelphia was conducted in secret. The public and the press had almost immediate access to sessions in the United States House of Representatives, but it was not until 1794 that spectators and reporters were allowed into the Senate chamber. While today access is guaranteed to nearly all sessions of Congress, much (maybe even most) congressional business is conducted by committees that frequently meet in secret.

Common law precedents exist that open certain public records to inspection by members of the public, but distinct limitations have been placed upon this common law right. For example, under the common law a person seeking access to a record must have an "interest" in that record. And most often this interest must relate to some kind of litigation in which the person who seeks the record is a participant. Also, only those records "required to be kept" by state law are subject to even such limited disclosure under the common law. Many important records kept by the government are not "required to be kept" by law. Hence, the common law must be found wanting as an aid in the process of news gathering.

The Constitution and News Gathering

The United States Constitution is another source of the law in this nation. Does this document provide any assistance to the citizen who seeks to scrutinize government records or attend meetings of government bodies? Surprisingly, perhaps, the First Amendment plays a rather insignificant role in defining the rights of citizens and journalists in the news-gathering process. The amendment was drafted in an age when news gathering was not a primary function of the press. The congressional records of the drafting and adoption of the First Amendment fail to support the notion that the protection of the news-gathering process was to be included within the scope of freedom of the press. The adoption of antecedents to the First Amendment, such as the free speech provisions of the Virginia Declaration of Rights, and the letters and publications of men like Adams, Madison, and Jefferson are also found wanting in support of this idea. On August 15, 1789, during the House debate on the adoption of the First Amendment, James Madison, its principal author in the Congress, stated that if freedom of expression means nothing more than that "the people have a right to express and communicate their sentiments and wishes, we have provided for it already" (in what was to become the First Amendment). "The right of freedom of speech is secured; the liberty of free press is expressly declared to be beyond the reach of this government; the people may therefore publicly address their representatives, may privately address them, or declare sentiments by petition to the whole body," Madison added. One is hard pressed to find within this description of the First Amendment guarantee of freedom of expression expansive notions about the right to gather news and information. The First Amendment was seen as a means by which the public could confront its government, not necessarily report on its activities.

The United States Constitution is a living document, and as Justice Oliver Wendell Holmes reminded us, each age should be the mistress of its own law. Courts are not precluded today from finding a right to gather news under the First Amendment, even if such a right was not thought to exist in 1791. Has this happened? Have the courts ruled that the First Amendment supports the right to gather news and information? The answer to this is not completely clear. There seem to be a small but growing number of court rulings that the First Amendment protects the rights of any citizen—not just reporters—to at least attend certain kinds of hearings or meetings, and of course attending such hearings or meetings is fundamental to news gathering.

The Supreme Court of the United States has considered the First Amendment and the right to gather news in several different contexts. In 1964 the Court ruled that the constitutional right to speak and publish does not carry with it the unrestrained right to gather information. This ruling came in an unusual case concerning the right of a United States citizen to travel to Cuba in violation of a State Department ban on such travel (*Zemel* v. *Rusk*, 1964). This ruling was regarded as the law until the 1970s.

Beginning in 1972 in a series of cases involving specific news-gathering problems, the Court attempted to shape the albeit narrow boundaries of the constitutional right to gather news and information.

In *Branzburg* v. *Hayes* in 1972 the High Court suggested for the first time that the United States Constitution provides at least a limited right to gather news and information. The case involved the assertions by a trio of journalists that reporters enjoyed the right under the First Amendment to refuse to reveal to a grand jury the names of confidential news sources, since such a revelation would interfere with their ability to gather news from other confidential sources (this case is discussed more on pages 321–22). Justice Byron White, who wrote the Court's opinion for the four-man plurality, disagreed with the reporters' arguments. But, he added, "Nor is it suggested that news gathering does not qualify for First Amendment protection; without some protection for seeking out the news, freedom of the press could be eviscerated." White could find no connection, however, between news gathering and the reporters' reluctance to reveal the names of confidential news sources. Two years later the High Court considered the right to gather news in federal and state prisons.

Access to Prisons

In *Pell* v. *Procunier* (1974) reporters in California attempted to interview specific inmates at California prisons. In *Saxbe* v. *Washington Post* (1974) reporters from that newspaper sought to interview specific inmates at federal prisons at Lewisburg, Pennsylvania, and Danbury, Connecticut. In both instances the press was barred from conducting the interviews. The United States Bureau of Prisons rule, which is similar to the California regulation, states:

> Press representatives will not be permitted to interview individual inmates. This rule shall apply even where the inmate requests or seeks an interview.

At issue was not access to the prison system. The press could tour and photograph prison facilities, conduct brief conversations with randomly encountered inmates, and correspond with inmates through the mails. Outgoing correspondence from inmates was neither censored nor inspected, and incoming mail was inspected only for contraband and statements that might incite illegal action. In addition, the federal rules had been interpreted to permit journalists to conduct lengthy interviews with randomly selected groups of inmates. In fact, a reporter in the *Washington Post* case did go to Lewisburg and interview a group of prisoners.

The argument of the press in both cases was that to ban interviews with specific inmates abridged the First Amendment protection afforded the newsgathering activity of a free press. The Supreme Court disagreed in a five-to-four decision in both cases. Justice Stewart's opinion was subscribed to by the chief justice, and Justices Blackmun, White, and Rehnquist. Justice Stewart wrote that the press already had substantial access to the prisons and that there was no evidence that prison officials were hiding things from reporters. Stewart rejected the notion that the First Amendment gave newsmen a special right of access to the prisons. "Newsmen have no constitutional right of access to prisons or their inmates beyond that afforded the general public," the justice wrote. Since members of the general public have no right to interview specific prisoners, the denial of this right to the press does not infringe upon the First Amendment.

The High Court did not disagree with the findings of the district court in the *Saxbe* case that face-to-face interviews with specific inmates are essential to accurate and effective reporting about prisoners and prisons. What the Court seemed to say was that while the First Amendment guarantees freedom of expression, it does not guarantee effective and accurate reporting. In fact, about five months after the *Saxbe* and *Pell* decisions on November 2, in a speech at the Yale Law School Sesquicentennial Convocation, Justice Stewart made this exact point:

> The press is free to do battle against secrecy and deception in government. But the press cannot expect from the Constitution any guarantee that it will succeed. There is no constitutional right to have access to

particular governmental information, or to require openness from the bureaucracy. The public's interest in knowing about its government is protected by the guarantee of a free press, but the protection is indirect. The Constitution itself is neither a Freedom of Information Act nor an Official Secrets Act. The Constitution, in other words, establishes the contest, not its resolution.

In 1978 the High Court split along similar lines on a case involving press access rights to a county jail. An inmate at the Santa Rita County, California, jail committed suicide in 1975. Following the death and a report by a psychiatrist that jail conditions were bad, KQED television in San Francisco sought permission to inspect and take pictures in the jail. Sheriff Houchins announced that the media could certainly participate in one of the six tours of the jail facility that were given to the public each year. However, the tours did not visit the disciplinary cells nor the portion of the jail in which the suicide had taken place. No cameras or tape recorders were allowed, but photographs of some parts of the jail were supplied by the sheriff's office.

Reporters at KQED took a jail tour, but were not happy at the limits placed upon them. Sheriff Houchins contended that unregulated visits through the jail by the press would infringe on the inmates' right of privacy, could create jail celebrities out of inmates that would in turn cause problems for jailers, and would disrupt jail operations. Houchins noted that reporters did have access to inmates—they could visit individual prisoners, could visit with inmates awaiting trial, could talk by telephone with inmates, could write letters to prisoners, and so forth. But KQED argued that it had a constitutionally protected right to gather news and challenged the limits (*Houchins* v. *KQED,* 1978).

Chief Justice Burger wrote the opinion for the court in the four-to-three decision in which neither Justice Blackmun nor Justice Marshall took part. "Neither the First Amendment nor the Fourteenth Amendment mandates a right of access to government information or sources of information within the government's control," Burger asserted. The chief justice seemed troubled by the argument of KQED that only through access to the jail could the press perform its public responsibility (*Houchins* v. *KQED,* 1978):

> Unarticulated but implicit in the assertion that the media access to jail is essential for an informed public debate on jail conditions is the assumption that the media personnel are the best qualified persons for the task of discovering malfeasance in public institutions. . . . The media are not a substitute for or an adjunct of government. . . . We must not confuse the role of the media with that of government. . . .

Looking back at the dictum in *Branzburg* that "news gathering is not without its First Amendment protections," Burger said this must be looked at in its context—forcing a reporter to disclose to a grand jury information received in confidence. "There is an undoubted right to gather news 'from any source within the law . . .' but that affords no basis for the claim that the First Amendment compels others—private persons or government—to supply information." Problems at the jail can be investigated by citizens' task forces or grand juries, Burger said, public bodies that can be coerced to disclose what they have discovered. There is no way to force a journalist who has been given special access to the jail to publish the information gained in such an inspection.

In 1980 the United States Supreme Court ruled that the First Amendment does provide the right for all citizens—press and public alike—to attend criminal trials (*Richmond Newspapers* v. *Virginia;* see chapter 7 for a full discussion of this case). But the Court's opinion, written by Chief Justice Warren Burger, was less clear on the larger question of a First Amendment right to gather news. As scholar Thomas Emerson recently pointed out, "The decision can be viewed as a very narrow one, limited to a situation where the information sought historically has been available to the public and the press. . . ." In other words, the High Court ruled there is the right for the public to attend criminal trials and nothing more. Or the opinion can be read more expansively, as Emerson notes, "On the other hand, the Supreme Court held, for the first time, that the First Amendment does compel the government to furnish some information." This surely can be interpreted as a limited First Amendment right for the public and press to gather information.

The eight justices who took part in the seven-to-one decision in *Richmond Newspapers* v. *Virginia* wrote a total of seven opinions: the Court's opinion, five concurring opinions, and a dissent. The multiple opinions make it difficult to determine both the depth and breadth of the Court's devotion to a limited constitutional right to gather news and information. But at least two unambiguous points were made by the decision in this case. All seven justices in the majority agreed that the right to attend criminal trials is a right that belongs to both journalists and nonjournalists. There seems little support among the members of the High Court for a special right of access or a special newsgathering right for members of the press. Also, whatever right to gather the news might exist within the First Amendment, it is not an absolute right. Chief Justice Burger made it clear that even the right to attend criminal trials is not absolute; in some cases, some limits upon attendance could be constitutionally applied.

Lower courts have added considerably more legal precedent to the notion that news gathering is protected by the First Amendment. In one of the earliest recorded decisions on the question, a federal district judge in Rhode Island ruled that when public records are restricted from examination and publication, "the attempt to prohibit their publication is an abridgement of the freedom of the speech and press" (*Providence Journal Co. et al.* v. *McCoy et al.,* 1950). The case involved two newspapers seeking to examine tax cancellation and abatement records. The Pawtucket city council gave permission to one newspaper (the paper that supported the city government in power) but refused to give similar access to an opposition newspaper. A U.S. Court of Appeals upheld the lower court ruling, but on grounds that denying one newspaper access to information given to another is a violation of the guarantee of equal protection of the laws, not necessarily a violation of the First Amendment. The lower court precedent, then, has limited value. In 1977 the Fifth U.S. Court of Appeals ruled that "Newsgathering is protected by the First Amendment," but nevertheless upheld a ban by the state of Texas against a reporter who sought to film the execution of convicted felon (*Garrett* v. *Estelle,* 1977). In 1981 a U.S. District Court in the nation's capital ruled that the White House staff could not totally exclude camera crews from the Cable News Network from the pool of television photographers covering the president because the First Amendment includes "a right of access to news and information concerning the operations and activities of government" (*CNN* v. *ABC et al.,* 1981). In 1984 the Third U.S. Court of Appeals extended the qualified First Amendment right of access to attend criminal trials outlined in the Richmond Newspapers case to civil trials (*Publicker Industries* v. *Cohen,* 1984; see chapter 7 for more on this case.) Finally, in 1985 a federal trial court in Utah ruled that the public and the press had a First Amendment right to attend a formal administrative fact-finding hearing held by the *Mine Safety and Health Administration* (MSHA) (*Society of Professional Journalists* v. *Secretary of Labor,* 1985). The hearing was held to investigate the causes of a mine fire that killed twenty-seven people. A federal statute said that the Secretary of Labor might hold an open hearing but that an open hearing was not required, and MSHA chose to close this fact-finding hearing. The First Amendment right is not without limits, the court said, but "It is doubtful that there are any governmental interests compelling enough to warrant complete closure of the MSHA hearings."

While these are not all the lower court rulings that speak to the question of First Amendment rights to gather news, these decisions are typical. Sometimes, courts grant what appears to be a First Amendment right to gather news, but in fact the courts are only acknowledging a reporter's First Amendment right to ask questions—a right of free speech. For example, the state of Washington, in an attempt to stop exit polling by the television networks, made it illegal for any person on an election day "to conduct any exit poll or public opinion poll with voters" within three hundred feet of a polling place.

It is a practice of network representatives to select a few polling places and ask a representative sample of voters leaving the polling place how they voted. The results of these exit polls are used for two general purposes; to gather detailed demographic data to use in analyzing vote totals and to help the networks project the winners before the polls have closed and votes are officially counted. Many persons in Washington state object because the networks use the exit polls and other data to project the winner of a presidential election before the polls in Washington and other western states are closed.

Since the state could not block the broadcast of the projections, it chose instead to try to impede the gathering of the information used for the projections. The state's efforts failed. A U.S. district court ruled in late 1985 that the law was a violation of the First Amendment. But the court did not find that the law impeded news-gathering rights; rather, the court said, it blocked the free speech rights of reporters to ask questions (*Daily Herald* v. *Munro*).

Why haven't courts more quickly and clearly moved to the position that the First Amendment protects news gathering? There are some obvious reasons. The consequences of establishing such an unambiguous right could, it is thought, arm the press with a key that it could use to unlock all doors and thereby give reporters access to all material held by the government, all meetings of government agencies and departments. Few believe this is a good idea, but not many seriously believe it would happen if a qualified but clear First Amendment protection of news gathering were enunciated.

There is perhaps a stickier problem, one outlined by Lynn C. Malmgren in a 1974 *Villanova Law Review* article. "The reluctance of the courts to recognize distinctly a news-gathering right in the press stems from a valid concern with the administrative problems and from the logical necessity of making the determination of what constitutes the press for the purposes of constitutional protection." If the right of the press to gather news is merely the same as the right of the public to gather news, then the press may go only where the public may go, Malmgren notes. But if the press has a special right, reporters would have access to many more areas than the public. In that case, who is a reporter? what is the press? Most court decisions so far specifically rule that it is the right of the press *and the public* to attend meetings, hearings, or trials that is guaranteed, not just the right of reporters. The spectre of all citizens clamoring to see records or attend hearings has irrationally frightened some judges out of granting any First Amendment rights to gather news and information.

SUMMARY

Access to information held by the government has been a problem faced by citizen and journalist alike for centuries. Changes in both the size and nature of government in recent years have exacerbated this age-old difficulty. The common law offers little assistance to persons attempting to inspect government records. The United States Constitution was drafted at a time when news gathering was not the central role of the press. There is little evidence to suggest that the right to gather news was intended to be guaranteed by the First Amendment. Federal courts have in recent years suggested that gathering news and information is entitled to some protection under the United States Constitution, but they have been stingy in granting such protection. The United States Supreme Court has limited the right of reporters to gather information at prisons and jails to the rights enjoyed by other citizens. And the High Court has also rejected the notion that the limited protection granted news gathering entitles journalists special rights to protect the identities of their confidential news sources. The Supreme Court did rule that all citizens have the right to attend criminal trials, and this ruling has been interpreted by some observers as suggesting that there is a First Amendment guarantee to gather news and information. The Supreme Court has also suggested, however, that any First Amendment right to gather news is a right enjoyed by all citizens, not just by the press, and that this right is not absolute.

FEDERAL STATUTES AND NEWS GATHERING

Neither the common law nor the Constitution has provided the clear and well-defined right of access to government information that most citizens believe is needed. Beginning in the early 1950s, there have been concerted efforts by press and citizen lobbying groups to pass statutes that guarantee to public and press alike the right to inspect records and other information held by the government and to attend meetings held by public agencies. These laws exist in almost every state. In addition, there are federal open records and open meetings laws. Let us look at the federal legislation first.

The Freedom of Information Act

Between 1789 and 1966 access to the records of the federal government was largely an unsettled question. Various housekeeping laws, administrative procedure statutes, had been passed by Congress, but none were aimed at providing the kind of access to government records that both the press and a large segment of the population believed necessary for the efficient operation of our democracy. Before 1966 the laws Congress passed were really laws authorizing information to be withheld, rather than laws forcing government agencies to open their files. Also, reporters could do little when requests for information were denied. In 1966 after many years of hearings and testimony and work, Congress adopted the **Freedom of Information Act** (FOIA), which was ostensibly designed to open up records and files long closed to public inspection. Today, hundreds of thousands of FOIA requests are made to the federal government each year.

Adopting a freedom of information law is one thing; the way the government administers and interprets that law is another. And since the early 1980s the administration of Ronald Reagan has treated the Freedom of Information Act in a hostile fashion. The president has taken actions that both inadvertently and directly slow down or stop the flow of information about government to the press and the people. One result of severe budget-cutting during Reagan's first term was the elimination of many government services aimed at providing information to the public. Agencies such as the Department of Agriculture and the Consumer Products Safety Commission lost funds used in the past to provide free pamphlets, brochures, and documents to the public. Libraries noticed a tremendous decrease in information coming to them from the federal government. The Defense Department clamped a lid on the release of unclassified information and permitted the military to bar reporters from accompanying American troops during the invasion of Grenada in 1983. Three American reporters already on the island were detained, and the government threatened to shoot other reporters who attempted to get to the island on their own.

The federal government has required more than 100,000 workers in the CIA, FBI, and other federal agencies to sign lifetime censorship contracts; the government must give approval before these people can ever write about their government service. The administration even went so far as to prosecute under espionage laws a researcher who gave the editors of the British publication *Jane's Defense Weekly* three photos, taken by an American satellite, of a partially-constructed Russian warship (see *U.S.* v. *Morison,* 1985).

In April of 1985 *Editor and Publisher* magazine listed fifty-one separate executive actions taken by Reagan or his staff to restrict access to information and limit freedom of the press. "The Reagan administration's policies are causing the most significant media access restrictions on government information since the end of voluntary censorship in World War II," noted Jack Landau, executive director of the Reporter's Committee on Freedom of the Press, the organization that compiled the list. Even presidential supporters appeared to be dismayed by the president's actions. The journal *presstime* [sic], a monthly publication of the American Newspaper Publisher's Association, certainly not a far-left organization, published a scathing special report on the president's information policies in April of 1985. The magazine quoted Wayne Lee, the editor and publisher of the *Enterprise,* a daily newspaper in Riverside, California, that twice endorsed Reagan for president. "He is a hell of a lot better than Jimmy Carter was or Walter Mondale would have been," Lee said. But when it comes to access to government information, his record is "deplorable," Lee continued. "And frankly, I don't understand it for a fellow who keeps talking about freedom and the fact that much of [this country's] freedom rests on the free access to information," the editor added.

An added problem has been caused by government budget cutting in the age of Gramm–Rudman, the federal budget-balancing law. Many federal agencies, forced to cut their staff, have not filled vacancies among employees who are supposed to fill Freedom of Information Act requests.

A hallmark of Reagan's information policies has been the attempt by his administration to make the Freedom of Information Act as unworkable as possible. The FOIA, as we will outline shortly, gives all citizens access to records and documents held by the federal government. The law specifically states, however, that information that falls into nine separate categories may be exempt from the provisions of the law; that is, an agency or department does not have to give a citizen access to information that falls into one of these nine categories. But the agency can give a citizen access to this material in many cases. And that was the rule when Jimmy Carter was president. Carter's Attorney General Griffin Bell wrote in a memo to all department heads, "The government should not withold documents unless it is important to the public interest to do so, even if there is some arguable legal basis for the withholding." Bell warned agency heads that the Department of Justice would defend FOIA suits only when "disclosure is demonstrably harmful."

When Reagan became president that policy was reversed. A memo from Attorney General William French Smith superseded Bell's memo and told department heads to comply only with the letter, not the spirit, of the law. If a document could be withheld, they were to withhold it. The Justice Department would defend all suits challenging an agency's decision "to deny a request submitted under the FOIA unless it is determined that the agency's denial lacks a substantial legal basis. . . ," Smith wrote.

Reagan has tightened up the classification of government documents (see pages 282–83), supported amendments to the FOIA that limit the effectiveness of the law, and has given at least tacit approval to actions by various agencies to avoid complying with the federal statute, according to a 1985 article in *Columbia Journalism Review* by Steve Weinberg. For example, when a reporter for an Arizona newspaper sought documents from the Immigration and Naturalization Service in El Paso, he was told the material was in Washington, D.C. When he sought the material in Washington, D.C., he was informed it was on the way to El Paso. And back and forth. It took four months for him to get four documents.

The law recognizes that news is perishable and requires an agency to respond to a request for information within ten days. But delays are common. On February 4, 1980, a reporter for the *Washington Post* sought information from the FBI on the death of Nelson Rockefeller. The FBI found two documents, both originated by the CIA, so it told that agency to respond to the reporter's request. It did—on July 11, 1984.

Most agencies say they do not have enough persons on their staffs to handle all the FOIA requests. But Weinberg reports in the *Columbia Journalism Review* that it is a common practice for agencies not to fill vacancies for persons to handle such requests. "It is not in our best interests to have a full staff. We would have to release too much information," said a spokesperson for the Drug Enforcement Administration. Agencies use many other tricks to slow down or stop the flow of information from the government to the press and the people. And the president seems to support such actions.

What all this means is that while the Freedom of Information Act is a reasonably good law and has been interpreted in a generally fair manner by the courts, that law will work only as well as the government wants it to work.

And the current administration is not keen on the law's working well at all. In the next few pages, as we attempt to outline the important provisions of the act, it is important to remember what has been pointed out in the preceding segment.

Agency Records

One can write an open records law in two basic ways. The first way is to declare that all of the following kinds of records are to be open for public inspection and then list the kinds of records that are open. The second way is to proclaim that all government records are open for public inspection except the following kinds of records and then list the exceptions. Congress approved the second kind of law in 1966, and it went into effect in 1967. The law was substantially amended in 1974 and again in 1976.

The United States Freedom of Information Act gives any person access to all the records kept by all federal agencies, unless the information falls into one of nine categories of exempted material. An agency has been defined under the law as:

> . . . any executive department, military department, government corporation, government-controlled corporation or other establishment in the executive branch of government (including the Executive Office of the President), or any independent regulatory agency.

The laws govern records held by agencies in the executive branch of government and all the independent regulatory agencies like the Federal Trade Commission, the Federal Aviation Agency, and the Securities and Exchange Commission. The law does not cover records held by Congress or the federal courts.

What is a record? While Congress did not specify the physical characteristics of a record, records include not only documents written on paper, but also films, tapes, and probably even three-dimensional materials such as weapons that have been used as evidence in criminal cases. The Ninth United States Court of Appeals ruled in 1979 that computer tapes are records for the purposes of the law (*Long* v. *IRS*).

Few disagreements have arisen about the definition of either an agency or a record. But there has been considerable litigation about the nature of an "agency record." Courts have ruled that there must be a connection between the agency and the record before the FOIA is applicable. If the agency creates the record and possesses and controls the record, it is an agency record under the law. Mere possession of a record created by others does not necessarily bring the material under the FOIA. A transcript of a congressional hearing that was in the possession of the Central Intelligence Agency for thirty years is not an agency record, according to the United States Court of Appeals (D.C.). The "record" had been created by Congress, which is not governed by the FOIA (*Goland* v. *CIA,* 1978). A report prepared by members of Ronald Reagan's staff prior to his inauguuration as president but possessed by a high official in the Department of Health and Human Services (HHS) is not an agency record, a United States district court recently ruled. "In this case, although copies of the report are physically located in HHS, the report was not generated by HHS, is not within the control of HHS, and indeed never entered the department's files or was ever used by the department for any purpose," Judge Gesell ruled (*Wolfe* v. *Department of Health and Human Services,* 1982).

Similarly, the United States Court of Appeals for the District of Columbia ruled in 1984 that telephone message slips and desk calendars were not agency records because neither were necessarily related to agency business. The message slips simply alerted an official that a call had been received; the desk calendars were created for personal convenience, to help officials organize personal and agency business appointments (*BNA* v. *Baxter* and *Environmental Defense Fund* v. *Office of Management and Budget,* 1984). What about records that were created by an agency but are no longer possessed by the agency? The Reporter's Committee on Freedom of the Press raised this question before the Supreme Court of the United States in 1980. At issue were transcripts and summaries of telephone conversations made by Henry Kissinger while he was secretary of state. When Kissinger left his post in government, reporters asked the State Department to see copies of these materials. The agency said it could not comply with the request because Kissinger had donated the material to the Library of Congress; the State Department did not possess the records. The Reporter's Committee sued, arguing that these were agency records which should be disclosed by the Department of State under the FOIA. Justice William Rehnquist, who wrote the Supreme Court's opinion, ruled that it was unnecessary to decide whether these telephone notes were agency records, since the covered agency—the Department of State— had not withheld the documents from the reporters. "The FOIA is directed only at requiring agencies to disclose those 'agency records' for which they have chosen to retain possession or control," Rehnquist added (*Kissinger* v. *Reporter's Committee,* 1980). While the facts in this case cloud the issue somewhat (were the telephone transcripts the personal property of Kissinger or something created by the agency?), the case strongly suggests that the Freedom of Information Act cannot be used to gain access to records no longer possessed by an agency.

One of the most vexing problems regarding the definition of agency records has to do with material created for an agency by a private consulting firm. Many persons argue that when the Congress amended the FOIA in 1974, it intended that the law cover all entities that "performed governmental functions and controlled information of public interest." This phrase was contained in a House of Representatives report (93rd Cong., 2d sess., H. Rept. 876) that focused on the amendment. This language surely would place many government consultants under the aegis of the FOIA, according to Anne Wright in an article in the *Georgetown Law Journal.* But the courts have not rigorously applied the law to consulting agencies, even though in some cases these firms do a tremendous amount of government work. Wright reports that in fiscal year 1979, the federal government spent $2.3 billion on consulting services. Seven federal agencies relied on consultants to meet more than 40 percent of their congressionally mandated reporting requirements, according to the legal scholar.

In 1980 the Supreme Court ruled that the FOIA does not normally apply to materials generated and retained by consulting firms. The National Institute of Arthritis, Metabolism, and Digestive Diseases (NIAMDD) hired private consultants to study the effectiveness of certain diabetes treatments. The consultants kept the raw data generated by the study, but NIAMDD had access to the data. The consultants concluded in their reports that the use of certain drugs in diabetes treatment increased the risk of heart disease. Access to the raw data was sought by persons outside government. The agency's refusal to grant access to the material was supported by the Supreme Court, which ruled that data generated by a privately controlled organization that has received federal grants are not agency records. Even though NIAMDD used federal money to have the consultants create the data in question, the High Court refused to agree that this amounted to "creating" the records themselves. "We agree with the opinions of the courts below . . . that an agency [the federal agency] must first either create or obtain a record as a prerequisite to it becoming an agency record within the meaning of the FOIA," wrote Justice Rehnquist for the majority of the Court (*Forsham* v. *Harris,* 1980).

Because of the importance to the news-gathering process of FOIA exemptions, of procedures for obtaining information under the FOIA, and of the potential for change in the Freedom of Information Act, all are treated here in separate sections, although all are subordinate to the overall discussion of the Freedom of Information Act.

FOIA Exemptions

Before the FOIA becomes applicable, then, the information that is sought must be considered an agency record under the law. Agency records may be inspected and copied by the public, unless they fall into one of the nine categories of exempt material. As noted previously, federal agencies are not required to withhold documents from disclosure, even if they fall within an exemption to the FOIA (*Chrysler Corp.* v. *Brown,* 1979). They may choose to disclose this information. But if records or documents properly fall under one of the nine exemptions, access to this material may be properly denied under the law.

Let us look at each exemption separately, try to illuminate its meaning, and note any important court interpretations of the language in the law. The Freedom of Information Act exempts the following nine categories of materials from disclosure.

Exemption 1: Matters specifically authorized under criteria established by an executive order to be kept secret in the interest of national defense or foreign policy and in fact properly classified pursuant to such an executive order. This exemption deals with a wide range of materials, from the highest secrets of state to more or less mundane matters. The United States Court of Appeals (D.C.) recently ruled, for example, that the army's compilation of combat units' operation readiness reports was properly classified as confidential and exempt from disclosure under the Freedom of Information Act (*Taylor* v. *Army,* 1982).

As originally adopted in 1966, this exemption excluded from disclosure any document or record that the president, through executive order, chose to classify in the name of national security. Courts, including the Supreme Court, ruled that there could be no challenge to the classification of the document or record, no judicial examination of whether the material was sensitive or even related to national security (see *Epstein* v. *Resor,* 1970 and *EPA* v. *Mink,* 1973). The exemption was abused by the administration, especially during the Nixon presidency, and was amended by the Congress in 1974. The change in the law has given the courts the power to inspect classified documents to determine whether they have been properly classified.

What is supposed to happen is this: The president (undoubtedly his staff) establishes criteria in an executive order for the classification of sensitive documents and records. Material is then classified according to the executive order by members of various government agencies such as the Department of Defense, the National Security Agency, and others. This material is exempt from disclosure. But a citizen seeking a document or record can challenge the classification of any document and ask a court to determine whether the material has been properly classified, using the criteria established by the president. A judge cannot question the criteria established by the executive branch but can only determine whether the records or documents were properly classified according to those criteria.

For example, a federal court was asked to determine whether the navy had properly classified videotape it had taken of the crash of a jet fighter aboard the USS *Nimitz*. The accident, which occurred in 1981, killed fourteen people and caused $100 million in damage to the carrier and other planes. A congressional investigation of the crash turned up evidence that flight-deck crew members may have been under the influence of drugs at the time of the incident. Since the navy routinely videotapes all carrier takeoffs and landings, there was tape of the accident. Reporter David Browde sought access to the videotape but was turned away. The navy said the material was exempt from release for national security reasons. Analysis of the videotape would reveal operational capabilities of the navy's supercarriers, Secretary of the Navy John Lehman said. Browde went to court, but Judge John Pratt ruled that the navy had shown that it had properly classified the videotape. The U.S. Court of Appeals refused to review the ruling (*Browde* v. *Navy,* 1983).

In fact, courts have been very reluctant to second-guess the administration on the classification of documents. The law states that a court *may* determine whether the material was properly classified; it does not state that the court *must* do so. And most courts refuse even to examine the documents. The Fourth Circuit Court of Appeals turned down a request that it privately examine specific secret materials to see whether the documents were classified properly. The court claimed it lacked the expertise to make such a judgment and told the complainant to file a complaint with the agency denying access originally (*Knopf* v. *Colby,* 1975).

In taking this tack the courts seemed to reflect the reluctance of Congress itself to view the FOIA as a means to reform the classification process or to bring about systematic review of individual decisions. The Senate-House Conference Committee report on the 1974 amendment, for example, noted:

> The executive departments responsible for national defense and foreign policy matters have unique insights into what adverse effects may occur as a result of public disclosure of a particular classified record. Accordingly, the conferees expect that federal courts . . . will accord substantial weight to an agency's affidavits concerning the details of the classified status of a disputed record.

Judicial reluctance to second-guess the executive branch on the classification of national security materials has become a much more serious problem since President Ronald Reagan sharply tightened the national security classification regulations. President Jimmy Carter had required government agencies to consider the public interest as well as the government interest before classifying any document. Under the Carter administration most documents automatically were declassified after six years unless the federal agency reviewed the material and requested reclassification for six more years. Also under President Carter, government agencies had to prove that "identifiable damage" to national security would result if the information were not classified.

President Reagan changed these policies in an executive order issued in April 1982 (Executive Order 12356). The order ended the explicit consideration of public interest before classification and directed officials to opt for the highest level of secrecy possible when classifying material. The order also permitted classification of materials if the agency could show "any damage," rather than "identifiable damage," to the national security. Material is no longer automatically declassified after six years. Reagan's executive order also permits the reclassification of material that has already been made public. The National Security Agency recently took documents off public shelves at a Virginia Military Institute library that had been available to the public for years and classified them (see *Peterzell* v. *Faurer,* 1986). These rules went into effect on August 1, 1982. Reagan added strong support for this executive order in March 1983 when he signed a directive ordering all federal employees with access to sensitive information to sign a nondisclosure agreement as a condition of gaining access to this information. The FBI was given enhanced authority to investigate so-called leaks, and federal employees could be forced to take lie detector tests during investigations of these leaks, under provisions of the presidential directive.

Exemption 2: Matters related solely to the internal personnel rules and practices of an agency. This exemption covers what are known as "housekeeping" materials: vacation schedules, coffee-break rules, parking-lot assignments, and so forth. Little harm would result if these materials were made public; the exemption is offered simply to relieve the agencies of the burden of having to maintain such material in public files.

The most controversial aspect of exemption two is whether it applies to agency staff manuals. For example, a citizen recently sought access to a Bureau of Alcohol, Tobacco, and Firearms staff manual entitled *Surveillance of Premises, Vehicles, and Persons.* The bureau released all but twenty pages of the manual, which it said described internal personnel rules and practices of the agency. The United States Court of Appeals for the District of Columbia ruled in favor of the agency in the lawsuit that followed. The court noted that during the debate on the FOIA in Congress, members spoke without contradiction that exemption two was designed to protect law enforcement investigatory manuals from disclosure (*Crooker* v. *Bureau,* 1981). Other federal courts agree (see *Hardy* v. *Bureau of Alcohol, Tobacco, and Firearms,* 1980).

Exemption 3: Matters specifically exempted from disclosure by statute (other than section 552b of this title) provided that such statute (a) requires that the matters be withheld from the public in such a manner as to leave no discretion on the issue, or (b) establishes particular criteria for withholding or refers to particular types of matters to be withheld. This exemption is designed to protect from disclosure information required or permitted to be kept secret by dozens of other federal laws. A wide range of records fall under this exemption, including census bureau records, public utility information, trade secrets, patent applications, tax returns, bank records, veterans benefits, and documents held by both the Central Intelligence Agency and the National Security Agency.

Courts generally ask three questions when determining whether exemption three applies to a specific record or document:

1. Is there a specific statute that authorizes or requires the withholding of information?

2. Does the statute designate specific kinds of information or outline specific criteria for information that may be withheld?
3. Does the record or information that is sought fall within the categories of information that may be withheld?

If all three questions are answered yes, disclosure can be legally denied.

In the mid-1980s the Central Intelligence Agency used both Congressional amendments and court action relating to this exemption to close off public scrutiny of much of its work. For the last several years, CIA officials have lobbied Congress for an amendment to the FOIA totally exempting the agency from the provisions of the law. They got something close to that in 1984 when Congress voted to exempt all operational files from release under the Freedom of Information Act. To be exempt a CIA file must deal with the conduct of foreign intelligence operations, background investigations of informants, liaison arrangements with foreign governments, or scientific or technical means of gathering foreign intelligence. The director of the CIA designates certain files as being exempt, using the criteria established by Congress. The law provides for judicial review of whether the files are properly designated, but as previously noted, judicial review has not worked well as it relates to national security documents and there is no reason to suspect it will work any better in this case.

In the spring of 1985, the Supreme Court ruled that another category of CIA material is not available for public inspection. From 1952 to 1966 the CIA funded 185 researchers at eighty universities to study the effects of mind-altering substances on humans. In 1963 the CIA's inspector general investigated the clandestine project and reported to the agency director that people were unwittingly being used as guinea pigs for some of the experiments. CIA files on the project were declassified in 1970, and Congressional reports on the project received publicity in middecade. John Sims, an attorney, in 1977 filed an FOIA request with the CIA, asking for the names of institutions and individuals who had participated in the experiments. The CIA would disclose only the institutions and individuals who agreed to the release of their names. The agency said that such names were exempt from disclosure under the National Security Act of 1947, which states, "The Director of Central Intelligence shall be responsible for protecting intelligence sources and methods from unauthorized disclosure." The institutions and individuals were intelligence sources, the agency argued.

The U.S. Court of Appeals ruled that an intelligence source was an individual or institution that provides the CIA with information on a confidential basis (*Sims v. CIA,* 1983). The Supreme Court disagreed, saying that this definition of an intelligence source was too narrow and that such a narrow definition of a source interferes with the broad authority granted to the director of the agency under the National Security Act, to protect all sources of information, not only those guaranteed confidentiality. The agency was free to withhold the information (*Sims* v. *CIA,* 1985). It is expected that more and more government agencies will go to Congress in the future to seek exemptions from the FOIA.

Exemption 4: Trade secrets and financial information obtained from any person and privileged or confidential. Two kinds of information are exempt from disclosure under this exemption—trade secrets and financial information. The trade secret exemption has not been heavily litigated, although recently the U.S. Court of Appeals in the District of Columbia fashioned a definition of a trade secret that considerably narrows the exemption. In litigation initiated by Ralph Nader's Public Citizen Health Research Project, the court said a trade secret is "an unpatented, commercial valuable plan, appliance, formula, or process which is used for the making, preparing, compounding, treating, or processing of articles or materials which are trade commodities, and that can be said to be the end product of either innovation or substantial effort." The court rejected a broader definition of a trade secret proposed by the Food and Drug Administration: "any . . . compilation of information which is used in one's business and which gives him an opportunity to obtain an advantage over competitors who do not know or use it" (*Public Citizen Health Research Group* v. *Food and Drug Administration,* 1983).

The "financial information" exemption applies only to information supplied to the government by individuals or private business firms. It is this second section of the exemption that has undergone the most thorough judicial interpretation. The *Miami Herald* recently sought records from the Small Business Administration (SBA) regarding loans made to small contractors that had become delinquent. The SBA attempted to block the disclosure by citing exemption four. Courts have interpreted exemption four to apply only if the disclosure of the information will impair the government's ability to obtain information in the future or cause substantial harm to the competitive position of the person from whom the information was obtained. The SBA failed to present any evidence that the delinquent borrowers would suffer competitive harm if this information were disclosed. In fact, there was no evidence presented that the borrowers were even in competition with anyone. A United States court of appeals ordered the material disclosed (*Miami Herald* v. *Small Business Administration,* 1982). The federal courts have rigorously applied the criteria outlined above in the *Miami Herald* case. To block disclosure the government must clearly demonstrate that the provider of the information will suffer considerably more than mere embarrassment or a small loss of business.

Exemption 5: Interagency and intraagency memorandums and letters which would not be available by law to a private party in litigation with the agency. This exemption is described in an FOI Service Center bulletin as designed to protect working papers, studies, and reports prepared within an agency or circulated among government personnel as the basis of a final agency decision. In addition, this exemption shields from disclosure communications between an agency and its attorney.

Two recent cases demonstrate the kinds of materials covered by exemption five. A request was made for material on the United States Air Force report on the use of herbicides in Vietnam. The government provided the final report prepared by the Air Force, but refused to give out portions of the first draft of the report, which were never included in the final report. The court of appeals upheld the government's refusal. The court said (*Russell* v. *Air Force,* 1982):

> There are essentially three policy bases for this privilege. First, it protects creative debate and candid consideration of alternatives, within an agency, and thereby improves the quality of the agency policy decisions. Second, it protects the public from the confusion that would result from premature exposure to discussions occurring before the policies affecting it had actually been settled upon. And third, it protects the integrity of the decision-making process itself by confirming that "officials should be judged by what they decided, not for matters they considered before making up their minds."

The portions of the first draft of the report sought by the plaintiff in the case were considerations, not decisions and part of the decision-making process designed to be protected by this exemption.

However, in another instance, the same court ruled against the government when it attempted to use exemption five. In the late 1970s the United States attorney general set up a task force to investigate charges that a Federal Bureau of Investigation (FBI) informant inside the Ku Klux Klan had committed illegal acts while in the Klan, including shooting a civil rights worker. A 302-page report was produced, and *Playboy* magazine sought a copy of the document. The FBI resisted, citing several exemptions including exemption five. The court ruled that while some parts of the report (i.e., names and identifying data) were exempt from the law under other exemptions (exemption seven), the entire report was not protected under exemption five. This exemption is designed to protect the deliberative process, to protect opinions and recommendations from which government decisions are made, the court said. It does not protect purely factual material appearing in documents in a form that is totally severable without compromising the private remainder of the documents (*Playboy* v. *Justice Department,* 1982).

In 1984 the U.S. Supreme Court ruled that confidential statements obtained during an Air Force investigation of an air crash are protected from disclosure under exemption five. The public is entitled to all such memorandums or letters that a private party could discover in litigation with the agency, wrote Justice John Paul Stevens for a unanimous court. But the material in question would not normally or routinely be open to discovery in a civil proceeding (the discovery process in litigation enables one party to gain access to evidence, testimony, and other material held by the other party, prior to the trial). The High Court ruled that exemption five incorporates the civil discovery privilege; Congress did not intend to create a situation in which litigants could use the FOIA to circumvent discovery privileges (*U.S.* v. *Weber Aircraft Corp.,* 1984).

Exemption five is also called the executive privilege exemption. **Executive privilege** is an old concept in the history of the republic. Since 1794, beginning with President George Washington, American chief executives have asserted that the president enjoys a common law privilege to keep secret all presidential papers, records, and other documents. Washington asserted the privilege when Congress called for all papers and records in the possession of the president that would facilitate its investigation of the negotiation of the Jay Treaty, a controversial agreement with Great Britain. Washington refused to comply with the congressional demand, citing executive privilege. Andrew Jackson refused to give Congress information relating to a boundary dispute in Maine. Millard Fillmore refused a request from the Senate that he provide that body with information regarding negotiations with the Sandwich (Hawaiian) Islands.

In modern times, however, the heads of agencies within the executive branch have asserted that they also enjoy a kind of limited executive privilege. Exemption five covers the kinds of documents—working papers, memorandums, and so forth—traditionally claimed exempt from public scrutiny by executive privilege. The purpose of the exemption is to protect the confidentiality of the decision-making process. However, exemption five is often used as a shield to avoid disclosing all manner of material totally unrelated to decision making. Legal memorandums, correspondence, minutes and transcripts, staff analyses, interpretations and opinions, and recommendations of experts and consultants have all been at one time or another declared to fall within the boundaries of exemption five.

In 1974 in *U.S.* v. *Nixon,* the Supreme Court sharply limited the boundaries of the traditional executive privilege. In this case several of the famous White House tapes were subpoenaed by the special prosecutor for use in the criminal trial of some of the Nixon aides. The former president argued that the tapes were protected by executive privilege. He said that revelation of the material on the tapes would damage the integrity of the decision-making process and that under our system of separation of powers, the courts were precluded from reviewing his claim of privilege. He also argued that even if his claim of absolute executive privilege should fail, the court should at least hold as a matter of constitutional law that his privilege superseded the subpoena.

However, in a unanimous opinion (eight-to-nothing, since Justice Rehnquist did not participate in the decision) the Burger Court rejected the notion of absolute privilege in this case. The Court said that an absolute privilege can be asserted only when the material in question consists of military or diplomatic secrets. When other kinds of information are involved, privilege of the president must be balanced against other values, in this case, against the operation of the criminal justice system. The need for the privilege must be weighed against the need for the information. Courts will have to make these decisions from private examination of the materials in question.

How does this decision affect exemption five? Since exemption five is based on the notion of the executive privilege and since the courts have said such an absolute privilege does not exist in the absence of military or diplomatic secrets, agencies that claim exemption five as reason to deny access will have to allow the courts to scrutinize the material in question and evaluate whether the need for secrecy outweighs the benefits of disclosure. The mechanical process of the past under which agencies could gain the exemption merely by asserting that the material in question fell under the purview of the fifth exemption is probably gone. Now when they are challenged, agencies will have to prove to a judge that the material does in fact come within the fifth exemption. Disclosure of much such material withheld in the past should be ensured.

Exemption 6: Personnel and medical files and similar files the disclosure of which would constitute a clearly unwarranted invasion of privacy. This exemption is designed to shield from public view personal and private information held in government files about millions of Americans. There has been considerable litigation involving exemption six, and it is possible to outline a fairly authoritative interpretation of its meaning.

The exemption protects "personnel and medical and similar files." What are similar files? They are files that contain highly personal information, similar to the kinds of personal information that can be found in medical and personnel files. In February 1981 the United States Court of Appeals (D.C.) suggested that "similar files" were files *like* medical and personnel files (*Washington Post* v. *State Department,* 1981). But fifteen months later the Supreme Court of the United States rejected that interpretation and said that that phrase "similar files" had a broad meaning and covered a wide range of different kinds of files. What is being protected from disclosure, Justice William Rehnquist wrote for the unanimous Court, is a kind of *information,* not a kind of *file.* An individual's medical and personnel files contain highly personal information about that individual. A file is a "similar file" if it contains the same kind of highly personal information (*State Department* v. *Washington Post,* 1982). Be careful here. Not every file that contains personal information will be considered a "similar file." "The test is not merely whether the information is in some sense personal, but whether it is of the same magnitude—as highly personal or as intimate in nature—as contained in personnel or medical records," according to the First United States Court of Appeals (*Kurzon* v. *Health and Human Services,* 1981; see also *Miami Herald* v. *Small Business Administration,* 1982).

Establishing that a file contains personal information is only the first step in the application of exemption six. The court must ask two additional questions:

1. Would the release of this information constitute an invasion of personal privacy?
2. If it will, is this invasion of privacy clearly unwarranted?

Whether an invasion of privacy is warranted or unwarranted will be determined largely by the public benefit that may be derived from the release of the information. The government normally carries the burden of proving that the release of certain information amounts to a "clearly unwarranted" invasion of privacy. But the person seeking the information generally will have to demonstrate that there is public interest in the release of the material. He or she cannot rely solely on the fact that the government has failed to meet its burden of proof. In a 1976 decision the Supreme Court said that exemption six does not protect from disclosure every incidental invasion of privacy, but rather "only such disclosures as constitute clearly unwarranted invasions of personal privacy" (*Department of the Air Force* v. *Rose,* 1976).

The U.S. Court of Appeals in the District of Columbia recently ruled that the release of records that list the description, quantity, and price of prescription drugs ordered for members of Congress by the U.S. Navy would not necessarily be an unwarranted invasion of privacy. The navy operates the Office of the Attending Physician to the United States Congress. Researchers for *Congressional Quarterly* sought access to the records. There was no attempt to gain access to the names of members of Congress who were given the prescription drugs. The navy contended, however, that researchers could put the list of the drugs together with other information and discover quite a bit about the personal health of the members of Congress. A federal district court granted a summary judgment to the navy based on this argument, but the court of appeals ruled that the navy would have to prove this contention before it could block release of the data.

The Supreme Court has said that the invocation of exemption six requires threats to privacy interests more palpable than mere possibilities. The court noted, "Even if each drug is only prescribed for a single disease, it is fanciful to assume that without more . . . [than the] knowledge that someone among 600 possible recipients was probably using the drug [only probably, because it might, of course, have been ordered merely to replenish an inventory], would lead to the conclusion that beneficiary X has disease Y." Even if release of the data did reveal information about the health of members of Congress, it is not necessarily an unwarranted invasion of privacy, the court said. The drugs are made available free to the beneficiaries, and the public has an interest in knowing such things as the extent to which the Office of the

Attending Physician prescribes name-brand drugs, as opposed to generic drugs, or whether drugs that the Food and Drug Administration says are ineffective are prescribed (*Arieff* v. *Navy,* 1983).

In another recent ruling a U.S. district court ordered the FBI to release the names of three FBI officials who had been censured for the bureau's domestic surveillance operations in the 1970s. Reporter Carl Stern got copies of the letters of censure, but the names were deleted. The court rejected the claim of invasion of privacy, noting that such considerations do not exist "when relatively high-placed officials entrusted with the performance of important public business actually jeopardize an agency's integrity by covering up government wrong doing" (*Stern* v. *FBI,* 1983).

Exemption 7: Investigatory records compiled for law enforcement purposes, but only to the extent that the production of such records would (a) interfere with enforcement proceedings, (b) deprive a person of the right to a fair trial or an impartial adjudication, (c) constitute an unwarranted invasion of personal privacy, (d) disclose the identity of a confidential source and, in the case of a record compiled by a criminal law enforcement authority in the course of a criminal investigation or by an agency conducting a lawful national security intelligence investigation, confidential information furnished only by the confidential source, (e) disclose investigative techniques and procedures, or (f) endanger the life or physical safety of law enforcement personnel.

The release of certain documents could seriously harm ongoing criminal or civil investigations being conducted by federal agencies. This exemption is designed to block the release of these documents. At one time many federal agencies used this exemption in a loose fashion to improperly shield a wide range of information. Exemption seven was amended in 1974, and now the law requires the government to prove that documents it seeks to withhold were compiled for specific criminal, civil, or other law enforcement proceedings and that disclosure would actually result in one of the six listed harms.

Courts follow a two-step approach in applying exemption seven:

1. Was the document an investigatory record compiled for law enforcement purposes?
2. If it was, would the release of the document have one of the six results specified in the exemption?

A good example of this approach came in *Cohen* v. *EPA.* Neil Cohen sought 142 names of persons and companies that had received notices from the Environmental Protection Agency regarding their potential liability for the release of hazard substances into the environment. The agency released six names but declined to reveal the other 136. It argued that these were law enforcement records and their release would interfere with enforcement proceedings. A federal district court agreed that these were law enforcement records but could not see how their release would interfere with the agency's attempts to enforce the environmental laws (*Cohen v. EPA*, 1983).

Summaries of investigatory records compiled for law enforcement purposes are also protected by exemption seven, according to a 1982 ruling by the Supreme Court of the United States. In 1969 the White House requested that the FBI summarize and transmit to the president information in its files concerning particular individuals who had criticized the administration. Howard Abramson sought to see these summaries in 1976. The FBI said the documents were shielded by exemption seven; these were investigatory records gathered for law-enforcement purposes. Abramson agreed that as long as the information was in the FBI files, it was exempt from disclosure but that when it was taken out of the files, summarized, and sent to the White House, it was no longer an investigatory record compiled for law enforcement purposes. The High Court disagreed in a five-to-four ruling. "We hold that information initially contained in a record made for law-enforcement purposes continues to meet the threshold requirements of exemption seven where that recorded information is reproduced or summarized in a new document prepared for a non–law enforcement purpose," Justice Byron White wrote for the majority. He said there was no question that exemption seven would shield the data if the FBI had given verbatim records to the White House. Summarization of this data does not withdraw the material from the protection of exemption seven. In a sharp dissent Justice William Brennan accused the majority of rewriting the law and said the Court was rejecting a logical and straightforward interpretation of the statute and replacing it with one less plausible (*FBI v. Abramson*, 1982).

Exemption 8: Matters contained in or related to examination, operating, or condition reports prepared by, on behalf of, or for the use of any agency responsible for the regulation and supervision of financial institutions. This is a little-used exemption that is designed to prevent the disclosure of sensitive financial reports or audits that, if made public, might undermine the public confidence in banks, trust companies, investment banking firms, and other financial institutions.

Exemption 9: Geological and geophysical information and data, including maps concerning wells. People who drill oil and gas wells provide considerable information about these wells to the government. This exemption prevents speculators and other drillers from gaining access to this valuable information.

Handling FOIA
Requests

Government departments must answer requests for records and documents within ten days. If an appeal is filed after a denial, the agency has only twenty days to rule upon the appeal. Each agency must publish quarterly, or more frequently, an index of the documents and records it keeps. If an agency charges for searching out records or for duplicating them, it must have a uniform schedule of fees (everyone is charged the same amount) and the charges must be fair and reasonable.

The cost factor has been used by agencies in an attempt to thwart FOIA requests. Attempts have been made to place heavy financial burden on persons seeking information. When Philip and Sue Long sought certain records from the Internal Revenue Service (IRS), the agency said that identifying data would have to be edited from the records and that the Longs would be billed for the editing costs—some $160,000. The Ninth Circuit Court ruled against the taxing agency and said that while it was permissible to charge persons seeking records for the cost of searching out the documents or duplicating them, the agency had to bear the costs of segregating the identifying data from the material that must be released under the law. As it turned out, the Longs wanted far fewer records than the IRS asserted, and the cost of editing was only a fraction of the initial estimate of $160,000 (*Long* v. *IRS,* 1979).

Agencies are required to report to Congress each year and must include in the report a list of the materials to which access was granted and to which access was denied and the costs incurred. If a citizen or a reporter has to go to court to get the agency to release materials and the agency loses the case, the agency may be assessed the cost of the complainant's legal fees and court costs. Finally, agency personnel are now personally responsible for granting or denying access, a requirement federal agencies object to strenuously. An employee of an agency who denies a request for information must be identified to the person who seeks the material, and if the access is denied in an arbitrary or capricious manner, the employee can be disciplined by the Civil Service Commission.

The Freedom of Information Act is not difficult to use. In an informative article in the *Columbia Journalism Review* ("The Revised F.O.I. Law and How to Use It"), longtime right-of-access proponent Sam Archibald offers some suggestions to journalists on making the law work:

1. Find out which agencies have the material in which you are interested. The *United States Government Manual* lists all federal agencies (Archibald writes), explains what they are supposed to do, and usually lists local addresses and telephone numbers.

2. Call or write the agency to get background information about the material and information in which you are interested.

3. When you have determined what records you seek, write an official request for the material. Address it to the head of the agency, describe as specifically as possible the material you seek, and state that the request is made under the Freedom of Information Act: 5 United States Code, Section 552 (see "Sample FOI Request Letter").

SAMPLE FOI REQUEST LETTER

Tele. No. (business hours)
Return Address
Date

Name of Public Body
Address

To the FOI Officer:

This request is made under the federal Freedom of Information Act, 5 U.S.C. 552.

Please send me copies of *(Here, clearly describe what you want. Include identifying material, such as names, places, and the period of time about which you are inquiring. If you wish, attach news clips, reports, and other documents describing the subject of your research.)*

As you know, the FOI Act provides that if portions of a document are exempt from release, the remainder must be segregated and disclosed. Therefore, I will expect you to send me all nonexempt portions of the records which I have requested, and ask that you justify any deletions by reference to specific exemptions of the FOI Act. I reserve the right to appeal your decision to withhold any materials.

I promise to pay reasonable search and duplication fees in connection with this request. However, if you estimate that the total fees will exceed $_____ , please notify me so that I may authorize expenditure of a greater amount.

(Optional) I am prepared to pay reasonable search and duplication fees in connection with this request. However, the FOI Act provides for waiver or reduction of fees if disclosure could be considered as "primarily benefiting the general public." I am a journalist *(researcher, or scholar)* employed by *(name of news organization, book publishers, etc.)*, and intend to use the information I am requesting as the basis for a planned article *(broadcast, or book). (Add arguments here in support of fee waiver)*. Therefore, I ask that you waive all search and duplication fees. If you deny this request, however, and the fees will exceed $___, please notify me of the charges before you fill my request so that I may decide whether to pay the fees or appeal your denial of my request for a waiver.

As I am making this request in the capacity of a journalist *(author, or scholar)* and this information is of timely value, I will appreciate your communicating with me by telephone, rather than by mail, if you have any questions regarding this request. Thank you for your assistance, and I will look forward to receiving your reply within 10 business days, as required by law.

(Signature)

Sample FOIA request letter, from *How to Use the FOI Act,* 2d ed., FOI Service Center Publication, Washington, D.C., 20005, 1980.

4. If your request is rejected, file an appeal with the head of the agency. Send along the copy of the rejection letter and make a strong argument as to why you think the material is not exempt.

5. If the appeal is rejected—and you really want to get the material—go to court. This final point, more than any other, needs to be emphasized. As long as government agencies are confident that the press and public will not bother with lawsuits, the tendency to withhold information will be reinforced. But strong sanctions can be applied against government officials who are found to have deliberately withheld material illegally. Sanctions can only be applied, however, after judicial determination of the matter. The application of this kind of pressure on a regular basis by the press and the public can have generally positive impact in the battle for open government.

Reporter Steve Weinberg, in an article in the *Columbia Journalism Review,* adds these additional tips for using the FOIA. Be specific in your request. Know exactly what you want. To do this you must study the agency indexes closely. Try to direct FOIA requests to regional or local offices when possible. It is easier to communicate with a local office, and very often the people who operate these offices are not as "hardened" as their counterparts in Washington. Offer to pay reasonable fees in your request letter; if not, the agency will write you back in ten days and ask if you are willing to pay the fees. This will simply delay any action on your request.

Potential Changes in the Freedom of Information Act

During each session of Congress, amendments to the FOIA are proposed. They generally come from those who wish to tighten the law, to make it harder to gain access to information. Several proposals have been introduced to increase the secrecy for law-enforcement, organized-crime, and Secret-Service records. Also, it has been proposed that businesses be given an avenue to object to the disclosure of sensitive corporate information before such information is released. The House Subcommittee on Government Operations approved an amendment to the law in 1986 that would give businesses additional protection from disclosure of information they have given to the government. Both the chemical and drug industries are fighting for this measure. If adopted, the law would permit businesses to designate any information they give the government as confidential. When a government agency got an FOI request for such information, it would have to notify the company. The company would have two weeks to file a request that the information not be given out. The agency would then be given two more weeks to make a decision on whether or not to honor the businesses' request. If the agency decides to release the information, the business would have two more weeks to file an appeal. Many expected this bill to reach the floor of Congress in the fall of 1986. In the last session of Congress Rep. Gerald Klecka, a Democrat from Wisconsin, introduced legislation that would amend FOIA exemptions for national security, internal personnel, and financial institution records to make it easier to obtain this material; expand the definition of "agency" and "records"; establish a system of financial penalties against agencies that refuse to comply with legal FOIA deadlines; authorize sanctions against government employees who mishandle FOIA requests; and require expedited access procedures to handle urgently needed information. This is the first time in many years that legislation aimed at providing greater access to information has been introduced.

Federal Open Meetings Law

In 1976 Congress passed and the president signed into law the Government in Sunshine Act, the **federal open meetings law.** The statute affects approximately fifty federal boards, commissions, and agencies "headed by a collegial body composed of two or more individual members, a majority of whom are appointed to such position by the president with the advice and consent of the Senate." These public bodies are required to conduct their business meetings in public. Notice of public meetings must be given one week in advance, and the agencies are required to keep careful records of what occurs at closed meetings. The law also prohibits informal communication between officials of an agency and representatives of companies and other interested persons with whom the agency does business unless this communication is recorded and made part of the public record.

Courts have strictly interpreted the requirement that the law only applies to bodies whose members are appointed by the president. In 1981 the United States Court of Appeals for the District of Columbia ruled that the Government in Sunshine Act did not govern meetings of the Chrysler Loan Guarantee Board, a body created by the Congress to oversee federal loan guarantees for the financially troubled automaker. Persons who serve on the board are not actually named by the president, but serve because they hold other federal offices (i.e., secretary of the treasury, comptroller general, chairman of the Federal Reserve). "If Congress had wanted to subject the board to the provisions of the Sunshine Act, it could have so provided when the board was established," the court noted (*Symons* v. *Chrysler Corporation Loan Guarantee Board,* 1981). A board or agency must also have some independent authority to act or take action before the law applies. A U.S. Court of Appeals ruled that the law does not apply to the president's Council of Economic Advisors (CEA). The sole function of the CEA is to advise and assist the president, the court said. It has no regulatory power. It cannot fund projects, even though it may appraise them. It has no function, saving advising and assisting the president. Hence, it is not subject to either the FOIA or the Government in Sunshine Act (*Rushforth* v. *Council of Economic Advisors,* 1985).

Even agencies or commissions that fall under the aegis of the law may meet behind closed doors. The 1976 law lists ten conditions or exemptions under which closed meetings might be held. The first nine of these exemptions mirror the exemptions in the Freedom of Information Act. The tenth exemption focuses upon situations in which the agency is participating in arbitration or is in the process of adjudicating or otherwise disposing of a case.

The court of appeals in Washington, D.C., recently ruled that agencies may not automatically hold budget deliberations behind closed doors. "The Sunshine Act contains no express exemption for budget deliberations as a whole. Specific items discussed at budget meetings might, however, be exempt and might justify closing portions of a commission meeting on an individual and particularized basis," Judge Skelly Wright ruled. In each case the agency must defend its closure of the meeting by demonstrating that the discussion would focus on material excluded from public disclosure by one of the ten exemptions (*Common Cause* v. *Nuclear Regulatory Commission,* 1982). The tenth exemption was recently used to block access to a meeting of the Nuclear Regulatory Commission. The NRC was discussing the reopening of the nuclear power plant at Three Mile Island in Pennsylvania. The federal district court ruled that this meeting would likely focus upon the final adjudication of the federal action involving the nuclear reactor and hence could be closed to press and public (*Philadelphia Newspapers* v. *Nuclear Regulatory Commission,* 1983).

There has been relatively little litigation under the Government in Sunshine Act, and reporters who work in Washington, D.C., report that compliance with the law is not good. The same problems existed in the early years of operation of the Freedom of Information Act. Constant pressure and frequent litigation against agencies that refused to comply with the FOIA finally made the law effective. The same pressure is needed to make the Government in Sunshine Act live up to its promise.

SUMMARY

Statutes provide public access to both federal records and meetings held by federal agencies. The federal records law, the Freedom of Information Act, makes public all records held by agencies within the executive branch of government and the independent regulatory commissions. Courts have given a broad meaning to the term *record* but have ruled that an agency must normally create and possess such a record before it becomes subject to the Freedom of Information Act. Nine categories of information are excluded from the provisions of the law. These include exemptions for national security, agency working papers, highly personal information, and law enforcement investigatory files. Agencies must publish indexes of the records they hold and must permit copying of these materials. It is important to follow specific procedures when making a Freedom of Information Act request to see certain records or documents.

The Government in Sunshine Act is the federal open meetings law. This law reaches about fifty agencies in the executive branch and the regulatory commissions. Members of these organizations are not permitted to hold secret meetings unless they will discuss material that falls into one of ten categories. These categories mirror the Freedom of Information Act exemptions but also include a provision that permits closed-door meetings to discuss attempts to arbitrate or adjudicate certain cases or problems. This is a newer law and does not seem to work as well as does the Freedom of Information Act.

STATE LAWS ON MEETINGS AND RECORDS

It is not as easy to talk about access at the state level as it is at the federal level, for we are dealing with hundreds of different statutes. (Most states have multiple laws dealing with access to meetings, access to records, and other access situations.) We can at best make a few generalizations. Harold Cross made some of the most astute generalizations in 1953 in his pioneering book *The People's Right to Know.* Cross was really the first scholar to present a comprehensive report on access problems. In his book he listed four issues or questions common to every case of access:

1. Is the particular record or proceeding public? Many records and meetings kept or conducted by public officers in public offices are not really public at all. Much of the work of the police, though they are public officers and work in public buildings, is not open to public scrutiny.

2. Is public material public in the sense that records are open to public inspection and sessions are open to public attendance? Hearings in juvenile courts are considered public hearings for purposes of the law, but they are rarely open to the public.

3. Who can view the records and who can attend the meetings open to the public? Many records, for example, might be open to specific segments of the public, but not to all segments. Automobile accident reports by police departments are open to insurance company adjusters and lawyers, but such records are not usually open to the general public.

4. When records and meetings are open to the general public and the press, will the courts provide legal remedy for citizens and reporters if access is denied?

The last question is probably not as important today as it was when Cross wrote his book in 1953, for at that time access to many public records and meetings in the states was based on the common law. Today this fact is no longer true. Access to meetings and records is nearly always governed by statute, and these statutes usually, but not always, provide a remedy for citizens who are denied access. This provision is more widespread in open meeting laws, which tend to be more efficient in providing access, than in open records laws, which are still weak and vague in many jurisdictions.

State Open Meetings Laws

Virtually all states have some kind of constitutional or legislative provision regarding the need for open meetings. All fifty states have specific statutes that mandate open meetings, and these laws range from good to awful. The need for **open-meeting laws** is obvious. There never was a solid common law right to attend the meetings of public bodies, and as noted earlier, the constitutional provisions regarding freedom of expression have proved inadequate with regard to access.

Many states have good laws with strong sanctions to be used against public officials who fail to live up to the legislative mandate. The Exxon Education Foundation recently released a study comparing all fifty laws on twenty-three different criteria and found the laws in Florida and Tennessee to be the best and the Pennsylvania law the weakest.

William R. Wright II, writing in a recent edition of the *Mississippi Law Review* ("Open Meeting Laws: An Analysis and a Proposal"), outlined the basic provisions of state open-meeting laws. According to Wright, the most vital provision of such a law is a strong, clear statement by the legislature to open up the deliberations and actions of the government to the people. If a provision of the law is questioned in court, a strong legislative declaration in favor of open access can be used to persuade a judge that if a section of the law is vague, it should be interpreted to grant access rather than to restrict access, since that is what the legislature wants.

In Washington the state's open meeting law begins as follows:

> The legislature finds and declares that all . . . public agencies of this state and subdivisions thereof exist to aid in the conduct of the people's business. It is the intent of this chapter that their actions be taken openly and that their deliberations be conducted openly.

State legislatures have usually written their open-meeting laws in one of two ways. Some state legislatures have declared that all meetings will be open, except specific meetings, and then list the meetings to be open. Other states list the agencies that must hold open meetings. Generally excluded from the provisions of an open-meeting law in either case are meetings of the legislature itself, of legislative committees, of parole and pardon boards, of law enforcement agencies, of military agencies such as the national guard, of public hospital boards, and so forth.

Wright says that a good law should specifically define a meeting by giving the number of members of the board or commission who must be present to constitute a public meeting (a quorum? at least two? etc.), by stating that all deliberative stages of the decision-making process are considered meetings and must be open to the public, and by stating that social gatherings and chance encounters are not considered meetings and are therefore excluded from the provisions of the law. Some laws are not this specific and merely refer to all meetings, all regular or special meetings, all formal meetings, or whatever.

The exclusion of chance meetings and social gatherings is often troublesome to the press, especially in small towns. It is not uncommon that all members of the school board or the city council happen to have dinner at the same restaurant just before a meeting. If the dinner is obviously a ploy to avoid the law, a suit can be brought against the members. Often it is difficult to prove that the dinner is anything other than a chance encounter or a social gathering. But a good law specifies that all gatherings at which public business is discussed must be open, not just official decision-making sessions.

Most open-meeting laws provide for closed or **executive sessions** in certain kinds of cases. Meetings at which personnel problems are discussed are an obvious example. A public airing of a teacher's personal problems could be an unwarranted invasion of privacy. The discussion of real estate transactions is another obvious example. When a school board considers buying a parcel of land for a new high school, premature public disclosure of this fact could cost the taxpayers money should the owner raise the price of the property or speculators buy it and force the school district to pay far more than it is worth. Meetings involving public safety are sometimes best conducted in private rather than in public. Usually laws will permit an official body to meet with its attorney behind closed doors if potential or actual litigation is on the agenda. This is merely an extension of the traditional lawyer-client privilege. Labor negotiations may also be held in private in about half the states. All but thirteen state open-meeting laws contain a provision that no final action can be taken at an executive session, that the board or commission must reconvene in public before a final determination can be made on any issue.

Most open-meeting statutes require not only that meetings be open to the public, but also that the public be notified of both regular and special meetings far enough in advance that they can attend if they wish. Time requirements vary, but normally a special meeting cannot be held without an announcement a day or two in advance.

Virtually all laws provide some kind of injunctive or other civil remedy if the law is violated; almost half the statutes provide for criminal penalties if the statute is knowingly violated. In many states any action taken at a meeting that was not public, but should have been public, is null and void. The action must be taken again at a proper meeting. Most laws provide fines and short jail terms for public officers who knowingly violate the law, but prosecution is rare.

While a few laws date from the nineteenth century, the open-meeting laws in most states are a relatively new phenomenon. Such laws, which owe their passage to strong, forceful pressure from the press, have developed largely since 1950. In 1959 only twenty states had such laws. Formation in the early 1970s of the public lobby Common Cause gave great impetus to the passage of open-meeting laws. In 1972 and 1973, alone, nine states passed such statutes. But after it had evaluated all of the nation's open meeting laws in 1973, the organization concluded that many states had inadequate laws. Common Cause defined an adequate law as one that covers both the legislative and executive branches, permits executive sessions only in extremely limited circumstances, and also includes provisions that void actions taken at illegally closed sessions.

One commentator recently noted that the lack of effectiveness of these laws "means that the reporter's most marketable skill is still very much in demand for covering local government. His or her special talent has been to ferret news from unexpected or well-cultivated sources." There is much truth in this statement with regard to open-meeting laws. Despite open-meeting legislation, one informal remedy is still very effective: to subject the commission or board that decides to meet in secret to public embarrassment. Reporters should never voluntarily leave a meeting they believe should be public. Rather, they should force public officials to escort them to an exit. Resistance is not advised, for criminal charges then might be levied against the reporter. If possible, a photographer should record the removal from the meeting. The photograph and the story can then be prominently featured on page one the next day. Public officials do not really like to meet in public, but they like even less to be pictured conducting "the public's business" behind closed doors. Voters begin to wonder what goes on in secret meetings.

State Open Records
Laws

Every state in the union also has some kind of **open-records law.** The access laws either follow the federal formula—all records are open except the following—or list the kinds of records that the public does have a right to inspect. In a useful article in the *George Washington Law Review,* attorneys Burt Braverman and Wesley Heppler ("A Practical Review of State Open Records Laws") outlined the basic dimensions of the state freedom of information laws.

Most state laws permit inspection of records by any person, but a few limit access to public records to citizens of the state. The reason persons want to see a record is normally considered immaterial when determining whether they can gain access to the record. The freedom of information laws provide access to records held by public agencies in the state, and normally these statutes provide a broad definition of these agencies. In Washington state, for example, an "agency" includes both state and local agencies. The law further states:

> State agency includes every state office, public official, department, division, bureau, board, commission, or other state agency. Local agency includes every county, city, city and county, school district, municipal corporation, district, political subdivision, or any board, commission or agency thereof, or other local public agency.

State access laws usually do not include the courts or legislature in the definition of agency.

Braverman and Heppler report that state laws follow either a liberal or conservative definition of a public record. *All records possessed by an agency* are deemed to be public records in those states with liberal definitions of a public record. But some state laws are more conservative and provide access only to those *records that are required to be kept by law.*

All state freedom of information laws provide exemptions to disclosure. Agencies *may* withhold material that falls under an exemption in some states; agencies *must* withhold this information in other states. Braverman and Heppler list the six most common substantive exemptions to the state open-records laws as follows:

1. Information classified as confidential by state or federal law
2. Law enforcement and investigatory information
3. Trade secrets and commercial information
4. Preliminary departmental memorandums (working papers)
5. Personal privacy information
6. Information relating to litigation against a public body

The attorneys report that although state laws vary widely, state courts have almost uniformly held that exemptions should be construed narrowly; that is, they should be read in such a way as to provide public access to the greatest amount of information. The federal Freedom of Information Act requires agencies to maintain an index of documents and records; not many state laws have the same requirement. But in every state except Indiana the right to inspect records includes the right to copy records. Procedures to gain access to state agency records follow the federal FOIA model. Two-thirds of the state statutes have provisions for judicial review of agency rulings where the state bears the burden to show that the record should remain undisclosed. But at least two states have tried to develop means that keep the question of access to records out of court.

Connecticut has established an independent commission to handle citizen appeals on denial-of-information requests. The three-member commission must meet within twenty days after receiving an appeal, hear the matter, and issue a ruling within fifteen days. The body can uphold the denial or make the agency provide access to the material. Either citizens or government agencies can appeal any decision by the commission to a court.

The New York State access law established a Committee on Public Access to Records. This committee has wide authority to issue regulations for the use of records and implementation of the new statute. There are seven members on the committee—three government officials and four persons appointed by the governor, two of whom must be from the media. The committee's function is different from the Connecticut commission, which acts as a review board. In New York the committee advises agencies and local government on access questions through guidelines, opinions, and regulations. It is supposed to recommend changes in the law when problems arise. In addition, to make the new law work more efficiently, the commission issues rules and guidelines: rules regarding the time and place records must be available, fees for copying, persons responsible for divulging records, and so forth. Finally, it is the job of the committee to ensure that the right of privacy of New York citizens is protected in connection with public access to the state's records. Some people criticize this last function, arguing that it makes little sense to make the same agency in charge of facilitating public access responsible for protecting the right of privacy.

This trend toward establishing public committees or commissions to handle access problems, to help interpret the law, and to issue guidelines is a very good one. It is far easier to complain to a commission when access is denied than to file a court suit. Committees like the New York Committee on Public Access to Records will make a state law far more meaningful and useful when a local government is dealt with. Access laws passed by states are often ignored at local levels because of ignorance or because citizens and press are unlikely to complain until a big issue arises. By providing guidelines and rules for local communities, a committee on public access immediately breathes life into an access law.

It is incumbent on all journalists and broadcasters to be as familiar as possible with the laws regarding access in their state. Knowledge of these kinds of laws is vital to efficient and complete reporting on government activities. Employees of public agencies are often as uninformed as average citizens about their responsibility to provide access to meetings, especially to records. Because of the normal adversary relationship between press and government, the natural tendency is to want to keep the reporter out of public documents and public meetings. Too often reporters are buffaloed by stubborn, uninformed, untruthful public employees who insist that they are not permitted by law to allow public inspection of certain records. If reporters know the law, they can recognize such bluffs on the spot and fulfill their responsibility to keep the public fully informed on the business and activities of government.

SUMMARY

All states have laws that govern access to public meetings and public records. Good state open-meetings laws have strong legislative declarations in support of public meetings, specifically define a public meeting by listing the number of members who must gather to constitute a meeting, and declare void all actions taken during a meeting that was improperly closed to the public. Most laws provide for closed sessions to discuss such matters as personnel actions, real estate transactions, and litigation.

State public-records laws tend to mirror the federal law. Both state and local agencies are governed by the laws that apply to most governmental bodies except the legislature and the courts. Most state laws govern all records kept by these agencies, but a few are applicable only to records that are required to be kept by law. Exemptions to state open-records laws include material specifically excluded by other statutes, law-enforcement investigatory information, working papers, and highly personal information. Most laws provide for access to the judicial system in case a request for data is rejected, but both New York and Connecticut have established commissions to act as arbiters in these matters.

LAWS THAT RESTRICT ACCESS TO INFORMATION

Just as there are laws that provide for public access to government-held documents, there are laws that specifically preclude access to government-held information. There are provisions in scores of federal laws alone that limit the right of access. Tax statutes, espionage laws, legislation on atomic energy, and dozens of other kinds of laws are filled with limitations on the dissemination of information (e.g., personal information on taxes, national security questions, and matters relating to nuclear weapons). But in addition to these kinds of laws, the federal government has adopted in the past decade at least three rather broad sets of regulations regarding information held by the government. All three were adopted in the name of protecting the right to privacy, a value that seems to have replaced national security as the most commonly asserted reason the government uses to keep things secret. While these regulations cannot be considered here in a comprehensive sense, persons who gather information for a living need to be aware of their implications.

General Education Provisions Act

An amendment to the General Education Provisions Act (1974) is aimed at increasing both the parental access to and the confidentiality of educational records. On the one hand, the law forces all federally funded schools and educational agencies to permit parents to inspect and review their children's educational records. On the other hand, the statute prohibits the distribution of personally identifiable information, excluding what is called directory data, to unauthorized persons without consent of the parents. The result is that student records or files must be kept confidential. This goal is hardly a hardship on the press in most instances. However, because of the stiff penalty in the law—possible loss to the school of federal funds—educators have occasionally overreacted and declared data that are actually unprotected by the statute to be confidential. In one absurd case a reporter-photographer indicated that school officials chased him off school property when he attempted to photograph children playing outside at recess. The officials cited the 1974 law as a reason that picture taking was no longer permitted on school property. Of course, instances like that are rare, and the significance of the law is its indication of the extreme interest in privacy today, rather than its threat to the legitimate news-gathering tasks of the press.

The Federal Privacy Law

The **Privacy Act** of 1974 has two basic thrusts. First, it attempts to check the misuse of personal data obtained by the federal government, the quantity of which has, of course, reached staggering proportions. Second, the law is intended to provide access for individuals to records about themselves that are held by federal agencies. The first objective of the law could be the more troublesome to the press.

The act requires that each federal agency limit the collection of information to that which is relevant and necessary, to collect information directly from the subject concerned when possible, and to allow individuals to review and amend their personal records and information. Also, under the act agencies are forbidden from disclosing what is called "a personally identifiable record" without the written consent of the individual to whom the record pertains. Since this section of the law is seemingly contradictory to the spirit of the federal FOIA, Congress was forced to clarify the responsibilities of federal agencies with regard to the law. A provision was added to the Privacy Act that declares that records required to be disclosed under the FOIA are not subject to the provisions of the Privacy Act and consequently cannot be withheld from inspection. To the government official with control of information, however, neither the Privacy Act nor the FOIA is unambiguous.

The difficulty in resolving aspects of the Privacy Act and the Freedom of Information Act is graphically illustrated by a recent case decided by the United States Court of Appeals for the District of Columbia. Frank Greentree was indicted and convicted in federal court on drug charges. He filed a civil suit to block state prosecution based on the same events. Greentree sought information from both the Drug Enforcement Administration (DEA) and the United States Bureau of Customs to assist him in his civil action. When the agencies refused to give him the material he sought, he filed both a Freedom of Information Act request and a Privacy Act request to get the information. The documents sought by Greentree were contained in something called the Investigations Record System, and this system of records has been declared to be exempt from the access provisions of the Privacy Act. Hence it was unavailable to Greentree through the federal privacy law. Because the information could not be released under the Privacy Act, the government argued that it was also unavailable under FOIA exemption three. Remember exemption three: it provides that the Freedom of Information Act does not apply to matters "specifically exempt from disclosure by statute." The material

*Discussion of the General Education Provisions Act and the Federal Privacy Law, pages 303–5, is adapted from Don R. Pember, "The Burgeoning Scope of 'Access Privacy' and the Portent for a Free Press," 64 *Iowa Law Review* 1155, 1979.

Greentree sought was exempt from disclosure under the federal privacy statute; therefore, the government argued, it was also exempt from disclosure under exemption three of the Freedom of Information Act. In two previous appellate court rulings this government argument was sustained. (See *Terkel v. Kelly*, 7th Circuit, 1979, and *Painter v. Federal Bureau of Investigation*, 5th Circuit, 1980.) But in Greentree the United States Court of Appeals for the District of Columbia denied the validity of this argument and ruled against the government. Judge Wald said that throughout its consideration of the Privacy Act, the Congress struggled to hold separate the Privacy Act and the FOIA. That effect was ultimately successful, he said. Judge Wald noted that section (b) (2) of the Privacy Act clearly states that "no agency shall disclose any record which is contained in a system of records . . . *unless disclosure of the record would be required under section 552 (The Freedom of Information Act) of this title* [author emphasis]." "We must conclude," Wald wrote, "that this section of the Privacy Act represents a congressional mandate that the Privacy Act *not* be used as a barrier to FOIA access." Congress could not have intended that a section of the Privacy Act could serve as a withholding statute under FOIA exemption three, the judge said. It is possible, he noted, that the information may not be available under exemption seven (the law enforcement exemption of the FOIA), but the government would have to prove that the material sought by Greentree was exempt from disclosure (*Greentree v. Customs Service*, 1982).

The Privacy Act imposes a cost on an agency if it releases a file that should remain private. To the bureaucrat, that presents a real dilemma, as was emphasized in the *Harvard Civil Rights/Civil Liberties Law Review* (1976):

> If government officials refuse to disclose the material, they risk being sued by the party who requested the file under the Freedom of Information Act. Under the FOIA the court may award to a successful plaintiff his costs and attorney's fees. If, on the other hand, agencies release material, they risk being sued under the Privacy Act by the person who is the subject of the file. In that case, the plaintiff might win by showing that the file was exempt from disclosure under FOIA. A successful Privacy Act plaintiff can collect not only his costs and attorney's fees, but also actual damage sustained because of disclosure.

Given this distinction between the statutes, it is easy to recognize that bureaucrats will choose to err on the side of caution—it is wiser to withhold the information and risk suit under the FOIA than possibly incur Privacy Act penalties.

Other conflicts exist in the administration of the two laws. Before passage of the Privacy Act, materials that were not required to be disclosed under the FOIA were nevertheless disclosable at the discretion of a government agency. Now, information falling under an FOIA exemption, and thus not required to be disclosed, will routinely be withheld out of fear of violating the Privacy Act.

In accordance with the broad scope of the Omnibus Crime Control and Safe Streets Act of 1968, the federal Law Enforcement Assistance Administration, an agency created by the Nixon administration to help local police forces fight crime, sought to develop a national computerized record-keeping system. The system that was established permits any police department in the nation to have access to the records of virtually all other police departments.

Congressional concern about the misuse of this record system led to limitations on access to the data. Police records have always contained a considerable amount of misinformation, information that is out of date, and information that is private. The centralized record-keeping system presents a problem referred to by some writers as the "dossier effect." The contrast between these computerized and centrally maintained records immediately accessible across the country and those police records of the past was sharp and immediately evident: fragmented, original-source records kept by a single police agency for a limited geographical area were not readily accessible because of their bulk and associated indexing problems. Hence, federal rules were adopted that require states, if they wish to participate in the national record-keeping system, to adopt rules that, among other things, limit the dissemination of some criminal history nonconviction data.

The *Code of Federal Regulations* ("Criminal Justice Information Systems") defines nonconviction data as follows:

> . . . arrest information without disposition if an interval of one year has elapsed from the date of arrest and no active prosecution of the charge is pending, or information disclosing that the police have elected not to refer a matter to a prosecutor, or that a prosecutor has elected not to commence criminal proceedings, or that proceedings have been indefinitely postponed, as well as all acquittals and all dismissals.

As a result of the state laws, press access to criminal history records kept by the police has been virtually eliminated unless data sought pertain to an incident for which a person is currently being processed by the criminal justice system, are conviction records, or are original records of entry, such as arrest records, that are maintained chronologically and are accessible only on that basis. Reporters can also obtain information about arrests not resulting in conviction, however, if they are aware of the specific dates of the arrests. The new laws have been in effect too short a time to determine whether they will substantially affect the press's ability to meet its societal responsibility to scrutinize and report on the criminal justice system. Nevertheless, potential problems are apparent. In commenting on the social desirability of press access to criminal records, Steven Higgins ("Press and Criminal Record Privacy") recently noted:

*Discussion of Criminal History Privacy Laws, pages 306–7, is adapted from Pember, "Access Privacy and Free Press."

On the one hand, the uncontrolled dissemination and publication of certain criminal history records can adversely affect the individual himself. On the other hand, the public and the press must have access to basic records of official action if they are to effectively scrutinize and evaluate the operations of the police, the prosecuting agencies, and the courts.

The ability to achieve that scrutiny is important. For example, it is possible to envision a situation in which a prosecutor is accused of favoring friends or certain ethnic or racial groups when deciding whether to prosecute arrested persons. Without access to arrest records that can be compared with prosecution records, such a charge would be difficult to investigate. Persons within the criminal justice system could gain access to the needed records, but history indicates that these people must be prodded before they take action. And, of course, prodding is the function of the press.

There is another related, more serious problem that should be of great concern to persons earnestly worried about invasions of privacy. If the press cannot obtain official criminal history records, which admittedly are sometimes incorrect, journalists will rely on their own record-keeping systems, which are much more frequently inaccurate. Newspapers and broadcasting stations usually build record systems—called morgues—by saving clippings from newspapers and film from newscasts. Errors in these original stories are seldom corrected. For example, suppose Jones was arrested in 1965 and charged with driving a stolen car. The local newspaper published incorrectly that he was arrested for car theft. Jones was never prosecuted. Fifteen years later he runs for the school board. The newspaper goes back into its own records—which it cannot verify with the police—and republishes its original error, that Jones was arrested for car theft. In such circumstances everyone—Jones, the press, the public—suffers.

To avoid such consequences, society would probably be served better if laws were passed that force law-enforcement agencies to continually monitor, update, and correct their criminal records but that nevertheless permitted public access to the records. Such laws could require, for instance, that when arrest data are released, disposition data must accompany the arrest data. There is, of course, no guarantee that the press or other agencies would publish the complete story—the arrest and the dismissal, for example, or the arrest and the subsequent acquittal—but no system that depends on a human element is risk free. In the end, public access to complete and accurate information is much to be preferred to a growing dependence on "private" media data banks.

State Statutes That Limit Access to Information

All states have statutes that limit access to information that would otherwise be available under a freedom of information law. Arizona, for example, has thirty-nine such laws. Some of these state statutes are aimed at blocking access to trade secrets; others limit access to information submitted to the state in compliance with environmental laws. The working papers of assessors, poll lists from prior elections, and reports from oil and gas companies are also frequently exempted from disclosure by a specific statute. State privacy laws are the most common kind of statutory limitation on the access to information.

Virtually every state has one or more statutes (sometimes this is the state's open-record law!) that limit access to government-held information on right-to-privacy grounds. While these laws are not traditionally thought of in the same terms as the tort of privacy (see chapter 4), they nevertheless have a similar impact. Tort law discourages the publication of private information by penalizing the press through the assessment of money damages. These statutes permit the state to institute civil or criminal action against the press for the publication of so-called private information or simply to bar access to this material so that it cannot be published.

Newspapers in Alabama can no longer get information regarding births and deaths from county officials. Citing state laws and rulings by the public health board, county officers say only persons who have a "valid and tangible interest" in these materials can gain access to them. Otherwise, publication of such information can be an invasion of personal privacy (*Birmingham News* v. *Roper,* 1978). In Vermont the press had to go to court to force the release of information relating to pardons granted several persons by a former governor of the state. Lower courts had ruled that the disclosure of such material might constitute an unwarranted invasion of the privacy of the persons pardoned. Yet it was only through the release of this information that citizens could evaluate the governor's actions in granting these pardons. The state supreme court finally opened up the records (*Doe* v. *Salmon,* 1977).

These two rulings are symptomatic of a wide range of privacy problems that have begun to haunt persons interested in access to information. In recent years fear of losing privacy has provoked passage of laws that impede the public's right to information. The press has generally failed to bring the negative aspects of these new privacy laws to the attention of the public, and now we all must suffer what may be severe consequences. Invasion of privacy statutes and invasion of privacy exemptions are perhaps the most common impediments to full access to government-held information in the United States today.

SUMMARY

All of the states and the federal government have laws that specifically exclude certain kinds of information from the public scrutiny. Some of these exclusions were noted in the discussion of exemption three of the Freedom of Information Act. Today, the right to privacy has been erected as a substantial barrier to access to information held by government agencies. The federal government has adopted a law protecting the privacy of student records. The Congress passed a federal privacy law, which often conflicts with the provisions of the Freedom of Information Act. The federal government has also insisted that states pass statutes that control access to criminal history records. Much privacy legislation has been passed by the states themselves, and today the right to privacy is being erected frequently to block access to public records.

ACCESS TO JUDICIAL RECORDS

Courts generally govern the access to information gathered through the judicial system. While the press and public have had some difficulty in recent years in gaining access to pretrial hearings and, in some instances, even in gaining access to trials (see chapter 7), it is a general rule that evidence introduced in a criminal or civil case is open to public inspection. It may be viewed, described, or photographed. But what if the evidence is a videotape of the defendant committing a criminal act or an audiotape of the defendant proposing an illegal deal? Can these tapes be broadcast over radio and television?

This is a recent access problem for both courts and broadcast journalists. The seeming litany of government "sting" and "scam" undercover operations has provided ample opportunity for this issue to be litigated. Thus far, the federal courts have not reached a consensus on the matter. In some instances courts have permitted this material to be copied and then broadcast or telecast. In other instances the courts have refused to allow such access to these materials. If there is a trend, it is toward giving the mass media access to such material.

The lack of resolution of this issue is at least partially the result of a decision by the Supreme Court of the United States. Tapes made by President Richard Nixon at the White House were used as evidence in many of the Watergate trials of the seventies. Broadcasters sought to make copies of these tapes and broadcast them. The High Court agreed that there is a generally recognized right to access to inspect the evidentiary record in a case, but this is not an absolute right. "The decision as to access is one best left to the sound discretion of the trial court, a discretion to be exercised in light of the relevant facts and circumstances of the particular case," the Court said (*Nixon* v. *Warner Communications,* 1978; see also *Nixon* v. *Carmen,* 1982).

Judges have been exercising their own discretion in these cases, and not surprisingly different judges have reached different conclusions. The courts have considered a variety of factors in reaching a decision on whether to permit the broadcast or telecast of these kinds of electronic recordings. Whether transcripts of the recordings have already been published is an important factor. Courts have also considered whether the broadcast or telecast of the material would enhance public understanding of an important historical or public occurrence. The rights of the defendant are also considered: Would the broadcast of this material prejudice the right to a fair trial? (See *U.S.* v. *Maddox,*

1982, where the court rejected a claim of potential prejudice, and *U.S.* v. *Bolen,* 1981, where the court denied broadcasters the right to telecast material because broadcast could interfere with the defendant's right to a fair trial.) Most courts will insist upon clear evidence that the broadcast or telecast of the videotape will harm the rights of the defendant or someone or something else. The Third U.S. Court of Appeals recently ruled that there is a strong presumption favoring such access and that this presumption is not outweighed by mere speculations on the potential impact the telecast of the material may have on related proceedings (*U.S.* v. *Martin,* 1984). In Washington State the Supreme Court voided a contempt citation against a radio station that had broadcast, in violation of a court order, tape-recorded testimony that had been placed into evidence because the trial court had "accepted the most superficial showing of justification and then shifted to KHQ [the radio station] the burden of proving that the prior restraint was not necessary. . ." (*Washington* v. *Coe,* 1984).

It is often important whether the tapes that are sought have been introduced into evidence. When John Hinckley was tried for the attempted assassination of Ronald Reagan, the television networks sought to televise the videotaped deposition given by actress Jodie Foster in the case. The court refused the request, noting that the testimony was never admitted into evidence. It was simply a statement from a witness; it just happened to be videotaped. No right existed to videotape and telecast the testimony of other witnesses. The videotaped deposition would not be an exception to that rule (in re *Application of ABC,* 1982). The New Mexico Supreme Court recently denied the press the right to copy and broadcast recordings of wiretaps that resulted in criminal indictments but were never played in open court or received into evidence (*New Mexico* v. *Brennan,* 1982). Who has been videotaped is also an important consideration when a court examines a request to broadcast the material. Videotapes of defendants and undercover police agents are more likely to be released than are recordings of innocent third parties. Jodie Foster was an "innocent witness" in the Hinckley case. She had been pulled into the case inadvertently. A United States district court in Minnesota rejected requests from broadcasters to air videotapes of a hostage recorded by her kidnapper. The court ruled that it would create serious hardship for the victim of the crime and would serve no proper purpose (in re *Application of KSTP,* 1980). A good way to outline the dimensions of this problem is to look at two different cases, one where access was granted and one where it was denied.

The government presented a considerable amount of evidence on both videotape and audiotape on Congressman John Jenrette and John Stowe in the Abscam trial. They were recordings of the defendants in the case making what the government alleged were illegal deals with undercover FBI agents. The networks sought to copy and broadcast these tapes. The United States district court refused the request, fearing that if the tapes were televised it would be difficult to later impanel an impartial jury should a retrial be ordered by a higher court. The United States Court of Appeals for the District of Columbia disagreed and promulgated this test:

> Access may be denied only if the district court, after considering the relevant facts and circumstances of the particular case, and after weighing the interests advanced by the parties in light of the public interest and the duty of courts, concludes that justice so requires. . . . The court's discretion must clearly be informed by this country's strong tradition of access to judicial proceedings. In balancing the competing interests the court must also give appropriate weight and consideration *to the presumption—however gauged—in favor of public access to judicial records* [author emphasis].

Several factors favored release of the tapes, the court concluded. They were admitted into evidence and played to a jury at a public trial. The tapes contained only admissible evidence. This was a trial where the defendant was a high public official charged with betraying the public trust. The court admitted a retrial *might* be a problem, but there was no evidence that if there were a retrial, impartial jurors could not be found. What about protecting innocent third parties who were also pictured or heard in the tapes? There were only one or two instances of that, and the trial court can delete these sections, the court said. The tapes must be released (in re *Application of NBC,* 1981).

The Fifth United States Court of Appeals reached the opposite conclusion in another 1981 decision. The speaker of the Texas House of Representatives, two attorneys, and a labor leader were all indicted in an alleged bribery scheme. The speaker and the two attorneys were tried and acquitted. Broadcasters wanted to air audiotapes that had been made during the FBI sting operation that resulted in the indictments. These were discussions between the defendants and FBI undercover operatives that had been secretly recorded. The trial court refused on the grounds that the broadcast might make it difficult for the fourth defendant to have a trial by an impartial jury. The Fifth United States Court of Appeals supported this decision. The court noted that while there is a right in this country to inspect and copy judicial records and documents, it is not an absolute right. The trial court may exercise considerable discretion in granting or refusing to grant access to material. Clearly, the concern that the fourth defendant's trial might be prejudiced if the tapes were broadcast is a legitimate concern, the court said. It is not the job of the appellate courts to second-guess the trial courts on these matters. Finally, the court said it could not agree with decisions by the District of Columbia Court of Appeals and other courts that there exists a strong presumption in favor of access to this kind of evidence. The court said it could not find a basis for that presumption (*Belo Broadcasting* v. *Clark,* 1981). Other courts have recently followed the rationale of the *Belo* case, giving wide discretion to the trial judge in such instances (see *U.S.* v. *Webbe,* 1986, and *U.S.* v. *Beckham,* 1986).

The differences between these rulings represent to a certain extent the differences in the cases. The retrial was a distant possibility in the first case; the trial of the fourth defendant was about to take place in the second situation. But these rulings also represent differences in judicial philosophy. And as long as the Supreme Court is content to let the lower courts use their discretion in making these decisions, different rules will be applied in different parts of the nation.

Gaining public access to government-held information has been a problem for about as long as democracy has existed as a form of government. With the development of a corps of professional information and news gatherers in this century, the problem has become more visible. Couple this fact with the enormous growth of government in the past half-century, and a problem of rather large proportions develops. Until the last twenty years, most journalists depended upon friendship with sources and upon skill and wile to get the news from governments. Many reporters argue that this is still the best way to find out what is going on. The law plays an ever-increasing role today in gathering news and information. Much of the process of getting the news and keeping it has been institutionalized by statute and court decisions. At the same time the law has raised serious impediments to information gathering, which the press has thus far had difficulty in hurdling. Many of the most important press-government battles in the next decade will be fought over these issues, and at present the question of who will be the winner—the press, the government, or the public—is far from being answered.

BIBLIOGRAPHY

Here is a list of some of the sources that have been helpful in the preparation of chapter 5:

Books

Adams, John B. *State Open Meeting Laws: An Overview.* Columbia, Mo.: Freedom of Information Foundation, 1974.

Cross, Harold. *The People's Right to Know.* New York: Columbia University Press, 1953.

Gerth, H. H., and Mills, C. Wright, eds. *From Max Weber: Essays in Sociology.* New York: Oxford University Press, 1946.

How to Use the Federal FOI Act. 2d ed. Washington, D.C.: FOI Service Center, 1980.

Marwick, Christine M., ed. *Litigation Under the Amended Freedom of Information Act.* 2d ed. Washington, D. C.: American Civil Liberties Union and Freedom of Information Clearing House, 1976.

Padover, Saul, ed. *The Complete Madison.* New York: Harper & Row, 1953.

Rourke, Francis E. *Secrecy and Publicity.* Baltimore: Johns Hopkins University Press, 1961.

Articles

Archibald, Sam. "The Revised F.O.I. Law and How to Use It." July/August *Columbia Journalism Review* 54, 1977.

Braverman, Burt A., and Heppler, Wesley. "A Practical Review of State of Open Records Laws." 49 *George Washington Law Review* 721, 1981.

"Criminal Justice Information Systems." 28 *Code of Federal Regulations,* section 20.3(K).

"The Definition of 'Agency Records' Under the Freedom of Information Act." 31 *Stanford Law Review* 1093, 1979.

"The Freedom of Information Act's Privacy Exemption and the Privacy Act of 1974." 11 *Harvard Civil Rights/Civil Liberties Law Review* 596, 1976.

Genovese, Margaret. "Reagan Administration Information Policies," April *Presstime* 14, 1985.

Higgins, Steven. "Press and Criminal Record Privacy." 20 *St. Louis University Law Journal* 509, 1977.

Malmgren, Lynn C. "First Amendment: Freedom of the Press to Gather News." 20 *Villanova Law Review* 189, 1974.

"National Security and the Public's Right to Know: A New Role for the Courts Under the FOIA." 123 *University of Pennsylvania Law Review* 1438, 1975.

Pember, Don R. "The Burgeoning Scope of 'Access Privacy' and the Portent for a Free Press." 64 *Iowa Law Review* 1155, 1979.

"The Rights of the Public and the Press to Gather Information." 87 *Harvard Law Review* 1505, 1974.

Scher, Jacob. "Access to Information: Recent Legal Problems." 37 *Journalism Quarterly* 41, 1960.

Weinberg, Steve. "Trashing the FOIA," January/February *Columbia Journalism Review* 21, 1985.

Wright, Anne H. "The Definition of 'Agency' Under the Freedom of Information Act as Applied to Federal Consultants and Grantees." 69 *Georgetown Law Journal* 1223, 1981.

Wright, William R. II. "Open Meeting Laws: An Analysis and a Proposal." 45 *Mississippi Law Review* 1151, 1974.

Cases

in re *Application of ABC,* 537 F. Supp. 1168 (1982).

Arieff v. *Navy,* 712 F.2d 1462 (1983).

Belo Broadcasting v. *Clark,* 654 F.2d 426 (1981).

Birmingham News v. *Roper,* 4 M.L. Rept. 1075 (1978).

BNA v. *Baxter, Environmental Defense Fund* v. *Office of Management of Budget,* 742 F.2d 1484 (1984).

Branzburg v. *Hayes,* 408 U.S. 655 (1972).

Browde v. *Navy,* 713 F.2d 864 (1983).

Chrysler Corp. v. *Brown,* 99 S.Ct. 1705 (1979).

CNN v. *ABC et al,* 518 F. Supp. 1238 (1981).

Cohen v. *EPA,* 575 F. Supp. 425 (1983).

Common Cause v. *Nuclear Regulatory Commission,* 674 F.2d 921 (1982).

Crooker v. *Bureau,* 670 F.2d 1051 (1981).

Daily Herald v. *Munro,* 747 F.2d 1251 (1985).

Department of the Air Force v. *Rose,* 425 U.S. 352 (1976).

Doe v. *Salmon,* 378 A.2d 512 (1977).

EPA v. *Mink,* 401 U.S. 73 (1973).

Epstein v. *Resor,* 296 F. Supp. 214 (1969), affd. 421 F.2d 930 (1970).

FBI v. *Abramson,* 102 S.Ct. 2054 (1982).

Forsham v. *Harris,* 100 S.Ct. 978 (1980).

Garrett v. *Estelle,* 556 F.2d 1274 (1977).

Goland v. *CIA,* 607 F.2d 339 (1978).

Greentree v. *Customs Service,* 674 F.2d 74 (1982).

Hardy v. *Bureau of Alcohol, Tobacco, and Firearms,* 631 F.2d 653 (1980).

Houchins v. *KQED,* 438 U.S. 1 (1978).

Kissinger v. *Reporter's Committee,* 100 S. Ct. 960 (1980).

Knopf v. *Colby,* 502 F.2d 136 (1975).

in re *Application of KSTP,* 504 F. Supp. 360 (1980).

Kurzon v. *Health and Human Services,* 649 F.2d 65 (1981).

Long v. *IRS,* 596 F.2d 362 (1979).

MacEwan v. *Holm,* 359 P.2d 413 (1961).

Miami Herald v. *Small Business Administration,* 670 F.2d 610 (1982).

in re *Application of NBC,* 653 F.2d 609 (1981).

New Mexico v. *Brennan,* 645 P.2d 982 (1982).

Nixon v. *Carmen,* 670 F.2d 346 (1982).

Nixon v. *Warner Communications,* 435 U.S. 591 (1978).

Painter v. *FBI,* 615 F.2d 689 (1980).

Pell v. *Procunier,* 94 S.Ct. 2800 (1974).

Philadelphia Newspapers v. *Nuclear Regulatory Commission,* 9 M.L. Rept. 1843
(1983).

Playboy v. *Justice Department,* 677 F.2d 931 (1982).

Providence Journal Co. et al. v. *McCoy, et al.,* 49 F. Supp. 186 (1950).

Public Citizen Health Research Group v. *Food and Drug Administration,* 704 F.2d
1280 (1983).

Publicker Industries v. *Cohen,* 733 F.2d 1059 (1984).

Richmond Newspapers v. *Virginia,* 100 S.Ct. 2814 (1980).

Rushforth v. *Council of Economic Advisers,* 762 F.2d 1038 (1985).

Russell v. *Air Force,* 682 F.2d 1045 (1982).

Saxbe v. *Washington Post,* 94 S.Ct. 2811 (1974).

Sims v. *CIA,* 709 F.2d 95 (1983), rev'd. 105 S.Ct. 1881 (1985).

Society of Professional Journalists v. *Secretary of Labor,* 11 M.L. Rept. 2474
(1985).

State Department v. *Washington Post,* 102 S.Ct. 1957 (1982).

Stern v. *FBI,* 9 M.L. Rept. 1789 (1983).

Symons v. *Chrysler Corporation Loan Guarantee Board,* 670 F.2d 238 (1981).

Taylor v. *Army,* 684 F.2d 99 (1982).

Terkel v. *Kelly,* 599 F.2d 214 (1979).

U.S. v. *Beckham,* 12 M.L. Rept. 2073 (1986).

U.S. v. *Bolen,* 8 M.L. Rept. 1048 (1981).

U.S. v. *Maddox,* 7 M.L. Rept. 2600 (1982).

U.S. v. *Martin,* 746 F.2d 964 (1984).

U.S. v. *Morison,* 604 F. Supp. 655 (1985).

U.S. v. *Nixon,* 94 S. Ct. 3090 (1974).

U.S. v. *Webbe,* 12 M.L. Rept. 2193 (1986).

Washington v. *Coe,* 101 WN.2d 364 (1984).

Wolfe v. *Department of Health and Human Services,* 539 F. Supp. 276 (1982),
aff'd. 711 F.2d 1077 (1983).

Zemel v. *Rusk,* 381 U.S. 1 (1964).

6

PROTECTION OF NEWS SOURCES AND CONTEMPT OF COURT

A merican journalists are no strangers to the confines of jail cells and prisons. In 1722 James Franklin, the less-publicized older brother of Benjamin Franklin, was jailed in a small cell for publishing a newspaper without the consent of the government of Massachusetts. He was the first of many American journalists to see the inside of a jail cell.

Today in the United States reporters are often jailed for disobeying court orders that instruct them to make public information they choose not to disclose. Journalists frequently want to keep the names of their news sources confidential. Some people tell things to reporters "off-the-record" with the expectation that this information will not be revealed. Often there is more to a story than fits in the newspaper or on the evening news. What remains is held in a reporter's notebook or a newspaper computer memory or a videotape cassette.

Most of us have little interest in what the journalist chooses not to reveal. For some, however, this information is valuable. A police agency might be interested in what a criminal suspect or a witness told a reporter off-the-record. A plaintiff in a libel suit might be interested in the name of the source of an allegedly libelous story. A prosecutor might be interested in film of a violent campus demonstration that was never aired on the evening news.

Reporters are often asked to reveal information they have gathered but chosen not to publish or broadcast. In many instances journalists comply with such requests. At times, however, they refuse. When this happens, the persons interested in getting this information often get a court order, called a **subpoena,** to force the journalist to reveal the name of the news source or to disclose the confidential information. Or government agents may get a warrant to search a newsroom or a reporter's home to find the information they want.

In our society the press is supposed to represent a neutral entity as it gathers and publishes news and information. When the government or anyone else intrudes into the newsroom or the reporter's notebook, it compromises this neutrality. A news source who normally trusts journalists may choose not to cooperate if government agents can learn the source's name by threatening the journalist with a court order. Television news crews will hardly be welcome at protest rallies if the demonstrators know that the government will use the film to identify and prosecute the protestors. The effectiveness of the reporter as an information gatherer may be seriously diminished if government agents or civil and criminal litigants can force journalists to reveal information they choose not to disclose. Society also may ultimately suffer because the flow of information to the public may be reduced.

This chapter is about the problems a reporter can face when government agents or other persons use the power of the judicial system to gain access to the news-gathering processes. We will study the problems of source confidentiality and newsroom searches. We will also look at recent judicial and legislative attempts to resolve these issues. Finally, we will examine the powerful weapon the government may employ to get its way in these disputes: the contempt power. ◆

NEWS AND NEWS SOURCES

If news and information are the lifeblood of the press, then news sources are one of the wells from which that lifeblood springs. Many journalists, especially those who consider themselves investigative journalists, are often no better than the sources they can cultivate. News sources come in all shapes and sizes. Occasionally their willingness to cooperate with a reporter is dependent upon assurances from the journalist that their identity will not be revealed. Why would a news source wish to remain anonymous? There are undoubtedly many reasons. Often the source of a story about criminal activities has participated in criminal activities and has no desire to publicize this fact. Frequently the source of a story about government mismanagement or dishonesty is an employee of that government agency, and revelation of his or her identity could result in loss of the job for informing the press of the errors made by the employee's superiors. Some persons simply do not want to get involved in all the hassle that frequently results when an explosive story is published; by remaining anonymous they can remain out of the limelight.

Journalists have always used confidential sources and obtained information that government officials sought to uncover. The earliest reported case of a journalist's refusal to disclose his sources of information took place in 1848 when a reporter for the *New York Herald* refused to reveal to the U.S. Senate the name of the person who had given him a secret copy of the treaty the United States was negotiating to end the Mexican-American War. He was held in contempt of the Senate and jailed. A United States Court of Appeals denied the journalist's petition for release (*Ex Parte Nugent,* 1848). But the issue of journalists protecting the identity of a confidential source surfaced infrequently in the next 120 years. In fact, from 1911 to 1968 only seventeen cases involving a reporter's confidential sources were reported, according to an article in the *California Law Review.*

But in the past twenty years, the issue has arisen far more often. A journalist who writes or broadcasts a story based on confidential information or confidential sources is confronted with official government inquiries about the name of the source or is called upon to reveal in a trial the nature of the information that was not published or broadcast. At this point the journalist's options are very limited. The journalist can tell the authorities what they wish to know, attempt to negotiate some kind of compromise with those seeking the information, attempt to attack the validity of the subpoena and have it quashed, or refuse to testify—and very likely be cited for *contempt of court* and be sent to jail.

Why has the problem arisen more frequently in recent years? The daily work of reporters and editors involves compiling and summarizing facts and events that often become the subject of court proceedings, government investigations, and legislative proceedings. Reporters are trained to be accurate observers, and they make ideal witnesses. In recent years many journalists have attempted to undertake intensive investigative reporting; and such stories have often provoked subsequent government investigations, in which the reporter is an ideal witness, and lawsuits, in which journalists are called upon to reveal confidential information to prove the truth of their accounts or that they acted responsibly in preparing the story. In such situations the reporter must usually provide the information that is sought or go to jail. This is a tough choice; reveal the identity of a source and you lose the ability to get the news from other sources who wish to remain anonymous. But a jail cell is unpleasant also.

The choice for society is not an easy one either. The interests that are involved in this dilemma are very basic to our system of government. Members of the United States Senate studied the issues involved in the reporters' claim to keep the names of news sources confidential. Former Senator Sam Ervin, chairman of the committee that looked into the problem, said he had never dealt with a more difficult problem during his years in Congress.

On the one hand, it is clearly the obligation of every citizen to cooperate with the government and testify before the proper authorities. This concept was so well established by the early eighteenth century that it had become a maxim. Wigmore, in his classic treatise on evidence (*A Treatise on the Anglo-American System of Evidence*), cites the concept thus: "The public has a right to everyman's evidence." The right to have witnesses and to compel them to testify is one of our cherished constitutional guarantees. The Sixth Amendment states, "In all criminal prosecutions, the accused shall enjoy the right to be confronted with the witnesses against him; and have compulsory process for obtaining witnesses in his favor." This is an important guarantee.

Suppose you were arrested for a crime you did not commit and that you had a witness who could prove you were fifty miles away at the time the crime was committed. How would you feel if your witness decided that he really did not have time to go to court and testify? that he was too busy? that he did not want to get involved? Your right to compel his testimony could be crucial to your freedom.

The Supreme Court has said on many occasions that it is a citizen's duty to testify. In 1919 the Court wrote as follows on the duties and rights of witnesses (*Blair* v. *U.S.*):

> [I]t is clearly recognized that the giving of testimony and the attendance upon court or grand jury in order to testify are public duties which everyone within the jurisdiction of the government is bound to perform upon being properly summoned, . . . the personal sacrifice involved is a part of the necessary contribution to the public welfare.

Most journalists do not dispute the immense societal value of the power to compel testimony. But they do argue that, on the other hand, in most cases involving a reporter's sources, society will benefit more if the reporter is not compelled to testify. Briefly the argument is this. The press is the eyes and ears of the people. Nothing should interfere with this role. The people must be informed; they must have access to the fullest information possible in order to operate properly as citizens in a democracy. Sometimes the only way a reporter can gain crucial information is to get it from an anonymous source. When a reporter is forced to reveal the name of a source, other potential sources will refuse to cooperate with journalists for fear that their identity will be made public as well. In the end it is society that will lose, as it is deprived of the information these sources might provide. At least this is the argument made by journalists.

Many reporters insist that news sources have dried up and will continue to dry up as long as there exists the potential that their identity might somehow be revealed. They cite studies by organizations such as the Reporters Committee of Freedom of the Press to support their argument. Other persons inside and outside the press dispute such evidence and note that only a small number of journalists use confidential sources regularly and that an even smaller number are ever called upon to reveal the identity of these sources. While recognizing the existence of a problem, these persons consider it a fairly small problem (Chamberlin, "Protection of Confidential News Sources: An Unresolved Issue").

CONSTITUTIONAL PROTECTION OF NEWS SOURCES

Big or small, the problem of a reporter's source confidentiality is an issue that the law has had to attempt to resolve. Doctors, lawyers, members of the clergy, and even accountants enjoy privilege that allows them to protect the confidentiality of discussions they have with patients, clients, or parishioners. Reporters seek a similar privilege and in the past ten years have made some headway in gaining such protection. An analysis of the depth and breadth of the reporter's privilege begins with the 1972 ruling by the Supreme Court of the United States in *Branzburg* v. *Hayes*.

The case was really three cases, *Branzburg* v. *Hayes*, in re *Pappas*, and *U.S.* v. *Caldwell*. Today, the Court's decisions are referred to collectively as the *Branzburg* ruling.

Paul Branzburg was a staff reporter for the *Louisville Courier-Journal*. In 1969 and 1971 he wrote two stories about drug use in Jefferson County, Kentucky. In the first story he described in detail his observations of two young men synthesizing hashish. When he was called before a grand jury, he refused to identify the two individuals in his story, citing both the Kentucky reporters' privilege statute, which he claimed exempted him from having to give testimony, and the First Amendment. A Kentucky appellate court rejected his First Amendment argument and ruled that while the state's statute afforded a reporter the privilege of refusing to divulge the identity of a confidential source, it did not give the reporter the right to refuse to testify about events he had witnessed personally. The second story was about drug use in Franklin County, Kentucky, and the court rejected Branzburg's arguments a second time when he refused to testify before a Franklin County grand jury. He appealed to the Supreme Court.

Paul Pappas was a reporter for a New Bedford, Massachusetts, television station. In July 1970 he was assigned to cover civil disturbances in an area near the headquarters of the local Black Panther organization. That afternoon he gained access to the Panther's headquarters and recorded and photographed a prepared statement read by one of the Black Panthers. He returned to Panther headquarters that evening and was allowed to spend three hours with members of the black militant organization as they waited for an anticipated police raid upon their headquarters—a raid that failed to materialize. As a condition of entry into Panther headquarters, Pappas had agreed not to disclose anything he saw or heard there. He was called to testify before a Bristol County grand jury, but he refused to answer questions about what had taken place inside the Panther headquarters, citing his privilege under the First Amendment. Massachusetts courts rejected his argument.

Earl Caldwell worked for the *New York Times* in 1970, an era in which there was significant public concern about the militancy of the Black Panthers. The press succeeded in fueling this fear by publishing masses of misinformation. Earl Caldwell, who was black, had gained the confidence of Black Panther leaders in Oakland, California, and consistently provided readers of the *Times* with accurate, illuminating accounts of the organization. It was probably natural, then, that when a federal grand jury began investigating the Panthers, Earl Caldwell was subpoenaed and told to bring his notes and audiotapes. Caldwell refused, arguing that giving information to the government would destroy his ability to report on the Black Panthers, that none of the leaders would ever again take him into their confidence or even talk with him.

A federal district court partially supported Caldwell's plea. It said that he would not have to answer questions unless in each case the government could demonstrate that "a compelling and overriding national interest" would be served by Caldwell's answer to a question and that no alternative means of getting the information was available. The court based its ruling on the strong First Amendment interests, which it said were at the core of the issue.

Caldwell and the *New York Times* were not satisfied, for the ruling still required the reporter to answer some questions. Since the proceedings were secret, the Panthers would never know which questions Caldwell answered and which questions he did not answer. Caldwell appealed to the Ninth Circuit Court of New York and again won. This time the court ruled that when it is shown that the public's First Amendment right to be informed will be jeopardized by requiring a journalist to submit to a secret grand jury interrogation, the government must respond by demonstrating a compelling need for even the witness's presence before attendance can be required. The court added that this case was very unusual, since most news sources are not as sensitive as the Black Panther organization and most reporters do not enjoy such unique trust and confidence of news sources. Still, the ruling was a significant First Amendment victory for the press. Such a victory, in fact, that the government appealed the ruling to the Supreme Court.

The Court was badly split in its decision on the three cases. Four justices voted against the constitutional privilege, four voted in favor of the constitutional privilege, and Justice Lewis Powell voted in favor of the constitutional privilege in some circumstances, but not in these cases. Let us look first at the votes against the privilege.

Justice Byron White wrote the opinion of the Court to which Chief Justice Warren Burger, Justice William Rehnquist, and Justice Harry Blackmun subscribed. White said that while the Court was sensitive to First Amendment considerations, the case did not present any such considerations. There were no prior restraint, no limitations on what the press might publish, and no order for the press to publish information it did not wish to. No penalty for publishing certain content was imposed. White wrote (*Branzburg* v. *Hayes*, 1972):

> The use of confidential sources by the press is not forbidden or restricted. . . .
> The sole issue before us is the obligation of reporters to respond to grand jury subpoenas as other citizens do and answer questions relevant to an investigation into the commission of crime. Citizens generally are not constitutionally immune from grand jury subpoenas; and neither the First Amendment nor other constitutional provisions protect the average citizen from the disclosing to a grand jury information that he has received in confidence.

Reporters are no better than average citizens, White concluded.

The four dissenters differed sharply with the other justices. Justice Douglas took the view that the First Amendment protection provides the press with an absolute and unqualified privilege. In any circumstance, under any condition, the reporter should be able to shield the identity of a confidential source. Justices Potter Stewart, William Brennan, and Thurgood Marshall were unwilling to go as far as Justice Douglas and instead proposed that reporters should be protected by a privilege that is qualified, not absolute. The three dissenters argued that the reporter should be able to protect the identity of the confidential source unless the government can show the following:

1. That there is a probable cause to believe that the reporter has information that is clearly relevant to a specific violation of the law
2. That the information sought cannot be obtained by alternative means less destructive of First Amendment rights
3. That the state has a compelling and overriding interest in the information

When the government cannot fulfill all three requirements, Justice Stewart wrote for the dissenters, the journalist should not be forced to testify.

With four votes against a constitutional privilege for journalists called to testify before a grand jury and four votes in favor of at least a limited privilege in such a circumstance, the vote of Justice Lewis Powell—the ninth member of the court—became critical. Powell concurred with Justices White, Rehnquist, and Blackmun and Chief Justice Burger in concluding that in the cases presented to the court, no First Amendment privilege existed. But Powell refused to accept the notion that the First Amendment might not provide the journalist with a privilege in other instances in which the reporter was asked to reveal the identity of a source. Powell said that no harrassment of news reporters could be allowed. A balance must be struck between freedom of the press and the obligation of all citizens to give relevant testimony. "The Court," Powell added, "does not hold that newsmen, subpoenaed to testify before a grand jury, are without constitutional rights with respect to the gathering of news or in safeguarding their sources." In short, Justice Powell added, "The courts will be available to newsmen under circumstances where legitimate First Amendment interests require protection." Justice Powell noted two years later in a footnote in another case (*Saxbe* v. *Washington Post*, 1974) that the Court's ruling in *Branzburg* had been an extremely narrow one and that news reporters were not without First Amendment rights to protect the identity of their sources.

Lower Court Rulings

The Branzburg decision, a bitter blow to many who believed that the recognition of at least a limited reporter's privilege was essential to the free flow of information in the society, failed to resolve the crucial First Amendment question. It left to the lower courts to decide on a case-by-case basis whether a reporter's privilege exists in various situations extending beyond the narrow facts of the Branzburg case. And in the past fifteen years, courts in most federal jurisdictions have recognized a constitutionally derived newsperson's privilege in all but those situations that mirror the Branzburg ruling. Courts in many states have done the same. The Third United States Court of Appeals noted with regard to Branzburg (*Riley* v. *Chester,* 1979):

> There, the Supreme Court decided that a journalist does not have an absolute privilege under the First Amendment to refuse to appear and testify before a grand jury to answer questions relevant to an investigation of the commission of a crime. No Supreme Court case since that decision has extended the holding beyond that which was necessary there to vindicate the public interest in law enforcement and ensuing effective grand jury proceedings.

Given this response by the lower courts, it is fair to assert, then, that today there exists a reasonably strong qualified privilege for journalists to refuse to reveal the names of confidential sources and other confidential information gained while gathering news. The successful application of this privilege depends upon several factors. What kind of a proceeding is involved is a key question. The privilege is more readily granted to a journalist involved in a civil suit than to one called before a grand jury, for example. And the privilege is qualified by various court tests, all of which mirror closely the test outlined by Justice Stewart in Branzburg. Is the information important? Is it clearly relevant to the proceedings? Is there somewhere else to get the information? In the next few pages we will attempt to sketch the rough outline of this reporter's privilege. It is important to remember, however, that without a binding Supreme Court ruling, the lower federal and state courts have been permitted to fashion their own rules; and there is distinct variance from state to state, federal circuit to federal circuit. Look to the court precedents in your region as the final authority in this matter.

Civil Actions

Most federal and state courts that have confronted the issue have granted to journalists involved in a civil action the qualified privilege to refuse to reveal the identity of a confidential source. The federal courts have found this privilege in the First Amendment. State courts have found the privilege in state statutes (see pages 334–37), the First Amendment, state constitutions, and even the common law.

The successful application of the privilege in these instances dates back to 1973, in the virtual shadow of the *Branzburg* ruling, when the Democratic party brought a civil action to win damages for the Watergate break-in. Ten reporters from the *New York Times, Washington Post, Washington Star-News, Time* magazine, and other publications were subpoenaed and told to bring their tapes, notes, letters, documents, and all other materials obtained during their reporting of the Watergate break-in. A United States district court quashed the subpoena, noting that the press is entitled to at least a qualified privilege to refuse to answer such questions under the First Amendment (*Democratic National Committee* v. *McCord*, 1973).

In 1977 the Tenth United States Circuit Court of Appeals refused to force filmmaker Arthur Hirsch to reveal confidential information he had obtained in connection with a civil action by the estate of Karen Silkwood against the Kerr-McGee Corporation. Hirsch was preparing a documentary film on the mysterious death of the young woman when he was subpoenaed by Kerr-McGee. The Tenth Circuit Court ruled that a limited First Amendment privilege protected the filmmaker and that before he could be required to answer questions, the trial court was bound to consider whether the party seeking the information had independently attempted to obtain the information elsewhere and had been unsuccessful, whether the information sought from the reporter went to the heart of the matter before the court, and whether the information was of certain relevance in the case. In this case Hirsch did not have to testify (*Silkwood* v. *Kerr-McGee*, 1977). Courts in many jurisdictions have made similar rulings, granting a reporter an exemption from the normal requirement to testify.

Normally a court asks three questions before determining whether the privilege should be granted to the journalist:

1. Has the person seeking the information (normally the plaintiff) shown that the reporter's information is of *certain relevance* in the case?

2. Does the information go to the heart of the matter before the court?

3. Can the person who is seeking the reporter's information demonstrate that there is no other source for this information?

If *all* three questions can be answered yes, the chances are good the reporter will be required to testify. But this is a heavy burden for the plaintiff or the defendant to meet, and in most instances journalists are being excused from testimony (see in re *Consumers Union*, 1978; *Riley* v. *Chester*, 1979; and *McGraw-Hill* v. *Arizona*, 1982).

In civil suits where the reporter is actually a party in the case, the courts have granted the privilege somewhat more grudgingly or not at all. A reporter can end up in a lawsuit either as a plaintiff or a defendant. If the reporter is a plaintiff in a lawsuit and has information that is critical to the case, it is unlikely that a court will permit the reporter to remain silent regarding these issues. When columnist Jack Anderson attempted to sue Richard Nixon and other former government officials for allegedly conspiring to deprive him of his civil rights, he refused to cooperate with the defendants seeking from him the names of confidential sources who gave the columnist information regarding the activities of Nixon and his White House associates. Citing the First Amendment, Anderson refused to reveal the names sought. But a federal district judge ordered him to give the information to the court if he hoped to continue his suit. The judge ruled that Anderson was attempting to use the First Amendment simultaneously "as a sword and a shield. . . . He cannot have it both ways. Plaintiff is not a bystander in the process, but a principal. He cannot ask for justice and deny it to those he accuses." Anderson was forced to withdraw his suit (*Anderson* v. *Nixon* et al., 1978).

A reporter usually ends up as a defendant in a lawsuit when a libel suit is filed because of something the reporter wrote or broadcast. Often the reporter based the libelous news report on confidential information or sources. It is important for the plaintiff in such a libel case to find out where the reporter obtained the information for the story to demonstrate that the journalist was negligent or that the material was published with actual malice (see pages 165–73 to refresh your memory about the meaning of these terms). It is much more difficult to predict how a court will respond to a plaintiff's demand that the reporter reveal confidential information in these kinds of instances. But some patterns have developed. For example, many courts insist that the plaintiff prove that the information sought is crucial to the matter of proving either negligence or actual malice. The 1972 ruling in *Cervantes* v. *Time* is a good example. The lawsuit was a $12-million libel action against *Life* magazine for publishing a story suggesting that the mayor of St. Louis, Alfonso Cervantes, had underworld connections. The mayor wanted to know the names of the sources in the Federal Bureau of Investigation and Justice Department who supplied the information to reporter Denny Walsh. Cervantes said he could not prove malice without these names.

However, the information about the mayor was a small part of the story, which was extremely well documented. The charges against Cervantes comprised only four paragraphs of the eighty-seven-paragraph story. The court of appeals ruled, "To compel a newsman to breach a confidential relationship merely because a libel suit has been filed against him would seem inevitably to lead to an excessive restraint on the scope of legitimate news-gathering activity." The court said that if the plaintiff was able to provide persuasive evidence that this information was crucial to the question of malice, the privilege might then have to give way. However, in this case, "The mayor has wholly failed to demonstrate with convincing clarity that either the defendant acted with knowledge of falsity or reckless disregard of the truth." There was just no reasonable probability that the plaintiff would succeed in proving malice.

In *Senear* v. *Daily Journal American,* the Washington State Supreme Court ruled that a reporter for the Bellevue (Washington) *Journal-American* enjoyed a qualified common law privilege to refuse to reveal the identity of a source for a story he had written about a labor dispute. The state's High Court ruled that the plaintiff could gain access to the information only if it could be shown that a libel claim against the newspaper had merit—it was not intended to merely harrass the newspaper; that the information sought went to the heart of the plaintiff's legal claim—it was critical to the cause of action; and that the plaintiff had exhausted other reasonable means to gain the information. Justice James Dolliver also noted that the trial court should determine that the reporter's interest in nondisclosure is supported by the need to preserve confidentiality, not simply a stance of noncooperation (*Senear* v. *Daily Journal American,* 1982).

In other libel suits, when reporters were asked to testify, the courts have ruled that the plaintiff need only show that there is a genuine issue of fact about the truth or falsity of the libelous material. It is not necessary to demonstrate that the reporter might have information that will resolve the issue. In a libel suit against the *Wall Street Journal,* the Massachusetts Supreme Judicial Court ruled that there was no privilege to protect the newspaper from revealing the name of the source of its story so long as questions material to the case remained to be resolved. "The obligation of newsmen, we think, is that of every citizen, *viz.,* to appear when summoned, with relevant written or other material when required, and to answer relevant and reasonable inquiries" (*Dow Jones* v. *Superior Court,* 1973). The New Hampshire Supreme Court ruled that a public-official libel plaintiff must satisfy the trial court that he or she has evidence to establish that there is a genuine issue of fact regarding the falsity of the publication. Once the plaintiff meets this burden, the privilege to withhold confidential information ceases to exist (*Downing* v. *Monitor Publishing Co.,* 1980). And the United States Supreme Court ruled in 1979 that plaintiffs may explore what the defendant was thinking about while preparing the story for publication or broadcast. The High Court ruled in *Herbert* v. *Lando* that as long as the public-figure libel plaintiff has a special burden of proof in a defamation case, denial of "discovery of editorial state of mind would make that burden unduly onerous." What this means is that the plaintiff can ask reporters or producers or editors if they had any doubts about the truth of the material when they published the story: Did they think they should check things a bit more before broadcasting the libelous charges? Were there other sources with whom they considered talking? And so forth.

On a few occasions in the past, courts have reacted sharply when a reporter refused to reveal the name of the source of a libelous story and have declared that such a refusal supports an inference that no source exists (see *Downing* v. *Monitor Publishing,* 1980; *Greenberg* v. *CBS,* 1979; and *Caldero* v. *Tribune Publishing Co.,* 1977, 1980). A court effectively strips away the libel defense for a newspaper or television station when it says there is no source for a libelous story. This is tantamount to saying the story was fabricated; the defendant will surely lose the case. Courts in Idaho did this on at least two separate occasions. In *Sierra Life* v. *Magic Valley Newspapers,* the trial judge completely struck the newspaper's defenses "as sanctions for their willful refusal" to obey his order to disclose confidential information and awarded almost $2 million to the plaintiff. The Idaho Supreme Court reversed this ruling and ordered the defenses reinstated, noting that at no time during the trial did the plaintiff show that its inability to discover the reporter's sources obstructed its ability to prove the falsity of the story (*Sierra Life* v. *Magic Valley Newspapers,* 1980). These kinds of dramatic court rulings are rare today. In most civil actions, especially when the reporter is not a party to the suit, a qualified privilege will protect the reporter's right to maintain silence about the identity of a news source.

Criminal Cases   Courts have granted the First Amendment privilege to reporters quite freely in civil actions in part, at least, because there is no competing constitutional right involved. In a criminal case, however, the privilege for the reporter must be balanced against the Sixth Amendment right of the defendant to compel testimony on his or her behalf. Consequently, it is somewhat less likely that a court will permit a reporter to refuse to answer questions about the identity of a confidential source or other confidential information. Courts most often apply slight variations of the Stewart test from the Branzburg case to determine whether or not the journalist will be compelled to testify.

In *United States* v. *Burke,* for example, the defendant was indicted for conspiracy in connection with a basketball point-shaving scheme at Boston College and attempted to impeach the testimony of the prosecution's chief witness, a reputed underworld figure. The defendant asked the court to subpoena the unpublished notes and drafts of *Sports Illustrated* reporter Douglas Looney, who had interviewed the witness. The Second U.S. Court of appeals quashed the subpoena, noting that a court may order reporters to reveal confidential sources only when the information is (1) highly material and relevant, (2) necessary or critical to the defense, and (3) unobtainable from other sources (*U.S.* v. *Burke,* 1983).

In New York a reporter interviewed a key prosecution witness before a murder trial and the defendant subpoenaed the notes from that interview. The New York Supreme Court refused to require the reporter to produce these notes because, it said, the defendant failed to show that the information sought was "highly material and relevant," "necessary to his defense," and "unavailable from other sources" (*New York* v. *Bova,* 1983). In 1982 authorities called a reporter to testify in a criminal case against a physician who was charged with violating federal drug laws. Reporter Patrick Malone had written a story about the use and misuse of the drug Quaalude. The story included several statements that Malone attributed to the defendant in the drug case. The government wanted Malone to testify, to verify that Dr. Frederick Blanton had made the statements attributed to him in the article. The trial judge ruled that Malone did not have to appear as a witness because the government had failed to show it had exhausted all efforts to get the information elsewhere or that there was a compelling need to get this information at all (*U.S.* v. *Blanton,* 1982).

Finally, in 1984 the Washington State Supreme Court ruled that an *Everett* (Washington) *Herald* reporter did not have to reveal the names of several confidential sources he had used to prepare an article about alleged cult activities at an eighty-acre farm near rural Snohomish, Washington. The owner of the farm, Theodore Rinaldo, had been convicted of statutory rape, assault, coercion, and intimidating a witness. A year after his conviction, several persons who had testified on Rinaldo's behalf at his trial stepped forward and admitted they had committed perjury. It was during his second trial for tampering with witnesses and other offenses that Rinaldo tried to force reporter Gary Larson to reveal the names of persons who gave the reporter information for six articles that had brought the activities at the farm to the attention of local authorities. Justice James Dolliver, speaking for the court, ruled that Rinaldo would have to show that the information was necessary or critical to his defense and that he had made a reasonable effort to get the material by other means. He could not make such a showing, and the subpoena was quashed (*State* v. *Rinaldo,* 1984).

There are, of course, instances in which courts recognize a qualified privilege for the reporter but still force testimony. The case of *Kansas* v. *Sandstrom* in 1978 provides a good example. Milda Sandstrom was charged with murder in connection with the death of her husband. Reporter Joe Pennington testified at the trial that a confidential source had revealed to him that at a party shortly before Thad Sandstrom was killed, one of the state's witnesses had threatened to kill Sandstrom. Pennington said the informant had heard about the threat from another person who attended the party but refused to reveal the name of the informant. The Kansas Supreme Court ruled that in this instance Pennington did not enjoy a First Amendment privilege to refuse to identify the confidential informant.

The state's High Court noted that lower courts that had applied the *Branzburg* ruling to criminal cases had generally concluded that the proper test for determining the existence of a reporter's privilege in a particular criminal case was to balance *the need of the defendant for a fair trial against the reporter's need for confidentiality* (author emphasis). "As a general rule, disclosure has been required only in those criminal cases where it is shown the information in possession of the news reporter is material to prove an element of the offense, to prove a defense asserted by the defendant, to reduce the classification or gradation of the offense charged, or to mitigate or lessen the sentence imposed," the court noted. In this case the trial court felt that the identity of the confidential informant could lead to information relevant to Mrs. Sandstrom's defense, the High Court said. That is a reasonable position to adopt, it was concluded.

In 1980 the Third United States Court of Appeals ruled that Jan Schaffer, a reporter for the *Philadelphia Inquirer,* had to testify about a conversation she had had with a prosecuting attorney before a criminal trial. The defendants in a government Abscam prosecution moved for a dismissal of the charges on the grounds that there had been massive pretrial publicity about the case that would prevent their getting a fair trial. The defendants charged that the publicity was the result of misconduct by the prosecutor, who they said had improperly given reporters details of the sting operation. The prosecutor admitted talking with reporters about the case, but the defendants sought the reporter's testimony to confirm the prosecutor's statements. The court, applying the three-part test, ruled that Schaffer would have to testify. The reporter obviously had the information—the prosecutor admitted talking with her about the case. There was a compelling need for the information—it was central to the defendant's charges of misconduct by the prosecutor. And the defense had attempted to get the information elsewhere—from the prosecutor himself. The reporter was the only source left (*U.S.* v. *Criden,* 1980).

The California Court of Appeals refused to quash a subpoena against the Columbia Broadcasting System (CBS) for media materials in a criminal prosecution against drug dealers. The material involved clandestine video-tapes and audiotapes made by the network (in cooperation with the Santa Clara sheriff's department) of meetings between narcotics officers and the criminal defendants (*CBS* v. *Superior Court,* 1978). Similarly, the First Amendment arguments made by reporter Myron Farber of the *New York Times* when he was called upon to produce material relevant to the defense in a New Jersey murder case were rejected by various state and federal courts (in re *Farber,* 1978). Farber, incidently, was pardoned by Gov. Brendan Byrne in 1982. His dispute with the New Jersey trial court had cost him forty days in jail and had cost the *New York Times* nearly $300,000 in fines.

Regardless of the outcome of some of these cases, what is important is that most courts have recognized that there is a qualified privilege for reporters to refuse to reveal the names of confidential sources in criminal cases as well as in civil suits.

Grand Jury Proceedings   While the qualified privilege for reporters to refuse to reveal the identities of confidential sources in civil and criminal actions has been recognized by most lower federal courts and state supreme courts that have considered the question, these same courts have routinely refused to extend the First Amendment privilege to grand jury proceedings. This is true even though the grand jury's power to force disclosure is not constitutionally guaranteed, as is the criminal defendant's right to compel a witness to testify. The obvious explanation for this reluctance on the part of judges is that the single U.S. Supreme Court precedent on the question focused upon grand jury testimony and of course in that case, *Branzburg* v. *Hayes,* the High Court ruled that no privilege existed. Only a few reported decisions exist in which appellate courts have quashed or partially quashed a subpoena requiring a reporter to appear and testify before a grand jury.

Two reporters for the Black Panther newspaper, Brenda Presley and Sherrie Bursey, were called to testify before a grand jury in 1972, shortly after the Branzburg ruling. They wrote a story about a speech by Panther leader David Hilliard in which he either did or did not threaten former President Richard Nixon. They were called to testify before several grand juries. Although the reporters always answered some of the questions, they refused to answer all queries regarding confidential information and information regarding management of the Panther paper. The government presented sufficient evidence to convince the district court that there was a compelling and overriding national interest, and the women were called to testify. They refused to answer fifty-six different questions. On appeal, the United States Ninth Circuit Court of Appeals of California ruled that the two reporters had to answer seventeen of the fifty-six questions (*Bursey* v. *U.S.*, 1972). The court said the women did not have to answer queries about the people who worked at the newspaper or about how the paper was edited, but they did have to answer questions about whether they had seen firearms and explosives at Panther headquarters and about whether the Panther leaders conducted discussions concerning violent activities. The government interests were legitimate and compelling, the court said, and infringement upon the First Amendment was incidental.

In 1982 a U.S. district court in Colorado quashed a subpoena that called for the testimony of a wire-service reporter before a grand jury investigating the illegal removal of some photographs by a Secret Service agent from the home of the parents of John Hinckley, Jr., the man who shot President Reagan. The agent allegedly illegally removed the photos from the home while it was being searched and passed the pictures on to United Press International. The judge ruled that the grand jury hearing was not really involved with a criminal prosecution but had been instituted as an administrative proceeding aimed at gaining evidence to support the firing of the Secret Service agent. The court ruled that the reporter would not have to honor the subpoena unless the government could show that the reporter had information that would go to the heart of a pending *criminal investigation* (in re *Grand Jury Subpoenas,* 1982).

Finally, in a very unusual case in 1985, the Third U.S. Court of Appeals ruled that the author of a book did not have to appear before a grand jury, because the government had failed to articulate a compelling interest in gaining the disclosure of the author's notes, documents, and other records. Antoni Gronowicz wrote a purported biography of Pope John Paul II, entitled *God's Broker.* Gronowicz alleged that much of the material in the book came from two hundred hours of interviews he had had with the Pope. The Vatican denied this, and the publisher withdrew the book from circulation. The Justice Department launched an investigation in Philadelphia with the aim of prosecuting Gronowicz for mail fraud because of his promotion of the book. What the government was attempting to do was prove whether the book was true or false. This is an improper motive, the court ruled. The First Amendment protects citizens from government prosecution for false speech. "We will not enforce the grand jury subpoena in this case, where the government's purpose is admittedly to prove the truth of the book," the court ruled (in re *Gronowicz*, 1985).

Outside of these three narrow rulings and a couple more, courts have required reporters to honor subpoenas issued for appearances before grand juries. If there is any good news in this state of affairs, it is that fewer such subpoenas are issued today than in the recent past.

Telephone Records

The names of confidential news sources, reporters' notes, news film, and photographs are not the only records that have been sought by government agents through the use of a subpoena. The records of toll telephone calls made by reporters have also come under government scrutiny in recent years.

The telephone company maintains subscriber records for toll telephone calls for about six months. For long-distance calls billed to the subscriber's telephone number, these records indicate the telephone number called, as well as the date, time, and duration of the call. The records are no secret; a copy of the monthly toll-call record is provided to each subscriber with each month's bill.

In 1974 the American Telephone and Telegraph Company (AT&T) announced that in the future it would not release these records to the government without a subpoena and, as a general policy, would seek to notify subscribers immediately when their individual records had been subpoenaed by a government agency. However, when records were subpoenaed pursuant to a felony investigation, the telephone company said it would not notify the subscriber of the subpoena as long as the government certified that an official investigation was being conducted and that notification to the subscriber could impede the investigation.

The Reporter's Committee for Freedom of the Press challenged the telephone company's policy of releasing *any* records to the government, arguing that the government could use such records to determine reporters' sources. Journalists raised both the Fourth Amendment and the First Amendment as bars to this cooperation between AT&T and the government.

The U.S. Court of Appeals seemed unpersuaded that this cooperation created a real problem and ruled against the Reporter's Committee. The Fourth Amendment claim lacked merit, the court said, because the constitutional prohibition against illegal search and seizure "does not insulate all personal activity from official scrutiny." The First Amendment claim was similarly rejected. The court asserted that the First Amendment offers no additional protections against good faith criminal investigations beyond that afforded by the Fourth and Fifth amendments (*Reporter's Committee* v. *AT&T,* 1978):

> The principle is clear. To the extent individuals desire to exercise their First Amendment rights in private, free from possible good faith law enforcement investigation, they must operate within the zone of privacy secured by the Fourth Amendment. When individuals expose their activities to third parties, they similarly expose these activities to possible government scrutiny.

SUMMARY

In recent years more and more reporters have been called to testify in legal proceedings. Often they are asked to reveal confidential information to aid police in criminal investigations, to assist in the defense of a criminal defendant, or to help a libel plaintiff establish negligence or actual malice. Failure to comply with a court order can result in a citation for contempt of court. The Supreme Court of the United States ruled in 1972 that reporters were like all other citizens; they did not enjoy a First Amendment privilege that permitted them to refuse to testify before a grand jury. Despite this High Court ruling, the lower federal courts and state courts have fashioned a constitutional-common law privilege that often protects a journalist who has been subpoenaed to testify at a legal hearing. The privilege is qualified. In many instances a court will not require a journalist to testify unless the person seeking the information held by the journalist can demonstrate that the reporter has information that is relevant to the hearing, that there is a compelling need for the disclosure of this information, and that there are no alternative sources for this information.

Courts tend to apply this three-part test differently in different types of legal proceedings. Journalists are most likely to escape being forced to testify in a civil suit, especially if the reporter is not a party to the suit in some way. Reporters are more likely to be forced to testify in a criminal case, but there are numerous examples of reporters being granted a qualified privilege to escape such testimony as well. Reporters called to testify before a grand jury, however, usually are required to honor the subpoena. The United States Court of Appeals has also ruled that the records of toll telephone calls made by journalists may also be subpoenaed to further legitimate law enforcement proceedings.

LEGISLATIVE AND EXECUTIVE PROTECTION OF NEWS SOURCES

While the courts have erected limited barriers to protect journalists from subpoenas issued by government agencies, the state legislatures and the United States Department of Justice have attempted to protect reporters as well. Twenty-six states have passed statutes that shield reporters in one way or another from subpoenas that might force them to reveal confidential information. There is no federal shield law, but the Department of Justice has developed an extensive set of guidelines that sharply limit when and how federal agents may use subpoenas against journalists. First, let us look at the state statutes.

Shield Laws

In 1896 Maryland granted journalists a limited privilege to refuse to testify in court proceedings. Since then, more than half of the fifty states have passed what the press refers to as **shield laws.** These laws set down in specific terms what the privilege entails, who may use it, and when it may be used. For example, the Alabama Shield Law provides:

> No person engaged in, connected with, or employed on any newspaper (or radio broadcasting station or television station) while engaged in a news gathering capacity shall be compelled to disclose, in any legal proceeding or trial, before any court or before a grand jury of any court, or before the presiding officers of any tribunal or his agent or agents, or before any committee of the legislature, or elsewhere, the sources of any information procured or obtained by him and published in the newspaper (or broadcast by any broadcasting station or televised by any television station) on which he is engaged, connected with, or employed.

Authorities who have studied the shield laws have found that they fail to give the news gatherer the same measure of protection as the First Amendment. Brian M. Cullen notes in the *Suffolk University Law Review:*

> Their disparate protection and their limited scope, as well as the narrow construction courts have accorded them, have permitted the frequent and arbitrary disclosure of confidential information. This lack of predictable protection has doubtlessly inhibited identity-conscious sources from revealing their stories to newsgatherers. Moreover, the state shield statute must give way whenever it conflicts with the Constitution.

Cullen and Douglas Frazer, in an article in the *The Journal of Criminal Law and Criminology,* recently summarized some of the features of these state laws. Most of the shield laws apply to all formal state proceedings, administrative and legislative hearings as well as trials and grand jury investigations. But few of the laws give a protection that exceeds, or is even equal to, that given by the constitutional privilege. Four state shield laws claim to be absolute—those in Arizona, Nebraska, New Jersey, and Ohio—but only the New Jersey courts have ruled on this interpretation. The remaining twenty-two laws are qualified in many ways. In four states—Alaska, Louisiana, New Mexico, and North Dakota—the shield law can be overcome by a mere judicial determination that justice or public policy requires the privilege to yield to some other interest. Most state shield laws protect only the identity of confidential sources or information that would reveal the identity of the source. The First Amendment privilege, on the other hand, extends to unpublished information, outtakes, notes, tape recordings, and even photos.

Other qualifications in the laws abound. A reporter waives the privilege upon the disclosure of any part of the confidential matter under the Nevada law. And in New York there must be an understanding of confidentiality between the source and the reporter before the law will apply. The shield laws usually apply only to professional news gatherers. The law in Oregon may be used by "persons engaged in any medium of public communication." State laws frequently exclude amateur news gatherers and free-lance writers. The Delaware law, on the other hand, protects "journalists, scholars, educators and polemicists." Frequently, the state laws restrict the privilege to professional journalists who work for specific kinds of mass media. In Illinois, for example, a newspaper reporter who wishes to use the privilege must work for a publication with a paid circulation, one that is published on a regular basis, and one that has been in operation for a full year prior to the assertion of the privilege. A reporter's own observations are frequently not considered privileged under the state statutes. In a few states the shield law will not protect the identity of a source unless the information given to the reporter by the source has been published or broadcast.

All these problems, plus the inconsistency from state law to state law, has made the statutes less than useful. A few cases will make this point.

In New York State an author who was preparing a book on organized crime was subpoenaed to produce the notes and tapes of his conversations with a witness in a murder prosecution. When he raised the state's shield law as a defense, the trial judge ruled that the law was inapplicable because the author of the book was not "a journalist engaged in gathering, preparing, or editing of news for newspapers, magazines, news agencies, press associations or wire service." The decision was later upheld by the state appellate court (*New York v. LeGrand*, 1979).

In Montana a reporter for the Associated Press telephoned a home where a gunman was holding two hostages. In a conversation with the reporter, which was tape recorded, the gunman admitted shooting a policeman. The audiotape was subpoenaed by the state, but the Associated Press refused to surrender it, citing the Montana shield law, which stipulates that no person employed by any news service for the purpose of gathering news may be required to disclose information gained through news gathering. A Montana district court ruled that the law protected only the reporter—not the Associated Press, which is an organization. The wire service had to surrender the tape (in re *Investigative File*, 1978).

In Maryland, home of the nation's oldest shield law, a reporter wrote a story about being offered a joint of marijuana by a clerk in a store. He was called by the grand jury and asked the name of the clerk and of the store. He refused to give the names and argued that the shield law protected him. The court said no, that in this case he had witnessed a crime and *he* was the source. The story was based on his firsthand account (*Lightman* v. *State,* 1972). Paul Branzburg got into trouble the same way, for Kentucky had a shield law. The courts ruled that Branzburg was a witness to a crime when he watched the hashish being synthesized. There was no other source. Two reporters in New York State found out the same thing. Stewart Dan and Roland Barnes of television station WGR-TV were inside Attica during the prison riots in 1972. They were questioned by a grand jury and asked what they had seen. They refused to tell, using the state's shield law as a defense. They lost. The court said the New York law protects news sources, not reporters who witness crimes (*People* v. *Dan,* 1973).

One of the most perplexing of all the shield law cases is the case of William Farr. The case is a classic example of how a shield law can sometimes prove to be absolutely worthless. In 1970 Farr, a reporter for the *Los Angeles Herald-Examiner,* was assigned to cover the trial of Charles Manson and his followers. A restrictive order was in effect during the trial prohibiting trial participants from releasing the content or nature of all testimony given at the trial. During the trial a witness gave a member of the prosecution a written statement that one of the defendants in the case, Susan Atkins, had confessed to the crimes for which she and the rest of the Manson clan were being tried. Copies of the statement were prepared and given to each of the attorneys in the trial. One of them gave a copy to Farr, who published it as part of a story in the *Herald-Examiner.* At the conclusion of the trial, the judge convened a special hearing to determine the source of Farr's story. Called as a witness, Farr refused to identify the attorney who had given him the copy of the statement. Farr argued that he did not have to testify because of the California shield law, but the court ruled that the privilege did not apply to Farr because at the time of the posttrial hearing, he had resigned from the *Herald-Examiner* and was working as a press aide to the Los Angeles district attorney. He was no longer a reporter. In addition, the California district court of appeals ruled that even if Farr were a working journalist, the shield law was inapplicable because its use would interfere with the right of the trial court to enforce its edicts and control the conduct of participants at the trial: "To construe the statute as granting immunity to petitioner, Farr, in the face of the facts here present would be to countenance an unconstitutional interference by the legislative branch with an inherent and vital power of the court to control its own proceedings and officers" (*Farr* v. *Superior Court,* 1971). In other words, the people of California have no business giving journalists this privilege if it interferes with the work of the courts. Bill Farr spent forty-six days in an eight-by-twelve-foot cell with no windows before the California court of appeals vacated the district court's contempt order. The state shield law was revised to prohibit judges from sentencing reporters to indefinite jail terms and to prevent a court from forcing reporters to reveal their sources after they leave journalism.

Obviously the shield laws are not all bad. There are numerous instances in which a law has in fact protected a reporter (see *Beach* v. *Shanley,* for example, where the New York Court of Appeals ruled that the state's shield law provided an absolute privilege to a reporter against disclosing the name of a confidential source to a grand jury, 1984). In addition, the number of subpoenas that were never sent to journalists simply because of the existence of a shield law cannot be calculated. Still, many reporters find it more to their liking to work to develop the limited First Amendment protection than to ask the government—the same government upon which they are expected to report—for a special protection. When push comes to shove, many reporters note, the government can strip away any protection it has given to the press. That cannot happen so easily with a privilege grounded in the First Amendment.

Federal Guidelines

As a kind of corollary to a shield law, the Department of Justice has adopted rules that define when and how a United States attorney can obtain a subpoena against a working reporter. Here is a summary of the guidelines:

1. The Department of Justice must attempt to strike a balance between the public's interest in the free dissemination of ideas and information and the public interest in effective law enforcement when determining whether to seek a subpoena for a journalist's confidential information.
2. All reasonable attempts should be made to obtain the information from alternative sources before considering issuing a subpoena to a member of the news media.
3. Negotiations with the news media to gain the information sought shall be pursued in all cases in which a subpoena to a member of the news media is contemplated.
4. If the negotiations fail (if the reporter won't provide the material voluntarily), the attorney general must approve the subpoena based on the following guidelines:
   a. There must be sufficient evidence of a crime from a nonpress source. The department does not approve of using reporters as springboards for investigation.
   b. The information the reporter has must be essential to a successful investigation—not peripheral or speculative.

c. The government must have unsuccessfully attempted to get the information from an alternative nonpress source.

d. Great caution must be exercised with respect to subpoenas for unpublished information or where confidentiality is alleged.

e. Even subpoenas for published information must be treated with care, because reporters have encountered harrassment on the grounds that information collected will be available to the government.

f. The subpoena must be directed to specific information.

Telephone Records

Rules one through three in the guidelines just listed apply when federal agents seek to subpoena the toll telephone records of members of the media as well. If the negotiations to get the records fail, the agents must seek permission from the attorney general to issue the subpoena. In such a case the following guidelines apply:

1. There should be reasonable grounds to believe that a crime has been committed, and that the information sought is essential to the successful investigation of that crime.

2. The subpoena should be directed at only relevant information regarding a limited subject matter and should cover a limited period of time.

3. The government should have pursued all reasonable alternative means before seeking the subpoena.

4. Reporters must be given timely notice that the government intends to issue a subpoena.

5. Information obtained through the subpoena must be closely guarded so that unauthorized persons cannot gain access to it.

These federal guidelines have worked well. In some federal cases judges have insisted that the government must demonstrate that it has followed these guidelines before it will force a reporter to testify (*U.S.* v. *Blanton,* 1982, for example). Some state and local law enforcement agencies have adopted rules similar to these federal rules. The federal guidelines apply to criminal cases, civil matters, and subpoena of telephone records. It is true that these guidelines do not completely protect the working journalist, but the guidelines often work better than shield laws, and they go a considerable distance in reducing animosity that was mounting between the press, the police, and the courts.

Newsroom Searches

Does a newsroom or a journalist's home enjoy any constitutional protection from a search by the police or federal agents? The Supreme Court of the United States refused to extend the First Amendment in such a manner in 1978

(*Zurcher* v. *Stanford Daily*). Since then, however, the Congress and many state legislatures have provided qualified legislative protection for premises where news and scholarship are produced. The lawsuit that resulted in the Supreme Court ruling stemmed from the political turmoil of the early seventies, a period that generated many of the previously discussed cases regarding reporters' sources.

In April of 1971 police were asked to remove student demonstrators who were occupying the administrative offices of Stanford University Hospital. When police entered the west end of the building, demonstrators poured out of the east end, and during the ensuing melee outside the building, several police officers were hurt, two seriously. The battle between the police and the students was photographed by a student, and the following day pictures of the incident were published in the *Stanford Daily* student newspaper. In an effort to discover which students had attacked the injured police officers, law enforcement officials from Santa Clara County secured a warrant for a search of the *Daily's* newsroom, hoping to find more pictures taken by the student photographer. It was hoped the pictures might provide visual evidence as to which students had battered the lawmen. There was no allegation that any member of the *Daily* staff was involved in the attack or other unlawful acts. No evidence was discovered during the thorough search.

This type of search is known as an innocent third-party search, or simply a third-party search. Police search the premises or a room for evidence relating to a crime, even though there is no reason to suspect that the owner of the premises or the occupant of the room is involved in the crime that is being investigated. Such searches are not uncommon, but in the lawsuit that followed, the student newspaper argued that this kind of search threatened the freedom of the press and should not be permitted unless police officials first obtain a subpoena—which is more difficult for lawmen to get than is a simple search warrant. The subpoena process would also provide the press with notice prior to the search and allow editors and reporters to challenge the issuance of the subpoena.

The newspaper argued that the unannounced third-party search of a newsroom seriously threatened the ability of the press to gather, analyze, and disseminate news. The searches could be physically disruptive for a craft in which meeting deadlines is essential. Confidential sources—fearful that some evidence that would reveal their identity might surface in such a search—would refuse to cooperate with reporters. Reporters would be deterred from keeping notes and tapes if such material could be seized in a search. All of this, and more, could have a chilling effect on the press, lawyers for the newspaper argued.

The Supreme Court, in a five-to-three ruling, disagreed with the newspaper. Justice Byron White ruled that the problem was essentially a Fourth Amendment question (i.e., was the search permissible under the Fourth

Amendment?), not a First Amendment question, and that under existing law a warrant may be issued to search any property if there is reason to believe that evidence of a crime will be found. "The Fourth Amendment has itself struck the balance between privacy and public need and there is no occasion or justification for a court to revise the Amendment and strike a new balance. . . ," White wrote. The associate justice conceded that "where the materials sought to be seized may be protected by the First Amendment, the requirements of the Fourth Amendment must be applied with 'scrupulous exactitude.' " He added, "Where presumptively protected materials are sought to be seized, the warrant requirement should be administered to leave as little as possible to the discretion of the officer in the field." But Justice White rejected the notion that such unannounced searches are a threat to the freedom of the press, arguing that the framers of the Constitution were certainly aware of the struggle between the press and the Crown in the seventeenth and eighteenth centuries, when the general search warrant was a serious problem for the press. Yet the framers did not forbid the use of search warrants where the press was involved, White asserted. They obviously believed the protections of the Fourth Amendment would sufficiently protect the press (*Zurcher* v. *Stanford Daily,* 1978).

The decision by the Supreme Court reinforced existing law on the question and did not represent a dramatic change in policy. But prior to the search of the *Stanford Daily* in 1971, there had been only fifteen police searches of newsrooms in this country, ever, according to Anthony Lewis, columnist for the *New York Times*. The Supreme Court ruling seemed to suggest the value of such searches to law enforcement agencies across the United States, for in the next ten years nearly twenty newsroom searches were conducted. What happened at KBCI-TV in Boise, Idaho, is typical. There was a riot at the Idaho State Penitentiary in July 1980. Inmates invited Bob Loy, managing editor of KBCI-TV, to meet with them to hear their grievances. Loy toured the facility with a cameraman, who shot videotape of the $15 million in damage at the prison. After the riot was quelled, County Prosecutor James Harris and police searched the KBCI newsroom for the videotapes taken at the penitentiary. The prosecutor obtained the search warrant on the grounds that he wanted to use the videotape in his prosecution of inmates for damaging the prison. After ninety minutes of what was described by *TV Guide* as "heavy-handed" searching, the tapes were found and confiscated. KBCI brought suit to have the search declared illegal and to get an injunction against future searches, but the case was dismissed by the Idaho district court, which cited the *Zurcher* ruling (*Reiss* v. *Harris,* 1980).

Incidents like these demonstrated the need for some kind of legislative relief, and Congress responded by passing the Privacy Protection Act of 1980. The law prohibits law officers and government agents from searching for or seizing materials that are in the hands of persons working for the mass media or persons who expect to publicly disseminate the material in some other manner (e.g., public speech). The statute designates two categories of material that are protected: work products and documentary materials. The law says a work product "encompasses the material whose very creation arises out of a purpose to convey information to the public." In layman's language work products are reporters' notes, unexposed film, outtakes, and so forth. Documentary materials are described as "materials upon which information is formally recorded," such as government reports, manuscripts, and the like. Congress based the statute on the commerce clause in the United States Constitution in order to extend the reach of the law to include state and local agencies, as well as federal law enforcement personnel. To obtain either work products or documentary materials, law enforcement agencies must obtain a subpoena; a search warrant will not do. There are, however, exceptions to the rule. A law enforcement agency may conduct a warranted search of a newsroom to find "work products" in either of the following two situations:

1. When there is a probable cause to believe that the person possessing such materials has committed or is committing a criminal offense to which the materials will relate
2. Where there is reason to believe that the immediate seizure of such materials is necessary to prevent the death of or serious harm to a person

A search warrant may be used instead of a subpoena to obtain documentary materials if either of the two conditions just listed are met or in either of these two situations:

1. There is reason to believe that the giving of notice pursuant to gaining a subpoena would result in the destruction, alteration, or concealment of such materials
2. That such materials have not been provided in response to a court order directing compliance with a subpoena, all other legal remedies have been exhausted, and there is reason to believe that further delay in gaining the material would threaten the interests of justice

In most instances, then, law enforcement personnel will be forced to seek a subpoena to gain access to information kept in a newsroom or a reporter's home. Many state legislatures have passed similar laws. Hence, the problem of newsroom searches has been significantly reduced.

How to Respond to a Subpoena

What should a reporter do if he or she is subpoenaed? Here are some tips from *The Seattle Times Newsroom Legal Guidebook,* prepared by P. Cameron Devore, Marshall Nelson, and other attorneys for the law firm of Davis, Wright, Todd, Reise and Jones in Seattle.

First, try to avoid the problem of a subpoena. Don't give a promise of confidentiality to a source without first carefully considering whether such a promise is actually needed to get the story. It may be wise to discuss the issue with an editor before agreeing to keep the name of a source confidential. Also, don't talk, even informally, with persons outside the newspaper about stories in which confidential information or sources are involved. Such discussions may constitute a waiver of the privilege you want to assert at a later date.

If you receive a subpoena, tell your editor immediately. Do not attempt to avoid being served with the subpoena. While a reporter is under no obligation to make the job easier for the person serving the subpoena, resistance to this service may result in the subpoena being abandoned and a search warrant issued in its place. Don't accept a subpoena for someone else, and don't volunteer information to the process server about the person being sought. If the subpoena calls for the production of notes or other documents, start compiling the material to give to your editor. Once the subpoena has been served, this material is considered evidence in the case. Destruction of such material to avoid having to produce it at a hearing will result in the court's holding you in contempt. Finally, don't panic. The law, as you have seen, is pretty much on your side these days.

SUMMARY

State legislatures and the federal government have adopted statutes and rules that offer some protection to journalists who hold confidential information sought by government agents and other individuals. Twenty-six states have adopted so-called shield laws, which provide a qualified privilege for reporters to refuse to testify in legal proceedings. While sometimes these statutes can be helpful, they are not without problems. There is a lack of consistency among the state shield laws. These laws have definitional problems that permit courts to construe them very narrowly if they choose to. The laws usually protect only what someone tells a reporter, not what a reporter personally sees or hears. Often courts see the statutes as legislative interference with judicial prerogatives and go out of their way to interpret the laws in the least useful manner.

The Department of Justice has adopted rules that govern when and how federal agents may subpoena journalists, records possessed by journalists, and telephone toll records. The rules require federal agents to strike a balance between the public's interest in the free flow of information and effective law enforcement. United States attorneys are instructed to attempt to obtain information from alternative sources or to negotiate with the journalist to get the material before seeking a subpoena. The attorney general must approve all subpoenas under guidelines outlined in these rules.

In response to a ruling by the United States Supreme Court that the First Amendment does not ban searches of newsrooms or reporters' homes, Congress passed the Privacy Protection Act of 1980. This act requires federal, state, and local police agencies who seek a journalist's work products or other documentary materials to get a subpoena for these materials rather than seize them under the authority of a search warrant. The statute does provide exceptions to these rules. For example, premises may be searched and materials seized under a search warrant if police believe the reporter has committed a crime, if there is reason to believe someone will be harmed if the materials are not seized, or if police fear the materials might be destroyed if a subpoena is sought.

THE CONTEMPT POWER

We have seen that reporters have been subpoenaed to testify in a wide range of legal proceedings. Television news departments have been ordered to surrender films and videotapes. Broadcast journalists have been required under court order to supply audiotape recordings to police and prosecutors. And, of course, if journalists refuse to cooperate, they face severe penalty under the courts' power to punish for contempt. What is the contempt power? Without a thorough understanding of the contempt power, it is difficult to truly appreciate the predicament journalists can find themselves in when asked to produce the name of a news source or other confidential information.

History of Contempt

In 1631 in England a British subject was convicted of a felony, not a very uncommon event. This particular subject was angered at being found guilty, and after the sentence was read he threw a brickbat at the judge. The brickbat missed the judge, but the man was quickly seized, his right hand was cut off and nailed to the gallows, and he was immediately hanged in the presence of the court (this story is recounted by Ronald Goldfarb in *The Contempt Power*).

While such judicial retribution is an uncommon exercise of the contempt power, it nevertheless is a representative example of the power of judges to control what goes on in their courtrooms. Even as the end of the twentieth century approaches, disobedience of or disrespect for the court is normally put down swiftly by exercise of the power of contempt. Any act that interferes with the orderly processes of justice is usually promptly stopped and the offender is quickly punished. While other governmental bodies (legislative bodies, for example) can use the contempt power, its use by judges, which is the subject of this chapter, is far more common today.

Does it not seem odd in what are supposedly representative democracies like the United States and Great Britain, countries in which the guarantee of civil liberties has long been part of the national heritage, that a single individual like a judge can wield such awesome power? The answer to that question is yes. But supporters of the contempt power point out that it is a necessary tool for judges to have to ensure the orderly function of the courts. Courts are an indispensable part of our governmental system. The courts make freedom of the press, freedom of speech, freedom of religion, and other civil liberties meaningful rights by protecting these constitutional guarantees. If the court system is impeded in some way, if judges are waylaid in their trek toward justice, society then suffers.

Even this rationale does not explain why judges and justices retain such extraordinary powers, powers that include summary punishment, when justice is stripped of many of the basic constitutional guarantees that the courts are supposed to protect. Nor does this rationale explain why supposedly intelligent men and women can believe that our court system, or any court system, can be infallible and should be free from citizen scrutiny and comment. The answers to these questions are, once again, found in the past.

In 1927 British legal scholar John Fox wrote in *The History of Contempt of Court*, "Rules for preserving discipline . . . came into existence with the law itself, and contempt of court has been a recognized phase of English law from the twelfth century to the present time." Order has always been essential to the administration of justice. Courts, after all, are where rational decision making must prevail. Yet the contempt power is peculiar to the common law nations. Judges in France or Holland or Italy do not enjoy such extraordinary latitude in dealing with disturbance, disobedience, and disrespect. The common law judges were able to assume such power because the first common law judge was the king himself. He was the administrator of justice. As Ronald Goldfarb points out in his important study of the contempt power, the people revered the king. Goldfarb writes, "This was but another, though not different, step from the sanctity of the medicine man, the priestly character of primitive royalty, and the Christian concepts of obedience." This legal scholar adds that the contempt power is clearly understandable, then, when viewed from the perspective of the age of its inception, "an age of alleged divinely ordained monarchies, ruled by a king totally invested with all sovereign legal powers and accountable only to God." In some instances resistance to the king was a sin, punishable by damnation. Being jailed or fined or tortured for being contemptuous of the king was really rather unimportant when compared with the fate offenders faced on judgment day in the hereafter.

When the king became too busy to hear all the cases coming before his court, he appointed ministers to sit in judgment throughout the realm. Logically, disrespect toward one of the king's judges should not be a serious offense, since the discourtesy was aimed at a mere mortal, not at a person divinely ordained to rule. But that was not the case, because while the king was not physically present in the courtroom, he was assumed to be there spiritually, guiding the hand of justice. Surely this assumption sounds like nonsense, but people will believe almost anything if the belief is important to them. In any case, disrespect or disobedience of the judge were considered to be disrespect or disobedience of the king or of the spiritual presence of the king. Punishment by the judge was as swift and as sure as punishment by the king would have been.

As representative democracy developed in England and royal influence on the government diminished, judges retained the contempt power, and it became institutionalized in common law courts in both Great Britain and the United States. Courts today rarely justify the exercise of the contempt power on the grounds that it protects the integrity of the judge. Today, protection of the authority, order, and decorum of the court is the usual reason given for the use of the contempt power, and sometimes it is protection of the rights of the litigants using the court to settle a dispute.

Kinds of Contempt

Historically, legal scholars have tried to classify the various kinds of contempt power judges have at their disposal into either civil or criminal contempt, but contempt seems to defy classification, or at least to defy consistent classification. Goldfarb refers to the "chameleonic characteristic" of contempt; that is, an action considered civil contempt in one court may be viewed as criminal contempt in another. Writing in the *Tennessee Law Review* (1971), Professor Luis Kutner notes the problem:

> The distinction between civil and criminal contempt is not clear-cut. The same act in different situations may be regarded as either civil or criminal. Contempt has been regarded criminal if the purpose is to punish the contemnor for his misconduct in the presence of the court or for conduct out of the court's presence challenging its authority, and the contemnor is fined a fixed amount or imprisoned for a definite term; it is regarded as civil if the primary purpose is to coerce compliance with a court order, usually for the benefit of an injured suitor, and the contemnor is imprisoned only until he complies. Whether the contempt is civil or criminal is determined by the judicial decision maker.

Despite the "chameleonic" nature of the contempt power, scholars frequently use the following method of classification. The classification is based on the purpose of the punishment: (1) punishment exacted to protect the rights of a private party in a legal dispute before the court and (2) punishment exacted to vindicate the law, the authority of the court, or the power of the judge. When the punishment is exacted for the first reason, the contempt is normally called a civil contempt. When the punishment is exacted for the second reason, the contempt is usually considered a criminal contempt. Here is a brief discussion of the types of contempt based on this classification scheme.

Civil Contempt

A **civil contempt** is not an affront to the court itself, but is more likely failure or refusal to obey a court ruling, decision, or order made to protect the rights of one of the litigants in the case. Normally, the punishment in a civil contempt suit is a jail sentence, which is terminated when the contemnor agrees either to do something or to stop doing something. For example, if a broadcasting station is sued for libel because it has broadcast a defamatory news story and the reporter refuses to divulge the source of the story under questioning by the plaintiff, the reporter can be held in civil contempt and can be put in jail and forced to stay there until he or she is willing to cooperate with the court. The court is protecting the rights of the libel plaintiff in this case. Civil contempt, then, is charged to obtain obedience to judgment, court orders, and court processes and is designed to protect the rights of the litigants in a case.

Criminal Contempt

Criminal contempt, on the other hand, is charged to protect the court itself, to punish a wrong against the court. Obstruction of court proceedings or court officers, attacks on court personnel, and deliberate acts of bad faith or fraud are all examples of criminal contempt. There are two kinds of criminal contempt—direct contempt and indirect contempt.

A **direct criminal contempt** is an action committed "in the presence of the court," that is, in the courtroom or near the courtroom. Generally two conditions underlie a direct contempt: first, the judge has actual personal knowledge of what occurred, and second, the act or action had a significant impact upon the judicial proceedings. The key seems to be the judge's personal knowledge of the events. In the instance of a direct criminal contempt, the judge is normally empowered to use what is called **summary contempt power.** When exercising summary power, the judge acts as prosecutor, jury, and judge. Suppose that in the midst of the trial, the defendant jumps on a table and begins to play an accordion. The judge can use summary power. "I accuse you of disrupting this trial by playing an accordion [the prosecutor's role], I find you guilty of disrupting the trial [the jury's role], and I fine you $200 [the judge's role]."

Summary punishment is the most onerous aspect of the contempt power, for the citizen is not allowed to exercise some of the basic constitutional guarantees that are normally a part of the criminal process. There is no jury trial. The accuser is also the judge and jury. The accused has no right to call witnesses in his or her behalf. Many authorities argue that because the summary power can normally be exercised only in a direct criminal contempt, an instance in which the judge has direct personal knowledge of what took place, the summary power is really not a threat to civil liberty. But this argument is questionable. Anytime one person can wield such power, a threat to civil liberties exists.

Any contempt conviction can be appealed. As in any other case, the appeal is taken to the next higher court in the state or in the federal system if the contempt stems from the action of a federal district judge. Normally, the punishment is held in abeyance until the disposition of the appeal is settled. It is possible, but not likely, that a reporter who has been jailed for a contempt might stay in jail during at least a portion of the appeal process. But usually the journalist is freed pending the results of the appeal. In the appeal process, however, the only record of the facts in the case is prepared by the judge who issued the citation. The appeal is based upon this factual record, the facts as seen by the trial judge.

The press infrequently gets involved in direct criminal contempt. However, if a photographer were to snap a flash picture in the midst of a trial, that photographer would undoubtedly find him- or herself in direct criminal contempt.

Indirect criminal contempt is sometimes called constructive contempt and can be described as misconduct that occurs apart from the trial or apart from the court but that still interferes with the proceeding.

Another definition of indirect criminal contempt is that it is a contempt about which the court or the judge has no firsthand knowledge or a contemptuous act that does not occur in the presence of the court. Comments published in a newspaper about the conduct of the court or of the judge in the midst of the trial can be constructive contempt. When during a trial a television station broadcasts the details of the defendant's confession after the judge has suppressed the information, the station commits an indirect contempt. Publication of false or grossly inaccurate stories about the proceedings of a court can be considered a constructive contempt. Any action that interferes with the administration of justice but that occurs away from the courtroom can be considered an indirect criminal contempt.

Limitations on
Contempt Power

Before the limits of the contempt power are discussed, it should be noted at this point that truth is not generally considered a limitation; that is, truthful criticism of the court, publishing truthful comments about a pending case, can be and frequently is regarded as contempt. As one author puts it, any adverse comment by the mass media, no matter how true, can interfere with the administration of justice and can be punished in most courts as contempt. The Supreme Court established this principle in the early years of this century when it upheld a Colorado court decision to punish the editor and publisher of a Denver newspaper for printing articles that questioned both the motives of the state's High Court and the manner in which two of the supreme court judges had been seated. The criticism was published as part of a commentary on a case pending before the state High Court. Justice Oliver Wendell Holmes, writing for the United States Supreme Court, said the comments were inappropriate because the case was being considered by the court. "When a case is finished," he wrote, "courts are subject to the same criticism as other people, but the propriety and necessity of preventing interference with the course of justice by premature statement, argument or intimidation hardly can be denied" (*Patterson* v. *Colorado,* 1907). Holmes added that the fact that the criticism is truthful is immaterial in a case of constructive contempt.

The early years of the twentieth century must be regarded as a high-water mark for the contempt power, because since that time the opponents of this power have succeeded in placing rather severe limitations upon its use. Make no mistake; it is not a sterile power. Judges can and still do use their contempt power. But in the last quarter of the twentieth century, judges throughout the United States have far less freedom in how they use this power than they had in the first quarter of this century.

Legislative Limits

One important limitation upon the power of the court to use contempt comes from legislatures. For example, for more than sixty years, the Congress has passed laws that limit use of the summary power by federal judges to dispose of contempt citations. The 1914 Clayton Antitrust Act, for example, requires that judges provide a jury trial in a contempt case when the contemptuous action is also a crime under federal or state law. In 1932, as a part of the Norris-LaGuardia Act, the Congress mandated jury trials for all constructive contempts arising out of labor disputes. The 1957 civil rights law provided for a jury trial for contempt when the sentence imposed exceeded forty-five days in jail. The 1964 civil rights law contains the same provision.

Court-Imposed Limits

The bench itself imposes limitations upon the use of the summary power. The *Federal Rules of Criminal Procedure* requires that in indirect contempt notice be given the contemnor and a hearing be allowed. In addition, there are the right to counsel, the right to cross-examine witnesses, the right to offer testimony, and in many instances the right to a jury trial. If the contempt citation is based upon criticism or disrespect of a judge, that judge is disqualified from the proceeding. Bail is also allowed. The courts and legislatures in many states also deem that a jury trial is a requirement in an indirect contempt.

In the instances just noted, the legislature or the bench itself grants the right to a jury trial. Is there a constitutional right to a jury trial in such cases? The United States Supreme Court has been grappling with this question since the 1960s.

In 1964 the High Court ruled that there is no constitutional right to a jury trial in a contempt case in upholding the contempt conviction of the governor of Mississippi, Ross Barnett, who willfully disobeyed an order of the Fifth Circuit Court of Appeals. As one might expect at that time and in that place, the substantive question involved was civil rights. However, a footnote to the Court's opinion states, "Some members of the Court are of the view that, without regard to the seriousness of the offense, punishment by summary trial without a jury would be constitutionally limited to that penalty provided for petty offenses" (*U.S. v. Barnett*, 1964).

Petty offenses generally carry a sentence of six months or less. What the Court seemed to be hinting at is that a jury trial is required constitutionally if the penalty exceeds more than six months in jail. A few years later in *Cheff v. Schnackenberg* (1966) the High Court specifically said what it had implied in the *Barnett* case—that sentences exceeding six months cannot be imposed in cases of criminal contempt without giving the accused a jury trial. Then in 1968, in *Bloom v. Illinois,* the High Court took the last step and ruled that criminal contempt is a crime in the ordinary sense and that since the United States Constitution guarantees the right to a jury trial in criminal cases, prosecutions by state courts for serious criminal contempts (those with more than a six-month penalty) must be heard by a jury.

One of the most interesting court-imposed limitations upon the power of contempt concerns judicial interpretation of the 1831 federal contempt statute. One of the first acts of the first United States Congress in 1789 was to establish a federal judiciary system. In doing so it gave federal judges the power "to punish by fine or imprisonment, at the discretion of said courts, all contempts of authority in any case or hearing before the same."

This broad authority to use the contempt power remained unchanged until the 1830s, when federal Judge James H. Peck arbitrarily punished an attorney who published an article critical of the judge. The judge's action resulted in his own impeachment. He was acquitted by a vote of twenty-two to twenty-one, but the trial prompted Congress to place a limit on the summary power. The 1831 law strictly limited federal judges' use of summary punishment to those contempts committed in the presence of the court "or so near thereto" as to obstruct the administration of justice. The change in the law, then, was designed to limit the power of federal judges. But by the Civil War this law had been forgotten, and federal judges once again used their summary power to punish a wide variety of contemptuous behavior.

Typical of this attitude was a decision by the Arkansas Supreme Court in 1855 that rejected a state statute limiting use of the contempt power and ruled that the power in courts to punish for contempt springs into existence upon the creation of the courts, that it is a part of the court's inherent power (*State* v. *Morrill*).

In 1918 a question over interpretation of the 1831 law came before the Supreme Court. Toledo, Ohio, was in the throes of a major dispute over a change in the transit fares. While a federal judge deliberated over the constitutionality of the change in the price of a streetcar ride, a local newspaper, the *News-Bee*, published unflattering remarks about him. After the judge ruled that the change in fare was unconstitutional, he found the newspaper in contempt and summarily fined the publisher. The newspaper appealed the action on the grounds that the judge lacked the authority to invoke a summary punishment, that summary punishment could only be used in cases in which the contempt is committed in the presence of the court or "so near thereto" as to create an obstruction of administration of justice. The *News-Bee* was published miles from the courthouse, not in the presence of the court nor "so near thereto." In other words, the *News-Bee* said that the 1831 law placed a geographic limitation upon the judge's use of the summary punishment. The high court disagreed. It ruled that the 1831 limitation placed a causal, rather than a geographic, limitation upon the use of the summary power (*Toledo Newspaper Co. v. U.S.*, 1918). Chief Justice Edward F. White wrote that *so near thereto* meant that any action that was in "close relationship" to the administration of justice could be punished summarily. In this case, the newspaper articles critical of the judge surely had a relationship to the case at hand.

The matter appeared settled, albeit wrongly. In 1928 Walter Nelles and Alice King, legal researchers, looked into the history of the 1831 law ("Contempt by Publication in the United States"). By their research these writers demonstrated that the 1831 measure was designed to limit the power of federal judges, not to enlarge it, as a majority of the Supreme Court had contended in the Toledo newspaper case in 1918.

In 1941 the Supreme Court had the opportunity to apply these research findings (*Nye v. U.S.*) in a case that did not involve the press. Instead, the case originated in a civil suit filed in federal district court against a patent medicine company. The plaintiff claimed that his son had died as a result of drinking the medicine. Agents from the patent-medicine maker plied the father with liquor one night and cajoled him into writing a letter to the judge, asking that the suit be dismissed. The judge was suspicious, investigated the request, and discovered the skulduggery by the drug company. He summarily fined the two men for their contemptuous behavior, despite the fact that their meeting with the plaintiff took place more than one hundred miles from the court. In an appeal to the Supreme Court, the convictions were overturned. Justice William O. Douglas, citing the legal research published by Nelles and King, noted that "so near thereto" has a geographic meaning, that before the summary power can be used, the misbehavior must be in the vicinity of the courtroom; that is, in physical proximity to the proceedings.

Justice Douglas did not indicate how close, but most experts today believe that a federal judge's right to use the summary power probably extends to the hallway outside the courtroom and perhaps even to the lobby of the building when a disturbance occurs. Conceivably a demonstration on the sidewalk outside the building can also be ruled to be in physical proximity if the disturbance is noisy and disturbs proceedings.

Through various means, then, during this century the summary power of judges has been limited, and in turn the limitations have reduced the contempt power. Through statutes that explicitly limit the use of the summary power and through court rulings that limit the severity of punishment that may be applied in the absence of a jury, the absolute power of judges has been trimmed. Nevertheless, the summary power is still a threat. And even six months in jail is a long time!

First Amendment
Limitations

The First Amendment was not raised as a barrier to contempt conviction until relatively modern times—in 1941 to be exact. In 1941, and again in 1946 and 1947, the United States Supreme Court ruled that freedom of the press to comment on the judiciary must be protected, except in those circumstances in which the commentary presents a serious threat to the proper functioning of the legal process. These three decisions—*Bridges* v. *California* and *Times Mirror Co.* v. *Superior Court, Pennekamp* v. *Florida,* and *Craig* v. *Harney*—stand as the bedrock support for the argument that the First Amendment protects the press in writing about the judiciary.

The first case, *Bridges* v. *California* and *Times Mirror Co.* v. *Superior Court* (1941), actually consisted of two appeals from decisions by California courts, and the cases were decided together as one case. In the first instance a newspaper, the *Los Angeles Times,* was ruled in contempt for publishing a series of anti-labor editorials. The trial court claimed that the editorials were aimed at influencing the disposition of cases before the court concerning labor unionists. In the second case, labor leader Harry Bridges was held in contempt of court when he publicly threatened to take the dockworkers out on strike if the courts attempted to enforce a judicial ruling going against Bridges and his union. While the spectre of a militant anti-labor union newspaper and a militant labor leader arguing on the same side of this question is remarkable, it is not as remarkable as the Court's decision, which voided both contempt citations.

In a five-to-four decision the High Court repudiated the idea that the contempt power is valid because it is deeply rooted in English common law. Justice Hugo Black wrote that even if this were the case, the idea ignores the generally accepted historical belief that "one of the objects of the Revolution was to get rid of the English law on liberty of speech and press." Black said that before a judge can use the contempt power to close off discussion of a case, there must be a "clear and present danger" that the discussion will produce interference with the proper administration of justice. In applying Holmes's famous World War I clear-and-present-danger sedition test to contempt, Black meant that only those threats to justice that are imminent or immediate can be punished. The substantive evil must be extremely serious and the degree of imminence extremely high before utterances can be punished, he wrote.

The government argued in these cases that commentary on a case is clearly proper, but only *after* the case is completed so that the course of justice cannot be influenced. Black rejected this notion, saying that it is while a trial is underway that the public interest about a case is highest. He wrote:

> We cannot start with the assumption that publications actually do threaten to change the nature of legal trials and that to preserve judicial impartiality it is necessary for judges to have a contempt power by which they can close all channels of public expression to matters touching on the pending cases.

It should be noted parenthetically that in using the clear-and-present-danger test to block contempt convictions, Justice Black made better use of those four words than did the High Court in its application of the test in sedition trials. For the clear-and-present-danger test indeed became an effective means of stopping contempt convictions against the press.

This concept was reinforced five years later when in the second case, *Pennekamp* v. *Florida* (1946), the court reviewed an appeal from the Florida Supreme Court involving a contempt citation against the *Miami Herald*. The *Herald* had been highly critical of the trial courts in Dade County, Florida, for many months. In at least two editorials, it was argued that the courts worked harder to protect the criminals than they worked to protect the people. But the newspaper's evaluation of the courts' performance was founded on serious misstatement of facts. The court found both the editor, John D. Pennekamp, and the newspaper in contempt and levied fines against them both.

The Supreme Court overturned the convictions, noting, "We are not willing to say under the circumstances of this case that these editorials are a clear and present danger to the fair administration of justice in Florida." Justice Stanley Reed wrote that while he could not precisely define clear and present danger, certainly the criticism of a judge's actions in a nonjury trial would not affect the legal process. What about the factual errors in the editorials? Justice Reed said the errors were quite immaterial. Free discussion, Reed said, is a cardinal principle of Americanism. Discussion after a trial ends might be inadequate and can endanger the public welfare. Freedom of discussion should be given the widest range compatible with the essential requirement of the fair and orderly administration of justice. "We conclude," Reed wrote, "that the danger under this record to fair judicial administration has not the clearness and immediacy necessary to close the door of permissible public comment. When that door is closed, it closes all doors behind it."

The following year, the Court once again reinforced the First Amendment barrier to the use of the contempt power in its decision in *Craig* v. *Harney* (1947), the third case. In this case a Texas newspaper had been highly critical of a judge who directed a jury to return a verdict against a well-liked citizen in a civil suit. The *Corpus Christi Caller-Times* was found in contempt of court, and again the High Court struck down the conviction. Justice William

O. Douglas admitted that in the Court's opinion the critical articles were unfair because they contained significant errors about what had actually occurred at the trial. "But inaccuracies in reporting," he wrote, "are commonplace. Certainly a reporter could not be laid by the heels for contempt because he missed the essential point in a trial or failed to summarize the issues to accord with the views of the judge who sat on the case."

Douglas wrote that it took more imagination than the Court possessed to find "in this sketchy and one-sided report of a case any imminent or serious threat to a judge of reasonable fortitude. . . ." Douglas added, "Where public matters are involved, the doubts should be resolved in favor of freedom of expression rather than against it."

The three cases just discussed—*Bridges, Pennekamp,* and *Craig,*—represent three strong statements in favor of a broad discussion of judicial matters, of trials, and of the legal process. To some degree they also represent a limitation upon the contempt power of the courts. The clear-and-present-danger test is a formidable hurdle for any judge to clear before punishing a newspaper or television station with a contempt citation. However, lest we get swept away by the Court's rhetoric, it is important to look at what was involved in each of these cases, or rather what was not involved. In none of the cases did the judge first issue an order banning certain kinds of publicity about the case. In none of the cases could a jury have been influenced by the media publicity. In none of the cases did the press publish or broadcast evidence or statements prohibited at the trial. As a matter of fact, all three cases involved the same question—commentary or criticism directed toward a judge. From these cases it is clear that the Supreme Court expects the nation's judges to be strong, not to bend in the wind of public opinion, not to be influenced by journalistic commentary. But the Court has never indicated that it has the same expectations with regard to juries. It has never said that a judge must allow the press free rein in its comments on a pending case with regard to material evidence or the credibility of witnesses. The caution, then, is not to read more into these decisions than is actually there. *Bridges, Pennekamp,* and *Craig* stand for almost unlimited discussion of pending nonjury cases. That is about as far as we dare go, however.

Interference with the trial process, however, especially in a jury trial, will usually not be tolerated, First Amendment or not. During a 1982 criminal trial in Boulder, Colorado, the members of a venire—a panel of persons being examined to determine whether they will be seated as jurors—were instructed, in the presence of the press, not to talk with reporters or anyone else about the trial. But after many citizens complained that they thought that the venire members were being intimidated by attorneys during the examination process, two reporters for the *Boulder Daily Camera* contacted some prospective jurors to ask if they felt they were being intimidated. This was brought to the attention of the court and fourteen provisionally qualified jurors were dismissed. The examination procedure had to be started all over again. An angry judge, who said reporters were aware of his order to the venire, found the two reporters in contempt of court. An appellate court upheld the citation, and the reporters were forced to reimburse the state and the parties for the costs incurred because of the additional four days of trial during which the reexamination of the venire took place. The reporters also had to pay the costs for their own contempt trial (in re *Stone, 1985*).

Present Status

The threat of a contempt citation is the judge's most potent weapon for enforcing an order issued by the court. Reporters and others must be sensitive to the notion that the violation of a court rule or court order can result in punishment for contempt. And in some jurisdictions the contempt citation will stand even if the court order or court rule that was violated is later declared illegal or unconstitutional by an appellate court. A case that dramatically makes this point is *U.S. v. Dickinson* (1972).

In November 1971 a hearing was underway in federal court in Baton Rouge, Louisiana. A VISTA worker had been indicted by the state on charges of conspiring to murder the mayor of Baton Rouge. The defendant complained that the state had no evidence in the case and that prosecution was merely an attempt to harass him. The hearing in federal court was to determine the motives of the state in the prosecution. Since it was possible that the charges would be sustained and that the VISTA worker would be tried later in criminal court, the federal judge ruled that there could be no publicity about what took place during the hearing. The press could report that such a hearing was taking place, but that was all. Reporters Gibbs Adams and Larry Dickinson of the *Baton Rouge Morning Advocate and State Times* ignored the order, published a story about the hearing, and were found in criminal contempt and fined $300 each.

Upon appeal, the United States Court of Appeals for the Fifth Circuit struck down the trial court's no-publicity order but at the same time upheld the contempt convictions. The court cited a 1967 Supreme Court ruling—*Walker* v. *Birmingham*—as precedent. In that case Martin Luther King and seven other clergymen were arrested and held in contempt for violating a Birmingham, Alabama, court injunction banning all marches, parades, sit-ins, and so forth. The High Court ruled that while the ban on marches and parades was unconstitutional, Dr. King and the other defendants should have challenged the ban in court rather than just violate it. The contempt citations stood.

The same logic was applied in the *Dickinson* case. Judge John R. Brown wrote (*U.S. v. Dickinson,* 1972):

> The conclusion that the District Court's order was constitutionally invalid does not necessarily end the matter of the validity of the contempt convictions. There remains the very formidable questions of whether a person may with impunity violate an order which turns out to be invalid. We hold that in the circumstances of this case he may not.

This decision perplexes many persons who cannot understand why the press, or anyone else for that matter, should be punished for not obeying an order that is not legal in the first place. It is probably best to have Judge Brown explain by quoting a lengthy passage from his opinion in the *Dickinson* case:

> We begin with the well-established principle in proceedings for criminal contempt that an injunction duly issuing out of a court having subject matter and personal jurisdiction *must be obeyed*, irrespective of the ultimate validity of the order. Invalidity is no defense to criminal contempt. "People simply cannot have the luxury of knowing that they have a right to contest the correctness of the judge's order in deciding whether to wilfully disobey it. . . . Court orders have to be obeyed until they are reversed or set aside in an orderly fashion. . . ."
>
> The criminal-contempt exception requiring compliance with court orders, while invalid nonjudicial directives may be disregarded, is not the product of self-protection or arrogance of judges. Rather it is born of an experience-proved recognition that this rule is essential for the system to work. Judges, after all, are charged with the final responsibility to adjudicate legal disputes. It is the judiciary which is vested with the duty and power to interpret and apply statutory and constitutional law. Determinations take the form of orders. The problem is unique to the judiciary because of its particular role. Disobedience to a legislative pronouncement in no way interferes with the legislature's ability to discharge its responsibilities [passing laws]. The dispute is simply pursued in the judiciary and the legislature is ordinarily free to continue its function unencumbered by any burdens resulting from the disregard of its directives. Similarly, law enforcement is not prevented by failure to convict those who disregard the unconstitutional commands of a policeman.
>
> On the other hand, the deliberate refusal to obey an order of the court without testing its validity through established processes requires further action by the judiciary, and therefore directly affects the judiciary's ability to discharge its duties and responsibilities. Therefore, "while it is sparingly to be used, yet the power of courts to punish for contempts is a necessary and integral part of the independence of the judiciary, and is absolutely essential to the performance of the duties imposed upon them by law. Without it they are mere boards of arbitration whose judgments and decrees would be only advisory."

While most members of the press accept this logic to a point, they argue that the press presents a special case because time is a crucial factor in news gathering. Had the reporters in the *Dickinson* case, for example, not disobeyed the order but instead appealed the decision to a higher court, the trial they were covering would have been over before the restrictive order could have been declared invalid.

Judge Brown said that timeliness is an important aspect of news and that an appellate court should grant a speedy review of such orders. "But newsmen are citizens too," he wrote. "They too may sometimes have to wait. They are not yet wrapped in an immunity or given the absolute right to decide with impunity whether a judge's order is to be obeyed or whether an appellate court is acting promptly enough." Although Judge Brown seemed to see the need for speed, nine months elapsed between the original contempt citation and his ruling in the court of appeals.

The reporters appealed the ruling to the Supreme Court, but the High Court declined to hear the matter. Many authorities interpret the refusal as approval by the Court of the Fifth Circuit Court decision (*U.S.* v. *Dickinson*, 1972).

The implications of *Dickinson* are rather frightening. In a paper entitled "Judicial Restraints on the Press," Professor Donald Gillmor quotes Dickinson's attorney:

> If the heavy burden which must be borne by the government to support any prior restraint can be met merely by the assertion of the possibility of a conflict . . . between constitutional rights, then freedom of the press as we know it would be held hostage to the fertile imagination of judges.

Many experts predicted that the precedent in *Dickinson* would be an open invitation to abuse by trial courts, and such prophecies were quickly realized.

In the summer of 1972, several persons were arrested on charges of conspiring to disrupt the 1972 Republican Convention in Miami. It is normal procedure in many courts to prohibit photography in the courtroom (more about this in a later section). Many newspapers and television stations use artists to make drawings of the proceedings. In the trial of the conspirators, the judge told the press that sketching would not be permitted in the courtroom if the sketches were intended for publication. As a way around the court order, an artist for the Columbia Broadcasting System attended the trial (without pad and pencil) and sketched scenes from memory after the court session. Four sketches were broadcast by the network, which was immediately held in contempt for violating the order. The trial court then issued an order that banned sketching both inside and outside the courtroom and forbade publication of any sketch of the courthouse "regardless of the place where the sketch is made." The Columbia Broadcasting System appealed the order and the contempt citation.

The court of appeals struck down the ban on sketching but upheld the contempt citation. Citing the *Dickinson* ruling, Judge Dyer wrote (*U.S.* v. *CBS*, 1974):

> That case stands for the proposition that before a prior restraint may be imposed by a judge, even in the interest of assuring a fair trial, there must be "an imminent," not merely a likely threat, to the administration of justice. The danger must not be remote or even probable, it must immediately imperil.

Despite the fact that the district court made no showing whatsoever that the sketching was obtrusive, disruptive, or an imminent threat to the administration of justice, the court said the order should have been challenged rather than disobeyed.

More recently, a federal judge in Rhode Island ruled *The Providence Journal* in contempt of court for publishing information about a reputed mob leader that had been obtained from an illegal government wire tape. The FBI had obtained the information illegally in 1962 and, in 1976, a U.S. Court of Appeals ruled that publication of the information would constitute an invasion of privacy. The matter arose again in 1985 and, on November 13, Judge Francis Boyle signed an order forbidding the publication of any of the information obtained from the wiretap. *The Providence Journal* published an article containing information from the wiretap on November 14. On November 19, Judge Boyle vacated his order forbidding the publication, acknowledging that it was likely to be found unconstitutional under the First Amendment. On March 17, 1986, however, he held *The Journal* and its editor, Charles Hauser, in contempt of court. He said the order should have been obeyed regardless of its legality. The newspaper was fined $100,000 and Hauser was sentenced to eighteen months probation and ordered to perform two hundred hours of public service work (in re *Providence Journal,* 1986).

The rule in the *Dickinson* case—that a contempt citation will stand even if the court order is later ruled invalid—is not accepted in all states or by all courts. For example, in a case similar to *Dickinson*, the Washington State Supreme Court ruled in an opposite fashion. In the Washington case a trial judge ordered the press to refrain from publishing reports about anything that occurred at a public trial when the jury was not in the courtroom. Two reporters from the *Seattle Times* violated the order and were found in contempt. The state's High Court said the court order was unconstitutional, that it violated the reporters' right to publish what happened in an open trial. The High Court also voided the contempt citation, ruling that the violation of a court order that was patently void on its face could not produce a valid judgment of contempt. "To sustain this judgment of contempt," Justice Walter McGovern wrote, "would be to say that the mere possibility of prejudicial matter reaching a juror outside the courtroom is more important in the eyes of the law than is a constitutionally guaranteed freedom of expression. This we cannot say" (*State* ex rel. *Superior Court* v. *Sperry,* 1971).

Similarly, an Illinois appellate court in 1977 rejected the reasoning in *Dickinson* when it voided a contempt citation issued against a newspaper for the violation of a court order. The paper had been sued for libel, and the trial judge presiding at the defamation suit issued an order prohibiting the newspaper from publishing any editorials in which the lawsuit was discussed. The judge said he was fearful that such material might prejudice jurors in the community. The newspaper and its publisher were held in contempt of court when a subsequent editorial was published. The Illinois court of appeals ruled that the court order was an unconstitutional restraint on freedom of the press and threw out the contempt citation as well. Justice Seidenfeld wrote that the

Dickinson case failed to clearly recognize the strong presumption against the validity of prior restraints on the press and the irremedial nature of the injury inflicted upon the press by the kind of ban on publication issued in the case. The Illinois court was not persuaded by the logic of the Fifth Circuit ruling. "If the case [*Dickinson*] stands for the rule that no order prohibiting pure speech may be disobeyed while in effect, we do not agree," wrote Justice Seidenfeld (*Cooper* v. *Rockford Newspapers*, 1977).

These state cases are important to consider alongside *Dickinson*. It must be remembered that each state can adopt its own rule regarding the viability of a contempt citation issued for the violation of a patently unconstitutional court order. Federal courts outside the Fifth Circuit are also not governed by the *Dickinson* **rule.**

Reporters who seek to protect the integrity of the news-gathering process from intrusion by the government must be extremely careful. Even the best attorneys have difficulty protecting a journalist from the contempt power of the judge. Myron Farber of the *New York Times* spent forty days in jail for contempt of court. William Farr of the *Los Angeles Times* spent forty-six days in a small cell for contempt of court. Both men worked for powerful news organizations and were ably represented by counsel. Yet each still spent more than a month in jail.

It is difficult for a reporter to raise the shield of the First Amendment in attempting to resist the power of a court to punish for contempt. While freedom of expression is the essence of a democratic state, the contempt power seems out of place in a democracy. Writing in "Contempt Power: The Black Robe—A Proposal for Due Process," Luis Kutner states the issue best:

> The contempt power, which arose as an extension of monarchial power, is incongruous in a nation dedicated to the principles of popular democracy . . . all contempts are examples of unlimited and arbitrary powers remaining as historical accidents and anomalies, inconsistent and incompatible with individual liberties and rights.

SUMMARY

The power of a judge to punish for contempt of court is a remnant of the power of English kings. Today, courts have broad powers to punish persons who offend the court, interfere with legal proceedings, or disobey court orders. Contempt has been roughly divided into the following two categories:

1. Civil contempt: The power of a court to obtain obedience to court orders and judgments to protect the rights of the litigants in a case
2. Criminal contempt: The power to punish a wrong committed against the court itself
   a. Direct criminal contempt: an action taken against the court in the presence of the judge (e.g., shouting obscenities at a judge)

b. Indirect or constructive contempt: an action taken against a court outside the presence of the judge (e.g., a newspaper editorial criticizing a court ruling)

Some limits have been placed upon the contempt power. Legislatures often restrict the kinds of sentences judges may impose for contempt or require a jury trial before a contempt conviction. The Supreme Court has ruled that before criticism of a court may be punished by contempt, it must be shown that the criticism created a clear and present danger of the likelihood of interference with the administration of justice. In some jurisdictions appellate courts have ruled that persons must obey even unconstitutional contempt orders (the *Dickinson* rule).

BIBLIOGRAPHY

Here is a list of some of the sources that have been helpful in the preparation of chapter 6:

Books

Fox, John. *The History of Contempt of Court.* Oxford: Clarendon Press, 1927.
Goldfarb, Ronald. *The Contempt Power.* New York: Columbia University Press, 1963.
Gordon, David. *Newsman's Privilege and the Law.* Columbia, Mo.: Freedom of Information Center, 1974.
Wigmore, John H. *A Treatise on the Anglo-American System of Evidence in Trials at Common Law.* 2d. ed. Boston: Little, Brown & Co., 1934.

Articles

Blasi, Vince. "Press Subpoenas: An Empirical and Legal Analysis." 70 *Michigan Law Review* 229, 1971.
Boyd, J. Kirk. "Legislative Response to *Zurcher* v. *Standford Daily*." 9 *Pepperdine Law Review* 131, 1981.
Chamberlin, Bill. "Protection of Confidential News Sources: An Unresolved Issue." 44 *Popular Government* 18, 1978.
"Comment: The Newsman's Privilege: Government Investigations, Criminal Prosecutions and Private Litigation," 58 *California Law Review* 1198, 1970.
Cullen, Brian M. "Circumventing Branzburg: Absolute Protection for Confidential News Sources." 18 *Suffolk University Law Review* 615, 1984.
Frazer, Douglas H. "The Newsperson's Privilege in Grand Jury Proceedings: An Argument for Uniform Recognition and Application." 75 *Journal of Criminal Law and Criminology* 413, 1984.
Goodale, James C. "*Branzburg* versus *Hayes* and the Development of a Qualified Privilege for Newsmen." 26 *Hastings Law Review* 709, 1975.
Guest, James, and Stanzler, Alan. "The Constitutional Argument for Newsmen Concealing Their Sources." 64 *Northwestern University Law Review* 18, 1969.
Kutner, Louis. "Contempt Power: The Black Robe—A Proposal for Due Process." 39 *Tennessee Law Review* 27, 1971.
Lewis, Anthony. "The Big Chill." *The New York Times,* Nov. 15, 1984.
Mullen, Lawrence J. "Developments in the News Media Privilege: The Qualified Constitutional Approach Becoming Common Law." 33 *Maine Law Review* 401, 1981.

Nelles, Walter, and King, C. W. "Contempt by Publication in the United States." 28 *Columbia Law Review* 401, 1928.

Newman, Craig A. "Qualified Privilege for Journalists *Branzburg v. Hayes:* A Decade Later." 61 *University of Detroit Journal of Urban Law* 463, 1984.

Cases

Anderson v. Nixon et al., 444 F. Supp. 1195 (1978).

Beach v. Shanley, 10 M.L. Rept. 1753 (1984).

Blair v. U.S., 250 U.S. 273 (1919).

Bloom v. Illinois, 391 U.S. 194 (1968).

Branzburg v. Hayes, 408 U.S. 655 (1972).

Bridges v. California and *Times Mirror Co. v. Superior Court,* 314 U.S. 252 (1941).

Bursey v. U.S., 466 F.2d 1059 (1972).

Caldero v. Tribune Publishing Co., 562 P.2d 791 (1977).

CBS v. Superior Court, 85 Cal. App.3d 241 (1978).

Cervantes v. Time, 446 F.2d 986 (1972).

Cheff v. Schnackenberg, 384 U.S. 373 (1966).

in re *Consumers Union,* 4 M.L. Rept. 2119 (1978).

Cooper v. Rockford Newspapers, 365 N.E.2d 746 (1977).

Craig v. Harney, 331 U.S. 367 (1947).

Democratic National Committee v. McCord, 356 F. Supp. 1394 (1973).

Dow Jones v. Superior Court, 303 N.E.2d 487 (1973).

Downing v. Monitor Publishing Co., 415 A.2d 683 (1980).

Ex Parte Nugent, 18 F. Cas. 471 (1848).

in re *Farber,* 394 A.2d 330 (1978).

in re *Farr,* 111 Cal. Rptr. 649 (1974).

Farr v. Superior Court, 99 Cal. Rptr. 342 (1971).

in re *Grand Jury Subpoena,* 8 M.L. Rept. 1418 (1982).

Greenberg v. CBS, 69 A.D.2d 693 (1979).

in re *Gronowicz,* 750 F.2d 223 (1985).

Herbert v. Lando, 441 U.S. 153 (1979).

in re *Investigative File*, 4 M.L. Rept. 1865 (1978).
Kansas v. *Sandstrom*, 581 P.2d 812 (1978).
Lightman v. *State*, 294 A.2d 149 (1972).
McGraw-Hill v. *Arizona*, 680 F.2d 5 (1982).
New York v. *Bova*, 118 Misc. 2d 14 (1983).
New York v. *LeGrand*, 4 M.L. Rept. 1897 (1979).
Nye v. *U.S.*, 313 U.S. 33 (1941).
in re *Pappas*, 266 N.E.2d 297 (1971).
Patterson v. *Colorado*, 205 U.S. 454 (1907).
Pennekamp v. *Florida*, 328 U.S. 331 (1946).
People v. *Dan*, 41 A.D.2d 687 (1973).
in re *Powers*, 4 M.L. Rept. 1600 (1978).
in re *Providence Journal*, 12 M.L. Rept. 1881 (1986).
Reiss v. *Harris*, No. 72454 (Idaho District Court, Ada County, 1980).
Reporter's Committee v. *AT&T*, 593 F.2d 1030 (1978).
Riley v. *Chester*, 612 F.2d 708 (1979).
Senear v. *Daily Journal-American*, 641 P.2d 1180 (1982).
Sierra Life v. *Magic Valley Newspapers*, 623 P.2d 103 (1980).
Silkwood v. *Kerr-McGee*, 563 F.2d 433 (1977).
State ex rel. *Superior Court* v. *Sperry*, 483 P.2d 608 (1971).
State v. *Morrill*, 16 Ark. 384 (1855).
State v. *Rinaldo*, 684 P.2d 392 (1984).
Toledo Newspaper Co. v. *U.S.*, 247 U.S. 402 (1918).
United States v. *Burke*, 700 F.2d 70 (1983).
U.S. v. *Barnett*, 376 U.S. 681 (1964).
U.S. v. *Blanton*, 534 F. Supp. 295 (1982).
U.S. v. *CBS*, 497 F.2d 102 (1974).
U.S. v. *Criden*, 633 F.2d 346 (1980).
U.S. v. *Dickinson*, 465 F.2d 496 (1972).
Walker v. *Birmingham*, 388 U.S. 307 (1967).
Zurcher v. *Stanford Daily*, 436 U.S. 547 (1978).

7 FREE PRESS AND FAIR TRIAL

People have complained about the abundance of crime news in American newspapers almost as long as American newspapers have existed, at least since the 1830s and 1840s when the newspaper evolved from being primarily a political journal to being a chronicler of public occurrences. For some as yet untold reason, both the press and the public seem to share a continuing fascination with the troubles and travails of humankind, especially the plight of persons caught up in the web of the law. For better than 150 years the press has provided Americans with a daily, weekly, and/ or monthly diet of crime news. Sometimes there was more crime news than at other times. Persons who complain that today reporters spend too much time writing about murder and kidnapping surely cannot remember the four decades between 1890 and 1930 when crime news was a staple of most American newspapers and the police reporter was the most important, envied man in the city room. Ben Hecht's remembrances in his play *Front Page* and his autobiography *A Child of the Century* are far more truthful than most journalists like to admit.

While some persons object to the publication of crime news because they believe it to be in bad taste, because they think such information is not relevant to present-day existence, or because they think the press should spend its time pursuing other news, other persons object to publication of crime news for another reason. Many people believe that the press— newspapers and broadcasting stations—interfere with the judicial process by the publication of such information.

The argument goes something like this: Every person accused of a crime has the right to a fair trial. According to the Sixth Amendment to the United States Constitution, a fair trial includes the right to an "impartial jury." Juries are selected from members of the community who read newspapers and watch television and listen to the radio. The trial process has built-in safeguards that protect accused persons. Certain kinds of information cannot be used as evidence against a suspected criminal. A past criminal record, for example, is immaterial in most trials. So are the results of examinations using the so-called lie detector. The court keeps this kind of information from the jury during the trial. What happens if the jurors read about these circumstances before the trial begins? What if they read, for example, that the defendant has a long record of convictions? What if they read that she refused to take a lie detector test? What if they read that he is an army deserter or that she operates a brothel? Does not the publication of such facts tend to prejudice jurors against the defendant? Many people believe that it does.

What is the solution? Is it to stop the press from publishing such facts? After all, the Sixth Amendment guarantees a fair trial, an impartial jury. This solution is fine—except for one problem: the First Amendment, which guarantees a free press, an unimpeded press, a press at liberty from governmental restrictions.

If this situation strikes you as a dilemma, it is. Justice Felix Frankfurter stated the problem quite succinctly in 1946 in his concurring opinion in the case of *Pennekamp* v. *Florida:*

> A free press is not to be preferred to an independent judiciary, nor an independent judiciary to a free press. Neither has primacy over the other; both are indispensable to a free society. The freedom of the press in itself presupposes an independent judiciary through which that freedom may, if necessary, be vindicated. And one of the potent means for assuring judges their independence is a free press.

The recent history of the free press–fair trial controversy in the United States has been the attempt to discover a way to balance these two very important constitutional rights. The attempt has not been completely successful. In those communities that solved the problem best, courts are forced to take extra care in shielding juries from publicity and in protecting defendants. The press also has to demonstrate its responsibility by exercising caution in publishing and broadcasting material about criminal and civil cases.

In this chapter the dimensions of both the problem and its solutions are sketched. First, the kinds of publicity many persons believe to be harmful to defendants are discussed, along with evaluation of the extent to which the mass media can in fact interfere with the trial process. In the remainder of the chapter the many schemes and ideas either proposed or enacted to solve the problem are outlined. It must again be remembered that in the free press–fair trial controversy, fifty-one different judicial systems are involved. That is, while the problem is clearly national, the solutions tend to be local or regional in scope. Consequently, generalizations about such a complex issue can sometimes be misleading. Reporters and broadcasters are urged to investigate the specific rules applicable to their state regarding publication of material about the judicial process. A simple way to do this is to talk to judges, members of bar associations, and veteran court reporters. ♦

PREJUDICIAL CRIME REPORTING

It is quite easy to find examples of the kinds of news stories that many people believe might prejudice potential jurors. For example, the *Los Angeles Times* ran a story a few years ago beginning this way:

> A television sportscaster, Stan Duke, shot and killed a radio commentator, Averill Berman, early Sunday at the Wilshire District home of Duke's estranged wife, police reported. Duke was booked on suspicion of murder.

Readers probably wondered why Duke was arrested for suspicion of murder when it was patently obvious from reading the lead that Duke had committed the crime—or had according to the *Los Angeles Times*. Under the American system of justice a person is presumed innocent until proved guilty. In other words the state had to prove that Duke shot and killed Berman.

A newspaper in Washington State ran a far less sensational story, but in its own way it could have been even more damaging. The *Yakima Herald-Republic* headlined the story: "Innocent Not Tried, Claims Prosecutor." The first sentence stated, " 'Because of the screening process built into the criminal justice system in this county, innocent men never go to trial,' John Moore, Yakima County Deputy Prosecutor, said Wednesday." The people of that county probably spent a considerable amount of time wondering why they had courts at all if only the guilty went to trial. All that was really needed was an administrator of some kind to hand out sentences and fines.

The first story was written in the flush of journalistic excitement brought on by a sensational murder. The second story was written by a reporter who should have challenged the outrageous statement on the spot. Numerous other specific examples can be cited, but probably a better idea is to summarize the kinds of information many people agree can possibly interfere with the defendant's right to a fair trial. The following was taken from lists published by the American Bar Association and various state press-bench-bar committees.

1. Confessions or stories about the confession that a defendant is said to have made, including even alluding to the fact that there may be a confession. The Fifth Amendment says that a person does not have to testify against him or herself. Therefore a confession given to police may be subsequently retracted and usually cannot be used against the defendant at the trial.

2. Stories about the defendant's performance on a test using a polygraph, or lie detector, or similar device, and about the defendant's refusal to take such a test. Most of this information is not permitted at the trial.

3. Stories about the defendant's past criminal record or that state the defendant is a former convict. This information is not permitted at the trial. It may seem entirely logical to some people that when someone has committed ninety-nine robberies and is again arrested for robbery the accused probably did commit the crime. As a matter of fact, past behavior is immaterial in the current trial for robbery. The state must prove that the defendant committed *this* robbery.

4. Stories that question the credibility of witnesses and contain the personal feelings of witnesses about prosecutors, police, victims, or even judges. To illustrate: in the Sam Sheppard case, which will be discussed a little later, the judge was quoted as telling a reporter—before the trial started—that he thought Sam Sheppard was "guilty as hell," and the remark was published (*Sheppard* v. *Maxwell,* 1966).

5. Stories about the defendant's character (he or she hates children and dogs), associates (he or she hangs around with known syndicate gunmen), and personality (he or she attacks people on the slightest provocation).

6. Stories that tend to inflame the public mood against the defendant. Such stories include editorial campaigns that demand the arrest of a suspect before sufficient evidence has been collected; person-on-the-street interviews concerning the guilt of the defendant or the kind of punishment that should be meted out after the accused is convicted; televised debates about the evidence of the guilt or innocence of the defendant. All these kinds of stories put the jury in the hot seat, as well as circulate vast quantities of misinformation.

One positive note should be made at this point. Stories like these are less common today. Most newspapers and broadcasting stations are much more sensitive to the problems that may be created by the careless publication of such inflammatory matter. Indeed, even though violent crime seems to be a matter of high visibility in the United States today, the mass media report on only a small percentage of the actual criminal activity in any community. Professor George Hough (in *Free Press and Fair Trial,* ed. Chilton R. Bush) at the University of Georgia documented this. After studying both court records and newspapers in Detroit for a 12-month period, Hough found that the newspapers reported only about 7 percent of all the felony cases in which warrants were issued. Hough also reported that during one 12-month period, only 3.4 percent of 9,140 felony cases ever resulted in a jury trial.

Still many American newspapers and broadcasting stations today do give heavy play to news of violent crime. Potentially prejudicial news does appear in the newspaper or is reported on television. Does the appearance of such stories have an impact upon the members of the community in such a way as to deny the defendant a right to a fair trial? This is a difficult question to answer. There are lots of opinions but little hard evidence on the matter. Let's examine briefly what we know about the issue.

Impact on Jurors

For more than twenty-five years, social scientists have attempted to systematically examine the question of the impact of published prejudicial material on potential jurors. A major difficulty in this research has been the inability of the researchers to study the behavior of real jurors in actual trials. The law will not permit this. (Recently a judge in Milwaukee, Wisconsin permitted a Public Broadcasting Service television crew to record jury deliberations and then broadcast a condensed version of the discussions on the *Frontline* series. This was a one-time event, however.) So researchers have instead conducted two kinds of studies: experiments in which they attempt to duplicate the trial process and surveys in which they interview nonjurors about actual crimes and criminal news.

The experiments have ranged from simple to elaborate and have often established some relationship between exposure to prejudicial material and the subject's increased willingness to find a hypothetical defendant guilty of a crime. But the findings are seriously flawed. The ersatz jurors know they are a part of an experiment; a real-life defendant's freedom or even life is not on the line. There was no robed judge to admonish these subjects to decide the case solely on the basis of the evidence presented at the trial and to insist that they ignore anything else they might have seen or read about the case. This is an important factor. In the single jury study done in recent times with real jurors and real trials, the researcher—Harry Kalven of the University of Chicago—reported, "We do . . . have evidence that jurors take with surprising seriousness the admonition [from the judge] not to read the paper or discuss the case with other people." The research cited by Kalven was part of a massive 1954 study in which actual jury deliberations were secretly recorded and studied. (Revelation of these practices prompted rules that permanently foreclosed the use of actual juries in such cases.) Finally, in real life a juror is not given newspaper articles about a defendant and then asked to judge that person guilty or innocent. This is what happened in the experiments and is patently phony. A trial, often a lengthy trial, will intervene in real life. So the experimental setting has been simply too unrealistic to determine whether or not the publication of prejudicial material may in fact cause problems for a defendant in real life.

Surveys conducted in some communities before the beginning of a major trial suggest that most persons are not affected by the publication of prejudicial pretrial material. Nearly two hundred persons were interviewed in one study before a sensational murder trial began in North Carolina, for example. Only twenty-three percent of the persons contacted said they believed the defendant in the case was guilty. One-fifth of the persons surveyed told researchers they had never even heard about the case before. Similar results were obtained in similar studies.

This whole question is complicated today by research on other aspects of mass media that suggests we tend to remember far less of what we see and hear on television and what we read in the newspaper than many people might presume. Advertising research has demonstrated this for years; and recently, researchers at the University of Maryland found that a significant percentage of the one thousand persons they telephoned could not remember news stories that had been prominently reported only the week before the interview. In summary, the research we have does not support the argument that prejudicial publicity will damage the right of a defendant to a fair trial. In a medium-to-large urban setting, it would indeed be rare if a jury of twelve citizens could not be found who knew little, even about a sensational crime, or who could not render a verdict based solely on the evidence presented in court. (See Pember, "Does pretrial publicity really hurt?")

The definition of an impartial juror used by the courts in the United States is about 180 years old and stems from a ruling by Chief Justice John Marshall in the trial of Aaron Burr. Charges that the jurors were biased were made at the trial. In 1807 Marshall proclaimed that an impartial juror was one free from the dominant influence of knowledge acquired outside the courtroom, free from strong and deep impressions that close the mind. *"Light impressions,"* Marshall wrote, *"which may fairly be supposed to yield to the testimony that may be offered, which leave the mind open to a fair consideration of that testimony, constitute no sufficient objection to a juror . . ."* [author emphasis] (*U.S. v. Burr,* 1807).

While this definition is fairly precise, modern courts nevertheless have to cope with the problem of applying the definition to specific situations. It is appellate courts that most often must apply Marshall's definition to cases in which convicted defendants ask for a reversal on the grounds that the jury is not impartial, as guaranteed by the Sixth Amendment. Indeed, reversal is one important, if costly, remedy the judicial system uses to cope with prejudicial publicity, that is, to simply reverse the guilty verdict and require that the defendant be retried.

Appellate courts appear to consider several factors in determining whether the defendant's trial was fair and impartial. Was there publicity about the case? Was the publicity prejudicial? Is there evidence that the jurors saw the prejudicial publicity? What kinds of information were contained in the publicity? It is not a simple task to uncover the answers to many of these questions, and not surprisingly, different courts often reach opposite conclusions in cases that appear to have similar facts. But even small differences in the facts can be important. For example, a United States court of appeals ruled in 1951 that a defendant's right to a fair trial was not damaged simply because a newspaper containing information about the case was found in a jury room. The judge had told the jury to disregard the contents of the news story and there was no evidence presented to the contrary (*Leviton v. U.S.,* 1951). Eight years later, however, the United States Supreme Court overturned a criminal conviction when evidence was presented that jurors had seen stories in newspapers, which were found in the courtroom, about a defendant's prior criminal record. The jurors told the judge they had read the stories but vowed they could decide the case solely on the evidence presented in court. The nation's High Court said it was not reasonable to believe that the jurors could be impartial in such a case (*Marshall v. U.S.,* 1959).

Appellate courts also pay attention to what the jurors tell judges in the pretrial questioning (voir dire) when they are asked about their knowledge of the case. Compare how the Supreme Court resolved these two appeals.

Leslie Irvin was arrested in connection with a series of sex murders. Statements that Irvin had confessed to all six killings received widespread publicity. At the trial, of 430 persons called as potential jurors, 375 told the judge that they believed Irvin was guilty. Of the twelve jurors finally selected, eight told the court they thought he was guilty before the trial started. The Supreme Court overturned the conviction, noting that in this case, in which so many persons so many times admitted prejudice, statements of impartiality could be given little weight (*Irvin* v. *Dowd,* 1961).

Fourteen years later Jack Murphy, the original "Murph the Surf," appealed his conviction for robbery and assault on the grounds that the jury had been prejudiced by extensive publicity about his previous criminal record and other extralegal exploits. The Supreme Court disagreed. Only twenty of the seventy-eight potential jurors who were questioned told the Florida trial judge they believed Murphy was guilty. The High Court said that this was not comparable to the evidence of hostility or overwhelming prejudice toward the defendant that was found in the Irvin case. The Constitution requires that the defendant have a "panel of impartial, indifferent jurors," ruled Justice Thurgood Marshall; "they need not, however, be totally ignorant of the facts and issues involved." It is sufficient that a juror can lay aside his or her impressions and personal opinions and render a considered opinion based on the evidence presented in court. Many people see this 1975 ruling in *Murphy* v. *Florida* as rejecting the often-asserted principle that publicity about a criminal case automatically results in bias toward the defendant.

In looking at the scores of decisions by appellate courts, one is persuaded that judges seem to have greater faith in jurors and the jury system than many social scientists who have studied these issues. Whether this is misplaced faith may never be known. Perhaps the answer is to be found in Professor Walter Wilcox's rhetorical question, "Could it be that the American jury confounds all the subtle nuances of the behavioral sciences and simply does its duty?" (in *Free Press and Fair Trial,* ed. Chilton R. Bush).

SUMMARY

The First Amendment to the United States Constitution guarantees freedom of the press; the Sixth Amendment guarantees every criminal defendant a fair trial. Many people believe these two amendments are in conflict because, often, publicity about a criminal case can prejudice a community against a defendant and make it impossible to find a fair and impartial jury in the case. The kinds of publicity that can be most damaging to a defendant include material about confessions or alleged confessions, stories about a past criminal record, statements about the defendant's character, and comments about the defendant's performance on scientific tests or refusal to take such tests.

Social science has not yet proved that such publicity does in fact create prejudice or that persons cannot set aside their beliefs about a case and render a verdict based on the facts presented at the trial. An impartial juror is not required to be free of all knowledge or impressions about a case; the juror must be free of deep impressions and beliefs that will not yield to the evidence that is presented in court during the trial.

COMPENSATING FOR PRETRIAL PUBLICITY

The law has many ways to minimize or even to eliminate the problem of prejudicial publicity in a criminal case. As a last resort a criminal conviction can be reversed by an appellate court if there is evidence that the trial was tainted by publicity.

Retrials cost the taxpayers money; considerable inconvenience results for witnesses, attorneys, and other participants. Defendants face continued hardship from uncertainty or even jail if they have not been released on bail. Most persons concerned with this problem consider reversal a remedy of last resort—something to do if all else fails.

Other remedies are considered far better in attempting to solve the problems that could result from pretrial publicity. These remedies fall into two broad categories:

1. Remedies that can be used by the trial court to compensate for the publication or broadcast of prejudicial publicity.
2. Remedies aimed at controlling the amount and kind of information that might be broadcast or published.

The remedies in the first category have existed for a long time and can be applied by trial judges with little difficulty in most instances. These include delaying the trial, moving the trial, carefully questioning the jurors to determine their biases, and other means. The impact upon both the judicial system and the press tends to be minimal when such remedies are applied.

The remedies in the second category can be more drastic and can cause serious problems, especially for the press. These remedies include issuing orders specifically limiting what can be published or broadcast, issuing orders that forbid participants in the trial process from talking about the case, and even barring public and press attendance at pretrial proceedings. This latter category also includes, however, nonbinding bench-bar-press guidelines, which have been adopted in many states and, of any of the remedies in either of the categories, seem to many persons to work the least hardship on both the press and the judicial system. A close examination of all these remedies follows.

Traditional Judicial Remedies

Trial judges have at their disposal a battery of procedural tools that can be used to alleviate the impact of prejudicial publicity.

Voir Dire

Before prospective jurors finally make it to the jury box, they must pass a series of hurdles erected both by the attorneys in the case and the judge. These hurdles are designed to protect the judicial process from jurors who have already made up their minds about the case or who have strong biases toward one litigant or the other. In a process called **voir dire,** each prospective juror is questioned prior to being impaneled in an effort to discover bias. Pretrial publicity is only one source of juror prejudice. If the prospective juror is the mother of a police officer, she is likely to be biased if the defendant is on trial for shooting a police officer. Perhaps the juror is a business associate of the defendant. Possibly the juror has read extensively about the case in the newspapers and believes the police are trying to frame the defendant.

Both sides in the case question the jurors and both sides can ask the court to excuse a juror. This procedure is called challenging a juror. There are two kinds of challenges: **challenges for cause** and **peremptory challenges.** To challenge a juror for cause, an attorney must convince the court that there is a good reason for this person not to sit on the jury. Deep-seated prejudice is one good reason. Being an acquaintance of one of the parties in the case is also a good reason. Any reason can be used to challenge a potential juror. All the attorney must do is to convince the judge that the reason is proper. There is no limit on the number of challenges for cause that both prosecutor and defense attorney may exercise.

A peremptory challenge is somewhat different. This challenge can be exercised without cause, and the judge has no power to refuse such a challenge. There is a limit, however, on the number of such challenges that may be exercised. Sometimes there are as few as two or three and sometimes as many as ten or twenty, depending upon the case, the kind of crime involved, the state statute, and sometimes the judge. This kind of challenge is reserved for use against persons whom the defense or the prosecution does not want on the jury but whom the judge refuses to excuse for cause. An attorney may have an intuitive hunch about a potential juror and want that person eliminated from the final panel. Or the juror's social or ethnic background may suggest a problem to the attorney. In obscenity trials, for example, defense attorneys often look for persons with college background, especially a liberal arts background; persons who are independent in their life-style, those who have had some exposure to pornography; and persons who have some artistic inclination. Studies have shown that Asian-Americans tend to be more tolerant of pornography than other ethnic groups. The prosecutor in an obscenity trial will look for other kinds of jurors. Less-educated jurors are more desirable, as are those with a religious background and persons who live close to the place where the pornographic material is distributed. Hispanic-Americans tend to be less tolerant of obscenity than most persons. An attorney will use the peremptory challenges to try to build the kind of jury he or she seeks. (See Seymour Wishman's *Anatomy of a Jury* for an interesting discussion of the elements involved in jury selection.)

Is voir dire a good way to screen prejudiced jurors? Seventy-nine percent of a large group of judges surveyed by Professor Emeritus Fred Siebert of Michigan State University said (in *Free Press and Fair Trial*, ed. Chilton R. Bush) that the questioning process was either highly effective or moderately effective in screening biased jurors. Most trial lawyers also agree, to a point.

It is difficult, however, to argue with critics who say that voir dire uncovers only the prejudice that the prospective juror is aware of or is not too embarrassed to admit. Biased jurors can lie when questioned about their biases. They may not even know their minds are made up about the defendant's guilt. But these kinds of objections attack the root of the entire jury system. The only way to find jurors who are not biased in even a small way is to lock up babies when they are born and raise them as jurors, isolate them from the rest of the world until they are adults, and then release them to act only as jurors at trials. Nobody wants this kind of system. The faith that most persons have in the effectiveness of voir dire is comparable to their faith in the entire jury system.

Change of Venue

Many judges and legal authorities describe a **change of venue** as an effective means of dealing with massive pretrial publicity. Imagine for a moment that John Smith is arrested for a series of six brutal murders committed in River City over a period of six weeks and highly publicized by the local press. When Smith is arrested, the local news media saturate the community with stories about the killings, about the arrest, and about Smith. Day after day the newspapers and broadcasting stations focus on one new angle after another. Soon most of the people in River City know more about the suspect's past than even the police and his parents know. One means to compensate for such publicity about a defendant in the community in which the crime takes place is to move the trial to another community. This procedure is called a change of venue. While the people in River City may be prejudiced against Smith by virtue of the reports in the news media, the people across the state in Ames have hardly heard of the matter. Therefore, the trial, including the prosecutor, the defendant, the judges, the witnesses, and assorted other trial participants, is moved to Ames for the month or two of its duration. The jury is selected from a panel of people who live in Ames. Seventy-seven percent of the judges surveyed think a change of venue is highly effective or moderately effective in controlling prejudicial publicity (*Free Press and Fair Trial*).

Change of venue is costly. Witnesses, attorneys, and other persons must be transported and housed and fed while the trial takes place in a distant city. The defendant must surrender the constitutional right to a trial in the district in which the crime was committed. Publicity about the case could appear in the media located in the community in which the trial is scheduled to be held, defeating the purpose of the change of venue. Often the effectiveness of the change of venue depends upon how far the trial is moved from the city in which the crime was committed. A trial judge in Washington State who was concerned about newspaper coverage of a local murder case granted a change of venue. But he moved the trial to an adjoining county, the only other county in the state in which the "offending" newspaper had significant circulation.

The move accomplished very little, and the judge ultimately was forced to close portions of the proceedings to the press (*Federated Publications* v. *Kurtz*, 1980). Used wisely, a change of venue can be an effective device to protect the defendant's right to a fair trial, especially for crimes committed in rural counties where the number of potential jurors is small and where news often travels faster by word of mouth than through the mass media. But there is normally ample opportunity in an urban area with a large population to find a panel of impartial jurors in even the most sensational criminal trials. A change of venue in such a case is normally a waste of money.

In some states it is possible for the defense to seek a change of veniremen rather than a change of venue. Instead of moving the trial to another city, the court will import a jury panel from a distant community. The judge and attorneys will visit the distant city, select a jury panel, and then transport the jurors to the community in which the trial will be held. This will cost the state less money, since all it must do is pay the expenses of twelve jurors for the duration of the trial.

Continuance

A **continuance** is somewhat like a change of venue. But the time of the trial, instead of the location, is changed. That is, the trial is postponed. Back to John Smith for a moment. A delay of six to nine months in his trial might have pushed the slayings to the back of the mind of the community. People rapidly forget information not vital to their lives. It is probably far easier to impanel an unbiased jury after a continuance of six months. But again there are problems. The defendant sacrifices his right to a speedy trial. While the right to a speedy trial is one of the myths we are content to live with in the United States, continuance nevertheless means an even longer delay than normal. If John Smith cannot make bail or if bail is not permitted, he spends the six months of the continuance in jail. Also, this scheme assumes that there will be little or no further publicity about the case. This assumption might be incorrect. The week before the continued trial is scheduled to begin the press may start publicizing the case again. It is hoped, of course, that other news will have pushed the interest in the case to the back of the newspaper by then. A continuance can work very effectively in cases of accidental publicity. A judge told of how, just as he was scheduled to begin hearing a malpractice suit on a Monday morning, the Sunday paper, quite innocently, carried a long feature story on the skyrocketing costs of physicians' malpractice insurance because of the large judgments handed down in malpractice suits. The article pointed out that physicians passed the additional charges along to patients. The story was widely read. Jurors, who also pay doctors' bills, might hesitate to award a judgment to an injured patient knowing that it would raise insurance rates and ultimately cost patients more. The judge therefore continued the case for two months to let the story fade from the public mind.

Once a jury is impaneled, its members are instructed by the judge to render their verdict in the case solely on the basis of the evidence presented in the courtroom. Judges believe that most jurors take this **admonition** quite seriously. Jurors are also warned not to read newspaper stories or watch television broadcasts about the case while the trial is being held. Often jurors are excused from the courtroom while the trial judge hears arguments from the attorneys or even testimony from witnesses. In such instances the court usually wants to determine whether certain evidence is admissible in the case before the evidence is presented to the jury. The press may publish or broadcast reports about this evidence, whether or not it is admitted in the case. It would accomplish very little to keep such evidence from the jury during the trial if jurors could watch news stories about it during the evening television newscasts.

The following admonition, which is one used by King County, Washington, superior court judges, is typical:

> Do not discuss this case or any criminal case or any criminal matter among yourselves or with anyone else. Do not permit anyone to discuss such subjects with you or in your presence. . . . Do not read, view, or listen to any report in a newspaper, radio, or television on the subject of this trial or any other criminal trial. Do not permit anyone to read about or comment on this trial or any criminal trial to you or in your presence.

There is evidence that jurors follow these instructions closely. In the single major study in which real jury deliberations were examined to determine the impact of mass media publicity on the trial process, researchers found that jurors listen carefully to the cautionary instructions given to them by judges. The coordinator of that research project, Harry Kalven, noted in a letter to the director of the American Law Institute:

> We do . . . have evidence that the jurors take with surprising seriousness the admonition not to read the paper or discuss the case with other people. . . . Our overall impression . . . is that the jury is a pretty stubborn, healthy institution not likely to be overwhelmed either by a remark of counsel or a remark in the press.

For cases in which a high level of publicity is expected, publicity that might prove hard for a jury to avoid, the court has another device: **sequestration of the jury,** which means that once it is impaneled, the jury is locked up. Jurors eat together, are housed at state expense at a hotel or motel, and are not permitted to visit with friends and relatives. Phone calls are screened, as is contact with the mass media. Jurors are allowed to read newspapers only after court officials delete stories that could be objectionable.

Sequestration is a costly process for both the state and the jurors. Sequestration for three or four days might be a lark, but the trials in which juries are normally sequestered are long trials, sometimes lasting as long as six months. Life can be seriously disrupted. The number of people who can afford the loss of income involved in such a situation is limited.

Although sequestered jurors are free from prejudicial publicity, attorneys fear the long quarantine produces a different kind of prejudice—prejudice against one or the other of the two sides in the case—wrought from keeping jurors away from friends and family for so long. Defense attorneys express this fear most often, feeling that jurors will tend to hold the defendant responsible for the inconvenience and therefore vote for conviction.

SUMMARY

Trial courts have many ways to compensate for the prejudicial pretrial publicity in a criminal case. Each citizen is questioned by the attorneys and the judge before being accepted as a juror. During this voir dire examination, questions can be asked of the potential jurors about the kinds of information they already know about the case. Persons who have already made up their minds about the defendant's guilt or innocence can be excluded from the jury.

Courts have the power to move a trial to a distant county to find a jury that has not been exposed to the publicity about the case that has been generated by local mass media. While such a change of venue can be costly, it can also be an effective means of compensating for sensational publicity about a case.

A trial can be delayed until the publicity about the case dies down. The defendant must waive the right to a speedy trial but, except in highly sensational cases, granting a continuance in a trial can thwart the impact of the massive publicity often generated in the wake of a serious crime.

Jurors are always admonished by the judge to base their decision on the facts presented in court and not to read or view any news stories about the case while they are on the jury. There is evidence that they take these warnings quite seriously.

In important cases it is always possible to lock up, or sequester, the jury after it is chosen to shield it from publicity about the trial.

The remedies just outlined have been used by trial judges for decades to reduce or eliminate the impact of prejudicial publicity. These remedies do not stop the publication of information about a criminal or civil case. They are used to compensate for the publication of prejudicial material. Such remedies are favored by the press because they have no direct impact upon the mass media.

However, many persons in the legal profession believe that compensating for publicity is a rather costly and sloppy way to solve the free press–fair trial dilemma. These compensatory remedies often create headaches for judges (extensive voir dire) or for trial participants (continuance, change of venue). They invariably cost all parties—especially the state—extra money, and they do not always completely compensate for massive publicity about a case, especially a sensational criminal case. Would it not be better if the press did not publish prejudicial information in the first place?

Agreements that attempt to limit certain kinds of publicity about criminal cases have been reached between the press and the courts in many states. These bench-bar-press guidelines are an effort to amicably resolve the free press–fair trial problem (these guidelines are discussed on pages 399–401).

But courts have also attempted other, more coercive means to limit publicity about criminal cases. Some trial judges have prohibited the press from publishing certain information about criminal cases. Violation of these orders, called restrictive orders by lawyers and judges and **gag orders** by journalists, can result in a citation for contempt of court. Other judges have barred journalists and other persons from attending pretrial hearings, and even trials, to keep out of the hands of reporters information that might prejudice a jury. No other aspect of mass media law has sparked more controversy in the past ten years than the restrictive-order–closed-courtroom issue. Since 1976 the Supreme Court of the United States has focused upon one or another aspect of this issue no less than eight times. Yet there is still no final resolution of the problems involved. This section of the text outlines these attempts to control the publication of information about criminal and civil matters. Restrictive orders are examined first; then the matter of closed courtrooms is discussed. Finally, we will outline the dimensions of bench-bar-press guidelines.

| RESTRICTIVE ORDERS TO CONTROL PUBLICITY | Can a trial judge constitutionally forbid the press from publishing information about a criminal case that it has obtained legally? The answer is yes, a judge can issue an order restricting the news media from publishing prejudicial pretrial information. But such a **restrictive order** can be issued only when there is evidence that publication of the material will create a clear and present danger of interfering with the defendant's right to a trial by an impartial jury. The Supreme Court has ruled that such a restriction is permissible only if the judge has determined that "the gravity of the evil, discounted by its improbability, justifies such an invasion of free speech as is necessary to avoid the danger" (*Nebraska Press Association* v. *Stuart*, 1976). In order for such an order to be issued, there must be sufficient evidence to reasonably conclude that the following conditions prevail: |

1. Intense and pervasive publicity concerning the case is certain.
2. No other alternative measure—such as a change of venue or continuance or extensive voir dire process—is likely to mitigate the effects of the pretrial publicity.
3. The restrictive order will in fact effectively prevent prejudicial material from reaching potential jurors.

Theoretically, then, a judge can bar the press from reporting on certain aspects of a trial. Practically, however, it is almost impossible for a judge to issue such an order today. It is simply too tough for a judge to meet the three-part Supreme Court test. In only a handful of instances in the past five years has an appellate court permitted a gag order aimed at the press to stand (see *KUTV v. Wilkinson,* 1984 for example). Before examining the contemporary gag orders let's look at why such judicial tools developed in the past twenty years. Our story begins with a bizarre murder case that in turn provided the inspiration for one of the nation's most popular television series of the mid-sixties, "The Fugitive," starring David Janssen.

The *Sheppard* Case

Sam Sheppard, a prominent Ohio osteopath, was arrested for the bludgeoning death of his wife Marilyn. The doctor professed his innocence in the case, claiming that an intruder had entered their home at night, knocked him unconscious, and killed his wife. The Sheppard story broke during the slow-news Fourth of July weekend in 1954 and immediately caught the fancy of the nation's press. The publicity in the case was massive, far more extensive than the simple slaying merited. The coroner's inquest was held in a school gymnasium and broadcast live to the community. Debates were held about Sheppard's guilt or innocence. At the trial the press—much of it national rather than local press—dominated the courtroom. Participants in the case—police, prosecutors, defense attorneys, and witnesses—appeared to try to outdo themselves in offering extraneous, often outrageous, statements to reporters, who dutifully published these comments. One appellate court later described the trial as a Roman holiday for the press, an orgy of sensation. Sheppard was convicted.

The United States Supreme Court rejected Sam Sheppard's first appeal that his trial was prejudiced by the massive publicity. But years later, in 1966, the High Court agreed to hear the doctor's plea. In a stinging rebuke of trial judge Blythin, the Court reversed Sam Sheppard's conviction for murder.*

Justice Tom Clark, who wrote the Supreme Court's opinion in the *Sheppard* case, came down hard on the press, noting that bedlam reigned during the trial and that "newsmen took over practically the entire courtroom,

*The state of Ohio chose to reprosecute Sheppard twelve years after the crime, but this time the middle-aged doctor was acquitted. Sheppard, who failed to reestablish his osteopathic career, died several years later.

hounding most of the participants in the trial, especially Sheppard. . . ." Justice Clark saved his sharpest criticism for Judge Blythin, who conducted the trial, and the other officers of the court for allowing the publicity about the case and the coverage of the trial to get out of hand. Here are some excerpts from Clark's opinion (*Sheppard* v. *Maxwell,* 1966):

> Bearing in mind the massive pretrial publicity, the judge should have adopted stricter rules governing the use of the courtroom by newsmen . . . the court should have insulated witnesses [from the media]. . . . The court should have made some effort to control the release of leads, information and gossip to the press by police officers, witnesses and the counsel for both sides. . . . And it is obvious that the judge should have further sought to alleviate this problem by imposing control over the statements made to the news media by counsel, witnesses, and especially the coroner and police officers. . . . The court might well have proscribed extrajudicial statements by any lawyer, party, witness or court official which divulged prejudicial matters . . . the court could also have requested the appropriate city and county officials to promulgate a regulation with respect to dissemination of information about the case by their employees. In addition, reporters who wrote or broadcast prejudicial stories could have been warned as to the impropriety of publishing material not introduced in the proceedings.

The Supreme Court made it quite clear in the *Sheppard* decision that it holds the trial judge responsible for ensuring that the defendant's rights are not jeopardized by prejudicial press publicity. While the Court was critical of the press's behavior, no suggestion was made that the judicial system launch an attack on the press. Nevertheless, at a meeting following the decision, a professor of law, in explaining the High Court's opinion in *Sheppard,* suggested that the Court had proposed that judges use the contempt power to control the press. Justice Clark, who was at the same meeting, told the assembled trial lawyers that the professor misinterpreted the court's ruling (Friendly and Goldfarb, *Crime and Publicity*):

> The Court never held up contempt and it may well be that it will never hold up contempt because the restraint is too stringent. . . . The Court's opinion never mentioned any guidelines for the press. . . . I am not proposing that you jerk a newspaper reporter into the courtroom and hold him in contempt. We do not have to jeopardize freedom of the press.

As we will see shortly, the remarks by Justice Clark were soon forgotten.

Restrictive Orders and the First Amendment

Two years after the ruling in *Sheppard* v. *Maxwell,* the American Bar Association (ABA) proposed that trial judges use court orders to control the public statements and activities of the many participants in a trial—the prosecutor, witnesses, defense attorneys, jurors, and others. The bar association also recommended that judges use the contempt power against any persons who knowingly violated a valid judicial order not to disseminate information about the case. No state court system ever officially adopted the ABA recommendations, but the suggestions were taken to heart by many individual judges. Restrictive court orders became a common tool for a judge who sought to control the publicity about a pending criminal trial. One observer estimated that in the ten years between 1966 and 1976, trial courts issued almost 175 restrictive orders, 39 of which prohibited the press from reporting or commenting on some aspect of a pending criminal case. In addition, nearly all of the federal courts adopted standing orders regarding publicity in criminal cases.

Use of Restrictive
Orders

There is no such thing as a typical restrictive order; in fact, that is one of the virtues seen in them by judges. Each order can be fashioned to fit the case at hand. They often tend to be quite comprehensive, as can be seen from the order issued by Judge William B. Keene for the Charles Manson murder trial (see pages 379–80). Orders aimed at the press usually limit the press coverage of certain specific details about a case; a defendant's confession or prior criminal record, for example. Orders aimed at the participants in a trial are usually much broader, forbidding comments by attorneys, witnesses, and others about any aspect of the case. In 1975 another sensational murder trial began, one that would ultimately bring the issue of pretrial publicity and gag orders before the Supreme Court.

Erwin Simants was arrested and charged in North Platte, Nebraska, with the murder of all six members of the Henry Kellie family. Like the Sheppard case, the arrest of Simants caught the eye of the national news media, and local Judge Hugh Stuart had his hands full with scores of reporters from around the state and the nation. Stuart responded by issuing a restrictive order barring the publication or broadcast of a wide range of information that he said would be prejudicial to Simants. The order was later modified by the Nebraska Supreme Court to prohibit only the reporting of the existence and nature of any confessions or admissions Simants might have made to police or any third party and any other information "strongly implicative" of the accused. The order was to stand in effect until a jury was chosen.

The press in the state appealed the publication ban to the United States Supreme Court, and in June 1976 the High Court ruled that Judge Stuart's order was an unconstitutional prior restraint upon the press (*Nebraska Press Association* v. *Stuart,* 1976). While all nine members of the Court agreed that the restrictive order in this case was a violation of the First Amendment, five members suggested that under the guidelines outlined at the beginning of this section (page 377), such an order might be proper. Chief Justice Burger wrote the opinion for the Court, in which he stressed that prior restraint was the exception, not the rule. There must be a clear and present danger to the defendant's rights before such a restrictive order might be constitutionally permitted, he said. But the Chief Justice did suggest that if the judge could demonstrate that the publicity about the case was intense and pervasive, that no other means could be used to compensate for such publicity, and that the

People of the State of California
Plaintiffs,

vs.

Charles Manson, et al.,
Defendants

No. A 253156
ORDER RE PUBLICITY

It is apparent, and this Court is going to take judicial notice of the fact, that this case has received extensive news media coverage as a direct result of its apparent public interest; further, it is equally apparent to this Court by reading various newspapers and weekly periodicals that this news media coverage is not limited to the County of Los Angeles, but has been extensive not only in the entire State of California but in the Nation as well, and of this fact the Court now takes judicial notice. This Court is of the firm conviction that the impossible task of attempting to choose between the constitutional guarantees of a free press and fair trial need not be made, but that they are compatible with some reasonable restrictions imposed upon pretrial publicity. It further appears to the Court that the dissemination by any means of public communication of any out-of-court statements relating to this case may interfere with the constitutional right of the defendants to a fair trial and disrupt the proper administration of justice. Some of the defendants now being for the first time before this Court, this Court now exercises its jurisdiction and assumes its duty to do everything within its constitutional powers to make certain that each defendant does receive a fair trial, and now issues the following orders, a violation of which will be considered as a contempt of this Court and will result in appropriate action to punish for such contempt.

It is the order of this Court that no party to this action, nor any attorney connected with this case as defense counsel or as prosecutor, nor any other attorney associated with this case, nor any judicial attache or employee, nor any public official now holding office, including but not limited to any chief of police or any sheriff, who has obtained information related to this action, which information has not previously been disseminated to the public, nor any agent, deputy, or employee of any such persons, nor any grand juror, nor any witness having appeared before the Grand Jury in this matter, nor any person subpoenaed to testify at the trial of this matter, shall release or authorize the release for public dissemination of any purported extrajudicial statement of the defendant relating to this case, nor shall any such persons release or authorize the release of any documents, exhibits, or any evidence, the admissibility of which may have to be determined by the Court, nor shall any such person make any statement for public dissemination as to the existence or possible existence of any document, exhibit, or any other evidence, the admissibility of which may have to be determined by the Court. Nor shall any such persons express outside of court an opinion or make any comment for public dissemination as to the weight, value, or effect of any evidence as tending to establish guilt or innocence. Nor shall any such persons make any statement outside of court for public dissemination as to the weight, value, or effect of any testimony that has been given. Nor shall any such persons issue any statement for public dissemination as to the identity of any prospective witness, or his probable testimony, or the effect thereof. Nor shall any such person make any out-of-court statement for public dissemination as to the weight, value, source, or effect of any purported evidence alleged to have been accumulated as a result of the investigation of this matter. Nor shall any such persons make any statement for public dissemination as to the content, nature, substance, or effect of any testimony which may be given in any proceeding related to this matter, except that a witness may discuss any matter with any attorney of record or agent thereof.

This order does not include any of the following:

1. Factual statements of the accused person's name, age, residence, occupation, and family status.

2. The circumstances of the arrest, namely, the time and place of the arrest, the identity of the arresting and investigation officers and agencies, and the length of the investigation.

3. The nature, substance, and text of the charge, including a brief description of the offenses charged.

4. Quotations from, or any reference without comment to, public records of the Court in the case, or to other public records or communications heretofore disseminated to the public.

5. The scheduling and result of any stage of the judicial proceeding held in open court in an open or public session.

6. A request for assistance in obtaining evidence.

7. Any information as to any person not in custody who is sought as a possible suspect or witness, nor any statement aimed at warning the public of any possible danger as to such person not in custody.

8. A request for assistance in the obtaining of evidence or the names of possible witnesses.

Further, this order is not intended to preclude any witness from discussing any matter in connection with the case with any of the attorneys representing the defendant or the People, or any representative of such attorneys.

It is further the order of the Court that the Grand Jury transcripts in this case not be disclosed to any person (other than those specifically mentioned in Penal Code Section 928.1) until 10 days after a copy thereof has been delivered by this Court to each defendant named in the indictment; provided, however, that if any defendant during such time, shall move the Court that such transcript, or any portion thereof, not be available for public inspection pending trial, such time shall be extended subject to the Court's ruling on such motion.

It is further ordered that a copy of this order be attached to any subpoena served on any witness in this matter, and that the return of service of the subpoena shall also include the fact of service of a copy of this order.

This order shall be in force until this matter has been disposed of or until further order of Court.

Dated: December 10, 1969

William B. Keene
Judge of the Superior Court

restrictive order would be effective in keeping the prejudicial information out of the hands of prospective jurors, such an order might stand. In Simants's case, Burger said, while there was heavy publicity about the matter, there was no evidence that Judge Stuart had considered the efficacy of other remedies to compensate for this publicity. Also, the small community was filled with rumors about Simants and what he had told the police. Burger expressed serious doubts whether the restrictive order would have in fact kept prejudicial information out of public hands.

Of the remaining four members of the Court, Justices Stewart, Brennan, and Marshall stated that such prior restraints against the press would not be constitutional under any circumstance. Justice White implied that he agreed with that notion, but since he was not compelled to answer that question in the case before the Court, he would wait until another day to face the issue.

Please note, the Supreme Court did not declare restrictive orders aimed only at *trial participants* to be unconstitutional. This issue was not raised in the trial, but it is assumed that courts have much broader power to limit what attorneys, police, and other trial participants can say about a case out of court. *Guidelines on Fair Trial/Free Press,* issued by the United States Judicial Conference, for example, specifically recommend that federal courts adopt rules that limit public discussion of criminal cases by attorneys and court personnel and suggests that courts issue special rules in sensational criminal cases to bar extrajudicial comments by all trial participants. But, in light of the ruling in *Nebraska Press Association* v. *Stuart,* the conference *Guidelines* states:

> No rule of court or judicial order should be promulgated by a United States district court which would prohibit representatives of the news media from broadcasting or publishing any information in their possession relating to a criminal case.

In both 1978 and 1979 the Supreme Court issued opinions in cases that had the effect of reinforcing the rule from the *Nebraska Press Association* decision that restrictions upon what the press may publish are to be tolerated only in very rare circumstances. In 1978 the High Court prohibited the state of Virginia from punishing the *Virginian Pilot* newspaper for publishing an accurate story regarding the confidential proceedings of a state judicial review commission (*Landmark Communications* v. *Virginia,* 1978). A Virginia State statute authorized the commission to hear complaints of a judge's disability or misconduct, and because of the sensitive nature of such hearings, the Virginia law closed the proceedings to the public and the press. The state argued that confidentiality was necessary to encourage the filing of complaints and the testimony of witnesses, to protect the judge from the injury that might result from the publication of unwarranted or unexamined charges, and to maintain confidence in the judiciary that might be undermined by the publication of groundless charges. While acknowledging the desirability of confidentiality, the Supreme Court nevertheless ruled against the state. Chief Justice Burger, writing for a unanimous Court, stated that the "publication Virginia seeks to punish under its statute lies near the core of the First Amendment, and the Commonwealth's interests advanced by the imposition of criminal sanctions are insufficient to justify the actual and potential encroachments on freedom of speech and of the press. . . ." The court did acknowledge that the state commission could certainly meet in secret and that its reports and materials could be kept confidential. But while the press has no right to gain access to such information, once it possesses the information, it cannot be punished for its publication. In this sense the Court followed the *Nebraska Press Association* rule limiting restraints placed upon the press's right to publish.

In 1979 the High Court declared unconstitutional a West Virginia statute that made it a crime for a newspaper to publish, without the written approval of the juvenile court, the name of a youth charged as a juvenile offender (*Smith v. Daily Mail Publishing Company,* 1979). Again Chief Justice Burger wrote the opinion for the Court and stressed the fact that once the press has legally obtained truthful information, it cannot be stopped from its publication. In this case two Charleston, West Virginia, newspapers published the name of a fourteen-year-old boy who was arrested for the shooting death of a fifteen-year-old student. Reporters for the newspapers got the name from persons who had witnessed the shooting. "If the information is lawfully obtained," the Chief Justice wrote, "the state may not punish its publication except when necessary to further an interest more substantial than is present here."

Restrictive Orders Today

Probably a dozen times a year appellate courts hear a case involving a restrictive order. Most of those aimed at the press are struck down, as noted previously. Orders aimed at the participants in the trial are usually allowed to stand if they are narrowly tailored. Let's look at some examples of recent cases.

The Utah Supreme Court struck down a gag order aimed at the Salt Lake City media that prohibited the media from referring to a defendant in a 1981 rape trial as the "Sugarhouse Rapist." Ronald D. Easthope, the man on trial, had been convicted in the early 1970s for a series of rapes in the Sugarhouse area of Salt Lake City. He was arrested again for rape after he was paroled. The state's High Court first outlined the three standards raised in the Nebraska Press Association case:

1. Did the publicity threaten his right to a fair trial?
2. Would measures short of the judge's restrictive order insure the defendant a fair trial?
3. Will the restraint on the press achieve the desired results?

The state High Court said the order was unconstitutional because the court had failed to consider any of these elements. The order was also invalid procedurally because the court had issued the order without notice or hearing. In addition, the state supreme court said it was hard to see how the term "Sugarhouse rapist" could harm Easthope, since he had admitted his previous crimes in open court (*KUTV* v. *Conder,* 1983).

The Arizona Supreme Court struck down a restrictive court order that blocked any courtroom sketching of the members of the jury unless the sketches were first approved by the court before they were telecast on the news. Applying the Nebraska Press Association test, the court said it could find little or no harm to the trial from the sketching. A few veniremen had expressed the fear of harm to their personal safety, but the vast majority of the 150 persons questioned had not. The trial court had not even considered other measures to cope with this limited threat. And finally, the order did not solve the problem. Newspapers could print sketches of jurors. Also the trial was open; anyone could attend and see who was on the jury. "Jury fear was neither significant nor imminent enough to justify the censorship, less restrictive measures would have sufficed, and the sketch order promised very limited success in tempering the media involvement," the court said (*KPNX* v. *Maricopa County Superior Court,* 1984).

And the Ninth United States Court of Appeals struck down a court order that barred CBS from showing videotape it had legally obtained of John DeLorean meeting with FBI undercover agents in what the government said was a drug transaction. The court agreed that there had been widespread publicity about the case but added that "both precedent and experience indicate that widespread publicity, without more, does not automatically lead to an unfair trial." To restrain the publication or broadcast of material "the publicity must threaten to prejudice the entire community so that twelve unbiased jurors cannot be found," the court ruled. Looking at the impact on a single viewer or reader is not sufficient. The trial court had also failed to consider other alternatives, short of the restrictive order. It had rejected without any explanation using the voir dire process to screen out jurors who had seen the film on television. It had also failed to consider the "prophylactic effect of emphatic and clear instructions to the jury," the Court of Appeals said (*CBS* v. *U.S. District Court,* 1984). (DeLorean was later acquitted of these charges at his trial.)

One recent case in which a restrictive order was upheld occurred in Utah, where that state's High Court permitted a trial court to bar the news media from reporting that a defendant was allegedly associated with organized crime. The press had reported such matters both before and after the trial began and the court had been forced to conduct a voir dire of the impaneled jurors. The court had asked the press to voluntarily restrain the publication of such material, but the news media had refused. The trial court said that waiver of a jury trial was too high a price for the defendant to pay and that sequestration of the jury during the long trial might prejudice the jury against the defendant. Strong admonitions to jurors might also result in such prejudice, the trial court concluded. The state supreme court ruled that the judge had met the burden of the Nebraska Press Association test and permitted the court order to stand (*KUTV* v. *Wilkinson,* 1984).

Court orders aimed at participants are more likely to be upheld. The Fourth U.S. Court of Appeals gave its approval to a restrictive order that prohibited several witnesses in a sensational criminal proceeding brought against several alleged members of the Ku Klux Klan and the Nazi Party from discussing their proposed testimony with reporters. The evidence supported the determination by the trial judge that there was a reasonable likelihood that the defendants would be denied a fair trial without this restriction on the witnesses, the court concluded (in re *Russell,* 1984). But even orders aimed at participants will be scrutinized carefully. A federal district court in California issued an order barring all attorneys in the espionage trial of FBI agent Richard Miller from making statements to the news media about any aspect of the case "that bears upon the merits to be resolved by the jury." The Ninth U.S. Court of Appeals ruled that the order was too broad. Many statements that bear upon the issues to be resolved by the jury present no danger to the administration of justice, the appeals court ruled. The district court must first determine what specific kinds of statements pose a real threat to the trial and then fashion a narrow restrictive order to proscribe them. The court of appeals then listed a half dozen kinds of comments that it might be permissible to block, regarding such matters as the identity or potential testimony of a witness or the contents of a statement made by the defendant (*Levine* v. *U.S. District Court,* 1985). And the Appellate Division of the New York Supreme Court ruled in 1986 that a court order to lawyers telling them to "refrain from any discussion of this case with the news media, to avoid any coverage of this case, or any attribution or any information in the media that would affect a fair trial of this case" was a violation of the First Amendment. The appellate judges ruled that the trial judge, who had told attorneys they could not even tell reporters what time court was supposed to convene, had not demonstrated that these extra-judicial statements by lawyers presented a "reasonable likelihood of a serious threat to the defendants right to a fair trial" (*NBC* v. *Cooperman,* 1986).

Restrictive orders that bar the press from publishing information about a criminal case have ceased to be a serious problem for journalists. Orders that limit what trial participants can say remain a nuisance, however, and probably do not serve the judicial system as well as many observers might imagine. Rumors tend to thrive in an atmosphere where the release of accurate information is stifled. Research has suggested that the publication of even massive amounts of factual information about a trial may reduce the likelihood of juror prejudice (see page 367). It would be better perhaps to provide journalists bound to publish something about a case with accurate and truthful statements rather than push them to report what is ground out by a rumor mill.

SUMMARY

In some instances trial courts have attempted to limit the publication of prejudicial information about a case by issuing court orders restricting what the press may publish or what the trial participants may publicly say about a case. These restrictive orders grew out of a famous United States Supreme Court decision in the mid-1960s that ruled that a trial judge is responsible for controlling the publicity about a case.

In 1976 the Supreme Court ruled that the press may not be prohibited from publishing information it has legally obtained about a criminal case unless these conditions are met:

1. Intense and pervasive publicity about the case is certain.
2. No other reasonable alternative is likely to mitigate the effects of the pretrial publicity.
3. The restrictive order will prevent prejudicial material from reaching the jurors (*Nebraska Press Association* v. *Stuart*).

Judges may, however, limit what trial participants say publicly about a case.

In two subsequent rulings the High Court reaffirmed its 1976 decision that confidential information legally obtained by the press may be published. These cases involved the name of a juvenile suspect in a murder case (*Smith* v. *Daily Mail*) and the names of judges whose conduct had been reviewed by a confidential state judicial commission (*Landmark Communications* v. *Virginia*).

CLOSED PROCEEDINGS

Trial judges were stripped of a potent weapon to control publicity about a criminal case when the U.S. Supreme Court barred the use of most restrictive orders aimed at the press. The state and federal judges quickly tried a new tack, the closing of trials and pretrial hearings to members of the press and the public. With the closing of these hearings, judges thus barred the press from gaining legal access to much of the prejudicial information that might be published or broadcast about a defendant. The damaging stories could not then be published, or so the judges argued. The closure of judicial hearings became the key First Amendment issue of the early 1980s. In the past eight years scores of appellate court decisions have been delivered on this question, including at least eight by the Supreme Court of the United States. From these decisions we can make the following generalizations: The courts have recognized a strong and virtually unqualified right for any citizen—including reporters—to attend a criminal or civil trial. And the courts have recognized a strong but qualified right for the press and public to attend pretrial hearings and gain access to most documents associated with a trial. Let's examine this issue, focusing first on the right to attend a trial and then on the right to attend pretrial and even posttrial hearings.

Closed Trials

In 1980 the Supreme Court of the United States ruled in a seven-to-one decision (Justice Powell took no part in this case) that the right of the public and the press to attend a criminal trial is guaranteed by both the common law and the First Amendment to the United States Constitution. The ruling, *Richmond Newspapers* v. *Virginia,* stemmed from a state court ruling in a Virginia criminal trial. In March 1976 John Stevenson was indicted for murder. He was tried and convicted of second degree murder, but his conviction was reversed. A second trial ended in a mistrial when a juror asked to be excused in the midst of the hearing. A third trial also resulted in a mistrial because a prospective juror told other prospective jurors about Stevenson's earlier conviction on the same charges. This was not revealed until after the trial had started. As proceedings were about to begin for the fourth time in late 1978, the defense asked that the trial be closed. The prosecution did not object and the court closed the trial. Richmond newspapers protested the closure to no avail. An appeal came before the United States Supreme Court in February 1980.

Chief Justice Burger wrote the Court's opinion, noting that "through its evolution the trial has been open to all who cared to observe." A presumption of open hearings is the very nature of a criminal trial under our system of justice, the Chief Justice added. While there is no specific provision in the Bill of Rights or the Constitution to support the open trial, the expressly guaranteed freedoms in the First Amendment "share a common core purpose of assuring freedom of communication on matters relating to the functioning of government," Burger wrote. "In guaranteeing freedoms such as those of speech and press the First Amendment can be read as protecting the right of everyone to attend trials so as to give meaning to those explicit guarantees," he added. The First Amendment, then, the Chief Justice noted, prohibits the government from summarily closing courtroom doors, which had been open to the public at the time that amendment was adopted.

But the Chief Justice refused to see the First Amendment as an absolute bar to closed trials. He noted that in some circumstances, which he explicitly declined to define at that time, a trial judge could bar the public and the press from a trial in the interest of the fair administration of justice. But, while the Court did not outline such circumstances, it was clear from both the tone and the language of the Chief Justice's opinion that in his mind such circumstances would indeed be unusual. Justices White, Stevens, Brennan, Marshall, Stewart, and Blackmun all concurred with the Chief Justice in five separate opinions. All but Stewart seemingly went further in guaranteeing access to trials than did Chief Justice Burger. Justice Rehnquist dissented.

In 1984 the Third U.S. Court of Appeals ruled that civil proceedings are also presumptively open to the public and the press. In *Publicker Industries* v. *Cohen* (1984), a lawsuit involving a corporate proxy fight, the court noted that a "survey of authorities identifies as features of the civil justice system many of those attributes of the criminal justice system on which the Supreme Court relied in holding that the First Amendment guarantees to the public and to the press the right of access to criminal trials. . . ." The right is not absolute, the court said, but absent a clear showing that closing the trial serves an important governmental interest and that closing the trial is the only way to serve this interest, the civil proceeding should be open. Numerous other federal and state courts have followed the rulings in the *Richmond Newspapers* and *Publicker* (see in re *Knight Publishing,* 1984, for example).

In most instances a trial will be presumed to be open and the burden on the person seeking to close the trial is indeed a high one. But there are occasions when a trial might be closed. Since 1980, courts have identified at least two such situations. The Vermont Supreme Court ruled in December 1981 that the ruling in the *Richmond Newspapers* case did not extend to juvenile proceedings. That is, the state may continue to hold such hearings—which are like trials—behind closed doors. The *Burlington Free Press* sought access to a juvenile proceeding in which a judge was to consider the status (adult or juvenile) of a fifteen-year-old boy who had murdered one young girl and assaulted another. Juvenile proceedings were supposed to be kept confidential under Vermont state law. The Vermont Supreme Court noted that there was no tradition of openness in these proceedings that mirrored the American tradition of public trials. In a juvenile proceeding there is no criminal conviction, often no punishment. "A juvenile proceeding is so unlike a criminal prosecution that the limited right of access described in *Richmond Newspapers* does not govern," the court ruled. In addition, there were many good reasons to keep such hearings closed, the court said. Publication of the name could impair the young person's opportunity for rehabilitation; confidentiality would protect the juvenile from carrying a stigma in the future. Publicity is often seen as a reward for a hard-core juvenile delinquent, the High Court added (in re *J.S.,* 1981). The Georgia Supreme Court made a similar ruling in 1984 but noted that both the press and the public must be given an opportunity to demonstrate that the public interest in an open proceeding overrides the interest of the state or the juvenile to close the hearing (*Florida Publishing* v. *Morgan,* 1984).

Access to juvenile proceedings is governed in most states by statute. Often reporters can gain access to such proceedings by promising not to reveal the names of the participants. Reporters who cover juvenile courts should know their statutory rights to attend such hearings.

Juvenile hearings are one common exception to the general rule of opening trials. Many states have laws that also close criminal trials when the juvenile victims of a sexual offense testify. In 1982 the Supreme Court ruled that a Massachusetts law that stated that the press and the public "shall" be excluded from the courtroom during such testimony was unconstitutional (*Globe Newspapers* v. *Superior Court,* 1982). The state argued that the law had two purposes: to encourage young victims to come forward to testify in such cases and to protect these young people from psychological harm once they come forward. The state law required the judge to close the trial when the victim testified; other portions of the trial could be closed at the judge's discretion. The flaw in the law, according to Justice William Brennan who wrote the Court's opinion, was that the trial judge was *required* to close the trial during the victim's testimony. Brennan agreed that protecting the physical and psychological well-being of a minor is a compelling interest:

> But as compelling as that interest is, it does not justify a mandatory-closure rule, for it is clear that the circumstances of the particular case may affect the significance of the interest. A trial court can determine on a case-by-case basis whether the closure is necessary to protect the welfare of a minor victim.

Under the statute the trial judge is not permitted to allow testimony in open court, even if the victim desires it, Brennan said.

Justice Brennan rejected the argument that a mandatory-closure law is more likely to prompt young victims of sexual assault to come forward to testify. He said there was no empirical support for this claim; in addition the argument was not logical. Reporters are permitted to attend the remainder of the trial, and can get the victim's name and details of the testimony from the transcript of the trial. The statute really does not do what the state thinks it should do, while it runs squarely against the presumption of open trials enunciated in the *Richmond Newspapers* case. Dissenters Burger and Rehnquist disagreed, arguing that the state has a long-standing right to protect juveniles, as well as a long tradition of excluding the public from trials involving victims of sexual assault. Justice Stevens also dissented because he said he believed the Supreme Court was improperly rendering an advisory opinion in the case, something the court is not suppose to do. (*Globe Newspapers* v. *Superior Court,* 1982).

Pretrial Hearings　　　　The closure of a trial, even before the ruling in *Richmond Newspapers,* was an uncommon occurrence. But the closure of a pretrial suppression hearing was not uncommon in the early 1980s. In fact, it became a routine practice in some courts. To comprehend the problem, a better understanding of pretrial suppression hearings is needed.

In most criminal cases the state and the defense will quarrel over the admittance of evidence at the trial. This evidence may be a weapon, a statement made by the defendant, the defendant's performance on a lie detector test, or something else of this nature. Usually the state will seek to have the evidence admitted at the trial, and the defense will attempt to block this effort. Fifty years ago this argument was normally carried out before the trial judge *after* the jury had been selected. The jurors were secreted in a safe place and did not hear the argument or the testimony that took place at such hearings. The judge would rule upon the admission of the disputed pieces of evidence and the trial would begin. The press attended such hearings, but of course the jurors were strongly admonished by the judge not to read or view or listen to anything about the case that might appear in the mass media. So if a judge ruled that the state could not introduce a weapon at the trial, and the press reported this ruling, the jurors would likely not see the story and never know such a weapon existed.

Evidentiary questions became somewhat more complicated following the numerous decisions regarding defendant's rights rendered by the Supreme Court in the 1960s. The pretrial hearing became more involved and often more lengthy. A practice soon developed of holding the hearing before the trial, often two or three weeks before the trial, even before a jury was chosen in the case. Press reports about the suppression hearing would circulate in the community. If a judge barred the introduction of an important piece of evidence in a trial, citizens in the community—all potential jurors—could read these stories. Those selected as jurors, then, might very well know that such evidence existed even though it was not introduced at the trial. Before the ruling in *Nebraska Press Association* v. *Stuart,* a judge could use a restrictive order to bar the press from publishing or broadcasting information about the evidence. With that option gone, judges began to close the pretrial hearings. Reporters were barred from these traditionally open proceedings. The press protested and important court cases resulted. The question was, Can a judge, with the agreement of the defendant and the state, close a pretrial hearing to the public and the press? Two constitutional amendments suggest that a judge cannot close such a hearing. The First Amendment guarantees to all persons the freedom of the press. And the Sixth Amendment states that "in all criminal prosecutions, the accused shall enjoy the right to a speedy and public trial. . . ." A public trial surely implies an open hearing.

It can be said with assurance today that there exists a qualified First Amendment right for the press and the public to attend a pretrial hearing. A 1986 Supreme Court ruling (*Press-Enterprise* v. *Superior Court*) clearly resolved the issue. But the nation's courts surely struggled to reach this determination and the legality of closing pretrial hearings was one of the most hotly litigated issues in the early 1980s. The story of what happened provides some interesting insights into the workings of the nation's judicial system. The starting point is the case of *Gannett* v. *DePasquale* (1979), one of the most confusing decisions handed down by the Supreme Court in the past half-century.

Gannett v. *DePasquale*

In 1976 the state of New York brought charges of second-degree murder and burglary against Kyle Greathouse and David Jones in connection with the slaying of a former Seneca County police officer. Considerable publicity surrounded the death of Wayne Clapp and the capture in Michigan of the two defendants. Before the trial began, both defendants sought to suppress statements they had given to police on the grounds that the statements had been given involuntarily. They also sought to suppress evidence that the police had uncovered as a result of those statements. Because of the intensive publicity surrounding the case, defense lawyers sought to close the pretrial hearings where arguments would be made to suppress the prejudicial evidence. The state agreed to this closure, and Judge DePasquale prohibited the press and public from attending the sessions. Gannett, which publishes both Rochester newspapers, appealed the judge's ruling. But the New York courts refused to overturn Judge DePasquale's order. The United States Supreme Court agreed to hear the case and in July 1979 sustained the trial judge's closure order.

The Court decision was fractured, and five separate opinions were written. Justice Potter Stewart's opinion for the Court drew support from only one other member of the tribunal, Justice John Paul Stevens. Chief Justice Burger, Justice Lewis Powell, and Justice Rehnquist each wrote a separate concurring opinion, and Justices Marshall, White, and Brennan concurred in a strong dissent by Justice Blackmun.

Justice Stewart said that if the defendant, the prosecutor, and the trial judge agree, a pretrial hearing can be closed to the public. Stewart suggested that a trial might be closed as well under the same circumstances. Stewart said that the right to a public trial guaranteed by the Sixth Amendment is a right belonging to a defendant alone. The defendant could choose to waive that right at any time and seek to have a closed hearing. Justice Stewart acknowledged that there is a legitimate public concern that the criminal justice system work properly. But, he said, "in an adversary system of criminal justice, the public interest in the administration of justice is protected by the participants in the litigation." If the state and the trial judge agree with the defendant, the hearing can be closed. Stewart said that the First Amendment was not a relevant issue in this case, but might be in some future case. However, he said that the Court would not decide in the abstract whether the press enjoyed a constitutional right to attend a pretrial hearing or a trial. Justice Rehnquist, who wrote a separate opinion, also based his support of the closure of the hearing upon the defendants' Sixth Amendment rights.

Chief Justice Burger agreed with Stewart that the Sixth Amendment's guarantee of a public trial did not guarantee the right of the people or the press to attend pretrial hearings. But Burger stressed that the same rationale did not necessarily apply to trials, as Stewart suggested. When the Sixth Amendment was drafted, suppression hearings were not a part of American jurisprudence, the Chief Justice noted. Similarly the common law rule, which mandated an open trial, did not envision the exclusionary rule and pretrial motions to suppress evidence. Hence, it is impossible to argue that the Sixth Amendment's guarantee of a public trial includes the guarantee of a public pretrial hearing.

The fifth member of the majority was Justice Lewis Powell. He was the only member of the High Court who, in his opinion, gave serious consideration to the guarantees of freedom of expression. Powell said there is a right under the First Amendment for the press and the public to attend pretrial hearings—but it is not an absolute right. The right of the press and the public must be balanced against the right of the defendant to a fair trial. When a closed hearing is requested, Powell wrote, the judge should consider whether there are other ways of protecting the defendant's right less damaging to the press than to close the hearing. The press must be allowed to make arguments opposing the closure of the courtroom before the order is issued, Powell said. The press can argue that a defendant's right can be protected in ways other than by closing a hearing. If in the end the trial judge is convinced by the evidence that closing the hearing is the only way to protect the defendant's right to a fair trial, the First Amendment right to attend the proceeding must then be sacrificed. Powell was the only one of the nine members of the Court to focus exclusively on the First Amendment, and the only justice who argued that there is a qualified right for the public and the press to attend such hearings. In this case, however, he said he was convinced that Judge DePasquale had determined that the only way to protect the rights of the defendants was to close the hearing. And Justice Powell accepted this determination by the trial judge.

The dissenters, led by a long and forceful opinion by Justice Blackmun, argued that the right to a public trial was put in the Constitution to protect the people as much as to protect the defendant. Blackmun wrote that the Sixth

Amendment guarantee of a public trial "embodies our belief that secret judicial proceedings would be a menace to liberty. The public trial is rooted in the principle that justice cannot survive behind walls of silence." He added (*Gannett v. DePasquale*):

> The public trial guarantee, moreover, ensures that not only judges but all participants in the criminal justice system are subjected to public scrutiny as they conduct the public's business of prosecuting crime. This publicity guards against the miscarriage of justice by subjecting the police, prosecutors, and judicial processes to extensive public scrutiny and criticism.

Blackmun argued that the public interest in both trial and pretrial proceedings cannot adequately be protected by the prosecutor and the judge, as suggested by Justice Stewart. "The specter of a trial or suppression hearing where a defendant of the same political party as the prosecutor and judge—both of whom are elected officials perhaps beholden to the very defendant they are to try—obtains closure of the proceeding without any consideration for the substantial public interest at stake is sufficiently real to cause me to reject the Court's suggestion that the parties be given complete discretion to dispose of the public's interest as they see fit," the justice wrote. The dissenters said that the Sixth Amendment does not impose an absolute requirement that all courts be open at all times. But before closing a hearing the judge surely must find that an open pretrial will cause irreparable damage to the defendant's right to a fair trial, that alternatives to closing the hearing will not protect the defendant, but that the closed hearing will ensure a trial by an impartial jury for the defendant.

The failure of the Supreme Court to clearly resolve the question of access to pretrial suppression hearings in the Gannett case led to considerable confusion in the lower courts. And for almost five years, the U.S. Courts of Appeal and state supreme courts were forced to forge their own answers to the question. But beginning in 1984, the Supreme Court issued the first of three decisions that would resolve the issue.

In January the High Court ruled, nine to nothing that the public and press hold a qualified First Amendment right to attend the pretrial voir dire proceeding. Remember, the voir dire process is the questioning of potential jurors for the trial. (See pages 370-71 for a fuller explanation of voir dire.) A California Superior Court in Riverside had closed all but three days of a six-week voir dire to protect the right of privacy of the jurors and the fair trial rights of the defendant. Chief Justice Burger wrote that the process of juror selection is a matter of importance, not simply to the adversaries but also to the criminal justice system. "No right ranks higher than the right of the accused to a fair trial. But the primacy of the accused's rights is difficult to separate from the right of everyone in the community to attend the voir dire which promotes fairness," he added. In some instances, Burger noted, the proceeding might be properly closed, but the presumption of openess may only be overcome by an overriding interest based on findings that closure is essential to preserve high values and is narrowly tailored to serve that interest. "The interest [is] to be articulated along with findings specific enough that a reviewing court can determine whether the closure order was properly entered," Burger said. In this case the judge's order was far too broad. Also, the judge had failed to articulate specific reasons for the closure and had failed to look to alternatives to closure as means of solving the problem (*Press-Enterprise* v. *Riverside Superior Court,* 1984).

Five months later the High Court was faced with another case involving a closed suppression hearing. In *Waller* v. *Georgia,* the state sought to close the pretrial suppression-of-evidence hearing to preserve the usefulness of the evidence (which was primarily wiretap evidence) against other persons not yet charged with a crime. But the defendant, Waller, insisted that the hearing be open. Justice Lewis Powell wrote the opinion for the unanimous court and ruled that under the Sixth Amendment, suppression-of-evidence hearing are presumptively open and surely cannot be closed against the wishes of the accused. In an aside Powell noted that in the earlier *Gannett* v. *DePasquale* ruling in 1979, a majority of the High Court had reached the same conclusion. He said he (Powell) had found such a presumptive right in the First Amendment, and Justices Blackmun, Brennan, Marshall and White had found such a right under the Sixth Amendment (*Waller* v. *Georgia,* 1984).

Finally, in the summer of 1986, the High Court completed fashioning the privilege it began in 1984. In a 7–2 ruling, the Court declared that there exists a qualified privilege for the press and the public to attend a pretrial hearing, even in the face of opposition from the defendant. A California trial court had closed the pretrial hearing for Robert Diaz, a nurse accused of killing as many as twelve patients in a hospital in which he worked. *The Riverside Press-Enterprise* protested the closure, but the California appellate courts ruled that while there was a First Amendment right for the public and press to attend a trial, no corollary right existed to attend a pretrial hearing. The U.S. Supreme Court disagreed. The preliminary hearing may be closed "only if specific findings are made demonstrating that first, there is a substantial probability that the defendant's right to a fair trial will be prejudiced by publicity, and, second, reasonable alternatives to closure cannot adequately protect the defendants fair trial rights," wrote Chief Justice Burger. Mere risk of prejudice does not automatically justify refusing public access to hearings, Burger stressed. If the judge makes specific findings that the probability of such prejudice does exist, the closure order must be tailored very narrowly to serve that interest. In other words, if only two-hours worth of testimony during a three-day pretrial hearing might cause the probability of prejudice, the hearing should be closed only during those two hours. Trial judges should use other means, where possible, to protect the defendant. "Through voir dire, cumbersome as it is in some circumstances, a court can identify those jurors whose prior knowledge of the case would disable them from rendering an impartial verdict," Burger added.

It should be noted that the requirement that the defendant or the state show that there is a "substantial probability" of prejudice, rather than a "reasonable likelihood," a standard used by many other courts, places a much heavier burden upon the person seeking to close the hearing. Hence, the High Court has made it extremely difficult for those who seek to overturn the presumption that the pretrial hearing will be open (*Press-Enterprise* v. *Riverside Superior Court,* 1986).

Given the case law generated by the Supreme Court on this issue, it is possible to fashion the following rule. To overcome the presumption of openness of the pretrial hearing the following must occur.

1. The party seeking closure must advance an overriding interest that is likely to be harmed if the hearing remains open. The right to a fair trial is such an interest.

2. The person seeking closure must demonstrate that there is a "substantial probability" that this interest will be harmed if the pretrial remains open.

3. The closure must be narrowly tailored and be no broader than necessary to protect that interest. For example, if there are several evidentiary questions to be settled, but publicity about only one of these issues might be harmful to the defendant, only the portion of the hearing that deals with that issue should be closed.

4. The trial court must consider reasonable alternatives to closure of the hearing.

5. The trial court must make adequate findings to support the closure. In other words, the judge must gather some facts and then specifically state the reasons for closure. This will permit an appellate court to examine whether or not the judge acted properly.

In the period between the High Court ruling in Gannett in 1979 and the more recent Supreme Court rulings, lower courts, faced sometimes with monthly requests for pretrial closures, were forced to try to resolve this issue on their own. Several U.S. Courts of Appeal and state supreme courts fashioned their own tests regarding access to pretrial hearings. Clearly, the newer Supreme Court rulings now set the boundary for determining when a judge may close a pretrial, but it is instructive to look at some of these lower court cases that provide a strong rationale for the open pretrial hearings. A federal trial judge in Philadelphia held an unannounced, closed evidentiary hearing in the trial of four defendants nabbed in one of the FBI's infamous Abscam investigations. The closure was justified on the grounds that if information discussed at the hearing were brought out and publicized, it would impair the defendants' right to a fair trial. The defendants in the case were three Philadelphia city councilmen and a private attorney. The Third United States Court of Appeals ruled that the closure order was improper (*U.S.* v. *Criden*, 1982). The public has the First Amendment right of access to pretrial hearings, the court ruled. "Who will protect the interests of the public and the press in these hearings if access is denied?" Chief Judge Seitz asked. "The defendant's interests will obviously not coincide with that of the press," he said. The government has the duty to ensure a fair trial, but is also interested in securing a conviction that will withstand appeal. The reversal of a conviction because of prejudicial publicity poses a risk to a successful prosecution. "We, therefore, cannot expect the government to vindicate the public's first amendement rights." Judge Seitz said that the trial judge could not be expected to be the "sole guardian of First Amendment interests even against the express wishes of both parties." No one has an interest to protect the rights of public and press in a closed hearing. "The public has some First Amendment right of access to information about how one of these great branches of our government conducts its business," he concluded.

In *U.S.* v. *Brooklier* (1982) a federal trial court barred the press and public from the suppression hearing and other evidentiary hearings in a case in which several persons were charged with violating federal racketeering laws. The court also partially closed the voir dire proceedings where potential jurors were questioned by attorneys before being chosen to serve on the jury panel. The Ninth United States Court of Appeals ruled the closures improper in this case, stating that before such a closure is proper, the accused must demonstrate that closure is "strictly and inescapably necessary in order to protect the right to a fair trial guarantee." To do this it is necessary to demonstrate the substantial probability of irreparable damage to the fair trial guarantee from conducting the hearings in public and a substantial probability that alternatives to closure will not adequately protect the right to a fair trial, and that the closure will be effective in protecting the rights of the accused. And in 1984 the Second U.S. Court of Appeals ruled that a U.S. District Court judge in Syracuse improperly closed a pretrial hearing. The defendant, Michael Klepfer, was indicted on charges of making false statements to government investigators and obstructing justice. He sought to exclude both the public and the press from his hearing, and the judge closed the proceeding. The court of appeals, noting that in *Richmond Newspapers* the Supreme Court had ruled that trials must be open, said, "It makes little sense to recognize a right of public access to criminal courts and then limit that right to the trial phase of a criminal proceeding, something that occurs in only a small fraction of criminal cases." Defendants in most criminal cases plead guilty and no trial is held. What happens at a pretrial hearing may have a decisive impact upon the outcome of the case. The trial judge must first consider alternatives to closure as a means of protecting the rights of the defendant, the court said. And the trial judge must articulate the basis for any closure order supplying sufficient details for appellate review, the court added (in re *Herald Co.,* 1984).

The privilege of attending a pretrial hearing is clearly a qualified one for the press and public, and can be overcome. A 1985 ruling in a sensational spy case shows that while difficult, the presumption of openness can be defeated. A suppression hearing in July of 1985 was closed when the government convinced a U.S. District Court judge that an open hearing might irreparably damage the fair trial rights of Arthur Walker, on trial for espionage. The Fourth U.S. Court of Appeals ruled that the trial judges had made a proper finding that publicity about the material at issue in the hearing was highly prejudicial to the defendant, especially in light of the public interest in the case. The district court concluded that there was no alternative to closure and that closure of the hearing would effectively protect Walker's rights. Finally, these findings were sufficiently articulated by the district court to permit review by the court of appeals. The hearing was closed (in re *Landmark Communications,* 1985).

Guidelines

The Department of Justice issued *Guidelines on Open Judicial Proceedings* in 1980. United States attorneys were instructed to ordinarily oppose any motions for the closure of any judicial proceeding. *Guidelines* states that before seeking closure or consenting to closure, the United States attorney must be satisified that these conditions are met:

1. No other alternative exists to protect the defendant's rights.
2. Closure will succeed in preventing harm to the defendant.
3. The degree of closure is minimized to the greatest extent possible.
4. The public is given adequate notice of the proposed closure.
5. Failure to close the proceedings will produce any one of the following effects:
    a. Substantial likelihood of the denial of the right of fair trial to the defendant.
    b. Substantial likelihood of danger to the safety of participants in the trial.
    c. Substantial likelihood that ongoing investigations will be seriously jeopardized.

A United States attorney must get authorization from the deputy United States attorney general before seeking to close a hearing or consenting to a motion to close the hearing made by another party in the case. Of course these rules apply only to litigation in which the Department of Justice is involved.

OTHER PROCEEDINGS

Courts have also been asked to rule on whether other aspects of the judicial process must be open to press and public. It is useful to note a few of these decisions, which tend to favor openness. The Third U.S. Court of Appeals ruled in 1985 that indictments and informations are open to the public and the press (*U.S. v. Smith,* 1985). The West Virginia Supreme Court ruled that under that state's constitution, attorney disciplinary hearings must be open (*Daily Gazette v. West Virginia Bar,* 1984). The Ninth U.S. Court of Appeals ruled in 1985 that a U.S. District Court erred when it sealed a postconviction motion to reduce a sentence together with the government's response. Such documents must be open, the court said, unless the proponents of closure demonstrate with specificity that compelling interests in support of closure override the presumption of access to such information (*CBS v. U.S. District Court,* 1985). And at least two U.S. Courts of Appeal have ruled that bail proceedings are presumptively open, the Fifth in *U.S. v. Chagra* (1983) and the First in re *Globe Newspapers* (1984). The court in the Globe case, however, permitted the trial judge to close the hearing because the closure order was narrowly tailored and the judge had considered, but reasonably rejected, alternatives to closure to protect the rights of the defendant. Finally, several courts have ruled that the public and the press have access to documents filed with the court in connection with a criminal trial. The Ninth U.S. Court of Appeals struck down a lower court order that sealed a large number of court records filed when the government prosecuted John DeLorean. There is a qualified right of access to pretrial proceedings, the court noted. "There is no reason to distinguish between pretrial proceedings and the documents filed in regard to them," the court said. Pretrial documents are often important to a full understanding of the way in which "the judicial process and the government as a whole are functioning," the court added (*AP v. U.S. District Court,* 1983).

The qualified right of access to judicial proceedings and documents has gone a long way to block attempts by courts to keep the public and the press out of the courtroom. Many trial judges, however, see closure as a simple solution to the problem of publicity about a criminal case. And often the motion for closure is made totally unexpectedly. What should a reporter do when faced with such a problem? Here are some tips for journalists from "*The Seattle Times* Newsroom Legal Guide" prepared by attorneys P. Cameron Devore, Marshall J. Nelson, and others at the Seattle law firm of Davis, Wright, Todd, Riese and Jones.

Call the editor immediately so he or she can contact the company's lawyer. Try informally to remind the lawyer who is proposing closure of the recent rulings and guidelines to provide for a presumptively open hearing. If that fails, the reporter should be prepared to make a formal objection to the closure, to try to hold the fort until legal help arrives. Reporters for *The Seattle Times* are prepared to read the following statement from a card they carry.

Your honor, I am _____, a reporter for *The Seattle Times,* and I would like to object on behalf of my newspaper and the public to this proposed closing. Our attorney is prepared to make a number of arguments against closings such as this one, and we respectfully ask the Court for a hearing on those issues. I believe our attorney can be here soon for the Court's convenience and will be able to demonstrate that closure in this case will violate the First Amendment and Article I, Section 10, of the Washington State constitution. I cannot make the legal arguments myself, but our attorney can point out several issues for your consideration. If it pleases the Court, we request the opportunity to be heard through counsel.

Such a statement would work in any court; simply cite the proper section of your own state constitution or any other relevant documents or guidelines. Reporters should be equipped to handle such an emergency.

SUMMARY

The public and the press have a right to attend trials and pretrial proceedings. While the right to attend a trial is not absolute, only in rare circumstances can such a proceeding be closed. Courts have permitted the closure of juvenile hearings, as well as that portion of the public testimony of a rape victim that might be embarrassing or cause unneeded anguish. The right to attend pretrial proceedings is qualified. The presumption that these hearings are open can only be overcome by a showing that there is an overriding interest that must be protected, that there is a "substantial probability" that an open hearing will damage this right, that the closure is narrowly tailored to deny access to no more of the hearing than is necessary to protect this interest, that the court has considered reasonable alternatives to closure, that closure of the hearing would in fact protect the interest that has been raised, and that the trial judge has articulated findings—which may be reviewed by an appellate court—that support the four points above. The Department of Justice and other agencies have promulgated guidelines supporting this presumption of openness, and courts have found that the press and the public have a right of access to a wide range of other judicial hearings and documents filed with the court.

BENCH-BAR-PRESS GUIDELINES

Both restrictive orders and the closure of court proceedings are admittedly effective ways of stopping publicity from reaching the hands of potential jurors, but they are equally dangerous in a representative democracy where information about how well government is operating is fundamental to the success of the political system. The bench, the bar, and the press in many states have found that cooperation, restraint, and mutual trust can be equally effective in protecting the rights of a defendant, while at the same time far less damaging to rights of the people.

In twenty-eight states the members of the bench, the bar, and the press have tried to reach a common understanding of the problems of pretrial news coverage and have offered suggestions as to how most of these problems might be resolved. These suggestions are usually offered in the form of guidelines or recommendations to the press and to participants in the criminal justice system. **Bench-bar-press guidelines** normally suggest to law enforcement officers that certain kinds of information about a criminal suspect and a crime can be released and published with little danger of harm to the trial process. The guidelines also suggest to journalists that the publication of certain kinds of information about a case (see the list of damaging kinds of statements on pages 365–66) can be harmful to the defendant's chances for a fair trial without providing the public with useful or important information. The guidelines are often presented in a very brief form; at other times they encompass several pages of text.

Bench-bar-press guidelines have existed in some states for more than twenty years. In some communities these guidelines work very well in managing the problems surrounding the free press–fair trial dilemma. A spirit of cooperation exists between press, courts, attorneys, and law enforcement personnel. In such communities it is rare to find a restrictive order or a closed courtroom. But most communities and states have found it takes considerable effort to make the guidelines work. Drafting the guidelines is only the first step. If after agreement is reached upon the recommendations, the bench, the bar, and the press go their separate ways, the guidelines usually fail as a means of resolving the free press–fair trial problems.

The state of Washington has one of the most successful bench-bar-press agreements in the nation. The Bench-Bar-Press Committee in Washington has been meeting regularly since 1966. In addition, the committee periodically sponsors day-long seminars around the state to educate attorneys, reporters, and judges in application of the guidelines. The Washington Supreme Court is very active in its support of the committee, and the chief justice sits as chairman of the committee. This has the distinct effect of getting both trial lawyers and other judges to attend the seminars.

Support by the state's leading newspapers is also helpful in getting reporters to attend. Discussion of libel and related press-law problems is also a device used to lure the press to meetings, so that a dose of free press–fair trial guidelines can be administered as well.

Also a subcommittee—called the liaison committee—of the state's bench-bar-press committee composed of a judge, an attorney, and a journalist acts as a special education group. The job of the committee is to respond quickly to immediate free press–fair trial problems. For example, a Seattle judge informed the press at the beginning of a trial that reporters would be excluded from certain portions of the trial. The reporters became angry, and the managing editor of one of the daily papers in Seattle immediately called the chairman of the bench-bar-press committee who in turn activated the liaison committee. The entire chain of events took about four hours. The judge who sat on the liaison committee called his colleague on the bench who had announced the trial closure. The committee member asked the judge whether he realized that by closing the trial he violated provisions of the bench-bar-press agreement. He then informed the judge that it was his experience that the press can be trusted in situations like these and need not be excluded from a trial. The peer pressure worked. The trial judge called reporters into his chambers and told them he had changed his mind, and the trial would be open. But he asked the press to refrain from reporting certain sensational details of the testimony. The reporters honored his request. In other instances judges complained about newsmen, and the journalist on the liaison committee successfully applied the same kind of educational pressure to his colleagues.

The spate of restrictive orders and closed courtrooms has tried the patience of many in the press, even in those states with bench-bar-press guidelines. Cooperation among the members of the bench, the bar and the press was in short supply even in the state of Washington after a couple of court rulings upholding the closure of a hearing (see *Federated Publications* v. *Swedberg,* 1981). But the establishment in the courts of a right of access to court proceedings has soothed the tension, and harmony seems to be returning, especially in those regions where the members of the press attempt to work with judges and lawyers to find a reasonable solution to these serious problems.

SUMMARY

In some states the press, attorneys, and judges have agreed to try to solve the problems surrounding the free press–fair trial controversy through voluntary bench-bar-press agreements. Such agreements usually contain suggestions to all parties as to what information should and should not be publicized about criminal cases. When the guidelines work, there is usually a cooperative, rather than a combative, spirit among the members of the press, the judiciary, and the bar. These guidelines often reduce or eliminate the need for restrictive orders or closed hearings.

CAMERAS IN THE COURTROOM

In 1976 journalists in all but two states were prohibited from bringing cameras or tape recorders into courtrooms. Today, only the District of Columbia, the federal courts, and nine states—Indiana, Louisiana, Michigan, Mississippi, Missouri, South Carolina, South Dakota, Vermont, and Virginia—ban such equipment from all judicial proceedings. In twelve states—Delaware,

Idaho, Illinois, Kansas, Maine, Minnesota, Nebraska, New York, North Dakota, Oregon, Texas, and Wyoming—recording equipment and cameras are allowed only in appellate courts. Cameras and tape recorders may be used at trials as well as appellate hearings in the remaining twenty-nine states—in Maryland and Pennsylvania on an experimental basis in civil but not criminal trials when this was written (see Richard Lindsey, *An Assessment of the Use of Cameras in State and Federal Courts*). And the Supreme Court of the United States has ruled that the use of recorders and cameras by journalists during a trial does not by itself deprive the defendant of the constitutionally guaranteed right to a fair trail (*Chandler* v. *Florida,* 1981).

This swift reversal of the rules regarding the use of cameras in the courtroom climaxed a forty-year struggle by the press for relaxation of prohibitions that were instituted in the 1930s. At that time the press had conducted itself in an outrageous fashion in covering the trial of Bruno Hauptmann, who was charged with kidnapping the baby of Charles and Anne Lindberg. The trial judge, who had great difficulty in controlling the press, ordered that no pictures be taken during the court sessions. But photographers equipped with large, bulky, flash-equipped cameras moved freely about the courtroom, ignoring the judge's orders and taking pictures almost at will. As a result of this travesty, the American Bar Association adopted rules prohibiting the use of cameras and other electronic equipment in courtrooms. The rules, known as Canon 35, were adopted in most states and were followed in practice in those states that did not adopt the rules (see Frank M. White, "Cameras in the Courtroom: A U.S. Survey").

After World War II when the photographic equipment became smaller and less obtrusive and faster film permitted photography indoors without flash equipment, the press began to agitate for changes in the rules. The television industry especially chafed under the proscriptions (the ABA rules had been amended in 1952 to include television), as they put broadcast reporters, who depended upon film to tell a story, at a distinct disadvantage in the competition with wordsmiths of the printed press. In the mid-1960s the United States Supreme Court had a chance to consider the constitutionality of the ban on cameras in the courtroom in a case that began in Texas, one of a handful of states that occasionally allowed photography and recording in the courtroom.

The defendant was Billie Sol Estes, who was accused of a salad oil swindle. The story was important in the Lone Star State; television was therefore permitted at the initial pretrial hearing, and still photographers were permitted throughout the trial. But there was disruption at the pretrial hearing. Twelve cameramen crowded into the tiny courtroom, cables and wires snaked across the floor, microphones were everywhere, and the distraction caused by this media invasion was significant. The situation improved during the trial when television and recording equipment was housed in a booth at the back of the courtroom. Estes appealed his conviction to the United States Supreme

Court on the grounds that he had been denied a fair trial because of the presence of the cameras and recorders. The court agreed with the salad oil magnate. "While maximum freedom must be allowed the press in carrying out this important function [informing the public] in a democratic society, its exercise must necessarily be subject to the maintenance of absolute fairness in the judicial process," wrote Justice Tom Clark for the majority (*Estes* v. *Texas,* 1965). The photography and broadcasting equipment simply created too many impediments to a fair trial.

However, experimentation with cameras in the courtroom continued. Telecasting equipment improved. Journalists demonstrated to judges that they could act responsibly if they were permitted access to courtrooms with their cameras and recorders. More and more states began to permit telecasts and broadcasts of criminal and civil trials, as well as of the oral arguments at appellate hearings. In the early eighties two former Miami police officers challenged the new rules in Florida that permitted cameras in the courtroom. They argued that television coverage of their trial in and of itself had deprived them of a fair trial. The Florida Supreme Court rejected their contention, and the United States Supreme Court agreed to hear the case. In a unanimous decision the High Court ruled that the mere presence of cameras in the courtroom or simply televising or broadcasting portions of a trial does not in and of itself cause prejudice to the defendant or interfere with the right to a fair trial. Chief Justice Burger wrote that at present "no one has been able to present empirical data sufficient to establish that the mere presence of the broadcast media inherently has an adverse effect on that [trial] process." It is true the presence of such equipment in the courtroom or the broadcast of a trial could endanger the defendant's right to a fair trial. But, Burger said, "an absolute constitutional ban on broadcast coverage of trials cannot be justified simply because there is a danger that, in some cases, prejudicial broadcast accounts of pretrial and trial events may impair the ability of jurors to decide the issue of guilt or innocence uninfluenced by extraneous matter." The Chief Justice said that in order to block the use of cameras and recorders at a trial, a defendant is going to have to demonstrate to the court how the trial will be adversely affected by the presence of this equipment. To overturn a conviction at a trial that has been televised, the defendant will need to show that the recording and photography equipment actually made a substantial difference in some material aspect of the trial. Proof that the jurors were aware of the cameras or that the presence of television cameras "told" jurors this was a big trial will not be sufficient to demonstrate prejudice, Burger wrote (*Chandler* v. *Florida,* 1981).

State courts have started to develop standards to assess complaints of prejudice from defendants who do not want their trials televised. In Florida, for example, the state supreme court has ruled that the trial court must hold an evidentiary hearing if a defendant or other participant in the trial protests the television coverage. Before cameras and recorders may be excluded, there must be a finding that electronic coverage of the trial would have important "qualitatively different effect" on the trial than would other types of coverage (*Florida* v. *Palm Beach Newspapers,* 1981). Another Florida case demonstrates how such a difference might be shown. The defendant in the case had previously been found incompetent to stand trial. Treatment subsequently rendered her competent to proceed with the case. Her attorneys, armed with testimony from psychiatrists, asserted that television cameras in the courtroom would adversely affect the defendant's ability to communicate with her counsel and she might lapse into psychosis. The Florida Supreme Court ruled that this kind of evidence satisfied the standard for excluding television cameras (*Florida* v. *Green,* 1981).

Cameras are not allowed in federal courtrooms, and federal judges have resisted all efforts to televise court hearings, even when the defendant sought to have cameras in the courtroom (see *U.S.* v. *Hastings,* 1983). The *Chandler* case stands for the principle that if the state decides to let cameras into the courtroom, their presence does not violate the constitutional guarantee of a fair trial. But nothing in the Court's opinion in *Chandler* suggests that states or the federal courts *must* permit cameras in the courtroom (see *Westmoreland* v. *CBS,* 1984 and *U.S.* v. *Kerley,* 1985).

State rules on the admission of cameras to the courtroom vary. In some states cameras will not be permitted unless various key trial participants agree. In more states the cameras are allowed upon the discretion of the judge. If a participant objects to the admission of cameras to the courtroom, the press must honor this objection and refrain from photographing or recording this individual. Most states have adopted guidelines that establish the number of still and motion picture cameras permitted in the courtroom at any one time. Rules often specify where the cameras may be placed, require that all pictures be taken with available light, and even set standards of dress for photographers and technicians. The press must often be willing to share the fruits of the photography through pooling agreements, since most states have guidelines limiting movement and placement of cameras to only when the court is in recess.

SUMMARY

Until recently cameras and recorders were banned from courtrooms in nearly all states. But today such equipment may be used during a trial in about two-thirds of the states. The Supreme Court has ruled that the mere presence of cameras or recorders in the courtroom does not prejudice the defendant's right to a fair trial (*Chandler* v. *Florida*). To block the use of the cameras or to seek the reversal of a conviction at a trial that has been televised or recorded, a defendant will have to offer specific proof that the use of the electronic news-gathering equipment will or did interfere with the right to a fair trial.

A good deal of space has been devoted to the free press–fair trial problem because it is an important problem and because it continues to be a problem. Within both the press and the law, sharp divisions regarding solution of the problem remain. Many years ago during a battle over a free press–fair trial issue in one southern state, the national office of the American Civil Liberties Union filed an amicus curiae (friend of the court) brief supporting a free and unfettered press, while the state chapter of the same civil liberties group filed a brief in favor of the court's position supporting a fair trial.

Most journalists probably agree that we need more, not less, reporting on the justice system in the United States. In *Crime and Publicity* Alfred Friendly and Ronald Goldfarb write:

> To shackle the press is to curtail the public watch over the administration of criminal justice. . . . The press serves at the gate house of justice. Additionally, it serves in the manorhouse itself, and all along the complicated route to it from the police station and the streets, to the purlieus of the prosecutor's office, to the courtroom corridors where the pressures mount and the deals are made.

The two authors also point out that we do not want a press that is free, more or less, just as we should not tolerate trials that are almost fair. "And to complicate the issue," they note, "it is evident that a free press is one of society's principal guarantors of fair trials, while fair trials provide a major assurance of the press's freedom."

Reporters dealing with the courts and the court system must be extremely sensitive to these issues. They should not be blinded as they clamor for news, to the sensitive mechanisms that operate in the courts to provide justice and fairness. At the same time they should not let the authoritarian aspects of the judicial system block their efforts to provide the information essential to the functioning of the democracy.

BIBLIOGRAPHY

Here is a list of some of the sources that have been helpful in the preparation of chapter 7:

Books

Advisory Committee on Fair Trial and Free Press. *Approved Draft Standards Relating to Fair Trial and Free Press.* New York: American Bar Association, 1968.

Barron, Jerome, and Dienes, C. Thomas. *Handbook of Free Speech and Free Press.* Boston: Little, Brown & Co., 1979.

Buddenbaum, Judith M., et al. *Pretrial Publicity and Juries: A Review of Research.* Research Report No. 11, School of Journalism, Indiana University, 1981.

Bush, Chilton R., ed. *Free Press and Fair Trial: Some Dimensions of the Problem.* Athens: University of Georgia Press, 1971.

Friendly, Alfred, and Goldfarb, Ronald. *Crime and Publicity.* New York: Random House, Vintage Books, 1968.

Gillmor, Donald M. *Judicial Restraints on the Press.* Columbia: Freedom of Information Center, University of Missouri, 1974.

Judicial Administration Division. *Courts and Community.* Salt Lake City: American Bar Association, 1973.

Pember, Don R. *Pre-Trial Publicity in Criminal Proceedings: A Case Study.* Unpublished Master's Thesis, Michigan State University, 1966.

White, Frank W. *Cameras in the Courtroom: A U.S. Survey.* 60 *Journalism Monographs,* 1979.

Articles

Gerald, J. Edward. "Press-Bar Relationships: Progress Since Sheppard and Reardon." 47 *Journalism Quarterly* 223, 1970.

Kline, Gerald, and Jess, Paul. "Prejudicial Publicity: Its Effect on Law School Mock Juries." 43 *Journalism Quarterly* 113, 1966.

Landau, Jack C. "The Challenge of the Communications Media." 62 *American Bar Association Journal* 55, January, 1976.

Lindsey, Richard P. "An Assessment of the Use of Cameras in State and Federal Courts." 18 *Georgia Law Review* 389, 1984.

Pember, Don R., "Does Pretrial Publicity Really Hurt?" *Columbia Journalism Review* 16, September/October, 1984.

Riley, Sam. "Pre-Trial Publicity: A Field Study." 50 *Journalism Quarterly* 17, 1973.

Simon, Rita. "Murders, Juries and the Press." May-June *Transaction* 40, 1966.

Trager, Robert, and Stonecipher, Harry W. "Gag Orders: An Unresolved Dilemma." 55 *Journalism Quarterly* 231, 1978.

Warren, Robert S., and Abell, Jeffrey M. "Free Press–Fair Trial, the Gag Order: A California Aberration." 45 *Southern California Law Review* 51, 1972.

Cases

AP v. *U.S. District Court,* 705 F.2d 1143 (1983).

in re *Application of NBC,* 653 F.2d 609 (1981).

Branzburg v. *Hayes,* 408 U.S. 655 (1972).

CBS v. *U.S. District Court,* 729 F.2d 1174 (1984).

CBS v. *U.S. District Court,* 765 F.2d 823 (1985).

Chandler v. *Florida,* 101 S.Ct. 802 (1981).

Daily Gazette v. *West Virginia Bar,* 326 S.E.2d 705 (1984).

Estes v. *Texas,* 381 U.S. 532 (1965).

Federated Publications v. *Kurtz,* 94 Wn.2d 51 (1980).

Federated Publications v. *Swedberg,* 96 Wn.2d 13 (1981).

Florida v. *Green,* 7 M.L. Rept. 1025 (1981).

Florida v. *Palm Beach Newspapers,* 7 M.L. Rept. 1021 (1981).

Florida Publishing v. *Morgan,* 322 S.E.2d 233 (1984).

Gannett v. *DePasquale,* 99 S.Ct. 2898 (1979).

Globe Newspapers v. *Superior Court,* 102 S.Ct. 2613 (1982).

in re *Globe Newspapers,* 729 F.2d 572 (1984).

in re *Herald Co.,* 734 F.2d 93 (1984).

Irvin v. *Dowd,* 366 U.S. 717 (1961).

in re *J.S.,* 438 A.2d 1125 (1981).

Kansas City Star v. *Fossey,* 630 P.2d 1176 (1981).

Kearns-Tribune v. *Lewis,* 10 M.L. Rept. 1737 (1984).

in re *Knight Publishing,* 743 F.2d 231 (1984).

KPNX v. *Maricopa County Superior Court,* 678 P.2d 431 (1984).

KUTV v. Conder, 668 P.2d 513 (1983).

KUTV v. Wilkinson, 10 M.L. Rept. 1749 (1984).

Landmark Communications v. Virginia, 435 U.S. 829 (1978).

in re *Landmark Communications*, 12 MLR 1340 (1985).

Levine v. U.S. District Court, 764 F.2d 590 (1985).

Leviton v. U.S., 193 F.2d 848 (1951).

Marshall v. U.S., 360 U.S. 310 (1959).

Miami Herald v. Lewis, 8 M.L. Rept. 2281 (1982).

Murphy v. Florida, 95 S.Ct. 2031 (1975).

NBC v. Cooperman, 12 M.L. Rept. 2025 (1986).

Nebraska Press Association v. Stuart, 96 S.Ct. 2791 (1976).

Page Corp. v. Lumpkin, 8 M.L. Rept. 1824 (1982).

Pennekamp v. Florida, 328 U.S. 331 (1946).

Press Enterprise v. Riverside Superior Court, 104 S.Ct. 819 (1984).

Press Enterprise v. Riverside Superior Court, 106 S.Ct. 2735 (1986).

Richmond Newspapers v. Virginia, 448 U.S. 555 (1980).

in re *Reussell*, 726 F.2d 1007 (1984).

Seattle Times v. Ishikawa, 640 P.2d 716 (1982).

Shepherd v. Florida, 341 U.S. 50 (1951).

Sheppard v. Maxwell, 384 U.S. 333 (1966).

Smith v. Daily Mail Publishing Company, 99 S.Ct. 2667 (1979).

Times-Picayune v. Marullo, 466 SO.2d 1291 (1985).

U.S. v. Brooklier, 685 F.2d 1162 (1982).

U.S. v. Burr, 24 Fed. Cas. 49 No. 14692g (1807).

U.S. v. Chagra, 701 F.2d 354 (1983).

U.S. v. Criden, 675 F.2d 550 (1982).

U.S. v. Hastings, 695 F.2d 1278 (1983).

U.S. v. Kerley, 753 F.2d 617 (1985).

U.S. v. Smith, 776 F.2d 1104 (1985).

Waller v. Georgia, 104 S.Ct. 2210 (1984).

Westmoreland v. CBS, 752 F.2d 16 (1984).

8 OBSCENITY

Issues involving mass media law tend to come in cycles. In the early 1970s much attention was focused upon the problems of reporters and their sources. At the end of that decade, trials and pretrials seemed to command the most attention. Today, libel actions are the center of much anguish and concern. One media law issue, however, always seems to be at hand—never really in the center spotlight, but just offstage, ready to catch our attention for a short time when there is a lull. It is the issue of the creation, sale, distribution, and use of obscenity and pornography. Whether about films or books or records or magazines, someone, somewhere, always seems to be protesting or complaining about the presence of erotic material in a community. And a surprisingly large number of these complaints end up in the courts.

Of course much of the fuss is not about real obscenity, a legally defined category of material that the Supreme Court has said is beyond the protection of the First Amendment. The discussion or debate or protest instead focuses upon other kinds of sexually oriented material, material that generally does fall within the shield of the First Amendment. There has been great concern about the contents of books in our school libraries (see chapter 2 for a discussion of this issue). Persons in some states object to the cablecast of R-rated movies via cable television (see chapter 11 for more on this issue). In the fall of 1985 the nation's news spotlight fell upon a group of concerned parents who were protesting the blatant sexuality of contemporary song lyrics and music videos. These protestors even succeeded in getting a hearing on the question before the Senate of the United States. The fact that the leaders of the Parents Music Resource Center were the spouses of the Secretary of the Treasury and three United States Senators certainly enhanced their abilities to catch the congressional ear so quickly on this issue. Little came of the public furor. The recording industry ably defended itself in the hearings, but agreed to put warning labels on phonograph records with sexually explicit or drug-oriented lyrics, a step sure to help the sale of many marginal record albums (note what being "banned in Boston" did to the sale of many books). And six months later the issue seemed to have disappeared. Finally, in 1986 the Attorney General's Commission on Pornography issued a report amidst controversy and soon found that it was forced to go to court to defend some of its actions. (see pages 447–49) So a general dissatisfaction on the part of a vocal minority with the kind of recordings, movies, television programs, and magazines that are available in the United States seems to be constantly gurgling just below the surface in this country, erupting occasionally here and there.

The focus of this chapter is obscenity, a somewhat narrower issue. Obscenity is not protected by the First Amendment. The books in school libraries, the R-rated movies on cable television, the song lyrics noted above and much of the material attacked by the Meese Commission on Pornography are protected by the First Amendment and are not technically or legally obscene. But we really don't have a good word for this other kind of material, so often it too is designated as obscenity. After a brief introduction to the subject, a short history of the law of obscenity in the United States is presented. We will see how the Supreme Court has defined obscenity. We will also focus upon some ways in which communities are attempting to control the distribution and sale of obscenities, means beyond the traditional criminal prosecution.

Definitions for obscenity can be found in many places. In reputable dictionaries among the meanings for the word *obscene* is "indecent, lewd, or licentious." In turn, we will find *licentious* to mean "lewd or lascivious." Further research shows that *lascivious* means "inclined to be lewd or lustful." *Lustful* proves to mean "having lewd desires." Finally, *lewd* turns out to mean "indecent or obscene." We have come full circle.

The courts themselves have been in a constant state of confusion over the matter of obscenity. In 1948 the Ohio Court of Common Pleas wrote (*State* v. *Lerner*):

> Obscenity is not a legal term. It cannot be defined so that it will mean the same to all people, all the time everywhere. Obscenity is very much a figment of the imagination—an indefinable something in the minds of some and not in the minds of others, and it is not the same in the minds of the people of every clime and country, nor the same today that it was yesterday and will be tomorrow.

Former justice of the United States Supreme Court John Marshall Harlan expressed a similar kind of frustration when he warned, "Anyone who undertakes to examine the Supreme Court's decisions since *Roth* which have held particular material obscene or not obscene would find himself in utter bewilderment" (*Ginsberg* v. *New York,* 1968). Harlan referred at least partially to the fact that between the *Roth* case in 1957 and 1968, when he wrote that comment, the High Court had published signed opinions in thirteen obscenity cases. Fifty-four separate opinions were published in those thirteen cases!

Social scientists have also entered the definitional fray. Probably the most well-known definition of pornography is that of Eberhard and Phyllis Kronhausen in their study *Pornography and the Law.* The researchers said that the main purpose of pornography is to stimulate an erotic response. They also listed several characteristics of pornography, among which were heavy emphasis on the physiological reponses of participants, heavy emphasis on aberrant or forbidden forms of sexuality, heavy sadism and passive submission, and unrealistic presentation of both sexual activities and sexual capacities. Anthropologist Margaret Mead defined pornography as "words or acts or representations that are calculated to stimulate sex feelings independent of the presence of another loved and chosen human being." But even these kinds of definitions contain little precision and little agreement. Sexual aberrations that stimulate some persons nauseate others. The clothed body is far more erotic to some people than is naked flesh.

The general governmental response to obscenity and pornography has been to pass laws against it. There are federal laws, state laws, city laws, county laws, township laws, and so forth. There are laws against importing obscenity, transporting it in interstate commerce, mailing it, or broadcasting it over the radio and television. There are laws against publishing it, distributing it, selling it, displaying it, circulating it, and even possessing it if you plan to distribute it, sell it, display it, or circulate it.

The fact that obscenity is such an elusive concept to define makes prosecution extremely difficult sometimes. An obscenity case is not like a bank robbery or like most other crime for that matter, where everyone agrees that a criminal act has occurred (e.g., a bank robbery) and the legal debate is about whether the defendant is the robber. In an obscenity case there is usually agreement that the defendant did commit the act (e.g., sold a book or showed a movie). The debate is over whether what the defendant did was a criminal act, whether the book was obscene or not.

The ambiguities in the law also make life less than certain for booksellers and theater operators. They really can never be certain whether a local jury will rule that the books in the morning mail are obscene and whether selling a copy of such books is a criminal act.

Professor Paul Freund neatly summarized many of the problems of obscenity in a speech before the Twenty-Ninth Annual Judicial Conference in 1966 (Federal Rules Decisions, 1966):

> The problem is rendered difficult, I think, because we are working with old statutes, based on outmoded, or at least unexamined assumptions, with poorly defined conceptions of the subject matter, directed at the protection of persons who don't want to be protected, without a very clear idea of why they need protection and from what.

Why is obscenity banned? For many persons this is the sixty-four-dollar question. Many police believe that pornography is somehow tied to sexual crimes, although there is very little evidence to support the notion. Many persons argue, as we will note later in this chapter, that dissemination of pornography and obscenity has a deleterious impact upon communities. This argument also has really little scientific evidence to support it. At the same time there is little evidence to support the argument of persons who oppose obscenity laws that distribution of the material has no impact at all. Some feminists suggest that pornography fosters violence against women. We will consider this argument in greater depth on pages 434–35. Probably the best reason to explain why obscenity is banned is that it has been banned for more than one hundred years, and once a good suppression is started, it is hard to stop. Once an obscenity law goes on the books, it usually stays there, often virtually unenforced. Nevertheless, legislators rarely vote for repeal of an obscenity law. To many constituents a vote for repeal is a vote for obscenity. That could be a heavy cross to bear during an election. ◆

EARLY OBSCENITY LAW

The Puritans were not the first to pass laws against obscene books and pictures. There is some confusion about obscenity laws during the colonial period, because many persons argue that pre-Revolutionary laws against blasphemy also prohibited obscenity. However, the best evidence available does not support this argument. Some of the other facts we know, or do not know, about pornography in the eighteenth and early nineteenth centuries are these.

Substantial amounts of pornography were in circulation at that time, some of it homegrown, much of it imported. As busy as he was, Benjamin Franklin still had time to write erotic literature.

We do not know whether the drafters of the Bill of Rights intended to include obscenity within the mantle of protection offered by the First Amendment. Various justices of the Supreme Court, including Justice Brennan in his opinion in 1957 in the famous case of *Roth* v. *U.S.,* have argued that the framers of the First Amendment never meant to protect obscene materials through the guarantees of free speech and press. While this assertion may sound logical, we have been unable to find any evidence to support it. Court records are devoid of evidence of obscenity prosecutions until 1815, when a man named Jesse Sharpless was fined for exhibiting a picture of a man "in an imprudent posture with a woman." Earlier, other persons were tried for offenses tied to obscenity, but they were tried under the common law for theological crimes against God, not for merely displaying erotic pictures. In 1821 Peter Holmes was convicted for publishing an edition of John Cleland's *Memoirs of a Woman of Pleasure,* better known to us as *Fanny Hill.* Although the book was first published in 1740, the prosecution in Massachusetts was based not on the original version, but on an edition in which Holmes added both more explicit text and pictures.

In the late 1820s and 1830s, the nation experienced the first strong attack on obscenity when several states passed laws limiting the distribution and sale of such material. Why should obscenity laws be passed at that particular period in our history? No one knows for certain, but numerous contemporary events and conditions may have been factors. This was a period of popular reform movements such as abolition, prohibition, and women's rights. It was also a time in which universal free education made great strides and more people were able to read, thereby increasing the market for erotic literature.

The changes in printing technology that made publishing of books and magazines less expensive could also have resulted in wider distribution and visibility of erotic material. The more visible and widespread such material became, the better target it also became for reformers. Laws were the result.

The first of dozens of federal laws was passed in 1842. It was a customs law and prohibited importation of obscene paintings, lithographs, engravings, and so forth. The law was amended many times to prohibit more and more kinds of materials. The first postal law was passed in 1865, but it was an ineffective measure because the government had no authority to exclude material from the mails, only to bring a prosecution after the shipment was delivered. In 1873 a more effective law was adopted. This was largely the handiwork of Anthony Comstock, whom some authorities have described as a zealous reformer who got a thrill from suppressing what other people liked. First it was liquor that Comstock sought to snuff out. Then he attacked prostitution. To him there was no such thing as erotic art, only pornography. With the help of the Protestant leaders in New York and the Young Men's Christian Association, Comstock succeeded in gaining passage, first, of a New York law against obscenity and then, in 1873, of a federal law, the so-called Comstock Law. After passage of the bill, Comstock was named a special agent for the Post Office Department, and he worked with his Committee for the Suppression of Vice for more than forty years to stamp out smut. As a kind of incentive the government gave Comstock a percentage of all the fines collected on successful prosecutions based on his work. It has been suggested that he may be the first man to have made a million dollars from pornography.

The 1873 law was simple: All obscene books, pamphlets, pictures, and so forth, were declared to be nonmailable. Violation of the law could result in a fine of $5,000 and five years in jail for the first offense and $10,000 and ten years for each offense thereafter. The Congress did not define obscenity, however, but left that to the courts.

After passage of this spate of laws in the late nineteenth century, the country underwent a seventy-year period of censorship of erotic material. Government censors tended to lump all erotic material together. They made no attempt to distinguish art from smut—Boccacio's *Decameron* from *The Dance with the Dominant Whip* or other junk literature. The Post Office Department banned books on sex education as well as medical journals that dealt with sexual problems. The *American Journal of Eugenics* (the study of hereditary improvement) was declared nonmailable at one point because it carried an advertisement for a book entitled *The History of Prostitution*. The *Journal* was not obscene, but the book advertised in its pages was considered offensive. The *Journal* therefore was not allowed to be sent through the mails.

In the 1930s the Post Office Department banned, among other books, John O'Hara's *Appointment in Samara,* Hemingway's *For Whom the Bell Tolls,* and nearly everything that Erskine Caldwell wrote. In the forties the list included *From Here to Eternity, Butterfield Eight,* and *Memoirs of Hecate County.* Lots of men's magazines, humor magazines, scandal magazines (e.g., *Confidential*), and even a skin diver's manual (because it contained pictures of several female divers with breasts exposed) were barred from the mails, and the publishers were often prosecuted.

The postal service used various devices in addition to prosecution as means of controlling pornography. It attempted to strip some publications of their second-class mailing subsidy because they failed to publish work that was for the public good. Obscenity was not for the public good, postal officials claimed. This ploy failed after a time (see *Hannegan* v. *Esquire,* 1946). The Post Office Department also used the mail block against publishers whose magazines contained solicitations for erotic materials. For example, if a magazine advertised that a reader could order an erotic book by sending $2 to the publisher, the postal service stopped delivering mail to the publisher in order to keep those book orders from being delivered. The publisher received no mail at all! Not an electric bill, not a bank statement, nothing. The courts declared this action illegal, but the post office continued the practice for several years (*Walker* v. *Popenoe,* 1945). According to Patricia Robertus in her study of the Post Office Department ("Postal Control of Obscene Literature 1942–1957"), postal regulations were so restrictive that in the early 1940s a magazine with the power of *Esquire* took advance copies of both stories and layouts to postal authorities to see whether they met postal standards of mailability. In some instances postal officials asked for changes and got them. This is informal prior censorship at its boldest.

Laws against importation were also prosecuted vigorously, and customs agents, until the 1930s at least, rarely discriminated between works that were art and works that were trash. Consequently, there are scores of horror stories of customs officials destroying art works, art catalogs, religious works, and other materials that they believed to be obscene.

This era of intense censorship of erotic or sexually oriented material parallels the struggle for freedom of the press that radicals and the organizers of labor unions endured (see chapter 2) with one exception: whereas the courts grew more tolerant of aberrant political and economic philosophy, they showed little tolerance for erotic materials. Except for striking down some of the Post Office Department's most outrageous censorship techniques, the Supreme Court stayed out of the fray, leaving the lower courts to work out the definition of obscenity and construct constitutional guidelines. That is, the Supreme Court stayed out until 1957, when it entered the controversy wholeheartedly (*Roth* v. *U.S.*) and has been there ever since, attempting to explain to judges, lawyers, censors, writers, artists, filmmakers, and other people what the term *obscenity* means when used by the Court. As you will no doubt conclude after reading the next section, the efforts of the Court in this endeavor have not been terribly effective.

Since 1957 when the United States Supreme Court ruled in *Roth* v. *United States* (pages 417–19) that obscenity falls outside the general protection granted to speech and press under the First Amendment, courts have been forced to attempt to define what is and what is not obscene. The ultimate responsibility has fallen to the Supreme Court as the final arbiter of the meaning of the Constitution. In the twenty years between 1957 and 1977, the High Court heard arguments in almost ninety obscenity cases and wrote opinions in nearly forty of the cases. The remainder of the cases were decided by **per curiam** rulings (this term is explained on page 26). Yet most observers agree that the Court has failed in the task of defining obscenity in a comprehensive and unambiguous fashion.

The Supreme Court borrowed and devised various tests in the past century in its frequent attempts to describe obscenity definitively. None of the tests have been satisfactory, but some were worse than others. The fatal defect in each test is that it is made up of words, words that have different meanings for different people. For example, the test in use today declares that if a work has serious literary value it is not obscene. What does "serious literary value" mean? A comic book may have serious literary value for some people. At the other end of the spectrum, even professors of literature haggle among themselves about whether some of the classics really have serious literary value. What we are faced with, therefore, is a dispute over not only the kinds of works that are obscene, but also the meaning of the words the courts use to define obscenity.

Three important legal tests of obscenity were developed during the past one hundred years or so. The *Hicklin* rule of the late nineteenth century was used by judges to define obscenity for more than seventy-five years. This rule was abandoned in the late fifties and sixties in favor of what was called the *Roth-Memoirs* test. Then in the early seventies the United States Supreme Court fashioned still another test, the *Miller* test, which supplanted the *Roth-Memoirs* definition of obscenity. We will examine the *Hicklin* rule and the *Roth-Memoirs* test to help explain the *Miller* test, which is currently the law in the United States. We will also look at some other obscenity problems faced by the Supreme Court, as well as at a report issued by a Presidential Commission on Obscenity and Pornography.

The *Hicklin* Rule

The first widely used American test of obscenity was the *Hicklin* rule. The United States Supreme Court borrowed the *Hicklin* rule from British law when it was called upon to undertake an early interpretation of the 1873 postal statute on obscenity. Benjamin Hicklin was the recorder of London who presided over an obscenity trial in that city in the 1860s. He ruled that the pamphlet in question was not obscene, but on appeal by the government, a higher court reversed the decision. Lord Chief Justice Alexander Cockburn handed down a ruling that included a definition of obscenity, a definition to which poor Benjamin Hicklin's name has been attached ever since (*Regina* v. *Hicklin,* 1868).

The *Hicklin* rule says that a work is obscene if it has a tendency to deprave and corrupt those whose minds are open to such immoral influences and into whose hands it might happen to fall.

Look at the elements of this test for a moment. First, a work is obscene if it has a tendency to deprave and corrupt. It does not have to deprave and corrupt, but only a tendency to deprave and corrupt is required; that is, it might deprave and corrupt. You can decide for yourself what *deprave* and *corrupt* mean. The second aspect of the test was even deadlier for authors and painters. Whom must the work have a tendency to deprave and corrupt? Those whose minds are open to such influences; in other words, anyone who runs across the book or drawing. Children's minds are obviously open to depravation and corruption from obscenity. Children might also run across such works in a library or at a bookstore. Therefore, the *Hicklin* rule comes down to this: If a book might have an impact upon a child or an extremely sensitive person, it is obscene and no one can read it. The *Hicklin* rule reduced the population of the nation to reading what was fit only for children.

In adopting the *Hicklin* rule American courts also decided that if any part of a book or play or magazine or whatever was obscene, the entire work was then obscene. Selected passages that might be harmful to children could result in an entire book or magazine being banned. The *Hicklin* rule was an extremely onerous test that was used for about seventy-five years. This test was what made prosecution of obscenity so easy in the twenties, thirties, and forties, and success in prosecution made government censors even more aggressive in rooting out "filth" and "smut."

In 1957 the Supreme Court wrote the obituary for the *Hicklin* rule when it declared that condemning the adult population to read only what children might safely read was unconstitutional (*Butler* v. *Michigan,* 1957). Various lower courts had tentatively reached this conclusion in the preceding fifty years, but the *Hicklin* rule remained law in most jurisdictions.

SUMMARY

Prosecutions for obscenity did not occur in this nation until the early nineteenth century. In the 1820s and 1830s many states adopted their first obscenity laws. The first federal law was passed in 1842. The government actively prosecuted obscenity in the wake of the Civil War, and in 1873 the Congress adopted a strict new obscenity law. Obscenity was defined by the Supreme Court as being anything that has a tendency to deprave and corrupt those whose minds might be open to such immoral influences and into whose hands it might happen to fall. This was called the *Hicklin rule*. The rule meant that if any part of a book or other work had the tendency to deprave or corrupt any person (such as a child or overly sensitive individual) who might happen to see the work, the material was obscene and no person could buy it or see it.

<table>
<tr><td>

ROTH-MEMOIRS
TEST

</td><td>

The 1957 decision in *Butler* was the first of a long series of High Court rulings that by 1966 had fashioned a new test for determining obscenity. Although it was not apparent in the beginning, the key cases, *Roth* v. *U.S.* in 1957 and *A Book Named John Cleland's Memoirs of a Woman of Pleasure* v. *Massachusetts* in 1966 (and a dozen or so lesser decisions in between), resulted in liberalizing the law with regard to obscenity (see, for example, *Manuel Enterprises* v. *Day,* 1962, and *Jacobellis* v. *Ohio,* 1964).

</td></tr>
</table>

In 1957 the High Court announced definitively that obscenity is not protected by the First Amendment. Justice William Brennan, who was to be the chief architect of the Court's new obscenity standards during the next nine years, wrote that while all ideas that have even the slightest redeeming social importance are entitled to the full protection of the First Amendment, obscenity and pornography were not included within this protection. In the *Roth* decision Brennan wrote, ". . . implicit in the history of the First Amendment is the rejection of obscenity as utterly without redeeming social importance."

By placing obscenity beyond the pale of First Amendment protection, the Court silenced those persons who believed the clear-and-present-danger test should be used for determining obscenity as well as for determining dangerous political speech. Since obscenity is not guaranteed the protection of freedom of the press, the clear-and-present-danger test does not apply. What is obscene then? In the *Roth* case Brennan said that a work is obscene if, to the average person, applying contemporary community standards, the dominant theme of the material, taken as a whole, appeals to prurient interest. The Court continued to reshape this test slightly until 1966, when in the *Memoirs* case the test evolved into the three-part definition that was used for nearly seven years. Under the *Roth-Memoirs* test, before a court can rule that a work is obscene, three requirements must be met.

First, the dominant theme of the material taken as a whole must appeal to prurient interest in sex. Implicit in this part of the test is the concept that the prurient (erotic) appeal of a book or film is determined by its impact upon the average man or woman, not upon a child or an extremely sensitive person. Also, the dominant theme of the work, not just selected passages or a few pages, must have this prurient appeal.

Second, a court must find that the material is patently offensive because it affronts contemporary community standards relating to the description or representation of sexual matters. Something that is patently offensive is something that is clearly indecent, and while we are hesitant to use this term, some people have argued that *patently offensive* means hard-core pornography. By contemporary standards the Court meant current standards, but the Court did not define what it meant by community: Were the standards local, state, or national?

Third, before something can be found to be obscene it must be utterly without redeeming social value. That means to have no social value at all.

Two aspects of this test should be noted: First, all three of these elements had to be present before something was obscene. Something that was patently offensive and had a prurient appeal was still not legally obscene if it had redeeming social value. All three elements must coalesce. Second, it was not a balancing test. Social value was not weighed against prurient appeal. If there was any social value at all, the material was then not obscene. And this fact, probably more than any other, made prosecution of obscenity cases very difficult. Utterly without redeeming social value is a difficult standard to prove. Some appellate court judges believed that if even only one or two persons found some value in a book or movie it was not *utterly* without redeeming social value. Consequently, the typical tack taken by defense attorneys was to bring in expert witnesses—psychiatrists, English professors, art critics, and the like—to testify that the work had some value as sexual therapy or as an example of a certain type of literature or art. Voila! Redeeming social value.

As liberal as the *Roth-Memoirs* standard was, it was not liberal enough for some civil libertarians. Absolutists argued that because of the First Amendment, the government had no business telling people what they could read or watch. The First Amendment prohibition says there is to be no law abridging freedom of speech and press means no law. Judge Jerome Frank, who heard the *Roth* case in the court of appeals, argued that restrictions against obscenity are extremely dangerous (*U.S.* v. *Roth*, 1956):

> If the government possesses the power to censor publications which arouse sexual thoughts, regardless of whether those thoughts tend probably to transform themselves into anti-social behavior, why may not the government censor political and religious publications regardless of any causal relation to probably dangerous deeds?

Justice Brennan, who constructed the *Roth-Memoirs* test, dismissed such criticism. There is no social value to obscenity, he said, and therefore society loses little if it is banned.*

*Of interest is the fact that Brennan turned his back on his own ruling some sixteen years later in his dissent in *Miller* v. *California* (1973) and in the *Paris Theatre* (1973) case when the aging justice wrote:

Our experience since *Roth* requires us not only to abandon the effort to pick out obscene materials on a case by case basis, but also to reconsider a fundamental postulate of *Roth*: that there exists a definable class of sexually oriented expression that may be totally suppressed by the Federal and State governments. Assuming that such a class of expression does in fact exist, I am forced to conclude that the concept of "obscenity" cannot be defined with sufficient specificity and clarity to provide fair notice to persons who create and distribute sexually oriented materials, to prevent substantial erosion of protected speech as a by-product of the attempt to suppress unprotected speech. . . .

SUMMARY

In the 1950s and early 1960s, the Supreme Court adopted a new definition or test, for obscenity, the *Roth-Memoirs* test. The test had three main parts:

1. The dominant theme of the material, taken as a whole, appeals to an average person's prurient interest in sex. This modified the *Hicklin* rule in two ways:
   a. Material that was offensive to children or overly sensitive persons was no longer declared obscene for all.
   b. The entire work, not just a part of a book or film, must be considered when determining whether it is obscene.
2. The material is patently offensive because it affronts contemporary community standards relating to sexual matters. It was assumed that there was a single, national standard that was applicable to all parts of the country.
3. The material is utterly without redeeming social value. It has no value at all.

CONTEMPORARY OBSCENITY LAW

In 1967 the Commission on Obscenity and Pornography was established, at least in part, because of the judicial and scientific uncertainty regarding the effects of obscenity on persons who consume it. The commission, which was made up of social scientists, religious leaders, and government officials, spent two million dollars and two years studying what some observers called the "puzzle of pornography." At the end of the study, a majority of the commission—twelve of the seventeen members—concluded that there is no evidence that viewing obscenity produces harmful effects and recommended that all laws restricting the consumption of such materials by consenting adults be repealed. Three members of the commission fielded a vigorous dissent and two others said they believed in the findings of the commission but did not believe these findings warranted the repeal of all laws.

The study was roundly criticized by persons who disagreed with its conclusions—rightly so in some cases. There were no long-range studies on the effects of exposure to pornography, for example, and no in-depth clinical studies. In some of the surveys people were asked blatantly foolish questions. For example, one survey asked people if they had experienced a breakdown in morals or had gone "sex crazy" from viewing explicit sexual material. Who would say yes to those questions? Patients at mental hospitals were questioned regarding the influence of pornography on sex crimes they had committed.

The single survey that received the widest publicity was the one that discovered that 60 percent of the persons questioned believed that adults should be able to read and watch whatever they want. However, to another question in the same survey, 73 percent of the respondents said that sex scenes in movies that merely titillate should be censored. Moreover, in 1969 both the Harris and Gallup polls found that about 80 percent of the people wanted stiffer controls on obscenity and pornography.

Regardless of what the commission found or of the flaws in its research, its recommendations were never adopted. The Senate rejected the report out of hand, and Richard Nixon, who was president at that time, vowed that so long as he was in the White House there would be no relaxation of the national effort to control and eliminate smut from our national life. Nixon noted that despite the commission's scientific evidence to the contrary, "Centuries of civilization and ten minutes of common sense tell us otherwise." Adding a phrase that would come back to haunt him in a different context four years later, Nixon said, "American morality is not to be trifled with."

The *Miller* Test

In 1973 and 1974, in apparent agreement with the president, the Supreme Court handed down a series of rulings that reshaped the legal test for obscenity. The central case in this group of decisions was *Miller* v. *California* (1973), a suit that emanated from California. Marvin Miller was convicted of violating the California Penal Code for sending five unsolicited brochures to a restaurant in Newport Beach. The brochures, which advertised four erotic books and one film, contained pictures and drawings of men and women engaging in a variety of sexual activities. The recipient of the mailing complained to police, and Miller was prosecuted by state authorities.

In *Miller*, for the first time since 1957, a majority of the Supreme Court reached agreement on a definition of obscenity. Chief Justice Warren Burger and four other members of the High Court agreed that material is obscene if the following standards are met:

1. An average person, applying contemporary local community standards, finds that the work, taken as a whole, appeals to prurient interest.
2. The work depicts in a patently offensive way sexual conduct specifically defined by applicable state law.
3. The work in question lacks serious literary, artistic, political, or scientific value.

As in the *Roth-Memoirs* test, the implications and ambiguities in these three elements create the need for fuller explanation. As a result of the *Miller* ruling and subsequent obscenity decisions handed down by the Burger Court since 1973, some guidelines have emerged. Before the guidelines are examined in detail, it is instructive to look at the rationale presented by Chief Justice Burger for his movement away from the *Roth-Memoirs* test to more conservative standards.

Justification

As noted previously, until 1973 the High Court had justified regulation of obscenity by arguing that because such material lacks social value it is not intended to be protected by the First Amendment. But in the *Miller* and subsequent decisions, Chief Justice Burger took a less neutral approach and asserted that not only did such material lack social value, but it was also harmful to society.

In *Paris Adult Theatre I* v. *Slaton* (1973), a ruling handed down at the same time the *Miller* decision was announced, the Chief Justice said that there is a clear justification for banning adults-only theaters, even if they do not intrude upon the privacy of others and even if patrons are properly warned of the kind of film they will see. The justification is, he said, "the interest of the public in the quality of life and the total community environment, the tone of commerce in the great city centers and, possibly, the public safety itself."

Ignoring the majority report from the President's Commission on Obscenity and Pornography, Burger noted that the minority report states that there is an arguable correlation between obscene material and crime. Even if there were no scientific evidence, the Chief Justice wrote, "We do not demand of legislatures 'scientifically certain criteria of legislation,' for unprovable assumptions underlie much lawful state regulation of commercial and business affairs." There need not be conclusive proof of a connection between antisocial behavior and obscene material for a state legislature to reasonably conclude that such a connection exists or might exist, Burger said.

The basic thrust of the Burger argument is a kind of quality-of-life argument that many thoughtful scholars have made for several years. In the *Paris Theatre* opinion, Burger in fact quoted Professor Alexander Bickel, who represented the *New York Times* in the *Pentagon Papers* case. In 1971 in *The Public Interest,* concerning justification for regulation of obscenity, Bickel wrote:

> It concerns the tone of the society, the mode, or to use terms that have perhaps greater currency, the style and quality of life, now and in the future. A man may be entitled to read an obscene book in his room, or expose himself indecently there. . . . We should protect his privacy. But if he demands a right to obtain the books and pictures he wants in the market, and to foregather in public places—discreet, if you will, but accessible to all—with others who share his tastes, then to grant him his right is to affect the world about the rest of us, and to impinge on other privacies. Even supposing that each of us can, if he wishes, effectively avert the eye and stop the ear (which in truth we cannot) what is commonly read and seen and heard and done intrudes upon us all, want it or not.

Perhaps the most literate spokesman for this point of view is Harry M. Clor in his book *Obscenity and Public Morality* (1969). The book came out at a time when the Warren Court was pushing the limits of permissibility farther and farther, and Clor was chided for even thinking about a change of direction by the Supreme Court. Now it appears that the Court has adopted his logic, if not his standards.

Clor argues that some kind of common ethos is needed in order to have a community and that the agencies that formerly provided this ethos—schools, churches, families—do not do it any longer. The law should set the example, he says. "It must be a task of modern government and law to support and promote the public morality upon which a good social life depends."

To enforce his argument Clor quotes Aristotle (in *Politics*):

> The education of a citizen in the spirit of his constitution does not consist in his doing the actions in which the partisans of oligarchy or the adherents of democracy delight. It consists in his doing the actions by which an oligarchy or a democracy will be enabled to survive.

Clor also cites Walter Berns (in *Freedom, Virtue, and the First Amendment*):

> Since the way of the community depends upon citizens of a certain character, it must be the business of the law to promote that character. Thus, the formation of the character is the principal duty of government.

Clor concludes his argument:

> It is generally understood that, whatever other purposes such laws may have, they are also designed to implement community ethical standards.

This is a thoughtful argument, and while many authorities disagreed with it, many others thought it seemed to make some sense in the chaotic 1980s. There is another side to the coin, however, and perhaps Justice Brennan expresses it best in his dissent in the *Paris Theatre* (1973) ruling:

> I am now inclined to argue that the Constitution protects the right to receive information and ideas, and that this right to receive information and ideas, regardless of their social worth . . . is fundamental to our free society. . . . This right is closely tied . . . to the right to be free, except in very limited circumstances, from unwarranted governmental intrusions into one's privacy. . . . It is similarly related to the right of the individual, married or single, to be free from unwarranted governmental intrusion into matters so fundamentally affecting a person as the decision whether to bear or beget a child . . . and the right to exercise autonomous control over the development and expression of one's intellect, interests, tastes, and personality.

The Meaning of *Miller*

The three-part obscenity test laid down by Chief Justice Burger in the *Miller* case has proved to be as elusive and unsatisfying as previous tests devised by the judiciary. It is best understood when reduced to its essential elements.

Community Standards

The first element of the test concerns community standards: To an average person, applying contemporary local community standards, the work, taken as a whole, appeals to prurient interest. While this standard resembles the *Roth-Memoirs* test, the Supreme Court emphasized that local rather than national standards are to be applied, which represents a departure from the earlier rulings. The Supreme Court had previously been silent on this question. In 1964 in *Jacobellis* v. *Ohio*, Justice Brennan subscribed to the notion that the applicable community standard was a national one. Only one other justice joined Brennan in this opinion, but as the only word on the subject, it led many observers to believe that the community standards applicable under the *Roth-Memoirs* test were national standards. The Chief Justice rejected this in *Miller*, arguing that it was silly to suggest that persons in a small town in Utah shared the same standards as persons living in Los Angeles.

The application of local standards has placed significant emphasis upon the trier of fact in the case. This can be the trial judge, but more often it is the jury. The Supreme Court expects the trier of fact to rely upon his own knowledge of the standards in the community to determine the applicable standards in an obscenity case. In 1974 in *Hamling* v. *United States,* Justice Rehnquist wrote:

> This Court has emphasized on more than one occasion that a principal concern in requiring that a judgment be made on the basis of contemporary community standards is to assure that the material is judged neither on the basis of each juror's personal opinion nor by its effect on a particular sensitive or insensitive person or group.

The matter of instructing jurors in the question of determining community standards surfaced quickly as a problem. Jurors are not supposed to rely on their own subjective preference; the jury is not a distillation of the standards of the community. The jurors are supposed to apply standards that they believe to be the prevailing ones in the community, standards that can be more conservative or more liberal than their own. Justice Rehnquist noted in his *Hamling* opinion that the jury should not judge the material on the basis of how it might affect a particularly sensitive person. Yet there are sensitive persons in every community. Do not their tastes matter, too?

In California a trial judge, in giving jurors instructions in an obscenity trial told them to consider the effect of the material upon members of the community as a whole, including children and sensitive persons. In 1978 in *Pinkus* v. *U.S.,* the Supreme Court ruled that the instructions to the jury had been faulty. In considering community standards, "Children are not to be included for these purposes as part of the 'community' . . . ," wrote Chief Justice Burger. However, instructing the jury to consider the impact of the material upon sensitive or insensitive persons is permissible, so long as these persons are looked at as a part of the entire community. Burger wrote:

> In the narrow and limited context of this case, the community includes all adults who comprise it, and a jury can consider them all in determining relevant community standards. The vice is in focusing upon the most susceptible or sensitive members when judging the obscenity of the materials, not in including them along with all others in the community.

In summary, then, the jury is most often the fact finder of community standards. The jurors are supposed to rely upon their knowledge of the standards of the adult members of the entire community to determine whether the material appeals to prurient interest or is patently offensive. The jurors are not supposed to apply their own standards. One commentator notes that this approach, which places such heavy emphasis on the jury, assumes that jurors know the prevailing standards in the community as well as have the needed exposure to "all manner of descriptions or representations of sexual matters, whether spoken, written or performed." This assumption is largely untested.

Which community is meant? Chief Justice Burger ruled in *Miller* that local community standards must prevail. Does this mean state, county, city, or neighborhood? In many instances state standards are the ones that apply. In some instances state High Courts have even ruled that cities and counties have no right to pass obscenity laws, since the states, through state statutes, have preempted the field of criminalizing obscenity (see *Spokane* v. *Portch,* 1979, for example). Yet for all practical purposes, since jurors are most normally drawn from county or city voting lists and jurors are expected to rely upon their knowledge of community standards, local standards are applied in determining the obscenity of the material.

In 1977 the Supreme Court was forced to consider an unusual case from Iowa that focused upon the role of the state in determining community standards. Between 1974 and 1978 Iowa state law prohibited only the distribution of obscene materials to minors. During this period Jerry Lee Smith used the United States postal service to distribute within Iowa several erotic magazines to adult recipients. His distribution did not violate state law, but he was charged with violating federal obscenity laws that prohibit the mailing of obscene material. At his trial Smith argued that since the state did not prohibit the distribution of such material to adults, his mailings had not offended the prevailing community standards. The federal trial judge nevertheless instructed jurors to draw upon their knowledge of the views of the people in the community to determine community standards. As part of their determination jurors could consider the state law, but the absence of statutes prohibiting the distribution of obscene material among adults was not a controlling factor in determining community standards. The Supreme Court, by a five-to-four vote, supported this position. The jury's discretion to determine community standards was not circumscribed by state law or the absence of state law (*Smith* v. *U.S.,* 1977). Justice Blackmun wrote that it would be inappropriate for a state legislature to attempt to freeze a jury to one definition of contemporary community standards. The state legislature can define within a statute the kinds of conduct that will be regulated by the state. It can adopt a geographic limit in the determination of community standards by defining the area from which the jury can be selected in an obscenity case. But it must leave to the jury the question of community standards. Blackmun also pointed out that this was a federal case. "The community standards aspects of the federal law present issues of federal law upon which a state statute such as Iowa's cannot have a conclusive effect," he added (*Smith* v. *U.S.*, 1977).

The question of applicable community standards is also an important factor in cases that involve the shipment of erotic material over long distances and its importation from abroad. Consider these hypothetical situations. A woman in New York mails obscene materials to another woman in Nebraska. She is arrested and tried. At her trial, do the community standards of New York or the standards of Nebraska apply? Here is another case. A man in Florida orders erotic material from Sweden. The material enters this country in Boston and is seized, and the United States customs service calls for a determination of whether the material is obscene. What community standards should apply? Those of Boston or of Florida? The answers to these questions are tentative, but case law suggests the following guidelines.

In cases involving violation of postal laws, the government may choose to try the case in the community in which the material was sent or received or in any district through which the material passed (see section on postal censorship, pages 442–44). Consequently, the applicable standards are the standards existing in the community in which the trial is held. In the hypothetical cases just given, if the government chose to prosecute the defendant in New York, the standards of that community would apply. If the government chose to prosecute in Nebraska, those community standards would apply. Recently a postmaster in Oregon asked a postmaster in Wyoming to use a false name and solicit by mail erotic material distributed by an Oregon man. The defendant sent the material to Wyoming, was arrested and tried, and Wyoming community standards were applied. The record showed that the defendant had never resided in, traveled through, or had any previous business contact in Wyoming—prior to the time he sent the erotic matter through the mails to the Wyoming postmaster. Still, the Tenth Circuit Court of Appeals concluded (*U.S.* v. *Blucher,* 1978):

> So long as *Hamling* is the law, publishers and distributors everywhere who are willing to fill subscriptions nationwide are subject to the creative zeal of federal enforcement officers who are free to shop for venue from which juries with the most restrictive views are likely to be impanelled. . . .

A similar decision was reached in *U.S.* v. *McManus* (1976).

In cases involving import laws and customs regulations, the community standards of the district in which the material was seized—not of the district in which the addressee lives—are normally the applicable standards. In the hypothetical case just cited, Boston standards rather than Florida standards would be applied. When customs officials seized hundreds of printed articles in New York, they sent notices to all 573 intended recipients advising them that the material would be destroyed within twenty days because it was obscene, unless the recipients made a claim challenging the government determination that importation of the material was illegal. Fourteen persons made such claims and sought hearings. None of these persons lived in New York, yet the Second Circuit Court of Appeals ruled that since the material was seized in New York and since the obscenity hearing would be held in New York, New York community standards should be applied (*U.S.* v. *Various Articles of Obscene Merchandise,* 1977).

If the first element of the *Miller* obscenity test appears to give the trier of fact (judge or jury) almost total power in determining what is and is not obscene, the second element, as interpreted by the Supreme Court, limits that power.

Patent Offensiveness

The second element of the *Miller* test says that a work is obscene if it depicts in a patently offensive way sexual conduct specifically defined by applicable state law. There are two basic parts to the test: (1) patent offensiveness as determined by community standards and (2) sexual conduct specifically defined by applicable state law. Each of the two elements is important.

Patent offensiveness is to be determined by the trier of the fact, the judge or the jury, using contemporary community standards. But that phrase is deceptive, because the courts have ruled that the discretion of juror or judge in determining patent offensiveness is not unlimited. The kinds of conduct that may be labeled "patently offensive" in a prosecution for obscenity are hardcore types of conduct. A 1974 Supreme Court ruling illustrates this seeming contradiction. In 1974 in *Jenkins* v. *Georgia* the Supreme Court was faced with the decision by a Georgia jury that the movie *Carnal Knowledge* was obscene. The film was an R-rated movie, and while it had scenes that included partial nudity, it contained no explicit sexual scenes usually associated with X-rated films. Nevertheless, because in the *Miller* ruling the United States Supreme Court had given communities the power to determine community standards and because this jury found that *Carnal Knowledge* violated those standards, the Georgia Supreme Court upheld the conviction.

The United States Supreme Court reversed the ruling, saying that the Georgia courts obviously misunderstood the *Miller* decision. The jury did have the right to determine local standards, but only those descriptions or depictions of sexual conduct that are patently offensive can be censored, regardless of local standards. Justice Rehnquist noted that in the *Miller* case Chief Justice Burger gave two examples of the kind of patently offensive material he was talking about. These examples included "representations or descriptions of ultimate sexual acts, normal or perverted, actual or simulated," and "representations or descriptions of masturbation, excretory functions, and lewd exhibition of the genitals." Rehnquist said that while this catalog of descriptions was not exhaustive, it was "intended to fix substantive constitutional limitations . . . on the type of material . . . subject to a determination of obscenity" (*Jenkins* v. *Georgia,* 1974). Therefore, under the second part of the *Miller* test, a jury is limited in what it can find to be obscene to what commentators call hard-core pornography.

The second element in the Miller test seems to be confusing in another way as well. Chief Justice Burger wrote that the descriptions or depictions of sexual conduct that are banned have to be specifically defined by the applicable state law as written or authoritatively construed. This sounds as though before a state can prohibit a description of a certain kind of sexual conduct, the state must pass a specific law defining that kind of material.

How specific does the applicable state statute have to be? Not very. The High Court approved an Ohio statute that defined material as being obscene if it contained a display or description of nudity, sexual excitement, sexual conduct, bestiality, extreme or bizarre violence, cruelty, brutality, or human bodily functions or eliminations.

What if a state law does not define obscenity? What if it merely prohibits "obscene materials"? This is really not a problem, according to Chief Justice Burger, who ruled that it is sufficient in such states if the state supreme court rules that the term *obscene materials* in the law means specific descriptions of sexual conduct. For example, the U.S. Supreme Court in 1977 upheld the conviction of an individual who had been found guilty of selling two sadomasochistic publications. The defendant argued that the state law did not specifically prohibit the sale of such material. But Justice White and four members of the High Court ruled that such an argument had no merit, that such material had been held to violate Illinois state law long before the *Miller* ruling, and that such authoritative construction of the statute was sufficient to meet the test outlined under *Miller.* The examples cited by Chief Justice Burger in the *Miller* ruling, according to Justice White, were not exhaustive, but simply illustrative of the kinds of materials that could be considered patently offensive (*Ward* v. *Illinois,* 1977). Since 1973 most state obscenity statutes have been found to comply with the *Miller* standards, because of either specific descriptive language in the statute or authoritative construction by the state's High Court.

Serious Value

To be obscene a work must lack serious literary, artistic, political, or scientific value. This is the third element of the *Miller* test. This element is designed to be a kind of check on the first two parts of the test, an effort to protect important works from obscenity prosecution. "The judicial role is more pronounced in the determination of the 'serious value' of the material, which is *not* [author emphasis] to be judged by the tastes of the average person or measured by community standards" (*Penthouse* v. *Mcauliffe,* 1981).

This standard is considerably narrower than the "utterly without re-deeming social value" standard of the *Roth-Memoirs* test. Both prosecutors and defendants often introduce "expert" testimony to persuade a judge that a film or book has some kind of serious value. Courts often have difficulty sorting out the conflicting statements from these witnesses because the Supreme Court has never defined "serious value" for the lower courts. In *Miller* v. *California* Chief Justice Burger warned lower courts to "always remain sensitive to any infringement on genuinely serious literary, artistic, political, or scientific value," but such an admonition does not help define the concept. Many courts have ruled that mere entertainment value in a film or book or the existence of a tenuous story line or the inclusion of an isolated idea are usually insufficient to redeem an otherwise obscene work (see *Penthouse* v. *Mcauliffe,* 1981, for example).

A United States district judge in Georgia defined serious value in this way when he was asked to determine whether the film *Caligula* was obscene (*Penthouse* v. *Mcauliffe,* 1981):

> We believe that by the phrase "serious value" the Supreme Court meant to extend constitutional protection to material which advocates ideas and in which the ideas are not used merely as a disguise or a sham for presenting obscenity. The ideas must be a substantial part of the material and treated in a nonfrivolous manner. . . . We do not believe that the "serious value" test of *Miller* was meant to extend protection only to works which are artistic successes or which include textual political commentary. All political views and ideas, including historical narrative and social criticism, are protected, as are all serious artistic and intellectual efforts, whether they appeal to the average person or not.

The judge ruled that the film, which portrays violence and explicit sex in telling the story of the life of Roman Emperor Caligula during his reign from A.D. 37 to A.D. 41, had serious political and artistic value.

The Supreme Court has also instructed lower appellate courts not to hesitate to closely scrutinize trial court judgments regarding "serious value." Justice Blackmun in *Smith* v. *U.S.* noted that the determination of whether a book or magazine or film lacks value "is particularly amenable to appellate review." Hence, while an appellate court should be reluctant to second-guess a jury on a determination of contemporary community standards, it should not be hesitant in making an independent determination that a work either has or has not literary, artistic, political, or scientific value (*Smith* v. *U.S.,* 1977).

The Impact of *Miller*

There was considerable speculation after the adoption of the more conservative *Miller* test by the Supreme Court that the nation would see an aggressive prosecution of the purveyors of obscenity. The single serious impediment to such prosecutions prior to *Miller,* the requirement that a work be utterly without redeeming social value, no longer blocked the often zealous local and federal authorities. But this, in fact, has not happened. Researchers discovered in 1977—four years after the promulgation of the *Miller* test—that prosecutors, judges, police officials, and defense attorneys reported a drop in the number of criminal prosecutions for obscenity (see "An Empirical Inquiry Into the Effects of *Miller* v. *California* on the Control of Obscenity"). And little appears to have changed since 1977.

Why? Some suggest that the *Miller* test is not really more conservative than the *Roth-Memoirs* test. Researchers Kenneth Mott and Christine Kellett have asserted in the *Suffolk University Law Review* that by defining community standards as local standards, the Supreme Court has seriously complicated obscenity prosecutions. They noted:

> The uniqueness of each smaller community makes it necessary for the state to move against a distributor or his agent in a separate action in each locality. Ironically, the desire of the Burger Court to give each community the privilege of setting its own standards has been defeated by the correlative duty of the community to prove the obscene nature of the material without relying on judgments of obscenity from other communities.

The result of this phenomenon has raised the cost of obscenity prosecutions and made them less attractive to budget-conscious public officials. The Los Angeles city attorney told researchers in 1977 that the average contested obscenity prosecution cost the city between $10,000 and $25,000. It costs much more today.

The increase in cost of prosecutions, the corresponding decrease in revenues at most levels of government, and the rise in numbers of other more serious crimes have forced prosecutors to be highly selective in moving against pornographers. This set of circumstances is another reason many observers believe that *Miller* has not wrought the anticipated change in the law. In the mid-1970s *New York Times* reporter James Sterba wrote, "The police say they have more important crimes to fight. Many local prosecutors comment that they have neither the time nor the money to spend cracking down on smut dealers." In 1977 prosecutors told New York University Law School researchers the same thing, and this circumstance leads to the conclusion that "despite the rising tide of sexually explicit materials, prosecutors have not committed more time and money to the battle against obscenity."

Finally, because of a legal-political phenomenon identified by political scientists as "compliance," there is some question whether the fine tuning that Chief Justice Burger did to the definition of obscenity really makes much difference on the streets, where pornography is sold and pornographers are arrested and tried.

Political scientists have proved "scientifically" a fact that good lawyers and judges have known for some time: simply because the United States Supreme Court says something is "the law" does not mean that it is "the law" at local levels, at least not right after a decision. Local noncompliance with Supreme Court rulings is not a new phenomenon, but it has become more apparent during the last quarter century. It is a function of the fact that a lawsuit is a dispute between two parties, and the resolution of that dispute by the courts technically affects only those two parties, not everyone else in a similar situation. If the Supreme Court rules that it is unconstitutional for the state of Maine to print a prayer on its license plates, the other forty-nine states would undoubtedly follow that ruling without being forced to, because it is really not a very important issue. However, if the Supreme Court tells Maine it cannot ban certain kinds of hard-core pornography, many other jurisdictions might be reluctant to follow that ruling until a court stops them from doing the same thing. Why? Because this issue seems to be more important. Technically, the states do not have to comply unless they are forced to by a court.

In a study of compliance with obscenity rulings in Oregon, Stephen L. Wasby wrote recently that one of the reasons for lack of compliance is the lack of agreement on what the Court intends by its opinion on the subject. "The development of Oregon obscenity policy," Wasby added, "gives evidence that the impact nationwide of a Supreme Court decision is by no means uniform. If there is as much variance in interpretation *within* one state as occurred in Oregon, certainly considerable variation must exist across the nation as a whole" ("The Pure and the Prurient: The Supreme Court, Obscenity and Oregon Policy").

What are the factors involved in compliance and noncompliance? Wasby identified several: role of the lawyers, legitimacy ascribed to the decision, direction of the decision, sentiment of the public, precision or ambiguity of the decision, decisiveness of the ruling, number of relevant opinions, and so forth.

What does compliance have to do with the impact of *Miller* on obscenity law? It has been suggested that local communities act largely unto themselves in prosecuting obscenity. The *Roth-Memoirs* test gave general guidelines for obscenity, which were followed as closely as possible. The changes in these guidelines wrought by the Burger opinion in *Miller* are too subtle to be reflected locally, where judges are forced to instruct juries in common language as to what is and what is not obscene. So sexually oriented materials that were protected by the First Amendment under the *Roth-Memoirs* test remain protected under the *Miller* test in most communities. And what was legally obscene under *Roth-Memoirs* remains obscene under *Miller*. While the changes in the law appear to be dramatic, except for the very few cases that are appealed and can be examined closely by high appellate courts, the changes in the law have had little impact for police, prosecutors, pornographers, and trial judges. The best definition of obscenity in any local community still remains what a local jury says is obscene and has changed little in the past fifteen years.

But some changes in obscenity law can be observed since the adoption of the *Miller* test. The Supreme Court is hearing far fewer obscenity cases than it did twenty years ago. Also, many communities have abandoned their attempts to regulate obscenity through criminal prosecution and today attempt to use civil suits or zoning regulations to control such erotic material (see pages 438–42 for a discussion of these means). Whether either of these changes is the result of *Miller* is unclear.

Selective Standards

Two other dimensions of the definition of obscenity that developed in the years prior to *Miller* seem to retain vitality today.

In 1966 in *Ginzburg* v. *U.S.,* the Supreme Court ruled that the manner in which material is marketed, advertised, and displayed can be a factor in determining whether a work is obscene or not. This case was the result of publisher Ralph Ginzburg's efforts to sell three different publications. In marketing these publications, Justice Brennan said, Ginzburg emphasized their erotic nature and thus was engaged in **"pandering"**—that is, in "the business of purveying textual or graphic matter openly advertised to appeal to the erotic interest of customers." This action can be a key factor in determining whether a publication or a film is obscene or not, Brennan said. Ginzburg's conviction was affirmed.

Richard Kuh, in *Foolish Figleaves,* cites as examples of pandering such schemes as using a provocative cover, using advertisements that list the previous bannings of the work, displaying the work along with other borderline items, and in various other ways promoting the erotic, deviant, or scatological appeal of the material. In 1977 in *Splawn* v. *California,* four members of the Supreme Court agreed with Justice Rehnquist's majority opinion that "evidence of pandering to prurient interests in the creation, promotion, or dissemination of material is relevant in determining whether the material was obscene." One year later, in writing for a seven-man majority, Chief Justice Burger noted, "We have held, and reaffirmed, that to aid a jury in its determination of whether materials are obscene, the methods of their creation, promotion, or dissemination are relevant. . ." (*Pinkus* v. *U.S.,* 1978). Hence it seems assured that if proof of pandering is introduced by the prosecution, the jury may consider it evidence in determining the obscenity of the books or films or magazines.

The Supreme Court has also ruled that states may adopt **variable obscenity standards** for juveniles and for adults; that is, material acceptable for sale to adults may not be acceptable for sale to children. A bookseller or a theater owner can be prosecuted for providing obscene material to young people. This is a standard that emerged in 1968 in *Ginsberg* v. *New York* and was upheld as recently as 1975 in *Erznoznik* v. *City of Jacksonville.* In the latter case the city forbade drive-in theaters to show movies in which female buttocks and bare breasts were shown if the theater screen was visible from the street. The ordinance, which was justified in part as a means of protecting the city's youth from exposure to such material, was defective according to the Supreme Court. The High Court said that laws aimed at setting variable standards of obscenity for adults and for children were permissible but must be carefully constructed. "Only in relatively narrow and well-defined circumstances may government bar public dissemination of protected materials to children," Justice Powell wrote. Banning the showing of nudity is simply not narrow enough; only materials that have significant erotic appeal to juveniles may be suppressed under such a statute, he added. A simple ban on all nudity, regardless of context, justification, or other factors, violates the First Amendment.

And of course the laws aimed at protecting children cannot substantially restrict what is available to adults. A Virginia statute prohibited the display for commercial purposes of sexually explicit material deemed harmful to juveniles. Materials that included nudity, sexual conduct, or described "sexual excitement" were included in the ban. Such a restriction affects many types of books that are perfectly legal to sell to adults. Booksellers who sold a wide range of books had one of four options under the statute. They could ban persons under eighteen from the store, but this would hurt the sale of books because the store would appear to be an adults-only facility, unattractive to many book buyers. Storeowners could establish adults-only sections in the store, but the ban covered so many different categories of works, this would be almost unworkable. For example, there would have to be two different photography book sections, one for "adults only" for the books that contained the occasional nude and one in the nonrestricted section.

Storeowners could refrain from stocking any book covered by the ban, but that would include a vast number of books, including some very popular bestselling works. Or these banned books could be carried behind the counter, again a problem by virtue of the tremendous number of books that would be restricted. The state defended the law under the Ginsberg standard in a suit brought by the American Booksellers, but the U.S. District Court said the statute was simply too broad and placed a substantial restriction upon adult access to protected material (*American Booksellers* v. *Strobel,* 1985; but see *Upper Midwest Booksellers* v. *Minneapolis,* 1985, where a more narrowly drawn ordinance aimed at protecting minors was upheld).

Child Pornography

In 1982 the United States Supreme Court unanimously upheld a New York statute aimed at limiting the distribution of child pornography. The state law prohibits any person from knowingly promoting a sexual performance by a child under the age of sixteen years by distributing material that photographically depicts such a performance. The statute explicitly defines sexual performance as sexual conduct and lists the kinds of conduct that are not permitted to be shown. Justice Byron White wrote that child pornography defined in the statute is unprotected speech and can be subject to content-based regulation. The state has a strong state interest in protecting the well-being of children. To help prevent the abuse of children who are made to engage in sexual conduct for commercial purposes, the state can prohibit the distribution of material that shows children engaged in such conduct, even if this material might not be obscene under the three-part *Miller* test. White said that when a judge considers photographic depictions of live sexual performances by children the *Miller* formulation should be adjusted in the following respects: "A trier of fact need not find that the material appeals to the prurient interest of the average person; it is not required that sexual conduct portrayed be done so in a patently offensive manner; and the material at issue need not be considered as a whole." The value of permitting live performances and photographic reproductions of children engaged in lewd sexual conduct is exceedingly modest, the Justice said. The law is aimed at stopping the sexual exploitation of children. One sure way to stop or at least reduce this exploitation is to ban the distribution of films in which children are depicted in sexual conduct. Distribution of written descriptions or other kinds of depictions (drawings) of children engaged in sexual conduct that are not otherwise obscene and that do not involve live performances are still protected by the First Amendment, White said (*New York* v. *Ferber,* 1982).

<table>
<tr><td>Pornography and Women</td><td>The most concerted but unsuccessful challenge to erotic material during this decade has come from an unlikely coalition of feminists and social conservatives such as the members of the Moral Majority. Ordinances drafted in Minneapolis, Indianapolis, Suffolk County, New York, and Los Angeles County, California, were aimed at blocking the sale and distribution of pornography on the grounds that it discriminates against women and fosters violence against women and children. The Minneapolis ordinance was drafted by two prominent feminists, Catherine MacKinnon, a professor of law at the University of Minnesota, and Andrea Dworkin, author of the 1981 book Pornography: Men Possessing Women.</td></tr>
</table>

Only the city of Indianapolis ultimately adopted such an ordinance, which created a civil cause of action for complainants aggrieved by any discriminatory practice prohibited by the ordinance, including the distribution of pornographic material. Complaints were to be investigated by the office of equal opportunity and if informal attempts to eliminate the discriminatory practice failed, a formal hearing could be held. Ultimately, the respondent in the case could face a court injunction blocking future discrimination, such as the distribution of certain magazines or books. Not even all feminist organizations supported the ordinance, which was highly controversial because of its definition of pornography. The ordinance went far beyond the traditional definition of obscenity or pornography. It declared that pornography shall mean the graphic sexually explicit subordination of women, whether in pictures or in words, that also includes one of the following:

1. Women are presented as sexual objects who enjoy pain or humiliation.
2. Women are presented as sexual objects who experience sexual pleasure in being raped.
3. Women are presented as sexual objects—tied up, cut up, mutilated, bruised, or physcially hurt—or as dismembered, truncated, fragmented, or severed into body parts.
4. Women are presented being pentrated by objects or animals.
5. Women are presented in scenarios of degradation, injury, abasement, or torture or are shown as filthy, inferior, bleeding, bruised, or hurt in a context that makes these conditions sexual.
6. Women are presented as sexual objects for domination, conquest, violation, exploitation, possession, or use or through postures or positions of servility, submission, or display.

Some observers noted that based on the final category alone, a large percentage of American advertising could be declared to be discriminatory, which it may well be, and hence be enjoined.

In June of 1984 an amalgam of booksellers, book distributors, publishers, and others sought to have the ordinance declared unconstitutional in federal court. Five months later U.S. District Judge Sarah Evans Barker granted the plaintiff's motion for summary judgment and ruled that the antipornography law was unconstitutional. The court ruled that the ordinance was unconstitutionally vague and that the kind of expression it sought to prohibit was protected by the First Amendment.

The proponents of the law had sought to avoid a confrontation with the First Amendment by arguing that the Indianapolis ordinance outlawed conduct, not expression. The law was aimed at stopping discrimination against women. And the Supreme Court, in *New York* v. *Ferber,* had recently approved of a New York State statute that was aimed at blocking a kind of onerous conduct, the use of children in sexual performances. But Judge Barker ruled that even if the court accepts the findings of the city that the distribution of pornography conditions members of society to subordinate women, the means by which the city attempts to combat this discrimination is through the regulation of speech. Speech may only be restrained, the judge noted, if it falls into one of those widely recognized categories of expression that may be constitutionally regulated: obscenity, profanity, libel, fighting words, etc. While the kind of material outlawed by the ordinance is somewhat akin to the erotic material prohibited by obscenity laws, the definition of pornography in the ordinance goes far beyond the definition of obscenity in the three-part *Miller* test.

Proponents of the ordinance argued that in the *Ferber* ruling the Supreme Court permitted the state to regulate nonobscene expression because of a compelling state interest in protecting children. But the judge refused to accept the analogy between the protection of children and the protection of women, noting that adult women, unlike children, are capable of protecting themselves from being victimized by pornography (*American Booksellers Ass'n. v. Hudnut,* 1985.)

The city appealed the ruling but lost when the Seventh U.S. Court of Appeals upheld the lower court ruling in August of 1985. Under the Indianapolis ordinance sexually explicit speech or expression is pornography or not, depending upon the perspective of the author, the court noted. Speech that subordinates women is pornographic, no matter how great the literary or political value of the work. Speech that portrays women in positions of equality is lawful, no matter how graphic the sexual conduct. "This is thought control," the court said. "It establishes an approved view of women, of how they may react to sexual encounters, of how the sexes may relate to each other. Those who espouse the approved view may use sexual images; those who do not, may not." The court added, "The power to limit speech on the ground that truth has not yet prevailed and is not likely to prevail implies the power to declare truth" (*American Booksellers Ass'n. v. Hudnut,* 1985).

The failure of this ordinance to pass constitutional muster will not end the debate over the question of pornography and women. But the law has also sparked sharp debate within the women's movement itself. Many found the coalition between ardent feminists and the conservative political right an unholy alliance that may in the end thwart other feminist goals. The Feminists Anti-Censorship Task Force, a group that opposed the ordinance, also questioned whether the images in books and magazines do actually cause violent acts against women and whether this type of law is the proper way to attempt to change the misogynist attitudes of many American males (see "Is One Women's Sexuality Another Women's Pornography? in *Ms.,* April, 1985, p. 37).

SUMMARY

The *Miller* test is used today by American courts to determine whether something is obscene. It has three parts. Material is legally obscene under the following conditions:

    1. An average person, applying contemporary local community standards, finds that the work, taken as a whole, appeals to prurient interest. This test requires the fact finder to apply local (usually state

or county) standards rather than a national standard. The judge or jury determines the standard, based upon their knowledge of what is acceptable in the community.

2. The work depicts in a patently offensive way sexual conduct specifically defined by applicable state law. Again, the fact finder in the case determines patent offensiveness, based upon local community standards. But the Supreme Court has ruled that only so-called hard-core pornography can be found to be patently offensive. Also, either the legislature or the state supreme court must specifically define the kind of offensive material that may be declared to be obscene.

3. The material lacks serious literary, artistic, political, or scientific value. This is a question of law, not of fact, to be decided in large part by the judge.

The three-part *Miller-Hamling* test is the test that courts must use in defining obscenity in all cases except those involving juveniles. The Supreme Court has ruled that states may use a broader definition of obscenity when they attempt to block the sale or distribution of erotic material to children or when they attempt to stop the exploitation of children who are forced to engage in sexual conduct by pornographic filmmakers. But the federal courts blocked an attempt by the city of Indianapolis to outlaw written and visual material that might result in discrimination against women or provoke violence against women and children.

STATE AND FEDERAL CONTROLS ON OBSCENITY

Various means can be used to regulate the dissemination of obscene materials, including criminal prosecution, passing nuisance and zoning laws, and regulating the types of films that can be shown. The federal government can also use postal censorship to prevent obscene materials from being disseminated. Let us look more closely at these measures for controlling obscene materials.

Criminal Prosecution

For more than one hundred years, the typical manner in which the state attempts to control obscenity has been a criminal prosecution. Such lawsuits are complicated, and to be successful in these cases, prosecutors must follow carefully prescribed paths in deciding whether material is obscene, in collecting and seizing evidence, and in making arrests. Often persons charged with exhibiting or selling obscene materials seek to plea bargain with the state to reduce the charge. Booksellers, theater owners, and other merchants who deal in pornographic materials often do not want to fight the government in an obscenity prosecution. They are not in the business to crusade for the First Amendment. Their goal is to stay out of jail and to return to selling books or showing movies. If the state can be convinced to reduce the obscenity charge in exchange for a guilty plea, the defendant can often get by with paying a fine instead of going to jail and be back in business within a few days of the arrest. Prosecutors seem amenable to such plea bargaining because, as one noted, "Our business is to stop public distribution of certain obscene materials, not put people in jail."

If a case goes to trial, the judge and the jury are the ones who must determine whether the material sold or exhibited is obscene. The fact finder in the trial—the jury or the judge if there is not a jury—determines parts one and two of the *Miller* test, prurient appeal and patent offensiveness. The judge normally rules on the serious value of the work as a matter of law. The instructions given to the jury by the judge are usually vitally important to the outcome of an obscenity case. The instructions, of course, tell the jury what the law is—in other words, how to determine whether the material is obscene. A trial judge generally bases the instructions both on a personal reading of the law and on personal experience. Judge David Soukup of the Washington State Superior Court, who has tried numerous obscenity cases, told researcher Kirk Anderson this about jury instructions:

> Basically the matter of deciding what to include in a set of instructions depends on what the judge himself feels is necessary such that the jury can make a knowledgeable and legally sound determination, a judgment that is predicated upon his own interpretation of the law and what it requires, in combination with what his practical experience tells him jurors need in order to best understand the criteria they must apply to the facts at hand. The result of this highly individualized process, which is also influenced by the judge's philosophy of his role under the law and his feeling about pornography in general, is that some judges will stick pretty close to the *Miller* test and the definitions of it provided by the Supreme Court, while others will attempt to embellish them by adding varying degrees of explanation arising from their own interpretations of the law. . . .

In addition to determining whether the material is obscene, jurors are also called upon to answer the question of whether the defendant was knowledgeable about the contents of what was being sold, distributed, or published. This is called scienter, or guilty knowledge. In a 1959 case, *Smith* v. *California,* the United States Supreme Court ruled that before a person can be convicted for selling obscene books the state has to prove that the seller was aware of the contents of the books, that he or she knew what they were about. The reason for this ruling is quite simple. As Justice William Brennan wrote more than twenty years ago, "If the bookseller is criminally liable without knowledge of the contents, . . . he will tend to restrict the books he sells to those he has inspected; and thus the state will have imposed a restriction upon the distribution of constitutionally protected as well as obscene literature . . ." (*Smith* v. *California,* 1959).

There has always been some confusion about exactly what a state or other jurisdiction must prove. For example, does the bookseller have to know the books are obscene? In the *Hamling* decision the Supreme Court tried to clarify this point by repeating that scienter merely means proving that the defendant has a general knowledge of the material in question—that it is a book about homosexuals, for example, or that the movie contains sadistic scenes. It is not necessary that the bookseller or the theater operator know that the material is legally obscene. Normally a prosecutor can demonstrate scienter without much trouble, but it is another question that the jury must decide.

What this process suggests is that, like other street crimes, the prosecution of obscenity in any community depends largely upon how the law is administered and interpreted *locally*. And within certain parameters, a community can read the books it wants to read, see the movies it wants to see, and buy the kinds of magazines it wants to buy. What the United States Supreme Court says about obscenity is relevant to most communities in only an indirect way. These practical realities regarding obscenity prosecutions suggest that the nation's appellate courts—especially the Supreme Court of the United States—probably spend far too much time contemplating this matter.

Civil Nuisance Suits

Some communities have attempted to block the sale or exhibition of obscene material through the use of civil nuisance suits. Initially some states attempted to use their general nuisance statutes to block the distribution of obscene material. More recently, however, nearly a dozen states and a great many cities and towns have passed nuisance statutes specifically aimed at obscenity. These laws operate in this fashion. The statutes or ordinances define nuisance to include obscenity and then define obscenity using the three-part *Miller* test. Prosecutors are authorized by the statute to maintain a civil suit to abate the nuisance, much as they would bring an action against a factory that is polluting the community. A hearing is held to determine whether the defendant in the suit is in fact maintaining a nuisance; that is, whether obscene materials are being sold or exhibited. The court will determine whether or not the material is obscene, using the *Miller* test. If the materials are found to be legally obscene, an injunction is issued to abate the nuisance; the materials can no longer be sold.

Few find fault with the procedure thus far. But then the court can issue a second injunction, called a blanket or "standards injunction." This injunction forbids the defendant to sell or exhibit any other comparable obscene material; that is, material that the court has not yet seen but that would be obscene under the law. If the defendant violates this injunction, he or she will be held in contempt of court. Some persons have argued that this second injunction—banning the sale of material that has not yet been declared legally obscene—is an illegal prior restraint. But the courts have generally disagreed.

North Carolina, for example, passed a nuisance statute aimed at theaters regularly showing pornographic films and at adult bookstores that had coin-operated film projectors (peep shows) showing explicit sexual activity or sold pictorial magazines or photographs showing similar activity. The statute defined obscenity using the three-part *Miller* test. The state is obliged to prove that a bookstore owner or theater operator whom it takes to court deals predominantly and in the regular course of business with such obscene material. If the court agrees that the material is obscene and that it is a principal or substantial part of the defendant's stock in trade, an injunction will be issued barring the future sale or exhibition of comparable material. If this injunction is violated, the individual can be held in contempt of court and fined or jailed. The Fourth United States Court of Appeals upheld the North Carolina law despite protests by the defendant that it was a prior restraint (*Fehlhaber* v. *North Carolina,* 1982).

It appears that courts have upheld the constitutionality of such nuisance laws because they view the contempt hearing, at which the merchant may be punished for violating the second or the "standards injunction," as being almost identical with a criminal prosecution. "The courts validate the injunction because its prohibition is substantively identical to the prohibition of a criminal obscenity statute and because the contempt proceeding is similar in structure to a criminal obscenity trial," wrote Steven T. Catlett in a recent issue of the *Columbia Law Review.* The courts reason that since the two regulatory techniques are similar, if one is constitutional, the other must be also, Catlett notes. In the contempt hearing the state must prove that legally obscene material was sold or exhibited in violation of the injunction. The defendant enjoys the same procedural safeguards as a defendant in a criminal case. And the same kinds of punishment—fine or imprisonment—will be applied.

The U.S. Supreme Court has not ruled directly on the question of whether such laws are constitutional or not. In 1981 the High Court struck down a Texas statute that allowed a court to issue a temporary restraining order against a theater owner barring as a nuisance the exhibition of a film even before a court determined that the film was obscene (*Vance* v. *Universal Amusement,* 1980). The court never considered the question of the constitutionality of the second injunction, the "standards injunction," in this case. But in a dissent, Justice White did discuss the question and concluded that the enforcement of the standards injunction was "functionally indistinguishable from a criminal obscenity statute." Hence it is constitutional.

Some still aren't certain that such laws should be permitted. Circuit Judge Phillips dissented in the Fourth United States Court of Appeals ruling approving the North Carolina law. He noted (*Fehlhaber* v. *North Carolina,* 1982):

> The key feature of this civil nuisance statute remains . . . the power it gives the state courts to enjoin, under the peril of a contempt sanction, the sale and exhibition of materials that no judicial tribunal has yet determined to be obscene. This is a violation of the principles enunciated by the Supreme Court in *Near* v. *Minnesota.*

Zoning Laws

In many communities, zoning regulations have been used instead to regulate adult bookstores, theaters, and news racks. Seattle passed a law in 1977 that requires all adult theaters to be located within a small area downtown. City officials said that the character and quality of Seattle neighborhoods could be preserved and protected by isolating this adult activity to a small area downtown. Detroit took just the opposite approach. A city law passed in 1972 prohibits adult theaters from being located within 1,000 feet of other adult theaters; adult bookstores, cabarets, bars, taxi dance halls, hotels, pawnshops, pool halls, secondhand stores, and shoeshine parlors or within 500 feet of areas zoned residential. The city did not want such businesses clustered together or near other types of "problem" businesses in the community. Both these statutes were upheld by the courts (*Northend Cinema* v. *Seattle,* 1978; *Young* v. *American-Mini Theaters, Inc.,* 1976).

The owners of these adult establishments have found that zoning, while perhaps inconvenient, provides them with a kind of safe haven from police harassment. They are normally permitted to operate their businesses without trouble unless they attempt to sell or exhibit material that is legally obscene (i.e., meets the definition of obscenity in the *Miller* test) or unless other criminal laws are violated as a result of the traffic into the adult establishments.

It must be remembered that these zoning schemes are aimed at regulating constitutionally protected material, not legally obscene material. Hence, there are clear limits that have been placed on such schemes. Foremost is the rule that a community cannot, under the guise of zoning, completely bar or even significantly reduce the number of bookstores, theaters, or newsstands that sell adult material. The ordinance in Detroit that was approved by the Supreme Court in the *Young* ruling did not substantially reduce the number of establishments selling adult material. And it left ample room for the introduction of new establishments. This point has been overlooked in some communities in which zoning regulations were used to try to close adult bookstores, theaters, and other businesses. In 1981 the Supreme Court struck down a Mount Ephraim, New Jersey, zoning regulation that effectively barred all live entertainment from the parts of the city zoned commercial. The High Court called the ordinance unreasonable and said that it excluded from the city a wide range of protected expression. The High Court also rejected Mount Ephraim's argument that its citizens had access to such entertainment, despite the zoning rules, because adult entertainment was readily available outside the city in nearby areas (*Schad* v. *Mount Ephraim,* 1981). The Sixth U.S. Court of Appeals threw out a Keego Harbor, Michigan, zoning law that prohibited adult theaters within five hundred feet of a tavern or bar, a church, or a school. There was no place in the small community that was not within five hundred feet of such an establishment (*Keego Harbor Company* v. *Keego*

Harbor, 1981). And the Eighth U.S. Court of Appeals voided a Minneapolis ordinance that effectively eliminated two-thirds of the adult bookstore locations in the city (*Alexander* v. *City of Minneapolis,* 1983).

These ordinances, which interfere with protected speech, must be strongly justified as furthering a substantial government interest. The city of Detroit provided a tremendous amount of data in defending its ordinance, data that demonstrated that concentrations of adult establishments caused neighborhood decay. The Detroit ordinance, then, was justified as preventing urban decay. Other communities have failed to do this, and their ordinances have been overturned. Keego Harbor, Michigan, provided little data at all to support its argument that the adult movie theaters created traffic problems and therefore had to be regulated by zoning. "When a city effectively zones protected activities out of a political entity, the justification required is more substantial than when the First Amendment burden is merely incidental as it was in *Young* v. *American Mini Theaters,*" the court noted (*Keego Harbor Company* v. *Keego Harbor,* 1981). Of course the First Amendment burden was incidental in *Young* because the law did not diminish the number of adult establishments. The Fifth U.S. Court of Appeals rejected a zoning ordinance adopted by the city of Galveston, Texas, modeled after the Detroit ordinance. The mayor and other city officials testified that they believed that the mere existence of adult theaters created crime and urban decay, but they offered no other evidence at the trial. "The paucity of evidence stands in sharp contrast to the facts of *American Mini Theaters* v. *Young,*" the court noted (*Basiardanes* v. *City of Galveston,* 1982). While a community must produce evidence to support its zoning regulation, it doesn't necessarily have to generate fresh evidence that relates directly to that community. It can rely upon the experience of other communities in the region. The city of Renton, Washington, a suburb of Seattle, relied upon the experience of other area cities (most notably Seattle) to justify its zoning statute. The U.S. Supreme Court ruled in 1986 that this was an acceptable practice. "The First Amendment does not require a city, before enacting such an ordinance to conduct new studies or produce evidence independent of that already generated by other cities," wrote Justice William Rehnquist, "so long as whatever evidence the city relies upon is reasonably believed to be relevant to the problem the city addresses" (*Renton* v. *Playtime Theatres,* 1986). Playtime Theatres owner Roger Forbes also objected to the Renton ordinance because, he argued, it forced all adult theaters to the outskirts of the community in an industrial area. In fact, only five percent of the entire city existed where the adult establishments were permitted; this made finding property very difficult, Forbes said. The seven-person Supreme Court majority was unsympathetic. "That respondents must fend for themselves in the real estate market, on an equal footing with other prospective purchasers and lessees does not give rise to a First Amendment violation," Justice Rehnquist wrote.

Finally, such a zoning ordinance must be narrowly drawn, so as not to restrict more speech than is necessary or to place a greater burden than necessary on the speech that is regulated. In the *Schad* case the city of Mount Ephraim had banned all forms of live entertainment, putting any sort of play or performance off-limits. This restricted more speech than needed to control adult entertainment. And the city of Galveston in the *Basiardanes* case defined an adult theater as any theater that regularly screened films that the state of Texas prohibited minors from seeing. Of course this includes all R-rated films. Again, the city went too far and banned too much expression. The city of Keego Harbor, on the other hand, might have used other methods—short of banning adult theaters—to handle its traffic problems, as Alfred X. Zen notes in the *Pepperdine Law Review*. "The court suggested that the increased ticketing of violators was a less intrusive means of serving the governmental interest involved," Zen wrote.

Zoning laws can be used to control the sale and exhibition of adult materials in a community. But only if they meet the three requirements outlined above: There can be no complete ban on such establishments or substantial reduction of the availability of such material in the community; a government must strongly justify—with evidence—such rules. And the laws must be narrowly drawn.

Postal Censorship

Use of the postal service to censor obscenity has a long tradition in the United States. In fact, it is largely through the postal system that the federal government becomes involved in the regulation of obscenity. The Post Office Department has long been an insensitive and moralistic censor of all sorts of material. Armed with congressional authority, as well as a nineteenth-century Supreme Court ruling that designated use of the mails a privilege and not a right (ex parte *Jackson,* 1878), the postal service has worked hard to keep the mails free of "smut," even smut in plain brown wrappers. While the government cannot tamper with first-class mail legally, publishers of magazines of all kinds—girly, nudist, art, anthropological, crime, true confessions—have long been plagued by postal inspectors. While the loss of much of this material would not be a severe blow to the nation's cultural heritage, it is still highly frustrating to publishers who must depend upon the postal service to deliver their wares. For most publications the Post Office Department runs the only game in town.

The Post Office Department has traditionally been plagued with administrative slovenliness that causes it to run afoul of the law. Federal courts have for years been telling the postal service that it cannot do this or that: institute a mail block, for example, deny due process of law in obscenity hearings, ban publications that do not contribute to "the public good," or force patrons to come to the post office to pick up mail from Communist countries.

In 1968 the postal service took a new tack in regulating certain kinds of obscene material, a tack designed to take the service off the legal hot seat. What is known as the Anti-Pandering Law, or Section 3008 of Title 39 of the United States Code, was put into effect by Congress. It was designed to stop the delivery of unwanted obscene solicitations to mail patrons' homes. This had been a problem for years, a real problem in many cases. Mailers were indiscriminate in sending out such material, and it was not uncommon for youngsters to receive lurid solicitations from publishers of magazines, books, and pictures.

Section 3008 allows postal patrons to remain free from such solicitations, but only after they have received such an advertisement. It works this way. Imagine that John Smith finds an advertisement for La Femme French postcards in his mailbox and is properly shocked. Under Section 3008 John can fill out a postal form, which is sent by the post office to the La Femme company, advising the mailer that Mr. Smith does not want to receive such solicitations in the future. If La Femme were to send John a subsequent mailing, the company could be subject to prosecution.

The interesting aspect of this law concerns the definition of obscenity—there is none. Postal patrons decide for themselves what is obscene. If they do not like the material, the dislike then is all that is needed. Once the notice is sent to the mailer, *any* subsequent mailing is a violation of the law. John might decide that a *Time* magazine solicitation or an advertisement for seat covers or a record club is obscene. There must be solicitation, but that is the only requirement.

The distributors of erotic material challenged this law, since to remove a name from a mailing list is quite costly. Also they argued that the law violated their First Amendment rights and that because the law did not define obscenity, it was too vague and therefore a violation of Fifth Amendment rights. But the Supreme Court unanimously supported the law. The Court said that Congress intended to give the postal patron the right to decide on the obscenity of an advertisement, and this right eliminates the Post Office Department from a censorship role.

As far as the First Amendment right to communicate (if there is such a right) is concerned, the High Court ruled that the right of privacy is also guaranteed by the Constitution. This law does impede the flow of ideas, information, and so forth. However, Chief Justice Burger wrote (*Rowan* v. *Post Office,* 1970):

> . . . today everyman's mail is made up overwhelmingly of material he did not seek from persons he does not know. And all too often it is matter he finds offensive. It seems to us that a mailer's right to communicate must stop at the mailbox of an unreceptive addressee. . . . We categorically reject the argument that a vendor has a right under the Constitution or otherwise to send unwanted material into the home of another.

A more recent addition to the postal laws operates on somewhat the same principle and has caused the pornography distributors even more headaches. Section 3010 of Title 39, United States Code, called the Goldwater Amendment to the Postal Reorganization Bill, allows mail patrons the opportunity to get off a pornographer's mailing list even before they receive the first solicitation. Under this law John Smith can fill out a form at his local post office asserting that he does not want to receive any sexually oriented advertising. The postal service periodically publishes computerized lists of the names and addresses of persons who have signed this form. After a person's name has been on the list for thirty days, it is illegal to send that individual sexually oriented advertising matter. Mailers who ignore this are subject to both criminal and civil penalties.

Where do the mailers get the lists of names? They have to buy the lists from the government. When the law went into effect a few years ago, the cost of a master list was more than $5,000. Of course supplements are published periodically, and they must be purchased as well.

Section 3010 is different from Section 3008 in that it defines sexually oriented material, whereas the Anti-Pandering Law lets postal patrons decide on their own. Here is how the statute defines sexually oriented material:

> . . . any advertisement that depicts in actual or simulated form, or explicitly describes, in a predominantly sexual context, human genitalia, any act of natural or unnatural sexual intercourse, or any act of sadism or masochism, or any other erotic subject directly related to the foregoing.

The law does not pertain to materials in which the sexually oriented advertisement comprises only a small and insignificant part of a larger catalog, book, or periodical. This statute was also upheld by the federal courts (*Pent-R-Books* v. *U.S. Postal Service,* 1971). This law also provides that any envelope containing an advertisement that falls within the definition just given must carry a warning on the outside as to the nature of the contents.

Both of these statutes have been widely used and have solved one of the most serious problems relating to pornography—its shipment to people who do not want it. However, neither of these laws precludes the possibility of criminal obscenity prosecution against advertisers for sending out such material, even to people who want it. The 1974 *Hamling* case was based on just such an advertisement.

Regulating Films

Courts have always treated movies differently than they treat books, magazines, and artwork. Films have been censored for a great many reasons, including obscenity. Initially the Supreme Court refused to include films under the protection of the First Amendment. In 1915 in the case of *Mutual Film Corp.* v. *Industrial Commission of Ohio,* Justice Joseph McKenna wrote for the Court that while, indeed, movies may be mediums of thought, so are many other things, such as circuses and the theaters. "It cannot be put out of view," the justice wrote, "that the exhibition of moving pictures is a business, pure and simple, originated and conducted for profit, like other spectacles, not to be regarded . . . as part of the press of the country or as organs of public opinion."

This was the law until the 1950s, when the High Court ruled that film is a medium protected by the First Amendment and cannot be censored by a state, except in cases of obscenity (*Burstyn* v. *Wilson*, 1952). This seemed to put moviemakers on the same footing as magazine publishers, with one exception. The courts permitted prior censorship with regard to motion pictures; that is, a theater owner or film distributor could constitutionally be required to present the film to a board of censors for approval before showing it in the theater. In 1961 a film distributor challenged this practice and lost. In a five-to-four ruling the Court said that there is no complete and absolute freedom to exhibit, even once, any and every kind of motion picture (*Times Film Corp.* v. *Chicago*).

While approving prior censorship for motion pictures, the High Court also demands, within the censorship system, procedures that protect the rights of theater owners. Concerning such, the Court struck down several film censorship systems (for example, in Maryland and Dallas) that took too long to reach a decision, placed the burden of proof on the theater owner rather than on the government, and so forth (*Freedman* v. *Maryland*, 1965 and *Interstate Circuit* v. *Dallas*, 1968). In 1965 when the Court struck down the Maryland censorship law in *Freedman* v. *Maryland*, it outlined the constitutional requirements of a permissible film ordinance. But the Court was unable to find an ordinance that passed muster until 1974, when it summarily affirmed the judgment of a three-judge panel that approved the revamped Maryland law.

The Maryland law that was approved in *Star* v. *Preller* (1974) had these provisions:

1. Every film, including those in coin-operated loop machines, must have a license from the state board of censors before it can be shown. Showing a film without a license is a crime, regardless of whether it is obscene.

2. Once a film is submitted to the censorship board, the board must either issue a license or initiate an action in court against the film within eight days.

3. In a court action to determine whether the film is obscene, the censorship board must prove the film is obscene. The film distributor does not have to prove that it is not obscene.

4. A hearing must be held in court within five days after the action is filed.

5. The court must issue a ruling within two days after the hearing is over. There is also a provision for expedited appeals.

6. The film cannot be shown until the hearing is completed.

Given the fact that prior restraint is allowed, the benefit of this ordinance is that a film must be licensed or declared obscene in a maximum of fifteen days. Moreover, the state bears the burden of proof in any hearing that results. Perhaps this seems like crumbs for a starving man, but this system is nevertheless far superior to those of yesterday, in which motion pictures were often tied up for months with the censors and the theater owner or film distributor was forced to go into court and try to prove a negative: that a movie was not obscene.

Most communities no longer operate film censorship boards. They are costly, and because the censors frequently abuse the system, these boards have a bad name. In Chicago, for example, the censorship board, which was comprised of police officers and the proverbial little old ladies in tennis shoes, once cut from a Walt Disney nature movie a scene showing the birth of a deer. Most communities proceed against obscene movies much as they do against obscene books—case-by-case prosecution.

Film prosecutions also present problems. In the case of an obscene book, an undercover officer can buy a copy of the suspect edition, and it can be scrutinized and later used as evidence if a criminal action results. But the price of a movie ticket includes only the right to look, not to take. So the police and the courts experienced many years of pushing and shoving over what was and was not legal. For a while the police merely seized all copies of the film. But the courts did not approve of that, because whether the film was obscene was for the courts to decide. If the jury decided the film was not obscene, seizure then constituted a clear case of prior restraint. So the police were forced to use other means. In some cities the police videotaped portions of the movie for use as evidence in a trial. But the quality of the tape was poor, and often theater owners who were arguing about the high technical quality of a film complained that the police copy made the picture look worse than it actually was.

In 1973 in *Heller* v. *New York,* the Supreme Court handed down rules that clarified the matter, even though the new policies did not satisfy many people on either side. Under the *Heller* rules a film cannot be seized by police as evidence until a warrant is issued by a neutral judge or magistrate who has viewed the film and has ruled that it is obscene. The hearing in which the judge issues the warrant is not an adversary hearing, because the theater owner is not represented. This warrant is called an ex parte warrant. Only the state is represented, and all that the warrant says is that one judge has seen the film and thinks it is obscene.

The Fifth United States Court of Appeals modified these rules in 1979 when it decided that a judge or magistrate can also issue a warrant for seizure of the film on the basis of a government agent's *detailed* affidavit describing the film's content. The judge or magistrate does not actually have to see the film in order to issue the warrant (*U.S.* v. *Middleton,* 1979). Whether the United States Supreme Court will agree with this ruling has not been tested. The High Court will not permit so-called open-ended warrants. A police officer in New York bought two films at an adult bookstore and permitted a judge to view them. The judge declared the films to be obscene and gave the police officer a warrant to seize all copies of the two films and other obscene materials at the store. Police raided the store and seized eight hundred different items. The names and descriptions of these items were filled in on the warrant *after* they were seized. The Supreme Court unanimously ruled that such a procedure was a violation of the Fourth Amendment. "Our society is better able to tolerate the admittedly pornographic business of petitioner [the store owner] than a return to the general warrant era," Chief Justice Burger wrote (*Lo-Ji Sales* v. *New York,* 1979).

Following seizure of a film, an adversary hearing—a trial—is held to determine whether the film is in fact obscene. During the period between seizure and final judicial determination of obscenity, the theater owner can continue to show the motion picture if he or she has a second copy. If no second copy is available, the state must then permit the exhibitor to make a copy of the film that was seized so that exhibition of the movie can go on. Therefore, the police get their evidence and the theater owner can keep showing the movie until the trial is over. The only serious problem is that it is expensive for the theater owner to make a second copy of the movie.

Informal Censorship

The legal control of obscene and other erotic materials troubled few citizens in the late 1980s. Indeed, these waters have substantially calmed since the hectic days of the 1960s and 1970s. Informal censorship, however, was becoming a serious problem in the eyes of many liberal and even moderate Americans. Attacks upon books in schools and public libraries was discussed in chapter 2 (see pages 87–90). And the attempt to censor record lyrics and music videos was noted earlier in this chapter. But perhaps the most audacious dacious attempt at informal censorship came as a result of the actions of the 1985 Attorney General's Commission on Pornography. President Reagan requested the formation of the eleven-person body in 1985 "to determine the nature, extent, and impact on society of pornography in the United States" and to make recommendations about ways that pornography might be more effectively contained. The Meese Commission, as it came to be known, held six public hearings to obtain testimony from approximately two hundred witnesses. It released its report in the summer of 1986. A majority of the commission members concluded that certain types of sexually explicit material are harmful, especially material oriented toward violent sex. This kind of material, the commissioners said, bears a causal relationship to sexual violence. Nonviolent pornography that depicts degradation, domination, subordination or humiliation also has an impact on fostering attitudes that women enjoy being raped, the commissioners said.

Two of the four women on the panel sharply disagreed with these conclusions, however. Columbia University psychology professor Judith Becker and Ellen Levine, editor of *Woman's Day,* said "The idea that eleven individuals studying in their spare time could complete a comprehensive report on so complex a matter in so constricted a time frame is simply unrealistic. . . . No self-respecting investigator would accept conclusions based on such a study." Others outside the commission also criticized the paucity (some said nonexistence) of evidence to support the commission's conclusions. But in the end, the Meese Commission recommended no new laws, only that existing federal and state laws be more vigorously enforced. Yet with state and federal prosecutors attempting to fight murder, rape, robbery, drug trafficking and other serious crimes with ever shrinking budgets, few believed the call for increased enforcement of obscenity laws would be widely heeded.

The most controversial aspect of the Meese's Commission's work, however, was its efforts (inadvertent or otherwise) to stop the flow of several popular men's magazines and sexually oriented films and TV programs. During testimony in Los Angeles in October 17, 1985, the Rev. Donald Wildmon, the executive director of the National Federation of Decency, a conservative Christian-based pressure group, said that certain American corporations were engaged in the sale of pornography, including *Playboy* and *Penthouse.* Among those Wildmon criticized were CBS; Time, Inc.; RCA; and Coca-Cola for the films and television programming they distribute, and K-Mart; Southland Corp. (7–Eleven stores); Dart Drug Co.; Stop N Go Stores; and other shops for carrying *Playboy, Penthouse,* and other "pornographic" magazines. The commission members seemed confused about whether Wildmon's testimony should be included in the final commission report, so they sent a letter to all twenty-six corporations. In part, the letter said ". . . the Commission received testimony alleging that your company is involved in the sale or distribution of pornography. The Commission has determined that it would be appropriate to allow your company an opportunity to respond to the allegations prior to drafting its final report section on identified distributors. . . . Failure to respond will necessarily be accepted as an indication of no objection (to the testimony)." The companies were not told that the allegations were based on the unsubstantiated testimony of one of two hundred witnesses.

Some companies were outraged. *Time,* Inc. responded: "We cannot believe the U.S. Department of Justice would lend its name to this slipshod and misguided effort." Others responded in a different fashion. Southland pulled *Playbody, Penthouse,* and *Forum* out of its 7–Eleven stores. The company denied, however, it was bending to commission pressure. *Playboy* and *Penthouse,* stung by the loss of distributors and already suffering a sales slump, went to court. In July, a U.S. District Court ruled that the letter sent by the commission threatened the First Amendment rights of the magazine publishers and distributors, and enjoined the publication in the commission report of the list of alleged pornography distributors. The court also ordered the commission to send a letter to all recipients of the first letter advising them that the original letter has been withdrawn and that no reply is required (*Playboy Enterprises* v. *Meese,* 1986).

While this seemingly ended the attempt by the Meese Commission to administratively censor publications, films, and television programming, and while it is likely that the impact of the commission's final report will be slight, attempts at informal censorship by often well-organized pressure groups are by no means over. Such groups continue to operate at many levels, totally outside the law and their impact will continue to be felt for many years.

SUMMARY

Criminal prosecution is not the only way in which communities have attempted to regulate the sale or exhibition of obscene or adult materials. Laws have been passed that permit a court, in a civil action to declare a business that deals in legally obscene materials to be a public nuisance. Continued sale or exhibition of obscene materials by a business deemed to be a public nuisance can result in a contempt-of-court citation. Many communities have attempted to use zoning regulations to control the sale and exhibition of nonobscene adult materials. These laws are permissible as long as they are well justified, do not totally exclude such material from the community, and are written to inhibit only the narrowest possible range of speech.

Federal regulations make it possible for postal patrons to block the delivery of solicitations for adult materials and other obscene publications. Communities may also censor films before they are shown, so long as they follow strict procedures laid down by the United States Supreme Court. Informal censorship remains a problem, however.

BIBLIOGRAPHY

Here is a list of some of the sources that have been helpful in the preparation of chapter 8:

Books

Berns, Walter. *Freedom, Virtue, and the First Amendment.* Chicago: Henry Regnery Co., Gateway Editions, 1965.

Clor, Harry M. *Obscenity and Public Morality.* Chicago: University of Chicago Press, 1969.

Kennedy, Michael, and Lefcourt, Gerald. "Trial Strategy in an Obscenity Case." In *Obscenity and the Law.* New York: Practicing Law Institute, 1974.

Kronhausen, Eberhard, and Kronhausen, Phyllis. *Pornography and the Law.* Rev. ed. New York: Ballantine Books, 1964.

Paul, James C. N., and Schwartz, Murray L. *Federal Censorship: Obscenity in the Mail.* Glencoe, Ill.: Free Press, 1961.

Robertus, Patricia. *Postal Control of Obscene Literature 1942–1957.* Ph.D. Dissertation, University of Washington, 1974.

Sunderland, Lane. *Obscenity, The Court, The Congress and the President's Commission.* Washington, D.C.: American Institute for Public Policy Research, 1974.

Wasby, Stephen L. "The Pure and the Prurient: The Supreme Court, Obscenity and Oregon Policy." In *The Supreme Court as Policy Maker*, edited by David Everson. Carbondale, Ill.: Public Affairs Research Bureau, Southern Illinois University, 1968.

Articles

Bickel, Alexander. "On Pornography: Concurring and Dissenting Opinions." 22 *The Public Interest* 25, 1971.

Blakely, C. "Is One Woman's Sexuality Another Woman's Pornography?" *Ms.,* April 1985, p. 37.

Catlett, Steven T. "Enjoining Obscenity as Public Nuisance and The Prior Restraint Doctrine." 84 *Columbia Law Review* 1616, 1984.

"An Empirical Inquiry Into the Effects of *Miller* v. *California* on the Control of Obscenity." 52 *New York University Law Review* 810, 1977.

Grunes, Rodney. "Obscenity Law and the Justices: Reversing Policy on the Supreme Court." 9 *Seton Hall Law Review* 403, 1978.

Leventhal, Harold. "1973 Round of Obscenity-Pornography Decisions." *American Bar Association Journal* 59, 1974.

Maag, Marilyn J. "The Indianapolis Pornography Ordinance: Does the Right to Free Speech Outweigh Pornography's Harm to Women?" 54 *Cincinnati Law Review* 249, 1985.

Mott, Kenneth, and Kellett, Christine. "Obscenity, Community Standards, and the Burger Court: From Deterrence to Disarray." 13 *Suffolk University Law Review* 14, 1979.

Shogue, Richard. "An Atlas for Obscenity: Exploring Community Standard." 7 *Creighton Law Review* 157, 1974.

Teeter, Dwight L., and Pember, Don R. "Obscenity, 1971: The Rejuvenation of State Power and the Return to Roth." 17 *Villanova Law Review* 211, 1971.

Teeter, Dwight L., and Pember, Don R. "The Retreat from Obscenity: *Redrup* v. *New York*." 21 *Hastings Law Journal* 175, 1969.

Yen, Alfred C. "Judicial Reviews of the Zoning of Adult Entertainment: A Search for the Purposeful Suppression of Protected Speech." 12 *Pepperdine Law Review* 651, 1985.

Cases

American Booksellers Ass'n. v. *Hudnut,* 598 F. Supp 1316 (1985); aff'd. 771 F.2d 323 (1985).

American Booksellers v. *Strobel,* 12 M.L. Rept. 1208 (1985).

Basiardanes v. *City of Galveston,* 682 F.2d 1203 (1982).

Burstyn v. *Wilson,* 343, U.S. 495 (1952).

Butler v. *Michigan,* 352 U.S. 380 (1957).

Erznoznik v. *City of Jacksonville*, 95 S.Ct. 2268 (1975).

ex parte *Jackson*, 96 U.S. 727 (1878).

Fehlhaber v. *North Carolina*, 675 F.2d. 1365 (1982).

Freedman v. *Maryland*, 380 U.S. 51 (1965).

Ginsberg v. *New York*, 390 U.S. 629 (1968).

Ginzburg v. *U.S.*, 383 U.S. 463 (1966).

Hamling v. *U.S.*, 418 U.S. 87 (1974).

Hannegan v. *Esquire*, 327 U.S. 146 (1946).

Heller v. *New York*, 413 U.S. 483 (1973).

Interstate Circuit v. *Dallas*, 390 U.S. 676 (1968).

Jacobellis v. *Ohio*, 378 U.S. 184 (1964).

Jenkins v. *Georgia*, 418 U.S. 153 (1974).

Keego Harbor Company v. *Keego Harbor*, 657 F.2d 94 (1981).

Lo-Ji Sales v. *New York*, 99 S.Ct. 2319 (1979).

Manuel Enterprises v. *Day*, 370 U.S. 478 (1962).

Memoirs v. *Massachusetts*, 383 U.S. 413 (1966).

Miller v. *California*, 413 U.S. 15 (1973).

Mutual Film Corp. v. *Industrial Commission of Ohio*, 236 U.S. 230 (1915).

New York v. *Ferber*, 102 S.Ct. 3348 (1982).

Northend Cinema v. *Seattle*, 585 P.2d 1153 (1978).

Paris Adult Theatre I v. *Slaton*, 413 U.S. 49 (1973).

Penthouse v. *Mcauliffe*, 610 F.2d 1353 (1981).

Pent-R-Books v. *U.S. Postal Service*, 328 F. Supp. 297 (1971).

People v. *Gitlow*, 195 A. D. 773 (1921).

Pinkus v. *U.S.*, 98 S.Ct. 1808 (1978).

Playboy Enterprises v. *Meese*, 13 M.L. Rept. 1101 (1986).

Regina v. *Hicklin*, L.R. 3 Q.B. 360 (1868).

Renton v. *Playtime Theatres*, 106 S.Ct. 925 (1986).

Roth v. *U.S.*, 354 U.S. 476 (1957).

Rowan v. *Post Office*, 397 U.S. 728 (1970).

Schad v. *Mount Ephraim*, 101 S.Ct. 2176 (1981).

Smith v. *California*, 361 U.S. 147 (1959).

Smith v. *U.S.*, 97 S.Ct. 1756 (1977).

Splawn v. *California*, 431 U.S. 595 (1977).

Spokane v. *Portch*, 92 Wn.2d 342 (1979).

Star v. *Preller*, 95 S.Ct. 217 (1974).

State v. *Lerner*, 81 N.E.2d 282 (1948).

Times Film Corp. v. *Chicago*, 365 U.S. 43 (1961).

Upper Midwest Booksellers v. *Minneapolis*, 602 F.Supp. 1361 (1985), affd 12 M.L. Rept. 1913 (1985).

U.S. v. *Blucher*, 581 F.2d 244 (1978).

U.S. v. *McManus*, 535 F.2d 460 (1976).

U.S. v. *Middleton*, 599 F.2d 1349 (1979).

U.S. v. *Roth*, 237 F.2d 796 (1956).

U.S. v. *Various Articles of Obscene Merchandise*, 62 F.2d 185 (1977).

Vance v. *Universal Amusement*, 445 U.S. 308 (1980).

Walker v. *Popenoe*, 149 F.2d 511 (1945).

Ward v. *Illinois*, 431 U.S. 767 (1977).

Young v. *American Mini-Theaters, Inc.*, 96 S.Ct. 2440 (1976).

9 COPYRIGHT

Pac-Man is a yellow, pie-shaped creature that once inhabited millions of video games in arcades and homes. The ravenous gobbler spent its entire technological life consuming pink dots, power capsules, and ghosts on electronic screens across the United States. In 1982 the feisty little creation of Midway Games overcame its biggest challenge when it vanquished K. C. Munchkin, a Pac-Man clone manufactured by North American Phillips. But it was not Pac-Man's metered mouth that devoured Munchkin; it was Midway's attorneys, armed with the law of copyright, who did the deed. A United States court of appeals ruled that the similarities between the two games far outweighed the differences, that Munchkin "captures the total feel and substance of Pac-Man," and that this was an infringement upon the Midway copyright on the popular game. A preliminary injunction was issued that blocked the sale of the North American Phillips game (*Advertising Age,* 17 May 1982).

Copyright is an area of the law that deals with immaterial property—property that a person cannot put hands on, that cannot be felt or touched or locked in a safe. The law of copyright is a close cousin to patent and trademark law. But each of the three protects something different. Copyright law protects "all original works of authorship fixed in a tangible medium of expression." This includes writings, paintings, music, drama, and other similar works. Patent law protects new and useful products and processes. A product is a physical entity; a process is a means to an end, a way of doing something. A trademark is a mark, a symbol, a word or words, or a phrase used by a manufacturer to distinguish that company's goods from the goods of another manufacturer. An example might help to distinguish between the three legal concepts. The word *Coke* is a trademark for the Coca-Cola Co.; the name distinguishes that soft drink from others that look about the same in a glass or bottle. The secret process by which Coke is made is protected by a patent. Finally, the pictures and words in a magazine ad or a television spot promoting Coke are protected by copyright law.

Plagiarism is another legal concept that is sometimes discussed in the same breath as copyright. But it is different as well. Plagiarism is the act of taking ideas, thoughts, or words from another and passing them off as your own. The notion of passing this material off as your own is critical in a case of plagiarism and is not found in copyright law. Similarly, plagiarism protects the theft of ideas, whereas copyright protects only the specific expression of these ideas. While all this sounds complicated, it is not. We will focus exclusively on copyright law in this chapter. Persons who work in the mass media do not need to become copyright attorneys to avoid lawsuits in the late 1980s. But writers and broadcasters should know both how to protect their own work from theft and how to avoid illegally taking the work of someone else.

Even copyright law covers a great many subjects that fall outside the scope of this book, which is law affecting the mass media. Hence, we will focus on a narrow range of subjects within the broader measure. First, the conditions creating the need for copyright laws and development of the law are discussed. Second, the kinds of works that may be copyrighted and the kinds that may not are considered. Third, how authors may protect their own work is discussed. Finally, the precautions that should be taken to avoid stealing the work of other persons, either inadvertently or advertently, are outlined. Also considered briefly are free-lance copyright and damages assessed in copyright suits. ♦

PROTECTING LITERARY PROPERTY

Law professor Paul Goldstein writes in the *Columbia Law Review* (1970), "Copyright is the uniquely legitimate offspring of censorship." British history from the late fifteenth century through the early eighteenth century partially substantiates this assertion. It is naive, however, to think of copyright as solely a limiting force on the production of written works. Protection of the rights of an author, after all, can give impetus to authors to write and publish more. There were really few legal problems in protecting literary property prior to the development of mechanical printing. Each hand-copied manuscript was the result of the labor of a copyist. It was an individual entity, a specific creation. As such, it was protected by the law of personal property. But the printing press, which permitted mass production of exact copies of a written work, changed the situation. The press produced both a piece of physical property—the book itself—and an immaterial property—the arrangement and organization of the words or ideas. The immaterial property was called literary property and was not protected by British law.

Roots of the Law

As noted in chapter 2, printing created many problems for the king. The Crown was fearful of the power of the press to rouse the passions of the people against the government. Therefore, in the sixteenth century the government sanctioned and supported the grant of printing privileges to certain master printers in exchange for loyalty and assistance in ferreting out antigovernment writers and publishers. In *The First Copyright Statute* Harry Ransom writes:

> The privilege had its origins in the Crown's patronage of specific printers. Warrants granting rights to print books or a specific book, usually for a certain term—two years, ten years, or the lifetime of the printer—were a

natural outgrowth of the system of appointing King's printers. The grant was a recognition of confidence in his printing and a protective guarantee of his right in copy. It was a means of extending royal control of the press through official choice of printers to be encouraged by patronage.

The first recorded privilege or royal grant was given in 1518, according to Professor Ransom. About forty years later the Stationers' Company was founded for much the same purpose. This was an organization of master printers chartered by the government to control, regulate, and protect printing. The company had sufficient power to regulate who did the printing and what was printed. The Crown cooperated with this guild, because it served as a useful tool for censorship. Some of the basic rudiments of copyright law were developed by the Stationers' Company. The company required printers to record the publication of their works in a registration book. While this device was used originally to keep track of what printers published, the registration book later became evidence in lawsuits over printing privileges. Registration of a book prior to publication of a pirated version substantiated a claim of ownership. It was in 1586 that a court first accepted the registration book as evidence of ownership.

What about the rights of authors, the persons who wrote the books published by the printers? In the sixteenth century authors had few rights. Generally when an author sold his manuscript to a printer or a bookseller, he sold all rights with it for a single fee. If the book sold well, the bookseller might further compensate the author, but the additional compensation stemmed from generosity, not from legal obligation. Ransom reports that many sixteenth-century authors were jailed for nonpayment of debt, others went hungry, and most had to undertake some kind of additional labor to keep body and soul together. If the author printed the work himself, he retained rights that would provide him a royalty, or he might make an agreement with a printer or bookseller to gain part of the proceeds of sales. Such arrangements were uncommon, and there was no organized royalty system.

In the seventeenth century litigation over the ownership of books increased, and with the increased litigation certain common law principles developed. A decree by the Star Chamber in 1637 asserted that all books that were published had to be registered in the Stationers' registration book, that the name of the printer or bookseller must appear in the published book, and that there was to be no infringement on the publishing rights of persons who held the printing privilege; that is, no theft of another person's work. In 1649 the government passed a law that provided a penalty—a fine—for anyone found guilty of reprinting works entered in the register.

More laws were passed and more cases tried in the second half of the seventeenth century. It soon became obvious, however, that problems of authors—who were becoming quite angry—and of booksellers and printers as well could not be solved by any measure short of a comprehensive law. Petitions began to appear at Parliament urging legislation to protect the rights of authors. In 1710 Parliament passed the first British copyright law: "An Act for the Encouragement of Learning, by Vesting the Copies of Printed Books in the Authors or Purchasers of Such Copies, during the Times therein mentioned." The law was passed in the eighth year of the reign of Queen Anne and hence became known as the Statute of Eight Anne.

The law gave the legal claim of ownership of a piece of literary property to the person who created the work or to a person who acquired the rights to the work from the author. The claim of ownership lasted for only fourteen years. The copyright could be renewed for fourteen more years, but after twenty-eight years the work fell into the public domain and could be copied by anyone. The copyright owner had to give nine copies to the government for use in libraries and had to register the book with the Stationers' Company. The most important aspect of this law was not the specific legal provisions, but the recognition by the British government that writers should enjoy the right of ownership in their creations. This concept is very important, for without it we might find ourselves with far less to read today. While most authors are motivated by a desire to inform and entertain, they must also subsist. By providing them the right of ownership in their work, authors are compensated in such a way as to encourage them to continue to write.

Clearly any law giving authors the right of ownership automatically limits copying and use of the literary property. This limitation is what Professor Goldstein means when he talks of censorship. A copyright law does in fact act as censorship, since it restricts the right to republish or copy books, articles, photographs, and any work that is copyrighted.

The Statute of Eight Anne did not go unchallenged. Booksellers were angered by the limit on ownership. (The law provided that the ownership in any work created before the statute was adopted would terminate in twenty-one years.) Publishers rushed into print with works the law ruled were in the public domain but that booksellers still claimed as literary property. The booksellers sought injunctions to stop what they called pirating. They argued that under the common law their ownership of a book was perpetual—it lasted forever. The Parliament could not take this away from them, they said. This dispute finally came before Britain's highest court, the House of Lords, in 1774. The House of Lords ruled that it was true that at common law the right of first printing and publishing lasted forever but that the statute superseded the common law, revoking the common law copyright in perpetuity for published works. The common law no longer applied. Twenty-eight years were the maximum for ownership of published literary property.

This case, *Donaldson* v. *Beckett,* established a very important point in copyright law: that the law treated an unpublished work differently from a published work. Eight Anne specifically applied to works that had been published. The House of Lords ruled that limited ownership applied to such works. However, the law did not embrace unpublished works, and hence the common law rule of ownership in perpetuity remained in force.

While our copyright laws are direct descendants of the British law, the British law had little impact in the colonies. The colonies had no separate copyright statute, but printing and publishing original books and pamphlets was not an active business prior to the Revolution. After the Revolution, of course, the British law did not apply.

Our first constitution, the Articles of Confederation, made no mention of the protection of literary property. Congress did, however, recommend that the states adopt legislation to protect the rights of authors. Several states did so before our present Constitution was adopted in 1789. In Article I, Section 8, of that document lies the basic authority for modern United States copyright law:

> The Congress shall have the power . . . To promote the Progress of
> Science and useful Arts, by securing for limited Times to Authors and
> Inventors the exclusive Right to their respective Writings and Discoveries.

This provision gives the Congress the power to legislate on both copyright and patent. The Congress did in 1790 by adopting a statute similar to that of Eight Anne. The law gave authors who were United States citizens the right to protect their books, maps, and charts for a total of twenty-eight years—a fourteen-year original grant plus a fourteen-year renewal. In 1802 the law was amended to include prints as well as books, maps, and charts. In 1831 the period of protection was expanded by fourteen years. The original grant became twenty-eight years with a fourteen-year renewal. Also, musical compositions were granted protection. Photography was given protection in 1865, and works of fine art were included five years later. Translation rights were added in 1870.

A major revision of the law was enacted in 1909, and as was previously noted, our current law was adopted in 1976. The 1976 federal law preempted virtually all state laws regarding the protection of writing, music, and works of art. Hence, copyright law is essentially federal law and is governed by the federal statute and by court decisions interpreting this statute.

What May Be
Copyrighted

The law of copyright gives to the author, or the owner of the copyright, the sole and exclusive right to reproduce the copyrighted work in any form for any reason. Before a copyrighted work may be printed, broadcast, dramatized, translated, or whatever, the consent of the copyright owner must first be obtained. The law grants this individual exclusive monopoly over the use of that material.

What kinds of works are protected? The federal statute lists a wide range of items that can be copyrighted:

1. Literary works
2. Musical works, including any accompanying words
3. Dramatic works, including any accompanying music
4. Pantomimes and choreographic works
5. Pictorial, graphic, and sculptural works
6. Motion pictures and other audiovisual works
7. Sound recordings

To quote the statute specifically, copyright extends to "original works of authorship fixed in any tangible medium of expression." The Congress has defined *fixed in a tangible medium* as that work which is "sufficiently permanent or stable to permit it to be perceived, reproduced, or otherwise communicated for a period of more than a transitory duration." Under these standards such things as newspaper stories or entire newspapers, magazine articles, advertisements, and almost anything else created for the mass media can be copyrighted. Performances, extemporaneous speeches, and improvised sketches are examples of materials that are not fixed in a tangible medium and are not protected by the federal copyright statute. But this does not mean that someone can film or record a performer's act, for example, without the performer's permission. This would be forbidden by other laws, such as the right to publicity (see chapter 4) and common law copyright.*

Copyright law is equally specific about what cannot be copyrighted:

1. Trivial materials cannot be copyrighted. Such things as titles, slogans, and minor variations on works in the public domain are not protected by the law of literary property. (But these items might be protected by other laws, such as unfair competition, for example.)

---

*Under the 1909 law the United States had two kinds of copyright protection: common law copyright and statutory copyright. Much as it did in eighteenth-century England, the common law protected any work that had not been published. Common law protection was automatic; that is, the work was protected from the point of its creation. And it lasted forever—or until the work was published. In order to protect published works, the author, photographer, or composer had to register the book or picture or song with the United States government and place a copyright notice on the work. The 1976 statute does away with common law copyright for all practical purposes. The only kinds of works protected by the common law are works like extemporaneous speeches and sketches that have not been fixed in a tangible medium. They are still protected from the point of their creation by common law copyright. Once they are written down, recorded, filmed, or fixed in a tangible medium in any way, they come under the protection of the new law.

2. Ideas are not copyrightable. The law protects the literary or dramatic expression of an author's idea—such as a script—but does not protect the ideas themselves.

3. Utilitarian goods—things whose purpose of existence is to produce other things—are not protected by copyright law, according to William Strong in *The Copyright Book*. A lamp is a utilitarian object whose sole purpose is to produce light. One cannot copyright the basic design of a lamp. But the design of any element that can be identified separately from the useful article can be copyrighted, according to Strong. The design of a Tiffany lamp can be copyrighted. The unique aspects of a Tiffany lamp have nothing to do with the utilitarian purpose of producing light; these aspects are purely decorative.

4. Methods, systems, and mathematical principles, formulas, and equations cannot be copyrighted. But a description, an explanation, or an illustration of an idea or system can be copyrighted. In such an instance the law is protecting the particular literary or pictorial form in which an author chooses to express her- or himself, not the idea or plan or method itself. Imagine, for example, that an individual develops a new method to teach people to type, the "X-System." The X-System is an idea and as such cannot be copyrighted. But the developer of the system can copyright instruction booklets, audiovisual materials, charts, drawings, and anything else used to describe or explain the X-System. These materials are considered "expressions of an idea" and are protected by the law. There is a limit, however, to how far the law will go in protecting such materials. You cannot protect the expression of an idea (through instruction books, charts, etc.) to the point where it prevents other persons from using the idea (the X-System of typing) at all.

Original Works

Can all books and motion pictures be copyrighted? Not really. The law specifically says that only "original" works can be copyrighted. What is an original work? In interpreting this term in the 1909 law, courts ruled that the word *original* means that the work must owe its origin to the author. In 1973 a court reporter, an employee of the court who transcribes the proceedings, attempted to claim copyright over a transcript he had made of some of the proceedings during the investigation of the death of Mary Jo Kopechne. This young woman drowned when a car driven by Senator Edward Kennedy went off a bridge and into a creek near Chappaquiddick, Massachusetts. In *Lipman* v. *Commonwealth* (1973), a federal judge ruled that the transcript could not be copyrighted. "Since transcription is by very definition a verbatim recording of other persons' statements, there can be no originality in the reporter's product."

In 1985 an organization called Production Contractors, Inc., or PCI, tried to block Chicago television station WGN from televising a Christmas parade on Thanksgiving Sunday. PCI, which put on the parade, sold the exclusive right to televise it to WLS. It claimed the parade was copyrighted, and WGN would be in violation of the law by televising it. A federal district court disagreed and ruled that a Christmas parade is not something that can be copyrighted; it is a common idea, not an event of original authorship (*Production Contractors* v. *WGN Continental Broadcasting,* 1985).

The work must be original. Must it be of high quality or be new or novel? The answer to both questions is no. Even common and mundane works are copyrightable. Courts have consistently ruled that it is not the function of the legal system to act as literary or art critic when applying copyright law. In 1903 Justice Oliver Wendell Holmes wrote in *Bleistein* v. *Donaldson Lithographing Co.,* "It would be a dangerous undertaking for persons trained only to the law to constitute themselves final judges of the worth of pictorial illustrations, outside of the narrowest and most obvious limits." Even the least pretentious picture can be an original, Holmes noted in reference to the posters involved in this case. Likewise, novelty is not important to copyright: the author does not have to be the first person to say something in order to copyright it. "All that is needed to satisfy both the Constitution and the statute is that the 'author' contributed something more than a merely trivial variation, something recognizably his own," one court ruled (*Amsterdam* v. *Triangle Publishing Co.,* 1951).

The key is how much of the author's own work is invested. In 1946 the *Philadelphia Inquirer* printed a copy of a map in connection with publication of a historical article. The map had been copyrighted by the Franklin Survey Company, which promptly sued for copyright infringement. The survey company had created the map by studying other maps; the company had done no surveying itself. It had obtained road numbers from the highway department and road names almost exclusively from other maps. There was no question that the Franklin Survey Company had spent a good deal of time assembling this material, but the fact was that the company did not create much of the material by its own labor. The court ruled that the survey company's copyright was invalid because the creative work by the plaintiff was not sufficient to make the map original (*Amsterdam* v. *Triangle Publishing Co.,* 1951). There must be at least a modicum of creative work in the map, the court said. Had Franklin not assembled this information in an original or unique fashion? This fact was immaterial, the court ruled. A map is protected only when the publisher gets some of the material "by the sweat of his brow." Originality is therefore the key; whether the work is novel or of artistic quality is not important.

Can an event or a fact be copyrighted? Suppose a reporter, Jane Adams, is standing next to a building that suddenly and violently collapses, killing scores of people trapped inside. Suppose the reporter is the only one who saw the building collapse. Can she write a news story about this disaster, copyright it, and then prohibit others from writing about the event as well? The answer is no.

This point was established in an interesting case. In 1917 the *New York Tribune* published a copyrighted story about the first large-scale use of submarine warfare by the Germans in World War I. The New York paper sold the republication rights for the story to the *Chicago Daily News*. Before the *Daily News* could print the story, the *Chicago Record-Herald* printed its own version of the story. The initial paragraph of the *Herald* version began, "The *Tribune* this morning in a copyrighted article of Louis Durant Edwards, a correspondent in Germany, says that Germany to make the final effort against Great Britain has plunged 300 or more submersibles into the North Sea."

The remainder of the *Herald* story was comprised of five additional paragraphs, each of which was almost an exact duplication of a paragraph from the much longer *Tribune* story. The *Tribune* sued for infringement of copyright. The *Herald* answered by saying that a newspaper cannot copyright the news. Lawyers for the defendant argued that all the newspaper did was make use of facts that were in the public domain.

The circuit court of appeals agreed that as such news is not copyrightable. If the *Herald* story had been merely a summary or statement of the *Tribune* story, the *Tribune* would then have no case. However, the *Herald* did not stick to just a summary of the facts but used parts of the article, including the literary style and quality. The article itself, the way the words were organized, the style—the creative aspects of the report—can be (and in this case were) protected by copyright. The court said (*Chicago Record-Herald* v. *Tribune Association,* 1921):

> This is plainly more than a mere chronicle of facts or news. It reveals a peculiar power of portrayal and a felicity of wording and phrasing, well calculated to seize and hold the interest of the reader, which is quite beyond and apart from the mere setting forth of facts. But if the whole of it were considered as stating news or facts, yet, the arrangement and manner of statement plainly discloses a distinct literary flavor and individuality of expression peculiar to the authorship, bringing the article clearly within the purview and protection of the copyright law.

The court ruled that the fact that the *Herald* gave the *Tribune* credit did not alleviate the theft. On the contrary, the court said, it might have conveyed to the public the incorrect idea that the *Herald* had got permission from the *Tribune* to use the story.

News cannot be copyrighted. But the style or manner of presentation can be protected. Consider the imaginary building-disaster story again. If reporter Jane Adams is the only one to witness the building collapse and publishes a copyrighted story about it, no one else can publish that story without permission. Other news media can report that Jane Adams reported in a copyrighted story that a building collapsed, killing many people. These news media can also summarize—note, summarize—the facts given by Adams in her story. This summary is not an infringement of copyright.

A case in Florida recently raised an interesting question about the difference between facts and expression of facts. Gene Miller, a Pulitzer-Prize-winning reporter for the *Miami Herald,* wrote a book entitled *83 Hours Till Dawn,* an account of the kidnapping of Barbara Mackle. Miller said he had spent more than 2,500 hours on the book, and many aspects of the kidnapping case were uncovered by the journalist and reported only in his book.

Universal Studios wanted to film a dramatization of the 1971 incident but was unable to come to terms with Miller on payment for the rights. The studio produced the so-called docudrama anyway, and Miller sued for infringement of copyright. The similarities between Miller's book and the Universal script were striking—even some of the errors Miller had made in preparing the book were found in the film. But Universal argued that it was simply telling a story of a news event, and as such the research that Miller had done in digging out the facts regarding the story was not protected by copyright law. A United States district court agreed with Miller's contention. "The court views the labor and expense of the research involved in the obtaining of those uncopyrightable facts to be intellectually distinct from those facts, and more similar to the expression of the facts than the facts themselves," the court said. The judge ruled that it was necessary to reward the effort and ingenuity involved in giving expression to a fact (*Miller* v. *Universal Studios,* 1978). But the Fifth United States Court of Appeals reversed the lower court ruling. "The valuable distinction in copyright law between facts and the expression of facts cannot be maintained if research is held to be copyrightable. There is no rational basis for distinguishing between facts and the research involved in obtaining the facts," the court said. To hold research copyrightable, the court said, is no more or less than to hold that the facts discovered as a result of research are entitled to copyright protection (*Miller* v. *Universal City Studios,* 1981). The court added: "A fact does not originate with the author of a book describing the fact. Neither does it originate with the one who 'discovers' the fact. The discoverer merely finds and records. He may not claim that the facts are 'original' with him, although there may be originality and hence authorship in the manner of reporting, i.e. the 'expression' of the facts."

The path followed by the Fifth United States Court of Appeals in the *Miller* case had been forged a year earlier by the Second United States Court of Appeals in a similar ruling. In March 1980 that court ruled that Universal Studios did not infringe upon the copyright of author A. A. Hoehling, who wrote *Who Destroyed the Hindenberg?* when it produced a film on the 1937 airship disaster. In writing his opinion Chief Judge Irving Kaufman noted that the Second Circuit Court had in the past refused "to subscribe to the view that an author is absolutely precluded from saving time and effort by referring to and relying upon prior published material. . . . It is just such wasted effort that the proscription against the copyright of ideas and facts . . . are designed to prevent" (*Hoehling* v. *Universal Studios,* 1980).

Misappropriation

While this chapter focuses upon copyright, an ancillary area of the law needs to be briefly mentioned, as it too guards against the theft of immaterial property. **Misappropriation,** or unfair competition, is sometimes invoked as an additional legal remedy in suits for copyright infringement. Unlike copyright, which springs largely from federal statute today, misappropriation, or unfair competition, remains a creature of the common law. One of the most important media-oriented misappropriation cases was decided by the Supreme Court seventy years ago and stemmed from a dispute between the Associated Press (AP) and the International News Service (INS), a rival press association owned by William Randolph Hearst. (INS merged with the United Press in 1958 and today represents the *I* in *UPI.*)

The Associated Press charged that the International News Service pirated its news, saying that INS bribed AP employees to gain access to news before it was sent to AP member newspapers. The press agency also charged that the Hearst wire service copied news from bulletin boards and early editions of newspapers that carried AP dispatches. Sometimes INS editors rewrote the news, and other times they sent the news as written by AP. Copyright was not the question, because AP did not copyright its material. The agency said it could not copyright all its dispatches because there were too many and they had to be transmitted too fast. The International News Service argued that because the material was not copyrighted, it was in the public domain and could be used by anyone.

Justice Mahlon Pitney wrote the opinion in the seven-to-one decision. He said there can be no property right in the news itself, the events, the happenings, which are publici juris, the common property of all, the history of the day. However, the jurist went on to say (*Associated Press* v. *International News Service,* 1918):

> Although we may and do assume that neither party [AP or INS] has any remaining property interest as against the public in uncopyrighted matter after the moment of its first publication, it by no means follows that there is no remaining property interest in it as between themselves.

Pitney said there was a distinct difference between taking the news collected by AP and publishing it for use by readers and taking the news and transmitting that news for commercial use, in competition with the plaintiff. This action is unfair competition, he said—interference with the business of the AP precisely at the point where profit is to be reaped.

In 1963 a Pennsylvania broadcasting station was found guilty of pirating the news from a local newspaper and reading it over the air as if it were the fruits of its own news-gathering efforts (*Pottstown Daily News Publishing* v. *Pottstown Broadcasting,* 1963).

The decision in both these cases was based on the doctrine of unfair competition, or misappropriation. Courts have applied the doctrine in various instances of fraudulent or dishonest competitive business practices, but particularly in those instances where one seller attempts to substitute his or her own products for those of a well-known competitor by counterfeiting a trade name, package design, or trademark. For example, the owner of the Acme Motel remodels that building in the guise of a Holiday Inn, calls the remodeled creation Holiday Inn, and attempts to lure weary travelers into this establishment on the basis of the reputation of the real Holiday Inn. This practice is considered unfair competition. In *Associated Press* v. *International News Service,* the Hearst wire service attempted to pass off Associated Press news as its own, and the court said the deception was unfair.

Another more recent case explores a different dimension of the problem. Orion Pictures bought the film rights to a French novel entitled $E = MC^2$ and prepared to make a film of the story entitled *A Little Romance.* Dell Publishing Company bought the translation rights to the same book and attempted to negotiate with Orion for a tie-in publicity campaign heralding the release of both the movie and the book. But Orion refused, claiming that the story had been changed so much in the film that it no longer resembled the book. Dell pushed on anyway and published the book using the movie title—*A Little Romance*—and the cover of the book stated "Now A Major Motion Picture." The promotional material for the book emphasized the tie-in with the film and was an attempt to boost sales of the book. Orion sued for unfair competition, arguing that the sale of the book could hurt the film. A federal judge agreed, noting that after he had read the book and seen the film he considered the motion picture to be substantially better than the novel. "It is the Court's belief that if one were to read the book first, the entertaining achievement of the film would not be anticipated." The court said that the Dell book, through its title and cover promotion, gives the impression that it is the "official novel" version of the film and therefore has similar content. This misleads the public and constitutes unfair competition (*Orion Pictures* v. *Dell Publishing,* 1979). The book company was attempting to trade on the name of the picture in promoting the book. This practice is illegal, even though the title of a film cannot be copyrighted.

| Duration of Copyright Protection | Any work created after January 1, 1978, will be protected for the life of the creator, plus fifty years. This allows creators to enjoy the fruits of their labor until death and then allows the heirs to profit from the work of their fathers, mothers, sisters, or brothers for an additional one-half century. After fifty years the work goes into what is called public domain. At that point it may be copied by any person for any reason without the payment of royalty to the original owner. The copyright on a work created by two or more authors extends through the life of the last author to die plus fifty years. A work for hire (i.e., where an author is paid to create a book for a corporation that then holds the copyright) is protected for seventy-five years after publication or for one hundred years after creation. |

Prior to 1978 works could be copyrighted for a term of twenty-eight years and then renewed for twenty-eight more years for a total of fifty-six years. The 1976 copyright revision prolongs the protection of works copyrighted before 1978 for a total of seventy-five years.

If the work is in its initial term of copyright, it is protected for the remainder of that term plus forty-seven years. That is, the owner of the copyright on a book that expires in 1991 can retain ownership of that book from the present time until 1991 plus forty-seven years. However, in order to gain this additional forty-seven years of protection, copyright holders must seek renewal as was required under the previous statute. Without renewal, copyright owners forfeit their ownership of the work, which will move into the public domain.

If the copyrighted work is in its renewal term—the second twenty-eight years under the old law—the work is protected for a total of seventy-five years. For example, a book that is in the fifteenth year of its second, or renewal, term has already been protected for one full term, twenty-eight years, and for fifteen years of the renewal term—a total of forty-three years. That book is protected for thirty-two more years from today, or a total of seventy-five years. No renewal request is needed.*

SUMMARY

American copyright law derives from rules and regulations established by the British government in the sixteenth and seventeenth centuries. The contemporary basis for the protection of immaterial property is contained in the United States Constitution, and since 1789 the nation has had numerous federal copyright statutes. The current law, adopted in 1976, gives to the author or owner of a work the sole and exclusive right to reproduce the copyrighted work in any form for any reason. The statute protects all original works of authorship

*Additional information concerning duration of copyright is available in circulars *R15A* and *R15T,* which are published by the Copyright Office, Library of Congress, Washington, D.C., 20559.

fixed in any tangible medium. Included are such things as literary works, newspaper stories, magazine articles, television programs, films, and even advertisements. Trivial items, utilitarian goods, ideas, and methods or systems cannot be copyrighted.

News events cannot be copyrighted, but stories or broadcasts that endeavor to describe or explain these events can be copyrighted. What is being protected is the author's style or manner of presentation of the news. Similarly, facts cannot be copyrighted, but works that relate these facts can be protected as expression. While news and facts cannot be copyrighted, anyone who attempts to present news or facts gathered by someone else as his or her own work may be guilty of breaking other laws, such as misappropriation, or unfair competition. In most cases copyrighted works are protected for the life of the author or creator plus fifty years. Different rules apply for works created before 1978 and for works made for hire.

FAIR USE

Owners of a copyright are granted almost exclusive monopoly over the use of their creations. The word *almost* must be used, for there are really four limitations upon this monopoly. Three of the limitations have been discussed already. First, the work must be something that can be copyrighted. There can be no legal monopoly on the use of something that cannot be protected by the law. Second, the monopoly only protects original authorship or creation. If the creation is not original, it cannot be protected. Third, copyright protection does not last forever. At some point the protection ceases and the work falls into the public domain.

The fourth limitation upon exclusive monopoly is broader than the other three, is certainly more controversial, and is concerned with limited copying of copyrighted material. This is the doctrine of fair use, which has been defined by one court as (*Triangle* v. *Knight-Ridder,* 1980):

> A rule of reason . . . to balance the author's right to compensation for his work, on the one hand, against the public's interest in the widest possible dissemination of ideas and information on the other.

This doctrine, then, permits limited copying of an original creation that has been properly copyrighted and has not yet fallen into the public domain.

Under previous copyright laws all copying of a copyrighted work was against the law. This absolute prohibition on copying constituted a hardship for scholars, critics, and teachers seeking to use small parts of copyrighted materials in their work. A judicial remedy for this problem was sought. It was argued that since the purpose of the original copyright statute was to promote art and science, the copyright law should not be administered in such a way as to frustrate artists and scientists who publish scholarly materials. In 1879 the United States Supreme Court ruled in *Baker* v. *Selden:*

> The very object of publishing a book on science or the useful arts is to communicate to the world the useful knowledge which it contains. But this object would be frustrated if the useful knowledge could not be used without incurring the guilt of piracy of the book.

The doctrine of **fair use** emerged from the courts, and under this judicial doctrine small amounts of copying were permitted so long as the publication of the material advanced science, the arts, criticism, and so forth.

The 1976 copyright law contains the common law doctrine of fair use. Section 107 of the new measure declares, "the fair use of a copyrighted work . . . for purposes such as criticism, comment, news reporting, teaching (including multiple copies for classroom use), scholarship or research is not an infringement of copyright."

In determining whether the use of a particular work is a fair use, the statute says that courts should consider the following factors:

1. The purpose and character of the use, including whether such use is of a commercial nature or is for nonprofit educational purposes
2. The nature of the copyrighted work
3. The amount and substantiality of the portion used in relation to the copyrighted work as a whole
4. The effect of the use upon the potential market for or value of the copyrighted work

These, then, are the factors that judges will take into account in determining whether a use is an infringement or a fair use. Fair use is perhaps the most confusing and complex part of the law, and the section of the law dealing with fair use became a major battleground for disputes between librarians and publishers. The librarians and other persons interested in photocopying of published works sought liberal rules under fair use. Publishers and copyright holders wanted tight rules against photocopying. The law seems to be a compromise, allowing for the photocopying of a single copy of a work for library use but with several qualifications of the general rule.

Purpose and Character of Use

Interestingly, the fair-use criteria included in the statute and just listed here (1 through 4) are very close to the criteria that courts used under the old common law fair-use doctrine. This is no accident. In a report issued by committees in the House and the Senate on Section 107, the legislators said that the new law "endorses the purpose and general scope of the judicial doctrine of fair use" but did not intend that the law be frozen as it existed in 1976. "The courts must be free to adapt the doctrine to particular situations on a case-by-case basis. Section 107 is intended to restate the present judicial doctrine of fair use, not to change, narrow, or enlarge it in any way."

Fair use is easiest to understand by looking at each of the four elements individually, as a judge would do in determining whether a particular use is a fair use. It is dangerous to assign relative weight to each of these elements, as in any given case a court may place more weight upon one than upon another because of the facts in the case, biases of the court, or any number of other reasons.

The purpose and character of the use—how the copyrighted material will be used—is very important. Courts look far more favorably upon noncommercial or nonprofit uses. The law specifically lists several categories of use that normally fall under fair use: criticism, comment, news reports, teaching, scholarship, and research. A book reviewer, for example, is clearly protected when quoting even long passages from a work being evaluated. A journalist could undoubtedly publish one or two stanzas from a poem by a poet named winner of a Pulitzer Prize. Yet if a poster publisher took the same two stanzas of poetry, printed them in large type on eleven-by-fourteen stock, and tried to sell them for $2.50 each, the publisher would be guilty of an infringement of copyright. The purpose of the use in the case of the journalist was to give readers an example of the poet's work, but the poster publisher simply wanted to make a few bucks.

Another dimension of purpose or character focuses upon the material itself and the public interest. In 1966 the Second Circuit Court of Appeals erected the public-interest dimension of fair use in a complex copyright suit involving America's best-known recluse, the late Howard Hughes. Random House planned to publish a biography of Hughes in which a series of articles about Hughes in *Look* magazine were quoted rather extensively. When he learned of the Random House project, Hughes, who manifested almost a compulsion about his privacy, formed a corporation called Rosemont, which bought the rights to the *Look* magazine story. Rosemont then sued Random House for using material from the series. All these events took place even before the book was published.

Judge Lumbard ruled in favor of Random House, noting that the purpose of the copyright laws was not to stop dissemination of information about publicity-shy public figures. It would be contrary to the public interest, he said, to allow a man to buy up the rights to anything written about him to stop authors from using the material. Lumbard said that at least the spirit of the First Amendment applied to the copyright laws and that the courts should not tolerate the use of the copyright laws to interfere with the public's right to be informed regarding matters of general interest. Rosemont (Hughes) protested that such copying might be appropriate if the work in question were a scholarly biography of Hughes but that the Random House venture was commercial. Judge Lumbard said this fact was immaterial (*Rosemont v. Random House*, 1966):

> Whether an author or publisher reaps economic benefits from the sale of a biographical work, or whether its publication is motivated in part by desire for commercial gain, or whether it is designed for the popular market, i.e., the average citizen rather than the college professor, has no bearing on whether a public benefit may be derived from such a work. . . . Thus, we conclude that whether an author or publisher has a commercial motive or writes in a popular style is irrelevant to a determination of whether a particular use of copyrighted material in a work which offers some benefit to the public constitutes a fair use.

The decision in *Rosemont* represented a bold new step forward in copyright law, a step that many authorities felt was long overdue. On its face the case could not have been equitably decided any other way. Hughes's attempt to buy up his own life story was so patently obvious that the entire suit was really a farce—a mild diversion for the idle rich. Many persons asked, Will the public-interest ruling stand?

Two years later a federal district court in New York used the standard to allow the copying of several frames of very famous motion-picture film. An amateur photographer named Abraham Zapruder happened to be filming President John F. Kennedy when he was shot by an assassin in Dallas in 1963. The film is crude but is the only film available. *Life* magazine bought the rights to the film from Zapruder for $15,000 with the stipulation that the magazine would allow government agencies to use it in connection with investigation of the president's death. *Life* had a tendency to buy the rights to important events, for example, signing contracts with all the astronauts for exclusive stories. The Zapruder film became (and remains) a central piece of evidence in the death of John Kennedy, and many persons who believe that the Warren Commission was wrong, that there was a conspiracy, that there was more than one gunman, use the Zapruder film to attempt to prove their thesis. In this case the defendant wanted to publish several frames of the film in his book proposing a multi-assassin theory. When *Life* refused permission to use the film, the author used the frames anyway. Was this fair use?

Life said no, but the court disagreed. The judge said that there was little damage to the magazine as a result of publication of the pictures, that customers purchased the book because of its thesis, not because of its pictures, and that without the photographs the author's thesis was at best difficult to explain. "There is a public interest in having the fullest information available on the murder of President Kennedy. Thompson [the author] did serious work on the subject and had a theory entitled to public consideration." The public interest won out over the magazine's property rights (*Time, Inc. v. Bernard Geis Associates*, 1968).

But the public interest standard enunciated in *Rosemont* and *Zapruder* is not without boundaries. Copyright law cannot be ignored or abandoned simply because there is great public interest in the reporting of an event or a story about an important person. Both the American Broadcasting System (ABC) and the Columbia Broadcasting System (CBS) discovered recently that the fair-use doctrine has limits.

While James Doran was a student at Iowa State University, he produced a twenty-eight minute biography of wrestler Dan Gable. The film was financed by Iowa State and the Gable family, and the university held the copyright. Doran worked for ABC as a videotape operator during the 1972 Olympic Games, during which Gable won a gold medal in wrestling. Doran told ABC about his film while network reporters were scrambling for some biographical film about Gable. ABC broadcast long segments of the film during its telecast of the Olympic Games, without first obtaining permission from Iowa State University. The network claimed that these broadcasts were fair use in the copyright infringement suit that followed. The network said it was engaged in the laudable pursuit of disseminating the life story of an important public figure involved in an event of intense public interest. But the Second United States Court of Appeals rejected this argument. The network could have used other, noncopyrighted material for its film biography of the gold-medal-winning wrestler. The film was used at least in part for commercial exploitation by the network, the court ruled. No fair use (*Iowa State* v. *ABC,* 1980).

CBS found itself in a similar mess in 1982 after it had broadcast a copyrighted compilation of Charlie Chaplin films on the occasion of the great comedian's death. Roy Export Company owned the rights to the motion pictures excerpted in the thirteen-minute montage. This compilation of segments from six of Chaplin's greatest films had been put together by Roy Export for a one-time telecast on NBC during the 1972 Academy Award presentations, which featured a special segment on Charlie Chaplin. CBS had tried to buy the rights to the compilation from Roy Export, but the company refused the offer. When Chaplin died, CBS nevertheless obtained a copy of the film compilation from NBC, which had kept a videotape of the Academy Awards ceremony, and broadcast it as a memorial biography of the great comedian.

When the network was sued for copyright infringement, it claimed its telecast of the material was fair use. Chaplin's death was newsworthy, and a biography of the comedian's life would be incomplete without showing excerpts from some of his greatest films, the network argued. But the Second United States Court of Appeals disagreed. "The showing of copyrighted films was not essential to CBS's news report of Charlie Chaplin's death or to its assessment of his place in history," the court ruled. Other films that were in the public domain were available, the court said. Also, the public is generally familiar with Chaplin's work.

CBS also argued that the 1972 Academy Awards ceremony was a very important news event, since it marked the return of Charlie Chaplin to Hollywood after a twenty-year exile in Europe following the Communist witch-hunts in the film industry in the early 1950s. Again the court rejected the network's ideas. "The audiovisual news event, if there was one, was Chaplin's appearance, not the showing of his work," the judge ruled. The showing of the copyrighted compilation of Chaplin's film exceeded fair use (*Roy Export Co. v. CBS,* 1982).

It is important to note the difference between these latter two cases and the earlier decision on the Zapruder film, for this difference is a key to understanding what are perhaps one set of limits to the public-interest standard in fair use. Assume for a moment that comparable public interest exists in all three events—the Kennedy assassination, Dan Gable winning an Olympic Gold Medal, and the death of Charlie Chaplin. There was considerable noncopyrighted material available for the networks to use in reporting the latter two events. The broadcast of the copyrighted films was not essential to telling an important news story. In the case of the Zapruder film, however, much of the book's argument about the Kennedy assassination was based upon the film taken by Zapruder. No suitable substitute existed. Courts in the future may use this criterion as an element in deciding whether the use of copyrighted material is fair use. The question will be, Was other noncopyrighted material available that could have been used to tell the story and thus serve the public interest?

Finally, the *Nation* magazine attempted to argue that its publication of an excerpt from the unpublished memoirs of Gerald Ford was fair use because the material contained information of great public interest. The article in *Nation* was approximately 2,250 words long and consisted almost entirely of paraphrases and quotations from portions of the 200,000 word draft memoirs, with little or no independent commentary. The article detailed Ford's recital of the events leading to the pardon of Richard Nixon, repeated stories about Henry Kissinger, John Connolly, and others, and closed with some of Ford's observations about Nixon's character. *Time* magazine had purchased the right to print prepublication excerpts from the manuscript and had already paid Ford $12,500, half of the promised sum for the prepublication privilege. An unidentified source gave a copy of the draft memoirs to Victor Navasky, the *Nation* editor, and the weekly published its article on April 9, 1979, a full week before the excerpts in *Time* were scheduled to appear. *Time* cancelled its publication of the excerpts and refused to pay Ford the additional $12,500. Harper & Row and the Reader's Digest Association, joint publishers of the Ford book (which was published in August of 1979) sued the *Nation* for copyright infringement.

A U.S. District court ruled that *Nation* had indeed infringed upon the copyright on the work held by the book publishers (*Harper & Row Publishers v. Nation Enterprises,* 1983). But the Second U.S. Court of Appeals overturned this decision, declaring the publication of the material by the *Nation* was a fair use. The appeals court ruled that all but 300 words of the 2,250 word article was uncopyrightable news and history. The court found that the only possible infringement was the use of verbatim passages from the memoirs that had not appeared previously in other publications. Because of the great public import in the material, the court said it could excuse the verbatim appropriation of copyrighted material as "lending authenticity to this politically significant material." The court added, "Where information concerning important matters of state is accompanied by minimal borrowing of expression, . . . the copyright holder's monopoly must not be permitted to prevail over a journalist's communication." This was a broad assertion of a public-interest element of the fair-use defense in a copyright action (*Harper & Row Publishers, Inc.* v. *Nation Enterprises,* 1983).

But the victory for *Nation* was shortlived, for the Supreme Court overturned the ruling by the court of appeals. Justice Sandra Day O'Connor, writing for the six-person majority, ruled that the promise of copyright would be an empty one if it could be avoided merely by dubbing the infringement a fair use because it contains news or information in the public interest. "In using generous verbatim excerpts of Mr. Ford's unpublished manuscript to lend authenticity to its account of the forthcoming memoirs, the *Nation* effectively arrogated to itself the right of first publication, an important marketable subsidiary right," O'Connor wrote. This was an important point in the ruling, for it surely narrowed the scope of the High Court's rejection of the public-interest component of fair use. The 1976 Copyright Act clearly recognizes the right of first publication for an author. The scope of fair use is narrowed where unpublished works are concerned. The Senate report that accompanied the 1976 law specifically states: "The applicability of the fair use doctrine to unpublished works is narrowly limited since, although the work is unavailable, this is the result of a deliberate choice on the part of the copyright owner. Under ordinary circumstances the copyright owner's 'right of first publication' would outweigh any needs of reproduction. . . ." Justice O'Connor wrote that the majority concluded that the unpublished nature of a work is a key, though not necessarily determinative factor, tending to negate a defense of fair use (*Harper & Row* v. *Nation Enterprises,* 1985).

The Supreme Court decision constituted a rejection of the public-interest element of the fair-use defense, but it was a narrow ruling and will be applicable in the future only in those instances when an infringement action is brought because of the alleged infringement of unpublished material. The decision does not alter earlier rulings such as *Rosemont* and *Zapruder,* both of which involved the alleged infringement of published material.

| Nature of Copyrighted Work | When the nature of the copyrighted work is considered, at least two important considerations of the protected work must be made. First, is the work still available? If a copyrighted book is out of print, unavailable for purchase, the user may have more justification for copying a portion of it than if it is readily available. The lack of the availability of the work cannot be used as an excuse for copying a work that has never been formally published. Second, what kind of work is it? Copying consumable materials like workbooks, exercise books, standardized tests, and so forth, is rarely if ever a fair use. If such materials could be copied freely, only a single workbook, for example, would ever have to be purchased. Copies could be made continuously, and the author would be deprived of justly earned royalties. The use of materials from publications like newspapers, news magazines, and reference books is less likely to be an infringement. Use of materials from these sorts of works is rarely harmful to the publisher—unless the copying is a persistent occurrence. |

Nature of Copyrighted Work

When the nature of the copyrighted work is considered, at least two important considerations of the protected work must be made. First, is the work still available? If a copyrighted book is out of print, unavailable for purchase, the user may have more justification for copying a portion of it than if it is readily available. The lack of the availability of the work cannot be used as an excuse for copying a work that has never been formally published. Second, what kind of work is it? Copying consumable materials like workbooks, exercise books, standardized tests, and so forth, is rarely if ever a fair use. If such materials could be copied freely, only a single workbook, for example, would ever have to be purchased. Copies could be made continuously, and the author would be deprived of justly earned royalties. The use of materials from publications like newspapers, news magazines, and reference books is less likely to be an infringement. Use of materials from these sorts of works is rarely harmful to the publisher—unless the copying is a persistent occurrence.

Amount of a Work Used

The amount and the substantiality of the portion used in relation to the copyrighted work as a whole—as stated—is a relative standard. Word counts, for example, do not mean very much. The use of five hundred words from a 450-page book is far less damaging than the use of three lines from a five-line poem. The question is always how much was used in comparison to the total size of the work. A court of appeals ruled that a novelist who copied twenty-four passages from a biography of the life of Hans Christian Andersen exceeded fair use. The passages were translations of Danish documents, and while the documents were in the public domain, the biographer had translated them into English. While twenty-four passages does not sound like very much, the court ruled that the defendant, who used the material in a novel based upon the life of Andersen, appropriated too much material to be considered a fair use. By using the fruits of the biographer's work, the translation of the Danish documents, the novelist was able to finish her work in far less time. She got much value from the plaintiff's work (*Toksvig* v. *Bruce Publishing Co.,* 1950).

It was the massive appropriation of copyrighted films that resulted in a successful suit for infringement against an educational services board in Erie County, New York. The educational board was sued by three corporations, including the Encyclopaedia Britannica, which made, acquired, and leased educational films. The defendant in the case rented films from various companies and then made videotapes of them for future use by the schools. Films broadcast on television were also videotaped for classroom use. Despite the nonprofit nature of the use of these materials, the court ruled that such activity was not a fair use. An important factor in the court's decision was that the educational services board used from five to eight full-time employees to do the copying and had made as many as ten thousand tapes per year since 1966. This was high-volume copying, and the court ruled it was not a fair use (*Encyclopaedia Britannica* v. *Crooks,* 1978). The issue of the amount of copying that can be done in the name of education arose again recently when nine book publishers sued New York University, nine of its professors, and an off-campus copy center for copyright infringement. The suit charged that the faculty members repeatedly copied major amounts from many popular works such as Truman Capote's *In Cold Blood* and *The Final Days* by Bob Woodward and Carl Bernstein. The publishers argued that such copying was done semester after semester. The publishers dropped their suit in April 1983 in return for a pledge from the defendant school and faculty to adhere to copying guidelines.

One of the toughest tasks a judge must face is measuring fair use when someone presents a parody of a copyrighted work. To be successful a parody must conjure up in the viewers' or listeners' minds the original work; hence, it must use some aspects of the original work. But how much of the original can be used? "Saturday Night Live," a National Broadcasting Company television program, presented a parody of a New York City public relations campaign. The city had even commissioned the writing of a song—"I Love New York"—as a theme for the campaign. The NBC "Saturday Night Live" parody ended with the singing of "I Love Sodom" to the tune of "I Love New York." The city claimed this was a copyright infringement, but the court disagreed. "A parody is entitled to conjure up the original. Even more extensive use would still be fair use, provided the parody builds upon the original, using the original as a known element of modern culture and contributing something new for humorous effect or commentary," the Second United States Court of Appeals ruled (*Elsmere Music* v. *NBC,* 1980). (See *MGM* v. *Showcase Atlanta,* 1981, for an example of a parody that went too far.) What is added to the copyrighted material is almost as important as how much of the original is used when determining whether a parody is a fair use.

It is important to remember that the amount of material that may be fairly copied is not an absolute but is always relative to the size of the total work from which the material is taken.

Effect of Use on Market The effect of the use upon the potential market for or value of the copyrighted work is the fourth criterion. While a cautionary note has been sounded against assigning relative weight to the four criteria, this final one—harm to the plaintiff—is probably given greater weight by most courts than any of the other three. In a Congressional Committee report on the 1976 law, the legislators noted that "with certain special exceptions . . . a use that supplants any part of the normal market for a copyrighted work would ordinarily be considered an infringement." And in the action by Harper & Row against *Nation,* Justice Sandra Day O'Connor noted that "This last factor is undoubtedly the single most important element of fair use" (*Harper & Row* v. *Nation,* 1985).

A group of song writers once sued *Mad* magazine for publishing parody song lyrics of their compositions. The publication appeared in the special bonus to the *Fourth Annual Edition of Mad* and was described by the magazine as "a collection of parody lyrics to fifty-seven old standards which reflect the idiotic world in which we live." The parody lyrics were written in the meter of the original songs and were to be sung to the melody of the standard versions. The parody lyrics to the song "The Last Time I Saw Paris" concerned a sports hero turned television pitchman, and the song was called "The First Time I Saw Maris." A song about a woman hypochondriac was sung to the tune of "A Pretty Girl is Like a Melody" and was called "Louella Schwartz Describes her Malady."

The judge asked, "How were the songwriters hurt?" In a negligible way, the court concluded. The parody of lyrics was not a theft. They were not about the same topic and did not have the same rhyme scheme. The parody lyrics were in the same meter as the original lyrics, which was necessary if the original songs were to be recognized and the lyrics were to fit the melodies. "We doubt," the court added, "that even so eminent a composer as plaintiff Irving Berlin should be permitted to claim a property interest in the iambic pentameter." The use by *Mad* of the song titles and references to their melodies was fair use, the court ruled (*Berlin* v. *E. C. Publications, Inc.*, 1964).

In 1977 a federal district court refused to grant a temporary order enjoining the publication of a cumulative 111-year name index of the 111 annually issued volumes of the *New York Times Index*. The *Times* index is organized alphabetically within each annual volume. The *Roxbury Index* of the annual *New York Times Indexes* was to be organized alphabetically over the 111 years from 1863 to 1974. The index of the *Times* index would be of great benefit to researchers. For example, using only the *New York Times Index* for material on Charles Evans Hughes, a researcher would have to look in more than forty annual volumes spanning the late Chief Justice's life. But with the *Roxbury Index,* a researcher would need only to look in a single volume under Hughes's name for all the references during the forty-five-year period. While this would be a great boon to researchers, there was no question that by its very nature the *Roxbury Index* included much material copied from the copyrighted *New York Times Index*. The court ruled, however, that the effect of the personal-name index on the market for the *New York Times Index* appeared "slight or nonexistent." As a matter of fact, persons could not use the *Roxbury Index* without also using the *New York Times Index,* so rather than being in competition with the annual index, the cumulative name index enhanced the value of the *New York Times* publication (*New York Times* v. *Roxbury Data Interface,* 1977).

The Fifth United States Court of Appeals ruled that it was fair use when the *Miami Herald* displayed copyrighted covers of *TV Guide* magazine in advertising for the newspaper's new television magazine. *TV Guide* had argued that such use was an infringement upon its copyright, since the advertisement for the *Herald* magazine was a blatantly commercial use of the *TV Guide* covers. The court conceded it was indeed a commercial use but noted that the use of the covers had absolutely no effect upon the potential market or value of the copyrighted *TV Guide* magazine covers. True, the advertisements for the *Herald* television magazine might hurt *TV Guide* sales, but the *advertising* did this, not the use of the covers of old editions of *TV Guide* (*Triangle Publications* v. *Knight-Ridder Newspapers, Inc.,* 1980). In this case the court said that the fourth factor, the effect of the use on the market for the copyrighted work, "is widely accepted to be the most important factor."

Finally, in the *Harper & Row* v. *Nation* case the Supreme Court looked at the direct economic impact of the publication of segments of the Ford memoirs in the *Nation*—the loss of $12,500 from *Time* magazine—as well as potential long-term losses. "More important," Justice O'Connor wrote, "to negate fair use one need only show that if the challenged use should become widespread, it would adversely affect the potential market for the copyright work."

The doctrine of fair use presented the nation in the 1980s with one of the most interesting copyright problems in decades, and the fourth element, the economic impact wrought by the unauthorized use, was crucial in the ultimate resolution of the issue. Is it fair use when the owner of a home videotape recorder copies television programs and motion pictures broadcast by television networks and local stations and then replays them for strictly personal use? Universal City Studios, Walt Disney Productions, and other program production companies brought suit in 1979 to stop such home recording. Named as defendants in the case were Sony Corporation of America and several distributors and sellers of the home video-recording equipment. Universal charged that the home copying of programs amounted to massive infringement of their copyrights on these programs. Sony and the other defendants argued that this was fair use of the material. The trial court ruled in favor of the defendants, noting that the copying was not undertaken for commercial purposes and that the harm to the plaintiffs in the case was purely speculative (*Universal City Studios* v. *Sony,* 1979). But the Ninth United States Court of Appeals reversed this decision and ruled against Sony. The court said such home recording was not fair use. The law states that *nonprofit educational* use may be fair use, but this is not the same as *noncommercial* use, the court said. The recording of entire programs was something certainly never contemplated when the fair-use standards were written, the court added. Finally, such copying could have a severe impact upon the plaintiffs. In the imminent future a large percentage of the nation's seventy-five million television households will have a videotape recorder, and massive amounts of copying will take place, the court predicted. Viewers would watch the playback of programs they had copied, rather than new programs; commercials would be deleted in the playback; and the audience for rerun programming would be significantly reduced, the court concluded (*Universal City Studios v. Sony,* 1981).

Sony appealed the decision to the Supreme Court, which, in 1984, reversed the ruling by the court of appeals. Taping television programs at home for showing at a different time (called time shifting) is a noncommercial, nonprofit activity, wrote Justice John Paul Stevens for the five-person majority. But even a noncommercial, nonprofit use may impair the copyright holder's ability to obtain rewards that Congress intended the holder to have, Stevens noted. Then the economic impact of the use on the copyright holder must be considered. A majority of the high court agreed completely with the trial court in its consideration of this factor. Universal City Studios and the other plaintiffs in the lawsuit had not shown that they had been harmed or might be harmed in the future because of such copying for home use. "Harm from time shifting is speculative and, at best, minimal," the justice wrote. "What is necessary is a showing by a preponderance of the evidence that some meaningful likelihood of future harm exists. If the intended use is for commercial gain, that likelihood may be presumed. But if it is for a noncommercial purpose, the likelihood must be demonstrated," he added. The motion picture and television program producers had failed to demonstrate this likelihood of harm. In fact, Stevens suggested, it was not implausible to suggest that time shifting, through the use of a video tape recorder, increased the number of viewers who might see a program (*Sony Corp. v. Universal City Studios,* 1984).

SUMMARY

While the copyright statute gives the author or owner of a copyrighted work an exclusive monopoly over the use of that work, there has been recognition that it is important in some instances for other persons to be able to copy portions of a protected work. No liability will attach to such copying if the use is what the law calls a "fair use."

A court will consider four factors when determining whether a specific use is fair use:

1. What is the purpose of the use? Why was the material copied? Was it a commercial use or for nonprofit educational purpose? Was the use intended to further the public interest in some way?

2. What is the nature of the copyrighted work? Is it a consumable item such as a workbook, or is it a work that might more likely be borrowed from such as a newspaper or magazine article? Is the copyrighted work in print and available for sale?

3. How much of the copyrighted work was used in relation to the entire copyrighted work? Was it a small amount of a large work? or was it a large portion of a small work?

4. What impact does the use have on the potential market or value of the copyrighted work? Has the use of the material diminished the chances for sale of the original work? or is the use unrelated to the value or sale of the copyrighted material?

While a court considers each of these items closely, most courts tend to give extra weight to item four. In a close ruling the impact on the market or value of the copyrighted work often becomes the most crucial question.

COPYRIGHT NOTICE AND INFRINGEMENT

In order for a work to be protected under the copyright law, it must contain what is called a **copyright notice.** The new law specifically prescribes the kind of notice required and states that it consists of three parts.

Proper Notice

A copyright notice must contain the word *Copyright,* the abbreviation *Copr.,* or the symbol © (the letter *C* within a circle; the symbol ℗ is used on phonorecords). The year of publication must also be included in the notice. For periodicals the date supplied is the date of publication. For books the date is the year in which the book is first offered for sale (e.g., a book printed in November or December 1991 to go on sale January 1992 should carry a 1992 copyright). The notice must also contain the name of the copyright holder or owner. Most authorities recommend that both the word *Copyright* and the symbol © be used, since the use of the symbol is required to meet the standards of the international copyright agreements. The symbol © protects the work from piracy in most foreign countries. A copyright notice should look something like this:

Copyright © 1989 by Jane Adams

The courts will be very strict with regard to the composition of the notice. Any old notice will not do. For example, a notice saying "This book was written by Jane Adams and is her property until 2005" will not qualify as proper notice. The new statute is virtually identical with previous statutes in prescribing the composition of the notice. In 1903 the Supreme Court ruled that since the statute states a specific way to give the reader proper notice, that is what the courts will demand. "In determining whether a notice of copyright is misleading, we are not bound to look beyond the face of the notice, and inquire whether under the facts of the particular case it is reasonable to suppose an intelligent person could actually have been misled" (*Mifflin* v. *H. H. White,* 1903).

The copyright notice can be placed anywhere that it "can be visually perceived" on all publicly distributed copies. (The rules are different for sound recordings, which by law cannot be visually perceived.) The Copyright Office of the Library of Congress has issued rules that implement the statutory description that the notice be visually perceptible. For example, the rules list eight different places where a copyright notice might be put in a book, including the title page, the page immediately following the title page, either side of the front cover, and so forth. For photographs, a copyright notice label can be affixed to the back or front of a picture or on any mounting or framing to which the photographs are *permanently* attached.*

The 1976 copyright law also provides that omission of the proper notice does not destroy copyright protection for the work if the notice is omitted from only a relatively small number of copies, if an effort is made within five years to correct the omission, or if the notice is omitted in violation of the copyright holder's express requirement that as a condition of publication the work carry a copyright notice.

At the same time the law protects persons who copy a work on which the copyright notice was inadvertently omitted. Such an innocent infringer incurs no liability—cannot be sued—unless this infringement continues beyond the time notice is received that the work has been copyrighted.

Registration

Proper notice is the only requirement that an author must fulfill to copyright a work. The work is then protected from the moment of creation for the life of the author plus fifty years. However, before a copyright holder can sue for infringement under the law, the copyrighted work must be registered with the federal government. To register a work the author or owner must do three things:

1. Fill out the proper registration form. The type of form varies, depending upon the kind of work being registered. The forms are available from the Information and Publications Section, Copyright Office, Library of Congress, Washington, D.C. 20559.
2. Pay a ten-dollar fee.
3. Deposit two complete copies of the work with the Copyright Office.

The statute gives an author or owner ninety days to get a work registered. What happens if the work is still not registered after ninety days and an infringement takes place? The owner can still register the work and bring suit.

*Additional information is available in the bulletin *Methods of Affixation and Position of the Copyright,* published by the Copyright Office, and in the *Federal Register,* vol. 42, no. 247, for 23 December 1977, pp. 64374–78.

But a successful plaintiff in such a suit cannot win statutory damages (see pages 489–90) or win compensation for attorney's fees. It is best to get into the habit of registering a work as soon as it is published or broadcast.

The requirement of notice is a very important one. It allows all the works that no one wants to copyright to fall into the public domain immediately. It also tells the reader whether a work is copyrighted, was ever copyrighted, or is still copyrighted. It also identifies the owner of the work and the date of publication. The change in the law that protects authors who accidently forget to include a copyright notice on their works is healthy and worthwhile. But writers and broadcasters should get into the habit of putting the notice on all material that they believe to be valuable, whether it is published or not.

Infringement

It is important for authors to know how to protect their own work. It is equally important to know how to avoid being sued for stealing someone else's copyrighted material. Such theft does not always result in a successful suit, or even in a suit at all. Many times the owner of the copyrighted matter is unaware of the theft. Other times the harm to the copyright holder is insignificant. In copyright, as in other areas of mass media law, who you are is often more important than what you stole. For example, if the *East Ames Morning Dispatch and World Advertiser* publishes in its entertainment section, without permission, one complete act of a Neil Simon play, the newspaper might get a nasty letter from Simon's attorney, but probably not much more. But if the National Broadcasting Company presents the same act on one of its shows, it will surely get slapped with a copyright suit. Publication of the play in a small newspaper has not harmed the playwright significantly, and in addition the paper probably does not have much money. But presentation of even a single act of the play on NBC can diminish Simon's future royalties, since it would probably lessen the number of future stage productions of the play.

The United States copyright statute does not really define infringement. The law states that anyone who violates any of the "exclusive rights" of the copyright holder is an infringer of the copyright. That statement is of little help to courts attempting to determine whether an infringement has taken place. Consequently, courts continue to rely upon the definition of infringement forged during the past 150 years. Courts look to a variety of criteria to determine whether an infringement has taken place. We will focus upon three of these criteria that seem to be the most important: originality, access, and copying and substantial similarity. The burden of proof falls on the plaintiff in a copyright suit, but of course the defendant will do everything possible to prove that no copyright infringement has occurred. So both sides normally present evidence.

Originality   One of the first questions the court asks in an infringement suit is whether the *plaintiff's* work is original. In other words, is the copyright on the plaintiff's book or article or film valid? If the copyright is not valid because the plaintiff's work is not original, no suit for infringement can be maintained. Many persons copyright material that is noncopyrightable. History, for example, exists for all to use in a book or story. Margaret Alexander brought a copyright suit against Alex Haley, claiming that he had copied portions of her novel *Jubilee* and her pamphlet *How I Wrote Jubilee* when writing his successful novel *Roots*. The court ruled in Haley's favor, noting that much of what the plaintiff claimed Haley had copied was material based on history—the westward movement in the United States, for example—and material that was in the public domain, such as folk customs that are an embodiment of black culture. "Where common sources exist for the alleged similarities, or the material that is similar is not original with the plaintiff, there is no infringement," the court ruled. Similarly, the court rejected the argument that Haley had copied Alexander's work when he used cliché language. "Words and metaphors are not subject to copyright protection; nor are phrases and expressions conveying an idea that can be, or is typically, expressed in a limited number of stereotyped fashions," noted the judge, citing the phrase "poor white trash" as an example of such an expression. In its ruling the court said that while certain conventional material appeared in both books, the material was not original with Alexander's works but belonged more generally to the nation's history or its idiomatic expressions. As such, illegal "copying" from the plaintiff had not occurred (*Alexander* v. *Haley,* 1978).

Judith Rossner, the author of the successful book *Looking for Mr. Goodbar,* sued CBS for copyright infringement in 1985 when the network produced the film "Trackdown: Finding Mr. Goodbar." Both Rossner's book and the TV movie are based on the murder in 1973 of Roseann Quinn by John W. Wilson. Rossner's book leads readers up to the point of the murder; the CBS movie purportedly tells the story of the capture of the killer. Rossner claimed the use of the term "Mr. Goodbar" in the title of the movie violated her copyright. But the United States District Court disagreed, noting that the term "Mr. Goodbar" had been used in newspaper stories about the killing before Rossner wrote her book. An author can't build a story around a historical incident and then claim exclusive right to the use of that incident, the court said. "To the extent that Rossner's character's were inspired by actual persons, she cannot prevent the future depiction of these characters through the individual creative efforts of others," the court ruled. The Mr. Goodbar concept was not original with Rossner; she could not claim it under copyright (*Rossner* v. *CBS,* 1985).

More recently, the author of a book entitled *Fort Apache* sued the producers of the film, "Fort Apache—The Bronx." Both the book and the movie focused upon the 41st Precinct of the New York City Police Department. Police officers had dubbed the South Bronx precinct Fort Apache because of the high incidence of violent crime in the area. Thomas Walker, a former police officer who was assigned to the 41st Precinct for fifteen months, wrote and published his book in 1976. The book was a series of stories about his work in the precinct, a narrative moving from one anecdote to the next with no real plot. The film, on the other hand, was intensely plotted, with several interrelated story lines, all taking place at once. Walker claimed the producers of the film had stolen his material, but the U.S. Court of Appeals disagreed. "To be sure, the book and the film share an identical setting, and police officers are central characters in both works," the court noted. "But the South Bronx and the 41st Precinct are real places known to the public through media coverage. Accordingly, the notion of telling a police story that takes place there cannot be copyrightable," the court ruled. The parts of the film that were similar to the book were not original with the book's author (*Walker* v. *Time-Life Films,* 1986).

Access

The second dimension of an infringement suit is access: the plaintiff must convince the court that the defendant had access to the copyrighted work. An opportunity to copy has to exist. If plaintiffs cannot prove that the so-called literary pirate had a chance to see and read the work, they are hard pressed to prove piracy. As Judge Learned Hand once wrote (*Sheldon* v. *Metro-Goldwyn-Mayer Pictures,* 1939):

> . . . if by some magic a man who had never known it were to compose anew Keats's, "Ode on a Grecian Urn," he would be an 'author' and if he copyrighted it, others might not copy that poem, though they might of course copy Keats's.

Here in contemporary terms is what Judge Hand said. If through some incredible coincidence a young composer were to write and publish a song called "Alfie" that was an exact duplicate of the song by Burt Bacharach and Hal David, it would not be an infringement of copyright. Publishing a song exactly like a copyrighted song is not infringement; copying a copyrighted song is infringement. Moreover, if the young composer could prove that he had lived in a cave since birth, had never listened to the radio or records, and had never watched television or gone to the movies, and if Bacharach and David could not prove that the defendant had had access to "Alfie," they would lose their suit. It must be obvious that such a coincidence can never occur, but this illustration nevertheless makes the point. The *plaintiff* must prove access to the stolen work. The smaller the circulation of the copyrighted matter, the harder it is to prove access.

Failure to prove the defendant had access to a copyrighted book was fatal to a lawsuit brought by Sonya Jason against the writers and producers of the film *Coming Home*. Defendants Jane Fonda and others stated that their film was conceived in the late 1960s, that a first draft of the screenplay was completed by late 1973 and was revised in 1977. Jason's book, *Concomitant Soldier,* was first printed in April 1974. Only 1,100 copies were printed. About 500 copies were sold in New Jersey, 100 were sold through the plaintiff's church, 200 copies were returned to the printer because they were defective, and the remaining copies were sold in southern California. Jason claimed that a copy of the book might have been given to Nancy Dowd, a screenwriter for the film, but there was no evidence that Dowd or anyone else connected with the film had seen the book. Jason was only able to prove that several hundred copies of *Concomitant Soldier* were sold in southern California where Fonda, Dowd, and others associated with the film lived and worked. "That level of availability creates no more than a 'bare possibility' that defendants may have had access to plaintiff's book," the court said. "In and of itself, such a bare possibility is insufficient to create a genuine issue of whether defendants copied plaintiff's book" (*Jason* v. *Fonda,* et al., 1981). It might be noted parenthetically that such copyright or plagiarism suits against successful films and television productions are becoming commonplace today. Most studios do not even open envelopes containing unsolicited manuscripts, to diminish the possibility of a plaintiff later showing access to a copyrighted story.

Copying and Substantial Similarity

Copying and substantial similarity are normally the final criteria examined by the court in an infringement suit. The court will first seek direct evidence that the defendant did in fact copy the plaintiff's work. If the defendant's work is a word-for-word replica of the plaintiff's work, copying is highly probable. Such cases are rare. A group aptly named Air Pirates, copied Walt Disney characters for posters and T-shirts. Instead of portraying Mickey and Donald and Pluto and the gang as their lovable Disney selves, the company translated the characters into what the court called "awful characters." Changing the nature of the character did not excuse the infringement, the court said (*Walt Disney Productions* v. *Air Pirates,* 1972). Disney still owned the characters. Changing the medium does not work either. A toy manufacturer cannot make a plastic doll in the likeness of a comic strip character without first getting permission of the copyright owner of the comic character.

More than likely there will be no direct evidence of copying. In such a case the courts then must determine whether the works in question are substantially similar. If they are similar and if the defendant had access to plaintiff's work, a court will normally presume that copying took place and an infringement occurred. More than just minor similarities must be present: the two works must be substantially alike. In *Folsom* v. *Marsh,* a very old copyright case involving the letters and documents of President George Washington, Justice Story wrote, "If enough is taken to diminish the value of the original or the labors of the original author are substantially appropriated," piracy occurs (*Folsom* v. *Marsh,* 1841). In a more recent statement of the same theme, the United States Ninth Court of Appeals said that the evaluation was "not an analytic or other comparison" of the works but rather "whether defendant took from plaintiff's works so much of what is pleasing to the audience that the defendant wrongfully appropriated something which belongs to the plaintiff" (*Sid and Marty Krofft Television Productions* v. *McDonald's Corp.,* 1977).

Courts frequently ask two questions in attempting to determine the substantial similarity of two works:

1. Is there substantial similarity in the *idea* between the two works? If there is not, the lawsuit ends. If the answer is yes, then the second question is applied.
2. Is there substantial similarity in the expression of this idea?

In seeking a similarity in the idea between the two works, courts rely upon what is called the "ordinary observer" test. A judge asks whether an average lay observer, rather than an expert, would recognize the alleged copy as having been appropriated from the copyrighted work. Let us look at some recent cases to see how substantial similarity is actually measured.

Artist Albert Gilbert painted a picture of two cardinals on an apple tree branch for the National Wildlife Art Exchange. Three years later he painted a picture of two cardinals on an apple tree branch for the Franklin Mint. National Wildlife Art Exchange, which held copyright to the first drawing, sued Franklin Mint for infringement. The United States Court of Appeals for the Third Circuit found similarities in the two pictures. Both contained two cardinals, one male and one female, in profile on apple tree branches in blossom. But there were differences as well. The male bird was on the top in one picture and on the bottom in the other; in one, the male was calm; in the other, he appeared aggressive. There was a large yellow butterfly in one; there was no butterfly in the other. The idea in both pictures was similar, the court ruled. But copyright does not protect thematic concepts. The expression of this concept—two cardinals on the branches of an apple tree—was different. "A pattern of differences is sufficient to establish a diversity of expression rather than only an echo . . . ," the court noted. The fact that the same subject matter may be present in two paintings—or in stories or plays for that matter—does not prove similarity and infringement of copyright (*Franklin Mint* v. *National Wildlife Art Exchange,* 1978).

The producers of two popular motion pictures sued for copyright infringement when programs with similar themes appeared on network television. Twentieth Century-Fox sued the producers of *Battlestar Galactica,* which Fox said was a copy of their successful film *Star Wars.* The trial court ruled that the basic idea in the two productions—a battle between good and evil in outer space—was indeed similar. But almost everything else about the two productions, including the story line and the main characters, was different. There was no copyright infringement, the trial court ruled (*Twentieth Century-Fox* v. *MCA,* 1980), but the Ninth United States Court of Appeals reversed the lower court ruling and ordered a trial in the case. "After viewing the *Star Wars* and *Battlestar* motion pictures, we conclude that the films in fact raise genuine issues of material face as to whether only the *Star Wars* idea or the expression of that idea was copied. At a minimum, it is a close enough question that it should be resolved by way of a trial," the court ruled.

Warner Brothers, the producers of the recent Superman movies, took ABC to court when the network broadcast "The Greatest American Hero." In both stories a character with superhuman powers battles the forces of evil. But the court ruled that Warner Brothers could not "claim a protected interest in the theme of a man dressed in a cape and tights who has the power to fly, resist bullets, crash through walls, break handcuffs, etc." The plaintiff must show that the concrete expression of the *Superman* idea has been appropriated. Warner Brothers could not do this. The characters in *Superman* and "The Greatest American Hero" are quite different. The hero of the ABC program is Ralph Hinckley, an ordinary man who reluctantly takes on abnormal abilities through a magic costume and is comically inept. Superman is naturally endowed with these powers, which he wields with grace and confidence. As a person Hinckley is the antithesis of the strong Superman character, the court said. In some ways the ABC show is a parody of Superman. "As a comedy that parodies American superheroes," Judge Motley wrote, " 'The Greatest American Hero' has a very different appeal from Superman, a real superhero, and plaintiffs have not sufficiently proven that it will reduce demand for movies and programs about Superman, and products bearing the Superman image" (*Warner Bros.* v. *ABC,* 1981).

Some courts have referred to the two parts of the test outlined above as an intrinsic, or subjective, test and an extrinsic, or objective, test. The intrinsic test is based on the response of the ordinary, reasonable person. Are the general ideas in the two works alike? In the extrinsic test the court attempts to objectively determine whether there are similarities in the two works in plot development, themes, characters, dialogue, mood, settings, and sequence of events. Expert witnesses may be used at this stage to assist the court. The Ninth U.S. Court of Appeals was recently asked to determine whether writer/director Michael Crichton had stolen a screen treatment for his film called *Coma,* which was based on a book by Robin Cook. Plaintiff Ted Berkik in 1968 wrote a fifty-four-page screen treatment for a story he called "Reincarnation, Inc." Crichton apparently saw the screen treatment but did not use it ten years later when he wrote the screen play for *Coma.* Berkik alleged that both the film and Robin Cook's book were taken from his screen treatment.

The court first applied the intrinsic, subjective test. Would ordinary, reasonable persons view Crichton's work as a copy of Berkik's work? The stories have certain similarities, the court noted. Both deal with criminal organizations that murder healthy young people and then remove and sell their vital organs to wealthy people in need of organ transplants. And in both stories courageous young medical professionals investigate and finally expose the criminal organization. But these similarities are at a high level of generality. When one applies the extrinsic test, the objective study of the parts of the two works, the similarity ends. The plots of the two stories develop differently; the settings are different. *Coma* is replete with medical terminology and is an old-fashioned detective story; "Reincarnation" is more of a romance. Yes, there are some similarities, but general ideas are not protected. Nor are situations and incidents that flow naturally from a basic plot premise, so-called scènes à faire. "These familiar scenes [depictions of the small miseries of domestic life or romantic frolics at the beach] and themes are among the very staples of modern American literature and film. The common use of such stock material cannot raise a trial issue of fact on the plaintiff's copyright claim," the appellate court ruled. "It merely reminds us that in Hollywood, as in the life of real men generally, there is only rarely anything new under the sun" (*Berkik v. Crichton*, 1985).

It is not impossible to demonstrate substantial similarity between two works. Universal City Studios successfully sued Film Ventures for copyright infringement when the company released a film called *Great White,* which was very similar to the movie *Jaws.* In this case the general idea of both films was obvious to an average filmgoer. But the similarities in the two pictures became even more apparent when the court objectively looked at the manner in which the ideas were expressed. Major characters were the same, the sequence of incidents was the same, the development and interplay of the major characters was the same, and even minor story points were the same. The court said the films were not identical but that "defendants have captured the total concept and feel of plaintiff's motion picture."

The court pointed to the following similarities in the films. In both films a local politician plays down the news of a great white shark in the interest of local tourism. Both films featured a salty English sea captain and a shark expert who go out to hunt the shark. The opening scenes of both films show innocent teenagers swimming on a beach who become the first victims of the shark. In both films a local fisherman's empty boat is found. In both films the shark approaches a small boat, bumps it hard, and causes a child to fall into the water. Finally, in both films the shark devours the English sea captain during the hunt but is finally killed when it swallows something that explodes in its stomach. "In light of the great similarity in expression, it would seem fair to conclude that the creators of *Great White* [which was titled *The Last Jaws* when it was released overseas] wished to be as closely connected with plaintiff's motion picture *Jaws* as possible." The court issued an injunction to stop the exhibition of *Great White* and set a hearing to consider the award of damages (*Universal City Studios* v. *Film Ventures,* 1982).

It is not easy to prove infringement of copyright; yet surprisingly, a large number of suits are settled each year in favor of plaintiffs. In such instances the obvious theft of the material would generally appall an honest person. An individual who works to be creative in fashioning a story or a play or a piece of art usually has little to fear. The best and simplest way to avoid a suit for infringement is simply to do your own work, to be original.

SUMMARY

To protect the copyright of a work the author or owner must give proper notice and register the work with the government. A proper copyright notice looks like this:

Copyright © 1989 by Jane Adams (use the letter ℗ for phonorecords)

Notice must be placed anywhere it may be visually perceived. Once notice is given, the work is protected. However, to gain the full benefits of the law, a work must be registered with the Copyright Office in the Library of Congress. The proper registration form along with ten dollars and two complete copies of the work must be sent to the Register of Copyrights.

When a plaintiff sues for infringement of copyright, the court will consider three important criteria. First, is the plaintiff's work original? If the plaintiff has attempted to copyright material that legitimately belongs in the public domain, the plaintiff cannot sue for infringement of copyright. Second, did the defendant have access to the plaintiff's work? There must be some evidence that the defendant viewed or heard the copyrighted work before the alleged infringement took place. Finally, is there evidence that the defendant actually copied the plaintiff's work? If no such evidence exists, are the two works substantially similar? In examining this latter issue, the court seeks to determine whether the ideas in the two works are similar. This is sometimes called an intrinsic, or subjective, test. If the general idea of the two works is similar, is the expression of these ideas similar as well? This is sometimes referred to as an extrinsic, or objective, test.

FREE-LANCING AND COPYRIGHT

What rights does a free-lance journalist, author, or photographer hold with regard to stories or pictures that are sold to publishers? The writer or photographer is the creator of the work; he or she owns the story or the photograph. Consequently, as many rights as such free-lancers choose to relinquish can be sold or given to a publisher. Beginning writers and photographers often do not have much choice but to follow the policy of the book or magazine publisher. Authors whose works are in demand, however, can retain most rights to the material for their future benefit. Most publishers have established policies on exactly what rights they purchase when they decide to buy a story or photograph or drawing. *The Writer's Market* is the best reference guide for the free-lancer. Here are some of the rights that publishers might buy:

1. All rights: The creator sells complete ownership of the story or photograph.
2. First serial rights: The buyer has the right to use the piece of writing or picture for the first time in a periodical published anywhere in the world. But the publisher can use it only once, and then the creator can sell it to someone else.
3. First North American serial rights: The rights are the same as provided in number 2, except the publisher buys the right to publish the material first in North America, not anywhere in the world.
4. Simultaneous rights: The publisher buys the right to print the material at the same time other periodicals print the material. All the publishers, however, must be aware that simultaneous publication will occur.
5. One-time rights: The publisher purchases the right to use a piece just one time, and there is no guarantee that it has not been published elsewhere first.

It is a common practice for publishers to buy all rights to a story or photograph but to agree to reassign the rights to the creator after publication. In such cases the burden of initiating the reassignment rests with the writer or photographer, who must request reassignment immediately following publication. The publisher signs a transfer of rights to the creator, and the creator should record this transfer of rights with the Copyright Office within two or three weeks. When this transaction has taken place, the creator can then resell the material. A ten-dollar fee must accompany either the original form or a certified copy of the transfer form when it is sent to the Register of Copyrights.

What if no agreement between the publisher and the writer or photographer is made? Neither the publisher nor the creator of the work should really be this careless, but if they are, it is generally presumed the publisher has purchased the following rights:

1. The right to use the material in that particular publication (an issue of *Sports Illustrated,* for example)
2. The use of the material in a collection of works from the publication (a book entitled *The Best Stories from Sports Illustrated,* for example)

3. Any revisions of the collection of works noted above (a second or third or fourth revision of *The Best Stories from Sports Illustrated,* for example)
4. The right to run the material again in a later issue of the same magazine or periodical

It is obvious that the creator gives away a considerable amount by not taking the time to ensure that his or her rights are protected. It is best for the writer or photographer to specifically stipulate what rights are being offered in the query letter to the publisher regarding the story or photograph. For example, the author might tell the publisher that "one-time North American rights" are being offered. In the absence of a subsequent formal or specific agreement, the existence of such an offer in the query letter could materially aid the writer or photographer in establishing the future ownership of the story or photograph. Free-lancers are also urged to beware of endorsements on payment checks from publishers. It is not uncommon for a publisher to include a statement on a royalty check to the effect that "the endorsement of this check constitutes a grant of reprint rights to the publisher." In order to cash the check, the writer must agree to grant the reprint rights. In such cases writers should quickly notify the publisher that such an agreement is unacceptable and demand immediate payment for the single use of the story. Other pitfalls too numerous to mention await the inexperienced free-lancer. The best advice is to understand exactly what you are doing at all times during the negotiation of rights. Take nothing for granted; just because you are honest and ethical does not mean everyone else is. And if questions come up, consult a qualified attorney. Legal advice is costly, but it can save a writer or photographer money in the long run.

DAMAGES

Plaintiffs in a copyright suit can ask the court to assess the defendant for any damage they have suffered, plus the profits made by the infringer from pirating the protected work. Damages can be a little bit or a lot. In each case the plaintiff must prove to the court the amount of the loss or of the defendant's profit. But, rather than prove actual damage, the plaintiff can ask the court to assess what are called statutory damages, or damage amounts prescribed by the statute. The smallest statutory award is $250, although in the case of an innocent infringement, the court may use its discretion and lower the damage amount to $100. The highest statutory award is $10,000. However, if the plaintiff can prove that the infringement was committed willfully, the maximum damage award can be as much as $50,000.

In addition the courts have other powers in a copyright suit. A judge can restrain a defendant from continued infringement, can impound the material that contains the infringement, and can order the destruction of these works. Impoundment and destruction are rare today.

A defendant might also be charged with a criminal offense in a copyright infringement case. If the defendant infringed upon a copyright "willfully and for purposes of commercial advantage or private financial gain," he or she could be fined up to $10,000 and jailed for not more than one year. The fines for pirating phonograph records and motion pictures are much higher: $25,000 and one year in jail for the first offense and $50,000 and up to two years in jail for subsequent offenses. Criminal actions for copyright infringement are rare today.

The law of copyright is not difficult to understand and should not be a threat to most creative persons in the mass media. The law simply says to do your own work and not to steal from the work of other persons. Some authorities argue that copyright is an infringement upon freedom of the press. In a small way it probably is. Nevertheless most writers, most authors, and most reporters—persons who most often take advantage of freedom of the press—support copyright laws that protect their rights to property that they create. Judge Jerome Frank once attempted to explain this apparent contradiction by arguing that we are adept at concealing from ourselves the fact that we maintain and support "side by side as it were, beliefs which are inherently incompatible." Frank suggested that we keep these separate antagonistic beliefs in separate "logic-tight compartments."

The courts have recognized the needs of society, as well as the needs of authors, and have hence allowed considerable latitude for copying material that serves some public function. Because of this attitude, copyright law has little, or should have little, impact upon the information-oriented mass media. No new law changes this situation.

BIBLIOGRAPHY

Here is a list of some of the sources that have been helpful in the preparation of chapter 9:

Books

Ball, Horace. *The Law of Copyright and Literary Property.* New York: Banks & Co., 1944.

Cambridge Research Institute. *Omnibus Copyright Revision.* Washington, D.C.: American Society for Information Science, 1973.

Kaplan, Benjamin, and Brown, Ralph S., Jr. *Cases on Copyright.* 2d ed. Mineola, N.Y.: Foundation Press, 1974.

Nimmer, Melville B. *Nimmer on Copyright.* New York: Mathew Bender & Co., 1963.

Pilpel, Harriet F., and Goldberg, Morton D. *A Copyright Guide,* 4th ed. New York: R. R. Bowker Co., 1969.

Ransom, Harry. *The First Copyright Statute: An Essay on An Act for the Encouragement of Learning, 1710.* Austin: University of Texas Press, 1956.

Strong, William. *The Copyright Book.* Cambridge, Mass.: The M.I.T. Press, 1981.

Articles

"Copyright: Hollywood Versus Substantial Similarity." 32 *Oklahoma Law Review* 177, 1979.

"Copyright Infringement and the First Amendment." 70 *Columbia Law Review* 320, 1979.

Goldstein, Paul. "Copyright and the First Amendment." 70 *Columbia Law Review* 983, 1970.

Holbrook, Lanny R. "Copyright Infringement and Fair Use." 40 *University of Cincinnati Law Review* 534, 1971.

Morrill, Stephen S. "*Harper & Row Publishers* v. *Nation Enterprises:* Emasculating the Fair Use Accommodation of Competing, Copyright and First Amendment Interests," 79 *Northwestern University Law Review* 587, 1984.

Nimmer, Melville B. "Does Copyright Abridge the First Amendment Guarantees of Free Speech and Press?" 17 *UCLA Law Review* 1180, 1970.

Schulman, John. "Fair Use and the Revision of the Copyright Act." 53 *Iowa Law Review* 832, 1968.

Shaw, David. "Plagiarism: a Taint in Journalism," *The Los Angeles Times,* July 5, 1984.

Yankwich, Leon R. "What Is Fair Use?" 22 *University of Chicago Law Review* 203, 1954.

Cases

Alexander v. *Haley,* 460 F. Supp. 40 (1978).
Amsterdam v. *Triangle Publishing Co.,* 189 F.2d 104 (1951).
Associated Press v. *International News Service,* 248 U.S. 215 (1918).
Baker v. *Selden,* 101 U.S. 99 (1879).
Berkik v. *Crichton,* 761 F.2d 1289 (1985).
Berlin v. *E. C. Publications, Inc.,* 329 F.2d 541 (1964).
Bleistein v. *Donaldson Lithographing Co.,* 188 U.S. 239 (1903).
Chicago Record-Herald v. *Tribune Association,* 275 F.2d 797 (1921).
Donaldson v. *Beckett,* 4 Burr. 2408 (1774).
Elsmere Music v. *NBC,* 623 F.2d 252 (1980).
Encyclopaedia Britannica v. *Crooks,* 447 F. Supp. 243 (1978).
Folsom v. *Marsh,* 2 Fed. Cas. 342, No. 4901 (C.C.D. Mass. 1841).
Franklin Mint v. *National Wildlife Art Exchange.* 575 F.2d 62 (1978).
Harper & Row Publishers v. *Nation Enterprises,* 557 F. Supp. 1067 (1983), revd 723 F.2d 195 (1983), revd. 105 S.Ct. 2218 (1985).
Hoehling v. *Universal Studios,* 618 F.2d 972 (1980).
Iowa State v. *ABC,* 621 F.2d 57 (1980).
Jason v. *Fonda,* et al., 526 F. Supp. 774 (1981).
Lipman v. *Commonwealth,* 475 F.2d 565 (1973).
MGM v. *Showcase Atlanta,* 7 M.L. Rept. 2190 (1981).
Mifflin v. *H. H. White,* 190 U.S. 260 (1903).
Miller v. *Universal City Studios,* 650 F.2d 1365 (1981).
New York Times v. *Roxbury Data Interface,* 434 F. Supp. 217 (1977).
Orion Pictures v. *Dell Publishing,* 471 F. Supp. 392 (1979).
Pottstown Daily News v. *Pottstown Broadcasting,* 192 A.2d 657 (1963).
Production Contractors v. *WGN Continental Broadcasting,* 12 M.L. Rept. 1708 (1986).
Rosemont v. *Random House,* 366 F.2d 303 (1966).
Rossner v. *CBS,* 11 M.L. Rept. 2321 (1985).
Roy Export Co. v. *CBS,* 672 F.2d 1095 (1982).
Sheldon v. *Metro-Goldwyn-Mayer Pictures,* 81 F.2d 49 (1939).

Sid and Marty Krofft Television Productions v. *McDonald's Corp.*, 562 F.2d 1157 (1977).

Sony Corp. v. *Universal City Studios*, 104 S.Ct. 774 (1984).

Time, Inc. v. *Bernard Geis Associates*, 293 F. Supp. 130 (1968).

Toksvig v. *Bruce Publishing Co.*, 181 F.2d 664 (1950).

Triangle Publications v. *Knight-Ridder Newspapers, Inc.*, 445 F. Supp. 875 (1978); affd. 6 M.L. Rept. 1734 (1980).

Triangle Publishing Co. v. *New England Newspaper Publishing*, 46 F. Supp. 198 (1942).

Twentieth Century-Fox v. *MCA*, 6 M.L. Rept. 2016 (1980).

Universal City Studios v. *Film Ventures*, 543 F. Supp. 1134 (1982).

Universal City Studios v. *Sony*, 480 F. Supp. 429 (1979); revd. 659 F.2d. 963 (1981).

Walker v. *Time-Life Films*, 12 M.L. Rept. 1634 (1986).

Walt Disney Productions v. *Air Pirates*, 345 F. Supp. 180 (1972).

Warner Bros. v. *ABC*, 523 F. Supp. 611 (1981).

10

REGULATION OF ADVERTISING

Americans are treated to scores of advertisements daily. Someone has estimated that each of us is exposed to at least 110 advertisements per day, and at least 76 of them register in our consciousness. People in the business tell us that advertising is the cornerstone of our capitalistic economic system. Low prices for consumers are dependent upon mass production, mass production is dependent upon volume sales, and volume sales are dependent upon advertising. Many economists support this theory. Critics of advertising argue that while people probably would pay more for some products without the savings wrought by mass production and advertising, they would pay less for many more products such as cosmetics and patent medicines, for which about half the purchase price of the product pays for large advertising expenditures. Critics also argue (not without challenge) that people buy more than they really need because of advertising. Regardless of who is right, it is a fact that scores of billions of dollars are spent each year on advertising. About four cents of every dollar spent by every man, woman, and child for goods and services goes to pay for advertising costs. Some companies in this country spend one dollar for every three dollars they earn in sales on advertisements for their products. Far more money is spent for advertising than for many social needs, a fact that makes advertising controversial.

Regulation of advertising is also controversial. Many persons argue that advertising deserves the same measure of First Amendment protection as other kinds of speech and that government interference with advertising is a serious violation of at least the spirit of freedom of expression. They say that our capitalistic system is based upon a laissez-faire economic theory in which consumers must compete in the marketplace like everyone else. Within bare limits (such as laws against selling dangerous medicines or tainted meat), the consumer must learn to shop carefully, read advertising closely, and be skeptical about any claim. Caveat emptor—let the buyer beware.

On the other hand, there are persons who consider purely commercial messages, those designed to convince consumers to purchase products, undeserving of First Amendment protection. Freedom of the press is designed to protect ideas, not the trivialities of advertising. Consumer information is the basis of our capitalistic system, they argue, and only those advertisements that inform truthfully and accurately should be published or aired. Each time they make a purchase, consumers should not have to worry that they are being lied to or deceived by the manufacturer.

The government should police unfair and deceptive advertising, just as it polices other fraudulent conduct such as extortion and phony land sales. Caveat venditor—let the seller beware.

In the last quarter of the twentieth century, advertisers find themselves somewhere between the two positions. A measure of regulation has been built into the law, as this chapter will show. We will take a brief look at the history of advertising regulation in the United States and consider some of the conditions making regulation necessary. Then we will consider the protection the First Amendment affords advertising claims and get a brief perspective of the means available to regulate unfair and deceptive advertising, including industry and governmental regulation. We will examine the Federal Trade Commission, the primary watchdog of advertising in this country. Its jurisdiction, its standards, its remedies to correct bad advertising, and its procedures are discussed. Finally, the various kinds of deceptive advertising are identified and discussed briefly, and the defenses an advertiser can use in a false-advertising suit are outlined. ✦

THE LAW, THE ADVERTISER, AND THE FIRST AMENDMENT

From a historical standpoint, the regulation of advertising is a fairly recent phenomenon in this country because advertising as we know it today is a relatively modern practice. True, the first American newspaper published more than two hundred ninety years ago contained advertisements, but these were really announcements by merchants that goods had arrived or that certain merchandise was now in stock. The announcements were embellished somewhat, of course, but the modern advertising pitch did not become a common affair until the last part of the nineteenth century. Advertising depended upon the mass marketing of goods, which depended upon the so-called industrial revolution and modern modes of transportation.

In the past one hundred years or so, the nation has moved gradually from having no regulations upon advertising to having hundreds of different kinds of laws whose purpose is to regulate advertising. While in this chapter we are primarily concerned with how false and deceptive advertising is policed, it must also be noted that today there are scores of other laws applicable to commercial messages of which advertisers and advertising agencies must be aware.

In the wake of the civil rights movement of the past two decades, a whole range of regulations whose purpose is to make advertisements comply with equal rights provisions have been adopted. In employment and housing advertisements, for example, it is illegal under federal, as well as under many state laws, to discriminate against persons because of sex, race, national origin, or marital status. The publication, as well as the advertiser, can be held liable for the violation of such laws. The Truth in Lending Law placed various credit disclosure requirements upon advertisers. There are numerous laws at both federal and state levels that prescribe certain rules for political advertising. The rates for political advertising are frequently limited. In many states newspapers and broadcasting stations must file the names of political advertisers with public disclosure commissions. In most states the name of the sponsor of a political advertisement must be included in the advertisement. Political party labels must also be conspicuous.

Other laws dictate what can and cannot be said in specific kinds of advertisements. For example, strict regulations apply to liquor advertising. The law requires the publication in a conspicuous type size of alcoholic content (86 proof) and kind (bourbon) of whiskey.

The provisions just given are but a few examples of how advertising laws have evolved to meet changing political and social conditions in the United States. It is sufficient to say that the advertiser must be both cautious and knowledgeable when preparing advertisements.

Need for Regulation

The first fact an advertiser must remember is that he or she must obey the laws that specifically regulate advertising messages *in addition* to all the other laws that regulate the mass media. In other words, an advertisement can be libelous and the advertiser can be sued for defamation. An advertisement can be obscene and can invade the privacy of a person. It can violate copyright law or violate the Federal Communications Act. It can violate a federal, state, or local advertising regulation.

The basic thrust of advertising regulation at all levels is to outlaw deceptive advertisements, advertisements that are dishonest or untruthful. Here is where the first—perhaps the biggest—problem arises. Whose standard of truth do we use? While this question is considered in greater detail later in the chapter, it is important to note at this point that there are persons who think that most advertising is dishonest, that the concepts of truth and advertising are antithetical in most instances. To demand advertising to be truthful, some argue, would be to stop most advertising. This argument is worth exploring for a moment.

Were a man to invent a truly unique product—such as an automobile that can be powered by tap water—advertising for such a product could simply be informative and tell consumers that this product is available. But if there were such a product, advertisements would not really be needed for long. Changes in the product might require advertising, but consumers rarely have to be convinced to buy a product with such obvious advantages. However, if you watch television closely and read the advertisements in newspapers and magazines, you will find that most advertising is not about products like the water-powered car. Most advertising dollars are spent on products that are not unique—headache remedies, toothpastes, automobiles, cosmetics, detergents, soda pop, and so forth. Because the differences between various brands of these products are usually marginal, the consumer must be given reasons to buy Bufferin rather than Bayer Aspirin or Anacin, Coke rather than Pepsi-Cola. Those who argue that there is little truth in advertising point to such advertisements and say that these advertisements manufacture differences that do not exist or are not important. They ask, who cares about such differences? and say that to promote them is dishonest.

There is considerable truth in such an argument, but not enough to halt a $100 billion-per-year industry. The regulators of advertising in the United States find it fairly easy to rationalize that such advertisements really do not hurt anybody, because consumers are smart enough to realize that their only purpose is to catch the attention, not to inform. What harm is done when one cigarette advertises that it is milder, another that it is longer, another that it is cooler, another that it is more masculine, and another that it is more feminine? No one believes these advertisements anyway. But can we be sure that consumers are skeptical of advertisements? As we will see, the law does not require that advertising actually inform, only that it does not deceive.

Advertising and the First Amendment

Commercial advertising enjoys a qualified First Amendment protection. But it was less than fifteen years ago that the Supreme Court ruled that the U.S. Constitution shielded advertising from most government regulation. Lawyers describe what has happened since 1975 as the development of the **commercial speech doctrine**. Because it is of recent origin, the dimensions of constitutional protection for advertising are still being outlined. But a few basic rules have emerged:

1. The First Amendment does not protect advertising for unlawful activities.
2. The First Amendment does not protect false, deceptive, or misleading advertising.

All other advertising is protected by the First Amendment. In order for the government to regulate such advertising it must satisfy these three requirements:

1. The government must assert a substantial state interest to justify the regulation.
2. The government must demonstrate that the regulation of the advertising directly advances this substantial state interest.
3. The regulation must be narrowly drawn, no more extensive than is necessary to serve the interest asserted by the state.

If the state can meet these three requirements, courts will normally permit the advertising in question to be restricted or banned altogther. But if the state interest advanced by the regulation is of little importance or the government fails to assert a substantial state interest at all, or if the ban on advertising is too broad (if it prohibits a wider range of commercial speech than is necessary to protect the important state interest), then the regulation will be stricken as a violation of the First Amendment. The application of these standards or tests by the courts, especially the U.S. Supreme Court, has been inconsistent, to say the least. In some cases, the courts have forced the government to carry a heavy burden of proving that there is a need for the regulation, that the regulation directly advances the governmental interest, and that there is not a less intrusive means to fix the problem. (See *Virginia State Board of Pharmacy* v. *Virginia Citizen's Consumer Council, Inc.,* 1976, for example.) In other cases, the High Court has uncritically accepted the government's rationale for regulation of the speech. (See *Friedman* v. *Rogers,* 1979, for example.) All this is said to warn readers that the case law emerging under the commercial speech doctrine some times seems to make little sense.

Growth of the Commercial Speech Doctrine

In 1942 the Supreme Court of the United States ruled that "the Constitution imposes no . . . restraint on government as respects purely commercial advertising." The decision came in an unusual case in which a man attempted to circulate handbills on a city street urging citizens to make a paid visit to a submarine he had moored at a nearby wharf (*Valentine* v. *Chrestensen,* 1942). Most authorities believed, despite the unusual nature of the case, that this decision settled the matter: advertising was not protected by the First Amendment. In 1964 the Supreme Court ruled that *political* or *editorial* advertising is protected by the First Amendment (*New York Times* v. *Sullivan*). But most authorities rationalized that the First Amendment is designed to protect political speech, and political advertising is certainly political speech. Hence, this was hardly a revolutionary decision.

It was not until the mid-seventies that the High Court ruled that *commercial* advertising enjoys the benefits of the First Amendment as well when it reversed the conviction of a Virginia newspaper editor who had been found guilty of publishing an advertisement that offered assistance to women seeking an abortion. Abortion was illegal in Virginia in 1971 when the advertisement was published. The Woman's Pavilion, a New York group, urged women who wanted an abortion to come to New York, where it was possible to have a legal abortion. Justice Blackmun wrote for the Court that speech does not lose the protection of the First Amendment merely because it appears in the form of a commercial advertisement. Blackmun distinguished this ruling from the High Court's ruling in *Chrestensen* by arguing that in that instance the Supreme Court merely upheld the New York ordinance as a reasonable regulation *of the manner in which commercial advertising can be distributed* [author emphasis]. Blackmun refused to open the door completely or to state explicitly how far this ruling opened the door. "We need not decide in this case," he wrote, "the precise extent to which the First Amendment permits regulation of advertising that is related to activities the state may legitimately regulate or even prohibit" (*Bigelow* v. *Virginia,*1975).

In 1976 the Supreme Court clarified and expanded the extent to which advertising is protected by the First Amendment in the case of *Virginia State Board of Pharmacy* v. *Virginia Citizens' Consumer Council, Inc.* The Court ruled that a Virginia statute that had the effect of prohibiting pharmacies from advertising the price of prescription drugs violated the guarantee of freedom of expression in the First Amendment. Justice Harry Blackmun wrote:

> Advertising, however tasteless and excessive it sometimes may seem, is nonetheless dissemination of information as to who is producing and selling what product, for what reason, and at what price. So long as we preserve a predominantly free enterprise economy, the allocation of our resources in large measure will be made through numerous private economic decisions. It is a matter of public interest that those decisions in the aggregate be intelligent and well informed. To this end, the free flow of commercial information is indispensable.

The High Court made it equally clear, however, that the government was completely free to continue to regulate commercial speech that is false, misleading, or deceptive or that proposes illegal transactions.

The next ruling on the commercial speech doctrine was handed down in 1977. The township of Willingboro, New Jersey, banned the display of For Sale and Sold signs on homes and lawns in the community. The motivation for the ban was the fear that such signs contributed to panic selling by white homeowners who feared that the township was becoming populated predominantly by black families and that property values would decline. The black population had increased in the community, while white homeowners moved elsewhere. Persons testified before the township council that "the reason 80 percent of the sellers gave for their decision to sell was that 'the whole town was for sale and they didn't want to be caught in any bind.' " Community leaders reasoned that banning For Sale signs might diminish the fear that "everyone is selling" and might also stabilize the population.

When the ban was challenged on First Amendment grounds, Willingboro attempted to justify the policy on two grounds: first, that homeowners had other means of communicating that their property was for sale, including newspaper advertising, and second, that the goal of the ban was to provide stable, racially integrated housing, two factors that the community and the region considered important. But Justice Thurgood Marshall and a majority of the Court rejected both arguments. Marshall wrote that advertising in the newspaper was not a satisfactory alternative because it was a costly and less-effective medium for communicating the specific message that a home was for sale. He added that while the goal of racial integration was important, so too were the goals asserted by the government in *Bigelow* and *Virginia Pharmacy*. Marshall asserted that the constitutional defect of the Willingboro For Sale-sign ban was basic (*Linmark Associates* v. *Township of Willingboro*, 1977):

> The Township Council . . . acted to prevent its residents from obtaining certain information. That information . . . is of vital interest to Willingboro residents, since it may bear on one of the most important decisions they have a right to make: where to live and raise their families. . . . If the dissemination of this information can be restricted, then every locality in the country can suppress any facts that reflect poorly on the locality. . . . *Virginia Pharmacy* denies government such sweeping powers.

A decision two years later demonstrated that there are limits to the high court's protection of commercial speech. The Court ruled that it was permissible for the State of Texas to constitutionally prohibit the practice of optometry under a trade name (i.e., Acme Optometrists). Customers could be misled or deceived through the use of such trade names, Justice Powell wrote for the majority of the high court. "The trade name of an optometrical practice can remain unchanged despite changes in the staff of optometrists upon whose skill and care the public depends when it patronizes its practice," Powell noted. The jurist added that the use of an optometric trade name is strictly a business use; it does not provide consumers with information or knowledge useful in making an economic decision (*Friedman* v. *Rogers*, 1979).

In 1980 the Supreme Court handed down its most definitive ruling on commercial speech, establishing clearly for the first time the guidelines outlined at the beginning of this section (see page 498). Central Hudson Gas and Electric Corporation asked the Supreme Court to invalidate a New York Public Service Commission rule that forbade utilities to publish or broadcast any advertising that promoted the use of electricity. The commission justified the rule as a means of promoting energy conservation. The High Court struck down the ban in an eight-to-one ruling. Justice Powell noted that the utility's advertising did not promote an unlawful activity. Also, the state ban was aimed at all such advertising, not merely deceptive or misleading advertising. When advertising is truthful and does not promote an illegal activity, Powell said, the Court must examine the regulation itself more closely. What are the substantial state interests that are asserted in this case? New York argued that advertising that promoted electrical service interfered with the state's effort to convince citizens to conserve energy. The advertising also fostered inequities in the utility's rate structures, the state said. Powell agreed that the ban on advertising did further the state's interest in energy conservation and that this was a substantial interest. But he said the link between advertising and inequitable rate structures was tenuous at best. In other words, the ban on the ads did not directly advance this state interest.

Was the rule no more extensive than necessary to serve the state interest in energy conservation? Justice Powell said the rule was too broad. It prohibited Central Hudson Gas and Electric from advertising more efficient electrical energy devices such as heat pumps and electric power as a backup for solar energy. The energy conservation rationale, as important as it is, cannot justify suppressing all promotional advertisements, including those that would cause no net increase in total energy use, Powell wrote for the majority. The state failed to show that a more limited restriction on content would not adequately serve the same state interests (*Central Hudson* v. *Public Service Commission,* 1980; see also *Consolidated Edison* v. *Public Service Commission,* 1980, discussed on page 103).

The High Court ruled in June 1983 that a federal statute that barred the mailing of unsolicited advertisements for contraceptives was unconstitutional when applied to a contraceptive manufacturer's mailing of informational pamphlets that promoted its products but also discussed important public issues such as family planning and venereal disease. Justice Thurgood Marshall, writing for the court, ruled that the government's interests asserted in support of the statute were insufficient to warrant the "sweeping prohibition" against mailing the advertisements. The government's interest in shielding persons from receiving mail that they are likely to find offensive "carries little weight," Marshall wrote. The government's second interest, aiding parents in directing the manner in which their children become informed about birth control, is substantial, Marshall conceded. But the statute goes too far, offering a "marginal degree of protection" only by "purging all mailboxes of unsolicited material that is entirely suitable for adults." (*Bolger* v. *Young Drug Products Corporation,* 1983)

The advertising of alcoholic beverages became an issue in the early 1980s as well. The Tenth U.S. Court of Appeals ruled that Oklahoma could require that cable television operators in that state delete all advertisements for alcoholic beverages contained in the out-of-state signals they retransmit to their subscribers. The state argued that the rule was designed to further its interest in discouraging the consumption of beer, wine, and liquor (*Oklahoma Telecasters Association* v. *Crisp,* 1983). The U.S. Supreme Court reversed this decision, however, but on the narrow grounds that the federal government had preempted the regulation of cable television and the state could not impose such a regulation on the electronic medium. The unanimous Supreme Court did not consider the First Amendment issue (*Capital Cities Cable* v. *Crisp,* 1984). Eight months earlier the Fifth U.S. Court of Appeals ruled that a Mississippi law that prohibited liquor and wine advertising on billboards, on newspapers printed and distributed in the state, and on radio and television stations operating within the state and that required state broadcasters to delete such advertising from incoming network programming was not in violation of the

First Amendment. The rule, the court said, had been shown to directly advance the substantial state interest in safeguarding the health of its citizens (*Dunagin* v. *Oxford,* 1984). Presumably, however, the subsequent ruling by the Supreme Court voids parts of the Mississippi ban, at least as it applies to broadcast media deleting commercials on incoming network programs, the exact issue in the *Crisp* case.

Finally, in an important ruling in mid-1986, the High Court ruled that Puerto Rico could restrict the advertising of casino gambling to persons who lived on the island, but continue to permit such advertising aimed at tourists (*Posadas de Puerto Rico Assoc.* v. *Tourism Co.,* 1986). Since 1948, Puerto Rico has permitted some forms of gambling, largely to enhance the tourist industry, but rules have prohibited the advertising of such games of chance to "the public of Puerto Rico." Puerto Ricans are not prohibited from gambling, local advertising for other types of gambling games is permitted (i.e., lottery and horse racing), and the casinos can maintain on-site advertising that can be seen by local residents. Still the state prohibited the casinos from promoting their games of chance among the people of the island territory.

A casino challenged the law as a violation of the First Amendment, but the U.S. Supreme Court, in a five-to-four ruling, upheld the regulation. The advertising was for a lawful activity and was not misleading, but Justice Rehnquist wrote that the government's interest in reducing the demand for gambling by Puerto Rican residents was a substantial interest. The regulations directly advanced this interest and the rule was no more intrusive than need be to accomplish this end. The casino argued that this was truthful advertising for a lawful activity. But Rehnquist responded that "the greater power to completely bar casino gambling necessarily includes the lesser power to ban advertising of casino gambling." In other words because the government could at will ban all gambling, it could certainly ban some advertising for gambling.

Some observers, such as attorney P. Cameron DeVore of Seattle, argue that the ruling in Posadas "cavalierly undermined the First Amendment foundation of the commercial speech doctrine." (See *Presstime,* August, 1986.) Others experts, such as New York attorney Leonard Orkin, said they believed the impact of the case would be minimal. "The Puerto Rico case is of interest because of the unusual legal question of whether it is acceptable to distinguish between local advertising and other advertising, not because of any broad impact it will have." (See *New York Times,* July 1, 1986.)

By the late seventies and early eighties, lower courts were also handing down rulings that helped shape the boundaries of the commercial speech doctrine. The federal District Court for Northern California struck down a state law that prohibited clinical laboratories from advertising to the general public (*Metpath* v. *Myers,* 1978). In Rhode Island a district court ruled that a statute that prohibited the broadcast of advertisements by persons who prepare income tax returns was unconstitutional (*Rhode Island Broadcasters* v. *Michaelson*, 1978). In Pennsylvania the state's supreme court invalidated the state law that prohibited "situation or job wanted" advertisements from listing the advertiser's race, color, religious creed, ancestry, age, sex, or national origin. The law was initiated as a good-faith effort to enforce the state's policy of fostering nondiscrimination in employment. While such a ban on persons seeking to hire workers was permissible, the ban on persons seeking work violated the First Amendment. Citing *Linmark*, the court ruled that "it is clear that commercial speech cannot be banned because of an unsubstantial belief that its impact is detrimental" (*Pennsylvania* v. *Pittsburgh Press*, 1979). And in 1983 a United States District Court in Minnesota ruled unconstitutional a Minnesota statute that prohibited the publication of any advertisement concerning the inducement of miscarriages or abortions, including the publication of truthful, nondeceptive advertisements for lawful abortion services (*Meadowbrook Women's Clinic* v. *Minnesota,* 1983).

Advertising Professional Services

The qualified constitutional protection for advertising just outlined is also applicable to advertising for professional services by doctors, dentists, lawyers, and other specialists. Yet the Supreme Court has demonstrated far greater concern for the potential deceptive nature of advertisements for such professional services. For example, while the High Court will clearly tolerate claims of quality service by plumbers, electricians, and piano teachers, lawyers and physicians may not make such claims in their advertisements. Such claims would be considered deceptive. Let us look briefly at the development of the rules regarding advertising by professionals.

In 1977 the Court struck down rules that prohibited lawyers from advertising and ruled that price advertising for routine legal services is protected by the First Amendment as long as it is not false or misleading. The High Court would not tolerate however, advertisements regarding the quality of legal services, Justice Blackmun wrote for the Court's majority. Such advertisements (Jones and Jones Lawyers win more acquittals in drunk driving cases than any other lawyers in town) are not susceptible to verification and "might well be deceptive or misleading to the public, or even false" (*Bates and Van O'Steen* v. *Arizona,* 1977).

The *Bates* decision left confusion in the minds of many attorneys about just how far a lawyer could go in advertising services and just how far state bar associations could go in limiting such advertising. Personal solicitation by attorneys has always been banned, and in 1978 the High Court ruled that such rules did not run afoul of the First Amendment. Such advertising is distinctly different from price advertising, wrote Justice Blackmun for a majority of the Court (*Ohralik* v. *Ohio State Bar Association,* 1978).

But four years later the High Court ruled that the Missouri Bar Association had read the *Bates* ruling too narrowly and adopted rules that were far too restrictive. State bar rules in Missouri permitted lawyers to advertise only the following information:

1. Name, address, and telephone number
2. Date and place of birth, schools attended, and foreign-language specialty
3. Office hours, fee for initial consultation, availability of fee schedule, credit arrangements, and fixed fees for certain specific routine legal services
4. Areas of practice

Under areas of practice the bar association listed twenty-three specialties that could be listed.

The association reprimanded an attorney who included in his advertisement the statements that he was licensed to practice in both Missouri and Illinois, that he was admitted to practice law before the Supreme Court of the United States, and that he also carried two legal specialties not listed among the twenty-three approved for advertising by the bar association. Justice Powell, writing for a unanimous Supreme Court, ruled that the Missouri bar regulations prohibited far more than was necessary to prevent misleading advertisements. Regulation of such advertisements is permissible "only where particular advertising is inherently likely to deceive or where the record indicates that a particular form or method of advertising has in fact been deceptive," Powell wrote. The state can regulate truthful advertisements only if a substantial state interest is asserted and the interference with speech and press is in proportion to the state interest served by the regulation. In this case the advertisements were not misleading, and no substantial state interest was asserted, Powell wrote (in re *R. M. J.*, 1982).

In 1985 the Supreme Court broadened to an even greater extent the right of attorneys to advertise when it ruled that lawyers could solicit business for particular lawsuits, so long as the advertisements were not deceptive (*Zauderer* v. *Office of Disciplinary Counsel*, 1985). The Ohio Office of Disciplinary Council had disciplined attorney Philip Q. Zauderer for various misconduct, including an advertisement soliciting female clients who had suffered injuries from the use of the Dalkon Shield intrauterine device. The ad contained a line-drawing of the Dalkon Shield, a violation of the state rules. It stated that Zauderer was currently representing women suing the manufacturer of the contraceptive device and that he was willing to represent other women in similar suits. The attorney said he would handle the case on a contingent fee basis, and that if the suit was not successful, "no fees would be owed by the client." Ohio said the ad amounted to a solicitation of business and was misleading as well because it failed to inform potential clients that they may be liable for court costs if their suit fails. The state defended its prohibition on such advertising by arguing that it was inherently too difficult for regulators to distinguish accurate legal advertising from misleading legal advertising. "Were we to accept the state's argument in this case, we would have little basis for preventing the government from suppressing other forms of truthful and non-deceptive advertising simply to spare itself the trouble of distinguishing such advertising from false or deceptive advertising," said Justice Byron White, speaking for five members of the court. "The First Amendment protections afforded commercial speech would mean little indeed if such arguments were allowed to prevail," he added. All eight justices ruled that the use of an accurate illustration was protected by the First Amendment, but in a six-to-two vote, the High Court affirmed the state's reprimand of Zauderer for failing to disclose to potential clients the likelihood that they would be assessed court costs if their suit failed.

SUMMARY	American advertising is regulated by scores of laws adopted by all levels of government. Persons in advertising must be aware of such rules, as well as of all other regulations (libel, invasion of privacy, obscenity, etc.) that restrict the content and flow of printed and broadcast material. Since the mid-1970s commercial advertising has been given the qualified protection of the First Amendment because much advertising contains information that is valuable to consumers. The government may regulate or prohibit advertising (1) that promotes an unlawful activity or (2) that is misleading or untruthful. The state may also regulate truthful advertising for lawful activities and goods if it can prove (1) that there is a substantial state interest to justify the regulation, (2) that such regulation directly advances this state interest, and (3) that the regulation is no more extensive than needed to serve that important governmental interest. Advertising by professionals such as attorneys and physicians may be regulated in a somewhat more restrictive fashion.
THE REGULATION OF ADVERTISING	The regulation of unfair and deceptive advertising is a most difficult task, for as previously noted, disagreement about what is and what is not unfair and deceptive is frequent. Society uses various means to control this kind of advertising. The industry—the advertisers, the advertising agencies, and the mass media—polices itself. Both competitors (of errant advertisers) and consumers use the courts to seek redress for false or unfair advertising. Cities and states also have laws that prohibit untrue and deceptive advertising. Regardless of all these efforts, the federal government is the primary agent in regulation of advertising. To understand why this is so, we must first examine the controls just mentioned.

Self-Regulation

The advertising industry takes self-regulation quite seriously in the 1980s. The industry has various codes that proscribe certain unfair and deceptive advertising practices. The **National Advertising Division** (NAD) of the Council of Better Business Bureaus and the National Advertising Review Board, both industry-sponsored groups, have been active in resolving complaints against advertisers. The NAD has resolved nearly three thousand challenges since it began operating in 1971. The mass media, the newspapers and broadcasting stations, usually have policies on the kinds of advertising they will and will not accept. The television networks, for example, all have commercial editors who screen advertisements before they are permitted on the air. ABC has fifteen such editors, CBS has eight, and NBC has six. Advertisements are scrutinized to determine whether they meet network standards for taste and in the case of specific claims about a product, truthfulness. These rules are quite tough. ABC, for example, rejects four out of every ten commercials it is asked to air, according to reporter Bill Abrams in an article in the *Wall Street Journal*. Also, legal counsel for the advertisers and the advertising agencies scrutinize every national advertisement published or broadcast.

Is self-regulation effective? The answer to this question depends upon whom you ask. Most people in the industry regard it as an effective tool to regulate deceptive or untruthful advertising. Consumer advocates often do not regard it quite as highly. Louis Engman, former chairman of the Federal Trade Commission (FTC), said in a speech to the American Bar Association in 1974, "The voluntary approach [to regulation] yields far more satisfactory progress in the development of compliance mechanisms than it does in the development of substantive standards." In other words, the industry sets up codes and panels and boards but has not been successful in establishing hard rules on what is and what is not deceptive advertising. Staff consultants to the Federal Trade Commission were even more critical in 1973 in the *Staff Report to the Federal Trade Commission:*

> . . . from the advertiser's perspective the purpose of marketing communications is ultimately to sell the product or the service. Thus, to the extent that the provision . . . [information that educates the consumer] conflicts with the ability of the advertiser to sell the product it is unlikely that he will indulge voluntarily in such "informational" communication.

At the very basis of self-regulation is the assumption that the advertiser and the consumer agree upon standards of deception and honesty, that they share a value system regarding the sale of consumer goods. Such agreement is perhaps beyond human facility at this point in its evolution. While newspapers and broadcasting stations do not necessarily share the advertisers' point of view, they tend to be more sympathetic to advertisers since they are, after all, the ones paying the bills.

Even those persons who do argue that self-regulation is an effective policing mechanism usually concede it is a tool that is more helpful to competing advertisers than to consumers. Remember, distinct groups of persons are concerned about the truthfulness of an advertisement. Consumers fear being cheated by deceptive advertisements that promise more than products or services can deliver. Competing business persons fear the loss of sales because of a competitor's deceptive advertising campaign. The interests of consumers and competitors surely overlap to some extent, but not completely. The consumer is concerned that all advertising is completely truthful and honest. Business persons are frequently concerned only that a competitor's advertising is as truthful as their own advertising.

Consider the claims made by pain relievers, for example. Medical researchers tell us that the cheaper, generic pain relievers work as well as the expensive, name-brand pain relievers. Consumers would surely want to restrict advertising claims that the name-brand drugs work more effectively than the generic version. But the manufacturer of Bayer aspirin has a much narrower concern—only that the makers of Bufferin not be able to claim that it is a more effective pain reliever than Bayer aspirin.

Competing advertisers themselves have found agencies such as the National Advertising Division (NAD) of the Council of Better Business Bureaus to be effective in controlling deceptive competitor claims. This is especially true in an era of advertising in which almost 25 percent of all advertisements compare one product to a specific competitor's product. At one time a kind of unwritten code of ethics within the industry would have prevented an advertiser from mentioning a competing brand. Television networks were also reluctant to broadcast such comparative advertisements. But the Federal Trade Commission (FTC) has actually encouraged such head-to-head comparative advertising in recent years on the theory that out of such conflicts the consumer will learn more about the weaknesses and strengths of the products advertised.

A tremendous growth in the number of complaints filed with the NAD is one direct result of the increase in comparative advertising in which one advertiser compares its product with a rival product. Coca-Cola, which manufactures Minute Maid products, complained to the NAD about advertisements by Country Time Lemonade Flavored Drink Mix stressing the idea that the peel of a lemon contains the richest flavor and that that is what makes Country Time taste like "good old-fashioned lemonade." Country Time contains lemon oil but no lemon juice. The NAD ruled the advertisements were not deceptive. Country Time then complained about an advertisement that said that Minute Maid Lemonade Crystals contain the juice of twenty lemons but that Country Time contains no lemon juice. After Country Time raised the issue, Minute Maid discontinued the advertisement. Next came an advertisement that proclaimed that Country Time tastes better than Minute

Maid. Minute Maid complained; the NAD asked for proof. Country Time provided the results of a blind taste test that showed its drink was preferred by 55 percent of the drinkers. Issue ended.

Sometimes the NAD rules that an advertisement is in fact deceptive. During the great laxative wars of the early eighties, Nature's Remedy ran an advertisement that said that a competitor, Ex-Lax, contains an artificial chemical, whereas Nature's Remedy has "natural active ingredients." The advertisement was accurate enough, but the NAD said it was misleading in our health-conscious society where words like "artificial" and "chemical" have taken on health-threatening connotations. Both laxatives had been certified by the federal Food and Drug Administration (FDA) as safe and effective.

When a complaint is made to the NAD, the agency reviews the allegations and normally asks the advertiser to submit evidence to support the claims. If the advertising claim is not supported by the data, the agency can ask that the advertisement copy be altered or the advertisement be withdrawn. While the NAD cannot punish an advertiser who refuses to comply, broadcasters and publishers normally refuse to run an advertisement declared deceptive by the NAD. If the NAD fails to resolve the controversy, an appeal can be made to a five-member panel of the National Advertising Review Board (NARD). This panel is drawn from fifty men and women representing national advertisers, advertising agencies, and the public sector. Advertisers can also make their initial complaint about a competitor's advertisement to the NARB.

Sometimes a competing advertiser does not believe a complaint to the NAD is sufficient to stop an advertisement or advertising campaign. Instead, a complaint is filed in court. That is another level of advertising self-regulation.

| Lawsuits by Competitors and Consumers | Lawsuits for false advertising claims traditionally have been rare. There is no deceptive advertising tort at common law. A plaintiff attempting to use the common law to establish a case for false representation was forced to prove that he had suffered an actual injury because of the false advertising claim. The federal Lanham Act, however, does provide a remedy for competitors who seek to block another advertiser's claims. The law is aimed at stopping unfair competition, and Section 43(a) of this measure makes it illegal for an advertiser to use a false description or representation of goods or services in selling a commodity. Remedies include civil damages and/or injunctive relief. A significant slowing of action against advertisers by the Federal Trade Commission (see pages 515–16) and an increase in aggressive comparative advertising has pushed a growing number of advertisers into the courtroom to complain that a competitor's advertising violates the Lanham Act. A lawsuit under this statute rarely gets beyond the preliminary injunction stage. The advertiser |

simply wants the competitor to stop making the false claim. Under the law, however, the individual or company challenging the ad must prove that it is false; the advertiser does not have to prove that the claim is truthful.

Typical of the cases brought under the federal statute is one that erupted during the analgesic wars of the late seventies. The American Home Products Company, the makers of Anacin, and Johnson & Johnson, manufacturers of Tylenol, sued each other over competing claims concerning their respective products' effectiveness. In what to many persons appeared to be a gross waste of time for the judiciary, a federal district judge plowed through masses of data purporting to prove one product was superior to the other. In the end, Johnson & Johnson won an injunction that stopped the makers of Anacin from claiming its product was superior to Tylenol for conditions "associated with inflammation or inflammation components" (*American Home Products* v. *Johnson & Johnson,* 1977).

In early 1981 Budget Rent-A-Car filed a suit against Hertz, accusing the competing rental car company of falsely claiming Hertz had lowered its rates to meet Budget's rates. Cuisinarts Inc., a manufacturer of home food processors, sued rival Robot-Coupé, claiming false advertising and misappropriation of Cuisinart's reputation. The suit succeeded in blocking some Robot-Coupé advertisements. Twinoaks Products, the maker of a toilet bowl cleaner, also went to court in 1981 to stop Vanish commercials that claimed that long-lasting toilet bowl cleaners, like Twinoaks' 120 Automatic Bowl Cleaner, are harmful to plumbing while Vanish is not. The most publicized suit of the early eighties stemmed from the multibillion dollar "burger wars" between McDonalds Restaurants and a host of competitors. Wendy's International and McDonalds both went to court to block Burger King television advertisements that claimed that people preferred the taste of Burger King burgers to those made by the other two fast-food franchisers. And in 1984 Procter and Gamble sued Chesebrough-Ponds for making the claim that "no leading lotion beats" its Vaseline Intensive Care Lotion. P & G claimed that its New Wondra skin lotion was better and wanted Chesebrough-Ponds to stop advertising its lotions as being equal to or superior to New Wondra.

The most significant Lanham Act decision in recent years involved U-Haul and Jartran, firms that rent trucks and trailers to consumers. In 1984 a U.S. District Court judge in Arizona enjoined an aggressive advertising campaign by Jartran aimed at U-Haul and then awarded U-Haul $20 million in compensatory damages, the first major damage award in the history of Lanham Act deceptive advertising cases. Many observers believed the U-Haul damage award will set more lawyers and their clients to dreaming of large damage awards and will significantly increase activity under the federal law.

It is extremely difficult if not impossible for a consumer to maintain a false advertising claim under the common law or the Lanham Act. In fact, the consumer is really left in the lurch when it comes to policing false advertising. Consumers can report false and deceptive advertising to the authorities, but as individuals they have few effective remedies at law for a deceptive advertisement. As George and Peter Rosden point out in their massive compendium *The Law of Advertising,* historically, common law courts have not been receptive to protecting consumers. "During the most formative period of common law," they write, "only a few goods in the marketplace were manufactured products so that the buyer was in an excellent position to judge for himself goods offered to him." Dairy products could be judged by their smell and texture; vegetables, meat, and fruit, by their looks. Judgments about wine, beer, and cloth were also easy to make. Protection was really necessary only in case of fraud such as watered beer. The basic slogan in those days was caveat emptor—buyer beware.

While today consumers are far better protected—they must be because of the thousands of consumer products about which they know little or nothing—there is little consumers can do themselves to attack the dishonest advertiser, short of reporting the advertisement to the proper authorities. Even if the law allowed a suit to redress an injury wrought by a false advertisement, where can a consumer find a lawyer to handle the case? Let us say you buy a certain toothpaste because the advertisements claim it will brighten your teeth and stop formation of cavities. If your teeth do not get brighter and you sue, your damages are for 94 cents. On a contingency fee the lawyer gets 40 percent, or about 38 cents. Even a suit over a $150 dental bill does not give an attorney-at-law much to work for, especially when a malpractice victim who wants to sue for $200,000 may lurk around the next corner.

The Rosdens point out that it is possible for a consumer to sue under product liability laws, but in such cases the advertisement must contain a commitment about the product that is not fulfilled after purchase by the consumer. For example, an advertisement for a carpet cleaning product states that it will not damage carpets, but after a consumer uses the product, a large hole appears in the rug. The consumer would be able to sue (if he or she could find a lawyer) for a new carpet.

A few states have also recently permitted consumers to sue advertisers under their unfair competition statutes. In late 1983 in California, for example, the state supreme court ruled that a group of parents of young children could sue General Foods, Safeway stores, and two major advertising agencies for damages allegedly caused by "a nationwide, long-term advertising campaign designed to persuade children to influence their parents to buy sugared cereals." Such rulings are not common, however, and this case never really came to fruition.

State and Local Laws   State regulation of advertising predates federal regulation by several years. This fact is not surprising when you consider that at the time the public became interested in advertising regulation—around the turn of the century—the federal government was a minuscule creature relative to its present size.

Harry Nims, a New York lawyer, drafted a model law called the *Printers' Ink* Statute (it was *Printers' Ink* magazine that urged passage of the law) in 1911. All but three states (Arkansas, Delaware, and New Mexico) have adopted one version or another of this law. Here is the text of the original law:

> Any person, firm, corporation or association who, with intent to sell or in any way dispose of merchandise, securities, service, or anything offered by such person, firm, corporation or association, directly or indirectly, to the public for sale, or distribution, or with intent to increase the consumption thereof, or to induce the public in any manner to enter into any obligation relating thereto, or to acquire title thereto, or an interest therein, makes, publishes, disseminates, circulates, or places before the public, or causes, directly or indirectly, to be made, published, disseminated, circulated, or placed before the public, in this State, in a newspaper or other publication, or in the form of a book, notice, handbill, poster, bill circular, pamphlet, or letter, or in any other way, an advertisement of any sort regarding merchandise, securities, service, or anything so offered to the public, which advertisement contains any assertion, representation or statement of fact which is untrue, deceptive or misleading, shall be guilty of a misdemeanor.

The general verdict is that these statutes have been fairly ineffective in dealing with false advertising. Enforcement, which is in the hands of attorneys general or local prosecutors, has been weak because these legal officers have many other statutes to enforce. When people are being murdered, robbed, maimed, or kidnapped, the fact that you or I have been deceived by an advertisement from a local furniture store seems relatively unimportant.

However, because of the consumer revolution of the last twenty years, cities, counties, and states have all strengthened their laws and their enforcement of false and deceptive advertising. In some areas prosecution is quite vigorous; in others, it is not. The laws vary from state to state, even from city to city. It is advised that persons involved in advertising obtain copies of all relevant laws regarding statutes in the area in which publication is made.

Most states do not do very well in policing false advertising statutes. Prosecuting false advertising claims is a rigorous, time-consuming chore. Big companies can afford good legal counsel to defend their advertising practices. The suits are complicated. In the time needed to begin a prosecution, the offensive advertising campaign has usually long since ended. Victory really brings little satisfaction. Outright fraud—used cars being sold as new—is usually promptly policed. However, it is costly, time-consuming, and of not much interest to the general public to take an automobile dealer to court for claiming that a used car gets twenty-two miles to a gallon of gasoline when it actually gets only fifteen miles.

The Federal Trade Commission

Here is the advertiser, surrounded by industry codes, media regulations, suits by competitors, and state and city laws and confused at best. But the worst is yet to come. The primary agent of the federal government for regulation of advertising is, of course, the Federal Trade Commission, which has a general mandate to police unfair and deceptive advertising. In addition to the Federal Trade Commission Act, federal regulations on advertising can be found in at least thirty-two other statutes. To name a few: the Communication Act, Federal Drug and Cosmetics Act, Consumer Credit Protection Act, Copyright Acts, Consumer Products Safety Act, Federal Cigarette Labeling and Advertising Act, Wool Products Labeling Act of 1939, and Plant Variety Protection Act. In addition, regulations can be found in the Age Discrimination Employment Act, Federal Seed Act, National Stamping Act, Savings and Loan Act of 1952, Securities Act, and Aid to Blind and Handicapped Act. Also postal regulations contain numerous provisions regarding the mailability of advertising matter.

Then there are specific statutes that limit such practices as using the United States flag for advertising purposes and using the name of the Federal Bureau of Investigation or its acronym FBI in an advertisement without the permission of the bureau. Rules exist that regulate the use of likenesses of United States currencies and securities in advertisements. Good books that give students a broad, comprehensive picture of this multitude of laws and regulations are available (the Bibliography at the end of this chapter has some suggestions). In the remainder of this chapter our discussion is mainly about the agency having primary responsibility for the creation and enforcement of advertising rules and regulations—the Federal Trade Commission—and also includes consideration of deceptive advertising.

The Federal Trade Commission was created in 1914 to police unfair methods of competition. As Congress conceived the agency, the FTC was to make certain that Company A did not engage in practices that gave it an unfair advantage over its competitive rival, Company B. One method of unfair competition is deceptive advertising. If Company A advertises that its widgets are four times quieter than any other widgets and they aren't, this claim gives Company A an unfair competitive advantage. What about the consumers, the people who buy widgets? As originally conceived, the FTC was not to worry about the effect of advertising on buyers, only on competitors. (This is the role played most prominently by the NAD and Lanham Act civil suits today.)

In the 1920s the agency began to flex its muscles illegally and cracked down on all kinds of deceptive advertising: advertising that endangered competition and advertising that merely cheated customers. Until 1931, that is. At that time the Supreme Court ruled in *FTC* v. *Raladam* that the FTC could not stop a false advertisement unless there was proof that the advertisement had unfairly affected the advertiser's competitors. While the ruling did not totally destroy the efficacy of the agency, it did slow it down and made action against false and deceptive advertising more difficult.

In 1938 Congress bolstered the power of the FTC when it passed the Wheeler-Lea Amendment to the Trade Commission Act giving the agency the authority to proceed against all unfair and deceptive acts or practices in commerce, regardless of whether they affected competition. This amendment gave the commission the power it had been seeking.

Today the FTC is one of the largest of the independent regulatory agencies. In addition to policing false advertising, the agency is charged with enforcing the nation's antitrust laws, the Flammable Fabrics Act, the Truth in Lending Law, the Fair Credit Reporting Act, and various labeling laws. The five members of the commission are appointed by the president and confirmed by the Senate for a term of seven years. No more than three of the commissioners can be from the same political party. The chairman, one of the five members of the commission, is named by the president. While the agency is located in Washington, D.C., it has regional offices in Atlanta, Boston, Chicago, Cleveland, Dallas, Kansas City, Los Angeles, New Orleans, New York, San Francisco, and Seattle.

The history of the regulation of advertising by the FTC is a mirror of recent political times. When conservatism swept the nation (in the fifties and early eighties), the agency did little to regulate American business. This inaction during the early fifties earned the FTC the nickname "Little Gray Lady of Pennsylvania Avenue." But during eras of liberalism and reform (most notably the late sixties and seventies), the agency has been aggressive in its posture against advertising and business in general. It is useful to briefly recount the recent history of the FTC and advertising regulation.

Under the leadership of two aggressive chairmen in the early seventies (Caspar Weinberger and Miles Kirkpatrick), the Federal Trade Commission actively sought to regulate advertising, pulling some of the nation's largest advertisers (Coca-Cola, ITT Continental Baking, etc.) on the carpet for allegedly deceiving consumers. In the early seventies the agencies developed several new regulatory methods, including advertisement substantiation, under which an advertiser must substantiate its claims, and corrective advertising, a scheme whereby advertisers must tell consumers previous advertisements were misleading (these powers are described fully on pages 525–29). In 1975 Congress greatly enhanced the agency's power by giving it the authority to issue trade regulation rules that could be used to curb deceptive advertising practices by an entire industry, not just by a single advertiser.

The FTC quickly sought to use these powers. Led by Michael Pertschuk, an industrious consumer advocate, the commission proposed rules that angered American business and in the end, the Congress of the United States. Included were regulations that would have forced funeral homes to furnish the bereaved with a complete price listing of all services and that required used-car dealers to put stickers on car windows spelling out just what might be wrong with used cars they hoped to sell. The FTC instituted antitrust actions against the giant citrus cooperative Sunkist Growers and tried to take away trademark protection for words such as *Formica* from the firms that developed these products. Perhaps the most controversial set of rules proposed were those that would have banned all television advertising aimed at young children, prohibited television advertising of sweetened foods aimed at older children, and forced advertisers of sugared products to broadcast a nutritional message to balance other statements in the advertisements for their products. The FTC contended that all advertising aimed at children is unfair because the youngsters are unable to intelligently evaluate product claims. Agency attorneys argued that since the advertisements were unfair, they could be stopped under the law.

The political mood in Washington was changing, however. The interest in the protection of consumers from predatory business practices was waning. President Jimmy Carter inaugurated a movement toward deregulation of business when he appointed Alfred Kahn to modernize government rules regulating airlines. And Carter's successor in the White House, Ronald Reagan, promised voters that he would get government off the back of business. Congress reflected this changing mood as well and adopted the Federal Trade Commission Improvements Act of 1980, which gave the nation's lawmakers the power to kill any FTC trade regulation rule if both the Senate and the House passed resolutions disapproving it. This congressional veto power was declared unconstitutional in 1982 because it violates the separation of powers established in the Constitution. The attempt by Congress to veto FTC actions nevertheless was a clear signal of the mood in the nation's capital. The FTC Improvements Act also included a temporary rule that prohibited the commission from issuing a trade regulation rule against advertising that was merely unfair. Advertising must be deceptive as well as unfair before the commission may adopt a rule prohibiting it. This, of course, killed the FTC's effort to regulate advertising aimed at children. In fact, in October of 1981 the FTC voted to abandon its attempt to regulate such commercial messages.

· New appointees to the FTC reflected Ronald Reagan's political conservatism. James C. Miller, a conservative economist, was named to head the agency. During his confirmation hearing Miller told the Senate that the FTC's Bureau of Consumer Protection had "an overly adversarial posture" toward business. This left little doubt about Miller's views on the regulation of advertising. Miller led the FTC during the first Reagan term, a period when the commission initiated fewer and fewer actions against national advertisers. Early in Reagan's second term, Miller was tapped to replace David Stockman as head of the White House Office of Management and Budget. Miller's successor had not been appointed as this chapter was being written. Regardless of who leads the agency, however, it is expected that the FTC will continue to display a very low profile with regard to advertising regulation for the fore-seeable future. Nevertheless, the commission still holds the most potent powers to regulate deceptive and untruthful advertising. And for that reason, if no other, it needs to be seriously considered.

SUMMARY

Self-regulation by the advertising industry has increased in recent years, especially because of the growth of comparative advertising practices. The National Advertising Division of the Council of Better Business Bureaus (NAD) provides the means for competitors to register complaints against advertising practices. Such self-regulation, however, is geared to the needs of competing advertisers, not consumers. Civil suits, brought by one advertiser against another under the Lanham Act, have also increased in recent years. Consumers find it difficult to use the courts to try to restrict false advertising or recover a judgment for damage that results from a false advertising claim.

Government regulation of advertising exists at all government levels, but the agency with the most power to control false and deceptive advertising is the Federal Trade Commission. After aggressively pursuing many national advertisers in the 1970s, this federal regulatory agency pulled in its horns. This is the result of both Congressional action aimed at limiting the power of the agency and the appointment of conservative, probusiness commissioners by the Reagan administration.

FEDERAL TRADE COMMISSION POWERS

The **Federal Trade Commission,** through practice and legal custom, has defined advertising as any action, method, or device intended to draw the attention of the public to merchandise, to services, to persons, and to organizations (see, for example, *Rast* v. *van Deman & Lewis Co.,* 1916, and *State* v. *Cusick,* 1957). Trading stamps, contests, freebies, premiums, and even product labels are included in this definition, in addition to more common product and service advertising.

Does the FTC regulate all advertising? Legally, no, it cannot. Practically, it can regulate almost all advertising. Because the agency was created under the authority of Congress to regulate interstate commerce, products or services must be sold in interstate commerce or the advertising medium must be somehow affected by interstate commerce before the FTC can intervene. While many products and services are sold locally only, nearly every conceivable advertising medium is somehow affected by or affects interstate commerce. All broadcasting stations are considered to affect interstate commerce. Most newspapers ship at least a few copies across state lines. Even when a newspaper is not mailed across state lines, it is very likely that some of the news in the newspaper comes across state lines or that the paper on which the news is printed, the ink and type used to print the news, or parts of the printing machinery travel across state lines. The federal government became quite adept at demonstrating that businesses affect interstate commerce or are affected by interstate commerce as it learned to enforce civil rights laws like the Public Accommodations Act. The motel owner who declared that he did not have to abide by the federal law because his business was a local operation soon discovered that if the chickens or apples he served in his restaurant were shipped in from out of state, the courts were willing to say that his motel operation was a part of interstate commerce.

There are some other requirements that must be met before the FTC can act. It must be shown that the agency is acting in the public interest, which is really not too difficult since false advertising generally has an impact upon the public. If the FTC says it is acting in the public interest, courts usually take its word for it.

Deceptive Advertising

Finally, an advertisement must be deceptive or untruthful. According to a 1983 policy statement issued by the FTC, three elements must be present before an advertisement will be considered deceptive. First, there must be a representation, omission, or practice that is likely to mislead the consumer. The ad or practice must be considered from the perspective of the reasonable consumer. And the representation, omission, or practice must be material. Let's consider each of these elements in greater detail.

There must be a representation, omission, or practice that is likely to mislead the consumer. Most deception involves written or oral misrepresentations or omission of material information. The commission will consider the entire advertisement, as well as all other elements in the transaction. The issue is whether the act or practice is likely to mislead rather than whether it causes actual deception. A deceptive statement may be made expressly, such as "Arcane Aspirin will cure the common cold," a blatantly false statement. Or it can be implied by juxtaposition of two statements or some other means. Listerine carried two messages on its label. "Kills Germs by Millions on Contact" immediately preceded the assertion "For General Oral Hygiene, Bad Breath, Colds and Resultant Sore Throats." The FTC ruled that by placing these two statements in close proximity, Warner Lambert conveyed the message that since Listerine can kill millions of germs, it can cure and prevent colds and sore throats. This is a deceptive statement (*Warner Lambert,* 1975, aff'd 1977). The omission of important or material information in an advertising claim can also be deceptive. For example, if a car dealer offers a current-year model car for sale but does not reveal that the car was previously owned, or used, such a statement would likely be considered deceptive. A reasonable consumer would consider the current-year model car to be a new automobile without further information. Similarly, for an advertiser to claim that 93 percent of all its watches that have been sold since 1952 still keep perfect time would be deceptive if the advertiser did not reveal that the watches have only been on the market for the last five years. Finally, the FTC ruled that a claim by the makers of Wonder Bread that its bread is fortified with vitamins and minerals to help children grow up to be big and strong was deceptive because it did not reveal that nearly all commercially baked bread is fortified with vitamins and minerals. The FTC argued that by not disclosing that Wonder Bread is really no different from other bread, the baking company omitted an important element; it told only half the story (in re *ITT Continental Baking Co.,* 1971).

The act or practice must be considered from the perspective of the reasonable consumer. The test is whether the consumer's interpretation or reaction is reasonable. When advertisements or sales practices are targeted to a specific audience, the commision will consider the likely effect of the ad on a reasonable member of that group. Advertising aimed at children, the elderly, or the terminally ill, for example, will be viewed from the perspective of a reasonable member of that group. "For instance, if a company markets a cure to the terminally ill, the practice will be evaluated from the perspective of how it affects the ordinary member of that group," the commission noted in its 1983 policy statement. The terminally ill consumer is likely to be far more susceptible to exaggerated cure claims than is a healthy person. Also, advertising aimed at a special vocational group, such as physicians, will be evaluated from the perspective of a reasonable member of that group. A well-educated physician might be better able to understand a complicated pharmaceutical ad than a typical average individual.

The advertiser is not responsible for every interpretation or behavior by a consumer. The law is not designed to protect the foolish or the "feeble minded," the commission has noted. "Some people, because of ignorance or incomprehension, may be misled by even a scrupulously honest claim," one commissioner noted in 1963. "Perhaps a few misguided souls believe, for example, that all Danish pastry is made in Denmark. Is it therefore an actionable deception to advertise Danish pastry when it is made in this country? Of course not," the commissioner noted (*Heinz* v. *Kirchner,* 1963). When an advertisement conveys more than one meaning to a reasonable consumer, one of which is false, the seller is liable for the misleading interpretation. Here is a classic example: "Jones Garage will put a new motor in your car for only $350." What does this claim mean? One meaning is that the garage will sell you a new motor and install it for only $350. But an equally reasonable meaning is that the garage will install a motor that you already own for only $350. If the second meaning is intended, the seller may very well be held responsible for the first meaning—which is false—as well.

The commission will evaluate the entire ad when it examines it for misrepresentation. Accurate information in the text may not remedy a false headline, because a reasonable consumer may only glance at the headline. If a television pitchman proclaims that a watch is 100 percent waterproof, the advertiser cannot qualify this claim in a long printed message in small type that crawls across the bottom of the TV screen while the announcer tries to sell the product (*Giant Food, Inc.* v. *FTC,* 1963). Similarly, an advertiser cannot correct a misrepresentation in an advertisement with point-of-sale information. A seller cannot advertise a vacuum cleaner as having a 100 percent money-back guarantee and then expect to qualify that claim in a tag that is attached to the product as it is displayed for sale in a store. Qualifying disclosures must be legible and understandable, the FTC has ruled.

"The commission generally will not bring advertising cases based on subjective claims (taste, feel, appearance, smell)," according to the 1983 guidelines. The agency says it believes the typical reasonable consumer does not take such claims seriously and thus they are unlikely to be deceptive. Such claims are referred to as **puffery** and include representations that a store sells "the most fashionable shoes in town" or a cola drink is "the most refreshing drink around."

Finally, the commission has stated that when consumers can easily evaluate the product or service, when it is inexpensive, and when it is frequently purchased, the Commission will scrutinize the advertisement or representation in a less critical manner. "There is little incentive for sellers to misrepresent . . . in these circumstances since they normally would seek to encourage repeat purchases," the 1983 statement proclaims. That means the advertiser of small, dry cell batteries, a relatively inexpensive product purchased often by most consumers, will be given a bit more leeway in advertising than the advertiser of a $600 home generator.

The representation, omission, or practice must be material. A material misrepresentation or practice is one that is likely to affect a consumer's choice of a product. In other words, according to the commission policy statement, "it is information that is important to the consumer." The FTC considers certain categories of information to be more important than others when deciding whether a claim is material or not. Express claims as to the attributes of a product are always considered material. Advertising claims that significantly involve health and safety are usually presumed to be material. Information pertaining to the "central characteristics of the product or service" are usually considered to be material. Information has also been found to be material where it concerns the purpose, efficacy, or cost of the product or service. Claims about durability, performance, warranties, or quality have also been considered material. An example of a claim that was not considered material is a statement made by Chevron in the advertising of a gasoline additive, F-310. In both television and print advertising, a company spokesman claimed to be standing in front of the Chevron research laboratories while he made the pitch for the product. In fact, he was standing in front of a county courthouse. The statement was false, but was it material? An FTC hearing examiner said it was not. The location of the spokesperson is immaterial to a consumer judging the product.

Demonstrations or mock-ups often become the subject of FTC inquiries, and the question of materiality is often raised. For many years a shaving cream manufacturer claimed that its product was so good that it could be used to shave sandpaper. In a TV demonstration Rapid Shave was spread on sandpaper and then, a few moments later, the sand was shaved off. The demonstration was phony. What the announcer shaved was not sandpaper, but sand sprinkled on glass. The FTC argued that this was deceptive and that the claim that Rapid Shave could be used to shave sandpaper was a material representation. The Supreme Court agreed, despite the plea from Colgate-Palmolive that the product really could shave sandpaper if it was left on the paper long enough. But because the sand and the paper were the same color, a TV demonstration did not work. Hence the company had to use sand on glass (*FTC v. Colgate-Palmolive Co.,* 1965). But the High Court did not say that all mock-ups were deceptive. Only those that are used to support a material product claim must be restricted. For example, plastic ice cubes may be substituted for the real thing in an advertisement for a soft drink because no claim about the quality of the ice cubes is involved. But plastic ice cubes can not be used in a television commercial aimed at selling ice cubes if the advertisement extolls the attributes of these marvelous, uniform-sized, crystal clear ice cubes. The phony ice cubes are being used to demonstrate a material claim for the product.

The adoption of the 1983 policy statement on deceptive advertising had been sought by the industry for many years. Until that time the FTC had proceeded to define deceptiveness on a case-by-case basis and the edges of the definition had surely become ragged. But the policy statement is controversial and was approved by a three-to-two vote. Consumer advocates believe the statement reflects a relaxation in the policing of advertising. It does reflect two important changes from previous definitions of deceptive advertising. First, the new statement says that an ad must be likely to deceive. In the past the FTC standard had been that an ad only have the tendency to deceive. Second, the new statement clearly states that advertising practices will be viewed from the perspective of a reasonable consumer. In the past the commission had viewed advertising from a somewhat broader perspective and had presumed its role was to protect the unthinking and the ignorant, as well as the ordinary consumer. But in fact, the notion of using a reasonable consumer as a standard had emerged in the seventies, even though it was not officially articulated by the FTC. For example, an advertising campaign by Hi-C suggested that its fruit drinks, which contain ten percent fruit juice, were as good or better than one hundred percent orange juice. The commission rejected allegations that the advertising was deceptive, implying in its ruling that the average consumer is smart enough to tell the difference between Hi-C and real fruit juice (in re *Coca-Cola,* 1973).

Some lawyers who represent advertisers take the cynical view that an advertisement is deceptive when the FTC says it is, regardless of the content of policy statements or other official pronouncements. There is undoubtedly some truth to this argument. If an ad is ruled to be deceptive, what happens next? Let's now look at the means the FTC has at its disposal to control or correct false and deceptive advertising.

Means to Reduce Deception

In 1973 a law professor named Richard Posner concluded a study of the FTC with the observation that the cardinal weakness in the agency was its lack of remedies to control false and misleading advertising. "To be sure," Posner wrote in his study for the American Institute for Public Policy Research, "it is possible that even though the commission's constructive activity is very small in any given year the very existence of the commission serves to deter a great deal of unlawful conduct. But it is unlikely that the FTC's power to deter is very great, given the limitations of its sanctions" *(Regulation of Advertising by the Federal Trade Commission).* But things changed dramatically in the ten years following Posner's study. New and potent remedies were added to the FTC arsenal. The agency became a power to be reckoned with by even the strongest business corporation. Indeed, it was the use of these powers that brought the wrath of Congress and the White House down upon the commission in the past four years. But even with its often immense powers, certain factors work against any agency that wishes to regulate advertising.

The commission's greatest enemy in dealing with false advertising is time, the time needed to bring an action against the advertiser. Advertising campaigns are ephemeral—here today, gone tomorrow. The average campaign does not last more than six or eight months. It frequently takes the commission much longer than that to catch up with the advertiser, to comply with all the due-process requirements involved in a hearing, and to ultimately decide whether there has been a violation of the law. By that time everybody has forgotten about the advertisement, and the advertiser is promising people a new pot of gold at rainbow's end.

Media historian and critic Erik Barnouw argues that contemporary regulation of advertising has another serious weakness as well—it is word oriented. Barnouw points out that by the time the FTC had won its campaign against the makers of Geritol (see page 524), the firm had switched to a more effective advertising strategy. The advertisements that got Geritol into trouble were word-oriented messages—promises that Geritol would be helpful to persons who felt tired and run-down. The new messages made no claims at all.

The television spots showed radiantly healthy young women who urged viewers to "take care of yourself, be the best you can." Then the actresses told the viewers that they took Geritol every day. Barnouw says, "The success of the campaign suggests the increasing irrelevance of most FTC review, which tends to be word oriented. In the new commercial dramaturgy, verbal promise is a secondary matter, vague and understated, while situation and imagery work on a more visceral level."

Less subtle examples of what Barnouw refers to can be seen in the advertisements for Sanka coffee and American Express. Sanka hired actor Robert Young for its slice-of-life messages. For years Young was popular on television as Doctor Marcus Welby. In these commercials actor Young (or is that Dr. Welby talking?) tells viewers that Sanka contains no caffeine and will not make them as nervous or jumpy as regular coffee. The message can have the ring of *medical* advice for many stalwart television viewers. And while Young was starring in the Welby television series, nearly a quarter of a million viewers wrote him asking for medical advice. Similarly, when Karl Malden suggests that carrying an American Express credit card is safer than carrying cash, who do viewers see giving them the advice? Karl Malden, actor, or police Lt. Mike Stone, a character Malden played on the successful television show "Streets of San Francisco"? Malden even wears a hat during the ad, a trademark of his performance as Mike Stone. Again, no verbal connection is made between the actor and the police officer during the advertisement. At this time, as Barnouw points out, the law cannot cope with such subtleties, since viewers make the crucial (and misleading) connections in their heads.

What remedies are available to the FTC to control false and misleading advertising? There is a wide range of remedies that begin with simple guidelines and end with the strong, industry-wide, rule-making power that got the agency into trouble with the Congress.

Guides

At the top of the list of remedies is the power of the commission to issue industry guides, which are really policy statements by the commission about potential problems. For example, if a cigar company wants to know whether it can legally advertise its cigars as "the coolest-burning cigar in town," it can ask the FTC for an opinion before launching the campaign. Normally the FTC will advise companies about the legality of proposed claims. In some cases the FTC issues an industry guide, which is merely an advisory interpretation of what the FTC believes the law to be on the subject. For example, the FTC has issued a guide on the use of the word *free* and similar representations in advertising. It has issued a guide for advertising private vocational schools and home study courses. It has issued a guide for the decorative wall paneling industry. There are many, many other guides. In a guide the commission tells the advertiser that statement X can be made, statement Y cannot be made, statement Z cannot be made without substantiation, and so forth.

The purpose of the guides is to help advertisers stay within the law. What happens when an advertiser fails to comply with the provisions of a guide? The FTC must proceed against the advertisement as it would against any other advertisement. The guides do not have the force of law. They are merely FTC opinions about what the law says. Deceptiveness still has to be proved in an FTC hearing.

Voluntary Compliance

Industry guides and advisory opinions apply only to prospective advertising campaigns, events that have not yet occurred. The next remedy on the ladder is voluntary compliance and is used for advertising campaigns that are over or nearly over. Imagine that the cigar company is nearing the end of its coolest-burning-cigar-in-town campaign. The FTC believes that the claim is deceptive. If the advertiser has had a good record in the past and if the offense is not too great, the company can voluntarily agree to terminate the advertisement and never use the claim again. In doing this, the advertiser makes no admission and the agency no determination that the claim is deceptive. There is just an agreement not to repeat that particular claim in future advertising campaigns. Such an agreement saves the advertiser considerable legal hassle, publicity, and money, all especially desirable since the advertising campaign is over or almost over.

Consent Orders

The next remedy seems to be similar to voluntary compliance but is more complicated and more binding. The remedy is called a **consent order** and is a written agreement between the commission and the advertiser in which the advertiser again makes promises concerning future advertising. The advertiser is asked to agree not to do certain things and may also be asked to do certain other things. If the advertiser signs the agreement, the FTC takes no further action.

Recently Ogilvy and Mather agreed to cease advertising that Aspercreme contains aspirin. Tomy Corporation agreed to discontinue representation that any collection of products (dollhouses, accessories, etc.) is a set unless depicted products can be bought as a set. Great North American Industries, Inc., agreed to halt claims that its engine oil additive will result in substantial fuel economy unless the claims were based on competent, scientific tests. These are typical of the kinds of consent orders drafted by the FTC.

As will be noted in the discussion of FTC procedures, there is considerable pressure on the advertiser to agree to a consent order. The chance of winning a case before the FTC is usually slim. The litigation is also costly. Finally, the publicity that results from such litigation often does the product more harm than any FTC sanction.

If after accepting the consent order the advertiser then violates the agreement, the company is subject to a severe fine, up to $10,000 a day while the violation continues (i.e., while the advertising campaign continues). RJR

Foods paid a $70,000 civil penalty for violating a 1973 order involving the disclosure of the fruit juice content in Hawaiian Punch. And R. J. Reynolds Tobacco Company was fined $100,000 for allegedly violating a 1972 order requiring a clear and conspicuous lettering in disclosing the health warning.

Cease and Desist Orders

What happens if the cigar company really believes that its cigar is "the coolest-burning cigar in town" and does not want to sign a consent order? The commission issues a **cease and desist order.** The advertisements must stop or the advertiser faces severe civil penalty: again, a fine of up to $10,000 a day. In the long-running (eleven years) Geritol case, for example, the commission issued an order in 1965 prohibiting the J. B. Williams Company from implying in its advertising for Geritol that its product can be helpful to persons who are tired and run-down (in re *J. B. Williams Co.,* 1965; in re *J. B. Williams Co.* v. *FTC,* 1967). The commission contended that medical evidence demonstrates that Geritol, a vitamin-and-iron tonic, helps only a small percentage of persons who are tired and that in most persons tiredness is a symptom of ailments for which Geritol has no therapeutic value. The J. B. Williams Company violated the cease and desist order (at least, that is what the commission alleged) and in 1973 was fined more than $800,000. A court of appeals threw out the fine in 1974 and sent the case back to district court for a jury trial, which the advertisers had been denied the first time around (*U.S.* v. *J. B. Williams Co.,* 1974). The jury was to decide whether the Geritol advertisements did in fact violate the cease and desist order. At a second hearing in 1976, the FTC won a $280,000 judgment against the patent medicine manufacturer.

In 1976 the manufacturer of STP was ordered to stop making false claims regarding the effectiveness of its oil treatment. In 1978 a court found that the advertisement violated the order, and a $500,000 fine was levied.

Standard Oil of California was ordered to stop claiming that its Chevron gasolines with F-310 produce pollution-free exhaust. The commission banned television and print advertisements in which the company claimed that just six tankfuls of Chevron will clean up a car's exhaust to the point that it is almost free of exhaust-emission pollutants.

In 1983 the FTC ordered the manufacturers of Bufferin, Excedrin, Bayer Aspirin, Cope, Vanquish, and Midol to stop claiming that these products were superior to or safer than similar products. The agency said that Sterling Drugs and Bristol-Myers Co., the patent medicine manufacturers, could only make such claims if they had well-controlled clinical tests to prove the claims. Such studies do not exist, the FTC said. The commission said that Bristol-Myers had wrongly claimed that doctors recommend Bufferin more than other nonprescription pain relievers. This claim was false, FTC Commissioner David A. Clanton said. The commission said that claims made by Sterling Drugs that Bayer Aspirin had greater purity, stability, freshness, and disintegration speed were also unproven. The order issued by the agency states that advertising claims must be proven by two well-controlled clinical studies, although other forms of proof may be acceptable on a case-by-case basis. This kind of substantiation is noted in the next section.

Few advertisers are willing to carry a case as far as the cease and desist order, and those that go that far frequently go beyond to a court of appeals to challenge the FTC's ruling. The appeal process is explored in the discussion of FTC procedures (page 533).

The pressure is heavy upon advertisers to voluntarily comply or to sign a consent order, especially since in neither case is there admission of wrongdoing and in both instances the legal processes will take so long that the offensive advertising campaign will probably be finished before the case is heard. Many people feel that the FTC does its job if it gains compliance voluntarily, for the mission of the agency is, after all, to stop deceptive advertising, not to punish advertisers. Other observers disagree, however, and argue that without stronger sanctions the advertiser is not motivated to refrain from future illegal acts. This kind of argument prompted the FTC to undertake new regulatory schemes, which we will now examine.

Substantiation

Advertising substantiation has been an important part of the FTC regulatory scheme since 1972. The basis of the program is simple: the commission asks advertisers to substantiate claims made in their advertisements. The FTC does not presume that the claims are false or misleading. The advertiser is simply asked to prove the claims are truthful. The substantiation process has been modified at least three times since it was initiated. Initially the commission demanded that all advertisers in a particular industry—such as soap and detergent makers—provide documentation for all their claims. This resulted in tremendous grumbling from advertisers, as well as mountains of studies and reports for the FTC. The agency was drowned in documentation. The process is streamlined today. Panels of experts scrutinize advertisements and target for documentation those claims that seem most suspect. The most recent commission policy statement on substantiation was issued in July 1984. Under this new policy express substantiation claims, such as "doctors recommend" and "specific tests prove," require the level of proof advertised. Otherwise, advertisers will be expected to have at least a "reasonable basis" for claims in their advertising, wrote attorney Thomas J. McGrew in a 1985 article in the *Los Angeles Daily Journal*. The degree of substantiation that will be deemed reasonable varies with "the type of claim, the product, the consequences of a false claim, the benefits of a truthful claim, the cost of developing substantiation . . . , and the amount of substantiation experts in the field believe is reasonable," the policy statement said.

On its face substantiation seems like a fairly benign regulatory tool. But from the standpoint of legal process, it has had a major impact upon regulation of advertising. It has shifted the burden of proof in a great many advertising cases from the FTC, which in the past had to prove that a claim was false, to the advertiser, who must now prove that the claim is truthful. If the case goes to litigation and a hearing, the burden reverts back to the FTC, which must then prove that the advertising claim is false or misleading. But most cases are settled far short of litigation through a consent agreement or a cease and desist order. Recently the agency issued an order against Sears, saying that specific claims made about its dishwashers were not proved. Advertisements for the Kenmore dishwashers claimed that no scraping or pre-rinsing of dishes was needed before loading them into the dishwasher. "It gives you freedom from scraping and pre-rinsing because it has two hot water jets to scour soft food off dishes, and a built-in stainless steel pulverizer that grinds up leftover food," the ads proclaimed. The FTC said that Sears had failed to substantiate this claim with competent, scientific tests. In 1982 the FTC issued an order against American Home Products Corporation because it had failed to provide the appropriate level of support for claims that Anacin and Arthritis Pain Formula were superior to other aspirin products. A year later the FTC ordered the makers of Bufferin, Excedrin, Bayer Aspirin, Cope, Vanquish, and Midol to stop claiming that these nonprescription pain relievers were superior or safer than other similar products. "I think we make it clear you just can't go around touting your product and claiming it works better than your competitor's without having some solid scientific support backing those claims up," wrote Commissioner David A. Clanton, author of the FTC decision.

Corrective Advertising

Corrective advertising is a highly controversial scheme, which the FTC first used in 1971 against the ITT Continental Baking Company. The scheme is based on the premise that to merely stop an advertisement is in some instances insufficient. If the advertising campaign is successful and long running, a residue of misleading information remains in the mind of the public after the offensive advertisements have been removed. Under the corrective advertising scheme, the FTC forces the advertiser to inform the public that in the past it has not been honest or has been misleading. One commentator called the scheme "commercial hara-kiri."

Under what circumstances will the FTC ask for corrective advertising sanctions? The commission has resisted issuing a specific policy regarding this question. For example, in 1979 it responded to a request for such a policy from the Institute for Public Representation in Washington, D.C., by saying it would continue to deal with corrective advertising problems on a case-by-case basis. In the past, however, the agency has adopted this rather vague standard for the imposition of corrective advertising:

> If a deceptive advertisement has played a substantial role in creating or reinforcing in the public's mind a false and material belief which lives on after the false advertising ceases, there is clear and continuing injury to competition and to the consuming public as consumers continue to make purchasing decisions based on the false belief.

In such a case, corrective advertising is appropriate, according to the FTC.

The FTC first attempted to force what it calls affirmative or corrective disclosures in 1950, but a court of appeals ruled that it lacked the power to do so under the Federal Trade Commission Act. The court ruled in *Alberty* v. *FTC* (1950) that the agency lacked the authority to encourage or require informative advertising. Ten years later, however, in *Feil* v. *FTC* (1960), the courts reversed the *Alberty* decision. The FTC threatened to use the remedy against the Campbell Soup Company to correct the misperception created when the company put clear marbles in the bottom of a bowl of vegetable soup to force the vegetables to the top (*Campbell Soup Co.*, 1970). The first corrective advertisement did not appear until 1971. As mentioned earlier, it was the result of a consent order signed by the ITT Continental Baking Company with regard to its advertising for Profile Bread. The television version of the advertisement was this:

> I'm Julia Meade for Profile Bread. And like all mothers I'm concerned about nutrition and balanced meals. So I'd like to clear up any misunderstanding you may have about Profile Bread from its advertising or even its name. Does Profile have fewer calories than other breads? No, Profile has about the same per ounce as other breads. To be exact Profile has seven fewer calories per slice. But that's because it's sliced thinner. But eating Profile Bread will not cause you to lose weight. A reduction of seven calories is insignificant. It's total calories and balanced nutrition that counts. And Profile can help you achieve a balanced meal, because it provides protein and B vitamins as well as other nutrients.

This corrective advertisement was in response to a Profile campaign that led some people to believe that one could lose weight by eating Profile Bread.

The commission required that corrective advertisements like this one constitute 25 percent of the advertising for Profile Bread during the year following the agreement. This is the typical percentage in a corrective-advertising agreement, although at times the FTC has agreed to allow advertisers to allot only 15 percent of their advertising budget for corrective advertisements.

Only a few other manufacturers of well-known nationally advertised products have been forced to make corrective disclosures. One was the company making Ocean Spray Cranberry Juice, which for years advertised that its cranberry juice had more food energy than other juices. Since food energy is really only another way of saying caloric value, the FTC ordered the juice maker to tell people that fact in a corrective ad (*Ocean Spray Cranberries,*

Inc., 1972). Neither the Profile advertisement nor the cranberry juice advertisement pleased all consumer advocates. Many thought the advertisements were too weak. In fact, studies showed that sales of Profile Bread were not hurt by the corrective campaign.

The FTC has been both tougher and more prepared to use the corrective-advertising device against small advertisers. Some corrective advertisements even have to include what lawyers dub "the Scarlet Letter," a statement by advertisers that the FTC found previous advertising to be deceptive. An example of such an order is the one agreed to by Wasem's Drug Store in Clarkston, Washington. The store marketed vitamin pills under its own name in advertising that the FTC deemed to be false and misleading. In the consent order the firm agreed to devote 25 percent of its advertising for one year to corrective advertising, to refrain from using the word *super* in the trade name of the vitamins, and to broadcast seven sixty-second corrective advertisements on seven consecutive days on local television stations. This is the corrective ad, including the Scarlet Letter:

> This advertisement is run pursuant to an order of the Federal Trade Commission. I have previously been advertising Wasem's Super B Vitamins and have made various claims which are erroneous or misleading. Contrary to what I told you previously, Super B will not make you feel better nor make you better to live with nor work with on the job. There is no need for most people to supplement their diet with vitamins and minerals. Excess dosages over the recommended daily adult requirement of most vitamins will be flushed through the body and be of no benefit whatsoever. Contrary to my previous ads, neither the Food and Drug Administration nor the Federal Trade Commission nor anyone else has recommended Super B or approved our prior claims. Super B Vitamins are sold on a money-back guarantee, so if you are not fully satisfied, then return them to me at Wasem's Rexall Drug Store in Clarkston for a refund.

But in an important ruling by the United States Court of Appeals in 1977, the future of the so-called Scarlet Letter was clouded. Warner-Lambert, the maker of Listerine mouthwash, was ordered by the FTC to stop claiming that its product prevents, cures, or alleviates the common cold. The agency also ordered the firm to include the following statement in its future advertisements: "Contrary to prior advertising, Listerine will not help prevent colds or sore throats or lessen their severity." Warner-Lambert challenged the entire order, arguing that the FTC had no power to force corrective advertising. United States Court of Appeals (D.C.) Judge Skelly Wright wrote on behalf of the two-to-one majority that the FTC does have the power to force corrective advertising statements in appropriate cases but ruled that the phrase "contrary to prior advertising" was superfluous and was intended to humiliate the company. Wright said that while humiliation might be appropriate for an "egregious case of deliberate deception," it was not appropriate here. The FTC has only the power to correct the problem, not to be punitive in its actions.

The firm was ordered to publish and broadcast the corrective claims in the next ten million dollars of its advertising for the mouthwash, which was the average annual sum spent on advertising between 1962 and 1972 when the complaint against Warner-Lambert was first issued. (The Supreme Court later refused to hear an appeal by the drug company.) While the ruling strongly upheld corrective advertising, the court of appeals nevertheless cast doubts on the propriety of the use of the so-called Scarlet Letter.

Nobody really knows whether these kinds of corrective advertisements are effective in ridding the consumer's mind of the falsity. Probably many buyers retain an unfavorable impression of the advertiser. Corrective advertising has been used only infrequently as a remedy in the past few years.

Injunctions

When Congress passed the Trans-Alaska Pipeline Authorization Act in 1973, attached to that piece of legislation was a bill that authorized the FTC to seek an injunction to stop advertisements that it believed violated the law. Attorneys for the FTC can seek these restraining orders in federal court. An injunction is clearly a drastic remedy and one that the agency has said it will not use often. Spokesmen for the FTC have said that the agency will use the power only in those instances in which the advertising can cause harm, in those cases where there is a clear law violation, and in those cases where there is no prospect that the advertising practice will end soon.

The first time the FTC used its new power was in 1973, when it sought and got a restraining order against several West Coast travel agents who promoted trips to the Philippines for "psychic surgery." The FTC said that many Americans were being fleeced by so-called psychic surgeons who supposedly performed bloodless operations on patients by using their minds rather than scalpels. The agency won its case. More recently the FTC won a preliminary injunction against the National Commission on Egg Nutrition to block advertising claims that no scientific evidence exists linking egg consumption to a higher risk of heart disease. A lower court ruled that an injunction was too severe, limiting public debate on the cholesterol issue and damaging the advertisers financially. But the U.S. Court of Appeals reversed the lower court ruling and granted the injunction (*FTC* v. *National Commission on Egg Nutrition,* 1977). The ruling by the court suggests that the FTC will be permitted to enjoin an advertising practice when the danger to the public is immediate.

Trade Regulation Rules

In January 1975 President Ford signed the Magnuson-Moss Warranty—Federal Trade Commission Improvement Act, the most significant piece of trade regulation legislation since the Wheeler-Lea Amendment in 1938. The new law did many things, but basically it greatly enlarged both the power and the jurisdiction of the FTC. Until the bill was signed, the FTC was limited to dealing with unfair and deceptive practices that were "in commerce." The new law expanded the jurisdiction to practices "affecting commerce." The change of a single word gave the FTC broad new areas to regulate. The law also gave the agency important new power. It is the vigorous use of this new power that caused the problems (discussed earlier) that the agency now has with the Congress.

Three sections of the act expanded the remedies the FTC can use against deceptive advertising. First, the agency was given the power to issue trade regulation rules defining and outlawing unfair and deceptive acts or practices. The importance of this power alone cannot be overestimated. In the past the agency had to pursue deceptive advertisements one at a time. Imagine, for example, that four or five different breakfast cereals all advertise that they are good for children because they contain nine times the recommended daily allowance of vitamins and minerals. Medical experts argue that any vitamins in excess of 100 percent of the recommended daily allowance are useless; therefore, these advertisements are probably deceptive or misleading. In the past the FTC would have had to issue a complaint against each advertiser and in each case prove that the statement was a violation of the law. Under the new rules the agency can issue a trade regulation rule—as it had done for nutritional claims—which declares that claims of product superiority based on excessive dosage of vitamins and minerals are false and misleading. If advertisers make such claims, they are in violation of the law. All the commission must prove is that the advertiser had actual knowledge of the trade regulation rule, or "knowledge fairly implied from the objective circumstances."

The advantages of the **trade regulation rules,** or TRRs as they are called, are numerous. They speed up and simplify the process of enforcement. Advertisers can still litigate the question, challenge the trade regulation rule, seek an appeal in court, and so forth. In most cases they probably will not go to that expense. Trade regulation rules should have a great deterrent effect, as they comprehensively delimit what constitutes an illegal practice. In the past after the commission issued a cease and desist order, businesses frequently attempted to undertake practices that fell just outside the narrow boundaries of the order. The TRRs are much broader and make it much harder for advertisers to skirt the limitations. Finally, via TRRs the FTC is able to deal with problems most evenhandedly. An entire industry can be treated similarly, and just one or two businesses are not picked out for complaint.

While the FTC has issued TRRs since 1962, it has done so sparingly, since it was unsure of its power to take this action. In 1974 a court of appeals upheld the right of the agency to promulgate such rules (*National Petroleum Refiners Association* v. *FTC,* 1974). This court decision was made law by Congress in the FTC Improvement Act. Since that time, according to one FTC representative, the commission has been busy promulgating rules, so that this aspect of regulation is more visible now.

The two other aspects of the new law that improved FTC remedies are these. The FTC may seek civil penalties against anyone who knowingly violates the provisions of a cease and desist order, even if that person was not originally the subject of the order. To wit: A Chemical Company sells a spray paint that is toxic if used in a closed area, but the product is advertised as being completely harmless. The FTC moves against the company and issues a cease and desist order that states that in the future the firm must not advertise the product as being completely harmless. B Chemical Company also sells a spray paint that has the same toxicity and is advertised the same way. If it can be shown that B Company was aware of the provisions of the order against A Company and continued to advertise its product as being completely safe, B can be fined up to $10,000 per day for violating the order, even though the order is not directed against B.

Finally, the new law gave the FTC the right to sue in federal court on behalf of consumers who have been victimized by practices that are in violation of a cease and desist order or by practices that are in violation of a TRR.

As you can see, the FTC has a potent array of remedies to use against the errant advertiser. But the agency must aggressively pursue deceptive and misleading advertising if these remedies are to act as deterrents. The commission did far more to police advertising in the early 1970s when it had fewer remedies than it does today, when it has many more sanctions. In a sense Professor Posner was wrong when he said that lack of remedies was the cardinal weakness in the FTC (see page 521). The will to use these remedies must exist before the FTC becomes an effective agent against misleading and deceptive advertising. For better or worse, such will seems to be lacking in the current era.

SUMMARY

The Federal Trade Commission has the power to regulate virtually all advertising that is deceptive or misleading. To be deceptive an advertisement must contain a representation, omission, or practice that is likely to mislead the consumer; the ad or practice must be considered from the perspective of a reasonable consumer; and the representation, omission, or practice must be material. The FTC has many remedies that may be applied to attempt to regulate deceptive or untruthful advertising:

1. Guides or advisory opinions that attempt to outline in advance what advertisers may say about a product
2. Voluntary agreements by advertisers to terminate a deceptive advertisement
3. Consent orders or written agreements signed by advertisers promising to terminate a deceptive advertisement

4. Cease and desist orders to advertisers to terminate a particular advertising claim, failure to comply with which can result in severe penalty

5. Substantiation of advertisements in which the advertiser must prove all claims made in an advertisement

6. Corrective advertising in which an advertiser must admit in future advertisements that past advertisements have been incorrect

7. Injunctive power to immediately halt advertising campaigns that could cause harm to consumers

8. Trade regulation rules that can be issued to regulate advertising throughout an entire industry

THE REGULATORY PROCESS

To understand the importance of the regulatory process, students should be familiar with procedures followed in a deceptive advertising case, be aware of the kinds of advertising that can be considered deceptive, and be familiar with the defenses to a charge of deceptive advertising.

Procedures

Most cases come to the attention of the FTC from letters written either by consumers or by competitors of the offending advertiser. The legal staff of the agency then does a preliminary investigation. If the complaint counsel, an FTC staff attorney, feels there is no substance to the charge, the case ends. But if the attorney believes there is a provable violation, he or she writes a memorandum to the commission. A proposed complaint and a proposed consent order accompany the memorandum. The agency has recently established an evaluation committee at the FTC to review prospective cases and weed out the weak cases that consume staff resources and time.

After the proposed complaint has been prepared by the staff and reviewed, the commissioners vote on it. If they agree with staff lawyers—and they normally do—the advertiser is notified that a complaint is about to be issued. The advertiser is given the opportunity to sign the consent order or to negotiate a more favorable consent order. At this point there can be three results. First, the advertiser can agree to the consent order, and the commission can vote to accept the consent order. Second, the commission can vote not to accept the order. Third, the advertiser can reject the consent order. If the first happens, the order is published and sixty days later is made final.

If either the commission or the advertiser rejects the consent order, a complaint is issued, and a hearing is scheduled before an administrative law judge, who works within the FTC and officiates at commission hearings. At the hearing that follows—which is a lot like an informal trial—the burden of proof rests upon the FTC staff lawyers—complaint counsels—to show a violation of the law. In a criminal trial for robbery or murder, the evidence must show "beyond a reasonable doubt" that the defendant is guilty. In a civil case, liability must be established by "preponderance of evidence." In a hearing before an administrative law judge, all the complaint counsel must show is that there is "substantial evidence" of a violation of the law. While what substantial evidence is, is hard to define, it is less evidence than is required in either a criminal suit or a civil suit. After the hearing the judge either orders the case dismissed or issues a cease and desist order. The decision is final unless either the complaint counsel or the advertiser appeals. If that happens, the entire commission decides the matter. Overruling an administrative law judge is not uncommon. For example, after the hearing on Chevron F-310 the commission overruled the judge's decision to dismiss the charges. More recently the commission overruled a judge's cease and desist order against several television advertisements for Dry Ban spray deodorant. The judge agreed with complaint counsel that the advertisements implied that the spray "went on dry" but in fact was wet when it hit the skin. The FTC disagreed and said that all the advertisement implied was that Ban went on the skin drier than other antiperspirant sprays. A court of appeals must finalize either a consent order or a cease and desist order, but this is a routine matter.

If the FTC dismisses the cease and desist order, the matter ends there. If it supports the order, the advertiser can still appeal to the courts for relief. This is not a common practice, however. It is difficult for courts to reverse an FTC ruling. There are only a handful of reasons that a judge can use to overturn the commission decision. The case goes to the court of appeals and there is no new finding of fact: what the FTC says is fact, is fact. The following are all instances in which a court can overturn a FTC ruling (1) "convincing evidence" that the agency made an error in the proceedings, (2) no evidence to support the commission's findings, (3) violation of the Constitution—for example, the agency did not provide due process of law, (4) the action goes beyond the agency's powers, (5) facts relied upon in making the ruling are not supported by sufficient evidence, and (6) arbitrary or capricious acts by the commission. Such an event is an extreme rarity. An appeal of an adverse ruling by a circuit court can be taken to the Supreme Court, but only if certiorari is granted.

The enforcement powers of the FTC are limited but can nevertheless be effective. Violation of either a cease and desist order or a consent order can result in a penalty of $10,000 per violation per day. A fine such as this can add up fast! As a result of the *Geritol* case, the agency can be forced into district court to prove to a jury that in fact the orders were violated. This action impedes the enforcement procedure, for a jury trial is time-consuming and costly. As an alternative the agency can go back to the court of appeals that finalized the consent order or the cease and desist order and seek a civil contempt citation against the advertiser. The penalty is then up to the judge and will probably be much smaller, since civil contempt damages are considered remedial and are not intended as a deterrent.

A question that is often raised about the regulation of advertising is whether or not an advertising agency has any responsibility in an FTC false-advertising case. In the 1940s the FTC announced that an advertising agency could be held jointly responsible with the advertiser for false advertising. The agency reasoned that if the agency was active in preparation of the advertisement and if it had relatively extensive product knowledge, it could be held accountable. So the extent of agency participation in the ad campaign will generally determine whether or not the agency will be held responsible, according to Marcella Tyler, who prepared a special report on the FTC for the Institute for Communication Law Studies at the Catholic University School of Law.

Special Problems

There are a few special problems regarding deceptive advertising that deserve special mention before we leave this topic.

Testimonials

Testimonials, ranging from Joe Namath advertising panty hose to "the average man" promoting a pain reliever, are a large part of the advertising business. Before 1932, when a company paid for a testimonial—any testimonial—that fact had to be revealed in the advertisement. This has not been the law for more than forty years, however (*Northam Warren Corp.* v. *FTC,* 1932). Today, within certain limits, paid testimonials are allowed. The testifier must have in fact endorsed the product (*Eastern Railroad Presidents' Conference* v. *Noerr Motor Freight, Inc.,* 1961). It is deceptive, as well as an invasion of privacy, for an advertiser to assert that astronaut Neil Armstrong eats X brand of breakfast cereal if Armstrong does not, in fact, endorse the product. A testimonial cannot be altered to change the meaning (see *FTC* v. *Standard Education Society,* 1937). Suppose this is a movie review: "This is the worst movie of the year. You can see it—but only if you want to make yourself ill." Now here is an advertisement for the movie citing the review: "The critics loved it. '. . . the movie of the year. See it. . . .' " The quotation is used out of context and this use is deceptive. An advertisement can note that a testimonial is unsolicited, but only if it is unsolicited (*FTC* v. *Inecto, Inc.,* 1934).

The FTC adopted a new set of rules for testimonial advertising in 1975. Experts who endorse products must now have the expertise to evaluate the products. The law is quite rigid concerning products that relate to health and safety. The FTC ruled that an "expert" endorsement by former astronaut

Gordon Cooper of a product that supposedly increased automobile performance, reduced smog emission, and cleaned an engine was improper. Cooper's skill related to space missions; he did not have the education or training to qualify as an "expert" in the field of automobile engineering (in re *Leroy Gordon Cooper,* 1979).

A celebrity or expert endorser must be a bona fide user of a product at the time of the endorsement. This means the individual must use the product more than "now and then," or "once in a while." And endorsers must use a product because they like it and approve of it. The advertiser can continue to use the endorsement only so long as there is good reason to believe that the endorser still uses the product.

When an organization—like the National Football League—endorses a product, there must be evidence that the endorsement represents the collective judgment of the members of the organization, not just the judgment of the executive director or the management council of the group.

Payment made to an expert or celebrity endorser does not have to be revealed as long as there is no representation made in the advertisement that the endorsement was given without compensation. Payment made to a non-famous endorser (the typical man on the street) need be revealed only if the endorser knows that a favorable review of a product might result in the use of the endorsement as an advertisement. Here is an example. An advertiser announces that it is looking for man-on-the-street endorsements for Snappy Soda and invites persons to taste it and give their reactions to the drink. The fact that the tasters know in advance that a favorable review might get them a lucrative television commercial could color their reactions to the drink. But if the advertiser secretly records an individual's reactions to Snappy Soda and has not told this person, such reactions might be used as a television endorsement. No disclosure of subsequent payment need be made.

Celebrity endorsements must also reveal a material connection between endorsers and products if one exists. Pat Boone was fined by the FTC for failing to meet this rule in his endorsements of Acne-Statin, a skin-blemish medication. Cooga Mooga Corporation, owned and operated by Boone for the purpose of promoting the performer's business interests, was one of several companies marketing and promoting the skin medication. Boone received twenty-five cents for each nine-dollar bottle sold. In this case Boone also implied that his four daughters had used the preparation successfully, which was not completely true, and that Acne-Statin was superior to other similar products, an expert evaluation he was not qualified to make (in re *Cooga Mooga, Inc. and Charles E. Boone,* 1978). This was the first time a celebrity had been held directly responsible for deceptive endorsement. The singer paid a large fine and was ordered to pay partial restitution to persons who had bought the product. The link between a product and a celebrity endorser does not have to be as direct as the connection between Boone and Acne-Statin to require disclosure. Former astronaut Gordon Cooper was paid for his endorsement of the previously noted automotive product on the basis of the number of devices sold. The more products sold, the more money he received. The FTC ruled that this was a material connection between the product and the endorser and should have been revealed in the endorsements (in re *Leroy Gordon Cooper,* 1979).

An endorser cannot make any statement that an advertiser cannot make; that is, the endorser also must have support for his or her conclusions. The makers of a cough syrup cannot honestly say that their product cures a cough. A housewife who endorses the cough syrup cannot make that statement either. If an endorser changes his or her view and decides the product is no good, the advertiser must stop using that testimonial.

Endorsements that claim to be from typical consumers must be made by consumers, not by actors playing the part of consumers. Laypersons cannot endorse the effectiveness of drug products. If an endorser says she removes facial hair safely with a depilatory, her experience must be typical of most consumers. She cannot be the exception to the fact that the product damages the skin of most women who use it.

Bait-and-Switch Advertising

One of the classic false advertising games is what is called **bait-and-switch advertising.** Here is the general idea. An appliance store advertises in the newspaper that it is selling a brand-new washing machine for $57. The advertisement is the bait to get customers into the store. When customers come to the store to grab up this bargain, the salespeople are very honest about the advertised washer and say that it is a pile of junk (and it probably is!): it has no dials, it tears fine fabrics, it tends to leak, its motor is loud, and so forth. However, over in a corner is a really good buy, a snappy model that is going for only $395 for only a few days. This high-pressure selling is the switch. If customers insist on buying the bait, chances are they will be told the machines have all been sold. The merchant had never intended to sell that model. The whole idea is to use the bait to lure into the store people who are in the market for washing machines, and then skillful, if not honest, salespersons switch customers to a more costly model via high-pressure selling—convenient monthly payments and so forth.

Bait-and-switch advertising is illegal. Technically the law says that it is deceptive to advertise goods or services with the intent not to sell them as advertised or to advertise goods and services with the intent not to supply reasonably expected public demand, unless limitation on the quantity is noted in the advertisement (see Title 16 *Code of Federal Regulations,* 238).

Bait-and-switch advertising is not the same as loss-leader advertising, legal in many places, in which a merchant offers to sell one item at below cost (the leader) in order to get customers into the store in the hope that they will then buy additional merchandise at regular cost. Supermarkets use this scheme and so do other retail outlets. Those states that outlawed this practice did so because of pressure from small merchants who cannot afford to sell anything at a loss and do not want to be put at a marketing disadvantage with high-volume sellers.

Free Offers

It is deceptive to be untruthful about matters of cost and price; to say that the price of an item is reduced when it is not; to advertise a factory discount price when it is not; to advertise a special introductory price when it is not. The use of the word *free* causes many problems. If a merchant gives a free toothbrush to all persons who come into the store, the merchant can advertise that free toothbrushes are being given away. The word *free* may be used in connection with mail-order giveaways, even if the customer is charged a small fee for postage and handling, fifteen or twenty-five cents. However, to advertise a free set of drinking glasses and then require people to pay three dollars postage and handling is illegal.

The word *free* can be used even when the customers are required to buy another item before getting the free item so long as this fact is made clear in the advertisement: a free toothbrush with every purchase of a tube of toothpaste. However, this rule applies only so long as the price of the toothpaste is not inflated to cover even partial cost of the toothbrush. The toothpaste must be sold at the regular price. The same limitation applies to two-for-one sales: the first item must be sold at regular price, not at an inflated price.

Defenses

The basic defense in any false advertising suit is truth; that is, proving that a product does what the advertiser claims it does, that it is made where the advertiser says it is made, or that it is as beneficial as it is advertised to be. While the burden is upon the government to disprove the advertiser's claim, it is always helpful for an advertiser to offer proof to substantiate advertising copy.

Another angle that advertisers can pursue is to attack a different aspect of the government's case rather than try to prove the statement true. For example, an advertiser can argue that the deceptive statement is not material to the advertisement as a whole, that is, it will not influence the purchasing decision, or that the advertisement does not imply what the government thinks it implies. For example, to say that a deodorant "goes on dry" does not mean that it is dry when it is applied, merely that its application is drier than that of other antiperspirants.

The success rate in defending false-advertising cases is not high. As for most legal problems, it is best to consult legal counsel before a problem arises and not after a complaint has been issued.

Advertising law is complicated, involved, and constantly changing. Even advertisers who set out to honestly follow the straight and narrow run into difficulty once in a while. The best way to cope with these problems is by thorough understanding of both the law and the way the law operates.

SUMMARY

Complaints against advertisers are prepared by the FTC staff and approved by a vote of the commission. Administrative law judges can hold hearings, which are somewhat like trials, to determine whether the FTC charges are valid. A United States court of appeals can review all commission orders. Advertisers need to take special care when dealing with testimonials and endorsements. The law outlaws bait-and-switch advertising in which customers are lured to a store with promises of low prices but then are pushed by salespersons to buy more expensive products.

BIBLIOGRAPHY

Here is a list of some of the sources that have been helpful in the preparation of chapter 10:

Books

Alexander, George. *Honesty and Competition.* Syracuse: Syracuse University Press, 1967.

Howard, John A., and Hulbert, James. *A Staff Report to the Federal Trade Commission.* Washington, D.C.: Federal Trade Commission, 1974.

Posner, Richard A. *Regulation of Advertising by the Federal Trade Commission.* Washington, D.C.: American Enterprise Institute for Public Policy Research, 1973.

Rohrer, Daniel M., ed. *Mass Media, Freedom of Speech, and Advertising.* Dubuque: Kendall/Hunt, 1979.

Rosden, George E., and Rosden, Peter. *The Law of Advertising.* New York: Matthew Bender & Co., 1975.

Articles

Devore, Cameron, and Nelson, Marshall. "Commercial Speech and Paid Access to the Press." 26 *Hastings Law Journal* 745, 1975.

Jones, Michael E. "Celebrity Endorsements: A Cause for Alarm and Concern for the Future." 15 *New England Law Review* 521, 1980.

Langworthy, Elisabeth A. "Time, Place, or Manner Restrictions on Commercial Speech." 52 *George Washington Law Review* 127, 1983.

McGrew, Thomas J. "Advertising Law: Inactive FTC, Activism in Courts." *The Los Angeles Daily Journal,* Jan. 17, 1985.

"Note: Corrective Advertising and the FTC." 70 *Michigan Law Review* 374, 1971.

Schuman, Gary. "False Advertising: A Discussion of a Competitor's Rights and Remedies." 15 *Loyola University of Chicago Law School,* 1983.

Townley, Rod. "No Hitting Below the (Money) Belt." August 7 *TV Guide,* p. 18, 1982.

Tyler, Marcella A. "Federal Trade Commission Regulation of Advertising Today." Institute for Communications Law Studies, Catholic University School of Law, 1984.

Zanot, Eric. "The National Advertising Review Board 1971–1976." 59 *Journalism Monograph* 1, 1979.

Cases   *Alberty* v. *FTC*, 182 F.2d 36 (1950).

American Home Products v. *Johnson & Johnson*, 436 F. Supp. 785 (1977).

Aronberg v. *FTC*, 132 F.2d 165 (1942).

Bates and Van O'Steen v. *Arizona*, 97 S.Ct. 2691 (1977).

Bigelow v. *Virginia*, 95 S.Ct. 2222 (1975).

Bolger v. *Young Drug Products Corp.* (citation pending).

Campbell Soup Co., 77 FTC 664 (1970).

Capital Cities Cable v. *Crisp*, 104 S.Ct. 2694 (1984).

Central Hudson v. *Public Service Commission*, 100 S.Ct. 2343 (1980).

in re *Coca-Cola Co.*, Docket No. 8839 (1973).

in re *Cooga Mooga, Inc. and Charles E. Boone*, 92 FTC 310 (1978).

in re *LeRoy Gordon Cooper*, 94 FTC 674 (1979).

Dunagin v. *Oxford*, 718 F.2d 738 (1984).

Eastern Railroad Presidents' Conference v. *Noerr Motor Freight, Inc.*, 365 U.S. 127 (1961).

Feil v. *FTC*, 285 F.2d 879 (1960).

Friedman v. *Rogers*, 99 S.Ct. 887 (1979).

FTC v. *Colgate-Palmolive Co.*, 380 U.S. 374 (1965).

FTC v. *Inecto, Inc.*, 70 F.2d 370 (1934).

FTC v. *National Commission on Egg Nutrition*, 570 F.2d 158 (1977).

FTC v. *Raladam*, 283 U.S. 643 (1931).

FTC v. *Standard Education Society*, 302 U.S. 112 (1937).

Giant Food, Inc., v. *FTC*, 322 F.2d 977 (1963).

Heinz v. *Kirchner*, 63 FTC 1282 (1963); affd. sub. nom. *Kirchner* v. *FTC*, 337 F.2d 751 (1964).

in re *ITT Continental Baking Co.*, 79 FTC 248 (1971).

Linmark Associates v. *Township of Willingboro*, 97 S.Ct. 1614 (1977).

Meadowbrook Women's Clinic v. *Minnesota*, 557 F. Supp. 1172 (1983).

Metpath v. *Myers*, 462 F. Supp. 1104 (1978).

National Petroleum Refiner's Association v. *FTC*, 340 F. Supp. 1343 (1972); revd. 482 F.2d 672 (1974).

Northam Warren Corp. v. *FTC*, 59 F.2d 196 (1932).

Ocean Spray Cranberries, Inc., 70 FTC 975 (1972).

Ohralik v. *Ohio State Bar Association*, 98 S.Ct. 1912 (1978).

Oklahoma Telecasters Association v. *Crisp*, 699 F.2d 490 (1983).

Pennsylvania v. *Pittsburgh Press*, 396 A.2d 1187 (1979).

Pittsburgh Press Co. v. *Pittsburgh Commission on Human Rights*, 413 U.S. 476 (1973).

Posadas de Puerto Rico Assoc. v. *Tourism Co.*, 106 S.Ct. 2968 (1986).

Rast v. *van Deman & Lewis Co.*, 240 U.S. 342 (1916).

Rhode Island Broadcasters v. *Michaelson*, 4 M.L. Rept. 2224 (1978).

in re *R. M. J.*, 102 S.Ct. 929 (1982).

State v. *Cusick*, 84 N.W.2d 544 (1957).

U.S. v. *J. B. Williams Co.*, 498 F.2d 414 (1974).

Valentine v. *Chrestensen*, 316 U.S. 52 (1942).

Virginia State Board of Pharmacy v. *Virginia Citizens' Consumer Council, Inc.*, 96 S.Ct. 1817 (1976).

Warner-Lambert v. *FTC*, 562 F.2d 749 (1977).

in re *J. B. Williams* v. *FTC*, 381 F.2d 884 (1967).

Zauderer v. *Office of Disciplinary Counsel*, 53 USLW 4587 (1985).

11 BROADCAST REGULATION

A communications revolution is underway in the world and nowhere is this more evident than in the American broadcasting industry. The popular press informs us daily about new broadcasting hardware, new transmission systems, and new software packages like laser discs. DBS, MDS, LPTV, STV, MMDS, SMATV, VCR—the communications world seems to have erupted with a nonstop flow of alphabetical marvels.

A revolution in the regulation of communications technology is also underway, generated in part by a need to confront the use of this emerging communications technology and in part by a radical revision in thinking about the relationship between the government and the broadcasting industry. After sixty years of rather strict government control of broadcasting, things are beginning to change. Traditional assumptions are being questioned; regulatory schemes are being abandoned. The result of this revolution is a complex and constantly changing mosaic, one that is difficult enough to understand, let alone describe.

The Federal Communications Commisssion, the government's primary agent of broadcast regulation, now reflects the strong impetus in the federal government to "get government off the back of business." Deregulation has become the dominant theme, at times the only theme, coloring the operation of the FCC. The agency has already relieved broadcasters of much of the onerous bookkeeping required in the past. Requirements that broadcasters devote time for nonentertainment programming and limit the number of commercial minutes each hour have been abandoned. The number of broadcasting properties any single individual can own has been sharply increased by the FCC. After a comprehensive reexamination of the fairness doctrine, which requires a broadcaster to cover controversial issues and to allow all sides to discuss them, the agency concluded that that requirement no longer serves the public interest and should be abandoned. This recommendation was part of a twenty-four-point legislative package presented to the Congress in 1986, which called for other sweeping changes (largely a relaxation of rules) in broadcast regulation as well.

Moves toward deregulation have resulted in renewed debate of the legal and philosophical justification for any broadcast regulation. Traditional assumptions, such as that the public owns the airwaves or that the physical limit on the number of broadcast signals requires government regulation of the industry, have been openly and vigorously challenged. Many have tried to justify the relaxation of rules on moral and legal grounds as well as with the traditional argument that government interference with radio and television is not good for the broadcasting business.

Congress, somewhat suspicious of the FCC's posture of aggressive deregulation, has asserted its authority and played an important role in the regulatory revolution. In adopting the comprehensive Cable Communications Policy Act of 1984, for example, it relieved the FCC of much of its regulatory authority over cable television, as well as outlined for the first time a national policy toward cable.

Finally, decisions by the federal courts have even further clouded the regulatory picture. Footnotes in a ruling by the U.S. Supreme Court (*FCC v. League of Women Voters of California,* 1984) suggest that the High Court may be willing to reexamine the constitutional implications of the fairness doctrine. At least two lawsuits have been brought to give the court this opportunity. And a U.S. Court of Appeals ruling in 1985 (*Quincy Cable v. FCC,* 1985) that declared that cable television is much more like a newspaper than a broadcasting station raises the possibility that most government regulation of the cable industry—including the 1984 federal statute—may be unconstitutional. This ruling voided rules that required cable television station operators to carry the signals of all television channels within their communities. Since this decision many other cable regulations have been challenged in court.

In this chapter we will attempt to describe contemporary broadcast regulation with both an eye to the past and an eye toward the future. First we will briefly recount the history of broadcast regulation in the nation. Next we will outline how the industry has been deregulated already and present a discussion of the arguments for and against this relaxation of rules. Possible implications of this deregulation will be suggested. In the third section current rules regarding the licensing of broadcast stations and program content will be explained. Finally, we will outline the development of cable regulation and discuss the Cable Communications Policy Act of 1984.

The regulation of telecommunications in America today is a massive and complicated affair. This chapter is necessarily limited to the regulation of broadcasting and video programming by cable and ancillary services such as multichannel multipoint distribution services (MMDS). No attempt will be made to cover the regulation of telephone and telegraph and the many interactive communication services available. Let's start by looking to the past to try to understand why our broadcasting system was not given the same First Amendment rights granted to the printed press. ◆

REGULATION HISTORY AND RATIONALE

The individuals who created our system of regulation of broadcasting adopted what some call a trusteeship model for a pattern. The model suggests that the broadcaster should act as a public trustee, using the valuable broadcast airwaves for the benefit of the public. It was no accident that this model was adopted. It was dictated in no small part by the early history of radio. Let us examine that history briefly. Then we can attempt to outline the basic rationale that supports this trusteeship model.

Development of Radio

Radio is not the invention of a single individual. Rather, it represents an accumulation of many ideas that emerged during the last years of the nineteenth century. At first only simple radio signals were transmitted. But gradually transmission of more complicated voice signals became possible. The basic hardware of radio had been developed by 1910, but the medium grew far differently than did the print medium. Remember, printing came at a time when people were groping for a means of spreading propaganda, and the printing press became a major weapon in the battle for religious freedom in England. The press was used as a means of spreading information and ideas. Radio has never really been dedicated to those ends. Initially it was a gadget that tinkerers built as a plaything for talking with friends and neighbors and for listening to strangers in distant places. The military was first to see the practical value of radio. The navy used radio as a means of keeping track of its ships out of port and for transmitting messages to captains on the high seas. The army too saw radio as an effective device for improving military communications. After World War I the armed forces made one concerted push to have the government take control of all radio communication, but the effort failed.

Aside from the military, few persons could see the practical side of radio, especially of radio broadcasting. The giant radio manufacturers were the first to reason that if they used radio to broadcast entertainment, people would want to buy radio sets. Commercialism took a big step forward in the early twenties when the concept of broadcasters selling broadcast time to sponsors developed.

Radio Act of 1912

The regulation of broadcasting in the United States dates from 1910, when Congress ruled that all United States passenger ships must carry a radio. Two years later the lawmakers passed the **Radio Act of 1912** in response to considerable pressure from the army and navy, which asserted that increasing numbers of amateur broadcasters interfered with military transmissions. The 1912 law required that all radio transmitters be licensed by the federal government and that operators of the transmitters be required to have a license. The secretary of labor and commerce, who was delegated the job of administering the law, was given authority to assign specific broadcast wavelengths to specific kinds of broadcasting (military wavelength, ship-to-shore wavelength, etc.). The secretary also had the power to determine the time periods when broadcasts could be carried, but he had no discretionary power to license. Anyone walking in the door and filling out an application could get a license.

Part of the problem in the early 1920s was the proliferation of licenses. Too many people wanted a license and too many radio stations wanted to transmit at the same time. In 1923 Secretary of Commerce Herbert Hoover decided to take things into his own hands when he refused to grant a license to an applicant, claiming that this discretion was inherent in the 1912 law. A federal court disagreed with the secretary, however. "The duty of issuing licenses to persons or corporations coming within the classification designated in the act reposes no discretion whatever in the Secretary of Commerce. The duty is mandatory," Judge Van Orsdel wrote (*Hoover* v. *Intercity Radio Co., Inc.,* 1923).

While Hoover was defeated in the courts, conscientious broadcasters and other persons concerned with the future of radio continued to urge the secretary to set up regulations to control broadcasting. At the Fourth National Radio Conference in 1925 (Hoover called yearly meetings to draft broadcasting regulations which Congress annually rejected), the secretary of commerce outlined his philosophy with regard to broadcast regulation. This philosophy remains today the basic foundation for the regulatory scheme:

> We hear a great deal about freedom of the air, but there are two parties to freedom of the air, and to freedom of speech for that matter. Certainly in radio I believe in freedom for the listener. . . . Freedom cannot mean a license to every person or corporation who wishes to broadcast his name or his wares, and thus monopolize the listener's set. We do not get much freedom of speech if one hundred fifty people speak at the same time at the same place. The airwaves are a public medium, and their use must be for the public benefit. The main consideration in the radio field is, and always will be, the great body of the listening public, millions in number, countrywide in distribution. There is no proper line of conflict between the broadcaster and the listener. Their interests are mutual, for without the one the other could not exist.

Under pressure from elements in the broadcasting industry and somewhat flush with the consensus that the annual radio conferences seemed to indicate, Hoover continued to act beyond his legal authority in regulating broadcasting. In 1926 his actions were again challenged, this time by Eugene F. McDonald who operated station WJAZ in Chicago on an unauthorized wavelength and at times not authorized by his license. His challenge to Hoover was joined in federal district court and Hoover lost. Judge Wilkerson ruled, "There is no express grant of power in the [1912] Act to the Secretary of Commerce to establish regulations" (*U.S.* v. *Zenith Radio Corp.,* 1926).

Hoover insisted that the attorney general appeal the ruling, but in a lengthy opinion Acting Attorney General William J. Donovan stated that he agreed with Wilkerson's interpretation of the law. Donovan wrote that while stations were required to have licenses to operate, the secretary of commerce had no authority to assign specific stations to specific wavelengths, to limit hours of operation, or to place limitations on the amount of broadcast power used by a station. Donovan added:

> It is apparent from the answers contained in this opinion that the present legislation is inadequate to cover the art of broadcasting, which has been almost entirely developed since the passage of the 1912 Act. If the present situation requires control, I can only suggest that it be sought in new legislation, carefully adopted to meet the needs of both the present and the future.

Hoover capitulated, and the chaos, which the secretary's illegal regulations had somewhat abated, returned to the airwaves. Finally, Congress could no longer ignore the mounting pressure and adopted federal legislation by passing the comprehensive **Radio Act of 1927.**

Radio Act of 1927

The nation had operated without substantial regulation of broadcasting for about twenty years, but nonregulation did not seem to work. A traffic cop was obviously necessary to make certain that broadcasters transmitted on assigned wavelengths, that they operated during assigned hours, and that they operated at assigned levels of power. Only with this kind of regulation could listeners use the medium. The Radio Act of 1927 created much more than a traffic cop however. As former FCC Commissioner Glen Robinson notes in *The Administrative Process,* "Even a cursory examination of the Act, however, indicates that the regulatory powers granted to the Federal Radio Commission (and later to the FCC) exceeded those minimally required to avoid electronic interference." The new law governed programming, licensing and renewal, and many other aspects of radio not associated with broadcast signals and electronic interference.

The years immediately following the passage of the new law brought order to broadcasting. The courts upheld the power of the federal government to regulate the broadcast media, and a system of regulations began to take shape. The 1927 act also provided the basic philosophical foundation for broadcasting regulation. The law asserted that the radio spectrum, the airwaves, belongs to the public and that broadcasters merely use this public resource while they operate a licensed station. The law established that the broadcaster must operate in "the public interest, convenience or necessity" at all times. This was the standard of conduct that would be used to evaluate licensees at renewal time. An independent agency, the Federal Radio Commission, was also established to supervise the regulation of broadcasting.

While the 1927 legislation was satisfactory in dealing with the problems of broadcasting, it became evident, following a study initiated by President Franklin D. Roosevelt in 1933, that the radio industry and the telephone and telegraph industries were interdependent. In 1934 Roosevelt urged Congress to adopt a new law that would be broad enough in scope to govern all these media. After extensive hearings and debates, the Federal Communications Act of 1934 was approved. This law has been amended frequently since 1934, but it stands as the basic regulation of the broadcast industry today (47 *United States Code*, Section 151, 1970).

Justification of Regulation

If we study this history closely, we can see that regulation of American broadcasting was really justified on three grounds: scarcity, public benefit, and fear. Let us examine each of these three justifications a bit more closely.

Scarcity

There is a real and absolute limit on the number of persons who can broadcast over the airwaves at any given time. What engineers call the broadcast spectrum—the roadways in the atmosphere on which broadcast signals travel—is finite. When the roads are filled, no one else can drive. When the full spectrum is being used, no one else can broadcast. Not everyone who wants to operate a radio or television station can do so. Someone must decide who shall be permitted to use this scarce resource. This need for an arbiter proved to be an important impetus to government licensing of broadcast stations.

Public Benefit

It is thought by many people that when a broadcaster uses the airwaves to transmit radio and television signals, the broadcaster is using a public resource that belongs to all persons in the nation. Some agency must administer this valuable public resource in behalf of the public. Someone must make certain that those individuals who do use the "public airwaves" serve the best interests of the people when they use this public resource. There must be some means to assure that the public gets some kind of value for permitting persons to make a profit by using a public resource.

Fear

The broadcast media are thought by many persons to be powerful and even potentially dangerous mass media. We can bring the electronic media into our homes with little or no effort by the mere flick of a switch. Once we buy a receiver, we do not even have to pay for what we receive. The broadcast media can be used to spread dangerous ideas to large numbers of persons almost instantaneously. They can harm a community or a nation by spreading false information about important issues. They can offend or even foster serious social problems; for example, violence on television and its possible influence on violence in our society. Vulnerable children have easy access to the content of broadcasting. Finally, broadcasters can use the electronic media solely for private gain and flood the airwaves with advertising and commercial promotions. This valuable communications device could be turned into a giant selling machine.

Under the trusteeship model, the government is assigned the responsibility of controlling broadcasting. Because of the scarcity of broadcast frequencies, the government must assign those frequencies to those persons who can best serve the nation. Because these frequencies are a public resource, the government must act to ensure that those broadcasters who use the scarce frequencies serve the public interest—the greatest good for the greatest number. And because broadcasting is powerful and could cause harm, the government must ensure that the electronic media are not used in an improper manner. Under the trusteeship model the government will maintain ownership of the public airwaves in behalf of the people and temporarily assign broadcast frequencies to private individuals who are expected to act as trustees for the public in the use of this valuable resource. The public interest will be served through government regulation of these trustees.

Challenge to the Trusteeship Model

The trusteeship theory and the entire structure of broadcast regulation constructed upon it is under challenge today. Some of the very premises of the theory are thought by many to be wrong. What follows is a condensation of the arguments that currently rage around the need for and wisdom of broadcast regulation.

Who Owns the Airwaves?

American broadcast regulation, as previously noted, is founded on the premise that commercial radio and television stations are using a valuable natural resource when broadcast signals are transmitted from their antennas to the radio and television sets of the listeners and viewers. The resource, the airwaves, is public property. No one can own it because it belongs to everyone. The public owns the airwaves, as the public owns the wild rivers and the mountains and the seas. But the Communications Act does not make that claim, as a memorandum from the National Association of Broadcasters (NAB) recently pointed out. In fact, both the House and the Senate in 1927 considered including language in the Radio Act stating that the public did own the airwaves, but such language was left out in favor of a provision that says the broadcaster does not gain ownership of the airwaves simply because he or she uses them. Both the Radio Act and the Communications Act, then, are founded upon the government's constitutional power to regulate interstate commerce, not upon the notion that the government is acting as a trustee on behalf of the true owners of the airwaves, the general public, the NAB argues. Others point out that while someone can touch, smell, or see a wild river, a mountain, or the sea—and thus get some value from it even though it is not developed—it is impossible to touch or smell or see the airwaves. Only when the airwaves are enhanced by the broadcaster do they have any value at all to the public. Hence, the analogy is imperfect and shouldn't be used as a justification for the regulation of broadcasting by the government in the name of the people.

Others argue, however, that even if the public doesn't own the airwaves, the broadcaster surely doesn't own them either. Yet when the broadcaster uses a portion of the spectrum, no one else may. If that isn't ownership, it is the next best thing. Consequently, someone must make certain that when that valuable portion of the spectrum is used, it is used in such a way that at least benefits the rest of us—those who can't use it. This is called serving the public interest. Through the Communications Act the people have given the broadcaster the exclusive right to use a portion of the airwaves, but on the condition that he or she serve the public interest. And that is what regulation is all about.

Regulation by the
Marketplace

FCC Chairman Mark Fowler is a strong advocate of what he calls "the marketplace approach" to regulation. "There is a growing national consensus that market-oriented solutions, in which consumers interact with market players unimpeded by the filters of government, are preferable to a system where the government attempts to regulate the marketplace," said Fowler. The FCC Chairman is suggesting that the best evidence of public interest is what the public will buy, what it will accept. How does a government agency, one that is generally isolated from the people by the huge federal bureaucracy, really know what the public wants? If a radio station broadcasts thirty minutes of commercials each hour and the public listens, that must be in the public interest. If the public doesn't listen, then it is not in the public interest. And that broadcaster will have to change this policy or go out of business. The marketplace determines the public interest.

But doesn't the majority of the public just want entertainment? Without regulation won't the minority of the viewers be denied the news and information programming they seek? Supporters of deregulation note that news and information programming on radio and television has increased substantially in the past decade—without government pressure. Broadcasters discovered that people watch and listen to news, so it is profitable for them to broadcast news. The marketplace approach has worked. Even if news programming were not successful, it is argued, the professionals in broadcast journalism would still insist that the news be covered and aired. Broadcast journalism has a long and strong tradition; it is not an infant any longer. The professionals will ensure that the public will continue to be served.

But there are critics of this notion, including Les Brown, editor of *Channels* magazine. Brown argues that quality programming—including news and information—will continue to be broadcast only so long as it is profitable. The professionals in the business are in a constant state of tension with the businesspeople in broadcasting, who are the dominant force and are concerned almost exclusively with surpassing last year's profits. "What keeps professional broadcast managers alive in the industry, and allows them to win some battles with the businessmen," Brown wrote, "is the statutory obligation to serve the public interest. You can't achieve great profit margins if you don't keep the license." Brown argues that professionalism will disappear when regulation disappears. If the broadcaster discovers the station can make more money showing reruns of "Days of Our Lives" than by presenting the news, the news will go.

Scarcity of Channels

There is an absolute limit on the number of radio and television signals that can be transmitted at any time in any community. A medium-sized town might have three television stations and a dozen radio stations. No one else can broadcast because there is no more space in the airwaves—the spectrum. This scarcity of broadcast space has been used to justify regulation of the industry by the government, as was noted previously. Those who use the precious resource must be certain to serve everyone in the community.

Mark Fowler and others argue that the scarcity argument makes about as much sense today as a law banning the use of automobiles because they might be dangerous to the horses being ridden up and down the public streets. The argument is out of date. Scarcity is no longer a factor. Take another look at that town with three television stations and twelve radio stations. There are also a daily newspaper and a handful of weekly papers. Several national newspapers (e.g., *USA Today* and *The Wall Street Journal*) are also distributed. There are magazines, books, pamphlets, and many other varieties of printed matter. Cable television is available in the community as well, giving residents access to dozens of channels. This is the communications "era of plenty"; there is no scarcity, Fowler argues.

Using scarcity of spectrum space as a justification for broadcast regulation is really a two-edged argument. One edge, that there are a limited number of broadcast channels available for viewing and listening by the public, is surely out of date today. The description above makes short work of such an assertion. But the other edge of this argument is not so easily dismissed. That is, there is a finite and limited number of broadcast properties for members of the public *to use for broadcasting,* not for listening or viewing. The fact that there are newspapers and magazines or books and national cable channels does not remedy the problem that not everyone who wants to can use a portion of the spectrum to broadcast his or her ideas or creative works.

Supporters of broadcast deregulation cannot deny the basic truth that only a few people—the owners of the broadcasting stations—can use the spectrum for broadcast purposes. They argue instead that the publishers control the content of newspapers and magazines. While the number of radio and television stations is limited by the physical constraints of the broadcast spectrum, the number of newspapers and magazines is limited by the practical constraints of economics. Not everyone who wants to can have a broadcast station; not everyone who wants to can have a newspaper or magazines. Yet the government has never used this fact as an excuse to regulate the printed press.

It is true that not everyone who wants to can own a *New York Times* or *Chicago Tribune,* supporters of continued government regulation argue. But most people can publish some kind of newspaper, pamphlet, or handbill. The scarcity argument simply doesn't apply to the printed press, it is asserted.

The First Amendment

Proponents of deregulation argue that the very concept of a free and uninhibited press is undermined by the regulation of broadcasting. The First Amendment simply cannot tolerate the kind of control currently exercised over radio and television by the government. The Supreme Court of the United States, of course, has disagreed with this argument, noting many times (see *Red Lion Broadcasting* v. *FCC,* 1969, for example) that because of the scarcity of the airwaves and the use by broadcasters of the public airwaves, it is the responsibility of the government to protect the interests of the public. Content regulations such as the fairness doctrine and the equal opportunity rule enhance freedom of speech by insuring that more, rather than fewer, views are heard. And the indirect censorship the government exercises by licensing broadcasters is simply the price we must pay to have a broadcasting system that will be responsive to the needs of the community. The First Amendment existed in 1927 when the first comprehensive broadcast legislation was adopted; surely the members of that Congress were aware of the guarantees of freedom of expression when the Radio Act was adopted, it is argued.

Recall, however, what was said in chapter 2 about the development of the meaning of the First Amendment, which did not really take place until the 1930s. Hence, broadcast regulation was conceived, was adopted, and took hold in an era when the scope of the First Amendment was largely undefined. The growth of news and public affairs programs in broadcasting did not take on serious proportions until the 1930s, as well. The First Amendment undoubtedly appeared in 1927 to be a limited impediment to the regulation of what was largely entertainment-oriented radio. By the time radio news took its proper place in the spectrum of programming, regulation of broadcasting was an established fact of life. Today, when the First Amendment means so much more and when broadcast news and information are so important to so many people, the regulation of the industry must be closely reexamined, it is argued.

There is no question that traditional First Amendment interests have been compromised through both regulation and the threat of regulation. President John F. Kennedy and the National Democratic Committee used the fairness doctrine and the FCC to try to silence right-wing radio critics (see Friendly, *The Good Guys, the Bad Guys and the First Amendment*). And many local television stations were intimidated when FCC Chairman Dean Burch requested copies of all analyses of televised speeches made by President Richard Nixon. Burch was the former chairman of the Republican party, hardly a disinterested observer of criticism of the embattled president. The GOP also organized license renewal challenges against television stations owned by the *Washington Post*, a major thorn in Nixon's side. And in 1984 the Central Intelligence Agency asked the FCC to consider refusing to renew the broadcast licenses of stations owned by ABC because the network had broadcast a news report highly critical of the agency, a report that CIA boss William Casey said violated the fairness doctrine. It has also been argued that many timid broadcasters simply refuse to exercise their full constitutional rights of free expression because they mistakenly fear government intervention. And this reduces, rather than enhances, the flow of news and information to the public.

The argument that broadcast regulation is wrong because of the First Amendment is perhaps the most difficult to challenge in some ways. It should be remembered, however, that there are really three distinct kinds of regulation of broadcasting. First, the government places limits on the accumulation of broadcasting properties; one person can own only twelve television, twelve AM radio, and twelve FM radio stations. Second, the government exercises control over who may use the airwaves for broadcasting; these are the licensing requirements. Finally, the Communications Act and FCC policies restrict the content of broadcast programming through rules such as the fairness doctrine and equal opportunity, as well as regulations regarding the broadcast of indecent material.

Each of these kinds of rules relates somewhat differently to the First Amendment. Limiting the number of broadcast properties any individual may own has few First Amendment implications. It is hard to argue that someone who owns thirty-six broadcasting stations is being denied freedom of expression because the government forbids that person from owning one more radio or television station. But there are those who will make that argument. Licensing regulations certainly have greater First Amendment implications. How these rules are written determines how serious these implications will be. The government can surely regulate the speakers in a public park so that four or five people don't try to speak at the same time in the same place—so long as all have a chance to speak sometime. Broadcast licensing rules could be written in the same fashion. But current rules are far more complex and because one applicant for a license is often selected over another on the basis of what kind of programs he or she proposes to broadcast, there is no question but that the government is acting as a kind of censor. Rules regulating content most clearly run counter to our traditional views of freedom of expression. Only those persons who are willing to accept the newer access theory of the First Amendment (see pages 52–53) or who view broadcasting as entirely different from the printed press can view the fairness doctrine and other similar rules as being a constitutional exercise of government power.

These then are the arguments for and against the deregulation of broadcasting. Before considering the implications of the changes, let's now briefly look at exactly how broadcasting has been deregulated.

The Deregulation of Broadcasting

Congress has played a very small role thus far in the deregulation of broadcasting. And important action by the courts has focused on cable television, a subject for discussion in another section of this chapter. The FCC has been the prime mover in deregulation, but the agency has been limited to relaxing only those rules that it, the commission, has adopted. The FCC cannot change rules that are a part of the Communications Act, which is a congressional statute. It can only ask that Congress change these rules, and it has done that.

Ownership Rules

Under previous rules no individual or company could own more than twenty-one broadcast properties, seven television stations, seven AM radio stations, and seven FM radio stations. Additionally, only five of the seven television stations could be VHF channels 2 through 13. The VHF stations are more powerful than UHF stations (channels 14 through 83), can reach a much wider audience, and are generally more profitable. Under new rules an individual can own as many as twelve AM radio and twelve FM radio stations. If two of each kind of the stations have fifty percent minority ownership, an individual or company can own fourteen of each. A single individual or company can own as many as twelve television stations; the distinction between owning VHF and UHF stations has been modified. If two of the stations are on the UHF band or if two have 50 percent minority ownership, the total number one individual may own is raised to fourteen. However, no owner may reach more than 25 percent of the total U.S. audience with his or her stations. Consequently, a company like Capital Cities/ABC, which owns eight television stations that reach 24.4 percent of U.S. television households, cannot own the maximum of twelve or fourteen stations. Congress has forced the FCC to abandon its plan to automatically abolish all ownership restrictions in 1990.

Licensing and Programming Rules

The FCC has not been able to make drastic revisions in the rules on licensing and relicensing. Congress has been petitioned by broadcasters, with the support of the commission, to modify the current regulations on relicensing broadcast stations and drop what is called the comparative hearing requirement. Currently, the FCC is supposed to hold a full hearing when a challenger seeks to gain a license currently held by a broadcaster (see pages 564–66). The commission is supposed to evaluate both the current license holder and the challenger on several criteria and award the license to the individual or company that will best serve the community interest. Under various congressional proposals this requirement would be abandoned. The broadcast license would automatically be renewed unless the commission finds that the actions of the current license holder demonstrated such serious disregard for the provisions of the Communications Act or FCC rules that the application for renewal should be denied. Only after the renewal is denied could the applications of challengers be considered. Congress has yet to take action on the proposal.

But while licensing rules per se have not been changed by the commission, many other rules that have an impact on relicensing have been relaxed. These are rules that govern performance standards for the broadcasters. By eliminating such standards the FCC has made it much easier for broadcasters to live up to the statutory mandate that they serve "the public interest, convenience and necessity." Commercial radio and television stations are no longer required to provide a minimum amount of local programming, informational programming, and nonentertainment programming. There are no longer limits on the number of commercial minutes per hour that may be broadcast. Requirements that broadcasters undertake a formal process of ascertainment to determine the needs and interests of their local community and then propose programming to meet these needs have also been dropped. Broadcasters are no longer required to keep program logs that list all programs, as well as the type and source of each program. Commission chairman Fowler has said that the agency has eliminated 84 percent of all bookkeeping formerly required. A myriad of other rules have been eliminated as well, including FCC policies concerning licensee distortion of audience ratings, conflict of interest, sports announcer selection, and use of a station for personal advantage in other business activities. The changes listed above represent a small portion of the regulations that have been dropped.

The agency has, where it is possible, relaxed rules regarding program content. In two separate actions the agency modified long-held rules regarding children's programming. In the past the broadcaster was required to demonstrate how the station had met the needs of various groups of child viewers, such as preschoolers, elementary-school-age children, and others. In 1984 the commission modified this rule and refused to adopt mandatory children's programming rules. The FCC said that the rules were not needed because the video market *as a whole* does not exhibit a clear failure to serve the needs and interests of the child. What this means in practical terms is this: If the needs of children are being met by a public television station in the community and through cable channels or other over-the-air stations, a broadcaster would not necessarily have to provide programming for young people. The decision was challenged, but the U.S. Court of Appeals upheld the ruling (*Action for Children's Television* v. *FCC*, 1985). In late 1984 the agency also reversed a ruling it had made in 1969 and announced that product tie-ins were permissible in television programming for children. Five years earlier the commission had ruled that the cartoon program "Hot Wheels" was "designed primarily to promote the sale of a sponsor's product, rather than to serve the public by entertaining or informing it." But in its most recent action, prompted by a petition from Action for Children's Television attacking shows such as "Smurfs" and "Pac Man," the FCC in a four-to-nothing vote said that product tie-ins were okay. There are nearly ten such programs on the air now as a result of the FCC decision.

The FCC cannot repeal the fairness doctrine; the equal opportunity rule, which provides for equal time on broadcasting stations for candidates for public office; and the candidate access rule, which gives candidates for federal office the opportunity to purchase commercial time on radio and television stations. But in fact the FCC has the power (and has used it) to apply these rules in such a way as to reduce their potency. For example, between the beginning of 1982 and the end of 1984, the FCC received more than fifteen thousand fairness doctrine complaints. Yet it issued only thirteen reprimands to broadcasting stations because of those complaints. Additionally, the Fowler-led FCC has only ruled against a broadcaster once in six years, when a station contested a fairness doctrine complaint. This was a decision against WTVH-TV in Syracuse, New York, in 1984 (see page 489).

Many persons argue that the commission has consistently undercut the intent of the equal opportunity rule. Under this regulation if a broadcaster allows one candidate for a particular office to use his or her broadcast facility, all other candidates for the same office must be given the same opportunity. But in recent years the FCC has declared that a candidate's news conference is not covered by the law and that debates between candidates may be staged by the news media without triggering the equal opportunity rules (see pages 579–80). By interpreting the rule in such a narrow fashion and the exceptions to the rule in such a broad fashion, the FCC has significantly reduced the effectiveness of this regulation.

Nevertheless, the FCC has asked the Congress to repeal all three measures—the fairness doctrine, the equal opportunity rules, and the candidate access rules. And legislation has been introduced to accomplish just that. No one knows whether it will pass. Deregulation is underway while the debate over its merits rages on. The final question that needs to be asked is, What are the implications of these policies?

What It May Mean   The relaxation of the rules on the ownership of broadcast properties is not viewed positively by many persons outside the communications industry. Owners of American mass media are happy to be able to add new radio and television stations to their broadcast chains or media conglomerates. In fact, the changes in the law set off a spate of buying and selling of broadcasting properties unparalleled in the history of the industry. But most neutral observers see the change as simply adding to the significant problem that already exists in this nation of fewer and fewer persons owning more and more of our mass media. This is responsible for the shrinking diversity of ownership (and content) in the mass media and the accumulation of incredible power by a small number of "media barons." The marketplace simply cannot control these emerging ownership patterns, any more than it controlled the shrinking of the number of American automakers to four or the accumulation of ninety daily newspapers by two different publishing chains. No good can come from this, most argue.

The implications in the change in licensing and program content rules are more difficult to assess. Few find fault with the elimination of the massive bookkeeping requirements—mostly busywork—that formerly saddled broadcasters. Changes in rules regarding the number of commercial minutes in radio and television are not likely to have too much impact. Advertisers are already unhappy with the number of commercial messages broadcast on commercial radio and television stations, and it is unlikely that they will stand for a substantial increase in this number. They fear that their own messages, which cost a lot today, will get buried even deeper in the commercial clutter apparent in prime-time television and drive-time radio.

The relaxation of rules on program content and the abolishing of the fairness doctrine and equal time rules could result in some substantial changes in broadcasting practices. We have already seen the sharp increase in children's programs with merchandise tie-ins that took place in the wake of the change of FCC policy on the matter. There are a good number of responsible radio and television station owners in this nation who likely will continue to serve their communities with quality and informative programming, whether or not the government requirements exist. In fact many of these stations may take a stronger role in news and documentary programming if the fairness doctrine and the threat of government review of programming are abolished. But the majority of American broadcasting stations will undoubtedly put profits ahead of product, as suggested by *Channels* editor Les Brown. Most of these stations have been doing that all along anyway, curbed only from wretched excess by the federal rules. If the massive proposals for change are approved, only public pressure—which until now has remained largely undefined and ill-directed—will exist to control these excesses.

There is a positive side to the deregulation of broadcast content, however. It removes the federal government from a position of being able to influence broadcasting as it has on occasion in the past. That is not an unimportant change. What the question of deregulation ultimately comes down to is a question of whom do you trust—government or the broadcaster? Those who trust the broadcaster will reluctantly support deregulation; those who distrust the broadcaster will oppose any relaxation of the rules. To many persons this represents a Hobson's choice, or no choice at all.

Whatever the success of the current effort toward deregulation, broadcast regulation is still a fact of life today. In the remainder of this chapter we will outline the law as it exists as this book is written. Those sections of the law that might be changed or abandoned will be noted.

SUMMARY

American broadcasting has been regulated almost from its inception. Regulation is based on what some call a trusteeship theory. This theory is based upon three pillars:

1. There is a scarcity of broadcast frequencies, and someone must decide who can best use these frequencies.
2. The broadcast spectrum is a valuable public resource. Users must be regulated to ensure that society gets the greatest benefit possible from radio and television.
3. Broadcasting is a powerful medium. Radio and television must be regulated so that they will not be used in a manner that could harm the public or be used solely for the profit of the users.

This trusteeship theory is under challenge today by persons who argue that there is no scarcity of communication channels and that even if scarcity existed, the government has never used that argument to regulate the printed press. They also argue that the public does not own the airwaves and that the First Amendment clearly calls for freedom of expression—including radio and television.

The FCC has already changed many rules regarding such things as the ownership of commercial radio and television stations, performance standards for broadcasters, the amount of commercial time permitted, and the keeping of broadcast logs. The agency has asked the Congress to abolish the fairness doctrine, the equal opportunity rules, and the candidate access rule. Congress has yet to act on such proposals, which could drastically affect the nature of broadcasting in the United States.

REGULATION THROUGH LICENSING

The broadcasting industry is regulated by the Federal Communications Commission, which accomplishes this primarily by the granting of licenses to broadcast and the renewing of those licenses.

Federal Communications Commission

The 1934 Federal Communications Act provided that a seven-member **Federal Communications Commission** regulate the broadcast industry. In 1982 Congress reduced the size of the commission to five members as an economy measure. Members of the FCC are appointed by the president, with the approval of the Senate, to serve a seven-year term. (In 1986 the Congress was considering a bill to reduce the term of FCC appointees to five years to give the Congress greater oversight of the Commission. Final action on the proposal was pending as this chapter was written.) One member is selected by the president to be chairman. No more than a simple majority of the commission (three members) can be from the same political party.

Like all administrative agencies, the FCC is guided by broad congressional mandate—in this case the federal Communications Act. The agency has the power to make rules and regulations within the broad framework of the Communications Act, and these regulations carry the force of the law. With regard to some matters the 1934 law is very specific. For example, Section 315—the equal opportunity provision (or equal time rule)—details regulations concerning the use of the broadcast media by political candidates. But in other areas Congress was eloquently vague. The mandate that broadcasters operate their stations in "the public interest, convenience or necessity" can mean almost anything a person wants it to mean. Consequently, the FCC developed rules like the Fairness Doctrine and the ascertainment rules in its effort to implement the public interest requirement.

Procedures

The commission employs a large staff and is divided into various divisions. The Mass Media Bureau, for example, deals exclusively with broadcasting and cable television problems. Other divisions work with telephone and telegraph problems and with safety and special services. Administrative law judges, who are assigned to the FCC by the Civil Service Commission, are independent of control and direction by the agency. The administrative law judges are responsible for conducting inquiries for the agency and have powers that are normally incident to conducting trials and hearings. Their decisions on matters such as controversy involving alleged violation of the Fairness Doctrine and license revocation are final unless an exception is filed by any of the parties in a case. If there is an exception, the FCC commissioners themselves normally hear the dispute and render a decision. Here is an example of this procedure.

Imagine that the National Rifle Association accuses television station KLOP of violating the Fairness Doctrine in presentation of material on gun control. The Fairness Doctrine requires that a broadcaster station, in its overall programming, fairly present all sides of a controversial issue. The National Rifle Association files a complaint with the FCC, which the Mass Media Bureau then investigates. Assume that after its investigation the Mass Media Bureau concludes that the station did violate the Fairness Doctrine. It then files a complaint with KLOP. The administrative law judge then conducts the hearing in the dispute. The Mass Media Bureau argues that the Fairness Doctrine was violated, and the station argues that it was not. Imagine that the judge decides that the station did not act fairly and rules against KLOP. This decision is final unless the station files an exception within thirty days. If the judge rules that the station did not violate the doctrine, the Mass Media Bureau can file an exception. The issue of whether KLOP violated the Fairness Doctrine then goes before the five commissioners, where oral argument is held and a decision is reached.

What happens if the FCC rules against KLOP? Is the matter finished? No. The station can ask a United States court of appeals (not the district court, since the FCC has already conducted its fact finding) to review the decision.

An appellate court cannot substitute its own judgment for that of the Federal Communications Commission. The judges do not review the factual record to see whether they reach the same conclusion. FCC decisions, like the decisions of all administrative agencies, cannot be overruled except for quite specific reasons. The court can check to see whether the petitioner (the party who brings the appeal) has been afforded due process of law. It can investigate various other issues. Were there procedural irregularities? Did the FCC make an adequate finding of the facts? Did the commission state the reasons for its decision? Are the findings of the agency supported by the evidence in the record? Did the action by the FCC conform to its congressional mandate or did it go beyond the authority granted in the Communications Act?

While theoretically these are the only kinds of issues a court can examine, courts on occasion have gone beyond these limits to examine the factual questions. Some judges have been reluctant to refrain from examining the substantive issues involved and sometimes have even reached conclusions different from those reached by the FCC. The United States Supreme Court is available for the final appeal.

We have briefly reviewed how the FCC operates. Other aspects of FCC procedures are considered when licensing and programming controls are discussed in detail. Let us next take a quick look at FCC powers as invested by the Communications Act of 1934.

Powers

An important aspect of the 1934 law is the affirmation of the philosophy in the 1927 measure, which established a privately owned broadcasting system operating over the public airwaves. This was a kind of compromise between establishing complete government control of broadcasting, as in most nations, and allowing the broadcasting industry to operate like most other industries, that is, with no government regulation.

The Congress approved the 1934 law under the authority of the commerce clause of the United States Constitution, which gives the federal legislature the exclusive power to regulate interstate commerce. This means that states, counties, and cities have no regulatory power over broadcasting stations. The federal government has *preempted* the law in this area. Under the

1927 act the question had arisen of whether this clause meant that the federal government lacked power to regulate broadcasters whose signals did not cross state lines, stations that were not engaged in interstate commerce. In 1933 in *FRC* v. *Nelson Brothers,* the United States Supreme Court ruled that state lines did not divide radio waves and that national regulation of broadcasting was not only appropriate but also essential to the efficient use of radio facilities.

While the Communications Act branded telephone and telegraph companies common carriers (because they are monopolies, they have to be common carriers; that is, they must accept business from anyone who wishes to use their services), broadcasting stations were not so designated. Because broadcasters are not common carriers, they may refuse to do business with anyone or any company. Broadcasters do not have to make their facilities available to all members of the public. In addition the commission lacks the power to set rates for the sale of broadcasting time. Broadcasting is founded on the basis of free competition among holders of broadcast licenses.

The Communications Act makes it clear that while broadcasters may freely compete, they in no way assume ownership of a frequency or wavelength by virtue of using it for three years or for three hundred years. When a license is granted, the broadcaster must sign a form in which is waived any claim to the perpetual use of a particular frequency.

Technically the FCC lacks the power to censor broadcasters. Section 326 of the Communications Act states:

> Nothing in this act shall be understood or construed to give the commission the power of censorship over radio communications or signals transmitted by any radio station, or condition shall be promulgated or fixed by the commission which shall interfere with the right of free speech by means of radio communication.

No censorship, then. At least that is what Section 326 states. But that is not the way this section has been interpreted. The FCC has chosen to interpret Section 326 (with the approval of the courts) to mean that it may not censor specific programs, that is, forbid a broadcaster to carry programs on radical politicians or programs that picture members of a minority group in a derogatory fashion. However, at license renewal time the agency can consider the kind of programming the licensee broadcasts, and if the agency finds the programming objectionable, this fact can be held against the licensee. The U.S. Supreme Court adopted this understanding of Section 326 in its 1978 ruling in *FCC* v. *Pacifica Foundation* when the Court sustained the agency's censure of WBAI-FM for broadcasting George Carlin's monologue "Seven Dirty Words" (see pages 572–73). Most people would call this censorship. Section 326, then, has limited meaning and is of limited value to broadcasters.

The commission has broad-ranging powers in dealing with American broadcasters. Section 303 of the Communications Act outlines some of the basic responsibilities of the agency, which include classification of stations, determination of the power and technical facilities licensees must use, and specification of hours during the day and night stations can broadcast. The FCC also regulates the location of stations, the area each station can serve, the assignment of frequency or wavelength, and even the designation of call letters. There are not many things that broadcasters can do without first seeking the approval or consent of the Federal Communications Commission.

The key powers held by the FCC, however, focus on licensing and renewal of licenses and the authority to regulate programming and program content. It is toward these powers that primary consideration is directed in the remainder of this chapter.

Licensing

Issuing and renewing broadcast licenses are perhaps the most important functions of the FCC. These functions are very important to broadcasters as well, for without a license there can be no broadcasting. Virtually everything the broadcaster does is tied in some way to having the license renewed. In addition to getting a license for a new station, the broadcaster must also seek FCC approval for most operational changes, such as increasing power, changing the antenna height or location, selling the station, transferring ownership, and so forth. Broadcasting licenses are granted to radio stations for seven years; a license to operate a television station lasts only five years.

The **licensing process** is very complex and loaded with small but important details. An applicant for a new broadcast license must complete an incredible amount of paperwork in order to be considered by the FCC. A person who is seeking a new broadcast license must first obtain a construction permit, permission to start building the station. Obtaining this permit is actually the biggest hurdle. If the permit is granted, if construction of the station conforms to technical requirements, and if the work is completed within the time specified in the permit, the license is routinely issued.

What kinds of qualifications must the prospective licensee meet? The applicant must be a United States citizen, must be capable of building and operating the station for one year without taking in any revenue, and must possess (or be able to hire people who possess) the technical competence to construct and operate a broadcasting station. The applicant must also be honest and open in dealing with the commission and must have generally good character. The applicant must meet the qualifications under the multiple-ownership rules. No individual may own more than twelve television stations (fourteen if two are 50 percent minority owned or UHF stations), provided the total number of stations can reach no more than 25 percent of U.S. households. Similarly, no one may own more than twelve AM and twelve FM radio stations. Again, fourteen of each kind of station may be owned if two of the stations have 50 percent minority ownership. This is an effort by the FCC to increase minority ownership of broadcasting properties. There are additional rules that limit ownership of multiple broadcasting properties and newspapers and broadcasting stations within a city or market area (these regulations are discussed in more detail in chapter 12). The applicant has to endeavor to ascertain the needs and interests of the people in the community to be served by the station and then prepare a programming scheme that will serve those needs and interests. If the applicant shows the commission that he or she is in compliance with these requirements and if there is no competing applicant or community protest against granting the permit, the permit to construct the station will be granted. The license then follows when construction is completed.

Competing Applicants

What happens when more than one person wants the same broadcast license? The government must decide who shall get it. The qualifications of both candidates are studied (a list of the kinds of criteria used by the FCC is given on page 565) and the most deserving gets the license.

An applicant for a new license might also be challenged by someone who already holds a broadcast license in the same area and believes that the local market cannot absorb another broadcasting station. The existing license holder can argue in one of two ways to try to convince the FCC not to grant the new license:

1. The addition of another broadcast signal will damage the quality of the owner's existing broadcast signal.
2. The addition of a new station will cause economic harm to the owner of the existing station. There is not enough advertising revenue in the community to support an additional station without harming the existing station.

The FCC can accept the second argument only if the station operator can show that the reduced revenues will *adversely affect program service*. Demonstrating a potential loss in profits is not sufficient. The United States Court of Appeals for the District of Columbia noted in 1958 that "to license two stations where there is revenue for only one may result in no good service at all" (*Carroll Broadcasting Co.* v. *FCC,* 1958).

Broadcast licenses are granted for limited periods of time. Television stations are licensed for five years; radio stations are licensed for seven years. These broadcast licenses must be renewed by the FCC before the broadcaster can continue to operate. The FCC recently established and the federal courts have affirmed a simplified renewal procedure that drastically reduced the documentation required by the commission in routine renewal cases.

To gain renewal of a license, the broadcaster must provide the FCC with data about the broadcast operation. This points out an important fact about renewal: the FCC does not conduct an independent investigation of the licensee. Rather, the broadcaster (and sometimes other interested parties) provides the commission with nearly all material relevant to the renewal. The data provided to the FCC focus upon technical matters, business matters, and programming matters. If the FCC is not satisfied with what it sees, it can schedule a formal hearing on the renewal application. A formal hearing is prerequisite to both nonrenewal and revocation of a license before expiration.

If a problem does arise during renewal, it often takes years for the FCC to resolve the matter. In 1975, for example, the FCC voted to strip the licenses from all the public television stations in Alabama because they had discriminated against blacks in the 1960s. By 1975, when the FCC took its action, these public broadcasting stations had solved the problems of the 1960s, served the minority community with high-quality programming, and were considered a model broadcasting operation with regard to the employment of minority persons. In 1976 the FCC voted to deny renewal to station WHBI in Newark, New Jersey, for failing to adequately supervise its programming. The action had started seven years earlier in 1969 when the station sought renewal of its license (*Cosmopolitan Broadcasting Corp.,* 1976).

The commission may refuse to renew a broadcast license if the licensee has violated any important provision of the Federal Communications Act or FCC rules. Stations that broadcast fraudulent advertising have been denied the renewal of their licenses (*May Seed and Nursery Co.,* 1936). The renewal of a license for a station that was used solely to promote the causes of its owner was denied (*Young People's Association for the Propagation of the Gospel,* 1938). If a station does not adequately supervise the programming it carries, its license may not be renewed (*Cosmopolitan Broadcasting Corp.,* 1976). Federal courts have ruled that denial of a license renewal does not violate the First Amendment. Acknowledging that a First Amendment issue might arise when a licensee is stripped of the power to broadcast, the United States Court of Appeals for the District of Columbia nevertheless ruled more than a half-century ago (*Trinity Methodist Church, South* v. *FRC,* 1932):

> This does not mean that the government, through agencies established by Congress, may not refuse a renewal of license to one who has abused it to broadcast defamatory or untrue matter. In that case there is not a denial of freedom of speech, but merely the application of the regulatory power of Congress in a field within the scope of its legislative authority.

The previous year another United States court of appeals judge had ruled that the commission had a perfect right to look to past programming practices of a renewal applicant to determine whether the license should be renewed. Invoking the biblical injunction "by their fruits ye shall know them," the court affirmed that past programming is a central issue in consideration of service in the public interest (*KFKB Broadcasting Association* v. *FRC*, 1931).

When a license renewal is denied, the broadcaster can appeal the FCC ruling to a United States court of appeals, and sometimes the court will reverse the decision by the agency. In one of the most widely publicized license renewal disputes of recent times, the United States Court of Appeals for the District of Columbia partially overturned a commission ruling that stripped RKO General, one of the nation's largest broadcasting chains, of television licenses in New York, Boston, and Los Angeles. The FCC had ruled in 1980 that the broadcaster and its parent company, General Tire and Rubber Company, had engaged in "extensive and serious" misconduct and could no longer be trusted as broadcasters. The agency upheld several charges that had been first levied against RKO General in 1974. The commission ruled that the renewal of licenses for stations WOR-TV in New York and KHJ-TV in Los Angeles were conditioned on the outcome of a hearing that was held to determine whether the license for WNAC-TV in Boston should be renewed. At the conclusion of the hearings on WNAC-TV, the FCC found misconduct in four areas and refused to renew any of the valuable licenses. RKO General appealed this decision. The Court of Appeals ruled that three of the four reasons given by the FCC for denial of the license renewal applications were invalid. The fourth reason—that RKO General had failed to be candid with the FCC during the Boston hearing about problems its parent company (General Tire) was having with the Securities and Exchange Commission—was sufficient to deny the renewal of the license for WNAC-TV, but not the television licenses for WOR and KHJ (*RKO* v. *FCC,* 1981). RKO General remained unsatisfied and sought to win back its Boston license through an appeal to the United States Supreme Court. But the High Court declined to hear the case. The FCC action against RKO General both angered and frightened radio and television station owners and spurred the broadcast industry in its efforts to win deregulation. By the end of 1985 RKO General had won renewal of the license for WOR-TV, but had not yet gained renewal at KHJ-TV.

Persons who seek to gain a new television license or renew an old one must in some manner consider the needs of the listeners and viewers in the community and show the FCC how they are being responsive to these needs. In the past the agency required that a broadcaster use formal ascertainment methods, which were quite specific and required the broadcaster to do a full study of the community and interview scores of community leaders and others. The FCC has dropped the formal ascertainment requirement for both radio and television stations.

The renewal of most broadcast licenses is a routine matter. There are instances, however, where members of the community ask the commission to deny the renewal of a broadcast license or another individual seeks to gain control of the license and operate a broadcasting station.

Public challenges to the renewal of a license are a relatively modern phenomena and today are quite rare. It wasn't until 1966 that citizens were even permitted to take part in the renewal process and, then, only after a U.S. court of appeals ordered the FCC to change its policies. A group of persons from Mississippi were blocked by the FCC in their attempt to stop the renewal of a television license for a station in Jackson, Mississippi, that citizens accused of racist policies. The FCC said the group lacked "standing" to take part in the hearing. "Standing" is a legal word that means a direct and substantial interest in the outcome of the hearing. Judge Warren Burger (who became the nation's chief justice) wrote in *Office of Communication, United Church of Christ* v. *FCC* (1966) that the action of the FCC:

> . . . denies standing to spokesmen for the listeners, who are often most directly concerned with and intimately affected by the performance of the licensee. . . . The theory that the commission can always effectively represent the listener interests in a renewal proceeding without the aid and participation of legitimate listener representatives . . . is one of the assumptions we collectively try to work with so long as they are reasonable and adequate. When it becomes clear, as it does to us now, that it is no longer a valid assumption which stands up under the realities of actual experience, neither we nor the commission can continue to rely upon it.

Recent FCC rulings have made it far more difficult for a citizen to challenge the renewal of a license. Because a station no longer is forced to keep many records that were at one time routine, it is often hard for a citizens' group to document its charges against the broadcaster. More important, however, the FCC has substantially lowered performance standards for radio and television stations. Stations no longer must program for children on a regular basis or broadcast nonentertainment programming, for example. This has sharply reduced the number of issues that a citizens' group might raise in challenging the renewal of the license.

More commonly the challenge to the licensee comes from another broadcaster who seeks the license for himself or herself. Since only one person can broadcast on the same frequency in the same community at the same time, the FCC must choose which of these two individuals should have the right to use the broadcast license.

Under the current law the FCC must hold what is called a **comparative license hearing** whenever there are two or more applicants for the same license. Broadcasters consider this an onerous rule and are seeking to have it changed. A bill has been introduced in Congress that would forbid the FCC to consider the application of another person for a license unless it first denies renewal of the license for the current license holder. Denial would only occur under the proposal (H.R. 1977, 99th Congress) if it were found that the actions of the licensee demonstrated serious disregard for the provisions of the Communications Act and FCC rules. This policy would ensure renewal of the license if the licensee has complied with the fairness doctrine, equal opportunity rules, technical regulations, rules on the broadcast of obscenity, and a handful of other strictures. Programming content would not be taken into account during renewal if this proposal became the law. The likelihood of passage of this measure is not considered good.

At the present time broadcasters must face the comparative renewal hearing. In the hearing the FCC attempts to determine which of the two license applicants will best serve the public interest. In 1965 the FCC outlined a list of seven items it said it would consider in looking at the applications from competing applicants:

1. Diversification of control of the media: Persons holding existing media (like a newspaper or a second broadcasting station) in the area or having significant media holdings elsewhere will not be considered as favorably as those without or with fewer media holdings.

2. Full-time participation in station operation by the owners: The FCC will favor working owners over absentee owners.

3. Proposed program service: What does the applicant propose to do with the frequency? Supposedly, applicants who plan to devote more time to programs on public affairs and education and information will be favored over those who plan to program heavily with entertainment.

4. The past broadcast record of the current license holder, as well as the record of other broadcasters who seek the license: If the past record is average, it is disregarded. If it is exceptional, with unusual attention to public needs and interests, or if it is especially poor with regard to serving the public interest, the past record then becomes a factor.

5. Efficient use of the frequency: This is a technical question and has to do with judicious use of the spectrum.

6. Character of applicant: Does the applicant have a record free of criminal prosecution? Is the applicant considered honest and trustworthy? and so forth.

7. Other factors: The report did not outline these additional factors.

Theoretically, based on these criteria, the best applicant in a comparative broadcast license hearing will be given the license. But theory does not always rule in such hearings, and the actions of the FCC with regard to competing applicants have often been erratic during the past two decades. It sounds quite simple to say that the FCC should score each applicant on seven criteria and announce a winner. But is it fair to compare the real programming records of an existing broadcaster with the promises of a challenger? Is it not possible that an individual who holds several broadcast properties might be better qualified—by virtue of this experience—to operate another station than someone without other broadcast holdings? Why should applicants' activities outside the broadcast industry be used against them in a comparative hearing? All of these questions, and many more we could list, raise difficult issues. And taking away a broadcast license is not a simple matter. The license holder has millions of dollars tied up in property and equipment that would be unusable without the license. Rulings by the FCC in comparative hearings reflect the problems inherent in these proceedings. And time and again the federal courts have overturned FCC decisions, adding to the confusion in this area. A recent ruling regarding a Florida broadcasting station is a good case in point.

Cowles Communication, Inc., held the license for a Daytona Beach television station, WESH-TV. In 1969 Cowles was challenged when it sought renewal of that license by a group entitled Central Florida Enterprises, Inc. Despite findings that the Cowles company had violated an FCC rule by moving a production studio without first getting permission, that some principals in the Cowles organization had pleaded no contest to charges of mail fraud for a *Look* magazine subscription scheme, and that Central Florida was rated more highly on the diversification and integration of ownership and management criteria, the FCC returned the license to Cowles after the comparative hearings. The commission concluded that Cowles had provided substantial service in the past, which should provide the owners with a "renewal expectancy." In 1978, nine years after the renewal application was filed, the United States Court of Appeals (D.C.) called the decision unreasonable and overturned it. The court said it was simply unfair to place so much weight upon past performance when the challenger was superior on other criteria (*Central Florida Enterprises, Inc.* v. *FCC*, 1978). "The fly in the analysis is that the Commission judges incumbents largely on the basis of their broadcast records," wrote Judge Wilkey, "to which there will be nothing comparable on the side of the challenger in any case." Four months later in an unusual statement, Judge Wilkey tried to clarify his earlier ruling in denying the FCC's petition to rehear the case:

> Our principal reason [for setting aside the renewal]. . . . was that the Commission's manner of balancing its findings was wholly unintelligible, based as it was said, on "administrative feel." Admittedly, licensing in the public interest entails a good many discretionary choices, but even if some of them rest inescapably on agency intuition . . . , we may at least insist that they do not contradict whatever rules for choosing do exist.

Wilkey added, however, that an incumbent broadcaster could be given an advantage in a comparative renewal hearing for meritorious service. The matter was remanded to the FCC for further action and again, the agency voted in favor of Cowles on the basis of the station's past service, indicating that in the interests of industry stability, a renewal expectancy is necesssary where meritorious service has been provided. The ruling was again appealed, but this time the court upheld the commission's action and said it approved of the FCC policy that renewal expectancy is a factor to be weighed with all other factors and that the better the past record, the greater the renewal expectancy weight (*Cowles Florida Enterprises, Inc.* v. *FCC,* 1982).

The prospect of a renewal challenge certainly causes apprehension among broadcasters, probably far beyond what it should. On only two occasions has the FCC ever taken away a broadcaster's license during a comparative renewal hearing.

SUMMARY

The five-member Federal Communications Commission has been established by law to regulate the broadcasting industry. The agency has the responsibility to supervise all over-the-air broadcasting as well as any other electronic communication that has an impact upon over-the-air communications. While the FCC is forbidden by law from censoring the content of broadcast programming, the agency nevertheless has considerable control over what is broadcast by radio and television. By licensing and relicensing broadcasting stations, the FCC can ensure that broadcasters meet certain standards, including programming standards.

Television stations are licensed for five years; radio stations are licensed for seven years. To gain a license to broadcast, an applicant must meet several important criteria that have been established by the Congress and by the FCC. When two or more persons seek the same license, the FCC must decide which applicant would best serve the public interest.

When a licensee seeks to renew a broadcast license, other interested persons may challenge the license holder. A citizen watchdog group may ask the FCC to deny the renewal of a license in order to force the broadcaster to change what group members believe to be onerous policies. Other persons who seek to use the broadcast license may also challenge the license holder at renewal time. Under current law the FCC must hold what is called a comparative hearing when such a challenge is made. Congress, however, is considering changing the law to protect license holders. Under a proposed new law a hearing would be needed only if the record of the current license holder contains serious deficiencies.

REGULATION OF PROGRAM CONTENT

The regulation of program content is not directly tied to license renewal, but the failure of a broadcaster to observe FCC rules regarding programming can certainly be considered at renewal time. Despite the rule against censorship in the Communications Act (see page 559), the commission has extensive control over a wide range of programming matters. Content controls range from specific federal statutes (the laws that prohibit the broadcast of obscenity) to rather vague commission guidelines (such as the policy statement regarding broadcasters' responsibility for phonograph records played over the air). Many programming rules are contained in the Federal Communications Act; others have been generated by the FCC under the agency mandate to regulate broadcasting in the public interest, convenience, and necessity.

The FCC has a wide range of sanctions with which to enforce these rules. These include, in order of magnitude, the following:

1. A letter of reprimand that is put in a licensee's file and may be material at renewal time
2. Cease and desist order, which is rarely issued but can be used to stop a broadcaster from doing something the commission does not believe should be done
3. Forfeiture or fine, which can range up to $20,000 for a serious violation (the FCC has asked the Congress to give it the authority to raise the limits on forfeitures to $1 million for serious violations)
4. Short-term renewal, from six months to two years, while the FCC studies the broadcaster's record to determine whether the license should be renewed at all
5. Nonrenewal or revocation of the license, the nuclear bomb of broadcast regulation (rarely used as a sanction)

Sometimes the commission will simply write a letter to a broadcaster inquiring about a programming practice. This letter alerts station management that the FCC is aware of the practice or even concerned about the practice. Often the letter of inquiry results in the station changing the programming practice. Some people call this "regulation by raised eyebrow."

Broadcasters have many programming responsibilities that are supervised by the FCC. In the broadest sense the radio or television station owner must carry programming that serves the needs of the community as they have been determined by the station. There was a time when the FCC required each and every broadcaster to carry a wide variety of programming: religious, educational, agricultural, news, sports, weather, and many other kinds. At renewal time a checklist was prepared to be certain the broadcaster fulfilled the station's responsibilities in all these areas. This is not done any longer, but a broadcaster is still expected to meet these kinds of needs if they exist in the community.

In a narrower sense, there are many simple little program rules that have been promulgated by both the Congress and the commission. Stations, for example, are required to identify themselves periodically. Broadcasters must announce when the station or program receives a gratuity in return for an advertising plug on the air. A station may not knowingly broadcast fraudulent advertisements. It is illegal for a station to broadcast a lottery (a lottery is a contest in which a person trades something of value for the chance to win a prize). The license for station WWBZ in Vineland, New Jersey, was not renewed in 1955 at least partially because it had broadcast information on lotteries—in this case horse races. Giving the race results from the local track as a part of the evening news is one thing, but broadcasting up-to-the-minute race results from racetracks around the country is something else altogether. At least the FCC thought so and ruled that such information is useful primarily to persons involved in illegal gambling (in re *Community Broadcasting Service, Inc.,* WWBZ, 1955). The broadcast or telecast of information about state lotteries, including live coverage of prize drawings, is considered news coverage as well.

At one time the FCC tried to ban two nationally broadcast game shows that were constructed around participation by viewers and listeners at home. A band played a melody and the emcee called randomly selected listeners. If the listeners could "name that tune" or tell the band to "stop the music," they won a prize. The commission said that the games were lotteries and were illegal for broadcast purposes. The Supreme Court disagreed, ruling that while the FCC may indeed regulate the broadcast of lotteries, these games were not lotteries (*FCC* v. *American Broadcasting Co.* et. al., 1954). To qualify as a lottery a contest must have three elements. First, there must be a prize for the winner. Second, the prize must be awarded to a person chosen wholly or partly by chance. Finally, winners must be required to furnish something of value—called consideration—in order to participate in the game. When participants must buy a product before they are allowed to play the game, have to ante up money, or have to send in a box top, they are furnishing consideration. The third element was missing from the musical game shows and is missing from nearly all televised game shows today. (Tickets to shows to get a chance to play the games are always free.)

Can the FCC control a broadcast station's format as part of its regulation of programming content? For many years the FCC resisted efforts by citizens' groups to force the agency to get involved when a radio station dropped one kind of music format, classical, for example, and adopted another format, let us say rock. But listeners went to federal court, and the FCC was ordered in 1970 to *review* a format change by a station when the abandonment of a unique format produced community protests (*Citizens Committee to Preserve the Voice of the Arts in Atlanta* v. *FCC,* 1970). The United States Court of Appeals in Washington, D.C., went one step further in 1974 and ordered the

FCC to *hold a hearing* whenever a unique format was being abandoned by a radio station and persons in the community objected (*Citizens' Committee to Save WEFM* v. *FCC,* 1974). A unique format would be one that no other station in the market used. The loss of this format would deny the citizens in the community access to a particular kind of music or programming. Normally it has been supporters of classical music who have protested when a local station drops the classical format. But in Seattle in 1981 New Wave rock fans mounted a protest when the community's only (at that time) New Wave station abandoned that format. Despite the earlier court rulings, the FCC continued to argue through the late seventies that the marketplace should determine the broadcaster's format; the government should not get involved. And in 1981 the Supreme Court of the United States supported the agency and overturned a lower federal court decision calling for a hearing on a format change. Justice Byron White, writing for the seven-person majority, stated, "We decline to overturn the commission's Policy Statement which prefers reliance on market forces to its own attempt to oversee format changes at the behest of disaffected listeners." Justice White warned the agency, however, to be alert to the consequences of its policies and stand ready to change its rules if necessary to serve the public interest more fully (*FCC* v. *WNCN Listeners Guild,* 1981).

Station breaks, lotteries, and format changes are all important content regulations. But it is in three other areas that the FCC exercises what many believe to be its heaviest hand in content regulation. Let us look at each of these areas—obscene material, political broadcasting, and public affairs broadcasting—separately and in some depth.

Obscene or Indecent Material

Broadcasters have a special set of problems concerning pornography. Section 1464, Title 18, of the *United States Code* gives the Federal Communications Commission the power to revoke any broadcast license if the licensee transmits obscene or indecent material over the airwaves. No station, however, has ever had its license revoked for broadcasting obscenity. Nor has the FCC denied renewal of a license solely on the grounds that the licensee broadcast pornographic or indecent material. The commission is quite hesitant to use its big guns in this area because of the immense constitutional questions involved. It is clearly a free-speech issue. Yet stations have been put on short-term renewal and have been fined, as will be noted momentarily.

Normally, when the FCC receives a complaint from a listener or viewer about a broadcast believed to contain obscene language or pictures, the agency responds with a form letter that includes the following statement:

> The broadcast of obscene, indecent or profane language is prohibited by a federal criminal statute. Although the Department of Justice is responsible for prosecution of federal law violations, the commission is authorized to impose sanctions on broadcast licensees for violation of this statute, including

revocation of the license or the imposition of a monetary forfeiture. However, both the commission and the Department of Justice are governed by past decisions of the courts as to what constitutes obscenity, and the broadcast of material which may be offensive to many persons would not necessarily be held by the courts to violate the statute.

Although the FCC approaches the problem of obscenity cautiously, the mere fact that it sends out even a form letter to a listener or viewer has an impact upon conservative broadcasters.

In 1975 the National Association of Broadcasters (NAB), following suggestions made by CBS president Arthur Taylor and at least condoned by the other networks, instituted what it called "the family hour." Stations that subscribe to the NAB Code of Good Practices were told that the hours from seven to nine each evening were to be set aside for family viewing and that programs with sexual overtones and excessive violence were taboo in this period. The censorship undertaken by the networks was heavy-handed. The word *virgin* was cut from one program (*innocent* was substituted). Censors began to look anew at Cher's navel and a braless guest on the "Phyllis" show was redressed before filming began. Programs that had been broadcast in the 8 P.M. time slot for several years were either moved or toned down to meet the new family-hour standards. But the rule was challenged by the creators of television programs. Writers and directors in Hollywood, where most television programs are produced, went to court, and in 1976 federal Judge Warren J. Ferguson of the District Court for Southern California ruled that the "adoption of the Family Viewing Policy by each of the three networks constituted a violation of the First Amendment." The judge ruled that the policy had been motivated by informal statements from the Federal Communications Commission, which threatened government action against the industry should not the family hour or something like it be adopted (*Writers Guild* v. *FCC*, 1976). The judge's conclusion is more than substantiated in Geoffrey Cowan's fascinating book *See No Evil*, the story of the genesis of the family hour.

A United States court of appeals later overturned the lower court ruling on the grounds that the federal district court had no jurisdiction in the case, that the Federal Communications Commission should have heard the issue (*Writers Guild,* v. *ABC,* 1979). The networks, however, made no effort to reestablish the policy.

Law professor Harry Kalven noted years ago in the *Michigan Law Review* that while a regulation may not directly interfere with free speech, "in operation it may trigger a set of behavioral consequences which amount in effect to people censoring themselves in order to avoid trouble with the law." Or what people believe will be trouble with the law. Such is the case with the regulation of obscenity in broadcasting. The family hour is a good example of this tendency.

In the past twenty years the FCC has considered several instances in which charges were made that obscene or indecent material was broadcast. In 1962 the commission refused to renew the license of radio station WDKD at least partially because a disc jockey at the station habitually told "off-color" or "indecent" jokes on the air (in re *Palmetto Broadcasting Co.*, 1962). A college radio station was fined $100 for broadcasting "indecent" four-letter words over the air in 1970 (in re *WUHY-FM, Eastern Educational Radio*, 1970). A $2,000 fine was levied against an Illinois radio station in 1973 for broadcasting a discussion between an announcer and a listener about oral sexual practices (*Sonderling Broadcasting Corp.*, 1973). The discussion stemmed from the station's call-in "topless radio" format. A federal court of appeals upheld the judgment two years later (*Illinois Citizens Committee for Broadcasting v. FCC*, 1975).

Undoubtedly the most significant decision on broadcast indecency came in 1978, when the Supreme Court upheld an FCC ruling that station WBAI in New York City had violated the federal law when it presented a recorded monologue on the English language by George Carlin. The recording, which was played in midafternoon after the announcer warned listeners that it might be offensive to some, contained seven four-letter words that were used many times. The record was played as part of a program on society's attitude toward language. The FCC got one complaint and as a result took action against the station on the grounds that it had broadcast indecent language. The agency defined indecent language as "language that describes in terms patently offensive as measured by contemporary community standards for the broadcast medium, sexual or excretory activities and organs, at times of the day when there is a reasonable risk children may be in the audience." The FCC said the WBAI broadcast met this definition.

Pacifica Foundation, which owns and operates the station, challenged the ruling, and in March 1977 the United States Court of Appeals (D.C.) overturned the FCC action, ruling that the commission's order was overbroad and vague. Two years later, however, the Supreme Court reversed the court of appeals and sustained the FCC ruling. Justice John Paul Stevens wrote the opinion for the Court, noting that because of its unique characteristics, broadcasting had traditionally received the least First Amendment protection of all media. Stevens said broadcast was uniquely pervasive, that it can have an impact upon persons not only in public, but also in the privacy of their own home. Prior warning cannot completely protect the listener or viewer, he added. Also, "The ease with which children may obtain access to broadcast material . . . amply justifies special treatment of indecent broadcasting," Stevens wrote. The majority denied that the order was vague or overbroad. Stevens said that the ruling would deter only the broadcast of offensive references to excretory and sexual organs and activities. "While some of these references may be protected, they surely lie at the periphery of First Amendment concern," he said.

The associate justice added that the Court's ruling did not involve Elizabethan comedy or even citizens band transmission. "We have not decided that an occasional expletive in either setting would justify any sanction . . . ," Stevens noted, adding that the FCC decision rested on a nuisance rationale—"putting the right thing in a wrong place." Stevens added, "Like a pig in a parlor" (*FCC* v. *Pacifica Foundation*, 1978).

Many observers were sharply critical of the Court ruling, noting that if broadcast standards were to be determined by what was fit for children to listen to, the court was then turning its back on its 1957 ruling in *Butler* v. *Michigan*. In that case the Supreme Court invalidated a Michigan statute that forbade the sale of erotic material to anyone if the material would be offensive to children (see page 416). Critics also argued that the High Court left too many loose ends in its ruling. Children can be present in the radio audience at any time of day or night. Does this mean such material can never be broadcast? Or can it be broadcast late at night when children are not expected to be listening? Who is a child? Many feared that given the timidity of the broadcast industry, the ruling would have a serious, chilling effect on radio stations, causing them to overreact and censor too much material.

In practical terms there is little government censorship of broadcast obscenity. The broadcasters censor themselves too well for obscenity to be much of a problem. The cases that do pop up tend to be from stations that are not in the mainstream of broadcasting—little educational stations, offbeat FM stations, and the like. The managers of these kinds of stations tend to believe the First Amendment means what it says and are not afraid to rock the boat. The vast majority of station owners and managers, however, are reluctant to even get into the boat.

It should be noted parenthetically that while the spirit of deregulation has descended full-blown upon the FCC, no one in a position of authority has suggested that regulations concerning the broadcast of obscene or indecent material be abandoned. Just the opposite is true. The success of the pay cable channels that broadcast adult movies has prompted many persons to attempt to close the loopholes in the law that permit these cable operators to transmit (not broadcast) R-rated films, which often include nudity. Utah, for example, adopted a criminal statute in 1981 to punish any person who distributed by wire or cable any pornographic or indecent material to subscribers. The United States District Court ruled that such a statute could only prohibit the distribution of hard-core pornography as defined in *Miller* v. *California* (see pages 420–21). The Utah statute was too broad because it defined indecent material to include nudity, which has not been ruled to be legally obscene by the Supreme Court. The state argued it sought to protect children from such adult fare. The court urged the legislators to read the rulings in *Butler* v. *Michigan* (see page 416) and *Erznoznik* v. *City of Jacksonville* (page 431) where the Supreme Court said that a state could not regulate materials for adults on the basis of what is fit for children. The judge added (*Home Box Office* v. *Wilkinson,* 1982):

> That's one of the nice things about TV—not just cable TV, but also regular broadcast channels that are allocated, licensed and regulated by the government. There is no law that says you have to watch. There is no law that says you have to purchase a television set. There is no law that says you have to subscribe to a cable TV service any more than you have to subscribe to the *Salt Lake Tribune.*

Subsequent rulings have reinforced the decision by the U.S. District Court (see *Cruz* v. *Fere,* 1983 and *Community Television* v. *Wilkinson,* 1985). The Cable Communications Policy Act of 1984 clearly states that all levels of government—federal, state and local—can prohibit, limit, and penalize the exhibition of obscene programming on a cable system. (However, a cable operator cannot be held liable for the obscene programming appearing on the public access channels.) But the law really did not resolve the matter of whether government may ban the broadcast of indecent programming on cable. Michael Myerson, writing in a recent edition of the *Georgia Law Review,* suggests that the Cable Act is open-ended on the question of indecency. Congress did not want to go beyond the Supreme Court in permitting indecent cable programming, yet it recognized that the federal courts have ruled that cable is different from over-the-air television and permitted indecent material to be cablecast. But if the Supreme Court were to rule that cable television could be treated like broadcast television for the regulation of indecency, the Cable Act will not preempt local laws, Myerson wrote.

SUMMARY

The FCC has broad control over the content of broadcast programming. To enforce this control the agency has a wide variety of sanctions, which include letters of reprimand, fine or forfeiture, and nonrenewal or revocation of broadcast licenses. Content regulations involve a wide range of broadcast programming. In the broadest sense the broadcaster must program to meet the needs of the community as determined through the previously discussed ascertainment procedures. But programming rules also involve simple regulations, such as the requirement to present station identification at various times of the broadcast day. Broadcasters are also prevented from broadcasting or promoting contests that are legal lotteries.

The FCC has chosen not to attempt to control the selection of format by a broadcaster. Citizens' groups have urged the FCC to hold hearings when a radio station drops one program format and adopts a new one. In the early seventies federal courts supported these citizen protests, but in 1981 the United States Supreme Court ruled that the government need not get involved when a broadcaster decides to switch from one format to another.

Federal law prohibits the broadcast of any obscene or indecent material. In 1979 the Supreme Court ruled that a radio or television station can be punished for broadcasting material that is not legally obscene, but is merely indecent. The court based its ruling on the fact that children might be present during the broadcast.

Several states have attempted to adopt laws that limit the transmission of indecent material, including adult R-rated films, over pay cable television. Federal courts have struck down these laws on the basis that only legally obscene material can be barred from such nonbroadcast television transmission.

REGULATION OF POLITICAL BROADCASTS

The guarantees of freedom of speech and freedom of the press were added to the Constitution in large measure to protect the political debate in this nation from interference by the government. Yet the Federal Communications Commission substantially regulates political broadcasting in this nation. How can we permit the government to have any control whatsoever over a kind of expression that is so important to the democratic system? Supporters of the federal regulation of political broadcasting argue that it is because political speech is so important that the government must ensure that broadcasters serve the public interest and not their own political interests in this area. Opponents of the political broadcast rules refer to this argument as Orwellian logic worthy of Big Brother in the frightening novel *1984*. Let us examine what controls the FCC exercises over political broadcasting.

Candidate Access Rule

Broadcasters cannot completely block candidates for federal office from buying airtime on the station to promote their candidacies because of the existence of the **candidate access rule.** Section 312 (a) (7) of the Federal Communications Act, adopted in 1971 by the Congress, states that a broadcast license can be revoked for willful and repeated failure "to allow reasonable access to or to permit the purchase of reasonable amounts of time for the use of a broadcasting station by a legally qualified candidate for federal elective office on behalf of his candidacy." This statute applies only to candidates for federal office: presidents and vice-presidents and United States senators and representatives. The FCC has asked the Congress to repeal this law in its effort to deregulate broadcasting.

Federal courts have provided two important interpretations of this statute. Both cases stemmed from the 1980 presidential election campaign. The Carter-Mondale Presidential Committee sought to buy thirty minutes of time on all three networks in early December 1979 for President Jimmy Carter to announce that he would be a candidate for reelection and to present a film outlining Carter's record as president. The request was made in October 1979. NBC refused. ABC said it could not reach a decision on the question. CBS offered two five-minute segments, one at 10:55 P.M. and one during the day. Privately, all three networks were fearful of breaking into their prime time entertainment schedules for a political broadcast. But publicly the broadcasters argued that the political campaign had not yet started; it was too early (the election was scheduled for November 1980) to begin to carry political programming.

The FCC ruled against the networks, the United States Court of Appeals (D.C.) ruled against the networks, and the Supreme Court of the United States ruled against the networks. The High Court ruled in its six-to-three decision that a broadcaster could not institute an across-the-board policy rejecting all requests from federal candidates for airtime. Chief Justice Burger wrote that once a political campaign begins, a broadcaster must give reasonable and good faith attention to access requests from legally qualified candidates (*CBS* v. *FCC,* 1981):

> Such requests must be considered on an individualized basis, and broadcasters are required to tailor their responses to accommodate, as much as reasonably possible, a candidate's stated purpose in seeking airtime. In responding to access requests, however, broadcasters may also give weight to such factors as the amount of time previously sold to the candidate, the disruptive impact on regular programming, and the likelihood of requests for time by rival candidates under the equal opportunities provision of Section 315 (a). These considerations may not be invoked as pretexts for denying access; to justify a negative response, broadcasters must cite a realistic danger of substantial program disruption—perhaps caused by insufficient notice to allow adjustments in the schedule—or of an excessive number of equal time requests.

Burger added that broadcasters must explain their reasons for refusing airtime or making limited counteroffers so the FCC can review these decisions if needed. Each of the networks had argued, however, that the 1980 presidential campaign had not really started. After all, the time period sought by Carter was eleven months prior to the election. In this case the networks should not be bound by Section 312, they asserted. The majority of the Supreme Court rejected this argument, noting the following evidence that the campaign had started:

1. Ten Republican candidates and two Democratic candidates had announced they were running for president.
2. The selection of delegates to the national political conventions had started in many states.

3. Many candidates were making speeches in an effort to raise money.
4. The Iowa caucuses to select convention delegates were scheduled for January, one month after the broadcast time sought by Carter.
5. Newspapers had been covering the national political campaign for at least two months.

Burger rejected the notion that Section 312 created a right of access to the media. None is created by this decision, he added. But a licensed broadcaster is "granted the free and exclusive use of a limited and valuable part of the public domain; when he accepts that franchise it is burdened by enforceable public obligations" (*CBS* v. *FCC,* 1981).

The Supreme Court's ruling means that a broadcaster cannot adopt an across-the-board policy of rejecting all requests for airtime. Each request must be considered individually, and can be rejected only if the broadcaster can demonstrate a good cause.

Section 312 implies that the candidate can seek to buy time on a station or ask for free time. Does this mean a broadcast station must *give* a candidate for federal office free time if fulfilling such a request would not interfere substantially with the broadcast schedule or would not prompt requests for equal time from other candidates? The United States Court of Appeals for the District of Columbia answered no when that question was asked. On March 14, 1980, then President Carter delivered a thirty-minute speech on the economic condition of the nation. The speech was carried on all three networks. This was four days before the presidential primary in Illinois. Senator Ted Kennedy, who was also seeking the Democratic nomination for president, requested that the networks *give* him thirty minutes of airtime to respond to the president's speech. The networks said they would sell Kennedy the time, but would not give it to him. Kennedy argued that they were obliged to provide him thirty minutes at no cost because of Section 312. The United States Court of Appeals (D.C.) supported the FCC's denial of Kennedy's request. The law does not confer upon a candidate the privilege of using a broadcaster's facilities without charge. Broadcasters may meet the demands of Section 312 by either giving the candidate free time or making time available for purchase, the court said. The networks had already given Kennedy's campaign considerable free time through its news coverage of the candidate (*Kennedy for President Committee* v. *FCC,* 1980).

Supporters of Section 312 see it as a means to permit candidates for federal office to use the important broadcast communication channels in this nation to talk to prospective voters. Opponents say it is government interference in broadcasters' operation of their business, and it can cause severe financial hardship if programming schedules are disrupted to facilitate political broadcasts. The FCC has asked Congress to abandon this law, but most observers do not believe Congress will repeal this statute.

When Congress adopted Section 312 in 1971, it also specified the highest rates that a broadcaster can charge a candidate for federal office for using station facilities. The general rule is: Forty-five days before a primary election and sixty days before a general election, the charge to a candidate cannot exceed the lowest rate the station charges its local advertisers for that particular time slot. At other times the rate must be "comparable" to what the station charges other advertisers. There are considerable details in these rules that are important but are too involved to outline here. Students who intend to enter broadcast sales should closely study Section 312 of 47 *United States Code.*

One final note. Section 312 applies only to candidates for federal office. However, a broadcast station has an obligation to serve the public interest. The FCC could surely find that a broadcaster who consistently refuses to provide access to candidates for state or local office was not properly serving the public interest.

Equal Opportunity Rule

Section 315 contains the equal opportunities or **equal time rule.** It has been a part of the Federal Communications Act since the law was passed in 1934. It was significantly changed by the Congress in 1959. Section 315 is not really difficult to understand. If a broadcasting station permits one legally qualified candidate for public office to use its facilities, it must afford equal opportunity to all other such legally qualified candidates for the same office. Section 315 also specifically prohibits the station from censoring material in broadcasts by political candidates. The FCC recently fined a Stamford, Connecticut, radio station $10,000 for censoring the paid political broadcasts of two mayoral candidates (see *Kuczo v. Western Connecticut Broadcasting,* 1977).

What does equal opportunity mean? It means equal time, equal facilities, and comparable costs. If John Smith buys one-half hour of television time on station KLOP to campaign for the office of mayor, other legally qualified candidates for that office must be allowed to purchase one-half hour of time as well. If Smith is able to use the station's equipment to prerecord his talk, other candidates must have the same opportunity. If the station charges Smith one hundred dollars for the one-half hour of time, the station must charge his opponents one hundred dollars.

The station does not have to solicit appearances by the other candidates; it merely must give them the opportunity to use the facilities if they request such use within one week of Smith's appearance. Finally, Section 315 clearly states that broadcasters do not have to allow any political candidates the use of their facilities if they so choose. However, if they allow one candidate to use the facilities, they must allow the same use to all seeking the same office. Of course the provisions of Section 312 of the Communications Act are relevant to use of a station's facilities by a candidate.

Section 315 states that "use" by one candidate of a broadcast facility entitles all opponents to "use" the facility as well. A key question then is, What does the word *use* mean? What constitutes an appearance by a candidate in the eyes of the law? It is easiest to begin by listing those things that do not constitute a use:

1. The appearance by a candidate in a bona fide or legitimate newscast does not constitute use of the facility in the eyes of the law. Section 315 will not be triggered. The FCC has ruled that appearances by political candidates on ABC's "Good Morning America," NBC's "Today" and the "CBS Morning News" are exempt from provisions of Section 315. The agency considers all three programs bona fide newscasts.

2. The appearance of a candidate in a bona fide news interview program does not constitute a use. The key words are *bona fide*. An appearance on "Meet the Press," which is a bona fide news interview show, is not use of a broadcasting facility. But an appearance on "Meet the Candidates," a public-affairs show created by a television station for the express purpose of interviewing candidates prior to an election is use because it is not a bona fide news interview show. The show was created especially for the election campaign by the station and is not broadcast when electioneering is not in progress.

3. The appearance of a candidate in the spot news coverage of a bona fide news event is not use. When candidate Smith is interviewed at the scene of a bad fire about the problems of arson in the city, this is not use in terms of Section 315. Political conventions are considered bona fide news events; therefore an appearance by a candidate at the convention can be broadcast without invoking Section 315.

4. The appearance of a candidate in a news documentary is not a use if the appearance is incidental to the presentation of the subject of the program. Example: During the spring months of the 1968 political campaign, CBS broadcast a documentary on reform of the federal income tax laws. An interview with Senator Robert Kennedy, who was leading a fight in the United States Senate for tax reform, was included in the program. At that time Kennedy was a candidate for the presidency, but his appearance in the documentary did not activate the equal opportunity rule because the program was about tax laws. Kennedy's appearance was incidental to that subject. A news documentary about Kennedy would have been a different story and would have triggered the Section 315 sanction. In the documentary the network was merely talking to Kennedy about a national problem on which he was an expert.

Debates between political candidates are considered bona fide news events, and the broadcast of these events will not initiate use of Section 315. This is true even if the broadcaster sponsors the debate, according to a 1984 ruling by the FCC. Prior to this ruling an outside third party had to sponsor the debate before it was considered a news event. In both 1976 and 1980, for example, the League of Women Voters sponsored presidential debates that included only the candidates from the Democratic and Republican parties.

Press conferences held by political candidates are also normally considered bona fide news events and are exempt from the provisions of Section 315. A press conference held by President Jimmy Carter in February 1980, several months after he announced he was a candidate for reelection, was broadcast live by all the television networks. Carter's opponent for the Democratic nomination, Ted Kennedy, sought time from the television networks under the equal opportunity rule. The networks said no. The FCC agreed with the broadcasters; the press conference was a bona fide news event. The agency had ruled in 1975 that all press conferences featuring political candidates were exempt from Section 315 as news events. Kennedy appealed the ruling to the United States Court of Appeals (D.C.) and lost. The court said that to determine whether the coverage of a news conference can be considered spot coverage of a bona fide news event three criteria must be examined:

1. Was the press conference broadcast live? Coverage of spot news should be live coverage.
2. Was there any evidence of favoritism on the part of the broadcaster? Did the station just carry Carter's press conferences and ignore his opponent's conferences?
3. Finally, did the broadcaster make a good-faith judgment that the news conference was a bona fide news event?

In this case the press conference was carried live, the networks had covered Kennedy press conferences, and it was obvious that a determination had been made by the broadcasters that this was an important news event (*Kennedy for President Committee* v. *FCC,* 1980).

With these exceptions, all other appearances by a candidate are considered use in the meaning of Section 315. A paid political broadcast, a spot announcement, and even a five-minute interview on the "Tonight Show" are all appearances that will invoke Section 315. Opposing candidates would have the right to ask for equal opportunity. During Ronald Reagan's campaigns for the presidency, stations had to refrain from showing his old movies and segments of "Death Valley Days" in which he appeared as the host (see *Adrian Weiss,* 1976). Pat Paulsen's quadrennial run for the White House forced television stations and networks to pull movies in which he appeared out of their libraries until the election was over. Once, Johnny Carson entertained the mayor of Burbank, California, on his program in recognition of the fame that town had gained by being the butt of a joke on Rowan and Martin's "Laugh-In." But Carson's staff had not done their homework, for the mayor was in the midst of a campaign for reelection. The National Broadcasting Company affiliate in Los Angeles was forced to give each of the mayor's dozen or so opponents equal time.

One of the most confusing aspects of Section 315 regards the FCC's definition of a legally qualified candidate. It is a long definition filled with lots of *ands* and *ors* and needs clarification.

A legally qualified candidate is any person (1) who publicly announces that he or she is a candidate for nomination or election to any local, county, state, or national office, *and* (2) who meets the qualifications prescribed by law for that office, *and* (3) who qualifies for a place on the ballot or is eligible to be voted for by sticker or write-in methods, *and* (4) who was duly nominated by a political party that is commonly known and regarded as such or makes a substantial showing that he or she is a bona fide candidate.

There should be no question about number one in the definition: the candidate must be an announced candidate. Number two merely states that the person must be eligible to hold the office to which he or she aspires. Henry Kissinger, for example, is not eligible to be president, since he is not a natural-born citizen. Despite the fact that he may be an announced candidate for that office, he is not a legally qualified candidate. Number three is self-explanatory: the person's name must appear on the ballot or he or she must be an eligible write-in or sticker candidate. Number four is the confusing qualification. Who knows what a substantial showing really is? What is a political party "commonly known and regarded as such"? Answers to these questions are judgment calls, and broadcasters with questions can solicit answers from the FCC. In fact, it is through the solicitation of such questions that the agency makes most of its Section 315 rulings.

Equal opportunity cases are rare. Normally the broadcaster asks the agency for guidance and then follows the recommendations of the commission. If there is a valid Section 315 complaint, the FCC usually just informs the licensee that candidate Adams is entitled to equal opportunity time and the station provides the time.

Many critics charge that a smart politician can refrain from announcing his candidacy for reelection, for example, and just make many television appearances and not be in violation of Section 315. That is true. But stations should be able to see what the candidate is doing and can refuse to allow appearances by an unannounced candidate, especially appearances that are clearly political in nature. A station that is not careful in this regard can be subject to problems at renewal time.

The FCC has granted two qualifications for the application of the equal opportunity doctrine, one of which appears much more important than it really is. The first qualification is broad: In primary elections, Section 315 applies to intraparty contests rather than to interparty contests. In a primary election, the contest is not Republicans versus Democrats, it is Republican versus Republican and Democrat versus Democrat. Only opponents can get equal opportunity. Imagine Jane Adams is a Republican candidate for governor. She is one of four Republicans seeking to win the primary. Six Democrats are also seeking to win the primary election and gain the nomination for the governorship in their party. Ms. Adams appears on KLOP for fifteen minutes. What are the station's obligations? The station is obliged to give equal opportunity to the other three Republican candidates, since they are the ones against whom Jane is running. The Democrats are not running against Ms. Adams at this time. While this qualification is broad, it makes a good deal of sense.

The second qualification turns out to be not much of a qualification at all, although it appears to be on its face. The only appearance that can trigger use of Section 315 is an appearance by the candidate. Under Section 315 appearances by friends, relatives, supporters, and so forth, do not require the station to give equal opportunity to opponents. However (this is an important however), the FCC has decided that such noncandidate appearances do require the station to provide an opportunity for appearances by supporters of the other legally qualified candidates.

This is known as the **Zapple rule** and was formulated a few years ago in response to a letter from Nicholas Zapple, formerly a staff member of the Senate Subcommittee on Communications. It was restated in the FCC's 1972 *Report Regarding the Handling of Political Broadcasts.* This is what the FCC said:

> The commission held in "Zapple" that when a licensee sells time to supporters or spokesmen of a candidate during an election campaign who urge the candidate's election, discuss the campaign issues, or criticize an opponent then the licensee must afford comparable time to the spokesmen for an opponent. Known as the quasi-equal opportunity or political party corollary to the fairness doctrine, the "Zapple" doctrine is based on the equal opportunity requirement of Section 315 of the Communications Act; accordingly, free reply time need not be afforded to respond to a paid program.

The Zapple rule is a fairly specific formulation of one part of what had been vague FCC policy for some time, that is, that during political campaigns, programs that do not invoke Section 315 fall under the ambit of the Fairness Doctrine. This means that licensees are required to play fair with all candidates. Broadcasters are therefore obliged to scrutinize even those programs that are exempt from Section 315, such as newscasts, to ensure that a balance of some sort is maintained.

Two last points need to be made about Section 315. First, since broadcasters are not permitted to censor the remarks of a political candidate, they are immune from libel suits based on those remarks. In 1959 the Supreme Court ruled that since stations cannot control what candidates say over the air, they should not be held responsible for the remarks. The candidate, however, can still be sued (*Farmers Educational and Cooperative Union of America v. WDAY,* 1959). Second, ballot issues like school bond levies, initiatives, and referendums do not fall under Section 315 but are treated as controversial issues under the Fairness Doctrine. The FCC has asked the Congress to repeal Section 315 as a part of its plan to deregulate broadcasting. It is not likely that the Congress will take this action.

SUMMARY

Several rules govern political broadcasts carried by radio and television broadcasters. Section 312 of the Communications Act states that broadcasters cannot have an across-the-board policy rejecting all paid and nonpaid appearances by candidates for federal office. A candidate's request must be evaluated and can be rejected only if it could cause serious disruption of program schedules or might prompt an excessive number of equal time requests. While this rule applies only to requests from candidates for federal office, the government's mandate that broadcasters operate their stations in the public interest may very well include similar standards for the treatment by broadcasters of requests for access to airtime from state and local candidates.

Section 315 states that if a broadcaster provides one candidate for office with the opportunity to use a station's broadcast facilities, all other legally qualified candidates for the same office must be given the same opportunity. The use of the station's facilities includes all appearances on the station with the exception of the following:

1. Bona fide newscasts
2. Bona fide news interview programs
3. Spot news coverage
4. Incidental appearance in a news documentary

Candidate press conferences and debates between candidates are considered spot news events. During primary elections Section 315 applies only to candidates from the same political party running against each other to win the party's nomination to run in the general election.

PUBLIC AFFAIRS PROGRAMMING AND THE FAIRNESS DOCTRINE

The FCC treads a bit softer when it comes to dealing with news programming. The commission normally gets involved in news programming through its enforcement of the Fairness Doctrine, which we shall consider shortly. There have been instances in which charges were made that stations and networks falsified the news. Congress also gets into such debates, as it did in the controversy over the CBS broadcast "The Selling of the Pentagon," but usually takes no action. The FCC is also reluctant to act in such cases. Distortion or falsification of news involves a good deal more than simply a news source disagreeing with the manner in which a news story was reported. The deliberate distortion rule states that the distortion or staging must be deliberately intended to slant or mislead—and this allegation must be supported by extrinsic evidence. For example, independent witnesses must testify that they saw the staging. Also, the distortion or staging must involve a significant part of the news event, not a minor or incidental part of the news report. The FCC has refused to investigate "inaccurate embellishments concerning peripheral aspects of news reports or attempts at window dressing which concerned the manner of presenting the news, as long as the essential facts of the news stories to which these presentational devices were related were broadcast in an accurate manner" (*Galloway* v. *FCC,* 1985).

Complaints were made to the commission about such programs as "The Selling of the Pentagon" and "Hunger in America." The Columbia Broadcasting System was accused of careless editing in the program on the Pentagon, editing that took quotations from various parts of a speech and made it appear that these separate statements were actually one statement. There were other questionable editing practices as well. In "Hunger in America" the same network showed viewers a baby that it claimed had died of malnutrition. While many babies do die each week of malnutrition, the one photographed by the network had, in fact, died of other causes. The response of the FCC in "The Selling of the Pentagon" case is typical of how that agency handles such complaints. "Lacking evidence or documents that on their face reflect deliberate distortion, we believe that this government licensing agency cannot properly intervene," the commission ruled. "As we stated in the 'Hunger in America' ruling, the commission is not the national arbiter of truth." While taking a hands-off action itself, the agency reminded broadcasters, "The licensee must have a policy of requiring honesty of its news staff and must take reasonable precautions to see that news is fairly handled. The licensee's investigation of substantial complaints . . . must be a thorough, conscientious one, resulting in remedial action where appropriate." From this statement one can presume that obvious and blatant staging of news will be considered a disservice to the public interest but that the FCC is not capable of evaluating or monitoring the editing techniques of thousands of news departments. Errors will have to be fairly serious and well documented before the commission will intervene.

The Fairness Doctrine

There is no aspect of broadcast regulation that is more controversial than the **Fairness Doctrine.** Some authorities consider it a flagrant affront to the First Amendment's guarantee of freedom of expression; others argue that the Fairness Doctrine is the only thing that makes freedom of expression a reality in broadcasting. In addition to being controversial, the doctrine is confusing.

The Fairness Doctrine is a broad doctrine, affecting some advertising (as will be noted later in this chapter), political campaigns, and political candidates, as was just noted briefly. Its primary thrust, however, is aimed at public-affairs programming and controversial public issues. In barest essentials the Fairness Doctrine involves a two-fold duty for broadcasters. First, broadcasters must devote a reasonable percentage of their broadcast time to the coverage of public issues. Second, the coverage of these issues must be fair in the sense that an opportunity for presentation of contrasting points of view is provided. What is so hard about that? Well, little words like *reasonable* and *public issues* and *fair* and *contrasting* are the troublemakers. These are the words that need to be clarified.

A quick look at the origin and status of the Fairness Doctrine is in order first. In 1927 and again in 1933, members of Congress tried to include a kind of Fairness Doctrine in federal legislation regulating broadcasting. All attempts failed, stopped either by the Congress itself or by presidential veto. In 1947 another attempt was made when a Senate bill to adopt a legislative Fairness Doctrine was introduced, but again the effort failed.

With or without a law, however, first the Federal Radio Commission (FRC) and later the Federal Communications Commission (FCC) ruled that balance and fairness were requirements of broadcasting that serves the public interest, convenience, or necessity. In 1929 in the *Great Lakes Broadcasting* case, the FRC ruled, "insofar as a program consists of discussion of public questions, public interest requires ample play for the free and fair competition of opposing views and the commission believes that the principle applies not only to addresses by political candidates but to all discussion of issues of importance to the public" (in re *Great Lakes Broadcasting Co.,* 1929). Sixteen years later in the *United Broadcasting* case, the FCC echoed the FRC. The commission agreed with the broadcaster's contention that a radio station is not a common carrier but noted also (in re *United Broadcasting Co.,* 1945):

> These facts, however, in no way impinge upon the duty of each station licensee to be sensitive to the problems of public concern in the community and to make sufficient time available, on a non-discriminatory basis, for a full discussion thereof. . . .

The first "official" announcement of what we know as the Fairness Doctrine was made in 1949 when the FCC issued the long report *In the Matter of Editorializating by Broadcast Licensees*. The report was the result of an extensive study that the commission undertook after broadcasters and other persons protested a 1941 ruling by the agency that licensees could not editorialize on their stations (in re *Mayflower Broadcasting Corp., WAAB,* 1941). The editorialization report stated that broadcasters had an affirmative responsibility to provide a reasonable amount of time for the presentation of programs devoted to the discussion and consideration of public issues. The report added that it was the licensee's responsibility to afford a reasonable opportunity for the presentation of all responsible positions on the matters discussed. The commission said that licensees would not be meeting their Fairness Doctrine responsibility if they refused to broadcast all controversial matter. The FCC also noted:

> . . . it is clear that any approximation of fairness in the presentation of any controversy will be difficult if not impossible of achievement unless the licensee plays a conscious and positive role in bringing about balanced presentation of the opposing viewpoints.

To the question that would surely be raised about the commission's role as censor in applying the Fairness Doctrine, the agency noted, "The duty to operate in the public interest is no esoteric mystery, but essentially a duty to operate a radio station with good judgment and good faith guided by a reasonable regard for the interests of the community to be served."

In 1959 when Congress amended Section 315 of the Communications Act to exclude news programming from the ambit of the equal opportunity rule, the legislators approved language in the measure that said that nothing in the amendment should be construed to relieve broadcasters "from the obligation imposed upon them under this Act to operate in the public interest and to afford reasonable opportunity for the discussion of conflicting views on issues of public importance." Many legal authorities, including the United States Supreme Court, consider this to be congressional sanction of the Fairness Doctrine, which, as we have seen, was created by the FCC. Other observers note that if this be the case the 1959 congressional action was at best tenuous authority for such broad legal powers as the Fairness Doctrine gives the FCC.

For years, while the Fairness Doctrine was in favor with the FCC, the agency argued strongly that Congress had in fact given statutory support to the doctrine by its 1959 action. But in the early 1980s, when the Mark Fowler-led FCC sought to deregulate the broadcast industry, some members of the commission argued that Congress had not approved the doctrine in 1959, that it was solely a creature of the commission, and that the commission could abandon the Fairness Doctrine any time it chose to. That argument did not win much support, so the agency instead asked Congress to repeal the Fairness Doctrine. In 1985, with Congress still lagging, the FCC conducted proceedings aimed at evaluating the Fairness Doctrine. A thirty-seven-page report was published in August following the inquiry in which the FCC said it had concluded that the Fairness Doctrine no longer served the public interest. "We have found," the commissioners wrote, "that far from serving its intended purpose, the doctrine has a chilling effect on broadcaster's speech." But the agency chose not to eliminate the doctrine, in light of pending legislation in Congress and potential court tests of the doctrine.

It has been previously noted that bills have been introduced in Congress to eliminate the Fairness Doctrine. A court challenge to the doctrine was initiated by television station WTVH in Syracuse, which the FCC ruled had violated the Fairness Doctrine in 1982 because of its unbalanced coverage of the nuclear power issue (see pages 588–89 for more on this case). More important to the FCC, however, was a 1984 Supreme Court ruling, *FCC* v. *League of Women Voters,* in which, in a pair of footnotes, the High Court said it might reconsider the constitutionality of the Fairness Doctrine if there were "some signal from Congress or the FCC" that new communications technology had invalidated the "scarcity rationale" or if the commission determined that the doctrine chills free speech. "The FCC virtually sent up signal flares to make both points in its August report," noted David Brollier in a 1986 article in *Channels* magazine. To give the High Court its chance, a group led by the Radio and Television News Directors Association launched a suit against the Fairness Doctrine in late 1985, a suit based on the FCC's announced conclusion that the doctrine no longer served the public interest but interfered with the broadcaster's right of free speech. Both the suit by WTVH and the RTNDA were pending as this section was being written.

The Fairness Doctrine was still the law as this chapter was being written, so it is important for students to have an understanding of this complex regulation. The best source of guidance on the doctrine is a 1974 FCC report that outlines in great detail how the commission expects the rule to work.

What the Doctrine Means

The first mandate of the Fairness Doctrine is that the broadcaster must provide adequate time for the discussion of controversial public issues. This means that if there are controversial public issues in the community, the broadcaster must set aside time to cover these matters. This is not an order that a broadcaster carry news and information programming, something the FCC has ruled is no longer a requirement. But if the issues arise, the broadcaster should devote time to an exploration of these issues. How much time? The agency has never specified an amount of time. "It is the individual broadcaster who, after evaluating the needs of his particular community, must determine what percentage of the limited broadcast day should be devoted to news and discussion or consideration of public issues," the FCC said.

An FCC ruling in 1976 helped clarify what is adequate time for the discussion of public issues. Representative Patsy Mink, the sponsor of an anti-strip-mining bill in Congress, asked a West Virginia radio station to broadcast an eleven-minute audiotaped discussion of her bill. The station refused, noting that it had not carried any pro-strip-mining broadcasts and consequently was not required to carry an anti-strip-mining program. Representative Mink complained to the FCC that the station had not fulfilled its obligations under the Fairness Doctrine to provide an adequate amount of time for a discussion of public issues. The station argued that it had covered the issue by presenting Associated Press news reports on the issue during its regular newscasts.

The FCC ruled against the station, reaffirming that "the Fairness Doctrine imposes two affirmative responsibilities on the broadcaster: coverage of issues of public importance must be adequate and must fairly reflect differing viewpoints." The commission noted that the requirement to present contrasting viewpoints would not make much sense without a corresponding obligation to cover issues of public importance. But what about the station's contention that the issue was covered via newscasts? Doesn't the broadcaster enjoy the discretion to fulfill Fairness Doctrine obligations in this manner? While acknowledging that the licensee was not obligated to address each and every issue that may be important to the public, the commission ruled (*Patsy Mink,* 1976):

> Where, as in the present case, an issue has significant and possibly unique impact on the licensee's service area, it will not be sufficient for the licensee as an indication of compliance with the Fairness Doctrine to show that it may have broadcast an unknown amount of news touching on a general topic related to the issue cited in a complaint. Rather it must be shown that there has been some attempt to inform the public of the nature of the controversy, not only that such a controversy exists.

The ruling should not be taken as standard policy for the FCC. The agency was specific in noting that the principle of the *Mink* case would be reserved for issues that are "critical and of great public importance." Still, the *Mink* ruling was the first time the FCC had taken such a strong stand on this issue.

What is a reasonable opportunity for opposing viewpoints? The Fairness Doctrine does not require—as does Section 315—one-to-one precision in granting time for opposing viewpoints. So long as all sides of the issue are reasonably aired, the strictures of the Fairness Doctrine will have been met. A U.S. Court of Appeals spoke to the question of balance in a 1983 ruling on a Fairness Doctrine complaint brought by the Democratic National Committee (DNC) against both NBC and CBS television networks. Both networks had broadcast a series of thirty-second paid spots, prepared by the Republican National Committee, that supported President Reagan's economic policies. The DNC argued that the networks did not balance these spots with material about the negative aspects of the administration's economic program. In hearing the complaint the FCC accepted the validity of the assertions by the Democrats that the spots, coupled with other reports on the administration, created a frequency of presentation ratio in which pro-administration views enjoyed a three-to-one advantage on CBS and a four-to-one advantage on NBC. But the FCC said this was not a glaring disparity; coverage was not out of balance. The Court of Appeals ruled that this was a reasonable conclusion on the part of the FCC and refused to overrule the agency. The balance required in the context of the Fairness Doctrine is measured not in terms of equal time or identical treatment, but rather in terms of fairness and reasonableness—with ample deference given to the broadcaster's conception of what reasonableness entails, the court said (*Democratic National Committee* v. *FCC,* 1983). But the commission did, in 1984, rule that Syracuse, New York, television station WTVH had failed to provide balanced coverage of the issue of whether or not the construction of a nuclear power plant would be in the economic interests of the state of New York. The television station had carried 182 minutes of paid advertising supporting construction of the plant but had provided no special coverage of the other side of the question. The FCC agreed with Liam Mahoney of the Syracuse Peace Council that, "Even the total amount of news programming [on nuclear-related issues, not just nuclear power] didn't equal the amount of advertising time bought by the utilities group." The station was given twenty days to respond to the FCC ruling but refused to comply with the order. Instead it mounted a court challenge to the Fairness Doctrine, as noted previously.

Do all viewpoints have to be aired? What about that fellow in the valley whose ideas are different from those of everyone else? No, it would be unreasonable to require the broadcaster to include all opinions. The commission requires an airing only of those viewpoints that have a significant measure of support or viewpoints that reflect the ideas of a significant segment of the community. But it is the duty of the broadcaster to make certain that these views are aired, and in this way the Fairness Doctrine is sharply different from Section 315. The Equal Opportunity Rule is a passive rule. The candidate must come forward and seek equal time. The Fairness Doctrine requires the active participation of the broadcaster, who has an affirmative duty to find someone to speak to all sides of the issue or present all sides of the issue himself.

What is a controversial issue of public importance? In actual practice the broadcaster decides what is controversial and what is not. Some of the factors which the FCC suggests that the licensee take into consideration when determining whether an issue is controversial include the following:

1. The degree of media coverage of the issue
2. The degree of attention the issue receives from government officials and other community leaders
3. The impact the issue is likely to have on the community at large

A ruling by the FCC, supported by the Court of Appeals (D.C.), indicates that a controversial issue is expected to be rather specific and narrow. A conservative political-action group calling itself American Security Council Foundation (ASCF) undertook a content analysis of CBS television news broadcasts in 1975 and 1976 and concluded that the network's coverage of the national security issue was not balanced. The group called the coverage "too dovish." The FCC rejected the complaint, noting among other things that ASCF had not defined a controversial issue with sufficient specificity in its complaint. The United States Court of Appeals upheld this ruling in 1979, arguing that the items included under the umbrella of "national security" were simply too diverse to be bunched together under a single national security heading. The ASCF looked at such items as NATO, détente with China and Russia, SALT treaties, amnesty for persons prosecuted during the Vietnam War for a wide range of offenses, the Vietnam War itself, Middle East issues, and others. "The issues analyzed by ASCF arose independently in time and were largely discussed and acted upon on an independent basis," the court ruled. "Consideration of the issues together, rather than individually, would not provide a basis for determining whether the broadcaster presented a reasonable balance of conflicting views, because views on any one issue do not support or contradict views on the others," the six-person majority noted. What does NATO have to do with détente in China? or what does amnesty have to do with SALT? the court asked. An issue is not a "particular, well-defined" issue for Fairness Doctrine purposes if the separate issues comprising it are so indirectly related that a view on one does not, in a way that would be apparent to an average viewer, support or contradict a view on any other (*American Security Council Foundation* v. *FCC*, 1979).

In 1980 the FCC dismissed a complaint made against all three networks by the National Committee for Responsive Philanthropy. The committee alleged that the networks had failed to balance the issue raised by broadcast of spot announcements urging persons to support the United Way fund drives ("Thanks to you, it's working."). The United States Court of Appeals for the District of Columbia upheld the commission action, noting that the committee's complaint failed to show that such announcements meaningfully addressed a controversial issue of public importance. The Fairness Doctrine only applies, the court said, when a broadcast statement amounts to advocacy of a position on one side of an ongoing public debate and obviously and substantially addresses that issue in a meaningful way (*National Committee for Responsive Philanthropy* v. *FCC*, 1981).

By and large it comes down to whether the broadcaster believes that an issue is important, is controversial, and does stimulate debate within the community.

How the Doctrine Works

The FCC does no monitoring for violations of the Fairness Doctrine itself but depends instead upon viewer and listener complaints. Organizations like Accuracy in Media (AIM), which take the pose of "professional media monitors," are popping up across the nation. Usually these groups have an axe to grind of one sort or another. Nevertheless, they do make complaints and have created problems for broadcasters.

The FCC requires that a Fairness Doctrine complaint contain the following items:

1. The name of the particular station involved
2. The particular issue of a controversial nature discussed over the air
3. The date and time when the program was carried
4. The basis for the claim that the station presented only one side of the question
5. Whether the station afforded or has plans to afford an opportunity for presentation of contrasting viewpoints

Complaints must present prima facie evidence of a Fairness Doctrine violation before the FCC will even seek a response from a broadcaster. Numbers one and three are simple to accomplish. Number two can be a problem, however, for the station may define the issue aired during the program somewhat differently than does the complainant, as we shall soon see. Number five requires that the complainant talk to the station before making a complaint, which is the only way the question can be answered. It is number four, however, that is the primary problem for unhappy viewers. The Fairness Doctrine does not require that a station present all sides of an issue within the context of a single program. What is required is that in its *overall programming* it make a balanced presentation of the issues. This month the station might present a program that is against abortion, and next month it may present one that is for abortion. Overall, the station has been fair. Therefore, in alleging that the station has presented only one side of an issue, the complainant has to have a pretty good idea of the station's overall programming—what has gone on in the past as well as what is going to happen in the future. This is a heavy burden for persons who seek to complain. Imagine seeing a one-sided gun-control program on television tonight. How certain are you that somewhere along the line in the past few months the station did not present the other side of the issue? maybe in a documentary? maybe during the news? maybe on a Sunday afternoon while you were watching a football game on another channel? While complaints are not foreclosed, they are difficult to make. More than 10,300 complaints and inquiries were submitted by the public to the FCC, in 1980, a typical year. Approximately 99 percent of the complaints were rejected outright because the complainant had not followed the proper procedure or had misunderstood the role of the Fairness Doctrine. Of the 1 percent of the complaints that were initially accepted, only about 15 percent were eventually resolved against the station. This amounted to less than twenty complaints, according to the National Citizens Committee for Broadcasting. The ruling against WTVH noted above was the first adverse ruling against a station in the more than six years that Mark Fowler chaired the commission.

If the complaint is forwarded to the station, the FCC letter asks the broadcaster these two questions:

1. Is the issue of controversial public importance in your viewing area?
2. Have you fulfilled your Fairness Doctrine obligations by presenting balanced programming on that issue?

If the broadcaster says that the issue is not controversial or not of public importance, the FCC must accept the answer unless there is evidence that the broadcaster is arbitrary or capricious in making the determination. So long as the broadcaster makes a good-faith judgment that the issue is not controversial, there is nothing the FCC can do. The broadcaster has the discretion to decide what is and what is not controversial. Furthermore the FCC cannot substitute its judgment for that of the broadcaster. Clearly if the broadcaster ignores overwhelming evidence that the people are interested or ignores the fact that a vigorous public debate is underway, the FCC can then rule that the determination is not made in good faith. But this is a very rare kind of ruling. Generally the agency takes the licensee's word.

In 1972 NBC broadcast a program entitled "The Broken Promise," a documentary about private pension plans. It was very critical of certain private pension plans and graphically showed how millions of Americans had been ripped off and cheated. Narrator Edwin Newman told viewers *that most private pension plans are good,* that they provide a real benefit to the workers. Most of the NBC program, however, dealt *with bad pension plans.*

A Fairness Doctrine complaint was lodged against the network by AIM. The FCC asked NBC whether the program dealt with a controversial issue. The network said no, and this was its reasoning. The program talked about bad private pension plans. There were no allegations that all pension plans were bad. In fact, quite the opposite: it was stated that most plans are good. NBC focused on the bad plans. Everybody agrees that some plans are bad. There is no controversy about that. Since the program focused only on the bad plans, it did not deal with a controversial issue.

The FCC did not accept this logic. But when the decision was appealed to a court of appeals, the agency had its hand slapped. The court said that so long as the network had made a good-faith judgment, NBC was to exercise discretion as to whether the issue was controversial (*NBC* v. *FCC,* 1974). The FCC could not come to a different conclusion on the basis of the same evidence. That was not permitted. What the agency must ask is this: Was there any evidence that could lead the network to decide that the issue was not controversial? And if there was, then NBC's determination was made in good faith.

Because the case took so long to get through the courts, the rulings by both the FCC and the court of appeals were in the end moot. The controversy disappeared when Congress passed its pension-reform bill. So the "Broken Promise" case is not a precedent. However, the rules have not changed. The case was cited to show how the rules work. If another case were to come along tomorrow, the same kinds of restrictions upon the FCC would exist. It is basically the broadcaster's decision whether the issue at hand is controversial and important.

If the licensee says the issue is controversial, the station must then tell the commission how it has fulfilled the Fairness Doctrine requirements or how it plans to fulfill its responsibilities. Here the FCC has a bit more discretion. However the key is still whether broadcasters *make a good-faith effort to provide balanced programming,* rather than whether they *provide balanced programming.* Unless the licensee is really out in left field, the commissioners are usually satisfied. It is only in outrageous cases that the FCC demands a hearing or demands that the broadcaster provide time for opposing viewpoints. Remember also that the initial burden of proof is upon the complainant to convince the FCC that a violation of the doctrine did indeed occur. Before the FCC even sends out a letter to the station, the complainant must provide "a reasonable basis for the conclusion that the licensee has failed in its overall programming to present a reasonable opportunity for contrasting views."

What happens if the FCC finds there has been a violation? A request may be made that the station provide time for airing opposing viewpoints, or a fine may be levied against the broadcaster. In extreme cases the broadcast license may not be renewed (see *Brandywine-Main Line Radio, Inc., v. FCC,* 1972). Denial of renewal generally results only when a pattern of flagrant abuses of the Fairness Doctrine can be shown. Few fairness complaints result in action of any kind against the station. Still, the time and trouble involved in answering such a complaint, especially one that evolves into a hearing and a court case like the NBC case just discussed, are quite onerous. Typical complaints may cost from $1,000 to $2,500 to answer. When a hearing is involved, expenses can easily reach into the tens of thousands of dollars. A West Coast television station won a Fairness Doctrine hearing that cost the broadcaster $20,000 to defend.

Advertising

The Fairness Doctrine has been applied to advertising for commercial products only one time, and the FCC has said since that application that it was a mistake to do it even once. In 1967 in response to a petition from a young attorney named John Banzhaf, the commission ruled that stations that carry advertisements for cigarettes must carry free public service messages showing the dangers of smoking as well (*WCBS-TV: Applicability of the Fairness*

Doctrine to Cigarette Advertising, 1967). The United States Court of Appeals (D.C.) sustained the ruling in *Banzhaf* v. *FCC* (1969). Cigarette smoking was a controversial subject. Later, of course, Congress passed a law that banned cigarette advertisements from the airwaves completely.

Following the *Banzhaf* ruling, other public interest groups sought to have broadcasters balance advertisements for gasoline and automobiles with messages about environmental protection. But the FCC did not agree to these proposals. The commission argued that the smoking decision was unusual, that smoking is a habit that can disappear, that the government urged the discontinuance of cigarette smoking, that government studies showed the danger of smoking, and so forth. In other words the problem of smoking is different from the problem of pollution. So the Friends of the Earth went to court, and in 1971 the Court of Appeals (D.C.) reversed the FCC ruling. The court said it could not see the distinction between the cigarette case and that case (in re *Wilderness Society and Friends of the Earth,* 1971):

> Commercials which continue to insinuate that the human personality finds greater fulfillment in the larger car with the quick getaway do, it seems to us, ventilate a point of view which not only has become controversial but involves an issue of public importance. Where there is undisputed evidence, as there is here, that the hazards to health implicit in air pollution are enlarged and aggravated by such products, then the parallel with cigarette advertising is exact and the relevance of *Banzhaf* inescapable.

The court said, however, that stations do not have to broadcast anti–big-car advertising, as in the cigarette advertisements case. The key is overall programming. If the licensees carry programming that discusses the environmental dangers of pollution and the diminution of resources, the Fairness Doctrine will be satisfied.

In its 1974 report the FCC discussed the application of the Fairness Doctrine to advertising. The commission said that it would apply the doctrine to editorial advertising—commercials that consist of direct and substantial commentary on important public issues—but not to product advertising, not even to controversial products. It said that the cigarette decision was a mistake; if it had to decide the case today, it would not make the same decision. "We believe that standard product commercials," the commissioners wrote, "make no meaningful contribution toward informing the public on any side of any issue." (This, of course, is a little different position than the Supreme Court has taken on the question of the value of advertising in the evolution of the commercial speech doctrine. See Chapter 11.) The courts have upheld this decision by the FCC, most recently in 1977 (*National Citizens Committee for Broadcasting* v. *FCC,* 1977). The commission also rejected a proposal by the Federal Trade Commission that the FCC require stations to offer rebuttal time to public interest groups to answer commercials that raise controversial issues, commercials that make claims that are based on disputed scientific premises, and commercials that are silent about the negative aspects of the advertised products (like too many aspirin can be harmful). The FCC said that almost all commercials raise controversial issues for some people, that such a "counteradvertising proposal" could have an adverse economic effect on broadcasting, and that it did not believe that the Fairness Doctrine was an appropriate vehicle with which to correct false and misleading advertising.

The case of *Public Media Center* v. *FCC* (1978) is an example of the kind of advertising to which the FCC will apply the Fairness Doctrine. In this case, in which eight California television stations were charged with violating the Fairness Doctrine for broadcasting commercials for the Pacific Gas and Electric Company advocating development of nuclear power without presenting the views of opponents of such development, the United States Court of Appeals (D.C.) upheld the commission ruling. The court also remanded the case to the FCC to clarify why it had not made the same ruling regarding four other stations that had also broadcast the same television commercials.

One additional note: the FCC has not applied the Fairness Doctrine to entertainment programs, even to controversial shows such as the two-part "Maude" episode concerning abortion (*Diocesan Union of Holy Name Societies of Rockville Centre and Long Island Coalition for Life,* 1973).

Personal Attacks and Political Editorials

While the Fairness Doctrine remains a nebulous policy that has been outlined almost on a case-by-case basis, the commission has drafted specific rules with regard to one portion of the doctrine—what are known as the **personal attack rules.** The agency has also enunciated specific rules governing political editorials. These rules are subsections of the Fairness Doctrine (see 32 Fed. Reg. 10303; 11531; and 33 Fed. Reg. 5362; 1967) and deal with a specific kind of one-sided presentation. Here are the rules:

Personal attacks
(a) When, during the presentation of views on a controversial issue of public importance, an attack is made upon the honesty, character, integrity or like personal qualities of an identified person or group, the licensee shall, within a reasonable time and in no event later than one week after the attack, transmit to the person or group attacked (1) notification of the date, time and identification of the broadcast; (2) a script or tape (or an accurate summary if a script or tape is not available) of the attack; and (3) an offer of a reasonable opportunity to respond over the licensee's facilities.
(b) The provisions of paragraph (a) of this section shall not be applicable (1) to attacks on foreign groups or foreign public figures; (2) to personal attacks which are made by legally qualified candidates, their authorized spokesmen, or those associated with them in the campaign, or other such candidates, their authorized spokesmen, or persons associated with the candidates in the campaign; and (3) to bona fide newscasts, bona fide news

interviews, and on-the-spot coverage of a bona fide news event (including commentary or analysis contained in the foregoing programs, but the provisions of paragraph (a) of this section shall be applicable to editorials of the licensee).

NOTE: The Fairness Doctrine is applicable to situations coming within [(3)], above, and, in a specific factual situation, may be applicable in the general area of political broadcasts [(2)], above.

Political editorials

(c) Where a licensee, in an editorial, (i) endorses or (ii) opposes a legally qualified candidate or candidates, the licensee shall, within 24 hours after the editorial, transmit to respectively (i) the other qualified candidate or candidates for the same office or (i) the candidate opposed in the editorial (1) notification of the date and time of the editorial; (2) a script or tape of the editorial; and (3) an offer of a reasonable opportunity for a candidate or a spokesman of the candidate to respond over the licensee's facilities: *Provided, however,* that where such editorials are broadcast within 72 hours prior to the day of the election, the licensee shall comply with the provisions of this paragraph sufficiently far in advance of the broadcast to enable the candidate or candidates to have a reasonable opportunity to prepare a response and to present it in a timely fashion.

The personal attack rules stem from FCC rulings in 1962 stating that when licensees broadcast what amounts to a personal attack upon an individual or group within the community, they have an affirmative obligation to notify the target of the attack of the broadcast and offer the target an opportunity to respond. In 1967 these earlier decisions were clarified and made more specific with the publication of the personal attack rules.

As you can see from the rules, the licensee's obligations are quite specific. It is important to remember that just naming someone in an editorial or commentary does not necessarily constitute a personal attack. On the other hand the rules apply to attacks made by everyone, not just by the station itself.

Paragraph (b) of the rules exempts attacks made by candidates and their followers upon other candidates and their followers. Newscasts, news interviews, and on-the-spot news coverage are also exempted from the personal attack rules but not from the more general provisions of the Fairness Doctrine. Paragraph (c) outlines licensee obligations with regard to editorial endorsements of candidates.

Soon after the personal attack rules were published, they were challenged in court. A small radio station in Pennsylvania challenged an FCC ruling requiring it to provide free time to Fred Cook, an author, who had been attacked by right-wing evangelist Billy James Hargis. The United States Court of Appeals for the District of Columbia upheld the constitutionality of both the personal attack rules and the Fairness Doctrine (*Red Lion Broadcasting Co.* v. *FCC,* 1967). While this case was being litigated, the Radio and Television News Directors' Association and other broadcasting organizations petitioned the United States Court of Appeals for the Seventh District in Chicago to review the constitutionality of the Fairness Doctrine. In this case the court of appeals struck down both the personal attack rules and the Fairness Doctrine as being in violation of the First Amendment (*Radio and Television News Directors' Association* v. *U.S.,* 1968). With two circuit courts at odds on the question, the Supreme Court had to decide the issue.

The argument made by opponents of the Fairness Doctrine, more specifically of the personal attack rules, was two-pronged. First, it was asserted that by forcing broadcasters to carry material, that is, the reply by the target of the attack, the government interfered with the First Amendment rights of broadcasters. Second, it was claimed that the Fairness Doctrine amounts to prior restraint as well. Here is the argument. A station has a public affairs budget of $5,000, just enough to produce and air a documentary opposing mandatory busing of children. The Fairness Doctrine requires the licensee to present both sides of the issue; therefore, the station has to produce a second documentary that outlines the favorable aspects of busing. But the station has no money for that and therefore cannot air the first documentary opposing busing. This government interference amounts to restraining the broadcast of the documentary opposed to busing. Hence, there is a violation of the First Amendment, there is prior restraint.

Whatever merit you may find in these arguments, the Supreme Court found little to recommend them. In a unanimous decision in 1969, the High Court upheld the constitutionality of both the personal attack rules and the Fairness Doctrine with the argument that the First Amendment operates as a command to the government to protect the public from one-sided presentations of public issues. Going back to the original congressional mandate that the broadcaster operate in the public interest, the Court said the public interest is served only when the community receives exposure to all sides of controversial matters. As far as the First Amendment is concerned, wrote Justice Byron White, the licensed broadcaster stands no better off than those to whom the licenses are refused (*Red Lion Broadcasting Co.* v. *FCC,* 1969):

> A license permits broadcasting, but the licensee has no constitutional right to be the one who holds the license or to monopolize a radio frequency to the exclusion of his fellow citizens. There is nothing in the First Amendment which prevents the government from requiring a licensee to share his frequency with others and to conduct himself as a proxy or fiduciary with obligations to present those views and voices which are representative of his community and which would otherwise, by necessity, be barred from the airwaves.

Later in the opinion Justice White asserted, "It is the right of the public to receive suitable access to social, political, esthetic, moral and other ideas and experiences, which is crucial here. That right may not constitutionally be abridged either by the Congress or by the FCC."

The decision in *Red Lion Broadcasting* declared that the Fairness Doctrine was a constitutional exercise of government. And this is where the law stood in late 1986, despite claims by the FCC that the doctrine no longer served the public interest. But some observers suggested that this mantle of constitutionality had cracked, that some members of the Supreme Court may have changed their minds on this question. The evidence of this is two footnotes in the 1984 ruling in *FCC* v. *League of Women Voters*. Justice William Brennan wrote the opinion in the five-to-four decision. In footnote 11 Brennan suggested that the High Court might reconsider its longstanding opinion that broadcast regulation was permissible if the FCC or Congress could show that with the advent of cable television and satellite television technology that the doctrine of spectrum scarcity was obsolete. In the following note Brennan said that if the FCC could show that the Fairness Doctrine has the effect of reducing rather than enhancing speech, "we would be forced to reconsider the constitutional basis of our decision" in *Red Lion.*

Critics of the doctrine insist that free speech is in jeopardy and point to a 1984 case in which the CIA asked the FCC to sanction ABC for a news broadcast. The network carried a story in which a Honolulu investment counselor claimed that he had been a covert CIA agent and that the agency had solicited someone to kill him. ABC aired the CIA's denial during the broadcast and later even seemed to back off the story when it reported that it could not corroborate the man's claim. But the CIA charged that the broadcast had been a violation of the Fairness Doctrine and asked the FCC to punish the network, even deny the renewal of licenses for the stations it owned. For the first time in the nation's history, one government agency was applying pressure to another arm of the government to censure a critical news organization.

The FCC dismissed the complaint in 1985 for the technical reason that the "allegations failed to establish prima facie complaints sufficient to initiate a Commission inquiry." But the commission did not say that it was impermissible for government agencies to file such complaints. The CIA recently refiled its complaint with the hope that it had corrected its previous technical deficiencies. The spy agency was joined in this action by the conservative American Legal Foundation, which already had two Fairness Doctrine complaints on file against CBS when it joined the CIA in the action against ABC.

The debate over the Fairness Doctrine continued while this chapter was being written, a debate that has resulted in making some fairly strange bedfellows. Ralph Nader-like public interest groups have been joined by big business (Mobil and General Motors) and right-wing activists like Phyllis Schlafly to fight to save the doctrine. Opposing them are a coalition of civil libertarians, media owners, and conservative members of Congress. Strange bedfellows indeed.

The First Amendment   Broadcasting stations are not common carriers; that is, they have the right to refuse to do business with anyone they choose. During 1969 and 1970 two groups, the Democratic National Committee and a Washington, D.C., organization known as Business Executives Movement for Peace, sought to buy time from television stations and networks to solicit funds for their protest of the Vietnam War and to voice their objections to the way the war was being prosecuted by the government. Broadcasters rebuffed these groups on the grounds that airing such controversial advertisements and programming would evoke the Fairness Doctrine, and they would then be obligated to ensure that all sides of the controversy were aired. Such action was a nuisance and could be costly. The broadcasters told the Democratic committee and the businessmen that one of their basic policies was not to sell time to any individual or group seeking to set forth views on controversial issues.

When this policy was challenged before the FCC, the commission sided with the broadcasters, noting that it was up to each individual licensee to determine how best to fulfill Fairness Doctrine obligations. But the United States Court of Appeals for the District of Columbia reversed the FCC ruling, citing the *Red Lion* decision that the right of the public to receive information is deeply rooted in the First Amendment. A ban on editorial advertising, the court ruled, "leaves a paternalistic structure in which licensees and bureaucrats decide what issues are important, whether to fully cover them, and the format, time and style of coverage. . . ." This kind of system, the court ruled, is inimical to the First Amendment (in re *Business Executives Movement for Peace* v. *FCC,* 1971):

> It may unsettle some of us to see an antiwar message or a political party message in the accustomed place of a soap or beer commercial. . . . We must not equate what is habitual with what is right or what is constitutional. A society already so saturated with commercialism can well afford another outlet for speech on public issues. All that we may lose is some of our apathy.

The victory of the businessmen and Democrats was short-lived, for by a seven-to-two vote, the United States Supreme Court overturned the appellate court ruling (*CBS* v. *Democratic National Committee,* 1973). Stations have an absolute right to refuse to sell time for advertising dealing with political campaigns and controversial issues. To give the FCC the power over such advertising runs the risk of enlarging government control over the content of broadcast discussion of public issues.

In response to the argument that by permitting broadcasters to refuse such advertising, we place in their hands the power to decide what the people shall see or hear on important public issues, Justice Burger wrote:

> For better or worse, editing is what editors are for; and editing is the selection and choice of material. That editors—newspaper or broadcast—can and do abuse this power is beyond doubt, but that is no reason to deny the discretion Congress provided. Calculated risks of abuse are taken in order to preserve high values.

The Court was badly fractured on this case and Justices Brennan and Marshall dissented. Only two other justices—Stewart and Rehnquist—joined the chief justice in his opinion. The remainder joined in overturning the court of appeals ruling, but for their own reasons. Broadcasters are required to present programming on public issues and to do so in such a manner as to ensure that all sides get a fair hearing. How this is to be accomplished is the business of the broadcaster. The Fairness Doctrine does not provide right of access to television or radio.

Finally the High Court used the First Amendment to strike down a Congressional statute that forbids all noncommercial educational broadcasting stations that receive money from the Corporation for Public Broadcasting from editorializing on any subject at all. The government attempted to justify the law on two grounds. It argued that a ban on editorials was needed to prevent noncommercial broadcasting stations from being coerced, as a result of getting money from the federal government, into becoming vehicles for government propaganda. Also, it said the law was needed to keep stations from becoming convenient targets for capture by private-interest groups wishing to express their own partisan viewpoints. These justifications were insufficient, wrote Justice William Brennan for the five-member majority. The ban on all editorials by every station that receives CPB funds is too broad and far exceeds what is necessary to protect against the risk of governmental interference or to prevent the public from assuming that editorials by public broadcasting stations represent the official views of government. "The regulation impermissibly sweeps within its prohibition a wide range of speech by wholly private stations on topics that do not take a directly partisan stand or that have nothing whatever to do with federal, state or local government," Brennan wrote. And the ban really isn't effective, since the very same opinions that cannot be expressed by the station's management may be aired by someone appearing on a program as a guest. Chief Justice Burger and Justices Rehnquist, White, and Stevens dissented (*FCC* v. *League of Women Voters,* 1984). Public broadcasting stations are still prohibited from endorsing political candidates, however.

SUMMARY

The government may also exercise control over the content of public affairs programs. While the FCC has thus far rejected complaints that television news coverage was slanted or staged, the agency does attempt to enforce the Fairness Doctrine. This rule states that a broadcaster must devote time for the discussion of controversial community issues and that the coverage of these issues must reflect contrasting community viewpoints on the issues. The Fairness Doctrine puts an affirmative responsibility upon the broadcaster to ensure that coverage is fair; it is insufficient for a radio or television station operator to present one side of an issue and then invite persons with opposing viewpoints to appear as a means of fulfilling Fairness Doctrine responsibilities.

The FCC has refused to define "adequate time" for the discussion of public issues. Affording a reasonable opportunity for opposing viewpoints means making certain that those views that reflect the ideas of significant segments of the community are aired. The broadcaster can decide what is a controversial issue of public importance. An examination of the media coverage of the issue, the impact the issue may have on the community, and the degree of attention the issue has received from community leaders may be used to guide the broadcaster in making this judgment.

It is difficult for a citizen to make an effective complaint against a broadcaster for violating the Fairness Doctrine. So long as the licensee has made a good-faith effort to present balanced coverage of important community issues, the FCC is reluctant to take action against the broadcaster. The Fairness Doctrine applies to editorial advertising (trying to sell an idea), but not to product advertising. A specific section of the Fairness Doctrine called the personal attack rules requires a broadcaster to notify a person or group that it plans to attack on the air and provide free time for the individual or group to respond to the attack.

The Supreme Court has ruled that the Fairness Doctrine does not violate the First Amendment, but some persons (including members of the FCC) believe the Court may be ready to change its mind on this question. Suits have recently been filed that challenge the doctrine under the First Amendment. The Supreme Court has ruled that broadcasters do not have to sell time to persons who wish to broadcast messages about controversial public issues. The Court has also ruled that a congressional ban on editorializations by public television stations is unconstitutional.

REGULATION AND NEW TECHNOLOGY

One of the most perplexing aspects of contemporary mass media law is the attempt by the government to regulate or control the bewildering array of new electronic information-transmitting technology that has burst upon the scene in recent years. In the pages that follow we will focus upon the regulation of the newer broadcast services, especially cable television. We will also briefly consider some aspects of the regulation of low-power TV (LPTV), multipoint distribution services (MDS), satellite master antenna television (SMATV), and private earth stations or dish antennas. No attempt is made to discuss the regulation of the many kinds of electronic data-transmission services or two-way nonbroadcast systems, just as regulation of telephone and telegraph is not a part of this book. Attempts to regulate the new mass media are coming at every level and occur at a pace equal to the introduction of the new technology. Comprehensive rules regarding such technology will take a long time to develop. Cable television has been around since the late 1940s, yet it was not until late 1984 that the Congress got around to adopting what might be called comprehensive cable television regulations. Readers interested in more information regarding the development and regulation of the new communications technologies are urged to look to magazines and other periodicals for the latest material.

Cable Television

Cable television is the oldest of the new technologies. Community antenna television (CATV), the forerunner of what we now call cable television, began in the late 1940s. The FCC first asserted jurisdiction over cable television in 1962; until then the industry was regulated by a hodgepodge of local and state rules. But from the very beginning the commission was forced to move tentatively toward the regulation of cable, because its jurisdiction was simply not clear. Cable is not broadcast; signals travel through wires, not the airwaves. There is no scarcity of spectrum, an important foundation for broadcast regulation. Cable is not a common carrier, as are telephone or telegraph; FCC authority to regulate these two-way communication devices does not clearly imply that the FCC has authority to regulate cable. At first rules were issued only for cable systems that used microwave relays as well as wire to transmit television signals. These microwave transmissions were similar to over-the-air broadcast and seemed to provide a jurisdictional foothold for the commission. These actions were sustained by the courts (in re *Carter Mountain Transmission Corp.,* 1962, 1963). In 1966 the agency issued rules that affected all cable systems, those that used the microwave relays and those that did not. Cable operators argued that the agency had no power to regulate cable transmission that did not use the broadcast spectrum, which was transmitted exclusively by wire. But the Supreme Court supported the FCC in a 1968 ruling. Justice Harlan wrote for the Court (*U.S. v. Southwestern Cable Co.,* 1968):

> The commission has been charged with broad responsibilities for the orderly development of an appropriate system of local television broadcasting. . . . The commission has reasonably found that the successful performance of these duties demands prompt and efficacious regulation of community antenna television systems [cable systems]. We have elsewhere held that we may not, "in the absence of compelling evidence that such was Congress' intention . . . prohibit administration action imperative for the achievement of an agency's ultimate purpose. . . ." There is no such evidence here, and we therefore hold that the commission's authority over "all interstate . . . communication by wire or radio" permits the regulation of CATV systems.

Justice Harlan added that the FCC can regulate cable television, at least to the extent "reasonably ancillary to the effective performance of the commission's various responsibilities for the regulation of television broadcasting."

Given a green light by the Supreme Court, the FCC began in the late 1960s and early 1970s to issue more and more wide-ranging regulations. The agency imposed equal time rules, sponsor identification rules, and the Fairness Doctrine upon all programming originated by cable casters. In addition, the FCC ruled that all cable systems having more than 3,500 subscribers would have to operate "to a significant extent as a local outlet by originating cable casting." In other words, the cable operators could no longer merely scoop the signals of other broadcasting stations out of the air and send them into a home via wire. They had to create programs themselves, which required programming facilities far beyond the needs of the simple automated services thus far originated by cable operators.

The Midwest Video Corp. challenged this rule. Again the Supreme Court upheld the authority of the FCC. In a five-to-four decision the Court ruled (*U.S.* v. *Midwest Video Corp.,* 1972):

> The effect of the regulation, after all, is to assure that in the retransmission of broadcast signals viewers are provided suitably diversified programming. . . .
> In sum, the regulation preserves and enhances the integrity of broadcast signals and therefore is "reasonably ancillary" to the effective performance of the commission's various responsibilities for the regulation of television broadcasting.

Cable television operators argued, as did Justice Douglas in a strong dissent, that the FCC was forcing them into the broadcasting business when they did not want to be licensed for that business. A majority of the Court disagreed, however, noting that the cable operators voluntarily engaged themselves in providing that service and that "the commission seeks only to ensure that it satisfactorily meets community needs within the context of their undertaking." Given this broad, sweeping power, the FCC issued a comprehensive set of cable regulations in 1972, the *Fourth Report and Order on Cable Television Service.*

In 1976 the FCC refined these rules to the extent that all cable systems with more than 3,500 subscribers carrying over-the-air broadcast signals had to develop a minimum twenty-channel capacity by 1986, had to make certain channels available for access by third parties, and had to furnish equipment and facilities for the creation and broadcast of this "access" programming. Again Midwest Video challenged the commission's ruling. This time the cable company won when the Supreme Court in April 1979 struck down the FCC order, saying that the commission was going beyond its authority. Justice Byron White, writing for the six-person majority, said that these rules were not reasonably ancillary to the effective performance of the commission's responsibility to regulate over-the-air television. White said the access rules transferred control of cable television from the cable operator to the public seeking to use the medium. "Effectively," White wrote, "the commission has regulated cable systems . . . to common carrier status," something which Congress has always rejected for broadcasting in the past (*FCC* v. *Midwest Video Corp.,* 1979). Earlier, the Eighth Circuit Court of Appeals had been even more critical of the commission when it struck down the cable access rules in 1978. The court said the FCC had no jurisdiction to promulgate such rules (*Midwest Video Corp.* v. *FCC,* 1978):

> Jurisdiction is not acquired through visions of Valhalla. An agency can neither create nor lawfully expand its jurisdiction by merely deciding what it thinks the future should be like, finding a private industry that can be restructured to make that future at least possible, and then forcing that restructuring in the mere hope that if it's there it will be used.

By 1980 the theme of deregulation, which was beginning to dictate changes in the regulation of broadcasting, also began to influence the regulation of cable television. In 1980 the FCC abandoned its rules that limited the number of distant signals a cable company could import for its subscribers. Distant signals are broadcast signals coming from more than thirty-five miles away from a cable system in a large market or more than fifty-five miles away from a cable system in a smaller market. The FCC also abandoned rules that stopped cable systems from transmitting programs carried by stations outside the area if the same programs were carried by local stations. These were called program exclusivity rules. While relaxing its own rules, the FCC worked to strengthen the local regulation of cable systems.

Then in the mid-1980s three things happened, two of which seemed to clarify the jurisdictional questions surrounding cable regulation and one that did exactly the opposite. Until 1984 the FCC jurisdiction to regulate cable had been justified because of the commission's statutory responsibility to regulate television generally. But in *Capital Cities* v. *Crisp* (see pages 502–3 for a fuller discussion of this case) a unanimous Supreme Court struck down an Oklahoma State ban on liquor advertising on cable TV on the grounds that the federal government had preempted this area of regulation. In its ruling the High Court suggested that the FCC had virtually unbounded authority over cable television. The High Court asserted that "the Commission's authority extends to all regulatory actions necessary to ensure the achievement of the Commission's statutory responsibilities." Those responsibilities were defined to include "ensuring that the substantial benefits provided by cable of increased and diversified programming are secured by the maximum number of viewers." (52 U.S.L.W 4803, 1984) This decision seemed to open the door that had been partially closed in *Midwest II* and seemed to signal the court's willingness to approve comprehensive cable regulation by the FCC.

Shortly after the Supreme Court ruling, Congress adopted the Cable Communications Policy Act of 1984, a comprehensive statute that firmly defined the jurisdiction and responsibilities of the FCC with regard to cable television. (The substance of this law will be outlined shortly.) In less than six months the commission's jurisdiction to regulate cable television had been clarified, first by the courts and then by the Congress.

In less than a year, however, the question of FCC jurisdiction to regulate cable was again clouded, this time by a 1985 ruling by the U.S. Court of Appeals for the District of Columbia, a ruling that cast a shadow over any government regulation of cable television. The case focused upon what are called the must-carry rules, FCC regulations that force a cable system to carry the signals of all commercial television stations within thirty-five miles of the community served by the system. The rules were originally adopted to protect local broadcasting. Many feared that if the cable operator could import signals into the community, local television stations would lose their audience and ultimately die. But the court of appeals ruled that the regulations violated the cable operator's rights of freedom of expression. "It is now clearly established that cable operators engage in conduct protected by the First Amendment," the court said. Government regulation of broadcasting has always been justified on the grounds of scarcity of broadcast signals in the spectrum, wrote Judge Skelly Wright. But such a rationale has no place in evaluating government regulation of cable television. Wright and the two other members of the court could find no other compelling reasons why the government should regulate the cable industry either. Cable television is much closer to film or the printed press than it is to broadcasting, Wright noted. The must-carry rules were designed to protect local broadcasters and in doing so are favoring certain classes of speakers over other speakers. Government cannot do this. Cable operators complained that on small cable systems, those with twelve or so channels, there were few channels left for cable network programming (MTV, CNN, and others) if the cable operator had to transmit all the local stations. They argued that this impinged upon their editorial discretion to program the channels that they wanted to program. The court agreed and noted that the rules also interfered with the wishes of the subscribers—who may want to watch something other than the local stations. Judge Wright pondered whether the rules were designed to protect localism in broadcasting, a worthy goal, or local broadcasters. Government assumes a heavy burden of justification for any rule that impinges upon the First Amendment. In this case the government failed to carry the burden, the court said (*Quincy Cable* v. *FCC,* 1985). It was the breadth of Judge Wright's opinion in the case, as much as the fact that the must-carry rules were declared unconstitutional, that prompted immediate and serious speculation about the meaning of the ruling. A week after the ruling, *New York Times* reporter Stuart Taylor, Jr., noted in an analytical article that the ruling in *Quincy* cast constitutional doubts on the validity of exclusive cable franchises and clouded the constitutionality of all governmental regulation of cable programming. (Author's note: In the summer of 1986, the FCC, with the support of the cable and broadcasting industries, adopted a set of revised must-carry rules that were scheduled to operate until the early 1990s. Under the new rules, cable systems must devote only a portion of their capacity to carrying local television signals. Systems with less than a 20-channel capacity must carry only a public broadcasting station; cable systems with between 21 and 27 channels must devote seven channels to local broadcast signals; and systems with more than 27 channels must devote 25 percent of their capacity to local television station signals. Local stations are defined as those located within 50 miles of the cable community.)

The Supreme Court, in 1986, added considerable fuel to speculation that the First Amendment may invalidate much cable regulation when it ruled that the operator of a cable television system engages in activities that "plainly implicate First Amendment interests." The case involved a California cable operator who could not get a franchise to wire a section of Los Angeles and challenged the right of the city to limit which cable operators could and could not wire the city. Writing for a unanimous Supreme Court, Justice Rehnquist said, "Cable television partakes of some of the aspects of speech and the communication of ideas as do the traditional enterprises of newspaper and book publishers, public speakers and pamphleteers." Obviously, none of the "traditional enterprises" listed by Rehnquist are regulated as heavily as cable television or broadcasting generally. The High Court made no ruling on the constitutionality of the city's franchising authority, but sent the case back for construction of a better factual record at a trial. But the message was clear. Not only were judges of the court of appeals beginning to look at cable television operators more as a newspaper than a broadcasting station, but members of the Supreme Court had some of the same ideas (*Los Angeles* v. *Preferred Communications,* 1986).

Cable Communications Policy Act of 1984

Until and unless the Supreme Court declares the Cable Communications Policy Act of 1984 (hereafter the Cable Act) unconstitutional, it is the law of the land and defines the ways in which government may regulate cable television. Congress adopted this statute because of the jurisdictional problems experienced by the FCC in regulating cable television. The statute was also adopted because cable regulation had become a patchwork crazy quilt of city, state, and federal rules, very confusing at best. Some believe, as well, that Congress was fearful that the FCC, in a rampant mood of deregulation, might abandon cable regulation as well, something that most members of Congress believed would be undesirable. Attorney Michael Meyerson points out in the *Georgia*

Law Review that to understand the law it is important to recognize that it is a compromise. Representatives of the cable industry and the cities—the government units that award cable franchises—negotiated for three years before a bill was drafted that both could find acceptable.

Purpose of the Law

The purposes of this legislation are enumerated in Section 601 of the Cable Act itself. They are as follows:

1. To establish a national policy concerning cable communciations
2. To establish franchise procedures and standards that encourage the growth and development of cable systems and that assure that cable systems are responsive to the needs and interests of the local community
3. To establish guidelines for the exercise of federal, state, and local authority with respect to the regulation of cable systems
4. To assure and encourage that cable communications provide the widest possible diversity of information sources and services to the public
5. To establish a process that protects cable operators against unfair denials of renewal by franchising authorities and that provides for an orderly process for consideration of renewal proposals

Jurisdiction and Franchises

The law clearly asserts federal jurisdiction over the control of cable but limits the FCC's broad discretion over cable policy. This is an indication that many members of the legislative body feared the commission would preempt local authority over cable television and then deregulate the industry. Consequently, under the new act most of the obligations imposed on the cable operator will come from local government rather than the FCC, but the local government must operate within the policy framework erected by the Congress in the Cable Act. The local government will be the "franchising authority" and grant the franchise to the cable operator.

While the statute outlines some policies regarding the content of the franchise, other matters—such as duration and timetable for construction of a system—are in the hands of the local government. The statute speaks of "services" and "facilities and equipment." *Services* generally means programming. *Facilities and equipment* refers to hardware of the system and the physical capabilities of the system, such as channel capacity, two-way or one-way, etc. Local governments are generally barred from establishing requirements for service or programming but are given a wide latitude to establish standards for equipment and facilities. The local government can insist that a cable operator provide broad categories of programming to meet the needs of children, different ethnic groups, or others and can insist that the cable operator provide public access channels for citizens to use. But critics of the law, such as Michael Botein of the New York Law School, point out that cable operators are permitted under the law to renege on these promises if they turn out to be "commercially impractical."

The act permits local govenment to charge a cable operator a franchise fee of up to 5 percent of the operator's gross revenues. But a recent ruling by the U.S. Supreme Court (see *Minneapolis Star and Tribune Co.* v. *Minnesota Commissioner of Revenue,* 1983) strongly suggests that there is a constitutional limit on such a fee that may be lower than the one set by statute. Observers, such as Michael Meyerson, suggest that any fee collected can only be used to finance the operation of the franchise system. It cannot be collected simply to raise revenue. So a local government may be forced to charge a lower fee if the 5 percent assessment generates too much revenue.

The act permitted local governments to regulate the rates a cable operator could charge for basic cable service for two years, until December 29, 1986. After that time the franchising authority could regulate the rates for basic service only if the cable system were without "effective competition" in the community. The act did not define effective competition but required the FCC to define the term within six months, and in mid-1985 the commission ruled that there was effective competition to a cable system in a community if there were three over-the-air broadcast channels available to viewers. Most communities meet this profile, so local government is largely without any power to regulate what the cable operator can charge for basic service—the local over-the-air channels, the public access channels, and whatever else the cable operator includes in the package. Regulation of charges for the premium or pay channels is not permitted under the law.

The law makes it somewhat easier for a cable operator to renew a franchise, another provision of the act that some critics don't like. A franchising authority can deny the renewal of a franchise if the cable operator has not "substantially compiled with the material terms of the existing franchise"—that is, has failed to live up to past promises—or if the cable operator's renewal proposal is not "reasonable to meeting the future cable-related community needs and interests." But the act also requires the local government to go through a set of formal procedures before it can deny a renewal, and critics charge that the burden of these procedures will tend to discourage cities from denying renewals.

Freedom of Speech

The Cable Act has established that third parties—that is, persons other than the cable operator or the local government—must have access to the cable system. Several means are provided for such access. The local franchising authorities are permitted to require that the cable operator provide public access and government and educational access channels. A public access channel is set aside for free public use on a nondiscriminatory, first-come, first-served basis. Neither the cable operator nor the government can censor what appears on such a channel. The franchising authority can prescribe limited content-neutral time, place, and manner rules for the public access channel, such as deciding that the access channel will give each user thirty minutes of time or that persons must sign up three days before the date they wish to use the channel. But that is about all. The government and educational channels are used either by schools or to broadcast public hearings or city council meetings. These channels are to be programmed as the government sees fit.

Commercial access channels must also be provided by the cable operator. The law provides that a certain number of channels must be set aside for use by "unaffiliated programmers" at reasonable rates. The cable operator cannot control the content of these programs. The number of channels that must be set aside for commercial access depends upon the number of activated channels in the cable system. An activated channel is one that is being used or is available for use. Systems with fewer than thirty-six channels need not have any commercial access channels; those with thirty-six to fifty-four channels must set aside 10 percent of the channels for commercial access. Systems with more than fifty-four channels must reserve 15 percent of these channels for commercial access. The cable operator can set the price and conditions of use for these channels, so long as they are "reasonable." Costs cannot have anything to do with content; that is, a cable operator cannot charge someone who puts on a conservative talk show $100 per hour and someone who puts on a liberal talk show $500. However, the cable operator can set different rates for different categories of program; i.e., news programs cost $50 per hour, movies $100 per hour.

As noted earlier the act permits all levels of government to prohibit and penalize the broadcast of obscene material over cable television. It is less clear about the broadcast of indecent material (see pages 570–74). However, the act requires that every cable operator provide upon the request of a subscriber a lockbox device that permits the subscriber to block out the reception of specific channels. This permits parents to control what children can watch when the parents are not at home. Local governments can control the cablecasting of obscenity over the commercial access channels, but it is much harder for the franchising authority to control the transmission of obscenity over the public access channels. Whoever runs the public access channels can ask a user to sign an agreement that he or she will not broadcast obscenity while on the air, and of course any programmer who does broadcast obscenity can be punished after the telecast. But the public access channels are supposed to be free from close government scrutiny. That is why the law relieves the cable operator of any liability for the broadcast of any obscenity, libel, false advertising, or invasion of privacy that appears on the access channels.

One purpose of the law is to make available to as many persons as possible the fruits of the burgeoning communications technology. The act deals with this issue in several ways. It does not permit a cable operator to redline; that is, refuse to wire one portion of a franchise area because the citizens are poor or most persons would not subscribe to the cable. The act makes legal the use of the private earth stations, the so-called dish antennas, to receive unscrambled satellite transmissions. Under the Communications Act such reception was often a violation of the law. However, cable channels and others who use satellite transmissions are permitted to scramble their signals under the new law—and many have begun to do so, much to the distaste of the 1.5 million dish owners. Both the FCC and local governments have the authority to regulate the use of the private earth stations in other ways. Local governments have attempted to use zoning rules or other regulations to keep the often unsightly and large antennas out of the community. But the FCC has ruled that local governments can only ban backyard or rooftop antennas when the TV receiving equipment violates "reasonable and clearly defined health, safety or aesthetic" considerations.

Protection of subscribers' right to privacy is a special concern in the Cable Act. The prospect of widespread use of two-way cable television—something that hasn't happened yet—gives the cable company the opportunity to gather an immense amount of data on subscribers. Products that are ordered via television, films that are watched, votes on public referenda are all recorded by the system's computer for legitimate reasons. But the use of this kind of data by the cable company for other purposes would surely violate the privacy of the subscriber. Yet there were no laws prohibiting such use. Users of one-way cable even provide the cable company with some kinds of information subscribers might not like to have widely known. The names of persons who subscribe to adult movie channels is one example. The Cable Act states that a cable company can only collect "personally identifiable information" for two purposes: (1) to obtain the information that is necessary to serve the subscriber and (2) to search for unauthorized reception of the cable signal. All personally identifiable information must be destroyed once it has been used for the purpose it was gathered, and the cable operator cannot disclose such information, even to government, unless the government can establish that it has a compelling reason to have this data that outweighs the subscriber's right to privacy. The subscriber must be told at least once a year what kind of data is being collected and is permitted to see this information and correct it if it is in error.

The Cable Act is a comprehensive attempt to provide both a cable policy and a regulatory framework. But it focuses almost exclusively on broadcast services. It says little about the regulation of data transmission over common carrier-type services; it skirts the issue of whether states, rather than the federal government, have a right to regulate such services. Can the FCC preempt the states in such regulation? What does the Crisp decision (see pages 502–3) mean in this regard? These are issues that are still very much alive.

<table>
<tr><td>Other Broadcast
Services</td><td>The FCC maintains the right to regulate other new broadcast services. Multipoint distribution services have the configuration of traditional over-the-air broadcasting stations and are controlled by the FCC rather than local government. An MDS is wireless cable; the operator transmits television signals via microwave signals to subscribers who are equipped with a special antenna and a device that converts the microwave signals to one that can be received through a television set. Operation of such systems is regulated by federal law. In 1983 the FCC decided to allocate eight microwave channels per market for commerical use, setting off a stampede for the MDS licenses. The FCC scheduled lotteries to determine which of the sixteen thousand applicants would get the thousand licenses, but it took two years for the lotteries to occur. Even then they were held under a legal cloud as minority and female applicants challenged the FCC licensing process.</td></tr>
</table>

The Cable Act has given the local governments some control over the regulation of satellite master antenna television. The SMATVs are really private cable companies that service large apartment and condominum complexes. The complex owner sets up antennas and provides residents with television services. Congress was concerned that these television viewers recieve as many of the benefits of cable television as regular cable subscribers and gave local government limited power to franchise such operations and establish levels of performance, as they can with cable operators.

In 1982 the FCC authorized the development of what is called low-power television, or LPTV. LPTV stations broadcast no more than ten miles in one direction. They are really neighborhood stations. The process of licensing these stations through lotteries has gone very slowly. As of September 1, 1985, only 109 such stations were licensed for the continental U.S., although more than 200 other LPTVs were licensed for Alaska. There is room for about 4,000 such stations in the lower forty-eight states and more than forty thousand applications have been filed. The FCC has drowned in these applications and even the use of a lottery selection process has not helped a great deal. The federal government is solely responsible for the regulation of such stations.

The regulation of these exotic new technologies is just beginning and in some ways government—and that means we the people as well as the bureaucracy—seems ill-prepared to handle the challenge we have been given. While the nation now has a cable policy, it still lacks a broader communications policy. And until that is developed, it will be difficult to use regulation in a "creative" rather than a "control" manner to insure the greatest benefits from these amazing new technologies for all the people.

SUMMARY

The power of the FCC to regulate cable television was a clouded issue for many years. Slowly, but surely, the commission, with the permission of the courts, moved to regulate this new technology. In 1984 both the Supreme Court and the Congress gave the FCC what seemed to be clear jurisdiction to set broad rules for government cablecasting. But a subsequent court of appeals ruling has cast some doubt on all government regulation of cable.

The Cable Communications Policy Act of 1984 is a comprehensive measure setting policies and standards for the regulation of cable television. Local governments are given the primary responsibility under this measure to regulate the cable systems in their communities. They may issue franchises, collect franchise fees, and renew franchises. Regulation of the cost of basic service, however, will no longer be common. The act also provides for the inclusion of public, government, and commercial access channels. It also makes provisions to protect subscribers' right to privacy. The FCC does retain the power to regulate other forms of communications technology, however, including MDSs, earth stations, and low-power television.

BIBLIOGRAPHY

Here is a list of some of the sources that have been helpful in the preparation of chapter 11:

Books

American Enterprise Institute, *Broadcast Deregulation.* Washington, D.C.: American Enterprise Institute for Public Policy Research, 1985.

Cowan, Geoffrey. *See No Evil.* New York: Simon & Schuster, 1979.

The First Amendment and Broadcasting: Press Freedoms and Broadcast Journalism. Transcript of the 1978 Edward R. Murrow Symposium. Washington State University, April 23–25, 1978.

Friendly, Fred. *The Good Guys, The Bad Guys and the First Amendment: Free Speech and Fairness in Broadcasting.* New York: Random House, 1976.

Geller, Henry. *The Fairness Doctrine in Broadcasting.* Santa Monica: Rand Corp., 1973.

Ginsberg, Douglas. *Regulation of Broadcasting: Law and Policy Towards Radio, Television and Cable Communications.* St. Paul: West Publishing Co., 1979.

Media and the First Amendment in a Free Society. Amherst: University of Massachusetts Press, 1973.

Pember, Don R. *Mass Media in America.* 5th ed. Chicago: Science Research Associates, 1987.

Robinson, Glen O., and Gelhorn, Ernest. *The Administrative Process.* St. Paul: West Publishing Co., 1974.

Articles

Bollier, David. "The Strange Politics of Fairness." *Channels* 46, January/February, 1986.

Botein, Michael. "Access to Cable Television." 57 *Cornell Law Review* 419, 1972.

Botein, Michael. "Who Came Out Ahead in the Cable Act." *Channels* 14, March/April, 1985.

Brown, Les. "Why Deregulation Won't Last." *Channels* 61, September/October, 1984.

"CATV Regulation: A Jumble of Jurisdictions." 45 *New York University Law Review* 816, 1970.

Chamberlin, Bill F. "The FCC and the First Principle of the Fairness Doctrine: A History of Neglect and Distortion." 31 *Federal Communications Law Journal* 361, 1979.

Fogarty, Joseph R., and Spielholz, Marcia. "FCC Cable Jurisdiction: From Zero to Plenary in Twenty-five Years." 37 *Federal Communications Law Journal* 113, 1985.

Houser, Thomas J. "The Fairness Doctrine: An Historical Perspective." 47 *Notre Dame Lawyer* 550, 1972.

Johnson, Timothy P. "Regulating CATV: Local Government and the Franchising Process," 19 *South Dakota Law Review* 143, 1974.

Marks, Richard D. "Broadcasting and Censorship: First Amendment Theory After *Red Lion*." 38 *George Washington Law Review* 974, 1970.

Meyerson, Michael. "The Cable Communications Policy Act of 1984: A Balancing Act on the Coaxial Wires." 19 *Georgia Law Review* 543, 1985.

Robbins, Vicky H. "Indecency on Cable Television—A Barren Battleground for Regulation of Programming Content." 15 *St. Mary's Law Journal* 417, 1984.

Robinson, Glen O. "The FCC and the First Amendment: Observations on 40 Years of Radio and Television Regulation." 52 *Minnesota Law Review* 67, 1967.

Simon, Jules F. "The Collapse of Consensus: Effects of the Deregulation of Cable Television." 81 *Columbia Law Review* 612, 1981.

Cases and Reports

Action for Children's Television v. FCC, 756 F.2d 899 (1985).

Adrian Weiss, 58 FCC2d 342 (1976).

American Security Council Foundation v. FCC, 607 F.2d 438 (1979).

Brandywine-Main Line Radio, Inc. v. FCC, 24 FCC2d 2218 (1970); 473 F.2d 16 (1972).

in re *Business Executives Movement v. FCC*, 450 F.2d 642 (1971).

Capital Cities v. Crisp, 52 U.S.L.W. 4803 (1984).

Carroll Broadcasting Co. v. FCC, 258 F.2d 440 (1958).

in re *Carter Mountain Transmission Corp.*, 32 FCC 459 (1962); affd. 321 F.2d 359 (1963); 375 U.S. 951 (1963).

CBS v. Democratic National Committee, 412 U.S. 94 (1973).

CBS v. FCC, 101 S.Ct. 2813 (1981).

Central Florida Enterprises, Inc. v. FCC, 598 F.2d 37 (1978).

Citizens Committee to Preserve the Voice of the Arts in Atlanta v. FCC, 436 F.2d 263 (1970).

Citizens' Committee to Save WEFM v. FCC, 506 F.2d 246 (1974).

Citizens Communication Center v. FCC, 447 F.2d 2101 (1971).

Citizens Communication Center v. FCC, 463 F.2d 822 (1972).

Commission en Banc Programming Inquiry, 20 P & F Rad. Regs. 1901 (1960).

in re *Community Broadcasting Service, Inc., WWBZ*, 20 FCC 168 (1955).

Community Television v. Wilkinson, 611 F. Supp. 1099 (1985).

Cosmopolitan Broadcasting Corp., 59 FCC2d 558 (1976).

Cowles Florida Enterprises, Inc. v. FCC, 683 F.2d 503 (1982).

Cruz v. Fere, 571 F. Supp. 125 (1983).

Democratic National Committee v. FCC, 717 F.2d 1471 (1983).

Diocesan Union of Holy Name Societies of Rockville Centre and Long Island Coalition for Life, 41 FCC2d 497 (1973).

In the Matter of Editorializing by Broadcast Licensees, 13 FCC 1246 (1949).

The Fairness Report, 39 Fed.Regs. 26372 (1974).

Farmers Educational and Cooperative Union of American v. *WDAY*, 360 U.S. 525 (1959).

FCC v. *American Broadcasting Co.* et al., 347 U.S. 284 (1954).

FCC v. *League of Women Voters*, 104 S.Ct. 3106 (1984).

FCC v. *Midwest Video Corp.*, 99 S.Ct. 1435 (1979).

FCC v. *Pacifica Foundation*, 98 S.Ct. 3026 (1978).

FCC v. *WNCN Listeners Guild*, 101 S.Ct. 1266 (1981).

First Report and Order on Microwave Served CATV, 38 FCC 683 (1965).

Fourth Report and Order on Cable Television Service, 37 Fed.Regs. 3251 (1972).

FRC v. *Nelson Brothers*, 289 U.S. 266 (1933).

Galloway v. *FCC*, 12 MLR 1443 (1985).

in re *Great Lakes Broadcasting* v. *FRC*, 3 FRC Ann. Rept. 32 (1929); 37 F.2d 993 (1930).

Home Box Office v. *Wilkinson*, 531 F. Supp.987 (1982).

Hoover v. *Intercity Radio Co., Inc.*, 286 F. 1003 (1923).

Illinois Citizens Committee for Broadcasting v. *FCC*, 515 F.2d 397 (1975).

Kennedy for President Committee v. *FCC*, 636 F.2d 417 (1980).

Kennedy for President Committee v. *FCC*, 636 F.2d 432 (1980).

KFKB Broadcasting Association v. *FRC*, 47 F.2d 670 (1931).

Kuczo v. *Western Connecticut Broadcasting*, 424 F. Supp. 1324 (1977).

Los Angeles v. *Preferred Communications, Inc.*, 106 S.Ct. 2034 (1986).

in re *Mayflower Broadcasting Corp., WAAB*, 8 FCC 333 (1941).

May Seed and Nursery Co., 2 FCC 559 (1936).

Midwest Video Corp. v. *FCC*, 571 F.2d 1025 (1978).

Minneapolis Star and Tribune Co. v. *Minnesota Commissioner of Revenue*, 460 U.S. 575 (1983).

National Citizens Committee for Broadcasting v. *FCC*, 567 F.2d 1095 (1977).

National Committee for Responsive Philanthropy v. *FCC*, 652 F.2d 589 (1981).

NBC v. *FCC*, 516 F.2d 1101 (1974).

Office of Communication, United Church of Christ v. *FCC*, 359 F.2d 994 (1966).

in re *Palmetto Broadcasting Co.*, 33 FCC 250 (1962).

Patsy Mink, 59 FCC2d 984 (1976).

Policy Statement on Comparative Broadcast Hearings, 1 FCC2d 393 (1965).

Policy Statement on Comparative Hearings Involving Regular Renewal Applications, 22 FCC2d 424 (1970).

Primer on Ascertainment of Community Needs, 27 FCC2d 650 (1971).

Primer on Ascertainment of Community Problems by Broadcast Applicants, 27 FCC2d 650 (1973); rev. 53 FCC2d 3 (1975).

Public Media Center v. *FCC*, 587 F.2d 1322 (1978).

Public Service Responsibility of Broadcast Licensees, (1946).

Quincy Cable v. *FCC*, 768 F.2d 1434 (1985).

Radio and Television News Directors' Association v. *U.S.*, 400 F.2d 1002 (1968).

Red Lion Broadcasting Co. v. *FCC*, 381 F.2d 908 (1967); affd. 395 U.S. 367 (1969).

RKO v. *FCC*, 670 F.2d 215 (1981).

Second Annual Report of the Federal Radio Commission (1928).

Second Report and Order on Microwave-Served CATV, 2 FCC2d 725 (1966).

Sonderling Broadcasting Corp., 27 P & F Rad. Regs. 285 (1973).
Trinity Methodist Church, South v. *FRC*, 62 F.2d 650 (1932).
in re *United Broadcasting Co.*, 10 FCC 515 (1945).
U.S. v. *Midwest Video Corp.*, 406 U.S. 649 (1972).
U.S. v. *Southwestern Cable Co.*, 392 U.S. 157 (1968).
U.S. v. *Zenith Radio Corp.*, 12 F.2d 616 (1926); 35 Op. Attys. Gen. 126 (1926).
WCBS-TV, 8 FCC2d 381 (1967); affd. Applicability of the Fairness Doctrine to
    Cigarette Advertising, 9 FCC2d 921 (1967); affd. *Banzhaf* v. *FCC*, 405 F.2d
    1164 (1969).
in re *Wilderness Society and Friends of the Earth*, 30 FCC2d 643 (1971); revd.
    Friends of the Earth v. *FCC*, 449 F.2d 1164 (1971).
Writers Guild v. *ABC*, 609 F.2d 355 (1979).
Writers Guild v. *FCC*, 423 F. Supp. 1064 (1976).
in re *WUHY-FM, Eastern Educational Radio*, 24 FCC2d 408 (1970).
Yale Broadcasting Co. v. *FCC*, 478 F.2d 594 (1973).
Young People's Association for the Propagation of the Gospel, 6 FCC 178 (1938).

12

REGULATION OF THE MEDIA AS A BUSINESS

The primary purpose of this book is to focus upon the censorship and regulation of what is printed in the press or broadcast over radio and television—the content of mass media communication. Yet mass media face other regulation as well, regulation based not on content, but on other criteria. In the United States newspapers, broadcasting stations, film companies, and magazines are usually private businesses, and as such these media businesses face the myriad rules and regulations confronting other businesses in this nation. Rules regarding minimum wages, maximum working hours, safety, health, taxation, and many other areas apply to the mass media as well as to automobile manufacturers, furniture companies, and beauty salons.

Two factors stand out regarding these rules. First, they are applied to the media regardless of content. Magazines that aim to contribute to the essential political debate in this country have to meet the same minimum wage rules as do true romance magazines, which appeal to the emotions. The makers of serious films must meet the same safety standards at their studios as do the makers of sleazy sex-oriented films. The point is this: Whereas in some areas the law is applied differently to businesses thought to serve the public interest than to those that do not, no such variable application occurs when the media are looked at as businesses.

Second, while the First Amendment has been at the center of our discussion of press regulation to this point in the book, the guarantees of freedom of expression mean very little when the media are regulated as businesses. The First Amendment might protect a newspaper that erroneously labels a politician a crook or a magazine that publishes the intimate secrets of the life of a public official, but it will not protect the publisher who fails to meet fire code regulations or the broadcaster who refuses to pay legitimate taxes. More than fifty years ago the Supreme Court made this abundantly clear when it upheld the constitutionality of the National Labor Relations Act, which at the time was under a First Amendment challenge launched by the Associated Press (AP). "The business of the Associated Press is not immune from regulation because it is an agency of the press," wrote Justice Owen Roberts for the five-man majority. "The publisher of a newspaper has no special immunity from the application of general laws" (*AP* v. *NLRB*, 1937). Broadcasting station operators and publishers often have to be reminded of this. In 1981 a United States district court in Massachusetts ruled that a newspaper has no First Amendment right to decline to participate in the quarterly financial report program of the Federal Trade Commission (FTC). The court said the FTC only sought financial data and did not intrude upon the exercise of editorial judgment (*U.S.* v. *Nanlo,* 1981). The press must meet all its legal responsibilities as a business, regardless of the First Amendment. ♦

GOVERNMENT AND THE MASS COMMUNICATION BUSINESS

No attempt will be made in this chapter to outline all the broad areas of regulation affecting the media as a business. Consideration of such rules more properly resides in a class in business law. But two areas of commercial regulation are considered, since both have implications beyond simple business regulation. The regulation of the ownership and operation of the media through antitrust laws and FCC policies is significant because it can have an important impact on who can own the press and, in some instances, the content of media communication. Taxation of the press will be noted briefly also, since on at least some occasions taxation has been used as a means to indirectly censor the press. These are the broad subjects to be covered in this short chapter.

Antitrust Laws and Newspapers

The government's primary weapon against economic concentration and restraint of trade in industry are the antitrust laws. The Sherman Act of 1890 and the Clayton Act of 1914 provide the legal bases for the Department of Justice to bring both criminal and civil suits against businesses that use monopolistic tactics to endanger free competition. The press is not immune from such legal pressure, yet surprisingly it has been an infrequent target of government antitrust action. One author notes that between 1945, when the Supreme Court ruled that the First Amendment did not shield the press from action by the government to stop monopolistic practices, and 1969, only twelve antitrust suits were initiated against the press. In 1976, when seventy-two different newspapers changed hands (most were bought up by newspaper chains), there were no antitrust actions against newspaper interests. Why? Catherine B. Roach offered one opinion in an article in the *Memphis State University Law Review:*

> Because of the structure of the communications industry—basically a collection of local circulation and advertising markets—anti-trust enforcers have encountered difficult problems of proof as to anticompetitive effects in relevant markets.

In an effort to explain some of the anticompetitive problems the federal government has sought to control in the press, here is a summary of some of the litigation in the past forty years.

Restrictive Membership Rules

As noted previously, it was in 1945 that the Supreme Court first gave approval to the prosecution of antitrust action against members of the press. The occasion was a suit by the government against the Associated Press, the giant news cooperative and wire service. Marshall Field had founded the morning

Chicago Sun and sought an AP membership for his newspaper. But under AP bylaws the owners of the rival *Chicago Tribune* were given the opportunity to approve or disapprove Field's application for membership. Without this approval, the applicant needed the consent of a majority of all AP members for the membership application to be accepted. These rules effectively kept newspapers that competed with AP members from getting the highly desirable membership and access to the AP wire service.

The federal government brought an antitrust action against the AP, charging that its membership laws resulted in an illegal monopoly in restraint of trade—a violation of the Sherman Act. Among the AP responses to the suit was the vigorous assertion that the Department of Justice lawsuit against the news cooperative represented a serious infringement upon the constitutionally guaranteed freedom of the press. But the High Court ruled that the Associated Press membership provisions were in fact a violation of the Sherman Act. Justice Hugo Black, writing for the majority, dismissed the argument that the AP was shielded from such legal action by the First Amendment. "Member publishers of the AP are engaged in business for profit exactly as are other businessmen who sell food, steel, aluminum or anything else people need or want," Black wrote. He said that the inability to buy news from the news agency could have serious effects upon a publication and actually endanger its ability to continue to operate successfully. And then Black penned one of his most memorable passages regarding freedom of the press (*AP* v. *U.S.*, 1945):

> The [First] Amendment rests on the assumption that the widest possible dissemination of information from diverse and antagonistic sources is essential to the welfare of the public, that a free press is a condition of a free society. Surely a command that the government itself shall not impede the free flow of ideas does not afford non-governmental combinations a refuge if they impose restraints upon that constitutionally guaranteed freedom. Freedom to publish means freedom for all and not for some. Freedom to publish is guaranteed by the Constitution, but freedom to keep others from publishing is not.

The First Amendment, then, provides no safe house for the business person who violates laws or rules designed to foster free competition. And as we have noted earlier, this generalization rings as true with regard to other commercial regulations as it does with antitrust laws.

Local Monopolies

Six years after the *AP* case, the Supreme Court heard arguments in another antitrust action involving the press. This case focused upon what was essentially a monopoly newspaper business in a medium-sized town. The newspaper refused to accept advertising from businesses that also used other community advertising media.

The *Lorain* (Ohio) *Journal* and the *Times Herald* were owned by the same publisher. The combined daily circulation of the two papers reached nearly 100 percent of the families in the community. The only print competition came from the weekly *Sunday News*. In 1948 a radio station began operation in the community. Shortly thereafter the publisher of the two daily papers announced that the newspapers would no longer accept advertising from businesses and industries in the community that also broadcast advertisements over the radio station. The Department of Justice brought an antitrust action against the Lorain Journal Company, charging that the publishing firm was attempting to monopolize interstate commerce and to force advertisers to boycott the radio station. Justice Harold Burton, writing for a unanimous Supreme Court, ruled that the newspaper's policy violated the Sherman Act, "A single newspaper, already enjoying a substantial monopoly in its area, violates the 'attempt to monopolize' clause [of the Sherman Act] . . . when it uses its monopoly to destroy threatened competition." A publisher has the right to refuse to publish any advertisement, but he cannot use this right as "a purposeful means of monopolizing interstate commerce." The First Amendment afforded the paper no special protection: "The injunction applies to a publisher what the law applies to others," Burton wrote (*Lorain Journal Co.* v. *U.S.*, 1951).

Two years later the Supreme Court was forced to scrutinize a tie-in, or combination advertising rate scheme, used by a New Orleans publisher. The Times-Picayune Company published both the morning *Times-Picayune* and the evening *States*. There was also a competing afternoon paper published in the city, the *Item*. Advertisers who wanted to purchase an advertisement in either the *Times-Picayune* or the *States* had to purchase an advertisement in both. The government brought a civil action against the Times-Picayune Company, charging that its forced combination advertising policy was an unreasonable restraint of trade.

The Supreme Court ruled in a five-to-four decision that the combination advertising rate was not a violation of the law. Justice Tom Clark admitted in his opinion for the majority that such an advertising scheme could hurt competition. Clark cited statistics that showed that of the 598 daily papers that had begun publication between 1929 and 1950, more than 225 of them survived at the end of that period. Of these 598, 46 dailies had encountered combination advertising-rate schemes like the one in New Orleans. Of those 46 papers, only 5 survived in 1950.

According to the Supreme Court, however, such an advertising-rate combination or "tying" arrangement was illegal only if a business with a dominant position in the market coerced its customers into buying an unwanted inferior product along with the desired product. The government argued that the *Times-Picayune* was the dominant, desired product and the afternoon *States* was the unwanted, inferior product that advertisers were forced to buy. The crucial questions in the case, according to Clark, were whether the *Times-Picayune* held a dominant market position and whether the *States* was really an inferior product. The five-man majority answered both questions negatively. The *Times-Picayune* had the greatest circulation, published the most pages, and had the highest amount of advertising, but it was not dominant in the relevant market—the advertising market. The morning paper carried about 40 percent of the classified and display advertising published by the three papers. If all papers had an equal share, the *Times-Picayune* would have still had about 33 percent. The circulation for the *Times-Picayune* was 190,000; for the *States*, 105,000; and for the *Item*, 115,000. The third paper, the *Item*, was flourishing, Clark wrote. He added, "The record in this case thus does not disclose evidence from which demonstrably deleterious effects on competition may be inferred." A majority of the High Court rejected the argument that the *Times-Picayune* was the desired product and the *States* was the inferior product. The products were identical, Clark added (*Times-Picayune* v. *U.S.*, 1953):

> Here . . . two newspapers under single ownership at the same place, time and terms sell indistinguishable products to advertisers; no dominant "tying" product exists . . . no leverage in one market excludes sellers in the second, because for present purposes the products are identical and the market the same.

Five years after the ruling, the Times-Picayune Company purchased the *Item* and created the *State-Item*, making it the only afternoon paper in the city.

Despite the loss in the *Times-Picayune* case, the Department of Justice pushed on with a similar antitrust action in Kansas City against a rate-combination, or tie-in, advertising policy. This time the government was successful in proving the market dominance of the Kansas City Star Company, something it could not prove with regard to the Times-Picayune Company.

The defendant owned the morning *Kansas City Times* and the afternoon *Kansas City Star*. The two papers were circulated to 96 percent of the homes in the area. In addition, the Kansas City Star Company published the *Sunday Star* and owned WDAF radio and WDAF-TV stations. Through all its holdings, the company received 94 percent of all advertising revenue spent in the area. The only competition in the print media field were weekly and suburban papers.

In order to subscribe to any one of the three Star Company–owned newspapers, a resident had to subscribe to all three: both dailies and the Sunday edition. Advertisers were also required to run advertising in all three newspapers. The Star Company used this monopoly power ruthlessly. Examples documented by the government included threats by the newspaper to stop the news coverage of a professional baseball player who bought space in a competing paper to advertise his florist shop. Also, it was reported that advertisers who failed to buy space in the defendant's newspapers received less favorable treatment in getting advertising on WDAF-AM and WDAF-TV. The United States Eighth Circuit Court of Appeals ruled that such circulation and advertising tie-ins violated the Sherman Act in light of the market dominance by the Star Company. With regard to the First Amendment the court said, "To use the freedom of the press guaranteed by the First Amendment to destroy competition would defeat its own ends, for freedom to print news and express opinions as one chooses is not tantamount to having freedom to monopolize" (*U.S.* v. *Kansas City Star,* 1957).

The conviction in this criminal antitrust action was just the beginning for the Star Company. A subsequent civil suit was settled by the firm through a consent order (this legal device is described on pages 523–24), under which the Star Company agreed to sell its broadcasting properties and to stop the tie-in policies with regard to advertising and circulation. Additional civil suits were generated by media competitors in the Kansas City area, and it is estimated that in the end the Star Company paid out several hundred thousand dollars in damages.

Chain Ownership

Ten years elapsed before a federal court again ruled in an important media antitrust action. And for the first time the government action against the press was initiated because of something other than newspaper policy regarding advertisers or subscribers. In this case the target of the federal suit had merely purchased a nearby newspaper.

Serious concern was generated by many thoughtful students of the media during the sixties with regard to the shrinking number of independently owned newspapers in the United States. Similarly, competition between papers in major cities shrunk rapidly to the point where communities with competing daily newspapers were considered unusual. The statistics tell the story graphically. In 1923 daily newspapers were published in nearly 1,300 American cities. Of that total, 502 cities had two or more competing daily papers. Forty years later in 1963, daily newspapers were published in 1,476 cities, but only 51 communities had competing papers. (By 1982 there were dailies in 1,536 cities, but in only 27 was there competition between daily newspapers.) Many feared the demise of the independent newspaper in the United States. The dearth of competition between papers in communities augured a less-vital press and fewer outlets for the publication of ideas and protests. The first real government response to these fears came in southern California when the Department of Justice brought a civil antitrust action against the Times-Mirror Corporation for purchasing a large newspaper company in an adjoining county.

Since 1948 the morning *Los Angeles Times* had had the largest circulation in California. It was an important force in southern California. In the mid-1960s the firm bought the Sun Company, which published the morning *Sun,* the afternoon *Telegram,* and the *Sunday Sun-Telegram* in San Bernardino County, which adjoins Los Angeles County on the east. Until its purchase by the Times-Mirror Corporation, the Sun Company had been the largest independent publisher in southern California. The government argued that the purchase of these newspapers by the Times-Mirror Corporation resulted in a restraint of interstate commerce, in violation of the Sherman Act, and had the impact of lessening competition in the area, which is a violation of the Clayton Act.

In ruling in favor of the government, Judge Warren Ferguson noted that the purchase of the Sun Company newspapers by Times-Mirror was only the latest of a series of actions that had reduced the number of independently owned California newspapers from 59 percent in 1952 to 24 percent in 1966. "The acquisition of the *Sun* by the *Times* was particularly anticompetitive," Judge Ferguson wrote, "because it eliminated one of the few independent papers that had been able to operate successfully in the morning and Sunday fields." Since the purchase of the Sun Company newspapers by the Times-Mirror Corporation, Ferguson noted, two daily newspapers had been closed and two more newspaper mergers in San Bernardino County had occurred. The federal district judge ruled that the acquisition of the Sun Company newspapers by the Times-Mirror Corporation "has raised a barrier to entry of newspapers in the San Bernardino County market that is almost impossible to overcome." Ferguson said that the market for new papers was effectively closed, and "no publisher will risk the expense of unilaterally starting a new daily newspaper there." The judge pointed to the fact that even the prestigious *New York Times* failed to break into the market with a West Coast edition of its successful newspaper. Divestiture was ordered by the court, and the Supreme Court affirmed this ruling one year later (*U.S. v. Times-Mirror Corporation,* 1968).

Following divestiture the Sun Company newspapers were purchased by the Gannett newspaper chain, the largest chain in the nation. Many persons questioned whether the people in San Bernardino County gained or lost as a result of the government lawsuit and the subsequent purchase of the paper by Gannett. Gannett ownership of the *Sun* and the *Telegram* did create a "second owner" in the community, but was the owner a better owner or as good an owner? Both the Times-Mirror Corporation and Gannett are absentee owners not living in the community in which the newspapers are published. But the Times-Mirror Corporation resided just over the county line and certainly was familiar with the problems and people in the area. Gannett has corporate offices in New York State, completely across the nation. The *Los Angeles Times* is one of the most prestigious newspapers in the United States. It remains speculative whether Gannett has fused this quality into the Sun Company newspapers. The opportunity did exist. However, few Gannett newspapers have risen above a mediocre or adequate level. Chances of producing a superior paper for the people of San Bernardino County seem significantly lower with the Gannett ownership. Finally, while the Times-Mirror Corporation is a large media corporation in its own right, its newspaper holdings remain miniscule compared with the growing Gannett chain, which by 1986 owned ninety-two daily newspapers in the nation. What was accomplished, many persons asked, by taking the Sun Company newspapers away from a small newspaper chain and giving it to a large one? The answers to these questions reflect directly on government antitrust policy, which appears to focus on the competition among economic units—advertisers and competing newspapers—rather than on the impact upon the reading public.

<table>
<tr><td>*Joint-Operating Agreements*</td><td>A year later the Justice Department's next major newspaper antitrust suit reached the Supreme Court. In this action the Department of Justice sought to break up the **joint-operating agreement** between the Citizen Publishing Company and the Star Publishing Company in Tucson, Arizona. The joint-operating arrangement had been in effect for nearly thirty years in Tucson, and similar agreements existed between newspapers in more than twenty other American cities. The arrangement was simple. Two independent newspapers merged their advertising, printing, and circulation operations to form a third company. The news departments of the two papers remained separate and independent. The third company, Tucson Newspapers Incorporated, handled all advertising and circulation and printing for the evening *Citizen* and the morning and Sunday *Star*. Profits were pooled and shared.</td></tr>
</table>

The joint-operating agreement had two clear impacts in the community. First, it provided lower costs for both papers and made it possible for two newspapers to be published in situations where only one might survive in pure head-to-head competition. At the same point, however, the lowered costs for the two newspapers made it difficult, if not impossible, for a third newspaper to compete. The government attacked several provisions of the arrangement as being violations of the Sherman Act. Specifically the lawyers for the Department of Justice argued that the setting of advertising and subscription prices by Tucson Newspapers was price-fixing. They also objected to profit pooling and to the fact that both the Star Publishing Company and the Citizen Publishing Company agreed not to engage in other media business in the area.

After considerable time in the lower courts, the Supreme Court in 1969 declared the arrangement to be a violation of the law (*U.S. v. Citizen Publishing Company,* 1969). Justice Douglas wrote that through a joint-operating agreement the two publishers had gained market control over the newspapers in Tucson. The Court did allow the *Star* and the *Citizen* to share some of the same facilities but struck down policies on profit pooling, establishment of joint-advertising and subscription rates, and other similar agreements.

In the months immediately following the ruling in the Citizen Publishing Company case, scores of bills were introduced in Congress to salvage the joint-operating agreement. If such policies were against the law, as the Supreme Court had ruled, then the law would have to be changed, the publishers argued. And it was. In 1970, after an intensive lobbying effort by the publishing industry, the Congress adopted the Newspaper Preservation Act. Taking a clue from Justice Douglas's opinion in the Citizen Publishing Company case, Congress enacted legislation that permitted newspapers to continue to function under joint-operating agreement so long as at the time at which the agreement is made, one of the two papers is in "probable danger of failing." Papers seeking to enter into joint-operating agreements in the future have to first gain permission from the attorney general if they expect to be exempted from the antitrust rules provided for by the law. The measure had the impact of legalizing the twenty-two agreements in effect in 1970, including the one that the Supreme Court had declared illegal in Tucson. The merits of the law have been hotly debated along lines similar to the debate over the joint-operating agreements themselves. While legalizing these agreements has ensured that in twenty-two cities, at least, newspaper news and editorial competition will survive, the law at the same time makes it practically impossible for other publishers to compete with the two monopoly papers that boast lower operating costs.

After several years of trying to compete with the *San Francisco Examiner* and the *Chronicle,* which have operated under a joint agreement since 1965, Bay Area publisher Bruce Brugman went to court in July 1971 and charged that the Newspaper Preservation Act violated his freedom of the press by encouraging journalistic monopoly. Brugman, who published the monthly *Bay Guardian,* told the court that his small paper had difficulty getting advertisers because of the lower joint-advertising rates set by the two newspapers. Many advertisers could not afford to or chose not to advertise beyond the two large San Francisco dailies. Federal district judge Oliver Carter showed little sympathy for Brugman's arguments, however, and in 1972 ruled that the congressional measure did not authorize a monopoly (*Bay Guardian Publishing Company* v. *Chronicle Publishing Company,* 1972). Carter wrote:

> Here the Act was designed to preserve independent editorial voices. Regardless of the economic or social wisdom of such a course, it does not violate the freedom of the press. Rather, it is merely a selective repeal of the antitrust laws. It merely looses the same shady market forces which existed before the passage of the Sherman, Clayton and other antitrust laws. Such a repeal, even when applicable only to the newspaper industry, does not violate the First Amendment.

The law regarding joint-operating agreements has changed little in the past fifteen years, although some litigation has ensued. In 1979 the E. W. Scripps Company sought Department of Justice approval of a joint-operating agreement between its *Cincinnati Post* and Gannett's *Cincinnati Enquirer.* For the first time a public hearing was held on the question. While the government ultimately agreed that the Scripps publication met the requirements of a failing newspaper, attorneys for the Department of Justice raised the interesting question of whether a newspaper could truly be termed "failing" when the parent company (Scripps) might be benefitting financially from the tax write-offs accorded by the *Post*'s losses. The matter was not pressed at that time by the government, and the application for the joint-operating agreement was approved.

A hearing was also held before the Department of Justice gave its approval to a joint-operating agreement between the *Seattle Times* and the *Seattle Post-Intelligencer*. Persons protesting the agreement argued that the Hearst Corporation, owner of the *Post-Intelligencer,* was not in danger of failing. They argued that Hearst had taken money out of the newspaper in order to put it in the position of a failing newspaper. They also argued that the corporation had made no effort to try to sell the newspaper so that another owner might keep it independent; in fact Hearst had rejected all offers to purchase the paper. The hearing judge rejected all contentions and approved the joint-operating plan. Attorney William French Smith also approved of the pact, despite arguments from the antitrust division of the Department of Justice that the *Post-Intelligencer* was not legally a "failing newspaper." A court challenge to Attorney General Smith's approval of the agreement was mounted, and in late August 1982 a United States district court ruled that Smith had acted improperly when he approved the joint-operating proposal. Judge Barbara Rothstein rejected plaintiff's contentions that the Newspaper Preservation Act was a violation of the First Amendment. But she did agree that before the *Post-Intelligencer* could qualify as a failing newspaper, there must be a showing by those persons seeking the approval of the agreement that no other viable alternatives existed for maintaining the newspaper's independent editorial voice. Hearst did not have an obligation under the law to try to seek out buyers for the paper. But in this case there was evidence that buyers were interested in the newspaper. Hearst would have to demonstrate that because of existing economic conditions and other factors, a new owner of the newspaper could not make the *Post-Intelligencer* succeed (*Committee v. Smith,* 1982). But less than one year later, the Ninth U.S. Court of Appeals reversed the district court ruling and held that the Hearst Corporation had met its burden of showing that the alleged alternative owners did not offer a solution to the financial difficulties experienced by the *Post-Intelligencer.* Six people did inquire into the possibility of buying the newspaper, but these were not offers. And these inquiries did not show that the *Post-Intelligencer* could in all probability be sold to a buyer who would continue its operation as an independent newspaper. The critical question in the case, the court of appeals opinion noted, was whether the newspaper was suffering losses that more than likely could not be reversed. There was no evidence that any new owner might be successful in reversing the *Post-Intelligencer's* financial difficulties. In fact, the court said, there was sufficient evidence in the record supporting a negative answer (*Committee for an Independent P–I v. Hearst,* 1983).

In 1986 *The Detroit Free Press,* owned by the Knight–Rider newspaper chain, and *The Detroit News,* owned by the Gannett Co., announced they would enter into a joint operating agreement. Many questioned how anyone could seriously contend that either paper was in danger of failing when their corporate owners were so prosperous. Nevertheless, owners of *The Free Press* and *The News* identified the former as the failing paper and sought permission to merge their production, circulation, and advertising operations. In August of 1986, an assistant U.S. attorney general recommended that a hearing be held to determine the need for the joint agreement. After studying the situation, he said he had concluded that a joint operating agreement does not appear necessary to maintain both editorial voices in Detroit. He noted that recently *The Free Press* had shown both advertising and circulation gains, and that the paper had yet to realize the promise of added revenue from an expanded and modernized printing plant. The newspaper did not appear to match the picture of a newspaper in a downward spiral, the traditional plight of a failing newspaper. True, *The Free Press* had lost $40 million in the past five years, but Assistant U.S. Attorney General Douglas Ginsberg noted that the losses came in an effort to achieve market dominance by offering cut-rate subscriptions and lower ad rates. "When a newspaper owner consciously and deliberately decides to sacrifice short-term profits in a quest for greater long-term profits, indeed potential monopoly profits, should a JOA be available as a 'second best' alternative?" Ginsberg asked. This issue was unresolved as this book went to press.

What most people regard to be the most serious anticompetitive newspaper phenomenon of the 1980s is the rapid growth of newspaper chains and the concurrent demise of the independent newspapers. But the Department of Justice seems unwilling to move against such acquisitions. The antitrust division of the department did investigate the merger of the Gannett newspaper chain with Combined Communications, a large broadcasting chain that also owned two newspapers. But following the investigation *Editor and Publisher* quoted the assistant attorney general for antitrust, John H. Shenefield, as saying:

> The antitrust laws do not flatly prohibit media conglomerates anymore than they prohibit other kinds of conglomerates. Under present law, some measurable impact on competition in some market must be proven before a merger or acquisition will be held to violate the antitrust laws. Indeed, the courts have been generally reluctant to condemn conglomerate mergers where such an impact has not been shown, regardless of the social or other objections that have been asserted.

In an effort to enhance the government's ability to attack the growth of the giant conglomerates, Senator Edward Kennedy introduced a bill in 1979 that, if enacted, would have prohibited companies with more than $2.5 billion in annual sales or more than $2 billion in assets from merging. In addition, under the Kennedy proposal companies with $350 million in annual sales or $200 million in assets could merge only if they could convince the government that such a merger would enhance competition or produce efficiencies of benefit to consumers. The Kennedy proposal would have had little impact upon media conglomerates, as most are not as large as the companies the Kennedy proposal sought to regulate. The Kennedy plan has not yet been adopted by the Congress.

Today the most common kind of antitrust action brought against a newspaper is brought by a competing publication. Serious wars are being waged in many communities between newspapers and competing free-circulation shoppers or direct-mail advertisers. For many years the newspaper was the only important carrier of print advertising in a community. Free-circulation shoppers developed in the 1950s and became a thorn in the side of many newspapers. The shoppers gave an advertiser total market coverage; newspapers, of course, were delivered only to subscribers. Recent changes in the postal laws caused the newspaper industry even more headaches. Formerly the U.S. Postal Service required postage on each piece of mail delivered. But the law has been revised. Today it is possible for a direct-mail company to insert several different advertisements in a single circular or wrapper and pay a single postage fee for the entire package. This is called marriage mail. The shoppers and marriage-mail packagers began to pull advertisers away from the newspapers. In retaliation many newspapers began offering advertisers their own total market service: a shopper or even a direct-mail package. This competition has resulted in a great many lawsuits in which the owner of a shopper or direct-mail operation has brought a civil action against the newspaper for antitrust law violations. Most of these suits never go to trial, but are settled. The newspapers have generally won the few that have gone to trial, but not in every case. A federal court in Virginia ruled against a daily newspaper that used illegal practices to try to kill a competing free-circulation weekly newspaper and shopper. The newspaper began issuing its own shopper and offered advertising rates below those in the weekly shopper, rates that were actually below the daily newspaper's costs. The federal judge ruled that the Sherman Act outlaws the use of monopoly power to destroy threatened competition. Below-cost pricing in and of itself is not illegal, the court ruled. But evidence of below-cost pricing along with evidence that advertisers who went into the daily newspaper's shopper got rebates and special tie-in rates for advertising in the daily paper does suggest monopolistic practices. There was also testimony in the case that the publisher of the newspaper had said that the weekly shopper would not be in business much longer. The court enjoined the publication of the daily newspaper's shopper unless its advertising rates were raised and all tie-in and rebate advertising arrangements were ended. That the daily newspaper already controlled 85 percent of all print advertising in the community was an important factor in the victory for the weekly publisher (*Advantage Publications* v. *Daily Press*, 1983).

<table>
<tr><td>

Broadcasting
Monopolies

</td><td>

The Department of Justice has carried the largest burden in attempting to control the competitive practices of the newspaper industry. But in broadcasting the Federal Communications Commission (FCC) has taken the lead in regulating the ownership of radio and television stations, and only recently has the Department of Justice moved against members of the industry.

</td></tr>
</table>

FCC Controls

The Federal Communications Commission has closely regulated the business practices of broadcasters by means of the license renewal procedures and other commission policies. Congress has passed statutes with regard to some matters such as the rates a broadcaster may charge a candidate for public office. The FCC itself has issued scores of rules regarding business and advertising practices. It has also been the FCC that has attempted to control both the growth of broadcast chains and other ownership practices of the members of the industry.

The commission's first rules on ownership were issued in 1940, when it declared that no single individual or company could own more than three television stations and six frequency modulation (FM) radio stations. Amplitude modulation (AM) radio ownership is not limited. These numbers were revised continually until 1954 when rules were adopted that stand today. A single individual or company cannot own more than twelve AM stations, twelve FM stations, and twelve television stations. If some stations are at least 50 percent minority owned or if two of the television stations are on the UHF rather than the VHF band, it is permissible for a single individual to own up to fourteen of each kind of station (see pages 560–61 for detailed information on this rule).

In 1968 the FCC adopted what is called its "one to a customer rule," which was modified in 1971 and is the rule that exists today. The commission will not permit any broadcasting company to own more than a single VHF television station in a given market or one AM-FM radio combination. The 1971 rule was applied prospectively; that is, the agency did not force the owners of existing very high frequency TV–AM-FM combinations to sell one of their properties. It simply announced it would no longer approve the formation of such combinations in the future. The agency took a more flexible position on the ultrahigh frequency TV–AM-FM combinations, announcing that it would rule upon requests for such combinations on a case-by-case basis in the future.

In 1975 the agency attempted to thwart what it saw as another problem: the ownership of broadcast properties by newspaper companies in the same city. The rules promulgated by the commission were rather simple but provoked a serious court battle. The commission said that in the future it would bar the ownership of a broadcast license by a newspaper operating in the same city. All but a handful of the existing newspaper-broadcast combinations were allowed to remain intact. However the FCC did seek divestiture in communities in which there was common ownership of the only daily newspaper and the only broadcasting station. Similarly, in communities where there was more than one broadcasting station, the agency sought to break up the common ownership of the only daily newspaper and the only television station. Sixteen such forbidden combinations existed, and the license holders were given five years to divest themselves of either the broadcasting property or the newspaper.

The National Citizens Committee for Broadcasting challenged the FCC rules, arguing that while it supported the prospective cross-ownership ban, the FCC should have forced *all* existing combinations to sell either their newspapers or broadcasting properties. In other words, the public interest groups opposed the grandfather clause in the FCC rules. The United States Court of Appeals (D.C.) agreed and ruled that the FCC must order divestiture of all the jointly owned newspaper-broadcast combinations except in "those cases where the evidence clearly discloses that cross-ownership is in the public interest" (*National Citizens Committee for Broadcasting* v. *FCC,* 1977). Judge McGowan wrote that "although we do not disturb the commission's prospective rules, we conclude that the divestiture order is inconsistent with its longstanding policy that 'nothing can be more important than insuring that there is a free flow of information from as many divergent sources as possible.' "

The FCC appealed the ruling by the court, and in 1978 the Supreme Court reversed the lower court decision. Justice Thurgood Marshall, writing for the unanimous Court, said the court of appeals was mistaken in ruling that the FCC could have no rational reason for not ordering divestiture of the existing combinations. The agency's arguments that it would disrupt the industry, that it would deny to many meritorious broadcast station owners the opportunity to continue service to the public, and that it would likely result in an increase in the growth of broadcast chains as locally owned broadcast properties were sold under the divestiture orders were substantial, Marshall argued. "We believe that the limited divestiture requirement reflects a rational weighing of competing policies," the justice concluded for the Court (*FCC* v. *National Citizens Committee for Broadcasting,* 1978).

Antitrust Action

Another important action aimed at broadcasters in the 1970s was a Department of Justice antitrust suit against the three major television networks: ABC, CBS, and NBC. The Department of Justice filed the actions in 1972, but the complaints were dismissed without prejudice. In 1974 the Justice Department refiled the actions, which asserted that the networks had violated the Sherman Act by trying to monopolize the programs shown in prime-time evening hours. The government originally sought a court order that would have accomplished the following:

1. Prohibited the networks from obtaining any interest (other than showing the program for the first time) in any entertainment television program, including feature films, made by others
2. Prohibited the networks from the syndication of such programs
3. Prohibited the networks from offering over a network any such programming produced by the network itself or any other network
4. Prohibited the network from offering any other commercial network programs it produced

The thrust of what the government sought was to take the television networks out of the program production business. Three years after the litigation began, NBC surprisingly agreed to sign a consent decree that was considerably more limited than the original order sought by the government. In the decree the network agreed to specific restrictions in bargaining with independent program producers, agreed not to acquire syndication rights or other distribution or profit shares in programs produced by others, agreed not to enter into reciprocal arrangements with either CBS or ABC in the purchase or sale of programming rights, and agreed to limit the broadcast of programs it had produced. Under the terms of the settlement, the network agreed that for the next ten years it would limit the broadcast of programs it produced itself to two-and-one-half hours per week during prime time, eight hours per week during daytime hours, and eleven hours per week during fringe hours. However, this programming limitation would only apply if both CBS and ABC either agreed to similar limitations or similar limitations were forced upon them through court order. CBS and ABC came to similar terms with the Justice Department. These agreements will expire in the early 1990s.

The Justice Department also attacked television trade association rules that it believed too monopolistic. A majority of television stations belong to the National Association of Broadcasters. The association promulgated an advertising code, that member stations were expected to follow. Rules included a limit on the number of commercials that could be broadcast each hour, the number of commercial interruptions in a particular program, and the number of different products that could be advertised in a commercial lasting less than one full minute. The latter rule, known as the multiple-product rule, prohibited a sponsor from advertising more than one product in a thirty-second commercial, the unit of time that has become the industry standard. The Justice

Department said the rule had the effect of compelling some advertisers to purchase more commercial time than they need or want and this prohibition artificially increased the demand for commercial time. Since all three networks and most television stations subscribed to the association code, the Justice Department said these rules violated the Sherman Act, that they were a restraint of trade.

A United States district court agreed in 1982 (*U.S.* v. *NAB*). The court noted that:

> . . . a relatively small business which is able to promote one successful product in a series of thirty-second commercials is precluded by that standard from using any portion of that thirty seconds to launch a second product, the sale of which will not, or not yet, support a commercial of its own.

The court noted that association member stations were monitored and code violations could result in discipline. The association argued that it was promoting the public interest in preventing overcommercialization of television. The court disagreed: "Congress has determined where the public interest lies when antitrust liability is at issue: it lies in fair and free competition" (*U.S.* v. *NAB*, 1982).

When the multiple-product standard was struck down, the association was forced to reexamine all its advertising rules. It apparently determined it was vulnerable to antitrust prosecution on other grounds as well, for it abandoned all enforcement of its advertising code. The association had dropped enforcement of its programming standards after the 1976 ruling that voided the family viewing hour. Consequently the National Association of Broadcasters completely closed its doors on such code enforcements in late 1982.

While these events were taking place in the broadcasting industry, the film industry was also under scrutiny by the government for anticompetitive practices that were first banned more than twenty-five years ago.

| Antitrust Laws and the Movies | The movie industry has faced government scrutiny for possible antitrust violations since the late 1930s. A succession of officials within the Department of Justice, including Thurman Arnold, Francis Biddle, and Tom Clark, attacked the Hollywood studios for a variety of commercial practices deemed to be anticompetitive. Particularly onerous was the fact that in the 1930s and 1940s most of the major studios owned vast chains of theaters. By controlling the film industry from the initial creative stages through the sale of popcorn during the exhibition of a film, the studios exercised powerful dominance in the media. Independent theaters found it extremely difficult to obtain good motion pictures to exhibit—the studios kept those for their own theaters. And independent filmmakers, of which there were few, found it difficult to compete with the large studios. A film made by a major studio was bound to be shown |

in a good theater—one owned by the film company—and generally costs at least were made. Independent producers had no guarantee that their films would be exhibited at all, let alone at a "good house."

Independent distributors and theater owners also faced a second problem: the block-booking policies of the major studios. Under **block booking** a distributor or theater owner was forced to "buy" a package of movies to exhibit. Generally this package included the popular and quality films the studio produced, but the package was also laced with a great many poorer films, often the lower grade B pictures that the Hollywood studios produced to keep their vast number of salaried technical employees busy and to develop new creative talent within the studio. Theater owners would often lose a considerable amount of money by exhibiting these second-rate films but had to take them as part of the package containing the good films that would be profitable to exhibit.

By the end of the 1940s, through a series of protracted antitrust litigations, the Department of Justice had succeeded in forcing the major studios to revise many of their policies. In 1948 the courts declared the block-booking practices to be a violation of the Sherman Act (*U.S.* v. *Paramount Pictures,* 1948). The studio policy of forcing independent theaters to charge minimum admission prices (so the independent owners could not undercut the admission prices at the studios' own theaters) was also declared illegal. Henceforth independent theaters were allowed to competitively bid for the right to show any of the films made by the major studios, and there could be no requirement that a theater had to take a bad picture to get a good one. The following year the studios agreed to sell their chains of theaters, a move that broke the backs of some of the weaker studios. By 1950 most of the serious anticompetitive practices the industry had developed in its fifty-year history had ended. But while this was a positive step for those in competition with the major studios, some students of film found that the government action hurt the creative end of the motion picture industry. Charles Higham in his book *Hollywood at Sunset* notes:

> . . . in practical terms the victory of the Department of Justice and the independents over wicked Hollywood had incalculably disastrous effects on the film industry and the very character of film entertainment itself. For confidence in a product, the feeling that it could flow out along guaranteed lines of distribution, was what gave many Hollywood films before 1948 their superb attack and vigor. Also, the block-booking custom, evil though it may have been, ensured that many obscure, personal, and fascinating movies could be made and released, feather-bedded by the system and underwritten by more conventional ventures.

Higham concluded that the successful antitrust action was a victory for justice, but a defeat for entertainment.

But the illegal practices by the major studios did not altogether cease after 1950. In 1962 the Department of Justice brought an action against Loew's, Inc., Screen Gems, and other film distributors for using the block-booking techniques in selling movies to television. In Washington WTOP-TV had complained that in order to get quality films such as *Casablanca, Sergeant York,* and *Treasure of Sierra Madre,* the station had to accept a large number of weak, less popular films. The Supreme Court followed its earlier precedents and declared the practice to be illegal under the Sherman Act (*U.S. v. Loew's, Inc.,* 1962). Even as late as 1978 the practice of block booking was found to exist in the film industry. Twentieth Century-Fox pleaded no contest to the charge of forcing theaters to exhibit *The Other Side of Midnight* in order to get the opportunity to book the studio's enormously popular *Star Wars.* The studio was fined $25,000 and assessed court costs of nearly $20,000.

The configuration of the film industry in the 1980s makes such illegal practices almost unnecessary, as the business is dominated by seven major studios that control the distribution of more than 80 percent of the films exhibited in the United States. The 1978 Task Force on the Motion Picture Industry reported that "major producers/distributors are effectively limiting competition by maintaining tight control over the distribution of films, both by their failure to produce more films and by their failure to distribute more films produced by others." As of today, this practice has not been investigated and probably is legal under our current interpretation of antitrust laws. The task force noted that there was no evidence of criminal intent on the part of the film companies, but they have nevertheless agreed to "tacitly limit production among themselves and . . . create sufficient barriers to entry to effectively squash new competition." Independent Hollywood producers are attempting themselves to beat this system by forming their own distribution systems, but it is a difficult and expensive task. Time will tell whether such schemes loosen the rein the major studios have over competition.

In addition to attempting to maintain control of distribution, the major studios are also getting back into the theater business. The Department of Justice has announced, informally at least, that it is no longer interested in enforcing the provisions of the consent agreement signed by the studios 40 years ago, prohibiting them from owning theaters. Quietly, the studios have started to reinvest in movie theaters and many predict they will soon all own substantial chains of the exhibition houses.

If the First Amendment has failed as a defense against antitrust action by the government, it has fared somewhat better as a means for blocking government taxes aimed at harrassing or hurting the press. And that is the next subject of this chapter.

Taxation and the Press
The First Amendment guarantees that the press shall be free from unfair and discriminatory taxes that have an impact upon circulation or distribution. In this area the classic case concerns a United States senator from a southern state and the daily press of that state (*Grosjean* v. *American Press Co.,* 1936).

During the late 1920s and early 1930s, the political leader of Louisiana was Huey P. Long. Long was a demagogue by most accounts and in 1934 held his state in virtual dictatorship. He controlled the legislature and the state house and had a deep impact upon the judicial branch as well. Long started his career by attacking big business—Standard Oil of California, to be exact. He became a folk hero among the rural people of Louisiana and was elected governor in 1928. In 1931 he was elected to the United States Senate, and many people believe that he would have attempted to win the presidency had he not been assassinated in 1935.

In 1934 the Long political machine, which the majority of the big-city residents had never favored, became annoyed at the frequent attacks by the state's daily newspapers against the senator and his political machine. The legislature enacted a special 2 percent tax on the gross advertising income of newspapers with a circulation of more than 20,000. Of the 163 newspapers in the state, only 13 had more than 20,000 subscribers, and of the 13, 12 were outspoken in their opposition to Long. The newspapers went to court and argued that the tax violated the First Amendment as well as other constitutional guarantees. The press won at the circuit court level on other grounds, but the state appealed. Then in 1936 the Supreme Court ruled in favor of the newspapers squarely on First Amendment grounds.

The state of Louisiana argued that the English common law, which it claimed the American courts had adopted after the Revolution, conferred upon the government the right to tax newspapers and license them if need be. Justice George Sutherland, who wrote the opinion in this unanimous Supreme Court decision, said however that such taxes upon newspapers were the direct cause of much civil unrest in England and were one of the chief objections Americans had had to British policy—objections that ultimately forced independence.

The justice wrote:

> It is impossible to concede that by the words "freedom of the press" the framers of the amendment intended to adopt merely the narrow view then reflected by the law of England that such freedom consisted in immunity from previous censorship. . . . It is equally impossible to believe that it was not intended to bring within the reach of these words such modes of restraint as were embodied in . . . taxation."

Sutherland asserted that the tax not only restricted the amount of revenue the paper earned but also restrained circulation. Newspapers with less than 20,000 readers would be reluctant to seek new subscribers for fear of increasing circulation to the point where they would have to pay the tax as well. The justice added that any action by the government that prevents free and general discussion of public matters is a kind of censorship. Sutherland said that in this case even the form in which the tax was imposed—levied against a distinct group of newspapers—was suspicious. He then wrote:

> The tax here involved is bad not because it takes money from the pockets of the appellees [the newspapers]. If that were all, a wholly different question would be presented. It is bad because, in the light of its history and of its present setting, it is seen to be a deliberate and calculated device in the guise of a tax to limit the circulation of information to which the public is entitled in virtue of the constitutional guaranties. A free press stands as one of the great interpreters between the government and the people. To allow it to be fettered is to fetter ourselves.

Therefore in *Grosjean* v. *American Press Co.,* the Supreme Court struck down a discriminatory tax against the press. An interesting footnote to the case concerns the opinion. Justice Sutherland's opinion is one of the most eloquent ever penned in defense of free expression. The justice was not normally such an articulate spokesman. What happened in this case? Speculation is that Sutherland's opinion incorporates a concurring opinion by Justice Benjamin Cardozo, perhaps the greatest writer ever to serve on the Court, and the eloquence of the *Grosjean* opinion is really Cardozo's, not Sutherland's.

Despite the fact that Justice Sutherland specifically noted in his opinion that the ruling in *Grosjean* did not mean that newspapers are immune from ordinary taxes, some newspaper publishers apparently did not read the opinion that way, but saw it instead as a means of escaping other kinds of taxes. After *Grosjean*, for example, unsuccessful attempts were made to have a sales tax in Arizona declared inapplicable to newspapers because it was a restriction on freedom of the press (*Arizona Publishing Co.* v. *O'Neil,* 1938). Since 1953 when the United States Supreme Court refused to hear an appeal from a California decision affirming the constitutionality of a general business tax on newspapers, the matter has been fairly well settled. The California case involved the *Corona Daily Independent,* which challenged a business tax imposed by the city of Corona. A license tax of thirty-two dollars had been levied for many years against all businesses. In 1953 the newspaper refused to pay the levy on the grounds that the tax violated its First Amendment rights to freedom of expression. The *Grosjean* case prohibited such taxation, lawyers for the publication argued. The trial court ruled in favor of the newspaper, but the California Appellate Court disagreed and reversed the ruling (*City of Corona* v. *Corona Daily Independent,* 1953). Justice Griffin wrote that there is ample authority to the effect that newspapers are not made exempt from ordinary forms of taxation. Justice Griffin said that the newspaper had not shown that the amount of the tax was harsh or arbitrary, that the tax was oppressive or confiscatory, or that the tax in any way curtailed or abridged the newspaper's right to disseminate news and comment:

> We conclude that a nondiscriminatory tax, levied upon the doing of business, for the sole purpose of maintaining the municipal government, without whose municipal services and protection the press could neither exist nor function, must be sustained as being within the purview and necessary implications of the Constitution and its amendments.

The United States Supreme Court refused to review the ruling in *City of Corona* v. *Corona Daily Independent,* and most people believed the refusal signaled concurrence with the opinion of the California court.

But in 1983 the U.S. Supreme Court did review an unusual tax placed on a handful of Minnesota newspapers. Since 1971 Minnesota had imposed a use tax on the cost of the paper and ink products consumed in the production of a publication. The law was amended in 1974 to exempt from the tax the first $100,000 worth of paper and ink used. After the exemption was adopted, only about fifteen newspapers in the state were forced to pay the tax. And the Minneapolis Star and Tribune Company ended up paying about two-thirds of all the revenues collected under the tax. The Star and Tribune Company challenged the tax, and in March 1983 the High Court ruled that the levy against the newspapers was invalid.

Justice Sandra Day O'Connor described the tax as a "special tax that applies only to certain publications protected by the First Amendment." She added: "A power to tax differentially, as opposed to a power to tax generally, gives a government a powerful weapon against the taxpayer selected." Such a tax could be used to censor the press, a clear violation of the First Amendment. The tax law is also deficient because it ends up hitting only a few of the newspapers in the state. "Whatever the motive of the legislature in this case," Justice O'Connor wrote for the Court's majority, "we think that recognizing a power in the State not only to single out the press but also to tailor the tax so it singles out a few members of the press presents such a potential for abuse that no interest suggested by Minnesota can justify the scheme" (*Minneapolis Star* v. *Minnesota Commissioner of Revenue,* 1983).

The basic rule of First Amendment law regarding taxes on the press is this: Newspapers, broadcasting stations, and other mass media must pay the same taxes as any other business. Taxes that are levied only against the press and tend to inhibit circulation or impose other kinds of prior restraints (such as very high taxes that keep all but very wealthy people from publishing newspapers) are unconstitutional.

Regulation of the commercial aspects of the mass media is not new. Yet surely as the media continue to grow as giant businesses and more and more take on the configuration of modern American industry, commercial regulation will increase. The Chief Justice of the United States suggested as much in 1978 in a concurring opinion in the case of *First National Bank of Boston v. Bellotti.* The case involved a Massachusetts state law that forbade banks and corporations from making contributions or expenditures for the purpose of "influencing or affecting the vote on any question submitted to the voters." The Court struck down the statute as running afoul of the First Amendment. Chief Justice Burger noted in his concurrence:

> A disquieting aspect of Massachusetts's position is that it may carry the risk of impinging on the First Amendment rights of those who employ the corporate form—as most do—to carry on the business of mass communications, particularly large media conglomerates. This is so because of the difficulty, and perhaps impossibility, of distinguishing, either as a matter of fact or constitutional law, media corporations from corporations such as the appellants [a bank] in this case.

John Oakes, editorial page editor of the *New York Times,* noted that Burger's opinion "may lead to a questioning of the need for special protection of the press as such, under a First Amendment that was in fact designed to insure the free flow of information and opinion, and not the accretion of corporate power." Oakes added, during a speech at the 1978 Conference on Media and the Public at the Washington Journalism Center, that the growth of concentration of the ownership of the media into fewer hands could lead to a grave dislocation between the press and the public:

> The quality of the product turned out by the conglomerates' publishing and broadcasting arms may be less important in the long run than the loss of public confidence in the press engendered by fears of "the sinister effect of riches" upon the institution of the press.

Oakes added that he feared that public disillusionment with the press could even adversely influence the judiciary's normal strong adherence to the guarantees of a free press.

SUMMARY

Mass media businesses are regulated by the government just like any other businesses, and the First Amendment offers no special protection from such regulation.

The government has brought many antitrust actions against mass media companies. Action by the Justice Department against newspapers has focused upon industry rules that limit the profitable entry into the newspaper business (the *AP* case) and upon discriminatory newspaper advertising and circulation rules. Antitrust law has been found to be largely ineffective to block the growth of vast chains of newspapers but has been used to stop concentration of ownership of newspapers in specific local areas. Congress adopted the Newspaper

Preservation Act in 1970, which permits monopolistic joint-operating agreements between newspapers in situations where one of the two papers is in danger of failing without such a cost-saving agreement. The law has been ruled to be constitutional by the federal courts.

The government has not used antitrust laws against the concentration of ownership in broadcast because the Federal Communications Commission has adopted ownership rules that limit such concentration, but many of these rules are currently under examination at the FCC and may be abandoned. The government has, however, forced the television networks to stop monopolizing the programs shown in prime time. It has also forced abandonment of industry codes that artificially increased the demand for advertising time on television.

Antitrust actions against the film industry in the late forties forced the major film production studios to sell off their chains of motion-picture theaters and prohibited them from such discriminatory practices as block booking the films they distributed.

While the courts have ruled that newspapers cannot be subject to discriminatory taxes that have the tendency to restrain circulation, publishers and broadcasters are expected to pay normal business taxes. The First Amendment cannot be raised as a bar to such levies.

BIBLIOGRAPHY

Here is a list of some of the sources that have been helpful in the preparation of chapter 12:

Books

Compaine, Benjamin M., ed. *Who Owns the Media?* White Plains, N. Y.: Knowledge Industry Publications, 1979.
Gerald, J. Edward. *The Press and the Constitution.* Minneapolis: University of Minnesota Press, 1948.
Higham, Charles. *Hollywood at Sunset.* New York: Saturday Review Press, 1972.
Oppenheim, S. Chesterfield, and Shields, Carrington. *Newspapers and Antitrust Laws.* Charlottesville, Va.: Michie Company, 1981.

Articles

Roach, Catherine B. "Media Conglomerates, Anti-Trust Law, and the Marketplace of Ideas." 9 *Memphis State University Law Review* 257, 1979.

Cases

Advantage Publications v. *Daily Press,* 9 M. L. Rept. 1761 (1983).
AP v. *NLRB,* 301 U.S. 130 (1937).
AP v. *U.S.,* 326 U.S. 1 (1945).
Arizona Publishing Co. v. *O'Neil,* 22 F. Supp. 117, affd. 304 U.S. 543 (1938).
Bay Guardian Publishing Company v. *Chronicle Publishing Company,* 344 F. Supp. 1155 (1972).
City of Corona v. *Corona Daily Independent,* 252 P.2d 56 (1953).
Committee for an Independent P–I v. *Hearst,* 704 F.2d 467 (1983).

Committee v. *Smith*, 549 F. Supp. 985 (1982).
FCC v. *National Citizens Committee for Broadcasting*, 436 U.S. 775 (1978).
First National Bank of Boston v. *Bellotti*, 98 S.Ct. 1407 (1978).
Grosjean v. *American Press Co.*, 297 U.S. 233 (1936).
Lorain Journal Co. v. *U.S.*, 342 U.S. 143 (1951).
Minneapolis Star v. *Minnesota Commissioner of Revenue*, 103 S.Ct. 1365 (1983).
National Citizens Committee for Broadcasting v. *FCC*, 555 F.2d 938 (1977).
Times-Picayune v. *U.S.*, 345 U.S. 594 (1953).
U.S. v. *Citizen Publishing Co.*, 394 U.S. 131 (1969).
U.S. v. *City Star*, 240 F.2d 643 (1957).
U.S. v. *Loew's, Inc.*, 371 U.S. 38 (1962).
U.S. v. *NAB*, 536 F. Supp. 149 (1982).
U.S. v. *Nanlo*, 7 M. L. Rept. 1950 (1981).
U.S. v. *Paramount Pictures*, 334 U.S. 131 (1948).
U.S. v. *Times-Mirror Corp.*, 274 F. Supp. 607 (1967); affd. 390 U.S. 712 (1968).

GLOSSARY

absolute privilege An immunity from libel suits granted to government officials and others based on remarks uttered or written as part of their official duties.

absolutist theory The proposition that the First Amendment is an absolute, and that government may adopt no laws whatsoever that abridge freedom of expression.

actual damages Damages awarded to a plaintiff in a lawsuit based upon proof of actual harm to the plaintiff.

actual malice A fault standard in libel law: knowledge before publication that the libelous material was false or reckless disregard of the truth or falsity of the libelous matter.

administrative agency An agency, created and funded by the Congress, whose members are appointed by the president and whose function it is to administer specific legislation, such as law regulating broadcasting and advertising.

admonition to a jury Instructions from a judge to a trial jury to avoid talking to other persons about the trial they are hearing and to avoid news broadcasts and newspaper or magazine stories that discuss the case or issues in the case.

Alien and Sedition Laws of 1798 Laws adopted by the Federalist Congress aimed at stopping criticism of the national government by Republican or Jeffersonian editors and politicians.

amici curiae "Friends of the court"; persons who have no legal right to take part in a lawsuit but are allowed to appear on behalf of one of the parties in a case.

appellant The party who initiates or takes the appeal of a case from one court to another.

appellate court(s) A court that has both original and appellate jurisdiction; a court to which cases are removed for an appeal.

appellee The person in a case against whom the appeal is taken; that is, the party in the suit who is not making the appeal.

appropriation In the law of privacy, use of a person's name or likeness without consent for advertising or trade purposes.

arraignment The first official court appearance made by a criminal defendant at which he or she is formally charged with an offense and called upon to plead guilty or not guilty to the charges contained in the state's indictment or information.

ascertainment A procedure established by the Federal Communications Commission that instructs broadcast licensees in the manner in which they are to determine important problems and issues in a community.

bait-and-switch advertising An illegal advertising strategy in which the seller baits an advertisement with a low-priced model of a product but then switches customers who seek to buy the product to a much higher-priced model by telling them that the cheaper model does not work well or is no longer in stock.

bench-bar-press guidelines Informal agreements among lawyers, judges, police officials, and journalists about what should and should not be published or broadcast about a criminal suspect or criminal case before a trial is held.

block booking An illegal scheme in which a motion-picture distributor requires a theater owner to book a poor film in order to book a popular film.

bond; bonding A large sum of money given by a publisher to a government to be held to ensure good behavior. Should the publisher violate a government rule, the bond is forfeited to the government, and the newspaper or magazine cannot be published again until a new bond is posted.

candidate access rule Section 312 of the Federal Communications Act, which forbids a broadcaster from instituting an across-the-board policy that denies all candidates for federal office the opportunity to use the station to further a political campaign.

case reporter(s) A book (or books) containing a chronological collection of the opinions rendered by a particular court for cases that were decided by the court.

cease and desist order An order issued by a court requiring the cessation of a particular behavior or practice.

challenge for cause The request by a litigant in a criminal or civil case that a juror be dismissed for a specific reason.

change of venue Moving a trial to a distant community in order to find jurors who have not read or viewed prejudicial publicity about the defendant.

citation The reference to a legal opinion contained in a case reporter that gives the name, volume number, and page number where the opinion can be found. The year the opinion was rendered is also included in the citation.

civil complaint A written statement of the plaintiff's legal grievance, which normally initiates a civil suit.

civil contempt That variety of contempt of court in which the act of disrespect or disobedience is aimed at one of the parties in the lawsuit, rather than at the court itself.

commercial speech doctrine The legal doctrine that states that truthful advertising for products and services that are not illegal is normally protected by the First Amendment to the United States Constitution.

common law Principles and rules of law that derive their authority not from legislation but from community usage and custom.

comparative license hearing A hearing to evaluate potential licensees when two or more persons seek the same broadcast license, as required by a Federal Communications Commission rule.

concurring opinion A written opinion by an appellate judge or justice in which the author agrees with the decision of the court but normally states reasons different from those in the court opinion as the basis for his or her decision.

consent A defense in both libel and invasion of privacy cases that provides that individuals who agree to the publication of a libelous story or the appropriation of their name cannot then maintain a lawsuit based upon the libel or the appropriation.

consent order or decree A document in which an individual agrees to terminate a specific behavior, such as an advertising campaign, or to refrain from a specific action, such as making a certain advertising claim.

constitution A written outline of the organization of a government that provides for both the rights and responsibilities of various branches of the government and the limits of the power of the government.

contempt of court An act of disobedience or disrespect to a judge, which may be punished by a fine or jail sentence.

continuance The delay of a trial or hearing; that is, the trial is postponed.

copyright That body of law which protects the works created by writers, painters, photographers, performing artists, inventors, and other persons who create immaterial property.

copyright notice The words "Copyright © 1989 by Don R. Pember," which indicate to a user that a work is copyrighted by the author or creator.

corrective advertising scheme Rules established by the Federal Trade Commission that require an advertiser to correct the false impressions left by deceptive advertising in a certain percentage of future advertisements.

court of chancery A specific court, maintained in some jurisdictions, that administers only the law of equity.

court's opinion The official opinion of an appellate court that states the reasons or rationale for a decision.

criminal contempt That variety of contempt of court in which the act of disrespect or disobedience is aimed directly at the court.

criminal history privacy laws State laws that limit the access of non-law enforcement personnel to criminal records maintained by states.

criminal libel A libel against the state, against the dead, or against a large, ill-defined group (such as a race) in which the state prosecutes the libel on behalf of the injured parties.

criminal suit A legal action brought by the state against an individual or group of individuals for violating state criminal laws.

criminal syndicalism laws Laws that outlaw advocacy, planning, or processes aimed at establishing the control over industry by workers or trade unions.

damages Money awarded to the winning party in a civil lawsuit.

defamation Any communication that holds a person up to contempt, hatred, ridicule, or scorn and lowers the reputation of the individual defamed.

defendant The person against whom relief or recovery is sought in a civil lawsuit; the individual against whom a state criminal action is brought.

demurrer An allegation made by the defendant in a lawsuit that even if the facts as stated by the plaintiff are true they do not state a sufficient cause for action.

devisable right A right that may be passed on to an heir.

Dickinson Rule A rule eminating from a decision by the Fifth United States Court of Appeals stating that even a patently unconstitutional court order must be obeyed until it is overturned by an appellate court.

dicta Remarks in a court opinion that do not speak directly to the legal point in question.

direct appeal The statutorily granted right of an aggrieved party to carry the appeal of a case to the Supreme Court of the United States. The High Court can deny this right if the appeal lacks a substantial federal question.

direct criminal contempt A criminal contempt that is committed in the presence of the court, that is, in the courtroom or near the courtroom.

dissenting opinion A written opinion by a judge or justice who disagrees with the appellate court's decision in a case.

en banc; sitting en banc A French term to describe all the justices or judges of an appellate court sitting together to hear a case. This situation is the opposite of the more typical situation in which a small group (called a panel) of judges or justices in a particular court hears a case.

Equal Time Rule Section 315 of the Federal Communications Act, which states that when broadcasters permit a legally qualified candidate for elective office to use their broadcasting facilities, all other legally qualified candidates for the same elective office must be given the similar opportunity.

equity A system of jurisprudence, distinct from the common law, in which courts are empowered to decide cases upon the basis of equity or fairness and are not bound by the rigid precedents that often exist in the common law.

Espionage Act A law adopted by the Congress in 1917 that outlawed criticism of the United States government and its participation in World War I in Europe.

executive privilege An asserted common law privilege of the president and other executives to keep presidential papers, records, and other documents secret, even from the Congress.

executive session A popular euphemism for a closed meeting held by a government body such as a city council or school board.

fair comment A libel defense that protects the publication of libelous opinion that focuses upon the public activities of a person acting in a public sphere.

Fairness Doctrine A Federal Communications Commission rule that requires that broadcasters devote a reasonable portion of broadcast time to the discussion of important public issues and that the coverage of these issues be fair in the sense that all important contrasting views on the issues are presented.

fair use A provision of the copyright law that permits a limited amount of copying of material that has been properly copyrighted.

false light That portion of privacy law which prohibits all publication or broadcast that falsely portrays an individual in an offensive manner.

FCC See Federal Communications Commission.

Federal Communications Act The law, adopted in 1934, that is the foundation for the regulation of broadcasting in the United States.

Federal Communications Commission A five-member body appointed by the president whose function is to administer the federal broadcasting and communications laws.

Federal Open Meetings Law (Government in Sunshine Act) A federal law that requires approximately fifty federal agencies and bureaus to hold all their meetings in public, unless a subject under discussion is included within one of the ten exemptions contained in the statute.

Federal Trade Commission A five-member body appointed by the president whose function it is to administer the federal laws relating to advertising, antitrust and many other business matters.

Fighting Words Doctrine A legal doctrine that permits prior censorship of words that create a clear and present danger of inciting an audience to disorder or violence.

FOIA See Freedom of Information Act.

Freedom of Information Act A federal law that mandates that all the records created and kept by federal agencies in the executive branch of government must be open for public inspection and copying, except those records that fall into one of nine exempted categories listed in the statute.

FTC See Federal Trade Commission.

gag order(s) A restrictive court order that prohibits all or some participants in a trial from speaking about a case or that stops publications and broadcasting stations from reporting on certain aspects of a case.

Government in Sunshine Act See Federal Open Meetings Law.

grand jury A jury whose function it is to determine whether sufficient evidence exists to issue an indictment or true bill charging an individual or individuals with a crime and to take such persons to trial. It is called a grand jury because it has more members than a petit, or trial, jury.

identification As used in a libel suit, the requirement that the plaintiff prove that at least one person believes that the subject of the libelous remarks is the plaintiff and not some other person.

impeachment A criminal proceeding against a public officer that is started by written "articles of impeachment" and followed by a trial. The House of Representatives, for example, can issue articles of impeachment against the president, who is then tried by the Senate.

indictment A written accusation issued by a grand jury charging that an individual or individuals have committed a specific crime and should be taken to trial.

indirect criminal contempt A criminal contempt committed outside the presence of the court, that is, not in the courtroom or near the courtroom.

information A written accusation issued by a public officer rather than by a grand jury charging that an individual or individuals have committed a specific crime and should be taken to trial.

intrusion An invasion of privacy committed when one individual intrudes upon or invades the solitude of another individual.

invasion of privacy A civil tort that emerged in the early twentieth century and contains four distinct categories of legal wrongs: appropriation, intrusion, publication of private facts, and false light.

joint-operating agreement An exemption to the federal antitrust law that permits two newspapers in a community to merge advertising, circulation, and printing functions but maintain separate editorial departments.

judgment of the court The final ruling of a court, which determines the outcome of a lawsuit. It is different from the verdict, which is the decision of the jury in a trial.

judicial decree A judgment of a court of equity; a declaration of the court announcing the legal consequences of the facts found to be true by the court.

judicial instructions A statement (often written) made by a judge to the members of a jury informing them about the law (as distinguished from the facts) in a case.

judicial review The power of a court to declare void and unenforceable any statute, rule, or executive order that conflicts with an appropriate state constitution or the federal constitution.

jury A group of men and women called together in a trial court to determine the facts in a civil or criminal lawsuit. It is sometimes called a petit jury to distinguish it from a grand jury.

legal brief(s) (brief) Written legal argument presented to the court by one or both parties in a lawsuit.

libel Published or broadcast communication that lowers the reputation of an individual by holding him or her up to contempt, ridicule, or scorn.

licensing process The process by which a government gives a publisher or a broadcaster prior permission to print a newspaper or operate a broadcasting station. Revocation of a license can be used as punishment for failing to comply with the law or the wishes of the government. Licensing of the printed press in the United States ended in the 1720s.

litigant A party in a lawsuit; a participant in litigation.

memorandum order The announcement by an appellate court of a decision in a case that does not include a written opinion containing the rationale or reasons for the ruling.

misappropriation Taking what belongs to someone else and using it unfairly for one's own gain; for example, attempting to pass off a novel as part of a popular series of novels written and published by someone else. It is often called unfair competition.

Missouri Plan A system used in some states by which judges are appointed to the bench initially and then must stand for reelection on a ballot that permits citizens to vote to retain or not retain the judge.

NAD See next entry.

National Advertising Division (NAD) of the Council of Better Business Bureaus An industry organization that evaluates and rules upon the truthfulness of advertising claims. Complaints are normally brought to the NAD by competing advertisers.

negligence A fault standard in libel and other tort law. Negligent behavior is normally described as an act or action that a reasonably prudent person or a reasonable individual would not have committed. In libel law, courts often measure negligence by asking whether the allegedly libelous material was the work of a person who exercised reasonable care in preparation of the story.

neutral reportage An emerging libel defense or privilege that states that it is permissible to publish or broadcast an accurate account of information about a public figure from a reliable source even when the reporter doubts the truth of the libelous assertion. The defense is not widely accepted.

nonjusticiable matter An issue that is inappropriate for a court to decide because the jurists lack the knowledge to make the ruling, because another branch of government has the responsibility to answer such questions, or because a court order in the matter would not likely be enforceable or enforced.

open meetings laws State and federal statutes that require that certain meetings of public agencies—normally in the executive branch of government—be open to the public and the press.

open records laws State and federal statutes that require that certain records of public agencies—normally in the executive branch of government—be open for inspection and copying by the public and the press.

opinion The written statement issued by a court that explains the reasons for a judgment and states the rule of law in the case.

oral argument An oral presentation made to a judge or justices in which the litigants argue the merits of their case.

original jurisdiction Jurisdiction in the first instance, as distinguished from appellate jurisdiction. A court exercising original jurisdiction determines both the facts and the law in the case; courts exercising appellate jurisdiction may only rule upon the law and the sufficiency of the facts as determined by a trial court.

pandering The business of purveying textual or graphic material openly advertised to appeal to the erotic interest of customers. This criterion is sometimes used in obscenity prosecution to determine whether the material in question is obscene.

per curiam opinion An unsigned court opinion. The author of the opinion is not known outside the court.

peremptory challenge A challenge without stated cause to remove a juror from a panel. Litigants are given a small number of such challenges in a lawsuit.

personal attack rules Specific rules issued by the Federal Communications Commission that outline the responsibilities of a broadcast licensee if and when an attack upon an individual or identifiable group is made during a radio or television broadcast. The licensee must inform the individual or group of the attack and provide an opportunity for a reply, among other requirements.

petitioner One who petitions a court to take an action; someone who starts a lawsuit, or carries an appeal to a higher court (appellant). This person is the opposite of a respondent, one who responds to a petition.

plaintiff An individual who initiates a civil lawsuit.

pleadings The written statements of the parties in a lawsuit that contain their allegations, denials, and defenses.

precedent An established rule of law set by a previous case. Courts should follow precedent when it is advisable and possible.

preferred position theory A theory on how the First Amendment should be interpreted that states that when the guarantees of freedom of speech and freedom of the press are balanced against other important rights, the rights of freedom of expression are to be given extra weight, to be preferred. Legally this proposition requires that persons who would restrict freedom of expression bear the burden of proving that such restrictions are justified and not a violation of the First Amendment.

pretrial hearing A meeting prior to a criminal trial at which attorneys for the state and for the defense make arguments before a judge on evidentiary questions; that is, whether a confession made by the defendant should be admitted as evidence at the trial. This type of hearing is sometimes called a suppression hearing.

Printers' ink statute A model law drafted in 1911 to control false or misleading advertising. Most states adopted some version of this model in the early twentieth century. Such laws are largely ineffective because they are not normally enforced.

prior restraint Prepublication censorship that forbids publication or broadcast of certain objectionable material, as opposed to punishment of a perpetrator after the material was published or broadcast.

Privacy Act A federal statute that forbids the disclosure of specific material held by federal agencies on the grounds that its release could invade the privacy of the subject of the report or document.

publication In libel law, exposing an allegedly libelous statement to one person in addition to the subject of the libel.

publication of private information In privacy law, publicizing embarrassing private information about an individual that is not of legitimate public concern.

puffery Often expansive hyperbole about a product that does not contain factual claims of merit. Normally puffery is permitted by the law (e.g., this is the best-looking automobile on the market today).

punitive damages Money damages awarded to a plaintiff in a lawsuit aimed not to compensate for harm to the injured party, but to punish the defendant for his or her illegal conduct.

qualified privilege In libel law, the privilege of the reporter (or any person) to publish a fair and accurate report of the proceedings of a public meeting or public document and be immune from lawsuit for the publication of libel uttered at the meeting or contained in the document.

Radio Act of 1912 The first federal broadcast law, which imposed only minimal regulation on the fledgling broadcast industry. Radio operators were required to have a license under this statute.

Radio Act of 1927 The first comprehensive national broadcast law, which provided the basic framework for the regulation of broadcast that was later adopted in the Communications Act of 1934.

reasonable access rule See candidate access rule.

reporter-source privilege The privilege asserted by a reporter to shield the identity of the source of confidential information used in a news story.

respondent The person who responds to a petition placed before a court by another person; the opposite of the petitioner. At the appellate level, the respondent is often called the appellee.

restrictive order A court order limiting the discussion of the facts in a criminal case both by participants in the case and by the press. See also gag order.

retraction In libel law, a statement published or broadcast that attempts to retract or correct previously published or broadcast libelous matter. A timely retraction will usually mitigate damages, and in some states that have retraction laws, plaintiffs must seek a retraction before beginning a lawsuit or they lose the ability to collect anything but special damages.

right of publicity An offshoot of privacy law that protects the right of persons to capitalize upon their fame or notoriety for commercial or advertising purposes.

right of reply A little-used libel defense that declares as immune from a lawsuit a libelous remark made against an individual in reply to a previously published libelous remark made by that individual.

Section 312 See candidate access rule.

Section 315 See equal time rule.

Sedition Act of 1918 An amendment to the Espionage Act adopted in the midst of World War I that severely limited criticism of the government and criticism of United States participation in the European war.

seditious libel Libeling the government; criticizing the government or government officers. It is sometimes called sedition.

sequestration of the jury Separating the jury from the community during a trial. Usually a jury is lodged at a hotel and members are required to eat together. In general, sequestration means to keep jurors away from other persons. The exposure of the jury to news reports is also screened to shield jurors from news reports about the trial.

shield laws State statutes that permit reporters in some circumstances to shield the name of a confidential news source when questioned by a grand jury or in another legal forum.

single mistake rule In libel law, a rule that states that it is not libelous to accuse a professional person or business person of making a single mistake (e.g., Dr. Alan Jones incorrectly diagnosed the patient's illness).

slander Oral defamation.

Smith Act A federal law adopted in 1940 that makes it illegal to advocate the violent overthrow of the government.

special damages Damages that can be awarded to a plaintiff in a lawsuit upon proof of specific monetary loss.

stare decisis "Let the decision stand." This concept is the operating principal in the common law system and requires that judges follow precedent case law when making judgments.

statute of limitations A law that requires that a legal action must begin within a specified period of time (usually one to three years for a civil case) after the legal wrong was committed.

statutes Laws adopted by legislative bodies.

statutory construction The process undertaken by courts to interpret or construe the meaning of statutes.

strict liability A doctrine in tort law that declares that a defendant is liable for even an unintentional and nonnegligent act that causes harm to a plaintiff. Libel law was formerly governed by the doctrine of strict liability.

subpoena A court document that requires a witness to appear and testify or to produce documents or papers pertinent to a pending controversy.

substantiation A Federal Trade Commission rule that requires an advertiser to prove the truth of advertising claims made about a product or service.

summary contempt power The power of a judge to find an individual guilty of a contempt of court and impose a sentence without giving the individual the benefit of a jury trial.

summary judgment A judgment granted to a party in a lawsuit when the pleadings and other materials in the case disclose no material issue of fact between the parties, making it possible for the case to be decided on the basis of the law by the court. A summary judgment avoids a costly jury trial.

survival statute A statute that permits an heir to continue to maintain a lawsuit though the plaintiff died after the suit was filed, but before it was resolved.

time, place, and manner restrictions or rules Rules, when justified by a substantial government interest, that can regulate the time, place, and manner of speaking or publishing and the distribution of printed material.

trade libel Product disparagement, and not considered true libel; disparaging a product as opposed to the manufacturer or maker of the product.

trade regulation rules Rules adopted by the Federal Trade Commission that prohibit specific advertising claims about an entire class of products. For example, makers of fruit drinks that contain less than 10 percent fruit juice cannot advertise these products as fruit juice.

trespass Unlawful entry upon another person's land or property.

trial court(s) Normally the first court to hear a lawsuit. This court is the forum in which the facts are determined and the law is initially applied, as opposed to an appellate court, to which decisions are appealed.

unfair competition See misappropriation.

variable obscenity standards A Supreme Court doctrine that permits states to prohibit the sale, distribution, or exhibition of certain kinds of nonobscene matter to children, so long as these laws do not interfere with the accessibility of this material to adults.

verdict The decision of a trial jury based upon the instructions given to it by the judge.

voir dire A preliminary examination the court makes of persons chosen to serve as jurors in a trial. Inappropriate persons can be challenged for cause or on the basis of a peremptory challenge by either side in the legal dispute.

writ of certiorari A writ by which an appellant seeks the review of a case by the Supreme Court of the United States. When the writ is granted, the Court will order the lower court to send up the record of the case for review.

Zapple Rule A corollary to the equal time rule that states that when the supporters of a legally qualified candidate are given time on a radio or television broadcast, the supporters of all other legally qualified candidates for the same office must also be given equal opportunity.

TABLE OF CASES

INDEX

Last Minute Approach

Honest Approach

Hollywood "

Exploitation "

Intellectual "

Lying "